Stanley Thornes (Publishers) Ltd

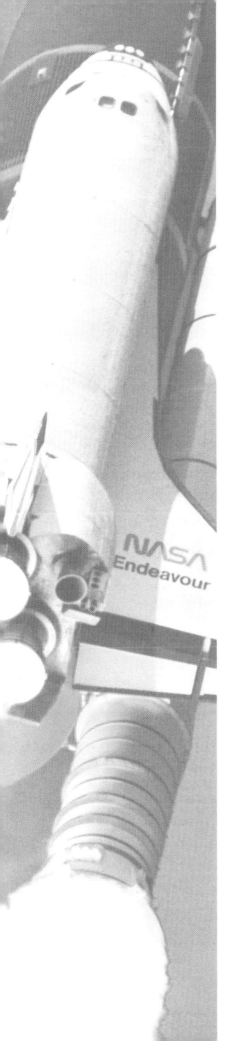

Advanced
Chemistry
for You

Lawrie RYAN

First published in 2000 by

Stanley Thornes (Publishers) Ltd
Delta Place
27 Bath Road
Cheltenham
GL53 7TH
United Kingdom

00 01 02 03 04 05 / 10 9 8 7 6 5 4 3 2 1

A catalogue record of this book is available from the British Library.

ISBN 0 7487-5297-8

Also available:

Advanced Biology For You   ISBN 0 7487 5298 6
Advanced Physics For You   ISBN 0 7487 5296 X

Typeset by TechSet Ltd, Gateshead, Tyne & Wear
Printed and bound in Italy by G. Canale & C.S.p.A., Borgaro T.se, Turin

Introduction

Advanced Chemistry for You is designed to support your studies in AS and A2 chemistry modules. It is suitable to use with any of the specifications offered by AQA, Edexcel and OCR as you will find all the essential concepts, written specifically for the latest AS and A2 examinations. In the best traditions of GCSE **Chemistry for You**, the text is as lively and interesting as possible, with a healthy smattering of humour to amuse you along the way!

Building on your previous work in chemistry, new ideas are introduced in a clear, straightforward way. The book is carefully planned so that each new concept is developed on a single page or on two facing pages. Pages with a red corner are needed for your core A2 modules and those without are the AS level pages. All the chapters, apart from one on polymers, are marked wholly as either AS or A2 to make reading, revising and answering questions as simple as possible. Importantly, the A2 chapters are linked to the AS chapters that they take on and develop further. This makes it easy to review your previous work before tackling the harder A2 units.

Each new chemical term is printed in bold text and key ideas are presented in a highlighted box. At the end of each chapter you will find a useful summary, ideal for revision. This is followed by questions to reinforce your understanding of the chapter. You can also use questions from recent past examination papers to practise your skills. These questions are at the end of each of the six main sections of the book. You can't miss them as they are coloured to match the chapters they refer to! In the last section of the book you will find guidance on study skills, exam technique, coursework and practical skills, together with advice on Key Skills in chemistry.

Throughout the book there are Chemistry at Work pages. These focus on showing how the concepts you learn about are relevant to all our lives... or will be, because we have tried to include some of the most exciting breakthroughs taken from 'cutting edge' chemical research.

If you enjoyed using GCSE **Chemistry for You**, I'm sure you'll like this book and will continue to understand chemistry and have some fun on the way to passing your exams. Good luck!

Finally, I must thank my family (Judy, Nina and Alex) for remaining so supportive throughout the course of this project.

Lawrie Ryan

Contents

Atoms and Structure

1. **Atoms and electrons**   **8**
   History of the atom
   Electron shells or energy levels
   Electrons in sub-shells
   Filling the sub-shells
   Chemistry at work: Atoms and electrons

2. **Atoms and the nucleus**   **18**
   Inside the nucleus
   Isotopes
   Relative atomic masses
   Mass spectrometer
   Mass spectra
   Chemistry at work: Atoms and their nuclei
   Chemistry at work: What's new in atoms?

3. **Calculations using the mole**   **29**
   Balancing equations
   Mole calculations
   Relative formula mass
   Moles in chemical equations
   Moles of gases
   The ideal gas equation
   Moles in solution
   Working out the formula
   Chemistry at work: Mole calculations

4. **Ionic compounds**   **46**
   Electron transfer
   More ionic compounds
   Dot and cross diagrams
   Properties of ionic compounds
   Explaining the properties of ionic compounds
   Chemistry at work: Ionic compounds

5. **Covalent bonding**   **56**
   Covalent bonding
   Double bonds
   Dative (or coordinate) bonds
   Shapes of molecules
   Giant covalent structures
   Chemistry at work: Bucky-balls
   Chemistry at work: More fullerenes
   Simple molecular structures
   Van der Waals' forces
   Polar molecules
   Hydrogen bonding
   Intermediate bonds

6. **Metals and structures**   **74**
   Metallic bonding
   Explaining the properties of metals
   Alloys
   Structure of metals
   Chemistry at work: 'Memory metals'

Further questions on Atoms and Structure   **82**

The Periodic Table

7. **The Periodic Table**   **88**
   History of the Periodic Table
   The modern Periodic Table
   Atomic structures and the Periodic Table
   Groups and periods
   Patterns in the Periodic Table
   Chemistry at work: Group 4 elements
   Periodicity
   Structure and periodicity
   Trends down a group: Group 1 – The alkali metals
   Chemistry at work: New elements

8.* **Periodicity and chemical properties**   **103**
   Oxides
   Structures of the oxides
   Chlorides across a period
   Chlorides with water
   Ions and the Periodic Table
   Periodicity and redox reactions
   Chemistry at work: Oxides

9. **Group 2 (s-block elements)**   **112**
   Group 2 elements – the alkaline earth metals
   Electronic structures
   Physical properties
   Reactions of the Group 2 metals
   Compounds of the Group 2 metals
   Chemistry at work: Compounds of the Group 2 metals

10. **Group 7 (p-block elements)**   **120**
    Group 7 elements – the halogens
    The halogens as oxidising agents
    Reactivity of the halogens
    Quantitative analysis

Reactions of the halogens and their compounds
Hydrogen halides
Oxidation number and the halogens
Oxohalogen compounds
Chemistry at work: Chlorine and its compounds
Chemistry at work: Bromine and iodine

11.*d-Block elements   132
Physical properties
Electronic structures
Variable oxidation number
Complex ions
Coloured compounds
More about ligands
Chemistry at work: Transition metal complexes
Redox reactions of transition metal compounds
Catalysis and the transition metals
Autocatalysis
Chemistry at work: Copper

Further questions on The Periodic Table   152

Organic Chemistry 1

12. Introduction to organic chemistry   158
Functional groups
Homologous series
Naming organic compounds
Structural isomers

13. Alkanes   166
Introduction
Physical properties of the alkanes
Reactions of the alkanes
Pollution from combustion
Substitution reactions of the alkanes
Chemistry at work: Petrol
Chemistry at work: Getting rid of waste

14. Alkenes   176
Introduction
Stereoisomers
Geometric isomerism in alkenes
Reactions of the alkenes
The mechanism of addition
Predicting products of addition
Mechanism of addition with halogens
Chemistry at work: Cracking
Chemistry at work: Use of ethene and epoxyethane

15. Halogenoalkanes (Haloalkanes)   187
Introduction
Reactions of the halogenoalkanes
Mechanism of nucleophilic substitution
Elumination reactions of halogenoalkanes
Chemistry at work: Uses of halogenoalkanes

16. Alcohols   195
Introduction
Physical properties
Reactions of the alcohols
Breaking the O—H bond
Nucleophilic substitution in alcohols
Dehydration reaction
Chemistry at work: Ethanol
Chemistry at work: Other alcohols

Further questions on Organic Chemistry 1   203

Organic Chemistry 2

17.*Aromatic compounds   209
The structure of benzene
The nature of the benzene ring
Attack on the benzene ring
Electrophilic substitution in benzene
Nitration
Sulphonation
Halogenation
Friedel–Crafts reactions
Addition reactions of benzene
Reactions of substituted arenes
Reactions in side-chains
Chemistry at work: Dyes
Chemistry at work: Aromatic compounds in agrochemicals

18.*Aldehydes and ketones   221
Introduction
Reactions of aldehydes and ketones
Nucleophilic addition to aldehydes and ketones
Condensation reactions of aldehydes and ketones
Chemistry at work: Aldehydes and ketones

19.*Carboxylic acids and related compounds   229
Introduction
Reactions of carboxylic acids
Acid chlorides
Acid anhydrides
Esters
Chemistry at work: Esters and carboxylic acids

20.*Organic nitrogen compounds 239
Introduction
Amines as bases
Reactions of amines
Amides
Nitriles
Amino acids
Optical isomerism
Chemistry at work: Proteins

21.†Polymers 250
Plastics
Properties of plastics
Addition polymers
Mechanism of addition polymerisation
Condensation polymerisation
Chemistry at work: New developments in plastics
Chemistry at work: New developments in polymers
Chemistry at work: Biodegradable plastics

22.*Organic synthesis 262
Synthetic routes
Calculating yields
'Stepping up' a homologous series
'Stepping down' a homologous series
Adding a carbon chain to an aryl compound
Summaries of organic reactions – alkenes, halogenoalkanes (Grignard reagents), alcohols, benzene, aldehydes, ketones, carboxylic acids, acid chlorides, esters, amines, amides, nitriles
Chemistry at work: Pharmaceutical drugs
Chemistry at work: Other drugs

23.*Organic analysis 274
Chemical analysis
Analysis using a mass spectrometer
Spectrometry
Ultraviolet and visible spectrometry
Infra-red spectrometry
Nuclear magnetic resonance (n.m.r.)
High resolution n.m.r.
Chemistry at work: Instrumental analysis

Further questions on Organic Chemistry 2 288

Energy and Rates

24. Enthalpy changes 295
Enthalpy changes (ΔH)
Enthalpy level diagrams
Working out enthalpy changes in solutions
Standard conditions
Using enthalpy cycles
Using enthalpies of formation
Average bond enthalpies
Chemistry at work: Enthalpy changes

25.*Lattice enthalpy 310
Calculating lattice enthalpies
Born–Haber enthalpy level diagram
Theoretical values of $\Delta H_{\text{lattice}}^{\ominus}$ compared with actual values
Lattice enthalpy and dissolving

26.*Entropy and free energy 318
Entropy
Calculating entropy changes
Free energy
Calculating changes in free energy

27. Kinetics – rates of reaction 325
Introduction
Investigating rates of reaction
Graphs and rates of reaction
Collision theory
Factors affecting rates of reaction
Effect of surface area
Effect of concentration
Effect of pressure
Effect of temperature
Effect of a catalyst
Catalysts in industry
Effect of enzymes
Chemistry at work: Immobilised enzymes

28.*Rate equations 338
Results from rate experiments
Rate equations
Order of a reaction
Finding out rate equations
Chemistry at work: Rapid reactions
Mechanisms and kinetics
Hydrolysis of bromoalkanes

Further questions on Energy and Rates 350

Equilibria and Redox

29. Equilibrium mixtures   **356**
Introduction
Closed systems and equilibrium
Affecting the position of equilibrium
Changing concentration
Changing pressure
Changing temperature and equilibrium
The Contact Process
The Haber Process
Making nitric acid in industry
Chemistry at work: Uses of nitric acid in industry
Chemistry at work: Building a chemical plant

30.* Equilibrium constants   **368**
Introduction
Values of K_c
Finding K_c by experiment
Gases at equilibrium (K_p)
The effect of changing conditions on K_c and K_p
Chemistry at work: Equilibria and growing crops

31.* Acid/base equilibria   **380**
Introduction
Neutralisation
The Brønsted–Lowry theory of acids and bases
pH values
Strong and weak acids
Dissociation constants (K_a)
pH of weak acids
pH of water
pH of alkalis
Indicators
pH curves
Choosing an indicator
Buffer solutions
pH of a buffer solution
Chemistry at work: Acids and bases

32. Redox: Extraction of metals   **398**
The Reactivity Series
Extracting metals with carbon
Extraction of iron
Iron into steel
Chemical reduction of other metal ores (tungsten, titanium and chromium)
Chemistry at work: Uses of tungsten, titanium and chromium
Extracting reactive metals
Extraction of aluminium
Recycling

33.* Redox: Electrode potentials   **407**
Introduction
Half cells
Cell diagrams
Standard electrode potentials
Using standard electrode potentials
Calculating $E^\ominus$ cell
Electrode potentials and corrosion
Chemistry at work: Preventing corrosion
Chemistry at work: Cells and batteries/Fuel cells

Further questions on Equilibria and Redox   **418**

Synoptic questions   **424**

Extra Sections

Study skills   **428**

Practical skills   **434**

Key Skills in Advanced Chemistry   **438**

Answers   **442**

Chemical tests   **458**

Periodic Table   **460**

Data pages   **462**

Index   **466**

Acknowledgements   **472**

Chapters marked * are usually not in AS level, only in A2. For the chapter marked † check the specification you are following.
For further details see: www.nelsonthornes.com/ac4u.htm

1 Atoms and electrons

▷ History of the atom

The Greeks were the first people to put forward the idea that all matter was made up from particles.
But it wasn't until the early 1800s that theories about atoms were really developed and taken seriously.

It was **John Dalton** who first tried to explain the great variety of substances by thinking of different combinations of atoms.
The word **'atom'** came from a Greek word meaning something that could not be split up. He thought of atoms as solid spheres, a bit like tiny snooker balls.
Dalton drew up a list of chemical elements. Look at the table opposite:
He believed these to be made from only one type of atom.
● Can you think of any of Dalton's ideas that we no longer believe?

At the end of the century, another scientist called **J.J. Thomson** was investigating the effects of high voltages on gases.
In one of his experiments he noticed some strange rays coming from the negative electrode.
Look at the experiment below:

Which substances above did Dalton mistakenly label as elements?
(There is a list of elements on page 89)

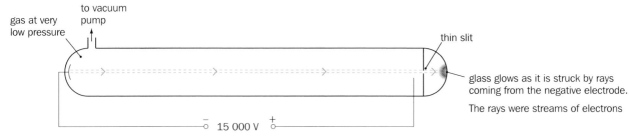

gas at very low pressure

to vacuum pump

thin slit

glass glows as it is struck by rays coming from the negative electrode.

The rays were streams of electrons

15 000 V

He carried out more work on these rays and found that they were made from tiny negatively charged particles. Their mass was much less than that of any atom.
To explain these results Thomson put forward a new model of the atom.
He said that the negative particles were **electrons**. He believed that they must have come from *inside the atoms* in his apparatus.
He also knew that atoms were neutral. They had no overall charge on them.
So he suggested that the electrons were embedded in a cloud of positive charge.
Look at his vision of an atom below:

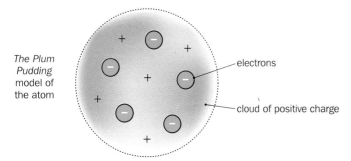

The Plum Pudding model of the atom

electrons

cloud of positive charge

People called this the Plum Pudding theory. Can you see why?
The positive cloud was thought of as the pudding mixture.
What would represent the electrons in this model?

The discovery of radioactivity at this time was important.
It gave scientists a new way to probe inside atoms.
In 1909 two students working with **Ernest Rutherford** did an experiment that would again change the way we think about atoms.
The students at Manchester University fired heavy radioactive particles (alpha particles) at a very thin gold foil.
They expected the alpha particles to crash straight through the foil.
After all, the atoms were thought to be mainly clouds of charge.

Can you imagine their surprise when some of the alpha particles were deflected? A few even bounced back off the atoms!
Their experiment is shown below:

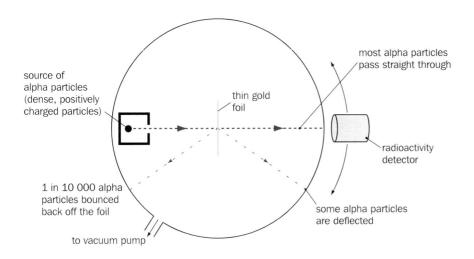

Rutherford explained their results by suggesting a new model of the atom.
He thought that the positive charge was not spread out in a cloud, as in the Plum Pudding theory. He believed that all the positive charge was packed into a very small, incredibly dense **nucleus** at the **centre of the atom**. So if one of the positively charged alpha particles struck the nucleus of an atom head on, it would be repelled away.
(See the diagram on page 18.)

But what about the electrons? Rutherford pictured them as flying around the nucleus at high speeds.
Look at his idea of the structure of an atom below:

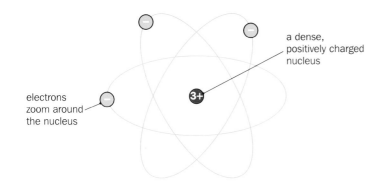

▷ Electron shells or energy levels

A few years after Rutherford put forward his theory of atomic structure, the model was refined again.
Niels Bohr was trying to explain atomic spectra.
These are the characteristic amounts of energy given out (or absorbed) by different atoms.

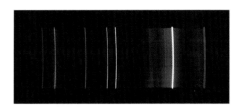

This is part of the atomic spectrum of helium

You can see part of an atomic spectrum by using a hand-held spectroscope to look at a discharge tube. The tube contains atoms of gas.
Their electrons have been excited by electrical energy.
Or you can look at a Bunsen flame through a spectroscope during a flame test on a metal compound. In this case, the electrons have been excited by heat energy from the flame.
You will see lines of intense colour in the spectrum.

Bohr explained the lines in atomic spectra by assuming that the electrons in an atom could only have **certain fixed energies**.
When excited, an electron jumps up to a higher **energy level**.
When it falls back again, the difference in energy is given out.
Sometimes we can see this as visible light energy.

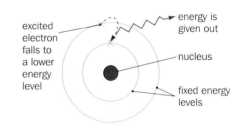

So in 1913 a revised model of the atom had the electrons occupying fixed energy levels or **'shells'**.
● Think back to your previous work on atoms. Can you remember how many electrons can fit into the first energy level (or shell)?

Look at this model applied to the atoms below:

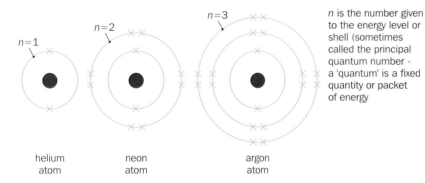

n is the number given to the energy level or shell (sometimes called the principal quantum number - a 'quantum' is a fixed quantity or packet of energy

The electrons fill up the energy levels (or shells) from the middle outwards.
They occupy the lowest energy level possible. When that is full, they start filling the next level up.

● Do you think it likely that this was the last development of the model?
You can see that each new model is needed to explain new observations.
Each model is useful for explaining some ideas, but not so good for others.
● What have you used the model shown above to explain?
(We will revise and extend our work on bonding in Chapters 4, 5 and 6.)

As you can imagine, there have been many refinements to our ideas about atoms throughout the last century. But the major change that we need to consider is the evidence for **sub-shells**.

Evidence for shells and sub-shells

As you know from the last page, atomic spectra give us
evidence that electrons occupy energy levels (or shells).
Look at one of the series of lines you get from atoms of hydrogen:

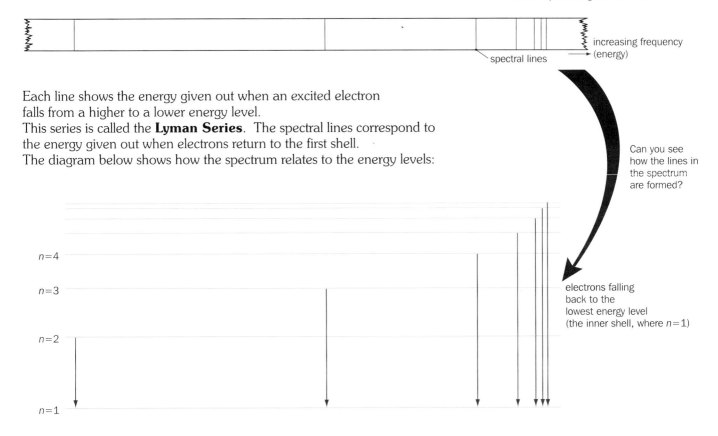

increasing frequency
(energy)

spectral lines

Each line shows the energy given out when an excited electron
falls from a higher to a lower energy level.
This series is called the **Lyman Series**. The spectral lines correspond to
the energy given out when electrons return to the first shell.
The diagram below shows how the spectrum relates to the energy levels:

Can you see
how the lines in
the spectrum
are formed?

$n=4$

$n=3$

$n=2$

$n=1$

electrons falling
back to the
lowest energy level
(the inner shell, where $n=1$)

If you use more sensitive apparatus to look at atomic spectra,
you can see some interesting details. What may appear to be single lines
are in fact two or more lines that are very close together.
So how can we explain these lines?

Look at the diagram opposite:
The energy levels (above $n = 1$) seem to be made up from
two or more shells. Their energy levels are very similar.
We call these **sub-shells**.

The diagram below shows you how the sub-shells are arranged:

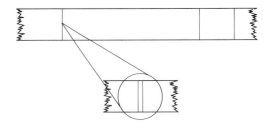

*A double line shown by 'high resolution
spectroscopy'. There must be two energy levels
(sub-shells) very close together to explain these
lines*

The sub-shells are labelled by letters s, p and d
(there are also f sub shells in large atoms)

*Notice how the sub-shells from the 3rd and 4th energy levels
overlap.

11

▷ Evidence from ionisation enthalpies

We can get further evidence of electron shells and sub-shells
from ionisation enthalpies (sometimes called ionisation energies).

> **Ionisation enthalpies measure the amount of energy
> needed to remove electrons from an atom.**

The ***first ionisation enthalpy*** refers to the removal of the first electron,
the ***second ionisation enthalpy*** to the second electron, and so on.

$$Na(g) \longrightarrow Na^+(g) + e^- \qquad \text{1st I.E.}$$
$$Na^+(g) \longrightarrow Na^{2+}(g) + e^- \qquad \text{2nd I.E.}$$

Each successive ionisation enthalpy tells us the energy needed to remove
one mole of electrons from the atom or ion we start with.

Look at the pattern you get as each of the electrons is stripped off
an atom of sodium:

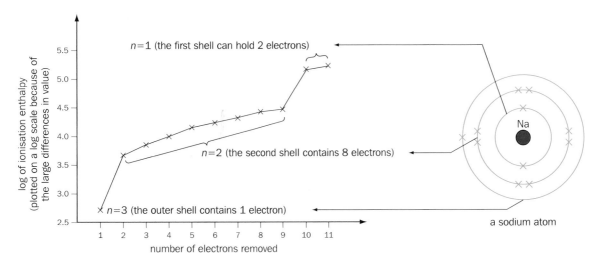

a sodium atom

Remember that electrons are negatively charged. They are attracted to
the positively charged nucleus.
Sodium's first electron is easiest to remove. Can you think why?
This electron is ***furthest away from the nucleus***.
It is also **shielded** by two inner shells of electrons from the attractive force
of the nucleus.

The second electron is much more difficult to remove.
This is because it is from a new shell which is nearer
to the nucleus.
The third electron is a little more difficult again. It is removed from
the same shell, but the same positive charge on the nucleus now has fewer
electrons to hold on to. So the mutual attraction is increased.

- Look at the graph above: How many electrons are removed from
  this second shell?
- How many electrons does a sodium atom have in total?
- Why is there another big jump between the 9th and 10th ionisation enthalpies?
- What pattern would you find if you plotted a similar graph for carbon
  (which has 6 electrons)?

This gives us further evidence for the main energy levels
(or quantum shells).
We can also get evidence for sub-shells using ionisation enthalpies.
This is explained on page 96.

She loves me; she loves me not

Electrons in sub-shells

You have seen how the sub-shells are arranged on page 11.
We will see how the electrons fill up these sub-shells
on the next page.
But first we need to know a bit more about them.
We can think of each sub-shell as being made up from
one or more **orbitals**.
The orbitals contain the electrons. They define the space
that an electron (or pair of electrons) can occupy.
You can see some diagrams of orbitals on page 15.

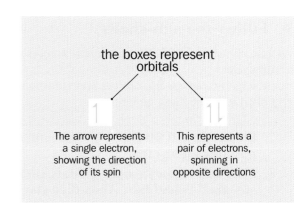

An orbital can hold a *maximum of 2 electrons.*
Each electron has a negative charge, so the electrons
in the same orbital will tend to repel each other.
However, they spin in opposite directions. This produces
a small magnetic force of attraction between the electrons.
You need to know that:

---

s sub-shells can hold 2 electrons (only 1 pair). There is only one orbital.
p sub-shells can hold 6 electrons (3 pairs). There are 3 orbitals.
d sub-shells can hold 10 electrons (5 pairs). There are 5 orbitals.

F subShells can hold 14 electrons (7 pairs) There are 7 orbits

We can think of the orbitals as boxes, waiting to be filled with electrons.
Look at the diagram opposite:

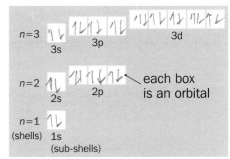

Short-hand electronic structures

Look at the diagram below, which shows the arrangement of electrons
in a sodium atom:

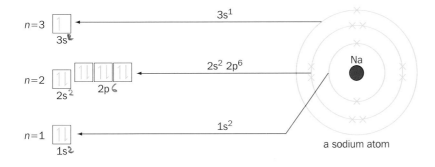

a sodium atom

This can be shown as: **$1s^2 2s^2 2p^6 3s^1$**

- What do you think the large numbers stand for? Orbits
- What do the small numbers above the line tell us? many in orbit

You can see that sodium has 2 completely filled shells
i.e. $n = 1$ and $n = 2$ shells. It has one electron in the 3rd shell, which
occupies the 3s sub-shell.

- Can you write the electron structures of the following atoms?
Use the shorthand shown above, showing the number of electrons in
each sub-shell:
helium (with 2 electrons), carbon (6 electrons) and neon (10 electrons).

$H = 1s^2$

$C = 1s^2 2s^2 2p^2$

$N = 1s^2 2s^2 2p^6$

13

▷ Filling the sub-shells

We have now seen how electrons are arranged
in sub-shells.
But in which order are the orbitals and sub-shells filled?
You need to know these *general* rules:

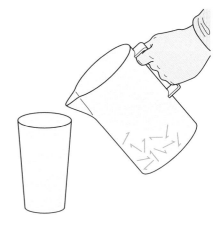

> **1. Electrons will fill the sub-shell with the lowest possible energy first.**
> **2. They will occupy empty orbitals singly until a sub-shell is half full. Then they start pairing up.**

Let's look at the first 10 elements:
The electron structures of some atoms are drawn for you.
- Can you draw some of the others?

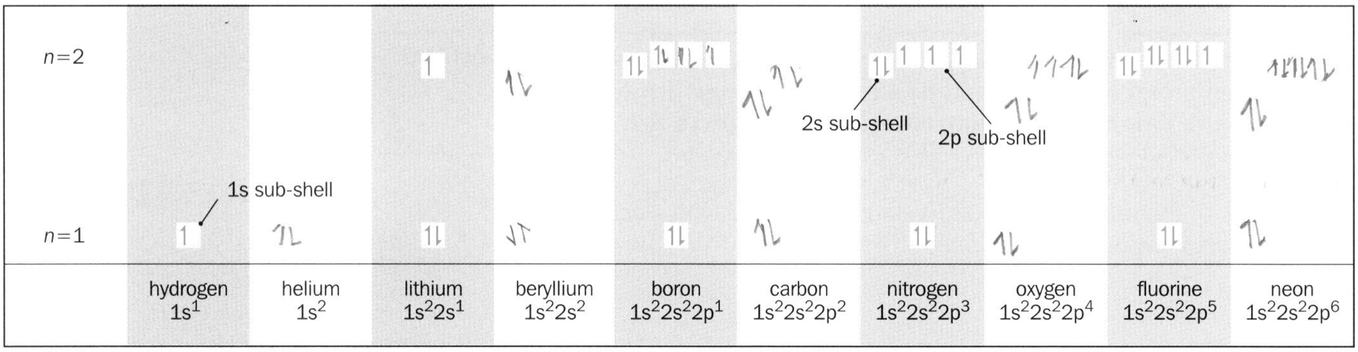

	hydrogen $1s^1$	helium $1s^2$	lithium $1s^2 2s^1$	beryllium $1s^2 2s^2$	boron $1s^2 2s^2 2p^1$	carbon $1s^2 2s^2 2p^2$	nitrogen $1s^2 2s^2 2p^3$	oxygen $1s^2 2s^2 2p^4$	fluorine $1s^2 2s^2 2p^5$	neon $1s^2 2s^2 2p^6$

(diagram showing n=1 (1s sub-shell) and n=2 (2s sub-shell and 2p sub-shell) orbital boxes with arrows representing electrons for each element)

The next atom is sodium. The 1s, 2s and 2p sub-shells are full,
so where does sodium's outer electron go?
(You can check your answer on page 13).
- Now you can try to work out the electron structure of:
magnesium (with 12 electrons),
sulphur (16 electrons), and
argon (18 electrons).

(handwritten notes)
Mg $1s^2\ 2s^2\ 2p^6\ 3s^2$
S $1s^2\ 2s^2\ 2p^6\ 3s^2\ 3p^4$
Arg $1s^2\ 2s^2\ 2p^6\ 3s^2\ 3p^6$

Larger atoms

Look back to page 11:
The bottom diagram shows us that the main energy levels
get closer together as you go further from the nucleus.
Can you see where sub-shells from different energy levels
start to overlap?

The 4s sub-shell is at a slightly lower energy level than the 3d sub-shell.
So what would you expect the arrangement of electrons
in a potassium atom, with 19 electrons, to be?
(Remember rule 1 above).

Can you see why potassium's electron structure is
$1s^2 2s^2 2p^6 3s^2 3p^6$**4s^1**?
(It is **NOT** $1s^2 2s^2 2p^6 3s^2 3p^6$**3d^1**.)

Half-full sub-shells

The rules for filling sub-shells are sometimes broken
with larger atoms.
As you know, full shells of electrons are very stable.
There is also some **added stability when a sub-shell is half full.**
● How many electrons are required to half fill:
an s sub-shell; a p sub-shell; a d sub-shell?
Look at the electronic structures of chromium and copper:

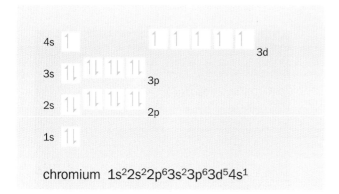

chromium $1s^22s^22p^63s^23p^63d^54s^1$

copper $1s^22s^22p^63s^23p^63d^{10}4s^1$

Why do these surprise you?
According to the rules, how would you expect
chromium's electrons to be arranged?
Chromium can achieve a half-filled sub-shell
by having only one electron in the 4s sub-shell.
This reduces repulsion between electrons to a minimum.

Would you expect copper's outer electrons to be arranged .... $3d^94s^2$?
By having the 4s sub-shell half full, copper atoms can have
a completely full 3d sub-shell. This is a more stable arrangement.

We can explain the stability of the full and half-full shells
by looking at the shapes of orbitals.
We can use mathematical calculations to find the most likely
positions of electrons in each orbital.
This gives us the following 'shapes' of the orbitals:

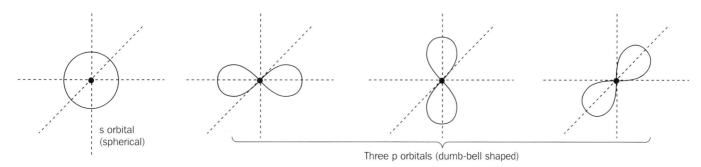

s orbital
(spherical)

Three p orbitals (dumb-bell shaped)

The five d orbitals are more complex, but are mainly dumb-bell shaped like p orbitals

When these are full the charge is spread evenly around the nucleus.
This makes an atom stable.
This is also true when *every* orbital in a sub-shell contains
only one electron, making it half full. Again, the charge is evenly distributed,
and repulsion between electrons is minimised.
So the atom is more stable than it would be with other
possible electron arrangements.

▷ Chemistry at work: Atoms and electrons

You have seen from pages 10 and 11 how excited electrons
can give out energy. By absorbing some energy,
electrons can jump into higher energy levels.
When they return to lower energy levels they give out
the difference in energy as radiation (which is sometimes visible light).
This has been very useful in a variety of applications:

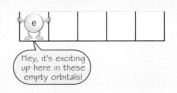

Hey, it's exciting up here in these empty orbitals!

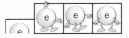

Lasers

The word laser stands for
light **a**mplification by **s**timulated **e**mission of **r**adiation.
A laser contains a tube with atoms ready to be excited.
The atoms can be anything from a noble gas to a ruby rod.
Their electrons are excited (for example by an ultraviolet flash lamp
or by electricity) and jump into higher energy levels.
When some fall back, the radiation is reflected up and down
the tube by mirrors at either end.
This causes a chain reaction and a high energy pulse of radiation
is produced. One of the mirrors is partially transparent and
lets the pulse escape from the tube.
Look at the photographs to see some uses of lasers.

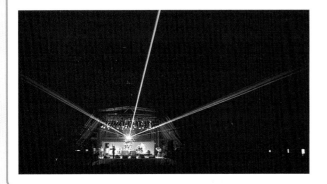

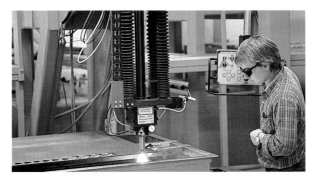

Luminescence

The electrons in some substances absorb energy,
then emit it as light. This is called luminescence.
You might have seen the glowing plastic tubes
on sale at seaside resorts. This phenomena is used
in safety sticks used to attract the attention of rescuers.
Some animals can also produce chemicals that emit light.

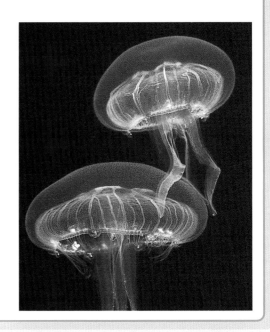

Summary

- Atoms consist of a positively charged nucleus, with negatively charged electrons orbiting the nucleus.
- The electrons orbit in shells or energy levels.
- Each shell is made up of sub-shells, e.g. s, p and d sub-shells.
- s sub-shells can hold a maximum of 2 electrons.
- p sub-shells can hold 6 electrons.
- d sub-shells can hold 10 electrons.
- (f sub-shells exist in the largest atoms, and these hold up to 14 electrons)
- Each sub-shell contains one or more orbitals. These hold a maximum of 2 electrons.
- When a pair of electrons occupy an orbital, the electrons spin in opposite directions.

▷ Questions

1 a) What is the charge on the nucleus of an atom?
   b) How many electrons can fit into the following:
      i) the 2s sub-shell, *2*
      ii) the 3p sub-shell, *6*
      iii) the 3d sub-shell? *10*
   c) What can you say about the spin of a pair of electrons occupying the same orbital? *opposite spin*

2 a) Describe the experiment that first suggested to scientists that atoms contain a nucleus.
   b) Why were the results of the experiment a surprise? *repelled*
   c) How was the model of the atom revised as a result of this experiment? *compact positive charge in center*
   d) Why was gold foil a suitable material to bombard in this experiment?
   e) Early investigators into atomic structure were at risk of getting cancer. Why? *Radiation*

3 a) Why do atomic spectra suggest that electrons orbit the nucleus in fixed energy levels or shells?
   b) What would you expect to see in an atomic spectrum if the electrons could possess any amount of energy at all?
   c) Look at the lines below from the atomic spectrum of hydrogen:

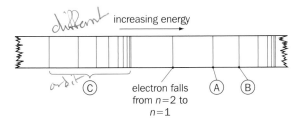

different   increasing energy →

orbit Ⓒ   electron falls
          from $n=2$ to
          $n=1$ Ⓐ   Ⓑ

   i) What does the letter n represent? *orbit*
   ii) What causes the line in the spectrum labelled A?
   iii) What causes the line in the spectrum labelled B?
   iv) What causes the series of lines labelled C?
   d) Sketch the spectra above, but extend your diagram to show the next set of lines. Explain your sketch.
   e) How can atomic spectra provide us with evidence of sub-shells?

4 a) What do we mean by the **first ionisation enthalpy** (or ionisation energy) of an atom?
   b) Look at the ionisation enthalpies of boron shown below:

	kJ mol^{-1}	log$_{10}$ I.E.
1st ionisation enthalpy	801	
2nd ionisation enthalpy	2427	
3rd ionisation enthalpy	3660	
4th ionisation enthalpy	25 026	
5th ionisation enthalpy	32 828	

Find the logarithm of each ionisation enthalpy to complete the table above.
Then plot a graph of log$_{10}$ (ionisation enthalpy) against the number of electrons removed.
(You can find a similar graph on page 12.)

   c) Explain the shape of your graph.
   d) Sketch the graphs you would expect if you did a similar thing for all the ionisation enthalpies of:
      i) sulphur (with 16 electrons), and
      ii) potassium (with 19 electrons).

5 a) Draw a sketch diagram showing the relative energies of the 1s, 2s, 2p, 3s, 3p, 3d, 4s and 4p sub-shells.

6 The electronic structure of sodium can be shown like this: $1s^2 2s^2 2p^6 3s^1$

   a) Use the same notation to show the arrangement of electrons in:
      i) nitrogen (7 electrons)
      ii) chlorine (17 electrons)
      iii) calcium (20 electrons)
      iv) titanium (22 electrons)
      v) chromium (24 electrons)
      vi) iron (26 electrons)
      vii) copper (29 electrons).
      viii) krypton (36 electrons)

   b) Explain the electronic structures you have given above for i) calcium, ii) chromium, and iii) copper.

17

2 Atoms and the nucleus

▷ Inside the nucleus

On page 9 we saw the experiment that prompted
Ernest Rutherford to suggest that there is a nucleus
at the centre of every atom.
Look back to the experiment carried out by his students,
Geiger and Marsden:

The diagram below shows Rutherford's interpretation:

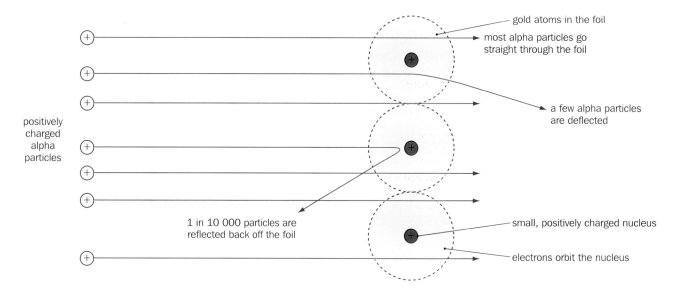

Protons

The nucleus of an atom is positively charged
and it is incredibly dense.

The positively charged particles in the nucleus
are called **protons**.
Atoms are neutral. They carry no overall charge.
Remember that an electron is negatively charged.
The size of this charge is equal to the size of the positive charge
on a proton.
Therefore we can say that in any atom the number of protons
is the same as the number of electrons.
This number is called the **atomic number** (or **proton number**).

> **Atomic number = the number of protons in an atom
> (which equals the number of electrons)**

Each chemical element has its own particular atomic number.
This corresponds to the element's position in the Periodic Table.

You can find out more about the Periodic Table in Chapter 7.

Neutrons

In the early days of exploring atomic structure, scientists came across a problem.
They had already found that a proton was 1840 times heavier than an electron.
In other words, the electrons' contribution to the mass of an atom
was negligible. The mass was concentrated into the nucleus.

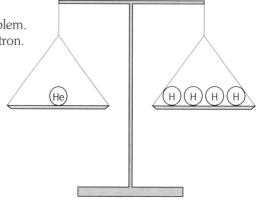

They knew that hydrogen had the lightest of all atoms, with just one proton
in its nucleus. Atoms of helium were the second lightest, with 2 protons.
Yet experiments had shown that helium atoms were 4 times heavier
than hydrogen atoms.
Why weren't the helium atoms twice as heavy as hydrogen atoms?
How could the difference be explained?

Helium is 4 times heavier than hydrogen

Scientists proposed that another type of sub-atomic particle must exist
inside the nucleus.
This particle must carry no charge, but have a mass equal to a proton.
They called the particle a **neutron**.

The problem with hydrogen and helium (and other elements) could now be solved.
The nucleus of a helium atom must contain 2 neutrons,
as well as its 2 protons.
This makes it 4 times as heavy as a hydrogen atom,
which has 1 proton and no neutrons.

It took years before experimental evidence for neutrons was discovered.
The fact that they were neutral made them very difficult to detect.
It wasn't until 1932 that James Chadwick solved the problem.
He did an experiment in which his observations only made sense
by assuming a stream of neutral particles were present in his apparatus.
Look at his experiment below:

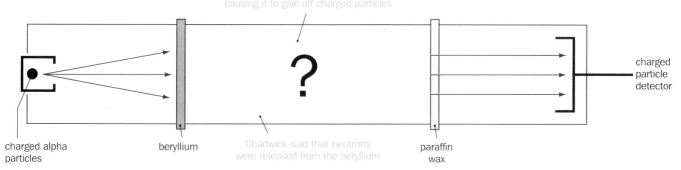

no charged particles could be detected here.
Yet something was crashing into the paraffin wax
causing it to give off charged particles

charged
particle
detector

charged alpha
particles

beryllium

Chadwick said that neutrons
were released from the beryllium

paraffin
wax

This shows how scientists are willing to use theories,
even without direct experimental proof, as long as the ideas
help them to explain things.

Summary of sub-atomic particles		
	Relative charge	Relative mass
Proton	+	1
Neutron	0	1
Electron	−	1/1840 (negligible)

▷ Isotopes

Representing atoms

On page 18 we defined the atomic number of an atom.
Each atom also has a **mass number**.
Remember that the mass of an atom is concentrated
in its nucleus, which contains protons and neutrons.
So we define the mass number of an atom as:

mass number = number of protons + number of neutrons

This is sometimes called the **nucleon number**, where a nucleon
is the name given to a proton or a neutron.

We now have two numbers that can give us all the detail
we need to know about an atom.
These can be shown like this:

mass number (A) ⟶ 35 **Cl** ⟵ chemical symbol

atomic number (Z) ⟶ 17

This shows that the chlorine atom has 17 protons,
17 electrons and 18 neutrons.

● Can you work out the number of protons,
   electrons and neutrons in:
   $^{14}_{7}N$, $^{31}_{15}P$ and $^{235}_{92}U$

You already know that the atoms of each element have
a unique atomic number.
However, atoms of the same element can have
different mass numbers.
Can you work out how this might happen?

Isotopes are atoms of the same element with different numbers of neutrons.

Let's look at an example:

Silicon (atomic number 14) has three isotopes, with mass numbers 28, 29 and 30.
These can be represented as:

^{28}Si ^{29}Si ^{30}Si   (also represented as silicon-28, silicon-29 and silicon-30)

This table shows the number of sub-atomic particles in each isotope:

Isotope	Protons	Electrons	Neutrons
^{28}Si	14	14	14
^{29}Si	14	14	15
^{30}Si	14	14	16

As you can see, the only difference is in the number of neutrons.
The chemical reactions of each isotope of silicon will be the same.
That is because chemical properties depend on the electronic structure
of an atom.
Each isotope here will have an identical electron arrangement of
$1s^2 2s^2 2p^6 3s^2 3p^2$.

There will be slight differences in some physical properties, such as
density.

*Isotopes are a bit like Easter eggs which have the
same chocolate shell but different numbers of
sweets inside!*

▷ Relative atomic masses

It is useful to have a way to compare the masses of elements.
This helps chemists to 'count' atoms, as you will see
in the next chapter.

However, we don't use the usual units of mass, i.e. kilograms or grams.
The masses of a proton and a neutron are almost the same.
This is about 1.66×10^{-27} kg. These are such small masses
that it is more convenient to use **atomic mass units (a.m.u.)**.
The exact measurement of the unit is $\frac{1}{12}$ of the mass of a ^{12}C atom.
The ^{12}C atom is exactly 12 a.m.u.

Notice that it says above that the masses of a proton and neutron
are **almost the same**.
Nowadays masses can be measured very accurately.
Look at the actual masses below:

proton = 1.007 276 a.m.u.
neutron = 1.008 665 a.m.u.

(Electrons have a mass of 0.000 549 a.m.u.
Can you work this out in kilograms?)

Using the unit, we can compare the mass of elements
on a **relative** scale.
The **relative atomic mass (A_r)** of ^{12}C is exactly 12.
Yet the relative atomic mass of the element carbon is 12.011.
Can you think why?

The answer lies in the isotopes present in a sample of carbon.
As well as carbon-12, there are also small amounts of carbon-13
and carbon-14.
These must be taken into account when we calculate
the relative atomic mass.

> **The relative atomic mass must take into account the relative proportions
> of each isotope present in a naturally occurring sample of the element.**

Let's look at the example of silicon in more detail:

A typical sample of silicon contains
92.23% silicon-28, 4.67% silicon-29 and 3.10% silicon-30.
What is the relative atomic mass of silicon?

Imagine we have 100 atoms of silicon.
We would have 92.23 atoms of ^{28}Si, 4.67 atoms of ^{29}Si and 3.10 atoms of ^{30}Si.

Now work out the average mass of these atoms:

$$\frac{(92.23 \times 28) + (4.67 \times 29) + (3.10 \times 30)}{100}$$

$$= \mathbf{28.11}$$

▷ Mass spectrometer

We can gain useful information about isotopes
from a **mass spectrometer**.
This instrument has helped scientists find out which isotopes
of an element are present in a sample.
It also shows the proportions of each isotope in the sample.
With this information you can then work out relative atomic masses.

Let's see how the mass spectrometer works.
There are five stages we need to consider:

(1) Vaporising the sample

(2) Ionising the sample

(3) Focusing and accelerating the ions

(4) Deflecting the ions

(5) Detecting and recording the ions

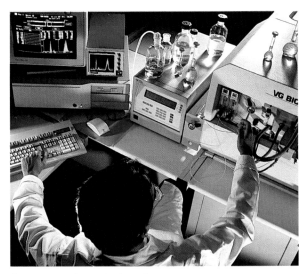

A mass spectrometer in action

Look at the diagram below:

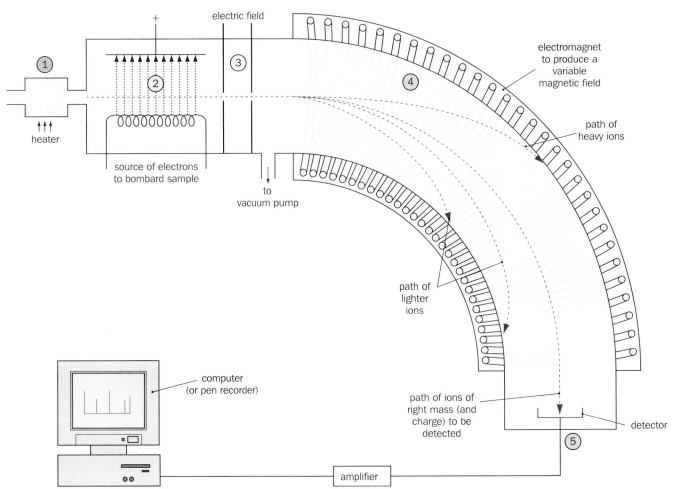

Let's see what happens in each section of the mass spectrometer:

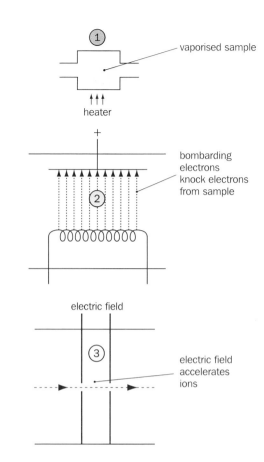

① Vaporising the sample

First of all the sample is heated to separate atoms or molecules of the sample from each other.

② Ionising the sample

Do you recall from previous work what an ion is?
You have probably met them when you considered ionic bonding.
Here's a quick reminder:
An ion is a charged particle, formed when an atom (or molecule, in the case of the mass spectrometer) loses, or gains, one or more electrons.

In the mass spectrometer, the sample is blasted with high energy electrons.
This knocks electrons from the atoms in the sample.
What charge will be on the ions formed if an electron is lost?
Remember that protons(+) balance out electrons(−) in an atom.
When one, or more, electrons is knocked off an atom
the protons now outnumber the electrons.
Therefore, the ion formed is positively charged.

③ Focusing and accelerating the ions

Electrically charged plates are used to focus the positive ions into a beam and direct them down the instrument.

④ Deflecting the ions

As you can see from the diagram, the beam of ions then enters a coil of wire. When the current is switched on it becomes an electromagnet. Its magnetic field deflects the charged ions as they pass through it.

Do you think that light ions are easier to deflect than heavy ions?
Think of a mixture of steel needles and nails dropped from the same height through the jaws of a magnet?
Which are more likely to stick to the magnet – the lighter needles or the heavier nails?

The extra momentum of the heavier ions makes them more difficult to deflect.

By varying the current passed through the coils, the strength of the magnetic field is changed.
In this way, all the ions with different masses are directed in turn into the detector.

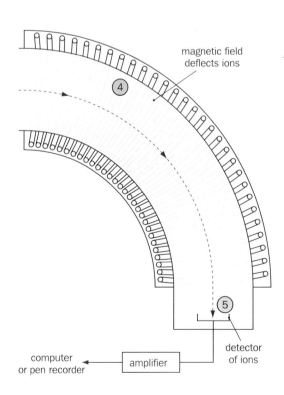

⑤ Detecting and recording the ions

As the positively charged ions hit the detector they cause electrons to move in a circuit. This produces a small pulse of electrical current that is monitored by a computer or a pen recorder.

The resulting set of lines can then be analysed and the relative atomic mass worked out.
You can see how this is done on the next page.

The mass spectrometer is now widely used to analyse carbon compounds. You can read about this on page 276.

▷ Mass spectra

You have seen on the last two pages
how the mass spectrometer works.
We can now look at the results we get from the machine.

Knowing the size of the electric and magnetic fields used,
the mass of the ions can be calculated.
However, as you know from page 21, chemists don't use
the actual masses for these small quantities.
It is more convenient to use **relative** masses.

The mass spectrometer is usually calibrated with ^{12}C.
Then the relative mass of each ion detected can be plotted.

What do you think happens to the current induced in the detector
if there is a lot of one particular ion?
The larger the current in the detector, the higher the peak recorded
in the mass spectrum. So the height of the peaks gives us
a measure of the relative proportions of each ion.

Example
Let's look at the mass spectrum of copper:

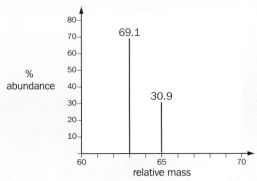

- What has caused the two peaks?
- What can you tell from the heights of the peaks?

The two peaks show the relative abundance of
$^{63}Cu^+$ and $^{65}Cu^+$ ions in a sample of copper.

Using this information we can work out the
relative atomic mass of copper, as shown below:
(The method is the same one we used on page 21 for silicon.)

Imagine you have 100 atoms of copper.
We would have 69.1 atoms of copper-63 and 30.9 atoms of copper-65.

Now we calculate the average (mean) mass of these atoms.

$$\text{relative atomic mass} = \frac{(69.1 \times 63) + (30.9 \times 65)}{100}$$
$$= \mathbf{63.5}$$

This is called the **weighted mean** because it takes
into account the relative proportions of each isotope.

Now let's see if you can interpret a more complex mass spectrum.
This is the trace recorded for the element germanium:

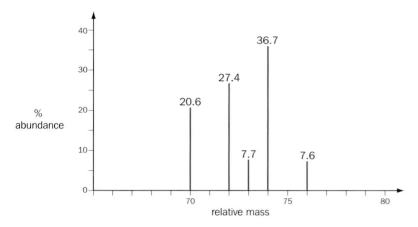

- Try to work out the relative atomic mass of germanium.
You can check your answer on page 442.

Ionising molecules

If we put molecules into a mass spectrometer, then we get
more peaks showing up.
Look at the trace from a sample of chlorine gas, Cl_2:

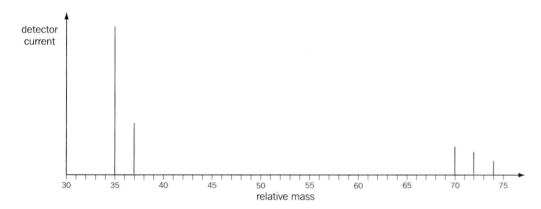

There are two isotopes of chlorine, ^{35}Cl and ^{37}Cl.
- In what proportions do the two isotopes exist?
- Work out the relative atomic mass of chlorine.
(Check your answer on page 442.)
- Can you explain the 3 peaks at 70, 72 and 74?

Remember on page 23 we said that an ion was formed from
an atom (or a *molecule*, in the case of the mass spectrometer).
When an electron is knocked from a Cl_2 molecule,
it forms a Cl_2^+ ion.
This Cl_2^+ ion could be made from:

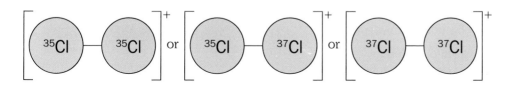

Does this explain the peaks at 70, 72 and 74?

▷ Chemistry at work: Atoms and their nuclei

No smoke without fire

We have met alpha particles on pages 9 and 18.
These radioactive particles can only travel a few centimetres through air.
However, they can cause a lot of damage to any living cells
they come into contact with.
Yet in most homes you can find a source of alpha particles
that can actually save your life.

An ionisation smoke alarm contains radioactive americium-241.
The alpha particles that it constantly emits knock electrons
from molecules in the air. The ions formed cause a small
current to flow between a pair of electrodes in the smoke alarm.
Sensitive electronic circuitry monitors the continuous current.

However, when smoke enters the gap between the electrodes,
the current is reduced. The circuitry detects the change
and the piercing alarm goes off.
So whether the smoke alarm saves you in a house fire,
or just tells you you've burned the toast again, you can thank
alpha particles for it!

The alpha particles in a smoke alarm could save your life

The next time you check the battery in your smoke alarm, you will probably see the words:

Caution Radioactive Material Am-241

Nuclear power

The fuel rods at the heart of a nuclear reactor contain uranium.
When an atom of uranium-235 absorbs a neutron, it splits
into smaller nuclei, and gives off more neutrons.
This is called **nuclear fission**. It releases about 50 times
more energy per atom than the burning of coal does.

Inside the reactor core, a chain reaction happens.
The energy is used to heat a stream of carbon dioxide gas.
The heated gas transfers its energy to water to make steam.
The steam then drives the turbines that generate electricity.

Control rods of boron or cadmium can be lowered between
the uranium fuel rods. These absorb neutrons and are used
to control carefully the chain reaction in the reactor core.
However, accidents can happen. Examples include the fire
at Windscale in the Lake District in 1957, or the even worse
disaster at Chernobyl in the Ukraine.
You can see what was left of the reactor after it exploded in 1986
in the photo opposite:
What are your views on nuclear power?

The radioactive cloud from Chernobyl drifted right over Western Europe

Uses of mass spectrometry

We have seen how chemists can use a mass spectrometer
to find relative atomic masses.
It was used on the American Viking space probe that landed
on Mars in 1976 and identified elements from their mass spectra.

On page 276 you can also see how we use it to analyse
unknown substances. It is used like this by forensic scientists
to test substances found at the scene of a crime.

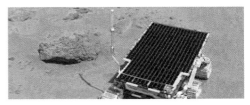

Mass spectrometry was used to identify elements on Mars

▷ Chemistry at work: What's new in atoms?

'Looking at' atoms

We can't **see** atoms even under the most powerful microscopes.
However, the latest developments do give computer-generated
images of atoms on the surface of a solid.
The technique, known as scanning probe microscopy,
can produce images like the one opposite:

We can even use the technology to move individual atoms around.
Can you see the initials of a famous company in the picture?

These were made by placing atoms of xenon in the gaps on the surface
of nickel.

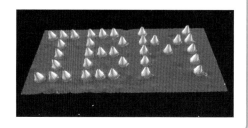

Strange things inside the nucleus

On page 19 we saw how neutrons were discovered in 1932.
Since then there have been other discoveries of weird
and wonderful particles.
Leptons and **quarks** are two groups of the smallest particles
of matter in the universe.

Members of the quark family are found in the nucleus of an atom.
They only exist when bound together.
Scientists now believe that a proton is made from two types of quark.
'Up quarks' carry a charge of $+\frac{2}{3}$ and have the mass of about 10 electrons.
'Down quarks' have a charge of $-\frac{1}{3}$, and have a mass twice that of an 'up quark'.
A proton is made up of two up quarks and one down quark.
Can you remember the charge on a proton?
Add up the charges on two 'up quarks' and one 'down quark'.
Does this produce the charge you would expect on a proton?

Neutrons contain one 'up quark'.
How many 'down quarks' do you think they contain?
Remember that neutrons carry no overall charge.

Other quarks discovered are called 'charm', 'strange',
'top' and – you've guessed it – 'bottom'!
It is thought that these only existed in the moments after
the Big Bang. They are now found only in cosmic rays
and in experiments done in particle accelerators.
Particle accelerators are used to investigate the building blocks
of matter. They produce high energy collisions
between sub-atomic particles. Then scientists search
for information in the aftermath of the collision.
Look at the diagram opposite:

The particle accelerator at Geneva contains over 4000 magnets
and has a circumference of 27 km.

Q *What did the posh duck say
to the atomic scientist?*

A *Quark, quark!*

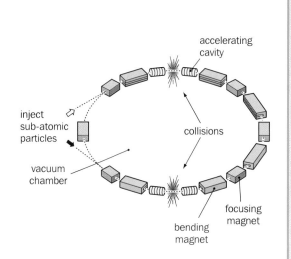

Summary

- The nucleus of an atom contains protons and neutrons.

	Relative charge	Relative mass
Proton	+	1
Neutron	0	1
Electron	−	1/1840 (negligible)

- Atomic number = the number of protons (which equals the number of electrons)
- Mass number = number of protons + number of neutrons

mass number $\longrightarrow A$

atomic number $\longrightarrow Z$ $X \longleftarrow$ chemical symbol e.g. $^{23}_{11}Na$

- **Isotopes** are atoms of the same element with different numbers of neutrons.
- The **relative atomic mass** of an element is the weighted mean mass of its naturally occurring isotopes.
- The mass spectrometer can be used to work out relative atomic masses.

▷ Questions

1 a) Which two types of fundamental particle do you find in the nucleus of an atom?
   b) Define **atomic number** and **mass number**.
   c) If two atoms are isotopes of the same element, how do they differ?
   d) Although mass numbers are always whole numbers, explain why relative atomic masses are often not.
   e) Which instrument is used to determine relative atomic masses?

2 How many protons, neutrons and electrons do you find in the atoms below? Draw a table to show your answers.

   a) $^{4}_{2}He$
   b) $^{40}_{20}Ar$
   c) $^{59}_{27}Co$
   d) $^{107}_{47}Ag$
   e) $^{166}_{68}Er$
   f) $^{235}_{92}U$
   g) $^{242}_{94}Pu$

   h) What do you notice about the number of protons compared with the number of neutrons as atoms get larger?
   i) Find out how this affects the stability of the atoms. (You might refer to page 100 for help.)

3 Calculate the relative atomic masses of the following elements. The relative abundance of their naturally occurring isotopes is given.
   a) Thallium, which contains 29.5% ^{203}Tl and 70.5% ^{205}Tl.
   b) Zirconium, which contains 51.46% ^{90}Zr, 11.23% ^{91}Zr, 17.11% ^{92}Zr, 17.40% ^{94}Zr and 2.80% ^{96}Zr.

4 Look at the diagram of the mass spectrometer below:

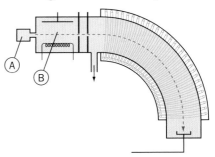

   a) What happens to the sample in the section labelled A on the diagram?
   b) What happens at B? Are the ions positive or negative? Explain your answer.
   c) Describe what happens to an ion as it follows the path shown by the dotted line.
   d) Describe the path of an ion that is lighter than the one shown above.
   e) How is the spectrometer altered to detect the complete range of ions produced?
   f) How does the current reading in the detector tell us the relative abundance of ions present?

5 Look at part of the mass spectrum of bromine below:

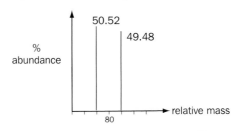

   a) Calculate the relative atomic mass of bromine.
   b) Can you explain the peaks also observed at 158, 160 and 162 in its complete mass spectrum?

28

3 Calculations using the mole

▷ Balancing equations

In this chapter we will look at the way chemists solve the problem of counting atomic and molecular particles that nobody can actually see!

Their calculations enable them to predict the amount of reactants needed to make a required amount of product.
This is an essential part of an industrial chemist's job.

Environmental chemists may have to work out the amount of pollutant in a sample of water or in the air.
Although more and more accurate sensors and instruments that can analyse samples are available, these skills are still important.

Chemists can work out exact quantities that will react together

Often calculations will involve chemical equations.
Do you recall how to balance chemical equations?
Remember that the number of atoms on either side of the equation must be the same.
In other words, no atoms can be created or destroyed in a chemical reaction.

As a reminder let's look at the reaction between hydrogen (H_2) and chlorine (Cl_2).
In sunlight the mixture of gases reacts violently to produce hydrogen chloride (HCl) gas:

$$H_2(g) + Cl_2(g) \longrightarrow HCl(g)$$

reactants   product

Can you remember what the letters in brackets represent?
Is this equation balanced?

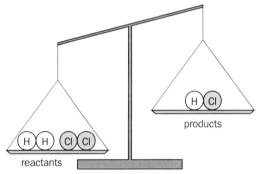

The atoms do not balance

When you count the number of atoms of reactants and product, you see that on the product side we are one H atom and one Cl atom short.
Remember we cannot change the formula of hydrogen chloride to H_2Cl_2 just to balance our equation!
But we can form 2 molecules of HCl in the reaction.

So the balanced equation becomes:

$$H_2(g) + Cl_2(g) \longrightarrow 2\,HCl(g)$$

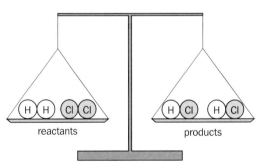

Balanced equation

You can practise balancing these equations:

1. $H_2(g) + O_2(g) \longrightarrow H_2O(g)$ $H_2O(l) + O$
2. $NaNO_3(s) \longrightarrow NaNO_2(s) + O_2(g)$ $NaNO_2(s) + O(g)$
3. $CaCO_3(s) + 2\,HCl(aq) \longrightarrow CaCl_2(aq) + H_2O(l) + CO_2(g)$
4. $2\,Na(s) + 2\,H_2O(l) \longrightarrow 2\,NaOH(aq) + H_2(g)$

▷ Mole calculations

On page 21 you saw that we can compare the masses of different elements.
Each element has a Relative Atomic Mass (R.A.M. or A_r).
The R.A.M.s help chemists to 'count' atoms.

As you know, atoms are too small to see.
Therefore, we have a big problem when we try to count them.
However, we can compare numbers of atoms quite easily.

Look at the approximate R.A.M.s in the table opposite:
Can you see that oxygen atoms are 16 times heavier than
hydrogen atoms?
Therefore, if you have 1 gram of hydrogen atoms and 16 grams of oxygen atoms,
you have the same number of hydrogen and oxygen atoms.
This is a lot of atoms!

The number of atoms in 1 gram of hydrogen is called a **mole.**
It is more accurately defined as the number of carbon atoms
in exactly 12 g of ^{12}C.

The mole is a number. It's like a dozen or a gross,
but an awful lot bigger. In fact, in 1 gram of hydrogen
there are about 602 000 000 000 000 000 000 000 atoms!
No wonder we can't see them!
This number is known as the **Avogadro constant**, and is written **6.02×10^{23}**.

Element	Approximate Relative Atomic Mass (R.A.M.) or A_r
hydrogen	1
carbon	12
nitrogen	14
oxygen	16
fluorine	19

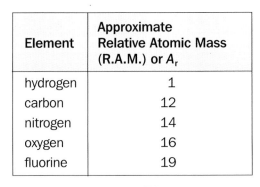

Amedeo Avogadro (1776–1856)

There are huge numbers of atoms even in test-tube reactions.
So it is more convenient to talk about moles rather than
the actual numbers involved.
Scientists weigh out substances, then say how many moles are present.
You need to know this equation:

$$\textbf{moles of atoms} = \frac{\textbf{mass}}{\textbf{R.A.M.}}$$

It's like cashing in 1p coins at the bank.
If you take 1000 1p coins to your bank, does the cashier
count out each coin?
The coins are weighed out on scales. The scales are calibrated to read
the mass of 100 1p coins as £1, so they tell the cashier how many
pounds (£'s) are on the scales.

Counting atoms takes its toll.
Just weigh them out then use the mole.

Example
How many moles of atoms are there in 4.8 g of carbon?

$$\text{moles} = \frac{\text{mass}}{\text{R.A.M.}} = \frac{4.8}{12}$$

$$= \textbf{0.4 moles}$$

Now try these yourself (the answers are at the back of the book):

● How many moles of atoms are there in:

1. 2.5 g of hydrogen   2. 3.6 g of carbon   3. 640 g of oxygen   4. 1.4 g of nitrogen   5. 0.57 g of fluorine?

(R.A.M.s (A_r): H = 1, C = 12, O = 16, N = 14, F = 19)

Changing moles to mass

You can rearrange the equation on the last page to get:

$$\boxed{\textbf{mass} = \textbf{moles} \times \textbf{R.A.M.}}$$

This tells us the mass of an element, if we know how many moles there are.

Example:
What is the mass of 0.05 moles of carbon atoms?

$$
\begin{aligned}
\text{mass} &= \text{moles} \times \text{R.A.M.} \\
&= 0.05 \times 12 \\
&= \textbf{0.6 g}
\end{aligned}
$$

If you find rearranging equations difficult, you can use the 'magic triangle'.

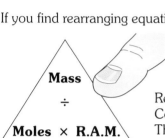

Read the question. See what you need to find out.
Cover that part of the triangle with your finger.
Then you have the equation you need!

Now you can try these:

What is the mass of:

6. 2 moles of H atoms   7. 5 moles of N atoms   8. 20 moles of O atoms
9. 0.5 moles of F atoms   10. 0.01 moles of C atoms?

Moles of molecules and compounds

You can use the same ideas for problems about molecules.
Once you have a list of relative atomic masses, you can work out the relative mass of any molecule.
You just need to know the chemical formula.

Let's look at carbon dioxide as an example:

The formula of carbon dioxide is CO_2.
Its molecules are made up of 1 carbon atom and 2 oxygen atoms.
The R.A.M. of carbon is 12.
The R.A.M. of oxygen is 16.

If we add up the R.A.M.s as in the formula, we get the **relative formula mass (M_r).**
(For some substances this number is called the **relative molecular mass**.)
So for CO_2 we have:

$$
\begin{aligned}
1 \text{ carbon} &= 1 \times 12 = 12 \\
2 \text{ oxygen} &= 2 \times 16 = \underline{+32} \\
& \ \ 44
\end{aligned}
$$

Therefore the relative formula mass (R.F.M.) of carbon dioxide is 44.

- How many times heavier than a hydrogen atom is a molecule of carbon dioxide?

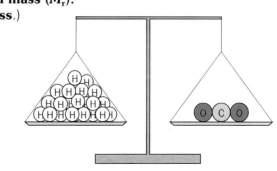

A CO_2 molecule is 44 times heavier than an H atom

▷ Relative formula mass

We can use relative formula masses to calculate the amount
of reactants and products in chemical reactions.
Before that, we need some practice using moles
and relative formula masses.
The equations are similar to those on the last page:

$$\text{moles} = \frac{\text{mass}}{\text{R.F.M.}}$$ or $$\text{mass} = \text{moles} \times \text{R.F.M.}$$

So the magic triangle becomes:

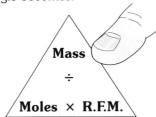

Mass

÷

Moles × **R.F.M.**

Example
How many moles are there in 0.8 g of copper(II) oxide (formula = CuO)?

Step 1 – Work out the R.F.M. by adding up the R.A.M.s:

$$\begin{aligned} \text{Cu} &= 64 \\ \text{O} &= +16 \\ \hline \text{R.F.M.} &= 80 \end{aligned}$$

Step 2 – Put information from the question and the R.F.M. into the equation:

$$\text{moles} = \frac{\text{mass}}{\text{R.F.M.}} \qquad \text{moles} = \frac{0.8}{80} = \textbf{0.01 moles}$$

● Now you can try these:
How many moles are there in:

1. 54 g of H_2O **2.** 1.7 g of NH_3 **3.** 4.8 g of CH_4 **4.** 0.14 g of C_2H_4 **5.** 32 g of NH_4NO_3?

Now let's try a harder example:

Example
What is the relative formula mass of
aluminium nitrate, $Al(NO_3)_3$?
(R.A.M.s: Al = 27, N = 14, O = 16)

Sometimes a formula has a number outside a pair of brackets.
This tells us that *all* the atoms inside the brackets
are multiplied by the number outside.
So in aluminium nitrate, we have:
1 aluminium, 3 nitrogens and 9 oxygens.

Now let's add up their R.A.M.s to get the answer:

$$\begin{aligned} 1\,\text{Al} &= 1 \times 27 = 27 \\ 3\,\text{N's} &= 3 \times 14 = 42 \\ 9\,\text{O's} &= 9 \times 16 = +144 \\ \hline & 213 \end{aligned}$$

*Chemists can 'count' atoms by weighing
substances*

Therefore the R.F.M. of aluminium nitrate is **213**.
In other words, 1 mole of aluminium nitrate weighs 213 g.

▷ Moles in chemical equations

Now we can look at an application of our work with moles:
Imagine that you are the manager of a chemical plant.
When a customer orders some of your product,
you need to know how much raw material you need
to order yourself.
This is where chemical equations help us out.

We can use balanced equations to predict
the masses of reactants and products.
Let's look at an example:

Example
Iron(III) oxide is heated with carbon in a blast furnace.
The iron(III) oxide is reduced to iron, and carbon monoxide is formed.
How much iron(III) oxide do you need to make 2240 tonnes of iron?
(1 tonne = 1000 kg)

Step 1: Write the balanced equation.

$$Fe_2O_3 + 3\,C \longrightarrow 2\,Fe + 3\,CO$$

Step 2: Write out the number of moles of reactants and products
from the balanced equation.

The equation above means that:
1 mole of iron(III) oxide reacts with 3 moles of carbon,
to make 2 moles of iron and 3 moles of carbon monoxide.

Step 3: Circle the information given and what you want to find out.

$$\boxed{Fe_2O_3} + 3\,C \longrightarrow \boxed{2\,Fe} + 3\,CO$$

So 1 mole of iron(III) oxide is needed to make 2 moles of iron.

Step 4: Convert the moles into masses (using R.F.M.s)

$$Fe_2O_3 \quad + \quad 3\,C \longrightarrow \quad 2\,Fe \quad + \quad 3\,CO$$
$$((56 \times 2) + (16 \times 3))\,g \qquad\qquad (56 \times 2)\,g$$
$$160\,g \qquad\qquad\qquad \longrightarrow \qquad 112\,g$$

Step 5: Use logical steps to arrive at your final answer.

So if we get 112 g of Fe from 160 g of Fe_2O_3, then
we'll get 112 tonnes of iron from 160 tonnes of Fe_2O_3.
So how many tonnes of Fe_2O_3 will give us 2240 tonnes of Fe?

*The reaction opposite is one of the changes
that take place in a blast furnace.*
You can read more about it on page 400

$\dfrac{160}{112}$ tonnes of Fe_2O_3 will give us 1 tonne of Fe.

Therefore, $\dfrac{160}{112} \times 2240 = $ **3200 tonnes of Fe_2O_3** will give us 2240 tonnes of Fe.

● Now you can try this problem:
A student burns 4.8 g of magnesium in oxygen.
What mass of magnesium oxide does she get?

MgO
24 16

▷ Moles of gases

As you know, gases are very light. It is difficult to weigh them.
However, it is quite easy to measure the **volume** of a gas.

Luckily for us, we can change the volumes of gases
straight into moles. There is no need to weigh the gas.

At room temperature (25 °C) and atmospheric pressure (1 atmosphere),
we can say that:

1 mole of any gas takes up a volume of 24 dm^3
(24 dm^3 = 24 000 cm^3)

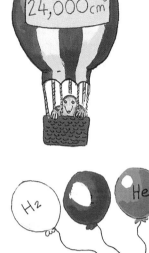

Using this information we can write this equation:

$$\text{moles of gas} = \frac{\text{volume of gas (in dm}^3)}{24}$$

In our experiments in the lab, we usually measure the volume of gas in cm^3.
In this case, the equation becomes:

$$\text{moles of gas} = \frac{\text{volume of gas (in cm}^3)}{24\,000}$$

The magic triangle is:

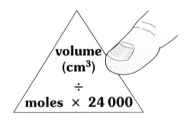

volume (cm^3)

÷

moles × 24 000

It's tricky weighing a gas!

Example
How many moles of hydrogen molecules are there in 48 cm^3 of the gas?

$$\text{moles} = \frac{\text{volume}}{24\,000} = \frac{48}{24\,000}$$

$$= \textbf{0.002 moles}$$

Now you can try these:
(Watch out for the units, dm^3 or cm^3!)

How many moles of gas molecules are there in:

1. 48 dm^3 of chlorine gas
2. 3 dm^3 of helium gas
3. 1.2 dm^3 of methane gas
4. 7200 cm^3 of oxygen gas
5. 4.8 cm^3 of nitrogen gas?

Notice that you don't need the relative atomic mass
or relative formula mass of the gases to work out
the problems above.

It's easier measuring volumes.

Volumes of gases

You can rearrange the equations on the last page to get:

volume of gas (dm³) = number of moles × 24	or	**volume of gas (cm³) = number of moles × 24 000**

Example
What volume of gas does 7 g of nitrogen gas occupy
at room temperature and atmospheric pressure?

Step 1: Work out the number of moles of gas molecules.
Remember that the formula of nitrogen gas is N_2.
Therefore, the R.F.M. of N_2 is $14 \times 2 = 28$.
So 1 mole of nitrogen gas weighs 28 g.

Use the equation $\quad \text{moles} = \dfrac{\text{mass}}{\text{R.F.M}}$.

The number of moles of nitrogen $= \dfrac{7}{28} = 0.25$ moles

Step 2: Now work out the volume of gas.

volume of gas (in cm³) $=$ moles $\times$ 24 000
$\qquad\qquad\qquad\quad = 0.25 \times 24\,000$
$\qquad\qquad\qquad\quad = \textbf{6000 cm}^3 \textbf{ of nitrogen gas.}$

How can quite large amounts of gas be stored in a small space?

- Now you can try these:
What volume do these gases occupy
at room temperature and pressure?
6. 4 g of H_2 7. 8 g of CH_4 8. 3.55 g of Cl_2 9. 0.002 g of He   10. 8.8 g of CO_2
Remember that you can check your answers at the back of the book.

Gases in equations

We can now predict, for example, the volume of gas produced in a reaction.

Magnesium ribbon fizzes in dilute sulphuric acid,
giving off hydrogen gas.
Using the ideas covered so far, we can answer the question below:
What volume of gas is given off if 2.4 g of magnesium reacts with excess acid?

Step 1: Write the balanced equation:

$\text{Mg(s)} + H_2SO_4\text{(aq)} \longrightarrow MgSO_4\text{(aq)} + H_2\text{(g)}$

Step 2: Circle what you are given in the question and what you want to find out.
This tells us that 1 mole of magnesium would give off 1 mole of hydrogen gas.

Step 3: Work out how many moles of magnesium we actually have:

$\text{moles} = \dfrac{\text{mass}}{\text{R.A.M.}} = \dfrac{2.4}{24} = 0.1$

Step 4: Work out how many moles of gas are given off by 0.1 mole of magnesium.
If 1 mole of magnesium gives 1 mole of hydrogen, then
0.1 mole of magnesium gives 0.1 mole of hydrogen gas.

Step 5: Calculate the volume that 0.1 mole of hydrogen gas will occupy.
volume of gas $=$ moles $\times$ 24 000 cm³ $= 0.1 \times 24\,000 = 2400$ cm³
So 2.4 g of magnesium will give off **2400 cm³ of hydrogen gas.**

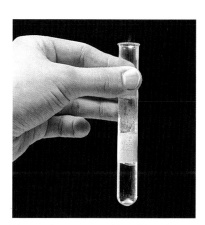

Magnesium reacts with acids, giving off hydrogen.
Can you remember the test for hydrogen gas?

▷ The ideal gas equation

Do you remember how the particles in a gas are arranged?
There are very small forces of attraction between the particles.
Here is a reminder of the different arrangements
in a solid, liquid and gas:

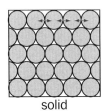

solid

*Particles in regular pattern.
They are fixed in position,
but do vibrate*

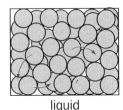

liquid

*Particles touching, but
they are free to slide
over each other*

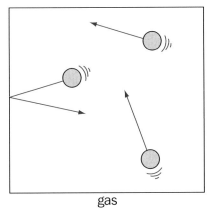

gas

*Particles zoom around with lots of
space between them*

Have you ever used a pump to blow up your bicycle tyres?
If you have, you will know that we can compress gases.
The pressure inside the tyre gets higher the more air
we pump into the tyre.
There is an inverse relationship between the pressure and volume
of a gas. In other words, if you increase the pressure of a fixed mass
of gas, its volume will decrease.

Experiments also show us that if we increase the temperature
of a gas, then its volume will also increase.
- Can you explain these observations in terms of the movement
  and arrangement of the particles in a gas?

We can show these relationships in an equation:

$$\frac{\text{Pressure } (P) \times \text{Volume } (V)}{\text{Temperature } (T)} = \text{a constant}$$

The value of the constant changes with the amount of gas we have.

If we have 1 mole of gas, it is called the **gas constant (R)**.
Its value is 8.314 J K^{-1} mol^{-1}.
(The Kelvin scale for measuring temperature is explained on page 298)

Temp. in kelvin (K) = Temp. in °C + 273

When we have a different number of moles of gas, the equation becomes:

$$\frac{\text{pressure } (P) \times \text{volume } (V)}{\text{temperature } (T)} = \text{number of moles } (n) \times R$$

We can write the equation as:

$$P \times V = n \times R \times T$$

or

PV = nRT

This is called the **ideal gas equation**.

	Units
Pressure	N m^{-2} (Pa)
Volume	m^3
Temperature	K

*Units in the ideal gas equation
(Pa = Pascal)*

Calculations using the ideal gas equation

Sometimes you are asked to work out a missing value
from the equation. You just have to put in the values given,
rearrange the equation, and do the sum!

Example
You have 2.5 moles of a gas that occupies 25 000 cm^3 at standard pressure,
assumed to be 100 000 N m^{-2}. What is the temperature of the gas?
(The gas constant is 8.314 J K^{-1} mol^{-1})

Using the ideal gas equation $PV = nRT$, we can rearrange it to find T:

$$\frac{PV}{nR} = T$$

Before we substitute in values, we need to change the volume into m^3
(1 cm^3 = 1 × 10^{-6} m^3)

$$25\,000\,\text{cm}^3 = 25\,000 \times 10^{-6}\,\text{m}^3 = 0.025\,\text{m}^3$$

Putting our known values into the equation we get:

$$\frac{100\,000 \times 0.025}{2.5 \times 8.314} = T$$

$$\mathbf{120.28\,K = T}$$

> It is useful to list the information
> given:
> $P = 100\,000$ N m^{-2}
> $V = 25\,000 \times 10^{-6}$ m^3
> $n = 2.5$ moles
> $R = 8.314$ J K^{-1} mol^{-1}
> $T = ?$

We can also use the ideal gas equation to find the relative molecular mass
of a gas or volatile liquid.
We can replace n in the equation with $\dfrac{\text{mass}}{M_r}$ (Remember from page 32 that moles = $\dfrac{\text{mass}}{\text{R.F.M.}}$)
So the equation becomes

$$PV = \frac{\text{mass}}{M_r} \times RT$$

Example
256 cm^3 of an unknown gas weighs 0.624 g at 298 K and a pressure of 101 325 N m^{-2}.
What is the relative molecular mass of the gas?

Re-arranging $PV = \dfrac{\text{mass}}{M_r} \times RT$

we get:

$$M_r = \frac{\text{mass} \times RT}{PV}$$

Substituting in the equation gives us:

$$M_r = \frac{0.624 \times 8.314 \times 298}{101\,325 \times (256 \times 10^{-6})}$$

$$\mathbf{= 59.6}$$

> It is useful to list the information
> given:
> $P = 101\,325$ N m^{-2}
> $V = 256 \times 10^{-6}$ m^3
> $mass = 0.624$ g
> $T = 298$ K
> $R = 8.314$ J K^{-1} mol^{-1}
> $M_r = ?$

The ideal gas equation only works exactly for ideal or perfect gases.
We assume particles in an ideal gas:

1. take up no space themselves
2. have no forces between their particles.

Neither of these can be true for real gases.
However, the errors are small, especially if the gas
is at a low pressure and high temperature. Can you think why?

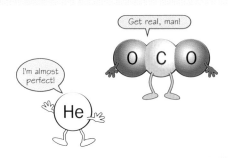

▷ Moles in solution

All bottles of solutions in a lab must be labelled.
Look at a bottle in your next experiment.
You will see that the label has the name of the solution.
Most will also show its concentration, such as 1M or 2M.
The concentration is sometimes called the **molarity** of a solution.

Is this a 1 mol dm⁻³ solution?

> **1M means that there is 1 mole of the substance dissolved in 1 dm³ (or 1000 cm³) of its solution = 1 mol dm⁻³**

Knowing this, and the actual concentration, we can work out the number of moles in any solution.

Let's look at an example:

Example
How many moles of sodium chloride are there in 200 cm³ of a 2.0 M solution?

2.0 M means that there are 2 moles in 1000 cm³ of solution.
200 cm³ is only a fifth of 1000 cm³.
Therefore, in 200 cm³ we will have a fifth of 2.0 moles, which is **0.4 moles**.

This type of logical thinking can be used to solve any moles calculation.

Here is a more difficult example:

Example
How many moles of sodium chloride are there in 22.0 cm³ of a 0.50 M solution?
Here are the logical steps:
In 1000 cm³ of the solution we have 0.5 moles.

So, in 1 cm³ of the solution we have $\dfrac{0.5}{1000}$ moles

So in 22.0 cm³ of the solution we have $\dfrac{0.50}{1000} \times 22.0$ moles

$$= \textbf{0.011 moles}$$

However, if you prefer to learn equations:

Or you can use a magic triangle again:

> **number of moles in a solution = concentration × $\dfrac{\textbf{volume of solution (in cm}^3)}{\textbf{1000}}$**

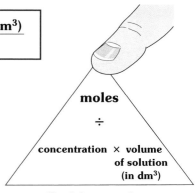

So in the first example:
the molarity (concentration) is 2.0 M, and
the volume of solution is 200 cm³.

Therefore, the number of moles $= \dfrac{2.0 \times 200}{1000} = 0.4$ moles

(Don't forget to change any volumes given in cm³ into dm³ by dividing by 1000)

Now you can try these:
● How many moles are there in:
1. 2 dm³ of 1.0 M sulphuric acid **2.** 500 cm³ of 2.0 M nitric acid
3. 250 cm³ of 1.0 M hydrochloric acid **4.** 10 cm³ of 0.50 M sodium hydroxide solution
5. 50 cm³ of 0.50 M sodium chloride solution?

Titrations

You can find out the number of moles that react together in solutions using a technique called **titration**.
In a titration experiment, you use a burette to add one solution to another.
You need a way to decide when the reaction is complete.
This is called the **end point** of the reaction.
How might you establish the end point in a reaction between an acid and an alkali?
Indicators are often used to determine end points in acid/alkali titrations.
Starch is used as an indicator in titrations that involve iodine.

A titration in progress

Example
You are given 50.0 cm^3 of sodium hydroxide solution of unknown concentration.
You decide to do a titration to find out the concentration of the solution.
Using methyl orange indicator, you titrate the alkali against a 0.10 mol dm^{-3} solution of sulphuric acid.
Having repeated the titration a suitable number of times, you find that:

It takes 22.3 cm^3 of 0.10 mol dm^{-3} sulphuric acid to neutralise 50.0 cm^3 of ? mol dm^{-3} sodium hydroxide solution.

Methyl orange

Step 1
Write the balanced equation for the reaction:

$$\text{(2NaOH(aq))} + \text{(H}_2\text{SO}_4\text{(aq))} \longrightarrow \text{Na}_2\text{SO}_4\text{(aq)} + 2\text{H}_2\text{O(l)}$$

Step 2
Circle the information given and what you need to find out.
This tells us that:
1 mole of sulphuric acid will neutralise 2 moles of sodium hydroxide.

Step 3
Find out how many moles of sulphuric acid there are in 22.3 cm^3 of 0.10 mol dm^{-3} sulphuric acid.
In 1000 cm^3 we have 0.10 moles.
So in 1 cm^3 we would have $\dfrac{0.10}{1000}$ moles

Therefore in 22.3 cm^3 we have $\dfrac{0.10}{1000} \times 22.3$ moles $= 0.00223$ moles

Methyl orange in excess alkali

Step 4
Work out how many moles of sodium hydroxide must be in the unknown solution.
We know from the balanced equation that:
1 mole of sulphuric acid will neutralise 2 moles of sodium hydroxide.
So 0.00223 moles of sulphuric acid will react with 0.00223×2 moles of sodium hydroxide.
Therefore we know that 0.00446 moles of sodium hydroxide are present in the 50.0 cm^3 of solution.

Step 5
Work out the concentration of the solution:
We need to know how many moles there would be if we had 1000 cm^3 of the unknown solution.
From Step 4 we know that:
In 50.0 cm^3 of solution we have 0.00446 moles of sodium hydroxide.

Therefore in 1 cm^3 we would have $\dfrac{0.00446}{50.0}$ moles of sodium hydroxide.

So in 1000 cm^3 we would have $\dfrac{0.00446}{50.0} \times 1000$ moles of sodium hydroxide

$= \mathbf{0.089 \; mol \; dm^{-3}}$ solution.

▷ Working out the formula

Empirical formulae

We can use moles to work out the formula of a compound.
The first step is to find out the mass of each element in the compound.
Then we can change the mass of each element into moles
and work out the simplest ratio.
This ratio is called the **empirical formula.**

Let's look at an example:

Example
A compound of nitrogen and hydrogen was broken down into its elements.
It was found that it contained 87.5% nitrogen and 12.5% hydrogen.
Its relative formula mass is 32.
What is the empirical formula of the compound?
(R.A.M.s: N = 14, H = 1)

Step 1:

Work out the **number of moles** of each element in the compound.
If you are given percentage masses, imagine you have 100 g of the compound:

$$\text{Remember that moles} = \frac{\text{mass}}{\text{R.A.M}}$$

$$\text{moles of N} = \frac{87.5}{14} = 6.25 \qquad \text{moles of H} = \frac{12.5}{1} = 12.5$$

Step 2:

Work out the **ratio** of the number of moles of each element,
to the **lowest whole numbers**.

N	:	H
6.25	:	12.5
1	:	2

> In actual experiments there is always some error involved in the results. So ratios such as 0.11 : 0.19 are taken as 1 : 2

We have twice as many H atoms as N atoms in this compound.
Therefore its **empirical formula is NH_2.**

This tells us the **simplest ratio of elements,** but the actual formula might be
NH_2 or N_2H_4 or N_3H_6 or N_4H_8 etc.
We can work out the actual formula at the top of the next page.

● Before that, see if you can work out the **empirical** formula
  of each of the compounds made from:

1. 75% of carbon and 25% of hydrogen
2. 828 g of lead and 64 g of oxygen
3. 2.4 g of carbon and 6.4 g of oxygen
4. 5.6 g of iron and 2.4 g of oxygen
5. 9.6 g of copper, 1.8 g of carbon and 7.2 g of oxygen.
(A$_r$ values: C = 12, H = 1, Pb = 207, O = 16, Fe = 56, Cu = 64)

Molecular formulae

So how do we know which formula is correct?
Look back to the start of the last example:
Which piece of information has not yet been used?

If you know the relative formula mass of the substance,
you can then establish the actual formula or **molecular formula**.

In this case we know the relative formula mass is 32.
The R.F.M. of the empirical formula NH_2 is $(14 + 2) = 16$
Therefore the molecular formula must be $(NH_2) \times 2$ because $16 \times 2 = 32$.
In other words, **the molecular formula is N_2H_4**.

Using results from experiments

You can work out the formula of a compound by
- splitting it up into its original elements, or
- making it from its elements.

In each case you need to measure the mass
of elements in the compound.

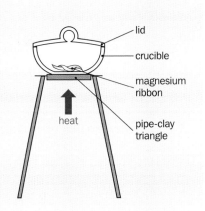

lid
crucible
magnesium ribbon
heat
pipe-clay triangle

Example – working out the formula of magnesium oxide
A student heated some magnesium ribbon as shown opposite:
The magnesium ribbons burns in air. It combines with the oxygen
to make magnesium oxide.

These are his results:

Mass of crucible + lid	= 25.00 g
Mass of crucible + lid + magnesium *before* heating	= 25.48 g
Mass of crucible + lid + magnesium oxide *after* heating	= 25.78 g

Step 1 – Work out the mass of each element in the compound.

Magnesium

Mass of crucible + lid + magnesium before heating	= 25.48 g
Mass of crucible + lid	= 25.00 g
Therefore, the mass of magnesium	= 0.48 g

Oxygen

Mass of crucible + lid + magnesium oxide after heating	= 25.78 g
Mass of crucible + lid + magnesium before heating	= 25.48g
Therefore, the mass of oxygen	= 0.30 g

Step 2 – Change the masses into moles.

Magnesium	Oxygen
$\dfrac{0.48}{24}$	$\dfrac{0.30}{16}$
= 0.02 moles	0.019 moles

Step 3 – Work out the ratio of moles of each element.

Mg		O	
0.02	:	0.019	
1	:	1	(taking experimental error into account)

Therefore the **empirical formula of magnesium oxide is MgO.**
- If the relative formula mass of magnesium oxide is 40,
  what is its actual formula?

▷ Chemistry at work: Mole calculations

Salty water

Have you ever been swimming in the sea?
If you have you will know the salty taste of sea water.
Do you know the chemical name for common salt?
We usually think of sodium chloride as the salt in sea water.
However, chemical analysis shows us that other chlorides,
such as magnesium chloride, are also present.

We can find the concentration of chloride ions in sea water
by **gravimetric analysis**.
We take a known volume of sea water and add excess
silver nitrate solution (acidified). An insoluble precipitate
of silver chloride is formed:

$$Ag^+(aq) + Cl^-(aq) \longrightarrow AgCl(s)$$

The precipitate is then filtered off and washed with distilled water.
Why do you think the silver choride is washed?
The silver chloride is heated to dryness and weighed.
We can then use the exact mass of silver choride to work out
the concentration of chloride ions in the seawater.
You can see how to do this below:

The Yangtse River burst its banks in 1998, flooding large areas of China. When millions of tonnes of floodwater entered the East China Sea the effects were noted 2500 km away. The salt content near the surface of the sea around Japan dropped by up to 20 per cent

Example
A 25.0 cm³ sample of seawater was treated with excess silver nitrate solution, then acidified.
After filtering, washing and drying, 1.940 g of silver chloride precipitate was produced.
Find the concentration of chloride ions in the seawater.

Firstly we find the number of moles of silver chloride (AgCl) produced:

Remember that moles $= \dfrac{\text{mass}}{\text{R.F.M}}$ (see page 32)

Using accurate relative atomic masses, the relative formula mass of AgCl $= 1 \times$ Ag $= 107.868$
$+ 1 \times$ Cl $= \underline{35.453}$
143.321

So we have:

$$\text{number of moles of silver chloride} = \frac{1.940}{143.321} = 0.014$$

We can see from the formula that 1 mole of AgCl contains 1 mole of Cl^- ions.
So there are 0.014 moles of chloride ions in 25.0 cm³ of seawater.
To find the concentration we need the number of moles in 1000 cm³ of seawater.
(See page 38.)
We can do this step by step:

In 1 cm³ we have $\dfrac{0.014}{25.0}$ moles

Therefore, in 1000 cm³ we would have $\dfrac{0.014}{25.0} \times 1000 = 0.56$ moles of Cl^- ions

So the **concentration of chloride ions is 0.56 mol dm^{-3}**

Sometimes solubility is given in grams per dm³.
We know that mass = moles × R.A.M. (see page 31).
So the mass of chloride ions dissolved in 1 dm³ of seawater = 0.56 × 35.453 = **19.85 g dm^{-3}**.

pH problem

An environmental scientist has been asked to investigate
the quality of water in a river where a number of dead fish
have been reported.
She collects a sample of water to analyse in the lab.
Her first tests suggest that the water is too acidic.
So she decides to find the exact concentration of acid (H^+ ions)
in the water by titrating against alkali.
The alkaline solution of sodium hydroxide is made up very accurately.
Its concentration is $0.0012 \, mol \, dm^{-3}$.
The results of her titration are shown below:

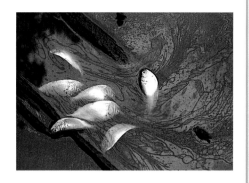

The scientist used $25.0 \, cm^3$ of the river water sample.
Having repeated the tests several times, she found that the end point
was reached when $15.8 \, cm^3$ of alkali (OH^- ions) had been added.

We can work out how many moles of OH^- ions reacted:

If we had $1000 \, cm^3$ of the solution it would contain 0.0012 moles of OH^- ions.

In $1 \, cm^3$ we would have $\dfrac{0.0012}{1000}$ moles

Therefore in $15.8 \, cm^3$ we have:

$$\frac{0.0012}{1000} \times 15.8 \text{ moles of } OH^- \text{ ions}$$

$$= 0.00002 \text{ moles}$$

The equation for the neutralisation of acid by alkali is:

$$OH^-(aq) + H^+(aq) \longrightarrow H_2O(l)$$

So we know that one mole of acid (H^+ ions) reacts with 1 mole of alkali (OH^- ions).
They react in the ratio $1 : 1$.

It follows that in the $25.0 \, cm^3$ sample of river water we must
have 0.00002 moles of H^+ ions.

In order to find its concentration we need to find out how many moles
there would be in $1000 \, cm^3$ of river water:

In $1 \, cm^3$ of river water we would have $\dfrac{0.00002}{25.0}$ moles of H^+ ions.

So in $1000 \, cm^3$ we would have $\dfrac{0.00002}{25.0} \times 1000$ moles of H^+ ions.

$$= 0.0008 \text{ moles}$$

Therefore the concentration of H^+ ions in the river was **$0.0008 \, mol \, dm^{-3}$**.

Although this seems a very low concentration of acid,
the pH of the river sample is only just above 3 (low enough to kill the fish!).

Summary

- $\text{moles} = \dfrac{\text{mass}}{A_r \text{ or } M_r}$ where A_r = relative atomic mass
M_r = relative formula mass (or relative molecular mass)

- $\text{moles of gas} = \dfrac{\text{volume in dm}^3}{24}$ at room temperature (298 K) and atmospheric pressure

- $\text{moles in solution} = \text{concentration} \times \dfrac{\text{volume (cm}^3)}{1000}$

Ideal gas equation:

$PV = nRT$ where P = pressure (N m^{-2} or Pa), V = volume (m^3), n = number of moles of gas
R = gas constant, T = temperature (K)

▷ Questions

1 Fill in the missing part of these equations:
   a) moles of atoms = <u>mass</u>
      ....
   b) At room temperature and atmospheric pressure:

   $\text{moles of gas} = \dfrac{\text{...............}}{24\,000}$

   c) $PV = n$ ....
   d) number of moles in solution

   $= \text{...........} \times \dfrac{\text{volume of solution (cm}^3)}{1000}$

2 a) What is the value of the Avogadro constant?
   b) What is the empirical formula of a substance?
   c) How is the empirical formula related to the actual formula of a substance?
   d) You are given the empirical formula of a substance.
   What other piece of information do you need in order to work out its actual formula.

Use the data pages at the back of the book to find the relative atomic masses you need to answer the following questions.

3 How many moles of atoms are there in:
   a) 28 g of nitrogen
   b) 1.6 g of oxygen
   c) 0.112 g of iron
   d) 0.04 g of helium
   e) 120 tonnes of calcium?
   (1 tonne = 1000 kg)

4 What is the mass of:
   a) 10 mole of silver atoms
   b) 2.5 moles of hydrogen atoms
   b) 0.1 mole of copper atoms
   c) 0.25 mole of carbon atoms
   d) 0.0015 mole of sodium atoms?

5 What is the relative formula mass of:
   a) water, H_2O
   b) ammonia, NH_3
   c) sodium bromide, NaBr
   d) potassium nitrate, KNO_3
   e) magnesium hydroxide, $Mg(OH)_2$?

6 How many moles are there in:
   a) 25 g of calcium carbonate, $CaCO_3$
   b) 0.64 g of sulphur dioxide, SO_2
   c) 3.42 g of aluminium sulphate, $Al_2(SO_4)_3$?

7 How many moles of gas are there in:
   (at room temperature and atmospheric pressure)
   a) 2400 cm^3 of chlorine
   b) 120 cm^3 of helium
   c) 96 cm^3 of nitrogen
   d) 24 cm^3 of methane
   e) 12 dm^3 of oxygen? (Be careful!)

8 How many moles are there in:
   a) 500 cm^3 of 0.10 M sulphuric acid
   b) 50 cm^3 of 2.0 M hydrochloric acid?

9 What mass of solid would you dissolve when making:
   a) 1000 cm^3 of a 0.25 mol dm^{-3} solution of sodium nitrate, $NaNO_3$
   b) 250 cm^3 of a 0.0100 mol dm^{-3} solution of potassium chloride, KCl?
   c) 10 cm^3 of a 0.020 mol dm^{-3} solution of calcium nitrate, $Ca(NO_3)_2$?

10 Balance these chemical equations:
   a) $H_2 + Br_2 \longrightarrow HBr$
   b) $Fe_2O_3 + Al \longrightarrow Al_2O_3 + Fe$
   c) $AgNO_3 + Cu \longrightarrow Cu(NO_3)_2 + Ag$
   d) $H_2O_2 \longrightarrow H_2O + O_2$
   e) $CH_4 + O_2 \longrightarrow CO_2 + H_2O$

11 Work out the empirical formula of the compounds that contain:
 a) 0.46 g of sodium and 0.71 g of chlorine
 b) 10 g of calcium, 3 g of carbon and 12 g of oxygen
 c) 7.8 g of potassium, 2.8 g of nitrogen and 6.4 g of oxygen
 d) 5.6 g of iron and 2.4 g of oxygen
 e) 2.73 g of carbon and 7.27 g of oxygen.

12 An oxide of copper was reduced in a stream of hydrogen gas as shown below:

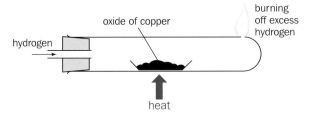

These were the results:
Mass of dish = 25.52 g
Mass of oxide of copper + dish (before reaction) = 29.52 g
Mass of copper left + dish (after the reaction) = 28.73 g

What is the empirical formula of this oxide of copper?

13 You want to find out the concentration of a solution of barium chloride. A white precipitate of barium sulphate is formed if you add sulphuric acid:

$$BaCl_2(aq) + H_2SO_4(aq) \longrightarrow BaSO_4(s) + 2\,HCl(aq)$$

You add excess sulphuric acid. The precipitate is filtered off, washed with distilled water, dried and weighed.
The mass of precipitate formed is 13.63 g.
If you started with 200 cm^3 of the barium chloride solution, what is its concentration?

14 Look back to page 42 to see how we use gravimetric analysis to find the concentration of chloride ions in sea water:
The same method was used to find the chloride ion concentration in the Dead Sea.

A 25.0 cm^3 sample from the Dead Sea gave 17.885 g of silver chloride precipitate.
Work out the concentration of chloride ions in the Dead Sea.

15 Look at the experiment opposite:
Work out the volume of hydrogen gas given off at room temperature and atmospheric pressure.

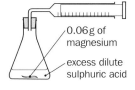

(1 mole of any gas occupies 24 000 dm^3 under these conditions.)

16 A student did an experiment to find out how much iron (in the form of Fe^{2+} ions) was in a particular type of 'health' tablet.
The student ground up the tablet, then dissolved it in water to make up 250 cm^3 of solution.
Next she took 25 cm^3 of the solution and titrated it against a solution of 0.00100 mol dm^{-3} potassium manganate(VII).
The end point is found by seeing when the first sign of a permanent purple colour is seen. The equation is:
$$5\,Fe^{2+}(aq) + \underset{purple}{MnO_4^-(aq)} + 8\,H^+(aq) \longrightarrow$$
$$5\,Fe^{3+}(aq) + Mn^{2+}(aq) + 4\,H_2O(l)$$

 a) **Explain** in terms of the reaction above, how the end point of the titration is found.

Having repeated the titration several times, the student found that it took 12.8 cm^3 of the potassium manganate(VII) solution to reach the mean end point.

 b) Calculate the number of moles of manganate(VII) ions in 12.8 cm^3 of 0.00100 mol dm^{-3} solution.
 c) Using the balanced equation, work out how many moles of Fe^{2+} ions there are in 25 cm^3 of solution taken from the dissolved tablet.
 d) How many moles of Fe^{2+} ions were there in the original 250 cm^3 of solution.
 e) What is the mass of iron in one of the 'health' tablets.

17 In this question you can find out the mass of argon gas in your bedroom.
We will use the ideal gas equation $PV = nRT$, rearranged to give:

$$n = \frac{PV}{RT} \quad \begin{array}{l} (R = 8.314\,J\,K^{-1}\,mol^{-1} \\ T = 298\,K,\ P = 100\,000\,Pa) \end{array}$$

 a) Measure the length, breadth and height of your room in metres. Multiply them together to get the volume in m^3.
 b) Now use the ideal gas equation to work out the number of moles of gas in your room.
 c) Argon makes up about 1 per cent of the atmosphere.
   How many moles of argon gas are there in your room?
 d) The relative atomic mass of argon is 39.9.
   What is the mass of argon in your room?
 e) Argon used to be called one of the Rare Gases.
   Do you think that this is a good name for argon?

45

4 Ionic compounds

This section explains the properties of materials.
To understand the ideas, you need to know about
the structure of atoms (see Chapters 1 and 2).

When we look at the Periodic Table (see page 89),
we find a group of elements with almost no reactions at all.
Can you remember the name of this group?
What can you say about the arrangement of their electrons?

The atoms of the very stable noble gases all have
full outer shells of electrons.
On page 15 we saw that when electron shells are full
the charge is spread evenly around the atom.
This makes an atom more stable.

In this chapter we will see how metals and non-metals
bond together in compounds.

▷ Electron transfer

Ionic bonds form between **metals and non-metals**.
Let's look at potassium fluoride as an example:

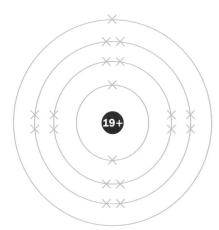

a potassium atom has 19 electrons (2.8.8.1)
$(1s^2 2s^2 2p^6 3s^2 3p^6 4s^1)$

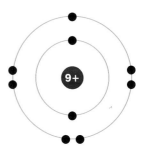

a fluorine atom has 9 electrons (2.7) $(1s^2 2s^2 2p^5)$

Both atoms can become stable by having full outer shells.
They will always take the easiest way to
get their outer shell full of electrons.

Notice that potassium has just 1 electron in its outer shell.
How do you think it could get a full outer shell?
Would it be easier for potassium to lose just 1 electron
or to gain 7 electrons?

Look at the fluorine atom above:
It has 7 electrons in its outer shell
How do you think it could get a full
outer shell?

46

When potassium reacts, it **loses** its one outer electron.
This leaves a full shell.
Where do you think that potassium's outer electron goes to?

Fluorine accepts the electron from potassium.
It **gains** the one electron it needs to fill its outer shell.
Look at the diagram below:

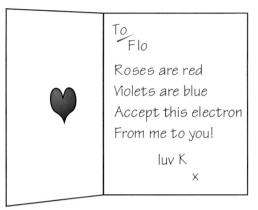

Atomic e-mail?

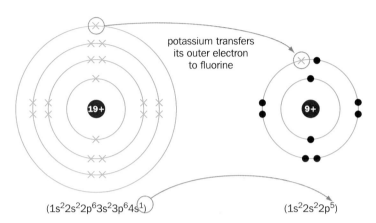

potassium transfers
its outer electron
to fluorine

$(1s^2 2s^2 2p^6 3s^2 3p^6 4s^1)$ $(1s^2 2s^2 2p^5)$

Remember that all atoms are neutral.
They have an equal number of positive protons
and negative electrons. So the charges cancel out.

However, after potassium has given an electron to fluorine,
the electrons and protons in both atoms no longer balance.

Let's add up the charges:

Potassium has: Fluorine has:
18 electrons $= -18$ 10 electrons $= -10$
19 protons $= +19$ 9 protons $\; = +9$
    $+1$ -1

The atoms, which we now call **ions**, become charged.
You can show how the electrons are arranged in ions like this:

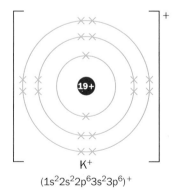

K^+
$(1s^2 2s^2 2p^6 3s^2 3p^6)^+$

F^-
$(1s^2 2s^2 2p^6)^-$

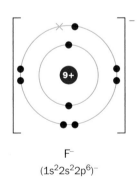

As you know, opposite charges attract.
Therefore, the K^+ ions and F^- ions are strongly attracted to each other.
This electrostatic attraction sticks the ions together,
and is called an **ionic bond**.

Millions of ions bond together in ionic compounds.
You can see a picture of the structure on page 51.

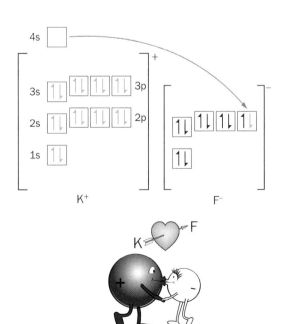

▷ More ionic compounds

We have looked at potassium fluoride as an example
of an ionic compound.
When potassium and fluorine react together,
each potassium atom gives one electron to each
fluorine atom.
The atoms combine with each other – one to one.
So the formula of potassium fluoride is KF.

Calcium is in Group 2 of the Periodic Table.
Therefore, we know that it has 2 electrons in its outer shell.
How could it get a full outer shell?
What do you think happens if calcium, instead of potassium,
combines with fluorine?
Look at the diagram below:

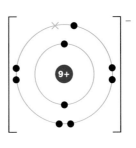

Ca atom
$(1s^22s^22p^63s^23p^64s^2)$

F atom
$(1s^22s^22p^5)$

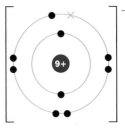 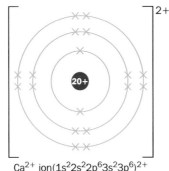 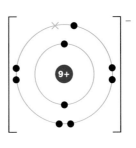

F⁻ ion $(1s^22s^22p^6)^-$ Ca²⁺ ion $(1s^22s^22p^63s^23p^6)^{2+}$ F⁻ ion $(1s^22s^22p^6)^-$

The calcium atom loses two electrons when it reacts.
Therefore, its ion has a 2 + charge, Ca^{2+}.

You can see that each calcium atom can combine with
two fluorine atoms.
So the formula of calcium fluoride is **CaF₂**.

Now let's look at magnesium reacting with oxygen:
An oxygen atom has 6 electrons in its outer shell.
How can it get a full outer shell?
Look at the diagram below:

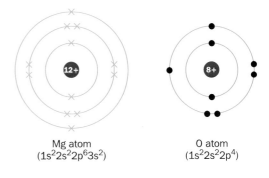

Mg atom
$(1s^22s^22p^63s^2)$

O atom
$(1s^22s^22p^4)$

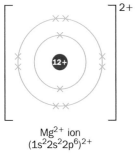 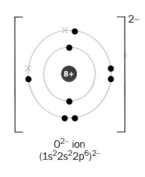

Mg²⁺ ion
$(1s^22s^22p^6)^{2+}$ O²⁻ ion
$(1s^22s^22p^6)^{2-}$

The oxygen atom gains two electrons, each with
a negative charge.
Therefore its ion has a 2− charge, O^{2-}.
It takes one magnesium atom to provide the electrons
required for one oxygen atom.
So the formula of magnesium oxide is **MgO**.

Ionic bonds are the **electrostatic forces of
attraction** between oppositely charged ions.

Working out the formula

You have now seen how three ionic compounds are formed.
Look at the ions that make up each compound:

potassium fluoride – K^+F^-
calcium fluoride – $Ca^{2+}(F^-)_2$
magnesium oxide – $Mg^{2+}O^{2-}$

Now add up the charges on all the ions in each compound.
What do you notice?

Ionic compounds are **neutral.**
The charges on their ions cancel each other out.
Knowing this, and the **charge on the ions**, we can work out
the formula of any ionic compound.

The scales of ionic changes always balance out

Notice that the metal always comes in front of the non-metal in the formula.
• Now see if you can copy and complete the table below:

	Chloride, Cl^-	bromide, Br^-	oxide, O^{2-}
Sodium, Na^+ Magnesium, Mg^{2+} Aluminium, Al^{3+}			

Polyatomic ions

Ions are charged particles. Sometimes the charge is carried
by a group of atoms. We call these **polyatomic ions**.
Common examples are shown in the table opposite:

We can also work out the formulae of compounds containing
polyatomic ions.

Polyatomic ion	Formula
sulphate ion	SO_4^{2-}
nitrate ion	NO_3^-
carbonate ion	CO_3^{2-}

Examples
Magnesium nitrate:
Magnesium ions have a 2+ charge, Mg^{2+}.
Nitrate ions have a 1− charge, NO_3^-.
The charge on 1 magnesium ion is balanced by
the charge on 2 nitrate ions.
$(2+) + (1- \times 2) = 0$
Therefore, they bond in the ratio 1 Mg^{2+} to 2 NO_3^-.
The formula is **$Mg(NO_3)_2$**.

The formula of magnesium nitrate is $Mg(NO_3)_2$

Aluminium sulphate is a little more difficult.
Aluminium ions have a 3 + charge, Al^{3+}.
Sulphate ions have a 2− charge, SO_4^{2-}.
So how many aluminium ions and sulphate ions
combine to balance each other out?
2 Al^{3+} ions will cancel out 3 SO_4^{2-} ions.
$2 \times (3+) = 6+$ and $3 \times (2-) = 6-$
$\qquad (6+) + (6-) = 0$
Therefore the formula is **$Al_2(SO_4)_3$**.

The formula of aluminium sulphate is $Al_2(SO_4)_3$

▷ Dot and cross diagrams

In order to save time, we can show the bonding in compounds by **dot and cross diagrams.**
These are a short-hand way to display the electrons in the outer shell of each ion (or atom) in a compound.

As you know, we cannot tell one electron from another.
They are all identical.
However, in dot and cross diagrams the electrons from each ion need to be distinguished from each other.
As the name suggests, we often use dots for the electrons from one atom and crosses for the electrons from a different atom.

Let's look at the examples we have met so far in this chapter:

Potassium fluoride

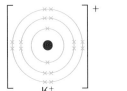
K⁺   F⁻

Dot and cross diagram

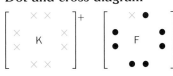

You could also represent the potassium ion as [K⁺]. Can you see why?

Calcium fluoride

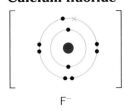 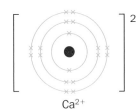 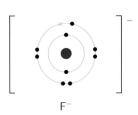
F⁻   Ca²⁺   F⁻

Dot and cross diagram

Magnesium oxide

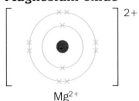 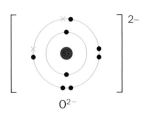
Mg²⁺   O²⁻

Dot and cross diagram

▷ Properties of ionic compounds

You have now seen how metals bond with non-metals.
Metals give electrons to non-metals. This means that:

These are ionic compounds

> **metal atoms always form positive ions, and
> non-metal atoms form negative ions.**

The attraction between the oppositely charged ions is the ionic bond.
Look at the photo of some ionic compounds:
Can you see any similarities?

Here is a list of the properties of ionic compounds.

They:

1. **are made of crystals (which can be split or cleaved along certain angles)**

2. **usually have high melting points**

3. **are often soluble in water**

4. **conduct electricity when molten or dissolved in water, but not when solid.**

Giant ionic structures

Scientists need to know how the ions are arranged in ionic compounds.
This helps to explain how ionic compounds behave.

They get their information by firing X-rays at a crystal.
The technique is called **X-ray crystallography.**
Look at the X-ray pattern opposite:
It is formed as the X-rays emerge from the crystal.
They are *diffracted* as they pass through the gaps between ions.
The X-rays are then detected on photographic film.
A computer is used to help us analyse the patterns.

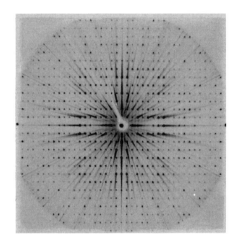

*The dots are the diffraction pattern of the X-rays
passing through a crystal of zeolite*

Scientists have found that the ions form **giant structures** or **lattices**.
Millions of positive and negative ions are fixed in position.
They are arranged in regular, repeating patterns.
Look at the diagram below:

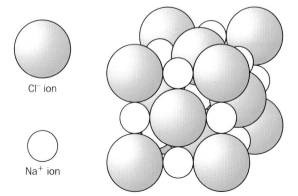

Cl⁻ ion

Na⁺ ion

'Space-filling' model

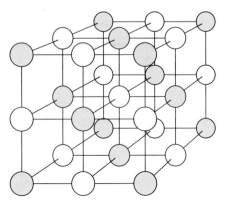

Sometimes the 'ball and stick' model is shown

▷ Explaining the properties of ionic compounds

We will now see how the properties of ionic compounds, listed on the last page, can be explained.

This is a crystal of sodium chloride

1. Regular angles in crystals that can be cleaved

Look at the photograph and diagram of sodium chloride opposite:

Can you see that the ions are arranged in a regular pattern?
This helps to explain the **regular angles** we see in the **crystals** of ionic compounds.

We can also imagine how the crystals can be cleaved along certain planes.

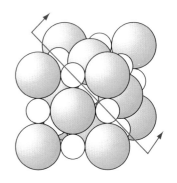

A crystal can be cleaved along its layers

2. High melting points

Why do you think that ionic compounds usually have **high melting points**?
Think about the changes that happen when a solid turns to a liquid:
Is there an orderly pattern in the particles that make up a liquid?
Consider melting an ionic compound:
We need to supply enough energy to make the ions vibrate so much that they break free from their fixed positions.

Remember that the oppositely charged ions attract, forming **strong ionic bonds.**
Imagine trying to separate all the ions in these **giant ionic structures**!
It takes a lot of energy to overcome all that electrostatic attraction.
That is why their melting points are high.

3. Solubility in water

Many ionic compounds **are soluble in water.**
To explain this we need to look at a water molecule in more detail:
The electrons in H_2O are not evenly spread around the molecule.
H_2O is said to be a **polar** molecule.
Look at the diagram opposite:

the oxygen end of a water molecule is slightly negative compared with the hydrogen end

One end of the molecule is slightly negative compared to the other end.
The reasons for this are discussed on page 68.

The polar water molecules are attracted to the ions.
Look at the diagram opposite:
Can you see how the water molecules align themselves differently with the positive and negative ions?
They pull the ions from the giant structure and the compound dissolves.

The ions in solution are surrounded by water molecules.
We call them **hydrated ions**.
You can read more about the process of hydration on page 107.

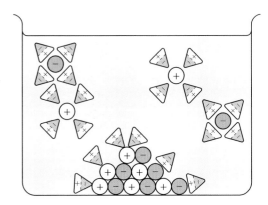

4. Electrolysis of ionic compounds

Do you recall from previous work how ionic compounds
can be split up into their elements?
Think about the extraction of reactive metals.
Do you remember about **electrolysis**?

> **Electrolysis is the breakdown of a
> substance by electricity.**

In experiments we find that *solid* ionic compounds do
not conduct electricity.
Yet if you melt the compound or dissolve it in water, they do conduct.
The compounds are called **electrolytes**.

So why do electrolytes conduct electricity?

We know that electrolytes are compounds made up of ions.
Remember that ions are charged particles.
Solids like sodium chloride contain ions, but they are
fixed in position.

Look at the top of the diagram opposite:
Their ions can't move between the electrodes. They can't
carry their charge through the solid.
However, when they are melted or dissolved in water,
the *ions become free to move around*.

Once the ions arrive at the electrodes:

> **Positive ions receive electrons and
> negative ions lose electrons.**

The diagram below shows what happens when molten lead bromide
is electrolysed:
(Notice that ions move through the electrolyte, not electrons!)

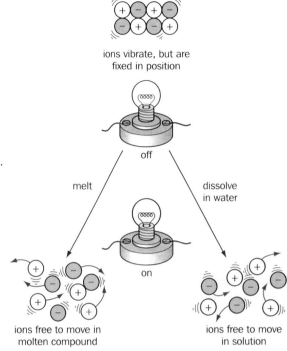

solid

ions vibrate, but are
fixed in position

off

melt

dissolve
in water

on

ions free to move in
molten compound

ions free to move
in solution

At the cathode (−) $\quad Pb^{2+} + 2e^- \longrightarrow Pb$
Lead ions, Pb^{2+}, gain two electrons.
They form lead atoms

At the anode (+) $\quad 2Br^- - 2e^- \longrightarrow Br_2$
Two bromide ions, Br^-, both lose their extra electrons.
They form Br_2 molecules

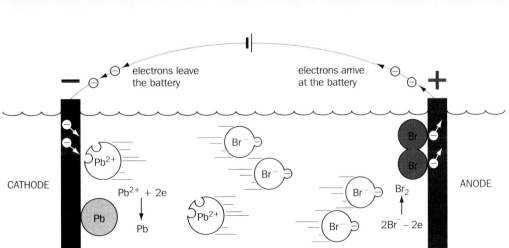

electrons leave
the battery

electrons arrive
at the battery

CATHODE

$Pb^{2+} + 2e$
$\downarrow$
Pb

$2Br^- - 2e$

Br_2

ANODE

▷ Chemistry at work: Ionic compounds

Sodium chloride – the tasty de-icer!

Sodium chloride is called 'common salt' and is referred to
as just 'salt' by most people.
It is widely used in the food industry to preserve and
enhance the flavour of foods.
Our word 'salary' comes from the Latin word for salt.
Roman soldiers were sometimes paid with bags of salt!

Even if you don't add salt to your food, dieticians are worried
about the levels of sodium ions we consume. They believe that
high concentrations of sodium ions lead to high blood pressure
and heart disease.

Just look at some of the labels of the food you eat every day.
How much salt do you eat in an average day?
Can you work out what fraction of the salt you eat is sodium?
(A_r of Na = 23, Cl = 35.5)

Salt is also used in winter to stop roads from freezing over.
The 'grit' that is spread from lorries contains impure sodium chloride.
It makes it more difficult for water molecules to bond together
to form ice.

Fluoride – chemical protection

Fluoride is added to many toothpastes in order to prevent tooth decay.
Look at the ingredients on your tube of toothpaste next time
you brush your teeth.
What is the name of the compound that contains the fluoride ions?
(It is worth knowing that all sodium compounds are soluble in water.)
What proportion of the toothpaste does the fluoride compound make up?

Some places have fluoride added to their water supplies.
Research shows this to result in many fewer fillings for children.
However, too much fluoride produces a mottling effect on teeth.
Larger doses of fluoride are actually toxic.
Is fluoride added to your water?
What are your views on the issue?

Magnesium oxide – hot stuff!

There are strong ionic bonds between the Mg^{2+} and O^{2-} ions
in magnesium oxide.
Both ions are relatively small and highly charged. We say that
they have a high **charge density**.
Remember that the ions are held together in a giant lattice.
This explains why magnesium oxide melts at over 2800 °C.
It is used in the bricks that line kilns.
You can find it inside any blast furnace, as it can stand
the high temperatures (around 1500 °C).

Summary

When metals react with non-metals they form **ionic compounds**.
Metal atoms give electrons to non-metal atoms.
This makes **positive metal** ions and **negative non-metal** ions.
The oppositely charged ions are stuck to each other by strong electrostatic forces of attraction.
This is called **ionic bonding**.

The ions are arranged in huge lattices, called **giant ionic structures**.
Ionic compounds:
- are made of crystals
- have high melting points
- are sometimes soluble in water
- conduct electricity when molten or dissolved in water, but not when solid.

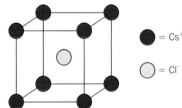

▷ Questions

1 Copy and complete:
.... compounds are made when metal atoms react with .... atoms.
The metal atoms donate one or more .... to the .... atoms.
Metal atoms always form .... charged ions, and non-metal atoms form .... charged ions.
These ions are arranged in .... ionic structures.
The ions are held together in the l.... by .... bonds, which arise from .... forces of attraction between .... charged ions.
The crystals formed have .... melting points and many will .... in water.
They conduct electricity when .... or when in solution, but not when they are .....

2 Which of these substances have giant ionic structures?
hydrazine, N_2H_4 iron(II) oxide, FeO
carbon dioxide, CO_2 zinc chloride, $ZnCl_2$
tin(II) bromide, $SnBr_2$ chlorine, Cl_2
sodium fluoride, NaF   ethanol, C_2H_5OH

How did you decide?

3 Explain, using diagrams to help, how these atoms transfer electrons when they form a compound together:
a) Lithium, Li (which has 3 electrons) and fluorine, F (which has 9 electrons).
b) Sodium, Na (which has 11 electrons) and oxygen (which has 8 electrons).

4 Here are 4 positive ions:
lithium, Li^+; ammonium, NH_4^+; barium, Ba^{2+}; and chromium(III), Cr^{3+}
Here are 4 negative ions:
iodide, I^-; nitrate, NO_3^-; sulphate, SO_4^{2-}; and phosphate, PO_4^{3-}
Draw a table like the one on page 49 to show the formulae of the compounds formed between pairs of ions.

5 Look at the Periodic Table on page 89.
a) What is the link between the group a metal is in and the charge on its ions? You can use sodium, magnesium and aluminium as examples.
b) Try to find a simple mathematical equation that will tell you the relationship between the group a non-metal is in and the charge on its ions. You can use oxygen and fluorine as examples.
c) Carbon (which has 6 electrons) never forms purely ionic compounds.
Why not?
d) Hydrogen (which only has 1 electron) can form both H^+ ions and H^- ions. Explain this.

6 Draw dot and cross diagrams to show how the electrons are arranged in these compounds:
a) magnesium fluoride,
(Mg has 12 electrons and F has 9 electrons).
b) lithium bromide
(Li has 3 electrons and Br has 35 electrons)
c) aluminium oxide
(Al has 13 electrons and O has 8 electrons).

7 The **coordination number** of an ion is the number of nearest neighbouring ions it is in contact with.
In a sodium chloride crystal (see page 51), the coordination number of the sodium and the chloride ions is 6. We say it has 6:6 coordination.
Look at the part of the lattice of caesium chloride below:

      ● = Cs^+
      ○ = Cl^-

a) What is the coordination number of the chloride ion?
b) Can you see how the lattice would continue? What will be the coordination number of the caesium ion?
c) What is the formula of caesium chloride?

5 Covalent bonding

In the last chapter we saw how metals react with non-metals to form ionic bonds.
Remember that when metal atoms react, they lose electrons, and non-metals usually gain electrons.

But think of all the compounds that are formed from just non-metals.
Common examples include water, carbon dioxide and methane.
Do you know which non-metals they contain?

Let's look at a molecule of hydrogen, H_2:
Both hydrogen atoms tend to gain electrons.
So how do their atoms bond to each other?
How can they both gain electrons to get full outer shells?
It can't be like ionic bonding because there is no metal atom to give away electrons.

Both hydrogen atoms can gain electrons **by sharing**!
If their outer shells overlap, they share some of each other's electrons.
This allows both atoms to get a full outer shell of electrons.
Look at the diagrams below:

The bonds between hydrogen and oxygen in H_2O are covalent

Both H atoms tend to gain electrons

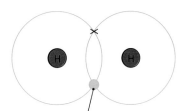

the shared pair of electrons in the covalent bond

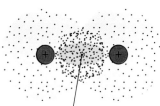

the electrons in the covalent bond are more likely to be found between the two nuclei

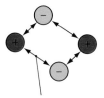

electrons between the nuclei hold the atoms together

'dot and cross' representation of the covalent bond

> Each *shared pair of electrons* forms a **covalent bond** between non-metal atoms.

Now let's look at the bonding in methane, CH_4:
one carbon atom and four hydrogen atoms overlap like this:

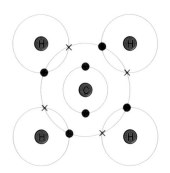

Count the electrons in the outer shell of each carbon and hydrogen atom in methane:

Can you see that the carbon now has 8 electrons in its outer shell?
How many electrons does each hydrogen have?
Has each hydrogen atom got a full outer shell?

Covalent bonds are sometimes shown like this:

$$\begin{array}{c} \quad\quad\text{H} \\ \quad\quad| \\ \text{H}-\text{C}-\text{H} \\ \quad\quad| \\ \quad\quad\text{H} \end{array}$$ where each line — is one bond (a pair of shared electrons)

This shows the number of covalent bonds clearly.
However, this type of diagram does not show the actual shape
of the molecule. We will look at the shapes of molecules on page 60.

Natural gas is mostly methane

You can also show the bonding using dot and across diagrams
(as we did for ionic bonding on page 50).
Notice that we only show the electrons in the outer shells:

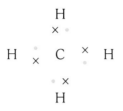

Let's look at another example of covalent bonding.
Chlorine gas does not exist as single atoms.
Remember that a chlorine atom has 7 electrons in
its outer shell. It needs 1 more electron to fill it.
Can it do this by sharing?

Two chlorine atoms bond together to make a Cl_2 molecule.
This is called a **diatomic** molecule.
Look at the diagram below:

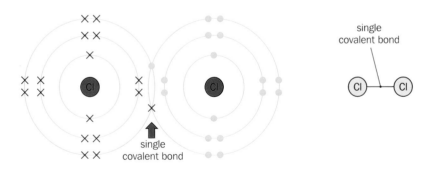

Chlorine used to be added to water in swimming pools to kill bacteria. A compound called 'Trichlor' has largely replaced it. Can you think why?

Count the electrons in the outer shell of each chlorine atom.
Do they both have 8 electrons?

The dot and cross diagram for a chlorine molecule is shown below:

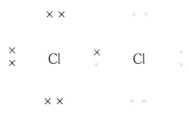

● Can you draw a diagram to show the bonding in
a hydrogen chloride molecule, HCl?

▷ Double bonds

Most people know that the formula of carbon dioxide is CO_2.
But do you know how the atoms are bonded together?

Carbon and oxygen are both non-metals, so they will
form covalent bonds with each other.
However, single covalent bonds, as shown below, would not make
each atom stable:

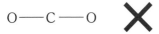

Carbon dioxide is used in some fire extinguishers

Can you see that this arrangement would leave carbon with only 6 electrons
in its outer shell? Would each oxygen atom have a full outer shell?

This problem is solved by forming **double** covalent bonds.
Remember that a single covalent bond is one pair of shared electrons.
So how many electrons will be needed for a double bond?
Look at the diagram showing the double bonds in CO_2 below:

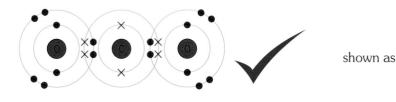

shown as

$$O = C = O$$
double covalent bond

Dot and cross diagram for CO_2

Count the electrons in the outer shell of each atom:
Can you see how each atom has achieved a full outer shell?
Count the electrons in each area of overlap:

Two pairs of electrons in the area of overlap form a **double covalent bond**.

Another molecule with a double bond

Do you recall the molecule ethene from your previous work?
Its formula is C_2H_4. It contains a double bond between its carbon atoms.
Look at the ways we can represent its bonding below:

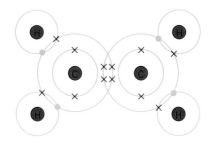

The double bond in ethene enables it to form poly(ethene). (See page 252)

How many electrons are in the area of overlap?
Can you see why we call this a double bond?
You can find out how the double bond affects the reactions
of ethene in Chapter 14.

▷ Dative (or coordinate) bonds

We have seen how we can describe a covalent bond
as a pair of *electrons* shared between two atoms.
In a few cases, both the electrons in the pair come from the **same atom**.
The resulting covalent bond is called a **dative (or coordinate) bond**.

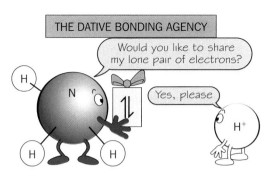

*Donating a pair of electrons to someone
can result in a strong bond forming!*

Example of dative bonding

Ammonium ions (NH_4^+) contain a dative bond.
We can only explain the bonding in NH_4^+ ions if we include
a dative bond.
The ammonium ion is formed when an alkaline solution of ammonia, $NH_3(aq)$,
reacts with an acid. The acid provides $H^+(aq)$ ions:

$$NH_3(aq) + H^+(aq) \longrightarrow NH_4^+(aq)$$

Look at the diagram of the NH_4^+ ion below:

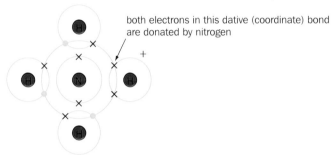

both electrons in this dative (coordinate) bond
are donated by nitrogen

The H^+ ion has no electrons of its own, so it accepts and shares
a non-bonding pair of electrons from the outer shell of the nitrogen atom.
This gives the hydrogen 2 electrons, filling its shell.
The dot and cross diagram is shown below:

$$H$$
$$_{\circ}\ ^{\times}$$
$$H \ _{\circ}^{\times} \ N \ _{\times}^{\times} \ H^+$$
$$^{\times} \ _{\circ}$$
$$H$$

The dative bond is usually represented by an arrow:

The direction of the arrow shows us which
atom the pair of electrons has come from.
It always points to the atom accepting the electrons.

*Water molecules are bonded to the Cu^{2+}
ions in this solution by dative (or
coordinate) bonds*

Studies have shown that there is no difference between any of the H atoms
in an NH_4^+ ion. So you will see the structure represented as:

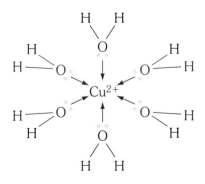

or even as

▷ Shapes of molecules

We can now look at the actual shape of covalently bonded molecules.

On paper everything looks flat, but many molecules have three-dimensional shapes.
We can predict the shape of a molecule like this:

1. Draw the dot and cross diagram for the molecule.

2. Count the number of electrons surrounding the central atom.

3. Divide this number by 2 to get the number of **electron pairs**. Electron pairs are negatively charged. They repel each other and get **as far apart as possible**.

4. Thinking in three dimensions, imagine the central atom in the middle of a football.
    The electron pairs point out towards the surface of the ball.

Where would you stick 2 pieces of tape so they are as far apart as possible? How about 3 or 4 pieces?

Let's consider some examples:

1. beryllium chloride, $BeCl_2$

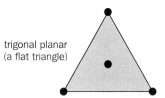

(notice Be does not have 8 electrons in its outer shell in this compound)

Cl ———— Be ———— Cl   180°

a linear molecule (in a straight line)

Another example: CO_2

2. boron trifluoride, BF_3

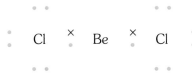

(again, B does not have a full outer shell)

F   120°
|
B
F   F

trigonal planar (a flat triangle)

Another example: $CO_3{}^{2-}$

3. methane, CH_4

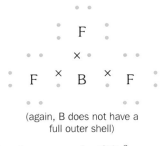

H
|
H – – – C   109.5°
H   H

tetrahedral (a pyramid with a triangle at the base)

Another example: $NH_4{}^+$

60

4. phosphorus(V) chloride, PCl_5

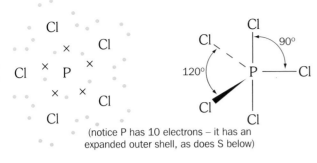

120°   90°

(notice P has 10 electrons – it has an
expanded outer shell, as does S below)

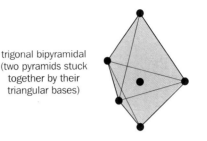

trigonal bipyramidal
(two pyramids stuck
together by their
triangular bases)

5. sulphur(VI) fluoride, SF_6

90°

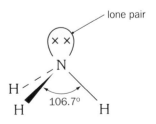

octahedral
(two pyramids stuck
together by their
square bases)

In the examples above the central atoms only have bonding pairs
of electrons repelling each other.
But what happens if we have a mixture of bonding
and non-bonding pairs of electrons?

**Non-bonding pairs of electrons
are called lone pairs.**

Let's look at ammonia (NH_3) as an example:

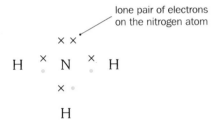

lone pair of electrons
on the nitrogen atom

You can see from the dot and cross diagram that there are 4 pairs of electrons
surrounding the nitrogen atom.
So what would you expect the H—N—H bond angles to be?
The perfect tetrahedral angles would be 109.5°.
However, the actual angles are found to be 106.7°.

This is explained by the stronger concentration of charge in a lone pair
compared with a bonding pair of electrons. The lone pair is held closer to
the nucleus of the central atom than the bonding pair. The bonding pair
is shared between two atoms and is attracted to both their nuclei.

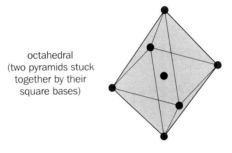

lone pair

106.7°

*The lone pair pushes the bonding pairs of
electrons slightly closer together than the
perfect tetrahedral angle, 109.5°
We describe the shape of NH_3 as*
pyramidal.
*Can you see why?
Can you predict the bond angles in H_2O?*

(See page 71)

So the force of repulsion can be summarised:

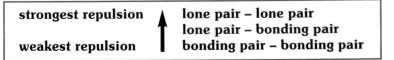

strongest repulsion		**lone pair – lone pair**
	↑	**lone pair – bonding pair**
weakest repulsion		**bonding pair – bonding pair**

This means that in the ammonia molecule the bonding pairs of electrons
are pushed closer together by the lone pair.

▷ Giant covalent structures

The covalent substances we have seen so far in this chapter have all been made of small molecules made from just a few atoms. However, some substances consist of giant three-dimensional networks of atoms. The atoms are fixed in position by covalent bonds. We call these **giant covalent structures.**

The great variety of life on Earth depends on carbon's ability to form covalent bonds with itself.
As the element, carbon atoms bond to millions of other carbon atoms in both diamond and graphite.

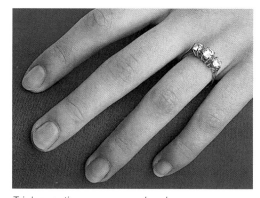
Trick question: name a molecule you can see with the naked eye.
Diamond can be thought of as a giant molecule made of millions of carbon atoms covalently bonded together

Carbon in the form of diamond

Do you know the hardest substance on Earth?
Look at the photo opposite:
Diamond's hardness makes it a very useful material.

Diamond is made from only carbon atoms.
How many covalent bonds can each carbon atom form?
Look at the diagram below:

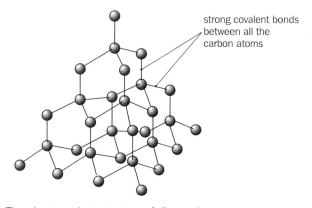

strong covalent bonds between all the carbon atoms

The giant covalent structure of diamond

The tip of this drill is lined with industrial diamonds. It is so hard because of its giant structure (the individual bonds between atoms are actually not as strong as those in CO_2!)

Each atom forms four strong covalent bonds with its neighbours.
The atoms are arranged in a giant three-dimensional lattice.

Does diamond have a high or a low melting point?
Can you explain why?

Another substance with a giant covalent structure is sand.
Its chemical name is silicon dioxide (SiO_2).
It melts at over 1500 °C.

Substances with giant covalent structures
are **not soluble in water.**
Their particles carry no charge (unlike those in ionic compounds).
So polar water molecules are not strongly attracted to them.
They can't provide the huge amounts of energy needed
to break the structures apart.
Substances with giant covalent structures **don't conduct electricity**.
There are no free ions or electrons to carry the charge.
(Graphite is an exception; see the next page).

> **Properties of giant covalent substances:**
> 1. **They have high melting points.**
> 2. **They are insluble in water.**
> 3. **They do not conduct electricity (graphite is the exception).**

Carbon in the form of graphite

Another form of carbon is graphite.
Diamond and graphite are **allotropes** of carbon.
Allotropes are different forms of the same element.
The carbon atoms in graphite are also held together
in a giant covalent structure.
However, some of its properties are very different from
a typical giant covalent substance, such as diamond or sand.

If you touch a lump of graphite, if feels smooth and slippery.
Your pencil contains graphite. As you move it across
your paper it flakes off, leaving a trail of carbon atoms.
Look at the diagram below:

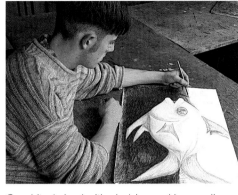

*Graphite (mixed with clay) is used in pencil
'leads'*

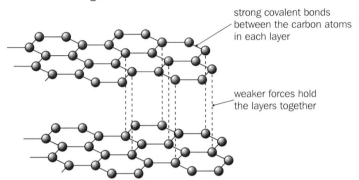

strong covalent bonds
between the carbon atoms
in each layer

weaker forces hold
the layers together

The giant covalent structure of graphite

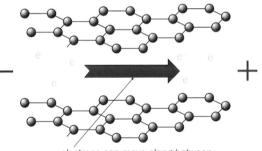

How many carbon atoms are joined to each other by strong covalent bonds?
Is this the usual number of bonds?
The fourth electron from each carbon atom is found in the gap between the layers.
These electrons hold the layers together by weak forces.
Therefore the layers can slide over each other easily.
Does this explain graphite's use in pencils?

Did you know that graphite is the only non-metal element
that conducts electricity well?
The electrons holding the layers together are only held loosely
to the carbon atoms.
They can drift along between the layers in graphite,
making it a good conductor of electricity (and heat).
Do you think that graphite conducts better along its layers
or across them?

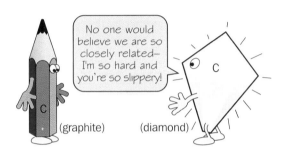

electrons can move along between
the layers in graphite

Graphite does not melt when you heat it.
At over 3000 °C it turns directly into a gas. We say it **sublimes**.
Why does it take a lot of energy for graphite to sublime?
Look at the photos of some other uses of graphite:
Which properties of graphite do they depend on?

*The tiles on the nose cone of the space shuttle
contain graphite*

*Lubricant oils sometimes contain
graphite. It can also be used as a
powder on moving parts in
machinery*

▷ Chemistry at work: Bucky-balls

For most of the last century, diamond and graphite were known as the allotropes of carbon. However, in 1985 a new form of carbon was discovered. Its molecules are made from 60 carbon atoms joined together. The atoms fold around, making a ball-shaped molecule, C_{60}.

Look at the photo opposite:

The new molecule looks just like a football! The carbon atoms form pentagons and hexagons, like the panels on a football.

Its full name is **buckminsterfullerene**. Scientists named it after an architect, Buckminster Fuller. In 1967, he designed a bucky-ball shaped building in Montreal, Canada.

The new allotrope of carbon was first made by simulating the conditions in the atmospheres of stars. The diagram below shows how we can make C_{60} molecules:

Sir Harry Kroto was awarded the Nobel Prize for chemistry in 1996 for his work in discovering C_{60}

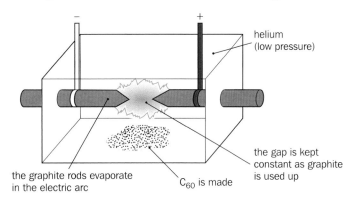

helium (low pressure)

the gap is kept constant as graphite is used up

the graphite rods evaporate in the electric arc

C_{60} is made

As new methods are found, 'bucky-balls' are getting cheaper. In 1999 the price was £25 per gram.

Since the discovery of C_{60}, more forms of carbon have been prepared. This family of carbon allotopes is called **fullerenes**. One is shaped more like a rugby ball, with the formula C_{70}. Look at the diagram opposite:

Others are larger cage-like structures, as shown below:

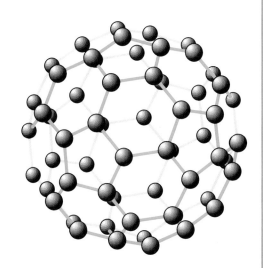

The original bucky-ball C_{60}

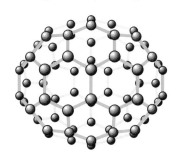

A molecule of C_{70}

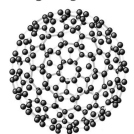

A molecule of C_{240}

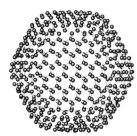

A molecule of C_{540}

▷ Chemistry at work: More fullerenes

Some other fullerenes are like 'balls within balls'.
Look at the diagram opposite:
These have been nick-named **'bucky-onions'**:
Can you see why?

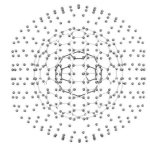

There are also a group of **'bucky-tubes'**:

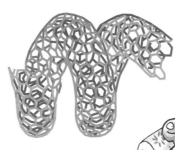

Potential uses

Bucky-TV

Researchers in the U.S.A. have found a way of lining up
'bucky-tubes' on the surface of glass. The 'bucky-tubes'
stick out at right angles from the glass which could
one day be used as flat screens for TVs or computer monitors.
The tubes could each fire electrons from the end sticking out
of the screen.
This would replace bulky cathode ray tubes used in most sets.
It promises to give us brighter pictures that you can view
from a wider range of angles.

Bucky-bulbs

Some bucky-balls glow in light.
Chemists in California have produced bucky-balls that light up
when an electric current is applied to them.
They predict that their discovery could eventually
be used in paints that could light up a room
or in windows that could glow at night just as if
the Sun were shining!

Bucky-strength

Israeli and American scientists have shown that
bucky-tubes can withstand pressures almost
a million times atmospheric pressure.
This makes them about 200 times stronger than
any other fibre. They believe the bucky-tubes can be embedded
in other materials like plastics to make incredibly strong materials.
These might be used, for example, in making bullet-proof vests.

Bucky-mules

Bucky-balls and cages can trap atoms or groups of atoms
inside their structures.
Scientists are trying to develop ways of using these 'molecular mules'
to carry drugs or radioactive atoms, used to treat cancer,
to the sites in the body where they are needed.

▷ Simple molecular structures

You already know that covalent bonds are strong.
So have you ever wondered why so many substances
with covalent bonds are so easy to melt or boil?

Let's take methane, CH_4, as an example.
It has a very low boiling point.
It boils at $-161\,°C$!
(Compare this with the values given for the
giant covalent structures in the table opposite.)

Giant Covalent Structure		Simple Molecular Structure	
Substance	Boiling pt. / °C	Substance	Boiling pt. / °C
diamond	4830	methane	−161
silicon	2355	water	100
sand (silica)	2230	chlorine	−35

By the time you get to room temperature (about $20\,°C$),
methane has already boiled and become a gas.
And yet it has strong covalent bonds holding
its atoms together, just like diamond.
So why is it so easy to boil methane?

To answer this question, you must realise that
no covalent bonds are broken when methane boils.
When it boils, individual CH_4 molecules move apart from each other.
They separate, but they are still CH_4 molecules.

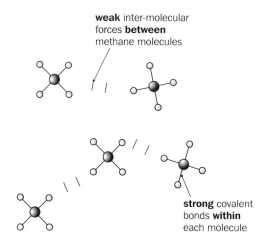

weak inter-molecular
forces **between**
methane molecules

strong covalent
bonds **within**
each molecule

Compare this with the giant covalent structures of diamond,
graphite or sand. To boil these, we have to break apart
the whole giant structure. Millions of covalent bonds
do have to break in these examples.

Substances, such as methane and water, have
simple molecular structures.
They have strong covalent bonds joining their atoms
within each molecule. However, they have only weak
forces between individual molecules.
We say that they have **weak intermolecular forces.**

Some solids with simple molecular structures

Look at the picture of iodine crystals opposite:
Iodine, I_2, has a simple molecular structure.
Its molecules are packed together in a regular pattern.
When heated very gently, it sublimes.
I_2 molecules escape from the lattice as a gas.
This shows how weak the forces are between its molecules.

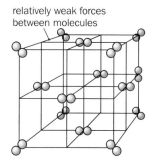

Iodine crystals sublime easily

relatively weak forces
between molecules

I_2 molecules arranged in regular pattern

Sulphur exists as S_8 molecules at room temperature.
These crown-shaped molecules are packed neatly
together to form crystals.
There are two crystalline forms of sulphur.
Its allotropes are called orthorhombic and monoclinic sulphur.
Both melt below $120\,°C$. This low melting point tells us
that sulphur also has a simple molecular structure.
Again, there are relatively weak forces **between** its molecules.

> **Substances with low melting points and boiling points have simple molecular structures**

▷ Van der Waals' forces

As you know, the forces of attraction between the molecules in a gas are very weak. They all have simple molecular structures. Other substances with simple molecular structures are either liquids at room temperature or solids with low melting points.

Although intermolecular forces are weak, there is always some force of attraction in all these substances. So how can we explain these weak forces?

Van der Waals' forces are weak

Molecules have no overall charge. They contain equal numbers of protons and electrons, unlike ions.
But think about our model of an atom, especially the electrons:
Are the electrons stuck in one place?
The protons are fixed in the nucleus, but electrons are moving constantly.
They move around the nucleus in their shells.

Imagine if we could take a photograph that showed the position of all the electrons in a molecule at any instant.
Do you think it likely that the electrons would be exactly evenly spread around the molecule?
The picture would be changing all the time.
We are very unlikely to find a perfectly uniform distribution of electrons around any of the atoms in the molecule.

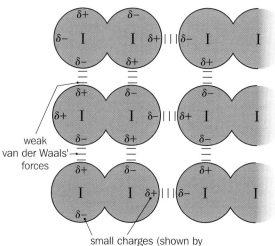

weak van der Waals' forces

small charges (shown by $\delta+$ and $\delta-$) on the I_2 molecules. They change constantly

These tiny imbalances of charge result in parts of the molecule being slightly positively or negatively charged at any moment in time.
They form **instantaneous dipoles** or **temporary dipoles**.
(Dipoles are a measure of differences in charge).

These instantaneous dipoles affect neighbouring molecules.
They cause a slight shift in the distribution of their electrons.
In other words, they **induce** a dipole in their neighbours.

In this way small forces of attraction are formed between molecules.
These are the weak intermolecular forces known as **van der Waals' forces**.

van der Waals' forces are caused by temporary induced dipoles.

Let's consider some van der Waals' forces in action:
We will look at the halogens from Group 7 in the Periodic Table.

Element	Atomic number	Molecules present	Boiling point/°C
fluorine	9	F_2	−188
chlorine	17	Cl_2	−35
bromine	35	Br_2	59
iodine	53	I_2	184

- Which halogen has the largest atoms and molecules?
- Does this element have the highest or lowest boiling point?
- Which halogen has the strongest van der Waals' forces between its molecules?
- What is the link between size of molecule and strength of intermolecular forces?

The more electrons there are in a molecule, the greater the opportunities for instantaneous dipoles to be set up within the molecule.
That is why iodine exists as a solid at room temperature, whereas fluorine is a gas.

The larger the molecule, the stronger the van der Waals' forces.

▷ Polar molecules

On the last page we saw how small imbalances of charge can form at any instant because of the movement of electrons in molecules. However, many molecules have **permanent dipoles**. One part of the molecule is always slightly positive or negative compared with another part. These are called **polar molecules**.

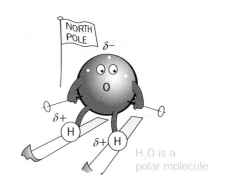

H_2O is a polar molecule

These permanent dipoles arise because molecules of compounds contain different types of atoms.
Do you think that the atoms of every element will have the same attraction for electrons?
Chemists use a scale called **electronegativity** to judge the ability of an atom to attract electrons to itself.

> **Electronegativity is a measure of how strongly an atom attracts electrons in a bond.**

Look at the values for the electronegativity of some elements in the table opposite:
The higher the number, the stronger the attraction for electrons.

Think back to the Cl_2 molecules on the last page:
On average, where would you expect to find the pair of electrons in the covalent bond holding the two Cl atoms to each other?
Do you think they would be drawn nearer one atom than the other?
In these molecules the electronegativity of each Cl atom is the same, so on average the electrons will be shared equally between atoms.

But what about molecules with different atoms?
Let's look at a molecule of hydrogen bromide, HBr.
Look at the table to see which is more electronegative, hydrogen or bromine?
Would you expect the atoms in HBr to share electrons evenly?
The pair of electrons in the covalent bond will tend to be drawn nearer the bromine atom.
Will this make the bromine end of the molecule slightly positive or negative compared with the hydrogen end?
Look at the diagram of HBr below:

Element	Electronegativity
hydrogen	2.1
carbon	2.5
chlorine	3.0
fluorine	4.0
bromine	2.8
iodine	2.5
oxygen	3.5
nitrogen	3.0

Electronegativity is based on a relative scale. It has no units

$$\overset{\delta+}{H} \longrightarrow \overset{\delta-}{Br}$$

The sign $\delta-$ (delta negative) means partially negative.
The $\delta+$ sign shows us which part of the molecule carries a partial positive charge.
The arrow on the bond shows the direction in which the electrons are drawn.
Can you see how polar molecules, like HBr, attract each other?
We can describe their intermolecular forces as attraction between permanent dipoles.

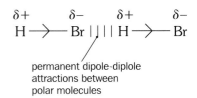

permanent dipole-diplole attractions between polar molecules

> **Polar molecules have permanent dipole–dipole forces of attraction between their molecules.**

The strength of the intermolecular forces depends on the size of the dipole set up within each molecule. But other factors, such as the size of the molecule, must also be taken into account.
Look at the boiling points of some hydrogen halides in the table opposite:
● Which has the highest boiling point?
● Which molecule has the strongest intermolecular forces?
● Would you expect this by just looking at the differences in electronegativities?
● How does the greater number of electrons in the large HI molecule affect its boiling point? (Think about the van der Waals' forces.)

Hydrogen halide		Boiling point/°C
H–Cl	hydrogen chloride	−85
H–Br	hydrogen bromide	−67
H–I	hydrogen iodide	−38

Symmetry of molecules

If we look at two other similar molecules, we can see the effect of symmetry on the polar nature of molecules.

Let's consider CCl_4 and $CHCl_3$:
As you can see from the table on the last page,
chlorine is more electronegative than carbon.
So the C—Cl bond will have a dipole.
Which way will the electrons in the bond be pulled?
The chlorine atom will be slightly negative compared with the carbon atom.
Cl will be $\delta-$ and C will be $\delta+$.

Now let's consider the shape of the molecule:
Can you work out the shape of the CCl_4 molecule
using the ideas on page 60?
Look at the picture below:

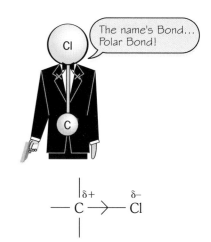

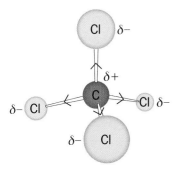

The charge is distributed evenly around the whole molecule
(despite the imbalance of charge within each bond).
So although the C—Cl bond is polar, CCl_4 is a **non-polar** molecule.

We can now compare CCl_4 with a molecule of $CHCl_3$.
Can you see the difference between the two molecules?
Like CCl_4, the central carbon atom in $CHCl_3$ is surrounded by
four bonding pairs of electrons. These four covalent bonds
will be arranged around the carbon atom in a tetrahedral shape.
Look at the picture below:

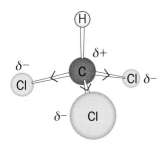

The C—Cl bond is polar in nature. The Cl atom has a stronger pull on the electrons in the covalent bond than the C atom

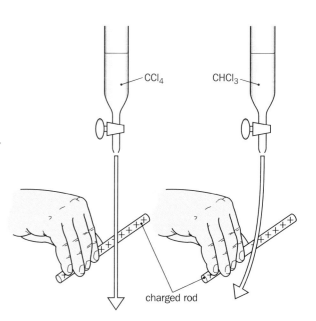

A thin stream of CCl_4 is not deflected by a charged rod. However, $CHCl_3$ is attracted towards the rod. This shows that CCl_4 is non-polar and $CHCl_3$ is polar

You can see that the top and bottom halves of the molecule do not match.
One end of the molecule carries a partial charge compared to the other end.
The end of the $CHCl_3$ molecule containing the three Cl atoms
is slightly negative compared to the H end of the molecule.
So $CHCl_3$ is a polar molecule.

▷ Hydrogen bonding

On page 74 we looked at the boiling points of HCl, HBr and HI.
Which had the lowest boiling point?
What was the pattern?
Now think about hydrogen fluoride, HF, the smallest hydrogen halide:
Would you expect its boiling point to be lower than that of HCl?

Look at the graph below:

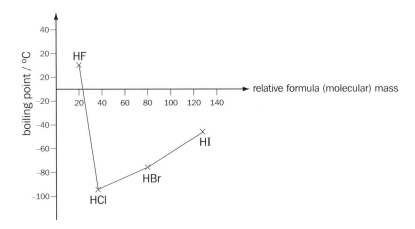

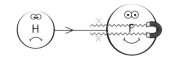

The electrons in the H—F
bond are nearer the F atom

The boiling point of hydrogen fluoride is unusually high.
So how can we explain this?
Look back to the table of electronegativities on page 68:
Which is the most electronegative element?
Fluorine is, in fact, the most electronegative of all the elements.
This sets up a very large imbalance of charge in the HF molecule.
The abnormally high dipole–dipole forces of attraction between its molecules
are called **hydrogen bonds**.

$$\delta+ \qquad\qquad \delta-$$
$$H \longrightarrow F$$

There is a strong dipole within the
HF molecule because of the large
difference in electronegativity
between H and F

> **Hydrogen bonds** are strong dipole–dipole forces between molecules.
> They occur in compounds containing a hydrogen atom bonded to
> a highly electronegative atom, such as fluorine, oxygen or nitrogen.

Look at the diagram below:

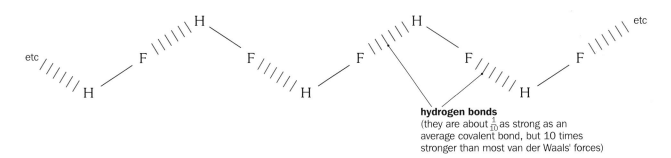

hydrogen bonds
(they are about $\frac{1}{10}$ as strong as an
average covalent bond, but 10 times
stronger than most van der Waals' forces)

In the solid and liquid states, we can think of hydrogen fluoride
being arranged in long chains.

Can you think of any other compounds that might form hydrogen bonds?

We know that water is a liquid at room temperature.
However, if we look at the boiling points of H_2S, H_2Se and H_2Te
(the other Group 6 hydrides), we would expect H_2O to be a gas.
H_2O has a much higher boiling point than expected for a molecule of its size.
Again, the high electronegativity of oxygen compared to hydrogen
leads to hydrogen bonding. This explains water's surprisingly high boiling point.

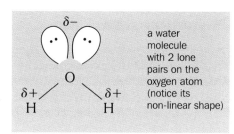

a water
molecule
with 2 lone
pairs on the
oxygen atom
(notice its
non-linear shape)

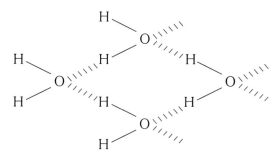

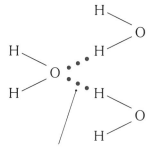

Sometimes hydrogen bonds are
represented by 3 dots

Hydrogen bonding explains many other properties of water.

Why does ice float on water? You would expect a solid
to be denser than its liquid.
But look at the structure of ice below:
It has a very open structure.
Each water molecule forms two hydrogen bonds.
Hydrogen atoms line up with the lone pairs of electrons on oxygen atoms
in neighbouring molecules.

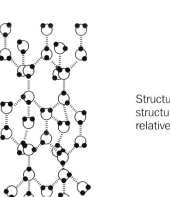

Structure of ice – its open
structure explains its
relatively low density

The relatively high boiling points of carboxylic acids can also be explained
by hydrogen bonding.
Let's compare ethanoic acid (CH_3COOH, $M_r = 60$) with
propanone (CH_3COCH_3, $M_r = 58$).
With similar relative formula masses and common atoms in each molecule,
we would expect similar boiling points.
However, the boiling point of ethanoic acid is more than 60 °C higher than propanone.
The hydrogen bonding in ethanoic acid in effect doubles the size of its molecules.
Look at the diagram below:

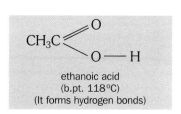

ethanoic acid
(b.pt. 118 °C)
(It forms hydrogen bonds)

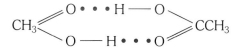

An ethanoic acid **dimer**
– hydrogen bonding holds ethanoic acid molecules
together in pairs

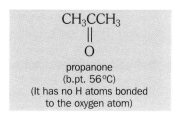

propanone
(b.pt. 56 °C)
(It has no H atoms bonded
to the oxygen atom)

The pair of molecules, joined by hydrogen bonds, is called a **dimer**.

▷ Intermediate bonds

In the last chapter you found out about ionic bonds.
We represented the ions as charged spheres, perfectly round in shape.
They were drawn as individual positive and negative ions
fixed next to each other in giant structures.
This model is the ideal picture of an ionic compound.

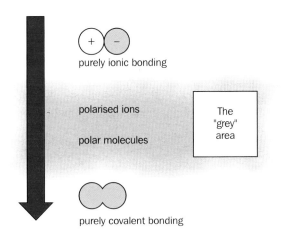

purely ionic bonding

polarised ions

polar molecules

The "grey" area

In Chapter 25 we shall see some evidence that suggests that
this perfect model is not always accurate.
Some compounds have **intermediate bonds**.
*They are ionic but have a degree of covalency
in their bonding*.

purely covalent bonding

These compounds are not made up of completely separate ions.
Their is some overlap between ions. As we have seen in this chapter,
this overlap is characteristic of covalent bonding.
We say that the ions are **polarised**.

The compounds with this type of bonding tend to have ions
that are very different in size and/or highly charged.

One example is lithium nitrate, $Li^+NO_3^-$.
Which ion is smaller in this compound?
We say that the lithium ion has a higher *charge density.*
Its charge is concentrated into a smaller volume than the large nitrate ion.
We can think of a small, highly charged Li^+ ion 'burrowing' into
the more diffuse electron cloud of the large NO_3^- ion.
So the lithium ion distorts the nitrate ion, producing some overlap between ions.
Therefore, the bonding is not purely ionic.

Let me snuggle in close!

Careful, you're distorting my electron cloud!

Li⁺ NO₃⁻

Summary

Non-metal atoms are joined together by **covalent bonds**.
A covalent bond is a shared pair of electrons between two atoms.
A double bond has two pairs of electrons in the area of overlap between atoms.

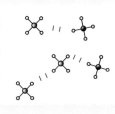

Covalent substances can have either:
● giant covalent structures, or
● simple molecular structures.
Giant covalent structures are huge three-dimensional networks of atoms.
Millions of atoms are all joined by strong covalent bonds.
This means that they have high melting points and boiling points.
They do not conduct electricity (except for graphite).
Simple molecular substances are made of individual molecules.
The atoms in each molecule are joined together by strong covalent bonds. However, there are relatively weak forces
of attraction *between* molecules.
These substances have low melting and boiling points and do not conduct electricity.

The forces between molecules (intermolecular forces or bonds) can be:
● **van der Waals'** forces (small temporary, induced dipole–dipole attraction) between non-polar molecules,
● **permanent dipole–dipole** attraction between polar molecules,
● **hydrogen bonding** in compounds containing a hydrogen atom bonded to nitrogen (e.g. ammonia), oxygen
(e.g. water) or fluorine (e.g. hydrogen fluoride). Hydrogen bonding can be thought of as abnormally strong
dipole–dipole attraction.

▷ Questions

1 Copy and complete:
Non-metal atoms bond to each other by .... electrons. These are called .... bonds. Each bond is a .... of electrons. The .... charged electrons in the bond are more likely to be found in between the two .... charged nuclei so that they bind the atoms together. Double bonds have .... electrons in the area of overlap between atoms.
Covalently bonded substances with high .... points and high boiling points have .... structures.
On the other hand, substances with low melting points and low boiling points have .... molecular structures. These have strong covalent bonds within each ...., but weak forces .... molecules.
The weakest inter.... forces are called van der .... forces. These arise from .... induced dipoles.
When a molecule is .... we have stronger permanent dipole–dipole forces of attraction between molecules.
.... bonding is a special case of 'stronger than normal' dipole–dipole interaction. The molecules contain one or more .... atoms bonded to a strongly .... atom such as ...., oxygen or .....
No covalently bonded substances conduct electricity, except .....

2 Fluorine forms diatomic molecules, F_2.
(Fluorine atoms have 9 electrons.)
Draw a 'dot and cross' diagram to show the bonding in an F_2 molecule.

3 Carbon exists as diamond and graphite.
a) What do we call different forms of the same element?
b) Name one other form of carbon.
c) Diamond and graphite have very different properties and uses. Refer to their structures to explain these differences.

4 The noble gases are monatomic gases with very low boiling points.
Here is a table showing their boiling points:

Noble gas	Atomic number	Boiling point/K
helium	2	4
neon	10	27
argon	18	87
krypton	36	121
xenon	54	166
radon	86	211

a) What do you think the word 'monatomic' means?
b) Name the type of forces between the atoms of a noble gas?
c) Explain how these weak forces arise.
d) What is the pattern in the table? Try to explain it.

5 a) Draw a 'dot and cross' diagram to show the bonding in an ammonia molecule, NH_3
(Nitrogen has 7 electrons and hydrogen has 1 electron.)
b) Ammonia is an alkali. It reacts with H^+ ions, forming the ammonium ion, NH_4^+.
What do we call the type of bond that forms between NH_3 and H^+?
c) Draw a 'dot and cross' diagram of the NH_4^+ ion.
d) Predict the shape of the NH_4^+ ion.

6 Negative ions carry extra electrons.
Look at the diagrams of the nitrate ion below:

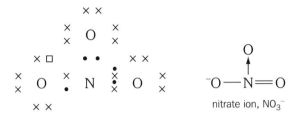

nitrate ion, NO_3^-

a) How is the extra electron in the nitrate ion shown in the 'dot and cross' diagram above?
b) Predict the shape of the nitrate ion.
c) Draw a 'dot and cross' diagram for the carbonate ion. CO_3^{2-}.
(Carbon has 6 electrons and oxygen has 8 electrons.)
d) Predict the shape of the carbonate ion.

7 Water is a covalent molecule. Its formula is H_2O.
(Hydrogen atoms have 1 electron and oxygen atoms have 8 electrons.)
a) Draw a 'dot and cross' diagram to show the bonding in an H_2O molecule.
b) How can you tell that water has a simple molecular structure?
Look at the melting points of the Group 6 hydrides:

Group 6 hydrides	M_r	Melting point/K
hydrogen oxide (water), H_2O	18	273
hydrogen sulphide, H_2S	34	188
hydrogen selenide, H_2Se	81	207
hydrogen telluride, H_2Te	130	225

c) Plot the melting points of the Group 6 hydrides against their relative formula mass.
d) Which hydride breaks the pattern?
e) Use your graph to predict the melting point of water if its intermolecular forces followed the pattern of the other Group 6 hydrides.
f) Explain the trend going from H_2S to H_2Se to H_2Te. Think whether dipole–dipole forces are more important or less important than van der Waals' forces between the molecules. (The electronegativity of the elements decreases going down a group.)
g) Explain water's surprisingly high melting point.
h) Why does ice have a lower density than liquid water?

6 Metals and structures

Metallic bonding

In the last two chapters we have looked at ionic and covalent bonding. However, the atoms in a metal are joined together in a different way.

Can you remember all the properties of metals?
Any ideas we have about the bonding and structure of metals must be able to explain their properties.

Most metals:
- have high melting and boiling points
- conduct electricity and heat
- are hard and dense
- can be hammered into shapes (they are malleable)
- can be drawn out into wires (they are ductile).

Metals are widely used in everyday life

Scientists have suggested a theory of metallic bonding shown in the diagram below:

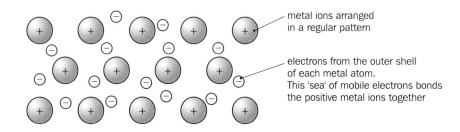

metal ions arranged in a regular pattern

electrons from the outer shell of each metal atom.
This 'sea' of mobile electrons bonds the positive metal ions together

Each metal atom gives up its outer electrons into a **'sea' of electrons**.
The electrons are said to be **delocalised**.
They are no longer associated with any particular atom.
In effect, the metal atoms become positive ions.
These ions are arranged in a **giant metallic structure**.

The electrons are free to drift about within the metal's giant lattice.
The negatively charged electrons attract the positive ions.
They act as the 'glue' that sticks the metal ions together.

There is no overall charge on the metal.
On average, the number of electrons near a particular ion at any time will equal the number of electrons it donated into the 'sea' of electrons.

▷ Explaining the properties of metals

Good conductors of electricity

A very important property of metals is their ability to conduct electricity.
The theory of metallic bonding on the last page can explain this property.

What do you think happens to the 'sea' of electrons
when a voltage is applied to a metal wire?
Remember that an electric current in a wire is caused by the flow of electrons
through the metal. Electrons move away from the negative terminal of a cell
towards the positive end. The outer electrons from each metal atom
are free travel through the metal in the 'sea' of electrons.
This is sometimes called the **conduction band**.
Look at the diagram opposite:

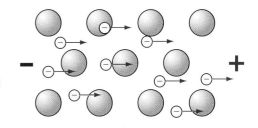

Good conductors of heat

The ease with which electrons move through a metal can also help to explain
why they are good conductors of heat.
As you heat one end of a solid its atoms will vibrate more vigorously.
The vibrations will be passed from atom to atom along the structure.
But metals conduct heat so well because the energy is transferred by
the faster movement of the free electrons in the 'sea' of electrons or
conduction band.

Metals conduct heat well

High density and high melting point

The ions in a metal are usually ***packed closely*** together.
The ions line up next to each other, leaving no gaps.
The row on top sits in the 'holes' or indentations in the first layer.
This is repeated layer by layer, building up a giant metallic structure.

In metal structures, the gaps are few,
A 'sea' of electrons acts as a glue!
Lining up, row upon row,
On top of each other, the ions do go.

This lack of space in the closely packed structure explains the high density
of ***most*** metals.
Can you think of any exceptions?
You can see the structure of the alkali metals at the bottom of page 77.

As you know from the last two chapters, when we have giant structures
it takes a lot of energy to break the millions of bonds holding the atoms together.
This explains the high melting point of most metals.
Again, there are some exceptions. Do you know any?

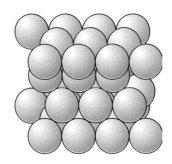

Part of a giant metallic structure

The density of gold is 18.8 g cm^{-3}

The melting point of gold is 1064 °C

▷ Alloys

We mix metals in order to improve their properties for a particular use.
The resulting mixture is called an **alloy**.
Alloys are made by melting the metals and stirring them together.

Metals can be hammered into different shapes, without smashing.
They are malleable.
They can also be drawn out into thin wires. They are ductile.

The fact that the metal ions are arranged in layers explains
why they are malleable and ductile.
When a force is applied to a metal, its layers of ions
can slide over each other.
However, if we add atoms of a different size to a pure metal,
the regular pattern of layers is disrupted. The layers can no longer
slide across each other as easily, and the metal is strengthened.

*To make an alloy the molten metals are mixed,
then allowed to set*

Look at the diagrams below:

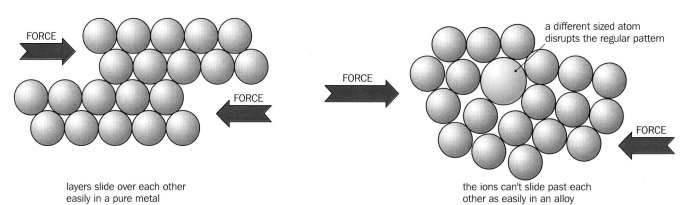

layers slide over each other
easily in a pure metal

a different sized atom
disrupts the regular pattern

the ions can't slide past each
other as easily in an alloy

The photographs below show some uses of alloys:

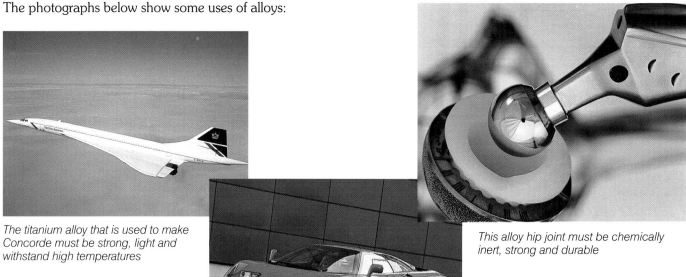

*The titanium alloy that is used to make
Concorde must be strong, light and
withstand high temperatures*

*This alloy hip joint must be chemically
inert, strong and durable*

These alloy wheels are shiny and resist corrosion

Structure of metals

As you know, metal ions are arranged in giant metallic structures.
We saw on page 75 how the layers sit on top of each other.
There are two ways of doing this:

1. Face-centred cubic close-packed structures

In these metals the first and fourth rows of ions lie directly in line.
They are sometimes called abc-type structures because there is
a repeating pattern in the position of the layers – abc abc abc etc.
Look at the diagrams below:

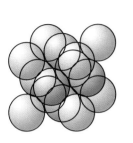

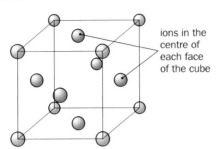

ions in the
centre of
each face
of the cube

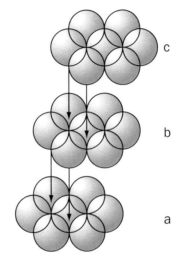

e.g. copper or gold

2. Hexagonal close-packed

In these metals the third row lines up above the first row.
It is also called an aba-type structure.
Look at the diagrams below:

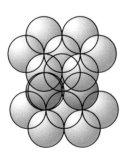

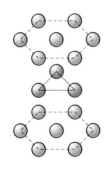

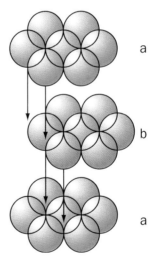

e.g. zinc or nickel

Body-centred cubic structures

A few metals do not have close-packed structures.
Metals, such as sodium, form more open structures.
The presence of more space between atoms results in low
densities for these metals.
Look at the diagrams below:

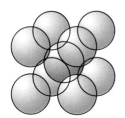

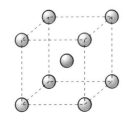

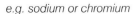

e.g. sodium or chromium

▷ Chemistry at work: 'Memory metals'

How can metals have a memory?
Memory metals are part of the latest research
to develop 'smart' materials. These are materials that
respond to changes in their environment.
Memory metals 'remember' their original shape.
They return to it by heating or cooling the metal.

We all know that metals change state if you heat them
to their melting point or melting temperature.
But fewer people know about a metal's **transition temperature**.
At this temperature a metal changes the way
its atoms are arranged.

Let's look at an example called Nitinol.
This is an alloy of nickel and titanium.
When heated up, the atoms take up
a compact cubic structure.
However, when we cool the alloy, it adopts a different arrangement.
These changes are at the atomic level. We can't see them.

So how does this give an alloy a memory?
We heat the object, in its desired shape, to its transition temperature.
Then we cool it, changing the arrangement of its atoms.
If we now bend the metal, we can change it back
to its original shape by warming it up.
Just imagine denting your car, then just washing it in hot water
to smooth it out again!

This type of Nitinol has a transition temperature, which is below room temperature, so it reverts to its original shape automatically. These sunglasses are expensive at the moment

Other alloys like this include mixtures of copper, zinc and aluminium
or copper, aluminium and nickel.
They are called 'shape memory alloys'.

Q. What does an alloy of nickel and titanium wear in bed?

A. a NiTi (if it remembers!)

Uses of memory metals

We are finding new uses for these metals all the time.
At the moment Nitinol has been used to:
- join hydraulic lines in fighter planes
(A Nitinol collar is stretched when cool, then slipped over the pipes
to be joined. When it is warmed the collar shrinks with great force,
forming a totally sealed joint)
- hold ligaments tightly to bones
- in veins as a sort of 'bird's nest' filter to trap blood clots.
(The heat of the body opens up the thin bundle of wire
when it's in position.)

Shape memory alloys are also used to make:
- braces for teeth
- thermostats on coffee pots
- fire sprinklers
- antennae for mobile phones
- under-wires for bras
- frames for spectacles and sun-glasses
(If you sit on your glasses and twist their frame,
they can change back to their original shape.)

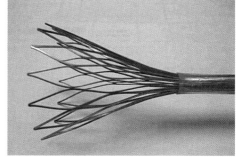

A Nitinol self-expanding stent is a surgical device that provides support when two tubular structures are joined

Future uses

American scientists are currently working on a project to make an artificial eel.
They are using Nitinol and plastics to make the body of the eel.
But why bother to make a robot that can swim on its own?
The US Defence Agency are funding further work.
They see its potential in finding mines at sea.
Armies of wriggling mechanical eels could locate mines which could then be blown up safely.

The researchers use Nitinol to imitate the movements of a sea eel.
Look at the diagram below:

Joseph Ayers is leading the work on robots to hunt mines

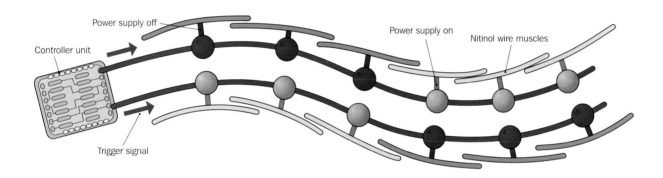

The Nitinol can be heated by passing an electric current through it. This heating makes the wire contract.
They carefully send the current down each wire in turn.
With the correct sequence of pulses down each side, the eel can swish its body.

At present the robot is attached to the side of its water tank.
There is a lot more work to do before it can actually swim.
Computer programmes have to be designed that can adjust the eel's movement in rough or calm seas.
The way a real eel keeps itself stable has to be studied further to inform the computer programmer's work.
Eventually instructions could be sent to the eels from buoys.

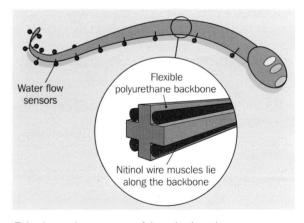

This shows the structure of the robotic eel

Besides searching for mines there are other potential uses.
Ideas include attaching chemical sensors and video cameras to the eels. They could then monitor pollution in the sea.
This would be useful around ship wrecks of oil platforms.
They would also give scientists a cheap way of gathering samples from the sea-bed or from deep ocean trenches.

The researchers are also thinking about developing an artificial lobster!
This could comb the sea-bed for mines.

Summary of metals

Metal ions are bonded together by a 'sea' of electrons.
Each metal atom donates its outer electrons into a conduction band.
The electrons in the conduction band are free to drift between the ions.
They move in one particular direction when an electric current flows.
Metal ions are arranged in giant structures. This explains why
most metals have high melting points.
The atoms are usually packed closely together in these giant structures.
This is why most metals have a high density.

The atoms in a metal can be arranged in a:

1. face-centred cubic close-packed structure,

2. hexagonal close-packed structure or

3. body-centred cubic structure (a more open structure).

Mixtures of metals are called alloys.
Alloys are blended to improve the properties of metals.
Their properties can be carefully matched to particular uses.

Metal atoms are usually close-packed

Summary of structure and bonding

In this section, we have now seen how atoms bond together.
We have also looked at how the atoms, ions or molecules are arranged
in structures.
The bonding and structure of a substance explain its properties.

Here is a summary of the last three chapters so that you can compare
the different types of structure and bonding:

Bonding	Ionic (between metals and non-metals)	Covalent (between non-metals)		Metallic (between metals)
Structures	giant ionic	giant covalent	simple molecular	giant metallic
Melting point	high	high	low	high
Conduct electricity	not when solid, but they do when molten or dissolved in water	no (except graphite)	no	yes
Example	sodium chloride	diamond	water	copper

▷ Questions on metals

1 Copy and complete:
A '....' of electrons bond metal ions together in ....
structures. Metals can .... electricity because these
delocalised .... are free to drift through the structure.
Most metals have .... melting points because it takes a
lot of energy to break down their .... structures.
Most metals are also .... because there is not much
space between their '....-packed' ions.
Some metals, such as .... , have a more open structure
called a ....-centred cubic structure.
Mixtures of metals are called .....

2 a) Make a list of the general properties of metals.
   b) Write down any metals you know that don't have
       the usual metallic properties. Do these metals have
       any uses related to their unusual properties? If so,
       explain them.
   c) Which property do **all** metals have in common?
   d) Draw a diagram to show how you would test the
       property given in c).

3 a) Describe how you can show the structure of a metal
       using a set of plastic balls.
   b) How can you arrange the balls in two different
       structures?
   c) What is each of these structures called?
   d) Name a third type of structure adopted by some
       metals.
   e) How does the structure in d) differ from those in
       your answer to c)?

4 a) Explain what we mean by 'metallic bonding'.
   b) Why are the particles in a giant metallic structure
       more correctly referred to as ions rather than atoms?
   c) Explain why metals are ductile, i.e. they can be
       drawn out into wires.
   d) An alloy can be made from two metals.
       In many cases the ions differ in size. In these cases
       the alloy is harder than the pure metal.
       Can you explain this?
   e) How would you make an alloy of aluminium and
       copper?
   f) Design a test you could do to show that the alloy in
       e) was harder than either copper or aluminium.

5 Sodium, magnesium and aluminium are in Groups 1, 2
   and 3 of the Periodic Table.
   Sodium has 11 electrons, magnesium has 12 and
   aluminium 13 electrons.
   a) Draw each atom showing the arrangement of
       electrons.
   b) All metal elements have metallic bonding.
       How many electrons do you think the atoms of
       each metal above donate into the 'sea' of electrons.
   c) Aluminium is the best conductor of electricity of the
       three metals. Sodium is the worst.
       Can you explain this?

▷ Questions on structure and bonding

1 Copy and complete:
There are three types of bonding – ionic, ...
(which includes dative or coordinate bonding)
and .....

.... bonds form between metals and non-metals.
The ions are arranged in .... structures, which have
high melting points. Sodium chloride is an example.
It does not conduct electricity when ...., as its ions are
fixed in position. However, when molten or .... in
water, the .... become free to move. It is electrolysed
as it conducts.

Covalent bonds form between two .... atoms.
These substances can have either a .... structure, like
diamond (with a .... melting point), or be made up of
simple ...., like water (with a .... melting point).
Neither type of structure conducts electricity.
The exception is .....

The ....-molecular forces in substances with simple
molecular structures can be put in order of strength
(for molecules of a similar size):

1. hydrogen ....   strongest
2. permanent dipole–.... forces
3. van der .... forces (which arise
    from temporary .... dipoles)   weakest
Substances with giant .... structures are the only ones
that conduct electricity when solid.

2 Look at this table:

Substance	Melting point / °C	Conducts electricity	
		when solid	when molten
A	−0.5	✗	✗
B	760	✗	✓
C	1800	✓	✓
D	114	✗	✗

Explain how you decide the answers below:
a) Which substance is a metal?
b) Which substance has a giant ionic structure?
c) Which substances are made up of relatively small
    individual molecules?
d) Which substance is a non-metal solid with a simple
    molecular structure?
e) Which substance is broken down into its elements
    as it conducts electricity?
f) What are the factors that could explain the
    differing melting points of substances A and D?

3 Put the following substances in order of their boiling
   points:
   ammonia (NH_3); methane (CH_4); zinc oxide (ZnO)
   Explain your answer.

Further questions on atoms and structure

▷ Atoms and electrons

1 a) i) What is meant by the term *atomic orbital*? [1]
      ii) Define the term *first ionisation energy*. [2]
   b) i) Sketch a graph of first ionisation energy against atomic number for the elements hydrogen to neon. Use the data at the back of the book. [2]
      ii) Explain the *general* trend in the first ionisation energies of the elements of the second period (lithium to neon). [2]
      iii) From the shape of your graph, and in the light of the electronic configurations involved, briefly explain the relative values of the first ionisation energies of each of the following pairs of elements. (Refer to pages 15 and 96 if necessary.)
      ● He and Li
      ● Be and B
      ● N and O [3]
   c) Write ionic half-equations to show the changes associated with each of the following.
      i) The molar first ionisation energy of sodium
      ii) The molar second ionisation energy of magnesium [2]
   d) State and explain how you would expect the value for the second ionisation energy of sodium to compare with each of the following:
      i) The first ionisation energy of neon
      ii) The second ionisation energy of magnesium [2]
      (AQA)

2 a) Define the second ionisation energy of fluorine. [2]
   b) Sketch a graph on axes like the ones below to show the successive ionisation energies of fluorine. Give reasons for the shape of the line you draw.

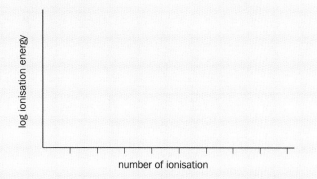

number of ionisation

[4]
(EDEXCEL)

3 The table below provides data on the successive ionisation energies of carbon

Ionisation number	1st	2nd	3rd	4th	5th	6th
Ionisation number/kJ mol^{-1}	1090	2350	4610	6220	37 800	47 300

a) Explain why each successive ionisation energy increases in value.
b) Write an equation to represent the 5th ionisation energy of carbon
c) Explain how these data can be used to provide evidence for the electronic configuration of carbon. [8]
(OCR)

▷ Atoms and the nucleus

4 A sample of lead consists of a mixture of three isotopes whose relative isotopic masses are 206.0, 207.0 and 208.0.
Use this example to explain the difference between the terms *relative isotopic mass*, and *relative atomic mass*. [5]
How are the units used for relative atomic masses and relative isotopic masses defined? [2]

5 a) How is the mass spectrum of an element produced? Explain how each of the following processes is involved.
      i) ionisation   ii) acceleration
      iii) deflection   iv) detection [4]
   b) The mass spectrum of a sample of magnesium contains three peaks with mass/charge ratios and relative intensities shown in the table:

mass/charge ratio	24	25	26
relative intensity	1	0.127	0.139

   i) Explain why magnesium gives three peaks in its spectrum. [2]
   ii) Use the information in the table to calculate an accurate value for the relative atomic mass of magnesium. [3]
   (AQA)

6 In terms of the numbers of sub-atomic particles, state one difference and two similarities between two isotopes of the same element. [3]

7 a) The table shows data relating to the relative isotopic abundance of the element titanium, Ti.

Isotope	^{46}Ti	^{47}Ti	^{48}Ti	^{49}Ti	^{50}Ti
% abundance	8.02	7.31	73.81	5.54	5.32

   i) Explain what is meant by the term *relative isotopic abundance*. [2]
   ii) Using the data from the table, calculate the relative atomic mass, A_r, of titanium. [2]

b) Bromine gas contains the isotopes ^{79}Br and ^{81}Br in almost equal proportions. Part of the mass spectrum of bromine gas, showing one of the peaks for the molecular ion, Br_2^+, is shown below:

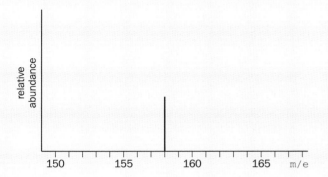

i) Copy the diagram and complete it to show the full spectrum of the molecular ion peaks of Br_2^+. [3]
ii) Explain the number of peaks present in your diagram. [1]
iii) Explain the ratio of the heights of the peaks shown in your diagram. [1]
(AQA)

8 a) Explain how a mass spectrometer works. [4]
b) Explain **two** uses of mass spectrometry. [2]
c) Chlorine, Cl_2, has two isotopes, ^{35}Cl and ^{37}Cl, present in the ratio $3:1$.
   i) How many peaks would you expect to see on a mass spectrum due to molecular chlorine? [1]
   ii) Identify the ion responsible for each peak.
   iii) The heights of the peaks on the mass spectrum depend on the relative abundances of the ions present. State, with reasons, which peak you would expect to be the highest. [1]
(OCR)

▷ **Calculations using the mole**

9 When a cake is baked, a gas is released which causes the mixture to rise. Baking soda is sodium hydrogencarbonate, $NaHCO_3$, which decomposes on heating to give carbon dioxide. Baking soda consists of dry $NaHCO_3$ mixed with a solid acid. When water is added to baking powder, carbon dioxide is produced.
a) Write an equation for the decomposition of baking powder to form sodium carbonate, water and carbon dioxide. [2]
b) Calculate the volume of carbon dioxide, at room temperature and atmospheric pressure, formed when 0.42 g of baking soda is heated. (1.0 mole of a gas occupies 24 dm^3 at room temperature and atmospheric pressure) [2]

c) Draw a labelled diagram of the apparatus you could use to heat 0.42 g of baking soda and measure the volume of carbon dioxide produced. [2]
(WJEC)

10 a) Calculate the number of moles and the mass of calcium hydroxide produced when 100 g of calcium oxide are treated with water and the yield is 84%. [4]
b) Assuming 100% yield, what mass of calcium reacts with water to produce the same mass of calcium hydroxide? Give an equation for the reaction. [2]

11 A fertiliser contains a mixture of ammonium sulphate and potassium sulphate. A sample of this fertiliser was warmed with an excess of aqueous sodium hydroxide (50 cm^3 of a 0.500 mol dm^{-3} solution) until the evolution of ammonia ceased:

$$(NH_4)_2SO_4 + 2\,NaOH \longrightarrow 2\,NH_3 + Na_2SO_4 + 2\,H_2O$$

The excess of sodium hydroxide was neutralised by 38.40 cm^3 of concentrated hydrochloric acid of concentration 0.500 mol dm^{-3}.

$$NaOH + HCl \longrightarrow NaCl + H_2O$$

(a) Calculate the number of moles of hydrochloric acid used to neutralise the excess sodium hydroxide. [2]
(b) Deduce the number of moles of sodium hydroxide that reacted with this number of moles of hydrochloric acid. [1]
(c) Calculate the number of moles of sodium hydroxide present in the original 50.00 cm^3 of 0.500 mol dm^{-3} solution. [1]
(d) Deduce the number of moles of ammonium sulphate present in the sample of the fertiliser. [1]
(e) Calculate the mass of ammonium sulphate present in the sample of the fertiliser. [2]
(AQA)

12 When phosphorus is burned in a limited supply of air, it forms two oxides, A and B. Oxide A contains 56.4% by mass of phosphorus.
a) Calculate the empirical formula of A. [3]
b) What additional information would you need to calculate the molecular formula of A? [1]
c) Oxide B has the molecular formula P_4O_{10}. Write an equation for the formation of P_4O_{10} from phosphorus and oxygen. Calculate the mass of P_4O_{10} formed by the complete oxidation of 3.2 g of phosphorus. [3]
(AQA)

83

Further questions on atoms and structure

13 a) When 0.25 g of sodium metal was added to 200 cm³ (an excess) of water, the following reaction occurred:

$$Na + H_2O \longrightarrow NaOH + \tfrac{1}{2} H_2$$

   i) Calculate the number of moles of sodium taking part in the reaction. [1]
   ii) Calculate the concentration in mol dm⁻³ of the sodium hydroxide solution which was formed. [1]
   iii) Calculate the volume of hydrogen formed at 300 K. Assume that hydrogen is insoluble in water at 300 K. [1]
   (Assume one mole of gas occupies 24 dm³ at 300 K.)

b) In another experiment, 25.0 cm³ of 0.183 mol dm⁻³ sodium hydroxide were neutralised by 13.7 cm³ of sulphuric acid according to the following equation:

$$2\,NaOH + H_2SO_4 \longrightarrow Na_2SO_4 + 2\,H_2O$$

Find the concentration of the aqueous sulphuric acid in mol dm⁻³. [2]

(AQA)

14 a) State the ideal gas equation.
b) A sample of a volatile liquid, of mass 0.148 g, vaporised to give a gas of volume 63.0 cm³ at a pressure of 1.01×10^5 Pa and a temperature of 100 °C.
Find the relative molecular mass of the liquid.
(The value of the gas constant, R, is $8.314\,J\,K^{-1}\,mol^{-1}$.) [2]

15 Sodium carbonate is produced in large quantities by the Solvay Process. In this process, ammonia and carbon dioxide are passed through a solution of sodium chloride, forming sodium hydrogencarbonate and ammonium chloride:

$$NaCl + H_2O + NH_3 + CO_2 \longrightarrow$$
$$NaHCO_3 + NH_4Cl$$

In the next stage, sodium hydrogencarbonate is thermally decomposed to form sodium carbonate.

$$2\,NaHCO_3 \longrightarrow Na_2CO_3 + H_2O + CO_2$$

Calculate the maximum mass of sodium carbonate which, theoretically, could be obtained from 546 kg of sodium chloride. [4]

(AQA)

16 Ammonium salts are widely used as fertilisers. One standard method for the analysis of ammonium salts (except the chloride) is to react them in a solution with methanal, HCHO. This forms a neutral organic compound together with an acid which can be titrated with standard alkali. For ammonium nitrate the equation for this reaction is:

$$4\,NH_4NO_3 + 6\,HCHO \longrightarrow$$
$$(CH_2)_6N_4 + 4\,HNO_3 + 6\,H_2O$$

15.0 g of a fertiliser containing ammonium nitrate as the only ammonium salt was dissolved in water and the solution made up to 1.00 dm³ with pure water. 25.0 cm³ portions of this solution were then treated with saturated aqueous methanal solution and allowed to stand for a few minutes.

The liberated nitric acid was then titrated with 0.100 mol dm⁻³ NaOH solution. The volume of NaOH solution used was 22.3 cm³. What percentage by mass of the fertiliser was ammonium nitrate? [4]

(EDEXCEL)

▶ Ionic compounds

17 This question is about the element barium and its compounds.
a) i) What are the two types of sub-atomic particle in the barium nucleus?
How many of each type are present? [2]
   ii) Draw 'dot-and-cross' diagrams to show the electron transfer process when barium chloride, BaCl₂, forms from atoms of its elements, showing outer-shell electrons only. [2]
b) Barium hydroxide reacts with dilute sulphuric acid. An experiment was carried out to find the equation for this neutralisation reaction.

1.0 mol dm⁻³ sulphuric acid was added to 50 cm³ of 0.10 mol dm⁻³ barium hydroxide solution using the apparatus shown in the diagram. The mixture was stirred after each addition.

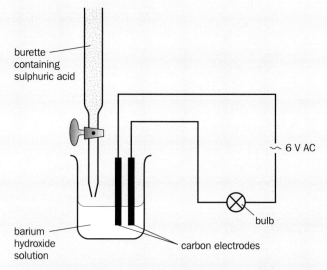

As the sulphuric acid was added a white precipitate was formed. After the addition of 5.0 cm³ of acid the lamp went out.
i) Suggest a reason for using alternating current (AC) rather than a direct current (DC) in the circuit. [1]

ii) Calculate the number of moles of acid and alkali used in the titration. [2]

iii) Deduce the equation for the reaction between barium hydroxide solution, $Ba(OH)_2(aq)$, and dilute sulphuric acid, including state symbols. [2]

iv) Explain why the lamp goes out when the endpoint of the reaction is reached. [1]

c) Barium nitrate gives a strong flame colour and is used in fireworks.

i) Give the formula of barium nitrate. [1]

ii) What colour do barium compounds give to fireworks? [1]

(EDEXCEL)

▷ **Covalent bonding**

18 a) i) Using the symbols $\delta+$ and $\delta-$, indicate the polarity of the covalent bonds in each of the following:

$$H_3C - Cl \qquad Cl - F \qquad H - Cl \qquad [3]$$

ii) Explain the term *electronegativity*. [2]

b) The formula below shows the structure of ethanoic acid when dissolved in benzene.

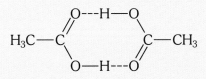

i) What do the broken lines represent in the formula? [1]

ii) What do we call pairs of molecules joined together in this way? [1]

iii) Calculate the apparent relative molecular mass of ethanoic acid when dissolved in benzene. [1]

19 The figure shows a graph of melting temperature against relative molecular mass for the hydrides shown in line **A** and line **B**.

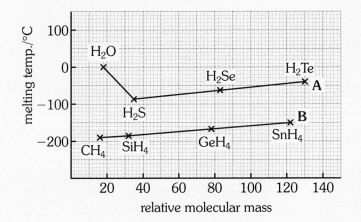

a) Explain the trend in the melting temperature of the hydrides represented by the line **B**. [1]

b) Explain why the first hydride in the group represented by line **A** has a higher melting temperature than the others. [1]

(WJEC)

20 The reaction between phosphorus and fluorine produces a compound of formula PF_3.

a) Give the electronic configuration of phosphorus.

b) Draw a diagram to show the shape of the PF_3 molecule, and state the bond angles present in it. Give the name of this shape.

c) Explain in terms of the electron pairs present, why the molecule has this shape.

(AQA)

21 Boron, nitrogen and oxygen form fluorides with molecular formulae BF_3, NF_3 and OF_2. Draw the shapes you would expect for these molecules, suggesting a value for the bond angle in each case.

22 White phosphorus melts at 317 K. In a mass spectrometer, white phosphorus gives only one peak at 124 in the region of the molecular ion.

a) What can you deduce from the fact that there is only one peak in the region of the molecular ion? Give the formula of the species responsible for this peak.

b) Explain in terms of structure and bonding why white phosphorus has a low melting point.

c) Explain why the melting point of silicon (1683 K) is higher than that of white phosphorus.

(AQA)

23 a) Copy the following table and complete it by giving, in each case, the formula of a molecule or ion which has the bond angle shown. Use a different molecule or ion for each angle.

Bond angle	90°	109° 28'	120°	180°
Formula				

b) i) Draw a diagram to show the structure of a water molecule and indicate the bond angle on your diagram.

ii) Explain why the bond angle in water is different from any of those in the table in part a).

iii) Draw a diagram to show how two water molecules attract one another by hydrogen bonding.

(AQA)

Further questions on atoms and structure

24 Draw dot-and-cross diagrams to show the bonding in each of the following:

NH_3 CO_2 HCl [3]

25 The diagram below shows how a water molecule interacts with a hydrogen fluoride molecule.

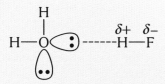

a) What is the value of the bond angle in a single molecule of water? [1]

b) Explain your answer to part (a) by using the concept of electron pair repulsion. [4]

c) Name the type of interaction between a water molecule and a hydrogen fluoride molecule shown in the diagram. [1]

d) Explain the origin of the $\delta+$ charge shown on the hydrogen atom in the diagram. [2]

e) When water interacts with hydrogen fluoride, the value of the bond angle in water changes slightly. Predict how the angle is different from that in a single molecule of water and explain your answer. [2]

(AQA)

26 a) i) State the shapes of the following molecules. Using the VSEPR (Valence-Shell Electron Pair Repulsion) principle, explain how the shapes of these simple molecules arise (diagrams are not required):

BF_3; CH_4; SF_6. [3]

ii) The bond angle HÑH in NH_4^+ is 109.5°;
The bond angle HÑH in NH_3 is 107°;
The bond angle HÔH in H_2O is 104.5°.

Explain these differences in bond angles in terms of repulsion between the different types of electron pairs. [3]

iii) Use the VSEPR principle to predict the shapes of the following molecules:

$BeCl_2$; BrF_5. [2]

(WJEC)

27 Ammonia, NH_3, and phosphine, PH_3, are the hydrides of the first two elements in Group 5.

a) i) Draw a dot-and-cross diagram for the ammonia molecule. [1]

ii) Sketch and explain the shape of the ammonia molecule. [3]

b) Some physical properties of ammonia and phosphine are given in the following table:

	Boiling temperature / °C	Solubility in water / mol dm^{-3}
Ammonia	−33	31.1
Phosphine	−88	8.88×10^{-4}

i) By reference to the nature of the intermolecular forces in both molecules, suggest reasons for the difference in boiling temperatures. [3]

ii) Suggest why ammonia is much more soluble in water than phosphine. [2]

(EDEXCEL)

28 a) Explain the following in terms of the bonding and structure of the substances being heated.

i) When a few crystals of iodine are gently warmed in a test tube a purple vapour is given off. [3]

ii) When a few crystals of sodium chloride are gently warmed in a test tube no change is observed. Very strong and prolonged heating is needed to melt the crystals. [3]

iii) Very strong heating fails to melt a sample of silicon dioxide. [3]

b) Molecules of the compound sulphur hexafluoride, SF_6, contain covalent bonds.

i) Explain the meaning of the term *covalent bond*. [1]

ii) Draw a diagram to show the shape of SF_6 and give a name for the shape. [2]

(AQA)

▶ Metals and structures

29 Explain carefully why copper conducts electricity, but diamond does not. [6]

30 Communication satellites are made of an alloy of titanium, containing small quantities of aluminium and vanadium, rather than parts made from alloys of iron. Data about aluminium, titanium, vanadium and iron are given in the table below.

Element	Atomic number	Melting point / K	Density / g cm^{-3}	Cost per tonne / £
Aluminium	13	933	2.70	1000
Titanium	22	1933	4.50	4700
Vanadium	23	2163	6.11	4800
Iron	26	1808	7.90	220

a) Describe, with the aid of a labelled diagram, a simple model of metallic bonding.

b) An alloy of iron, containing a small amount of vanadium, shows increased resistance to wear and is stronger at high temperatures than the titanium alloy. However, despite their similar properties in other respects, the titanium is preferred for use in satellites. Using data from the table answer the following:

i) State another advantage of the iron–vanadium alloy over the titanium alloy.

ii) Suggest why the titanium alloy is preferred for use in satellites.

▷ Structure in general

31 A crystal of iodine, heated gently in a test tube, gave off a purple vapour. A crystal of sodium chloride, heated to the same temperature, remained unchanged.

a) Name the type of bonding or interaction which occurs
   i)   between atoms in a molecule of iodine;
   ii) between molecules in a crystal of iodine.

b) Give the formula of the species which is responsible for the purple colour in the vapour.

c) Explain why iodine vaporises at a relatively low temperature.

d) Explain, in terms of its bonding, why the sodium chloride crystal did not melt or vaporise.

e) Describe what happens to the particles in sodium chloride when the solid is heated above room temperature but below its melting point.

f) Explain why the heat energy needed to vaporise sodium chloride (171 kJ mol^{-1}) is greater than the heat energy needed to melt it (29 kJ mol^{-1}).

32 a) Describe, with the aid of diagrams, the bonding and structure of i) iodine and ii) diamond.

b) State and explain the effect, if any, of heat on separate samples of solid iodine and of diamond.

c) Sodium chloride and caesium chloride have different crystal structures. Describe, with the aid of diagrams, the structure and bonding found in each solid. State the lattice type and coordination number in each and explain why these two salts have different crystal structures.

d) Copper has a high electrical conductivity. Draw a diagram to show the bonding in copper and use it to explain its high electrical conductivity.

(AEB)

33 a) State the meaning of the term **coordination number** of an ion in a crystal structure. [1]

b) The structures of sodium chloride and caesium chloride are shown below. What is the coordination number of the **chloride** ions in **each**?

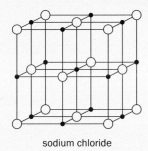
sodium chloride

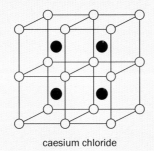
caesium chloride

[1]

c) Explain why
   i)   Sodium chloride is soluble in water, and
   ii) ethanol is soluble in water while hydrocarbons are not. [3]

(WJEC)

34 The electron density distributions for three species, hydrogen (H$_2$), hydrogen chloride (HCl), and lithium fluoride (LiF), are shown below.

Which species is represented by each of the following electron density distributions? Indicate the type of bonding present in each.

a)

b)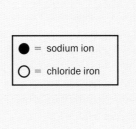

c)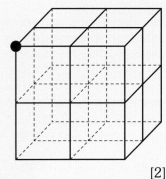

[3]

(WJEC)

35 The isotopes of three elements (**X**, **Y** and **Z**) are listed below.

$^{23}_{11}$**X**; $^{19}_{9}$**Y**; $^{12}_{6}$**Z**

(**X**, **Y** and **Z** are not the elemental symbols.)
Which combination of two elements will form

a) an ionic bond, and

b) a covalent bond? [1]

(WJEC)

36 a) Complete the diagram below to show the structure of sodium chloride using the given key to represent sodium and chloride ions.

● = sodium ion
○ = chloride iron

[2]

b) Showing outer shell electrons only, draw a 'dot and cross' diagram of i) MgCl$_2$ ii) PCl$_3$.

c) Draw a diagram to show the expected shape and bond angles in a molecule of PCl$_3$.

d) Phosphorus also forms a pentachloride, PCl$_5$, which is thought to exist in the solid form as [PCl$_4$]$^+$[PCl$_6$]$^-$.
Suggest the shapes of these two ions:
[PCl$_4$]$^+$
[PCl$_6$]$^-$ [2]

(OCR)

7 The Periodic Table

▶ History of the Periodic Table

Around 200 years ago, scientists were busy discovering as yet unknown elements.
However, they struggled to find any patterns that linked the different elements.

Wolfgang Döbereiner had some early success in grouping
similar elements in sets of three.
He called these triads. One triad was formed by calcium, strontium and barium.
Look at their relative atomic masses opposite:
Döbereiner found that the relative atomic mass of the middle element
was roughly the average of those of the other two elements.
However, only a few triads could be found.

Element	Relative atomic mass
calcium	40
strontium	88
barium	137

A real breakthrough was made around 1865 by John Newlands.
He put the elements in order of atomic mass.
He found that every eighth element was similar.
Unfortunately, his pattern only worked for the first 15 or so
of the elements known at that time. After that, he could see no links
between the rest of the elements.
Other scientists made fun of his ideas. They suggested that he could
have done better by sorting the elements into alphabetical order!

In 1869 the problem was solved by a Russian called Dmitri Mendeleev.
He also tried putting the elements in order of atomic mass.
He started making a table of elements. New rows were started so that
elements which were alike could line up together in columns.
He wanted a table of regular (periodic) patterns.

However, Mendeleev was not afraid to take risks.
When the pattern began to go wrong, he would leave a gap in his table.
He claimed that these gaps were for elements that had not yet been discovered.
He even changed the order round when similar elements didn't line up.

Dmitri Mendeleev (1834–1907)

As you might expect, at first people doubted his 'Periodic Table'.
However, he used his table to predict the properties of elements which could
fill the gaps. Then in 1886 the element germanium was discovered.
This new element closely matched Mendeleev's predictions.
Look at the table opposite:
Other scientists finally accepted his ideas.

Although Mendeleev's table was widely accepted, there was one thing
that he could not explain.
Why did he need to change the order of atomic masses sometimes
in order to make the pattern carry on?

	Mendeleev's predictions	Germanium
R.A.M.	72	72.6
Density	$5.5 \, \mathrm{g\,cm^{-3}}$	$5.35 \, \mathrm{g\,cm^{-3}}$
Colour	light grey	dark grey

The answer lies inside the atoms. The atoms of elements in the Periodic Table
are not arranged in order of mass. It is their number of protons (atomic number)
that really matters.
Look at the modern version of the Periodic Table on the next page:

▶ The modern Periodic Table

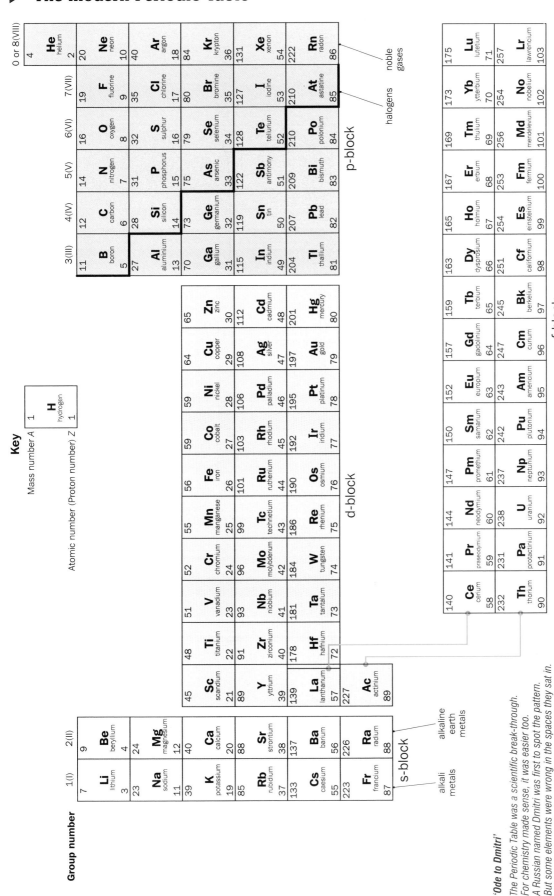

'Ode to Dmitri'

The Periodic Table was a scientific break-through.
For chemistry made sense, it was easier too.
A Russian named Dmitri was first to spot the pattern.
But some elements were wrong in the spaces they sat in.
"I know," thought Dmitri, "I'll just leave gaps."
And a stroke of genius had just come to pass.
Some of the elements were as yet undiscovered.
So he made predictions from the properties of others.

A few years later when germanium was found,
Scientists agreed his ideas were sound.
Even now we use the table on which we never dine.
Still based on that discovery in 1869.

▶ Atomic structure and the Periodic Table

You can see on the last page that there are four main blocks in the Periodic Table.
These are called s, p, d and f-blocks. Do these letters remind you of anything?
Let's look at the electronic structure of an atom from the s, d and p blocks:

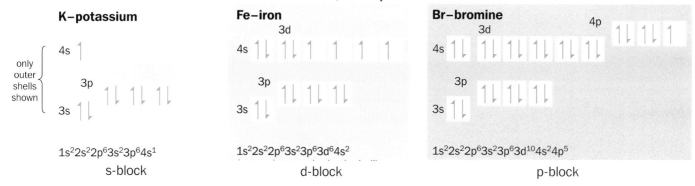

K–potassium

only outer shells shown

$1s^22s^22p^63s^23p^64s^1$

s-block

Fe–iron

$1s^22s^22p^63s^23p^63d^64s^2$

d-block

Br–bromine

$1s^22s^22p^63s^23p^63d^{10}4s^24p^5$

p-block

The electronic structures of the first 36 elements are shown below:

Atomic number

1	H $1s^1$	
2	He $1s^2$	
3	Li $1s^22s^1$	s-block elements
4	Be $1s^22s^2$	
5	B $1s^22s^22p^1$	
6	C $1s^22s^22p^2$	
7	N $1s^22s^22p^3$	p-block elements
8	O $1s^22s^22p^4$	
9	F $1s^22s^22p^5$	
10	Ne $1s^22s^22p^6$	
11	Na $1s^22s^22p^63s^1$	s-block elements
12	Mg $1s^22s^22p^63s^2$	
13	Al $1s^22s^22p^63s^23p^1$	
14	Si $1s^22s^22p^63s^23p^2$	
15	P $1s^22s^22p^63s^23p^3$	p-block elements
16	S $1s^22s^22p^63s^23p^4$	
17	Cl $1s^22s^22p^63s^23p^5$	
18	Ar $1s^22s^22p^63s^23p^6$	
19	K $1s^22s^22p^63s^23p^64s^1$	s-block elements
20	Ca $1s^22s^22p^63s^23p^64s^2$	
21	Sc $1s^22s^22p^63s^23p^63d^14s^2$	
22	Ti $1s^22s^22p^63s^23p^63d^24s^2$	
23	V $1s^22s^22p^63s^23p^63d^34s^2$	
24	Cr $1s^22s^22p^63s^23p^63d^54s^1$	(remember the stability of the half-filled sub-shell, discussed on page 15)
25	Mn $1s^22s^22p^63s^23p^63d^54s^2$	
26	Fe $1s^22s^22p^63s^23p^63d^64s^2$	d-block elements
27	Co $1s^22s^22p^63s^23p^63d^74s^2$	
28	Ni $1s^22s^22p^63s^23p^63d^84s^2$	
29	Cu $1s^22s^22p^63s^23p^63d^{10}4s^1$	(this arrangement fills copper's 3d sub-shell)
30	Zn $1s^22s^22p^63s^23p^63d^{10}4s^2$	
31	Ga $1s^22s^22p^63s^23p^63d^{10}4s^24p^1$	
32	Ge $1s^22s^22p^63s^23p^63d^{10}4s^24p^2$	
33	As $1s^22s^22p^63s^23p^63d^{10}4s^24p^3$	p-block elements
34	Se $1s^22s^22p^63s^23p^63d^{10}4s^24p^4$	
35	Br $1s^22s^22p^63s^23p^63d^{10}4s^24p^5$	
36	Kr $1s^22s^22p^63s^23p^63d^{10}4s^24p^6$	

▶ Groups and periods

Do you recall from previous work how we label the columns and rows in the Periodic Table?

Groups

There are eight groups in the s and p-blocks of the Periodic Table.
A group is a **vertical column**.
All the elements in a group have similar properties.
They are a 'chemical family'.

Look at the Periodic Table on page 89:
Some groups have special 'family' names. Can you find Group 7 (VII)?
What is the group called? Have you met any elements from this 'family' before?
Which other groups have a 'family' name?
The rest of the groups are just known by their group number.

Can you see a link between the group number and
the total number of electrons in the outer shell?

Although iodine has 53 electrons, you know it has 7 electrons in its outer shell because it is in Group 7

Group number in the Periodic Table equals the number of electrons in the outer shell.

Therefore all the atoms of elements in the same group have the **same number of electrons in their outer shells**.

Example
Group 1

Li	$1s^2$	$2s^1$
Na	$1s^22s^22p^6$	$3s^1$
K	$1s^22s^22p^63s^23p^6$	$4s^1$

Example
Group 7

F	$1s^2$	$2s^22p^52s^22p^5$
Cl	$1s^2 2s^22p^6$	$3s^23p^5$
Br	$1s^22s^22p^6 3s^23p^63d^{10}$	$4s^24p^5$

Remember it is the electrons in the outer shell that take part in chemical reactions. This explains why elements in the same group have **similar chemical properties**.
They undergo similar reactions.

Periods

Periods are the **rows across** the Table.
You read the Periodic Table like a book. Start at the top, and work your way down, reading from left to right.
So there are two elements in the 1st period, H and He.
The 2nd period has eight elements, starting with Li.

- Which is the last element in the 2nd period?
- Can you count how many elements are in the 3rd period?
- Can you work out a link between atomic structure and the number of elements in each period?
- Is there a link between the number of electrons a sub-shell can hold and the width of each block in the Periodic Table?
  So how many electrons do we need to fill an *f* sub-shell?

Examples
Si is in Group 4 (IV).
It is in the 3rd period.

Sr is in Group 2 (II).
It is in the 5th period.

▶ Patterns in the Periodic Table (Group 4)

Metal and non-metal elements

92 elements are found naturally on Earth. The elements after uranium in the Periodic Table are only made in nuclear reactions. Some are so unstable that they exist only for a fraction of a second before splitting up.

The elements can be sorted into 2 sets – the metals and the non-metals.
Over three-quarters of the elements are metals.
The elements in the s, d and f-blocks are all metals.

The elements in the p-block can be either metals, non-metals or metalloids (sometimes known as semi-metals).

For example, we can look at Group 4:

C	carbon	**non-metal**
Si	silicon	Silicon and germanium are metalloids or **semi-metals**.
Ge	germanium	They are on the border-line between metals and non-metals.
Sn	tin	**metal**
Pb	lead	**metal**

Silicon is the most well-known metalloid.
It behaves like a metal in some ways, but like a non-metal in others.
For example,
• it is a semiconductor (it does conduct electricity, but not as well as a metal)
• it is shiny like a metal, but
• it is brittle like a non-metal.

Silicon chips have made it possible to make circuits incredibly small

This shows us that science is not always 'black and white'.
The metalloids (or semi-metals) are a 'grey' area.
However, we can draw an imaginary line
in the Periodic Table to divide the metals and non-metals.
You can think of the line as a staircase.
Below stairs you find metals, above stairs you find non-metals.

> The oxides of tin and lead are **amphoteric** (see page 104). They behave as both acids and bases.

				metals
H 1 hydrogen				non-metals
				semi-metals or metalloids

Li 3 lithium	**Be** 4 beryllium										**B** 5 boron	**C** 6 carbon	**N** 7 nitrogen	**O** 8 oxygen	**F** 9 flourine	**Ne** 10 neon	**He** 2 helium
Na 11 sodium	**Mg** 12 magnesium										**Al** 13 aluminium	**Si** 14 silicon	**P** 15 phosphorus	**S** 16 sulphur	**Cl** 17 chlorine	**Ar** 18 argon	
K 19 potassium	**Ca** 20 calcium	**Sc** 21 scandium	**Ti** 22 titanium	**V** 23 vanadium	**Cr** 24 chromium	**Mn** 25 manganese	**Fe** 26 iron	**Co** 27 cobalt	**Ni** 28 nickel	**Cu** 29 copper	**Zn** 30 zinc	**Ga** 31 gallium	**Ge** 32 germanium	**As** 33 arsenic	**Se** 34 selenium	**Br** 35 bromine	**Kr** 36 krypton
Rb 37 rubidium	**Sr** 38 strontium	**Y** 39 yttrium	**Zr** 40 zirconium	**Nb** 41 niobium	**Mo** 42 molybdenum	**Tc** 43 technetium	**Ru** 44 ruthenium	**Rh** 45 rhodium	**Pd** 46 palladium	**Ag** 47 silver	**Cd** 48 cadmium	**In** 49 indium	**Sn** 50 tin	**Sb** 51 antimony	**Te** 52 tellurium	**I** 53 iodine	**Xe** 54 xenon
Cs 55 caesium	**Ba** 56 barium	**La** 57 lanthanum	**Hf** 72 hafnium	**Ta** 73 tantalum	**W** 74 tungsten	**Re** 75 rhenium	**Os** 76 osmium	**Ir** 77 iridium	**Pt** 78 platinum	**Au** 79 gold	**Hg** 80 mercury	**Tl** 81 thallium	**Pb** 82 lead	**Bi** 83 bismuth	**Po** 84 polonium	**At** 85 astatine	**Rn** 86 radon

Explaining metallic/non-metallic properties of elements

Do you remember the charge on the ions of a metal? Are they positive or negative?

The tendency for an element's atoms to lose electrons, forming positive ions, can be thought of as a measure of its metallic character.

On the other hand, ions formed by non-metals are negatively charged.
What do we call an atom's tendency to attract electrons to itself?
We looked at electronegativity on page 68.
Do you think non-metals are more electronegative than metals?
So what pattern would you expect to see in electronegativity going across a period?
Compare your answer with the graph below:

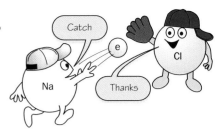

Metal atoms tend to lose electrons. Non-metal atoms tend to gain electrons

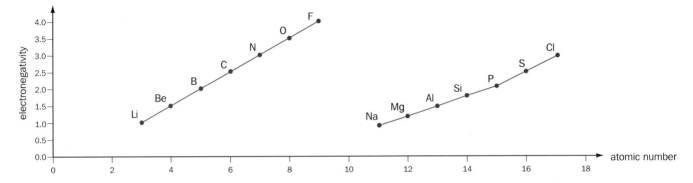

As you go across a period any electrons attracted to an atom would be added to the same shell, but the positive charge on the nucleus is increasing. This increases the pull on the electrons, making the atoms smaller. Therefore the atoms of non-metals, on the right-hand side of a period, are more electronegative.
Does this agree with the table below?

2nd period Common ion	Li 1+	Be 2+	B no ions	C	N 3−	O 2−	F 1−	Ne no ion
3rd period Common ion	Na 1+	Mg 2+	Al 3+	Si no ions	P	S 2−	Cl 1−	Ar no ion

We have also looked at ionisation enthalpies (page 12).
These are a measure of the energy needed to remove electrons from atoms.
Let's look at the first ionisation enthalpies of the Group 4 elements that we listed on the last page. Look at the table below:

Element	First ionisation enthalpy/kJ mol^{-1}
carbon (C)	1086
silicon (Si)	789
germanium (Ge)	762
tin (Sn)	709
lead (Pb)	716

- Does this agree with the theory that elements get more metallic going down a group? Which elements don't quite follow the trend?
- Why is it usually easier for atoms to lose electrons as we go down a group?

An atom of lead is much larger than an atom of carbon.
Therefore its outer electrons are further from the attractive force of the nucleus.
These outer electrons are also shielded from the nucleus by more full inner shells of electrons.
These two factors generally make it easier for atoms to form positive ions as we go down a group.

The elements of Group 4 all form covalent compounds, i.e. they are typical non-metals. But tin and lead also form Sn^{2+} and Pb^{2+} ions, i.e. they are typical metals. For example, lead forms the salt $PbCl_2$ but also has a simple molecular chloride, $PbCl_4$.

Carbon

Diamonds are forever!

We all know about the use of diamonds in jewellery.
If you have ever looked in a jeweller's shop,
you will know how expensive they are.

Diamonds have ideal properties for gemstones.
A well-cut diamond reflects light better than
any other gem (it has 'brilliance').
It also disperses white light into
the colours of the spectrum (it has 'fire').

The cutting edge

Diamond is the hardest of all substances.
It is used on the edges of drills for oil wells.
(Look back to the photo on page 62.)
It also lines circular saws used to cut metal,
stone and other hard materials.

A new process can now fuse together tiny
diamonds. So instead of metal coated in diamonds,
you can now use a solid diamond tool on a lathe.
This can cut and shape the hardest materials.
Diamond coated surgical instruments are used
for delicate operations, like those on the eye.

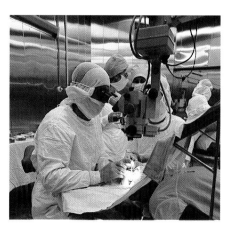

This eye surgeon is using a diamond-coated scalpel

Diamond sinks?

Which type of materials are the best conductors of heat?
Most people would say that metals were.
However, diamond is a better thermal conductor!
On the other hand, it is a poor electrical conductor.
This leads to its use in electronics to get rid
of heat produced in circuits.

Lead in your pencil?

We have already talked about graphite's use in pencils
on page 63. It is mixed with clay to make it harder.
You know that there are different grades of pencil,
such as H, HB, or 2B. Do you know which makes
the darkest lines on paper? How do you think the
amount of clay varies in each type of pencil?
Which type needs sharpening most often?
One thing's for sure – there's no lead in a pencil!

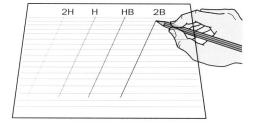

Slippery customer

Graphite feels very slippery. It can be used as a powder
to lubricate metal parts on machinery.
When would you need to use solid graphite rather than oil?
Remember that graphite only turns to a gas at over 3500 °C!
In some lubricants, graphite is added to oil to
improve its properties.

Graphite into diamond!

The diamonds used in cutting and grinding tools
are called industrial diamonds.
They are not mined from the ground, like gemstone diamonds.
They are made in factories from graphite.
Graphite is squeezed in a press and heated.
A metal is used as a solvent and as a catalyst.
The temperature is about 1400 °C in the press,
and the pressure is 60 000 times normal air pressure!
The diamonds are made in a few minutes.
Under these conditions anything containing carbon,
even wood, changes into diamonds!
The diamonds made are small and unattractive.
Manufacturers can vary the sizes to suit the use
by changing conditions.

Silicon and germanium chips

Both these semiconductors are used in the microelectronics industry.
The silicon chip has enabled us to integrate thousands
of transistors into a tiny space. For example, the first computers
occupied large rooms and had only a fraction of the memory
of today's PCs.

Silicon is also used in solar cells, producing electricity
from the sun's energy

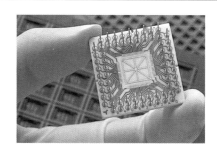

Tin protection

'Tin cans' have very little tin in them!
Cans are made from steel, with a very thin
coating of tin. The tin layer, which is only a few
thousandths of a millimetre thick, stops the steel from rusting.
Steel sheet passes quickly through a plating solution
with anodes made from blocks of tin.

Object at the cathode: $Sn^{2+} + 2\,e^- \longrightarrow Sn$

If the coating is scratched, the can will soon corrode.
This lets in bacteria from the air, which can cause food poisoning.
People can get botulism, which is sometimes fatal.

Making connections

Have you ever used a soldering iron?
Solder is used to join up parts of electrical circuits.
This alloy is made from lead and tin.
It has a low melting point for a metal.
Why is this important?
The solder is made into thick wire. It melts when
held against the hot soldering iron.
Other alloys melt at even lower temperatures (about 70 °C).
These are used in automatic fire sprinklers.

Periodicity

On page 93 we saw how the electronegativity of elements varies going across a period. This type of *repeating trend* across the Periodic Table is called **periodicity**.

We can look at other properties of the elements to demonstrate periodicity.
Plotting the first ionisation enthalpy of successive elements we get this graph:

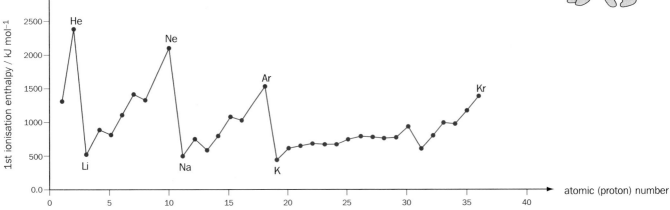

In general, ionisation enthalpies increase going across a period.
The graph of atomic radii below helps to explain this trend:

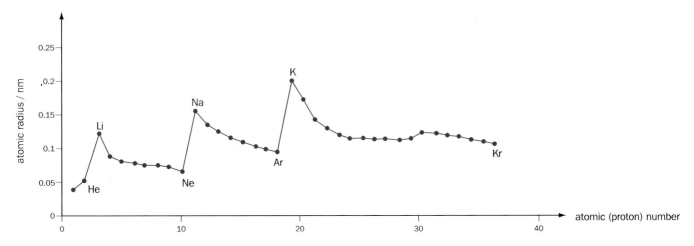

The atoms get smaller as you go across a period.
Successive electrons are filling the same shell, but the positive charge on the nucleus is increasing steadily. This attracts the negative electrons more strongly until a shell is full. Then a new period begins as the next electron enters a new shell further from the nucleus.

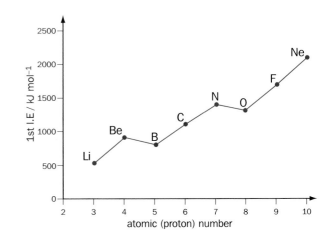

Look more closely at the trend in ionisation enthalpies across the second period shown opposite:
Is there a smooth pattern across a period?
The pattern we get going across each period gives us further evidence for the existence of sub-shells.
Look at the pattern across the 2nd period:
Can you explain the small peak at beryllium (Be)?
And what about the peak at nitrogen (N)?
The stability of full s sub-shells and half-filled p sub-shells, making it more difficult to remove electrons, explains this repeated trend.

96

▶ Structure and periodicity

Look at the graphs showing trends in the melting points
and boiling points of the elements:

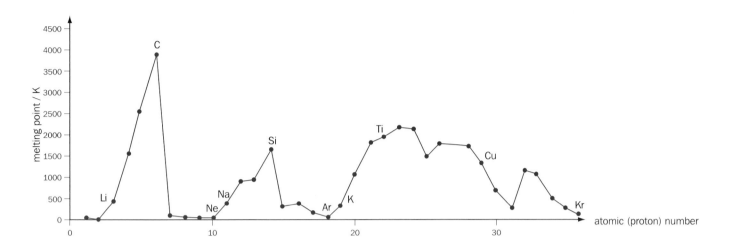

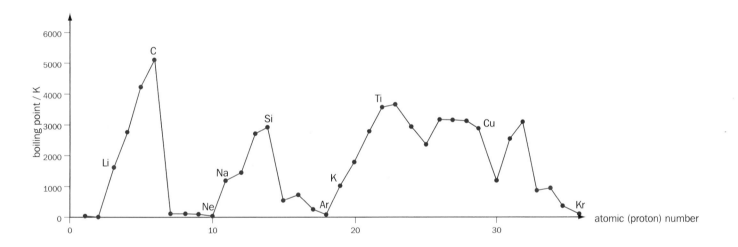

We can explain the repeating trends across periods
by looking at the structure of the elements:

2nd period Structure	Li (lithium)	Be (beryllium)	B (boron)	C (carbon)	N (nitrogen)	O (oxygen)	F (fluorine)	Ne (neon)
	giant metallic	giant metallic	giant covalent	giant covalent	simple molecular	simple molecular	simple molecular	simple molecular
3rd period Structure	Na (sodium)	Mg (magnesium)	Al (aluminium)	Si (silicon)	P (phosphorus)	S(sulphur)	Cl(chlorine)	Ar (argon)
	giant metallic	giant metallic	giant metallic	giant covalent	simple molecular	simple molecular	simple molecular	simple molecular

As you can see, the giant structures appear at the start of a period.
This explains the high melting points and boiling points.
The line falls steeply after Group 4 because the remaining groups
contain elements made of simple molecules, e.g. N_2, S_8, Cl_2.
- We could also plot the electrical conductivity of the elements.
- What pattern do you think we would get?

▶ Trends down a group: Group 1 – The alkali metals

The metals in this first group don't have many uses as the elements themselves. They are too reactive.
However, you will certainly use some of their compounds every day.

Li	lithium
Na	sodium
K	potassium
Rb	rubidium
Cs	caesium

Group 1 elements are metals, but they have some unusual properties.

Why are the alkali metals stored under paraffin (oil)?

Physical properties

Can you remember why sodium, and the other alkali metals, are unusual metals?
They have **low melting points** and are **very soft**.
They can be cut with a knife. Look at the photo opposite:

The graph below shows how their melting points change with increasing atomic number:

Sodium is a soft metal

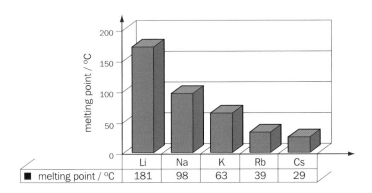

■ melting point / °C	Li	Na	K	Rb	Cs
	181	98	63	39	29

- Can you see a trend going down the group?
- What can you say about the melting points of the alkali metals as we go down the group?

For metals, the elements in Group 1 also have **very low densities**.
Look at their densities on the graph below:

The alkali metals can be cut with a knife

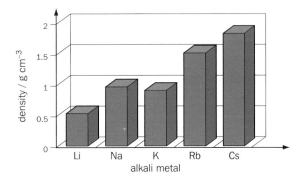

- What is the *general* trend going down the group?
- Which element breaks the pattern?

Chemical properties

The alkali metals are the most reactive group of metals in the Periodic Table.
Look at the photo of caesium reacting with water:

Lithium fizzes on the surface of the water, giving off hydrogen gas.
Sodium gets hot enough to melt itself as it reacts.
Potassium gets so hot that it ignites the hydrogen gas given off.
It burns with a lilac flame.
Can you see a pattern in reactivity going down the group?

Caesium reacts explosively with water!

> ## The alkali metals get *more reactive* as you go down the group

The Periodic Table is very useful. Its groups make chemistry easier!
You only have to learn the reactions of one element in a group.
The others are usually similar. For example,

lithium + water $\longrightarrow$ lithium hydroxide + hydrogen
                          (alkaline solution)

$$2\,Li(s)\ +\ 2\,H_2O(l)\ \longrightarrow\ \ \ 2\,LiOH(aq)\ +\ H_2(g)$$

Knowing this, we know the equations for the other alkali metals:

sodium + water $\longrightarrow$ sodium hydroxide + hydrogen

$$2\,Na(s)\ +\ 2\,H_2O(l)\ \longrightarrow\ \ \ 2\,NaOH(aq)\ +\ H_2(g)$$

etc.

*The Group 1 metals form alkaline solutions
(soluble hydroxides) with water*

We can explain the patterns in reactivity by looking at
the atomic structure of the elements.

Why are the alkali metals (from Group 1) so reactive?

Like most atoms, they react to get a full outer shell.
As the elements, they have just one electron in their outer shells.
So when they react, they want to lose that one electron,
leaving a full outer shell. (See ionic bonding, Chapter 4.)
Look for the alkali metals on the graph of ionisation enthalpies on page 96:
Group 1 elements are so reactive because it is so easy for them
to get rid of just one electron.
● Why do you think that sodium, from Group 1, is more reactive
  than its neighbour from Group 2, magnesium?

Why do the metals get more reactive as we go down Group 1?

The outer electron gets easier to remove as you go down the group.
Remember that electrons are negative. They are attracted to
the positive protons in the nucleus. As you go down the group,
the atoms get bigger. Therefore the outer electron
gets *further away from the attractive force of the nucleus*.
There are also more inner shells full of electrons between the outer electron
and the nucleus. This has a *shielding effect* on the outer electron,
again reducing the attraction between it and the nucleus.

These two factors make it easier for an electron to be removed from a
larger atom.

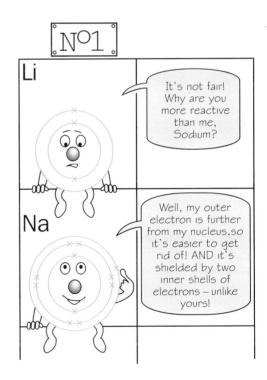

▶ Chemistry at work: New elements

You might know that the heaviest atoms occurring naturally on Earth belong to uranium (atomic number 92).
But Enrico Fermi, one of the early pioneers into nuclear reactions, suggested that heavier atoms could be made.
Using uranium as a target, neutrons could be fired and absorbed into the heavy nucleus. The extra neutron should break down in the nucleus, producing another proton. His theory proved correct. Element 93 was made in 1940.
American scientists at the Lawrence Berkeley National Laboratory in California created elements 94 to 101 in the years before 1955. Look at the names given to their discoveries:

In 1934 Enrico Fermi suggested how to make new elements

Atomic number	Element
93	neptunium
94	plutonium
95	americium
96	curium
97	berkelium
98	californium
99	einsteinium
100	fermium
101	mendelevium

Alchemists in the Middle Ages wasted their time trying to turn lead into gold.
They really needed a heavy ion accelerator!

Then the Russians, who also became a nuclear power and had access to uranium, joined the race. They still work from the Joint Institute for Nuclear Research in Dubna.
Both countries made the elements 102 to 106. But arguments started about who should name the new elements. Yet it wasn't until 1997, having consulted chemists around the world, that IUPAC (the International Union of Pure and Applied Chemistry) finally named them:

New elements created by fusing smaller atoms

Atomic number	Element
102	nobelium
103	lawrencium
104	rutherfordium
105	dubnium
106	seaborgium

Atomic number	Element
107	bohrium
108	hassium
109	meitnerium
110	unnamed

In the 1970s German scientists entered the race to create new atoms.
A new technique was needed to make element 107 and beyond, and the Germans perfected it using a heavy ion accelerator.
They managed to make the elements opposite:
It took 10 years to create element 110 by smashing together lead (atomic number 82) with nickel (atomic number 28).
It existed, like most of these giant creations, for a matter of microseconds – just long enough to be detected and verified.

Scientists have now progressed to element 114 with some excitement!
The Russians from Dubna have calculated that 'an island of stability' exists for some isotopes of element 114. So far they have made one isotope, containing 175 neutrons, that lasted all of 20 whole seconds!
The peak of the island is thought to be at 114 protons and 184 neutrons.
We shall have to wait and see!

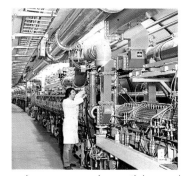

Researchers use massive particle accelerators

Summary

- The Periodic Table arranges the elements in order of **atomic number**.
- Elements with similar properties line up in vertical columns.
  These columns are called **groups**.
  The atoms of elements in the same group have the same number of electrons in their outer shells.
- A row across the Periodic Table is called a **period**.
- There are four blocks of elements in the Periodic Table.
  These are the s-block, p-block, d-block and f-block elements.

Key

Mass number A — 1 / **H** hydrogen

Atomic number (Proton number) Z — 1

0 or 8(VIII)

1(I)	2(II)											3(III)	4(IV)	5(V)	6(VI)	7(VII)	4 **He** helium 2
7 **Li** lithium 3	9 **Be** beryllium 4											11 **B** boron 5	12 **C** carbon 6	14 **N** nitrogen 7	16 **O** oxygen 8	19 **F** fluorine 9	20 **Ne** neon 10
23 **Na** sodium 11	24 **Mg** magnesium 12											27 **Al** aluminium 13	28 **Si** silicon 14	31 **P** phosphorus 15	32 **S** sulphur 16	35 **Cl** chlorine 17	40 **Ar** argon 18
39 **K** potassium 19	40 **Ca** calcium 20	45 **Sc** scandium 21	48 **Ti** titanium 22	51 **V** vanadium 23	52 **Cr** chromium 24	55 **Mn** manganese 25	56 **Fe** iron 26	59 **Co** cobalt 27	59 **Ni** nickel 28	64 **Cu** copper 29	65 **Zn** zinc 30	70 **Ga** gallium 31	73 **Ge** germanium 32	75 **As** arsenic 33	79 **Se** selenium 34	80 **Br** bromine 35	84 **Kr** krypton 36
85 **Rb** rubidium 37	88 **Sr** strontium 38	89 **Y** yttrium 39	91 **Zr** zirconium 40	93 **Nb** niobium 41	96 **Mo** molybdenum 42	99 **Tc** technetium 43	101 **Ru** ruthenium 44	103 **Rh** rhodium 45	106 **Pd** palladium 46	108 **Ag** silver 47	112 **Cd** cadmium 48	115 **In** indium 49	119 **Sn** tin 50	122 **Sb** antimony 51	128 **Te** tellurium 52	127 **I** iodine 53	131 **Xe** xenon 54
133 **Cs** caesium 55	137 **Ba** barium 56	139 **La** lanthanum 57	178 **Hf** hafnium 72	181 **Ta** tantalum 73	184 **W** tungsten 74	186 **Re** rhenium 75	190 **Os** osmium 76	192 **Ir** iridium 77	195 **Pt** platinum 78	197 **Au** gold 79	201 **Hg** mercury 80	204 **Tl** thallium 81	207 **Pb** lead 82	209 **Bi** bismuth 83	210 **Po** polonium 84	210 **At** astatine 85	222 **Rn** radon 86
223 **Fr** francium 87	226 **Ra** radium 88	227 **Ac** actinium 89															

d-block

p-block

halogens   noble gases

s-block

alkali metals   alkaline earth metals

140 **Ce** cerium 58	141 **Pr** praseodymium 59	144 **Nd** neodymium 60	147 **Pm** promethium 61	150 **Sm** samarium 62	152 **Eu** europium 63	157 **Gd** gadolinium 64	159 **Tb** terbium 65	163 **Dy** dysprosium 66	165 **Ho** holmium 67	167 **Er** erbium 68	169 **Tm** thulium 69	173 **Yb** ytterbium 70	175 **Lu** lutetium 71
232 **Th** thorium 90	231 **Pa** protactinium 91	238 **U** uranium 92	237 **Np** neptunium 93	242 **Pu** plutonium 94	243 **Am** americium 95	247 **Cm** curium 96	245 **Bk** berkelium 97	251 **Cf** californium 98	254 **Es** einsteinium 99	253 **Fm** fermium 100	256 **Md** mendelevium 101	254 **No** nobelium 102	257 **Lr** lawrencium 103

f-block

- The elements can be divided into metals and non-metals (with a few semi-metals or metalloids in between).
- Metals are good conductors of heat and electricity.
  They are shiny, malleable (can be hammered into shapes) and ductile (can be drawn out into wires).
  Most are hard, dense and have high melting points.
- Iron, cobalt and nickel are the magnetic metals.

- Most **non-metal** elements are gases.
  They have low melting and boiling points.
  They are poor conductors of heat and electricity.
  If solid, they are usually dull and brittle.

- We see repeating (periodic) patterns in the physical properties of the elements with increasing atomic number.
  This is called **periodicity**.
- These patterns or trends are related to the elements' bonding and structure:

2nd period Structure	Li (lithium) giant metallic	Be (beryllium) giant metallic	B (boron) giant covalent	C (carbon) giant covalent	N (nitrogen) simple molecular	O (oxygen) simple molecular	F (fluorine) simple molecular	Ne (neon) simple molecular
3rd period Structure	Na (sodium) giant metallic	Mg (magnesium) giant metallic	Al (aluminium) giant metallic	Si (silicon) giant covalent	P (phosphorus) simple molecular	S (sulphur) simple molecular	Cl (chlorine) simple molecular	Ar (argon) simple molecular

▶ Questions

1 Copy and complete:

The elements in the Periodic Table are arranged in order of atomic .....

The vertical columns in the s-block and p-block are called .....

The atoms of elements in the same group have the same number of .... in their .... shells.

The rows across the Periodic Table are called .....

There are four blocks of elements in the Periodic Table.

These are the **s-block, p-block,** .... and .... elements.

We can divide the elements into **metals** and **non-metals**

(with a few semi-metals or ....).

Metals are good conductors of .... and electricity.

They are shiny, malleable (can be .... into shapes) and ductile (can be drawn out into ....).

Most are hard, dense and have .... melting points.

Iron, ... and .... are the magnetic metals.

Most non-metal elements have .... melting and boiling points.

They are poor conductors of .... and .....

There are .... (periodic) patterns in the physical properties of the elements with increasing atomic number.

We call this .....

These trends are related to the elements' .... and structure.

Metals are found on the .... of a period and non-metals on the .....

2 Use the Periodic Table on page 89 to answer the questions below.

Which element:

a) has the lightest atoms?

b) is in Group 2 and in the 3rd period?

c) is in Group 6 and in the 2nd period?

d) is the first listed in the d-block?

e) has 3 completely full inner shells and 7 electrons in its outer shell?

f) is the alkali metal with the lightest atoms?

g) has atoms with one more proton than Si (silicon)?

h) has the smallest atomic radius in the 4th period?

i) is the alkaline earth metal in the 5th period?

j) is the halogen with the largest atomic reading?

3 Write down the electronic structure (or configuration) for the atoms listed below:

a) Li (atomic number 3) f) Cr (atomic number 24)

b) F (atomic number 9) g) Co (atomic number 27)

c) S (atomic number 16) h) Cu (atomic number 29)

d) Ca(atomic number 20) i) Zn (atomic number 30)

e) Sc (atomic number 21) j) Kr (atomic number 36)

4 This question is about Group 4 in the Periodic Table.

a) Name two metalloids in the group.

b) Name the non-metal.

c) Name the two metals.

d) Explain the difference between the 1st ionisation enthalpies of carbon and lead.

e) How does the difference in d) help to explain the increasing trend in metallic character going down the group?

5 Describe the general pattern observed going across a period when we look at:

a) melting points

b) electronegativities

c) electrical conductivity

d) atomic radii (the size of the atoms)

e) 1st ionisation enthalpies.

6 Explain each of the trends you described in question 5.

7 Look at the graph below:

It shows how the standard enthalpy of vaporisation (the energy required to vaporise a mole of each element) varies for the first 18 elements.

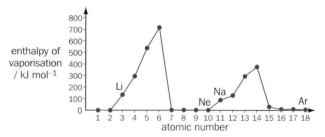

a) Descibe the trend going across a period.

b) Explain the trend, referring to the structures of the elements.

8 Look at chlorine's position in the Periodic Table.

a) How many ways can you find to relate its position to its atomic structure?

b) Why does bromine undergo similar reactions to chlorine?

9 This question is about the elements in Group 1.

a) What are the Group 1 elements commonly known as?

Why do you think we call them this name?

b) Which is the least reactive element in the group? Explain why.

c) Write the word and symbol equation for the reaction of Rb (rubidium) with water.

d) Predict what you would see in the reaction in c).

e) In what ways are the Group 1 elements unusual metals.

8 Periodicity and chemical properties

In the last chapter we saw how the properties of elements vary
in repeating patterns when we arrange them in order of atomic number.
These trends can be explained by an element's position in the Periodic Table.

In this chapter we shall see if there are similar patterns
in the compounds of the elements.

▶ Oxides

From your previous work, you know that most elements can react with oxygen
to form compounds called **oxides**.
Some examples are shown below:

sodium + oxygen $\longrightarrow$ sodium oxide (plus some sodium peroxide, Na_2O_2)
$4\,Na(s) + O_2(g) \longrightarrow 2\,Na_2O(s)$

magnesium + oxygen $\longrightarrow$ magnesium oxide
$2\,Mg(s) + O_2(g) \longrightarrow 2\,MgO(s)$

carbon + oxygen $\longrightarrow$ carbon dioxide
$C(s) + O_2(g) \longrightarrow CO_2(g)$

sulphur + oxygen $\longrightarrow$ sulphur dioxide
$S(s) + O_2(g) \longrightarrow SO_2(g)$

Sulphur also forms another oxide, sulphur trioxide, SO_3.

$2\,SO_2(g) + O_2(g) \rightleftharpoons 2\,SO_3(g)$

This reaction is largely responsible for acid rain.
The sulphur dioxide released when fossil fuels burn
reacts with oxygen in the air. The SO_3 formed then reacts
with water droplets to make sulphuric acid.

$SO_3(g) + H_2O(l) \longrightarrow H_2SO_4(aq)$

This shows us that some oxides are acidic.

On the other hand, we get quite a different solution
when sodium oxide reacts with water:

sodium oxide + water $\longrightarrow$ sodium hydroxide
$Na_2O(s) + H_2O(l) \longrightarrow 2\,NaOH(aq)$
a strong alkali

In general, we can say:

> **Metal oxides tend to be basic, whereas non-metal oxides tend to be acidic.**

Sodium reacts vigorously when heated
and placed in oxygen as shown above.
Potassium reacts even more vigorously
and produces some of the superoxide
$(K^+O_2^-)$

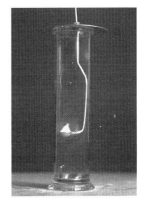

Sulphur reacts less vigorously than
sodium with oxygen. It burns with a gentle
blue flame

Oxides of sulphur contribute towards
acid rain

▶ Oxides across a period

Look at the results of an experiment below that shows
the pH of oxide solutions from the 2nd and 3rd period elements:

2nd period	Li₂O	BeO	B₂O₃	CO₂	NO₂	O₂	OF₂	Ne (no oxide formed)
pH of solution	14	insoluble	6	5	2	–	1	–
3rd period	Na₂O	MgO	Al₂O₃	SiO₂	P₄O₁₀	SO₃	Cl₂O₇	Ar (no oxide formed)
pH of solution	14	11	insoluble	insoluble	2	1	3	–

- Why are no pH values given for some oxides?
- Can you see any general trends going across a period?

The insoluble oxides can still have acidic or basic natures
even though you can't test their pH values.
You can find out by seeing if they react with acids or alkalis.
Let's consider silicon dioxide as an example.
Look at the equation below:
Remember that all alkalis contain OH⁻(aq) ions.

$$SiO_2(s) + 2\,OH^-(aq) \longrightarrow SiO_3^{2-}(aq) + H_2O(l)$$

alkali   silicate ion

Silicon dioxide reacts with concentrated alkali.
Therefore it behaves like an acid.
(An acid has no effect on silicon dioxide.)

Now let's look at aluminium oxide, which is also insoluble in water.
Look at the equations below:
Remember that all acids contain H⁺(aq) ions.

$$Al_2O_3(s) + 6\,H^+(aq) \longrightarrow 2\,Al^{3+}(aq) + 3\,H_2O(l)$$

acid

$$Al_2O_3(s) + 2\,OH^-(aq) + 3\,H_2O(l) \longrightarrow 2\,Al(OH)_4^-(aq)$$

alkali   aluminate ion

Aluminium oxide reacts with both acids and alkalis.
It behaves like a base and an acid.
Oxides that are both acidic and basic in character
are called **amphoteric**.
Beryllium oxide reacts in a similar way.

We can now see the pattern across the Periodic Table:

*Aluminium oxide is found naturally
in the ore bauxite.
The bauxite is an orange-brown colour.
We extract aluminium metal from it*

2nd period	Li₂O	BeO	B₂O₃	CO₂	NO₂	O₂	OF₂	Ne (no oxide formed)
Acid/base nature	base	amphoteric	acid	acid	acid	–	acid	–
3rd period	Na₂O	MgO	Al₂O₃	SiO₂	P₄O₁₀	SO₃	Cl₂O₇	Ar (no oxide formed)
Acid/base nature	base	base	amphoteric	acid	acid	acid	acid	–

base

amphoteric

weak acid

strong acid

▶ Structures of the oxides

We can relate the periodic patterns in the properties of the oxides
to their structures.
Look at the boiling points of the oxides plotted below:

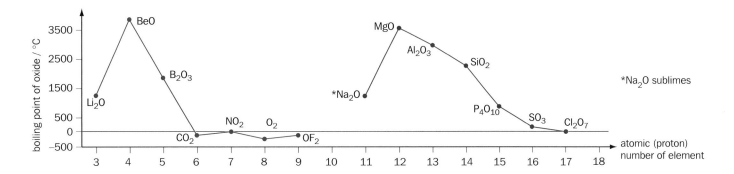

- What happens to the boiling points as we go across
  the 2nd and 3rd periods?

These trends can be explained by the structures of the oxides.
Can you recall the type of bonding between metal and non-metal elements?
These compounds form giant ionic structures.
The metal oxides are located early on in a period.

Why does SiO_2 have such a high boiling point
for a non-metal oxide?
How do non-metal atoms bond to each other?
Remember there are two types of structure for covalently bonded compounds.
The giant covalent structures, like silicon dioxide, have very high boiling points.
The simple molecular structures, such as carbon dioxide, have low boiling points.
Can you remember why?

Here are the structures of the oxides of elements in the 2nd and 3rd periods:

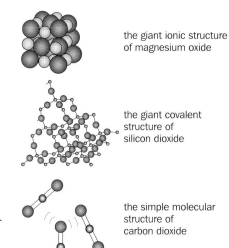

the giant ionic structure
of magnesium oxide

the giant covalent
structure of
silicon dioxide

the simple molecular
structure of
carbon dioxide

2nd period	Li_2O	BeO	B_2O_3	CO_2	NO_2	O_2	OF_2	Ne (no oxide formed)
relative boiling point	high	high	high	low	low	-	low	—
conduction of electricity when molten / liquid	good	quite good	poor	none	none	–	none	–
structure	giant ionic	giant ionic	giant covalent	simple molecular	simple molecular	–	simple molecular	–
3rd period	Na_2O	MgO	Al_2O_3	SiO_2	P_4O_{10}	SO_3	Cl_2O_7	Ar (no oxide formed)
relative boiling point	high	high	high	high	low	low	low	—
conduction of electricity when molten / liquid	good	good	good	none	none	none	none	–
structure	giant ionic	giant ionic	giant ionic	giant covalent	simple molecular	simple molecular	simple molecular	–

- Look at the table.
How can we distinguish between the giant ionic and the giant covalent structures?

▶ Chlorides across a period

As with the oxides on the last page, we can also find repeating patterns with the chlorides as we go across the Periodic Table. Look at the way that elements from the 3rd period react when we heat them in dry chlorine gas:

	Na	Mg	Al	Si	P	S
Reaction when heated in dry chlorine	reacts very vigorously to form NaCl	reacts vigorously to form $MgCl_2$	reacts vigorously to form Al_2Cl_6	reacts slowly, to form $SiCl_4$	reacts slowly, to form a mixture of PCl_3 and PCl_5	reacts slowly. to form a mixture of SCl_2 and S_2Cl_2

- What is the trend in reactivity across the period?

Now look at the formulae of the 2nd and 3rd period chlorides:

2nd period	LiCl	$BeCl_2$	BCl_3	CCl_4	NCl_3	Cl_2O (Cl_2O_7)	FCl	Ne (no chloride formed)
3rd period	NaCl	$MgCl_2$	$AlCl_3$ (Al_2Cl_6)	$SiCl_4$	PCl_3 (PCl_5)	S_2Cl_2 (SCl_2)	Cl_2	Ar (no chloride formed)

(Formulae in brackets are other forms of the chloride)

- Do you notice what happens to the number of chlorine atoms in each compound as we cross a period?
- Can you plot a graph to show the trend?
- Can you relate the trend to the electronic structures of the elements in each period?
- What type of bonding would you expect in the chlorides of
  a) metals, and
  b) non-metals?

Let's look at the boiling points of the chlorides:

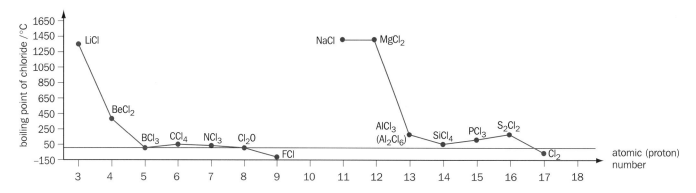

- What patterns can you see?
- Which chlorides seem to have giant structures?

We can relate the trends in boiling points to the structures of the chlorides:

2nd period	LiCl	$BeCl_2$	BCl_3	CCl_4	NCl_3	Cl_2O (Cl_2O_7)	FCl	Ne (no chloride formed)
structure	giant ionic	giant	simple molecular	simple molecular	simple molecular	simple molecular	simple molecular	–
3rd period	NaCl	$MgCl_2$	$AlCl_3$ (Al_2Cl_6)	$SiCl_4$	PCl_3 (PCl_5)	S_2Cl_2	Cl_2	Ar (no chloride formed)
structure	giant ionic	giant ionic	simple molecular	simple molecular	simple molecular	simple molecular	simple molecular	–

▶ Chlorides with water

Now we can see what happens when we add the chlorides to water.
Look at the photo opposite:
Some chlorides, like that of phosphorus, react violently with water:

$$PCl_3(l) + 3\,H_2O(l) \longrightarrow H_3PO_3(aq) + 3\,HCl(aq)$$

The reaction is called **hydrolysis** (breakdown by water).
The hydrochloric acid produced forms a strongly acidic solution.
This is a typical reaction of non-metal chlorides with water.

$$2\,S_2Cl_2(l) + 2\,H_2O(l) \longrightarrow 3\,S(s) + SO_2(aq) + 4\,HCl(aq)$$

$$SiCl_4(l) + 2\,H_2O(l) \longrightarrow SiO_2(s) + 4\,HCl(aq)$$

(However, look at the box opposite for CCl_4 plus water)

Some chlorides of metals, such as sodium chloride, simply dissolve in water, forming neutral solutions:

$$NaCl(s) \xrightarrow{\ H_2O\ } Na^+(aq) + Cl^-(aq)$$

Look at the table below. It is a summary of what we see when chlorides from the 3rd period are added to water:

Phosphorus(III) chloride reacts vigorously with water. If exposed to air it is hydrolysed by the water vapour present

As $SiCl_4$ reacts with water, we would also expect CCl_4 to be hydrolysed. In fact, there is **no reaction**. The two liquids form immiscible layers. But why? With $SiCl_4$, initial attack by H_2O involves the O atom donating a lone pair into an empty 3d orbital on the Si atom. However, there are no equivalent 2d orbitals on a C atom, so H_2O does not attack CCl_4.

3rd period	NaCl	MgCl$_2$	AlCl$_3$ (Al$_2$Cl$_6$)	SiCl$_4$	PCl$_3$ (PCl$_5$)	S$_2$Cl$_2$	Cl$_2$	Ar (no chloride formed)
Observations when added to water	solids dissolve		chlorides react with water, giving off fumes of hydrogen chloride (HCl)				–	–
pH of solution formed	7	6.5	3	2	2	2	–	–
Bonding	ionic	ionic	ionic/ covalent	covalent	covalent	covalent	–	

As you go across the period, the bonding becomes less ionic and more covalent in character.
The bonding in aluminium chloride is intermediate – in this case, it is covalent with a degree of ionic nature. (See page 72.)
The acidic solution formed is due to the HCl dissolving in the water.
But another factor is the high charge density on the aluminium, Al^{3+}, ion.

When any ion dissolves in water it becomes surrounded by H_2O molecules. (See page 52.)
Look at the diagram opposite:
Because of its small size and high charge, the electrons in the water molecules are drawn towards the Al^{3+} ion. This weakens the O—H bonds in water and H^+ ions are lost. It is $H^+(aq)$ ions that make a solution acidic.

$$[Al(H_2O)_6]^{3+}(aq) \rightleftharpoons [Al(H_2O)_5OH^-]^{2+}(aq) + H^+(aq)$$

The pattern in the bonding of the *oxides* is similar to the chlorides.
Look back to the table at the bottom of page 104:

- What evidence can you find for any intermediate nature in the bonding in aluminium oxide?

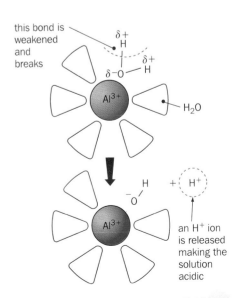

this bond is weakened and breaks

an H^+ ion is released making the solution acidic

▶ Ions and the Periodic Table

Think about what happens to atoms when they become ions.
Is the ion formed bigger or smaller than the original atom?
Are some ions bigger and others smaller?

Remember that metal atoms lose electrons so that they are left with
a full outer shell. In effect, they lose their outer shell completely.
So how will the size of the positive ion formed compare with
the size of its atom?

On the other hand, non-metal atoms tend to gain electrons.
These fill up their existing outer shell. The negative ion formed
now has more electrons but still only has the same positive charge
on its nucleus holding them in.
How do you think this will affect the size of the ion formed?

Look at the table below:
It shows how the atomic radius and the ionic radius vary
going across the 2nd and 3rd periods.

2nd period	Li	Be	B	C	N	O	F	Ne
atomic radius / nm	0.134	0.125	0.090	0.077	0.075	0.073	0.071	0.065
ionic radius / nm	Li^+ 0.074	Be^{2+} 0.027	B^{3+} 0.012	no ions formed	N^{3-} 0.171	O^{2-} 0.140	F^- 0.133	no ions formed
3rd period	Na	Mg	Al	Si	P	S	Cl	Ar
atomic radius / nm	0.154	0.145	0.130	0.118	0.110	0.102	0.099	0.095
ionic radius / nm	Na^+ 0.102	Mg^{2+} 0.072	Al^{3+} 0.053	no ions formed	P^{3-} 0.190	S^{2-} 0.185	Cl^- 0.180	no ions formed

- What pattern can you see going across the period in the size of
  a) the atomic radii, and
  b) the ionic radii?
- Can you explain these trends?

▶ Periodicity and redox reactions

You might recall from your previous work the terms **reduction** and **oxidation**.
You need to remember that:

> **Oxidation is the loss of electrons.**
> **Reduction is the gain of electrons.**

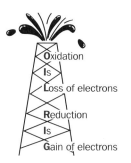

In chemical reactions whenever something is reduced something else must be oxidised.
So chemists use the abbreviation 'redox' to describe such reactions.

From the definitions above, it follows that:

> **Reducing agents give electrons.**
> **Oxidising agents accept electrons.**

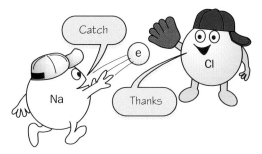

Reducing agents **reduce** their number of electrons.

● *Which is the reducing agent here?*

Using what you know already about the Periodic Table, where will we find the best reducing agents? These will be those atoms with the greatest tendency to give away electrons.

How about the best oxidising agents? This will be linked to an atom's electronegativity. (See pages 68 and 93.)
Look at the general trends below:

```
                                          ────────────────────▶  best oxidising agents

        Li      Be      B       C       N       O       F

        Na                                              Cl

        K                                               Br

        Rb                                              I

best
reducing  ▼ Cs                                          At
agents
```

● *Which two elements would you like to see react together?*

● Can you see a link between these trends and those in atomic radii on the last page?

We have already explained why it becomes increasingly easy to lose electrons as you go down a group. (See pages 93 and 99.)

It becomes more difficult to lose electrons as we go across a period. This is because the atoms get smaller. Therefore the electrons in the outer shell are nearer to the attractive force of the nucleus. However, this means that it becomes increasingly easy for atoms to attract electrons into their outer shell as we cross a period.

So the best oxidising agents will be found in the top right-hand corner of the Periodic Table, whereas the best reducing agents will be found in the bottom left-hand corner..

A party that's guaranteed to go with a bang!

▶ Chemistry at work: Oxides

An oxide of a metal – a steely oxide

You can get a variety of different steels, but all of them
contain mainly iron. The iron is extracted from its oxides,
Fe_2O_3 or Fe_3O_4 – a mixture of **FeO** and **Fe$_2$O$_3$** – in a blast furnace.
One problem with iron and steel is rusting.
Rust is a hydrated form of iron(III) oxide.
So the metal tends to return to its original state as an oxide.
More expensive stainless steels do not rust.
What other ways do we have to prevent iron from rusting. (See page 414.)

Car bodies are made from steel

An oxide of a metalloid – a sandy oxide!

Did you know that glass is made mainly from sand (**SiO$_2$**)?
It was probably discovered by accident in the sand underneath an ancient fire!
The first glass object has been dated at about 4500 BC.
The Egyptians used glass containers around 3000 BC.

Limestone ($CaCO_3$) and sodium carbonate (Na_2CO_3) are the other raw materials.
You have seen some of the uses of common salt (sodium chloride)
on page 54. Sodium carbonate is another useful product made from salt.
Recycled glass (cullet) can make up to 30% of some glass-making mixtures.

Recycling glass

There are many different types of glass. Scientists have
tried changing the glass-making mixture. They've also
found ways of treating the glass to change its properties.
For example, windscreens are made like a glass sandwich
– with a thin sheet of plastic as the filling! This is called
laminated glass.
How does this help if a stone hits your windscreen?
Look at the table opposite:

Do all these types of glass have any properties in common?

Have you taken any glass to be recycled at a bottle-bank?
The bottles are sorted out into different colours.
Brown bottles get their colour from iron impurities
in the sand that it's made from.
On page 138 you will see that the transition metals
form coloured compounds. Adding small amounts
of their metal oxides makes coloured glass.

Type of glass	Use
soda-lime	windows
boro-silicate	test-tubes, beakers, etc. (heat-proof, chemical resistant)
lead-crystal	decorative glasses, bowls and vases
glass fibres	fibre optics, fibreglass
optical glass	lenses in spectacles, cameras, projectors, etc.
glass ceramic	opaque oven-ware

An oxide of a non-metal – a fire-fighting oxide!

Some fire extinguishers give off carbon dioxide gas.
They are good at putting out electrical fires.
They smother the fire, starving it of oxygen.
Why don't we use water on electrical fires?

Can you think of a problem with using
a carbon dioxide extinguisher outdoors on a windy day?
Look at the photo opposite:
Fire crews at a 'plane crash spray foam on to fires.
The carbon dioxide gas is trapped in the foam,
so it stays on the fire.

Summary

Oxides

2nd period	Li$_2$O	BeO	B$_2$O$_3$	CO$_2$	NO$_2$	O$_2$	OF$_2$	Ne (no oxide formed)
Acid / base nature	base	amphoteric	acid	acid	acid	–	acid	–
Structure	giant ionic	giant ionic	giant covalent	simple molecular	simple molecular	–	simple molecular	–
3rd period	Na$_2$O	MgO	Al$_2$O$_3$	SiO$_2$	P$_4$O$_{10}$	SO$_3$	Cl$_2$O$_7$	Ar (no oxide formed)
Acid / base nature	base	base	amphoteric	acid	acid	acid	acid	–
Structure	giant ionic	giant ionic	giant ionic	giant covalent	simple molecular	simple molecular	simple molecular	–

Chlorides

2nd period	LiCl	BeCl$_2$	BCl$_3$	CCl$_4$	NCl$_3$	Cl$_2$O (Cl$_2$O$_7$)	FCl	Ne (no chloride formed)
Structure	giant ionic	giant	simple molecular	simple molecular	simple molecular	simple molecular	simple molecular	–
3rd period	NaCl	MgCl$_2$	AlCl$_3$ (Al$_2$Cl$_6$)	SiCl$_4$	PCl$_3$ (PCl$_5$)	S$_2$Cl$_2$	Cl$_2$	Ar (no chloride formed)
Structure	giant ionic	giant ionic	simple molecular	simple molecular	simple molecular	simple molecular	–	–

▶ Questions

1 Copy and complete:
The oxides and chlorides of the second and third .... have giant .... structures on the left-hand side of the Periodic Table, but simple .... structures on the right-hand side.
The oxides move from being .... to acidic as we cross a period. Those oxides that display both acidic and basic properties are called .... oxides.

2 a) Use sodium oxide as an example of a metal oxide, and sulphur as an example of a non-metal oxide, in order to show how oxides can be classified as acidic or basic.
b) Show with equations why we describe aluminium oxide as amphoteric.

3 a) Make a table showing the formulae of the oxides of the 3rd period, Na to Cl.
b) Why haven't we included argon in the table?
c) Work out from the formulae the number of moles of oxygen per mole of element for each oxide in your table. For example, in Na$_2$O, we have 0.5 moles of O per mole of Na.
d) Plot a graph showing the pattern as in c) as we cross the period.
e) Repeat parts a), c) and d) for the oxides of the 2nd period.
f) Can you explain the difference in the trends across the 2nd and 3rd periods?

4 a) Describe the trend in the melting and boiling points of the oxides as we go across the 3rd period.
b) Do the same for the chlorides of the 3rd period.
c) Explain the trends in terms of the structure and bonding of the oxides and chlorides.

5 a) How does the behaviour of the chlorides of the 3rd period differ when we add them to water?
b) Relate the trend across the period in part a) to the bonding in the chlorides.
c) Explain why aluminium salts are acidic.
d) Explain why SiCl$_4$ is attacked by water but CCl$_4$ is not.

6 a) Which element has atoms with the smallest atomic radius in the 3rd period? Explain why
b) Explain why metals form ions with a smaller radius than their original atom, whereas non-metal ions are larger.
c) Which elements in the 3rd period do not form ions? Explain why in each case.

7 Which two elements from the 2nd and 3rd periods:
a) would you add together to get the most vigorous reaction?
b) form amphoteric oxides?
c) form no oxides or chlorides?
d) form chlorides with the formula XCl$_4$?
e) have oxides that react with water to produce a solution with a pH value of 14?

▶ Group 2 elements

All the elements in Group 2 are metals.
They are commonly known as the **alkaline earth metals**.

You are probably familiar with at least one of the Group 2 elements.
Magnesium ribbon is often used in science lessons to show how
some metals burn in air and react with dilute acid.

Another Group 2 element is calcium.
Many people know that calcium is essential for healthy teeth and bones.
But how many realise that it is not the element itself present
in foods such as milk and cheese.
Calcium itself is a reactive, grey metal!

The other Group 2 elements – beryllium, strontium and barium –
are relatively unknown (although you might have heard of barium meals).
You can read more about the uses of Group 2 elements
and their compounds on page 118.

*Magnesium powder is used in fireworks
and distress flares*

▶ Electronic structures

Do you know how many electrons are in the outer shell
of each Group 2 metal?
As you have seen on page 93, the group number equals
the number of electrons in the outer shell.
Look at the electronic structures opposite:

Be	$1s^2 2s^2$
Mg	$1s^2 2s^2 2p^6 3s^2$
Ca	$1s^2 2s^2 2p^6 3s^2 3p^6 4s^2$
Sr	$1s^2 2s^2 2p^6 3s^2 3p^6 3d^{10} 4s^2 4p^6 5s^2$
Ba	$1s^2 2s^2 2p^6 3s^2 3p^6 3d^{10} 4s^2 4p^6 4d^{10} 5s^2 5p^6 6s^2$

- Can you see why these elements belong in the s-block?
- How many electrons do they have to lose to achieve a full outer shell?

All the Group 2 metals form ions with a 2+ charge.
Look at the ionisation enthalpies below:

Element	1st ionisation enthalpy / kJ mol^{-1}	2nd ionisation enthalpy / kJ mol^{-1}
beryllium	900	1800
magnesium	740	1450
calcium	590	1150
strontium	550	1060
barium	500	970

- Can you see the pattern going down the group?
- Which element do you think will be most reactive?
- Predict the 3rd ionisation energy of magnesium.
  You can check your answer in the data on pages at the
  back of the book.
  Can you explain why it is so high?

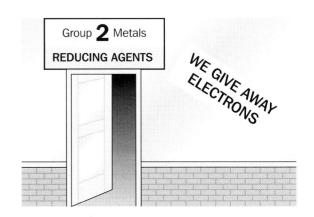

Group **2** Metals

REDUCING AGENTS

WE GIVE AWAY ELECTRONS

We can plot the sum of the first two ionisation enthalpies on a graph.
This gives us an idea of how easily the 2+ ions are formed:

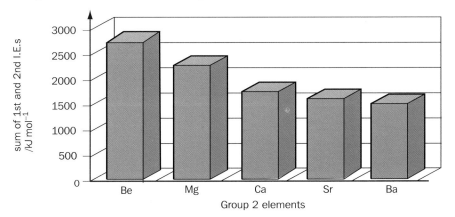

Beryllium (Be)

Magnesium (Mg)

Calcium (Ca)

- What is the trend going down Group 2?

> **Group 2 metals form ions more easily as we go down the group.**

▶ Physical properties

You will have used magnesium ribbon before in experiments.
However, you might not have seen the other Group 2 metals.
Look at the photos opposite:

- Why do you think we store strontium and barium under oil?
- Does this agree with the ionisation enthalpy data on the last page?

The metals are more dense than their Group 1 neighbours,
but less dense than most other metals.
They also have higher melting points than Group 1 metals.
Look at the graphs below:

Strontium (Sr)

Barium (Ba)

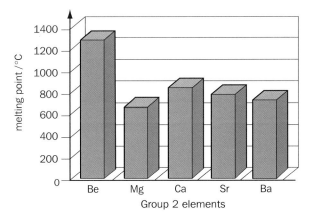

- What is the general trend in melting points going down Group 2?
  Which element breaks the pattern?
- Why do you think that Group 2 metals have higher melting points
  than their Group 1 neighbours?
(Think about metallic bonding and the number of electrons donated
into the 'sea of electrons').
- What is the trend in densities going down Group 2?

> **Group 2 metals have relatively low densities and melting points
> compared with most metals.**

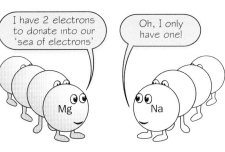

▶ Reactions of the Group 2 metals

Reactions with oxygen

Would you expect to find any of the Group 2 metals
occurring as the element naturally?
Although they're called the alkaline earth metals, they are too reactive
to find as the metals themselves in the Earth's crust.

You know how magnesium reacts when heated in air.
It can be used in fireworks and distress flares.

magnesium + oxygen $\longrightarrow$ magnesium oxide

$$2\,Mg(s) \quad + \quad O_2(g) \quad \longrightarrow \quad 2\,MgO(s)$$

But can you predict how the other members of the group
will react with oxygen compared with magnesium?
You can work out the answer by looking at the table on page 112.
It becomes easier for the atoms to lose their 2 outer electrons
as we go down the group.
Therefore:

*Magnesium is used in some distress
flares. It burns with a bright white flame*

The Group 2 metals get more reactive as we go down the group.

However, they are less reactive than their neighbouring metals in Group 1.
Can you explain why?

So the Group 2 metals' reactions with oxygen will be similar,
but differ in how vigorous they are.
The reaction of barium with oxygen is very rapid:

barium + oxygen $\longrightarrow$ barium oxide

$$2\,Ba(s) + O_2(g) \longrightarrow 2\,BaO(s)$$

Some barium peroxide (BaO_2) will also form.

Reactions with water

The trend is also found when we look at the reactions with water.
Beryllium, at the top of the group, hardly reacts at all with water or steam.
Magnesium reacts very slowly with water:

magnesium + water $\longrightarrow$ magnesium hydroxide + hydrogen

$$Mg(s) \quad + \quad 2\,H_2O(l) \longrightarrow \quad Mg(OH)_2(aq) \quad + \quad H_2(g)$$

The magnesium hydroxide formed is not very soluble.
Its solution is weakly alkaline. Hence its use to treat indigestion
by neutralising excess acid in the stomach. It is called an **antacid**.

However, if you react magnesium with steam, you see a vigorous reaction.
Look at the diagram opposite:
The equation is:

magnesium + steam $\longrightarrow$ magnesium oxide + hydrogen

$$Mg(s) \quad + \quad H_2O(g) \longrightarrow \quad MgO(s) \quad + \quad H_2(g)$$

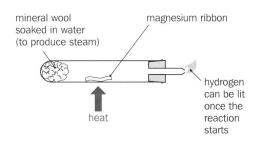

mineral wool
soaked in water
(to produce steam)

magnesium ribbon

heat

hydrogen
can be lit
once the
reaction
starts

Calcium reacts readily in cold water.
Look at the photo opposite:

calcium + water $\longrightarrow$ calcium hydroxide + hydrogen

$Ca(s) + 2H_2O(l) \longrightarrow Ca(OH)_2(aq) + H_2(g)$

Once again the hydroxide is only sparingly soluble,
forming a weakly alkaline solution.
You will have come across this solution when testing for
carbon dioxide gas. Can you remember its common name?

$Ca(OH)_2(aq) + CO_2(g) \longrightarrow CaCO_3(s) + H_2O(l)$

limewater

milky suspension
of fine particles of insoluble
calcium carbonate

Calcium reacting with water

If more CO_2 gas is passed into the milky suspension, it goes colourless again:

$CaCO_3(s) + CO_2(g) + H_2O(l) \rightleftharpoons Ca(HCO_3)_2(aq)$

The calcium carbonate reacts to form soluble calcium hydrogencarbonate.

As we carry on down the group, the reactions of the metals with water
become more and more vigorous.
The hydroxides formed get **more soluble as we descend the group**.
So their solutions become more strongly alkaline.
Look at the table at the bottom of the next page for actual values.

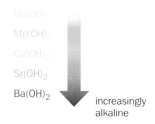

increasingly
alkaline

Reactions with acid

Can you recall the general equation if a metal reacts with an acid?
Remember that we always get a salt and hydrogen gas.
For example,

magnesium + sulphuric acid $\longrightarrow$ magnesium sulphate + hydrogen

$Mg(s) + H_2SO_4(aq) \longrightarrow MgSO_4(aq) + H_2(g)$

The reaction with any acid can be shown as an **ionic equation**.
This type of equation does not include any ions that
remain unchanged in the reaction. These are called **spectator ions**.
Look at the equation below:

$Mg(s) + 2H^+(aq) + SO_4^{2-}(aq) \longrightarrow Mg^{2+}(aq) + SO_4^{2-}(aq) + H_2(g)$

It shows all the ions, atoms and molecules present.
Can you see which ions don't change?
These spectator ions are left out of the ionic equation:

$Mg(s) + 2H^+(aq) \longrightarrow Mg^{2+}(aq) + H_2(g)$ ionic equation

So when calcium reacts with an acid we can write:

$Ca(s) + 2H^+(aq) \longrightarrow Ca^{2+}(aq) + H_2(g)$

How will this reaction differ from that of magnesium with acid?
Once again we find that the metals react more vigorously
as we go down the group.

- How could you collect the hydrogen gas?
- How could you test that the gas was hydrogen?
- Name the salt formed when calcium reacts with
  a) dilute hydrochloric acid,
  b) dilute nitric acid.
- Why would it be dangerous to react strontium or barium with acid
  in the lab?

Magnesium reacting with dilute acid

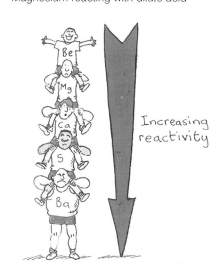

Increasing
reactivity

*The most powerful reducing agent in
Group 2 is found at the bottom of the
group*

▶ Compounds of the Group 2 metals

The alkaline earth metals are too reactive to occur naturally
as the elements themselves.
However, their compounds are commonly found in the Earth's crust.
The carbonates of magnesium and calcium are particularly abundant.

Their compounds are mainly ionic, but those of beryllium
have a high degree of covalent character.
● Can you explain why?
The effects of an ion with a high charge density were covered on page 72.

*These white cliffs are made mainly of
calcium carbonate*

Flame tests

Like the compounds of Group 1 metals, calcium, strontium
and barium produce brightly coloured flames when their compounds
are put in a Bunsen flame. Can you remember why this happens?

On page 10 we saw how electrons can absorb energy and jump into
empty, higher energy levels. When these excited electrons fall back into
lower energy levels, they give out energy.
For some elements this energy lies in the visible range of light
and we get characteristic colours.
Look at the table below, which shows the results for the s-block elements:

A flame test on a compound of strontium

Group 1	Flame colour	Group 2	Flame colour
lithium	scarlet red	beryllium	no colour
sodium	bright yellow	magnesium	no colour
potassium	lilac	calcium	brick red
rubidium	red	strontium	crimson red
caesium	blue	barium	apple green

Oxides and hydroxides

The first part of the name '*alkaline* earth' metals comes from
the chemical properties of their oxides and hydroxides.
The oxides form hydroxides when added to water:

calcium oxide + water $\longrightarrow$ calcium hydroxide

$$CaO(s) + H_2O(l) \longrightarrow Ca(OH)_2(aq)$$

As with any soluble ionic oxide, the reaction can be summarised as:

$$O^{2-}(s) + H_2O(l) \longrightarrow 2\,OH^-(aq)$$
hydroxide ions (which make a solution alkaline)

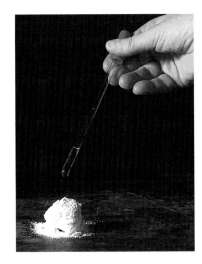

Calcium oxide reacts vigorously with water

We often use these compounds of calcium and magnesium
to neutralise acids.
Examples include treatments for *excess* stomach acid,
preventing the escape of acidic gases in industry and neutralising acidic soil.

Look at the solubilities of the hydroxides in the table opposite:
● Do they get more soluble or less soluble as we descend the group?
● Would you expect their solutions to get more alkaline
as we go down the group? (See page 115.)

Hydroxide	Solubility at 298 K/ (mol / 100 cm³ of water)
$Mg(OH)_2$	2.0×10^{-5}
$Ca(OH)_2$	1.5×10^{-3}
$Sr(OH)_2$	3.4×10^{-3}
$Ba(OH)_2$	1.5×10^{-2}

Carbonates

Calcium carbonate is the most common Group 2 carbonate.
It is found as limestone, chalk and marble. It is also occurs, together with magnesium carbonate, in the rock called dolomite. You can read about some uses of calcium carbonate on page 118.

Beautiful limestone landscape in the Derbyshire Peak District

The carbonates are **insoluble** in water, but do react in acidic solutions. For example:

magnesium carbonate + hydrochloric acid $\longrightarrow$ magnesium chloride + water + carbon dioxide

$$MgCO_3(s) + 2\,HCl(aq) \longrightarrow MgCl_2(aq) + H_2O(l) + CO_2(g)$$

- How could you test that the gas given off was carbon dioxide?
This test relies on the fact that calcium carbonate is insoluble in water.

- Can you work out what happens in the test?
(We saw on page 115 that limewater is a solution of calcium hydroxide.)

The fact that calcium carbonate reacts with acid has a major influence on the lives of millions of people in this country.
Hard water contains dissolved calcium or magnesium ions.
These can enter our water supplies when water, acidified naturally by carbon dioxide in the air, reacts with carbonates in rock.

This hot water pipe has furred up because of hard water

If you heat Group 2 carbonates, they break down into the oxide and give off carbon dioxide gas:

calcium carbonate $\longrightarrow$ calcium oxide + carbon dioxide

$$CaCO_3(s) \longrightarrow CaO(s) + CO_2(g)$$

This is the important reaction that takes place in a lime kiln.
The calcium oxide has many uses in making products for the building industry.

> **The carbonates become increasingly stable as we go down the group.**

Nitrates

Like all other nitrates, these compounds are **soluble** in water.

When we heat them, they decompose. Look at the photo opposite:
Do you know the name of the brown gas given off?

magnesium nitrate $\longrightarrow$ magnesium oxide + nitrogen dioxide + oxygen

$$2\,Mg(NO_3)_2(s) \longrightarrow 2\,MgO(s) + 4\,NO_2(g) + O_2(g)$$

> **Like the carbonates, the nitrates increase in thermal stability as we descend the group.**

This can be explained by the greater polarisation of the negative ions (anions) in compounds containing the smaller Group 2 ions. The small 2+ ions have a higher charge density and 'burrow' into the larger anion.
They tend to draw electrons from the nitrate or carbonate ion, weakening its bonds.

waste air and carbon dioxide gas

limestone (calcium carbonate)

fire-brick

1500 °C

hot air $\longrightarrow$ $\longleftarrow$ hot air

lime (calcium oxide)

A lime kiln

▶ Chemistry at work: Compounds of the Group 2 elements

Neutralising acid

Have you ever had indigestion? The 'burning' feeling
comes from too much hydrochloric acid in your stomach.
You can cure the pain quickly by taking a tablet.
The tablet contains an **alkali** which gets rid of the acid.
'Milk of Magnesia' can be taken as a suspension
containing basic magnesium oxide. This neutralises
the excess acid:

$$MgO(s) + 2\,HCl(aq) \longrightarrow MgCl_2(aq) + H_2O(l)$$

Other remedies can use calcium carbonate ($CaCO_3$)
as the active ingredient.

$$CaCO_3(s) + 2\,HCl(aq) \longrightarrow CaCl_2(aq) + CO_2(g) + H_2O(l)$$

Farmers use this on a larger scale!
If soil is too acidic, crops will not grow well.
They can spread powdered limestone or chalk (both forms of $CaCO_3$)
on the soil to neutralise it.
Lime, calcium hydroxide – $Ca(OH)_2$ – can also be used.

Blast off!

Do you remember from page 54 how magnesium oxide
is used to line the inside of kilns?
Beryllium oxide is also used as a refractory (heat resistant) compound.
It melts at over 2500 °C. It also has the lowest density
of all the Group 2 oxides.
The end of a rocket has to withstand high temperatures,
and be strong and light. For these reasons BeO is used
as one of the materials in the nose-cones of rockets.

The caring compounds!

Can you remember the trend in the solubility of the Group 2 hydroxides?
Unlike the hydroxides, ***the solubility of the sulphates
decreases as we descend the group.***
Barium sulphate is practically insoluble.
In fact its ions are used to test for sulphate ions:

$$Ba^{2+}(aq) + SO_4^{2-}(aq) \longrightarrow BaSO_4(s)$$
white precipitate

Doctors use an insoluble suspension of barium sulphate in order to X-ray
the soft tissue of the digestive tract. Since barium ions (like calcium
in your bones) have lots of electrons, they scatter X-ray radiation.

Another Group 2 sulphate used in hospitals is calcium sulphate.
It occurs in nature as gypsum, $CaSO_4.2H_2O$.
When heated to just below 100 °C, some of the H_2O is driven off
and we get Plaster of Paris. This is used to keep broken limbs in place.
A paste of Plaster of Paris sets in a two-stage chemical process,
expanding slightly as it hardens.
This expansion enables us to record fine details in moulds.
When would this be useful to a forensic scientist?

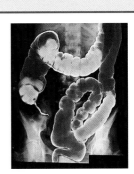

X-ray after a 'barium meal'

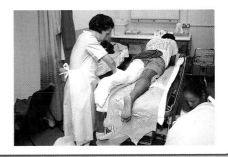

Summary

- The s-block is made up from Group 1 and Group 2 metals.
- Both groups get more reactive as we descend the group, with a group 1 metal more reactive than its neighbour in Group 2.
- The s-block metals have relatively low densities and low melting points compared with other metals.
- Most have characteristic flame colours. (See page 116.)
- Their oxides are basic, and if soluble in water, they react to form an alkaline solution:

$$O^{2-}(s) + H_2O(l) \longrightarrow 2\,OH^-(aq)$$

- The hydroxides of the Group 2 elements get more soluble and more alkaline as we descend the group.
- Their carbonates and nitrates get more stable as we descend the group.

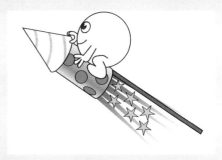

▶ Questions

1 Copy and complete:

Groups 1 and 2 make up the ....-block of the Periodic Table. Group 1 are known as the .... metals and Group 2 are called the alkaline .... metals.

Group 1 and 2 metals both get .... reactive as we descend the group (with Group 1 metals .... reactive than their neighbour in Group 2).

Most Group 1 and 2 elements have characteristic .... colours. For example, lithium is scarlet, sodium is ...., calcium is ...., strontium is .... and .... is apple green. The oxides are ...., and if soluble in water, they react to form an .... solution containing .... ions.

The hydroxides of the Group 2 elements get .... alkaline with increasing atomic number, and the carbonates and nitrates get more .... as we descend the group.

2 This question is about the Group 2 elements:

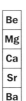

Be
Mg
Ca
Sr
Ba

a) Which one has the lowest 1st ionisation enthalpy? Explain why.

b) Which one is most likely to form compounds with a high degree of covalency in its bonding?

c) Which one has the highest melting point?

d) Which one has the lowest density?

e) Which two are commonly found as carbonates in rocks?

f) Which one is most reactive?

g) Which one forms the most soluble hydroxide in water?

h) Which one is found in limestone, chalk and marble?

i) Which one is essential for healthy teeth and bones?

j) Which one has a flame test colour of crimson red?

k) Which one's electronic structure ends in $...4s^2$?

l) Which one forms the least soluble sulphate?

3 a) Explain how electrons are involved in producing an element's characteristic flame colour.

b) Why doesn't magnesium have a flame colour?

c) Give the equation for the reaction of calcium oxide with water.

d) How are calcium compounds useful to farmers?

4 Lithium and magnesium have many similarities in their chemistry.

a) Why is this similarity sometimes referred to as an example of a 'diagonal relationship'?

b) Name another pair of elements from Groups 1 and 2 that should be similar according to this relationship.

c) Write the equation for the decomposition of magnesium nitrate by heating.

d) Predict the equation for the decomposition of lithium nitrate by heat.

5 Using your knowledge of the other Group 2 elements, answer these questions about radium (Ra). It is a radioactive element that lies beneath barium in Group 2.

a) Will the 1st ionisation enthalpy of radium be higher or lower than barium's?

b) In which sub-shell will we find the outermost electrons in a radium atom?

c) What will be the charge on a radium ion?

d) Write down the formula of:
   i)   radium oxide   ii) radium hydroxide
   iii) radium carbonate   iv) radium nitrate

e) Predict what you would *see* if you added radium to water.

f) Write the word and symbol equations for the reaction of radium with water.

g) Which of these pairs of compounds will be more stable when heated:
   i)   magnesium nitrate or radium nitrate
   ii) calcium carbonate or radium carbonate?

h) What can you predict about the solubility of
   i)   radium hydroxide, and
   ii) radium sulphate?

We call Group 7 (VII) elements the **halogens**.
The name comes from Greek words meaning 'salt-makers'.

The halogens and their compounds have had both
good and bad effects on the world.
Chlorine gas has had a bad reputation since it was used
as the first chemical weapon in the First World War.
Its compounds are also used in biological nerve gases.

However, chlorine's use in killing bacteria in **drinking water**
has saved millions of lives around the world.
It has greatly reduced the number of cases of cholera.

Halogen-based **pesticides** have reduced deaths caused
by diseases carried by insects, such as malaria. They
also reduce the loss of crops in storage.
On the other hand, these compounds can also harm other
wildlife in the food chain.

You can read more about the uses of the halogens on pages 128 to 130.

Chlorine

Bromine

Iodine

Halogens
are toxic

▶ Group 7 elements – The halogens

Halogen	Halogen molecule	Colour	State at 25 °C	Boiling point / °C
F – fluorine	F_2	pale yellow	gas	−188
Cl – chlorine	Cl_2	yellow / green	gas	−34
Br – bromine	Br_2	orange / brown	liquid	58
I – iodine	I_2	grey / black	solid	183

Look at the table above:
Notice that all the halogens form **diatomic** molecules.
In other words, 'two-atom' molecules, like F_2 and Cl_2.
By looking at their electronic structures, we can explain why.
Look back to the cartoon on page 93:
All the halogen atoms have 7 electrons in their outer shells.
On page 57 we saw how two chlorine atoms bond together
by a single covalent bond.
Look at the similar dot and cross diagram for fluorine opposite:
Can you see how both atoms achieve a full outer shell?

single covalent bond

The diatomic fluorine molecule (F_2)

You can also see some patterns in the table above
as you go down the group:
● Do the halogens get darker or lighter in colour?
Look at their boiling points:
● What is the pattern?
  Can you explain this pattern?
(Think about the van der Waals' forces between molecules.
Look back to page 67 if you need help.)
● Using the table, can you make some predictions about astatine
  (the radioactive element at the bottom of Group 7)?

Friend or foe?

That depends how
you use us!

▶ The halogens as oxidising agents

All the halogens are *oxidising agents*.
They accept electrons, forming **halide** ions.
How many electrons do you think an atom of a halogen
accepts when it forms its ion? What charge will it carry?

> **Fluor*ine*** forms **fluor*ides***, **chlor*ine*** forms **chlor*ides***,
> **brom*ine*** produces **brom*ides***, and **iod*ine*** turns into **iod*ides***.

- What would you call the halide ion formed by astatine?

Remember that metals lose electrons when they react.
So it follows that the halogens will react with many metals.
These reactions are examples of **redox** reactions. (See page 109.)
(Remember OIL-RIG – oxidation is loss, reduction is gain.)

In order to perform the reactions with chlorine,
you can make some of the gas in the lab.
Look at the apparatus opposite:

Chlorine can be made by dropping concentrated hydrochloric acid
on to damp potassium manganate(VII).
Its reaction with sodium is commonly used as an example
of the general reaction:

> **metal + halogen ⟶ metal halide**

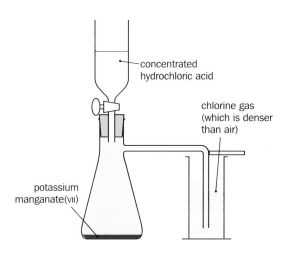

concentrated
hydrochloric acid

chlorine gas
(which is denser
than air)

potassium
manganate(VII)

In this case, each sodium atom loses an electron.
This can be shown in a *half equation*:

$$Na \longrightarrow Na^+ + e^-$$

So the sodium atom acts as a reducing agent, giving away an electron.
(Remember RAGE – reducing agents give electrons.)
In this process the sodium atom itself gets oxidised (OIL!).
Each chlor***ine*** atom accepts an electron, forming a chlor***ide*** ion:

$$Cl + e^- \longrightarrow Cl^-$$

So the chlorine atom acts as an oxidising agent,
and in the process is itself reduced. (RIG!)
But you know that chlorine exists as diatomic molecules.
Therefore the half equation is more correctly written:

$$Cl_2 + 2\,e^- \longrightarrow 2\,Cl^-$$

By adding up the two half equations, we get the full equation
for the redox reaction.
But before we do this we must make sure that the numbers of electrons
given and accepted are equal. In this case, we need to double
everything in the sodium half equation:

$$2 \times (Na \longrightarrow Na^+ + e^-) = 2\,Na \longrightarrow 2\,Na^+ + 2e^-$$

We can now add up the half equations to get the full redox equation.
The 2 electrons in front and behind the arrow cancel out:

$$
\begin{aligned}
2\,Na &\longrightarrow 2\,Na^+ + 2e^- \\
+ \quad Cl_2 + 2e^- &\longrightarrow 2\,Cl^- \\
\hline
2\,Na + Cl_2 &\longrightarrow 2\,Na^+Cl^-
\end{aligned}
$$

This equation, shows the charges on the ions formed.

*Sodium and chlorine react vigorously to
form sodium chloride (common salt)*

The normal balanced equation is shown below:

$$\text{sodium} + \text{chlorine} \longrightarrow \text{sodium chloride}$$
$$2\,Na(s) + Cl_2(g) \longrightarrow 2\,NaCl(s)$$

▶ Reactivity of the halogens

The halogens are the most reactive group of non-metals
in the Periodic Table.
But is there a pattern in their reactivity?
You can look at their redox reactions with metals to answer this.

Fluorine will oxidise iron readily when the gas comes into contact
with the metal.
Chlorine will also react vigorously with iron wool,
but you need to heat the iron.
You can see this reaction opposite:

$$\text{iron} + \text{chlorine} \longrightarrow \text{iron(III) chloride}$$
$$2\,Fe(s) + 3\,Cl_2(g) \longrightarrow 2\,FeCl_3(s)$$

Iron reacting with chlorine

- Has the iron been oxidised or reduced? What is acting as the oxidising agent?
- Can you write half equations for the reaction?
  Now add them to get an ionic equation.

It takes longer for bromine vapour to oxidise the iron,
and with iodine the reaction is slower again.

This, plus evidence from other experiments like the ones described below, show:

> **The reactivity of the halogens decreases as we descend Group 7.**

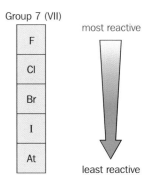

Displacement from solution

We can put the halogens into competition with each other to see
which is more reactive.
It can help us to judge their relative power as oxidising agents.
You do this by adding solutions containing the halogen elements
to solutions of other halide ions.
For example, you can add chlorine solution to a solution of potassium bromide.
- What do you think will happen? Will chlorine be a strong enough
  oxidising agent to remove the extra electron from each bromide ion (Br^-)?
Look at the diagram opposite:
Bromine molecules dissolved in water turn the solution yellow.
- Is chlorine a stronger oxidising agent than bromine?
We can show the reaction by two half equations:

$$Cl_2 + 2\,e^- \longrightarrow 2\,Cl^-$$
$$2\,Br^- \longrightarrow Br_2 + 2\,e^-$$

When we add them up, remember that the electrons cancel out:

$$Cl_2 + 2\!\!\!/\,e^- \longrightarrow 2\,Cl^-$$
$$+ \quad 2\,Br^- \longrightarrow Br_2 + 2\!\!\!/\,e^-$$
$$\overline{Cl_2 + 2\,Br^- \longrightarrow 2\,Cl^- + Br_2}$$

If you do the same with a solution of potassium iodide, what will happen?
- Can you write the half equations for the reaction?
Now add them up to get the ionic equation.

> **The halogens decrease in strength as oxidising agents as we
> descend Group 7.**

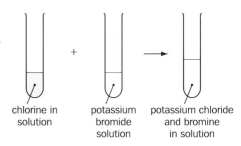

Chlorine is more reactive than bromine.
It can displace bromine from solution:

$$Cl_2(aq) + 2\,KBr(aq) \longrightarrow 2\,KCl(aq) + Br_2(aq)$$

You may be bigger
but I'm more reactive!

▶ Quantitative analysis

Have you ever been swimming and thought that
there was too much chlorine in the water?
Well, we can work out how much chlorine is present in a swimming pool.
We can use the displacement of iodine from a solution of iodide ions
to find out the concentration of many oxidising agents,
including chlorine. You can see the method below:

Step 1: Add a known volume of the oxidising agent
to excess potassium iodide solution.
This makes sure that all the oxidising agent has reacted.
Iodine is formed, which turns starch solution blue/black.

$$2\,I^- \longrightarrow I_2 + 2\,e^-$$

Step 2: Titrate against a known concentration of thiosulphate solution.

$$I_2(aq) + 2\,S_2O_3^{2-}(aq) \longrightarrow 2\,I^-(aq) + S_4O_6^{2-}(aq)$$

The iodine is used up as shown above. The end point is indicated
when the blue/black colour of the starch indicator disappears.

You can then calculate how much iodine was present.
From this you work backwards to find out how much oxidising agent
caused that much iodine to be formed in Step 1.
You can see one of these calculations on page 129.

Why do the halogens get less reactive as we go down Group 7?

An atom of a halogen has seven electrons in its outer shell.
It can gain one electron to fill its outer shell.
Look at the table below:

Halogen	Atomic radius / nm
fluorine	0.071
chlorine	0.099
bromine	0.114
iodine	0.133

- What pattern can you see?

A fluorine atom is a lot smaller than an iodine atom.
Therefore, an electron entering the outer shell of a fluorine atom
is much nearer to the attractive force of the nucleus.
The incoming electron is attracted more strongly.
An electron coming into the outer shell of iodine will also be shielded
from the nuclear attraction by more inner shells full of electrons.

Can you remember the scale we use to judge the tendency of an atom
to attract electrons to itself in a compound?
Look at the table of electronegativities below:

Halogen	Electronegativity
fluorine	4.0
chlorine	3.0
bromine	2.8
iodine	2.5

- What is the pattern going down the group?
- Does this agree with our explanation of why reactivity decreases as we descend the group?

You can estimate how much chlorine is in the water using the method opposite

Chlorine leak

More than 30 children, some as young as three, were taken to hospital suffering from breathing difficulties, skin irritations and vomiting after too much chlorine apparently leaked into a swimming pool in the Hillsborough Leisure Centre, Sheffield.

This story appeared in the Times on 4/8/99. Pools now use solid compounds, such as 'Trichlor', to make the bactericide HOCl in the water instead of handling cylinders of toxic chlorine which used to be dissolved directly into water.

123

▶ Reactions of the halogens and their compounds

Identifying halogens and halide ions

The halogens are easy to tell apart by their physical appearance.
(See the table on page 120.)
In terms of chemical properties, you probably link chlorine and its compounds
with their use in household bleach.

The test for chlorine gas relies on its ability to bleach damp indicator paper.
In fact all the halogens are **bleaching agents**.
The bleaching properties are related to their oxidising power.
Therefore, they are *less effective bleaches as we go down the group*.

The halogens can oxidise the dyes in fabrics

The **halide ions** are identified by precipitation reactions with **silver nitrate solution**.
The ionic equation below shows the general reaction:

$$Ag^+(aq) + X^-(aq) \longrightarrow Ag^+X^-(s)$$ (where X is Cl, Br or I)

Look at the table below. It shows what happens when we add silver nitrate solution,
$AgNO_3(aq)$, followed by ammonia solution, $NH_3(aq)$:

Halide	Colour of silver halide precipitate	Effect of adding dilute ammonia solution
fluoride	none formed (silver fluoride is soluble)	soluble
chloride	white	soluble
bromide	cream	insoluble
iodide	yellow	insoluble

Silver chloride precipitate

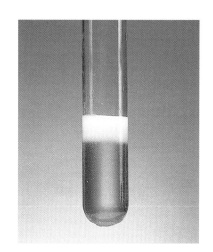

Silver bromide precipitate

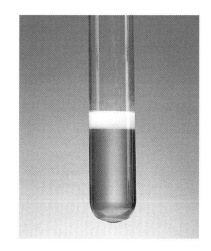

Silver iodide precipitate

Silver bromide is used in photographic film.
It breaks down in sunlight, as does silver chloride:

$$2\,AgBr(s) \longrightarrow 2\,Ag(s) + Br_2(g)$$

The small deposits of silver create the dark areas
on a black and white negative.

This can be used to distinguish between silver chloride and
silver bromide. A precipitate of silver chloride turns
a greyish purple colour in sunlight.
Silver bromide turns a yellowy green colour.

Silver bromide is used in photographic film

▶ Hydrogen halides

You all know the formula HCl. Asked what this stands for, many people say hydrochloric acid. But strictly speaking, you should say hydrogen chloride. Like the other hydrogen halides, this is a gas and shows its acidic properties when dissolved in water:

$$HCl(g) + H_2O(l) \longrightarrow H_3O^+(aq) + Cl^-(aq)$$

An excess of $H_3O^+(aq)$ ions, which we sometimes represent as $H^+(aq)$, make a solution acidic.

Hydrogen halides are formed by reacting a solid halide (such as NaBr) with concentrated phosphoric(v) acid (H_3PO_4):

$$3\,NaBr(s) + H_3PO_4(l) \longrightarrow Na_3PO_4(s) + 3\,HBr(g)$$

Look at the diagram:

HF dissolves in water to make a weak acid. However, the hydrofluoric acid made can react with the sand in glass. This etches the surface of the glass

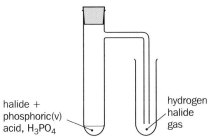

halide + phosphoric(v) acid, H_3PO_4

hydrogen halide gas

They fume on contact with air. They react with the moisture, forming acids:

$$HBr(g) + H_2O(l) \longrightarrow H_3O^+(aq) + Br^-(aq)$$

It is cheaper for us to use concentrated sulphuric acid to make HF or HCl:

$$NaCl(s) + H_2SO_4(l) \longrightarrow NaHSO_4(s) + HCl(g)$$

- What would you use to prepare some hydrogen fluoride (HF) gas?

But concentrated sulphuric acid is quite a powerful oxidising agent. So we can't use it to prepare HBr or HI. We find that as HBr or HI are formed, they are oxidised by the sulphuric acid. Look at the equation below:

$$2\,HBr(g) + H_2SO_4(l) \longrightarrow Br_2(l) + SO_2(g) + 2\,H_2O(l)$$

Further reduction also produces some hydrogen sulphide gas (H_2S). This toxic gas smells like bad eggs!
The same thing happens with hydrogen iodide.

- What mixture of products would you get if you added concentrated sulphuric acid to sodium iodide?

> **It gets easier to oxidise the hydrogen halides as we go down the group.**

Look at the table opposite:
- So can you explain why HI is a stronger acid than HF?
  Why is it easier to oxidise (remove hydrogen from) HI?

> **The strength of the H—Halogen bond decreases down the group.**

	Bond enthalpy / kJ mol^{-1}
H— F	568.0
H— Cl	432.0
H— Br	366.3
H— I	298.3

The hydrogen halides form clouds of white smoke with ammonia gas:

$$HCl(g) + NH_3(g) \longrightarrow NH_4Cl(s)$$

This can be used to test for the gases.

▶ Oxidation numbers and the halogens

You will have noticed how we use Roman numerals in brackets when naming some compounds.
These numbers tell us the **oxidation number** (or **oxidation state**) of an element in the compound.
For example, sodium chlorate(V) tell us that the oxidation number of chlorine in this compound is $+5$.

Oxidation numbers help us to decide the extent to which an element is reduced or oxidised.
There are some rules to follow when assigning oxidation numbers.
These are shown in the box below:

Oxidation number rules

1. The oxidation number of:
   a) any uncombined element is 0 (zero),
      for example, the oxidation number of Cl in Cl_2 is 0,
   b) any simple ion equals its charge,
      for example, Br has an oxidation number of -1 in Br^-,
      or Ca has an oxidation number of $+2$ in Ca^{2+}.

2. The **sum of the oxidation numbers**:
   a) in any compound equals 0 (zero),
      for example, in NH_4Cl we have
      $$(-3) + [4 \times (+1)] + (-1) = 0$$
      $$\quad N \qquad H_4 \qquad\quad Cl$$
   b) in any polyatomic ion equals the charge on the ion,
      for example, in ClO_3^-, each O has an oxidation number of -2
      (see rules in 3. below), so Cl must be $+5$,
      i.e. $(+5) + [3 \times (-2)] = -1$
      $$\quad Cl \qquad\quad O_3$$

3. You need to know that in compounds, the oxidation number of:
   any Group 1 metal is $+1$,
   any Group 2 metal is $+2$.
   Al is $+3$,
   H is $+1$ (except in metal hydrides, e.g. NaH,
        where it is -1),
   O is -2 (except in peroxides and in OF_2),
   F is -1.

Example
sodium chlorate(V), $NaClO_3$

$$\overset{+1}{Na} \quad \overset{+5}{Cl} \quad \overset{(-2) \times 3}{O_3}$$

Total $= +1 + 5 - 6 = 0$

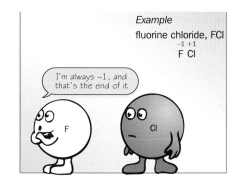

Example
fluorine chloride, FCl
$$\overset{-1\ +1}{F\ Cl}$$

I'm always -1, and that's the end of it

Chlorine can exist in a range of oxidation states, from -1 to $+7$:

Oxidation number	Example
$+7$	ClO_4^-, Cl_2O_7
$+6$	ClO_3
$+5$	ClO_3^-
$+4$	ClO_2
$+3$	ClO_2^-
$+1$	ClO^-
0	Cl_2
-1	Cl^-

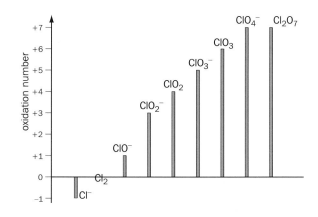

Bromine has the same range, and iodine exhibits all except the +4 and +6 oxidation states.
They can do this by expanding their outer shell (octet), using its empty d orbitals.
For example, look opposite at how chlorine's electrons are arranged in the +5 oxidation state:

Iodine can also exist in the +1 oxidation state, as I^+ ions.
This shows its slightly metallic character.

Fluorine, as the most electronegative element, only exists in the 0 oxidation state in F_2, and as -1 in its compounds.
- Why can't fluorine expand its outer octet?

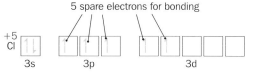

5 spare electrons for bonding

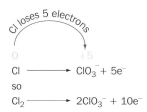

- What would be the arrangement of chlorine's electrons in the +7 oxidation state?

Oxidation numbers and half equations

Do you remember adding half equations on page 121?
Changes in oxidation numbers help us to decide how many electrons are involved in each half equation.
The examples we have looked at so far are straightforward.
It's quite easy to see that changing Cl_2 into two Cl^- ions requires us to add 2 electrons. But what about changing Cl_2 into two ClO_3^- ions? Using oxidation numbers helps here.
Each chlorine atom in Cl_2 has an oxidation number of 0 (zero).
The oxidation number of Cl in ClO_3^- is +5.
So each Cl must lose 5 electrons in changing from a Cl atom to a ClO_3^- ion.
Two Cl atoms change when Cl_2 is oxidised to two ClO_3^- ions, making 10 electrons lost overall.

Cl loses 5 electrons

$$Cl \longrightarrow ClO_3^- + 5e^-$$
so
$$Cl_2 \longrightarrow 2ClO_3^- + 10e^-$$

▶ Oxohalogen compounds (halates)

As we saw on page 124, chlorine is often associated with bleaches.
The gas bleaches damp litmus paper.
When it reacts with water, it forms hydrochloric acid and chloric(I) acid:

$$Cl_2(aq) + H_2O(l) \longrightarrow HCl(aq) + HClO(aq)$$

Bleach is made by reacting chlorine with alkali (sodium hydroxide) at 15 °C:

$$Cl_2(aq) + 2OH^-(aq) \longrightarrow Cl^-(aq) + ClO^-(aq) + H_2O(l)$$
chlorate(I) ion

The chlorate(I) ion decomposes in sunlight to form oxygen:

$$2ClO^-(aq) \longrightarrow 2Cl^-(aq) + O_2(g)$$

Why do you think that bleaches are sold in opaque plastic bottles?
If you use warm alkali (at 70 °C), you get chlorate(V) ions formed:

$$3Cl_2(aq) + 6OH^-(aq) \longrightarrow 5Cl^-(aq) + ClO_3^-(aq) + 3H_2O(l)$$

This is an example of a **disproportionation** reaction.
It can be thought of as 'self reduction–oxidation'.
Chlorine (Cl_2) is both *reduced* (to Cl^-) *and oxidised* (to ClO_3^-) in the same reaction.
- Which of the other reactions shown above are examples of disproportionation?

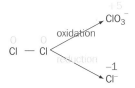

Chlorate(I) ions, $ClO^-(aq)$, are used in bleaches. The active compound is sodium chlorate(I), NaClO

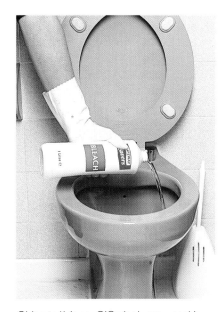

*This is **disproportionation***

127

▶ Chemistry at work: Chlorine and its compounds

Making chlorine

Chlorine, sodium hydroxide and hydrogen are made
by the electrolysis of brine (sodium chloride solution).
This is done in a **diaphragm cell**.
Look at the diagram opposite:

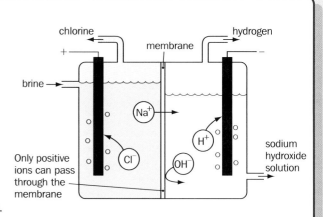

The cell uses titanium anodes and steel cathodes,
which are surrounded by a porous asbestos diaphragm.
Chlorine is given off at the anode.

anode (+) reaction: $2\,Cl^-(aq) \longrightarrow Cl_2(g) + 2\,e^-$

The chlorine rises up through the brine and is piped away.
The cathodes are hollow steel gauze fingers coated in asbestos.
Sodium hydroxide and hydrogen formed inside them
are led away separately:

cathode (−) reaction: $2H^+(aq) + 2e^- \longrightarrow H_2(g)$

Removal of H^+ ions during electrolysis leaves an excess
of OH^- (hydroxide) ions around the cathode.

The brine is kept at a higher level in the anode compartment
compared with the cathode compartment. This lets it
percolate through the diaphragm from anode to cathode.
The design keeps the chlorine and hydrogen gas separate and
keeps the sodium hydroxide solution in the cathode compartment.

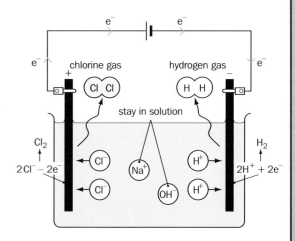

The drawback of the diaphragm cell is that the solution produced
contains only 10% sodium hydroxide. We find that there is
about 15% sodium chloride mixed in the solution.
The solution has to be evaporated to remove the less soluble
sodium chloride.
The final solution contains 50% sodium hydroxide
and less than 1% sodium chloride.

Whiter than white!

Of all the chlorine manufactured, about 20 per cent is used to make
disinfectants and bleaches.
Chlorine is a cheap industrial oxidising agent. It is used
to bleach paper, although it is not used directly as itself.
When we dissolve it in water we get chloric(I) acid (HOCl).

$$Cl_2(g) + H_2O(l) \rightleftharpoons HOCl(aq) + HCl(aq)$$

It is the chloric(I) acid that acts as the oxidant.
It can oxidise the complex organic molecules that make up
coloured dyes, and turn them into colourless products.

$$\underset{\text{(coloured)}}{HOCl + dye} \longrightarrow \underset{\text{(colourless)}}{HCl + oxidised\ dye}$$

Chlorine bleaches paper

However, people are getting worried about the harmful products
in rivers near paper-mills, probably formed by reactions involving chlorine.

Water without bugs

Have you ever smelled chlorine from your water at home
when you turn the taps on full?
Chlorine is used in the water industry to sterilise our water supplies.
The **chloric(I) acid** (HOCl) formed in the water acts as a **bactericide**.
It is lethal to bacteria, and so rids our drinking water
of harmful micro-organisms.

We first used chlorine to sterilise water in 1905.
It was introduced to combat an epidemic of typhoid fever in Lincoln.
Modern water treatment involves the processes shown below:

There are still many people who have to drink untreated water

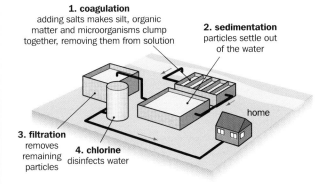

1. coagulation
adding salts makes silt, organic
matter and microorganisms clump
together, removing them from solution

2. sedimentation
particles settle out
of the water

home

3. filtration
removes
remaining
particles

4. chlorine
disinfects water

Once the water is free from any solids, chlorine is
added to kill off any bacterial micro-organisms.
The water in a treatment works is adjusted to a pH of
7.3, although more HOCl(aq) would be present at
lower pH's.

$$HOCl(aq) \rightleftharpoons H^+(aq) + OCl^-(aq)$$

If H^+ ions are removed by raising the pH, more HOCl
splits up to replace them. However, more acidic
conditions would dissolve harmful substances from
the pipes.
(Equilibrium reactions are discussed in detail in
Chapter 29).

Most chlorine is removed chemically, but some is left
in the water.
Why do you think that is?
The water companies have to take care that the water
is kept free from bacteria during its journey to homes
and industry.

HOCl is a bactericide

The amount of dissolved chlorine has to be carefully monitored.
Chemists can use the redox reaction with iodine
to work this out. We described the method on page 123.
Look at the example below:

An analyst from a water company collected a 500 cm^3 sample of water.
She added excess potassium iodide to the sample.
The iodide ions (I^-) react with any chlorine molecules:

$$2\,I^-(aq) + Cl_2(aq) \longrightarrow 2\,Cl^-(aq) + I_2(aq)$$

The iodine is then titrated against sodium thiosulphate,
using starch as an indicator of the end point.
Can you remember how we can tell when we've reached the end point?
She found that it took 7.0 cm^3 of 0.00100 mol dm^{-3} sodium thiosulphate
solution.
The reaction between iodine and thiosulphate can be shown by
this ionic equation:

$$I_2(aq) + 2\,S_2O_3{}^{2-}(aq) \longrightarrow 2\,I^-(aq) + S_4O_6{}^{2-}(aq)$$

Her calculation is shown opposite:

Number of moles of
thiosulphate:
$$\frac{7 \times 0.001}{1000} = 7 \times 10^{-6} \text{ moles}$$
∴ Number of moles of I_2
(as 2 moles of thiosulphate
react with 1 mole of I_2)
$$= \frac{7}{2} \times 10^{-6} = 3.5 \times 10^{-6}$$

1 mole of iodine was formed
from 1 mole of Cl_2
∴ concentration of $Cl_2 =$
$3.5 \times \mathbf{2} \times 10^{-6}$
(as we used a 500 cm^3 sample)
$= \mathbf{7 \times 10^{-6} \ mol \ dm^{-3}}$

▶ Chemistry at work: Bromine and iodine

Bromine from the sea

On page 42 we saw how much sodium chloride is dissolved in seawater.
But there are lots of other salts dissolved in the seas,
especially the Dead Sea in Israel.
Its waters contain relatively large amounts of magnesium bromide.
Bromine is extracted from this and Israel is the biggest
exporter of bromine and its compounds in the world.
So how do they get the bromine from the seawater?

Once again, redox reactions are important in halogen chemistry.
First of all, though, we have to get rid of most of the other salts
dissolved in the water. You can do this by evaporating off
some of the water. The less soluble salts crystallise out,
and you are left with a solution containing plenty of bromide ions.
Turning bromide (Br^-) ions into bromine (Br_2) molecules
is where the redox reaction comes in!
Chlorine is bubbled through the concentrated solution of bromide ions.
We saw on page 122 that chlorine will displace bromide ions from solution:

$$Cl_2(aq) + 2\,Br^-(aq) \longrightarrow 2\,Cl^-(aq) + Br_2(aq)$$

- Which substance is acting as an oxidising agent?

The bromine produced is not very soluble in water,
and soon forms a separate layer beneath the water.
The bromine can then be tapped off.

The chlorine for the reaction is made by electrolysing seawater.
The bromine formed has to be distilled to purify it,
making it ready to be made into compounds.
Its compounds are used to make pesticides, flame retardants and drugs.

The Dead Sea is rich in dissolved salts, including magnesium bromide

Bromine is a dangerous cargo to transport

Iodine and health

We all need a small amount of iodine in a healthy diet.
Insufficient can result in people getting goitre. This is a condition
in which the thyroid gland in the neck swells up.
Iodide ions are converted into hormones in the thyroid gland.
An underactive gland in children can result in slow mental
and physical development. The child is treated with
the iodine-containing hormones.

Have you heard of the town Chernobyl?
In 1986 there was a terrible accident at its nuclear power plant.
Radioactive iodine-131 was one of the isotopes released into the air.
People had to take tablets of non-radioactive iodine-127
to ensure that their bodies had enough iodine. This meant that
they would not need to absorb any of the radioactive iodine.
However, many people did get cancer as a result of the accident.

Iodine is a mild oxidising agent. That's why we use it
as an antiseptic on cuts. We apply it as a solution called
tincture of iodine (iodine mixed with potassium iodide solution and ethanol).
It is also used before operations. Look at the photo opposite:

Radioactive iodine-131 was released at Chernobyl

Iodine can be used before operations

Summary

- The elements of Group 7 are called the **halogens**.
- They exist as diatomic molecules, e.g. F_2.
- Their boiling points increase as we go down the group.
- They form ions with a $1-$ charge (called halide ions), e.g. Cl^-.
- In gaining electrons they act as oxidising agents.
- They get less reactive as we descend the group and are less powerful oxidising agents.
- We test for halide ions using silver nitrate solution.
  The silver halide precipitates formed (or not in the case of fluorides)
  can be distinguished by colour and their solubility in ammonia solution.
- Hydrogen halides can be made by reacting a sodium
  halide with concentrated phosphoric(V) acid.
  (HF and HCl can be made using concentrated sulphuric acid and the sodium halide.)
- Chlorine, bromine and iodine have variable oxidation numbers
  in oxohalogen compounds.

► Questions

1 Copy and complete:
   Group .... elements are called the halogens. Their
   molecules are ...., e.g. the formula of a bromine
   molecule is ....
   Fluorine has the .... boiling point of the halogens. It is
   the .... reactive element and is the .... oxidising agent
   in the group. It forms ions with a .... charge.
   We can test for the presence of halide ions using ....
   nitrate solution. For example, chlorides give a ....
   precipitate which dissolves in .... solution.
   We can prepare samples of hydrogen halides by
   adding concentrated .... acid to the appropriate
   sodium halide.

2 a) Make a table showing the atomic number, colour
       and boiling points of the halogens (fluorine to
       iodine).
   b) Draw a graph of boiling point against atomic
       number for the halogens. (Read part c) first!)
   c) Estimate the boiling point of astatine, At.
   (Its atomic number is 85 and it lies beneath iodine in
   Group 7).
   d) Predict the colour of astatine.
   e) What will be the formula of an astatine molecule?
   f) Draw a dot and cross diagram showing the
       bonding in an astatine molecule.

3 A white solid gives a bright yellow flame test.
   When it is dissolved in dilute nitric acid and silver
   nitrate solution is added we get a cream, off-white
   precipitate.
   The precipitate is insoluble in ammonia solution.
   a) Name the white solid.
   b) Write an ionic equation to show the precipitation
       reaction described above.
   c) Give one use of the precipitate and explain why it
       can be used for that purpose.

4 Hydrogen chloride gas can be made by adding
   concentrated sulphuric acid to solid sodium chloride.
   a) Write an equation to show the reaction.
   b) Draw the apparatus you can use to collect the gas.
   c) Why can't we collect the gas 'over water'?
   d) What would you see if ammonia gas met
       hydrogen chloride gas. Explain your observations
       with an equation.
   e) Why can't we use the method to make
       hydrogen bromide or hydrogen iodide?
   f) How would you change the method to prepare
       a sample of hydrogen iodide?

5 a) What is a disproportionation reaction?
   b) Give an equation involving chlorine which shows
       this type of reaction. Show the changes in the
       oxidation state of the chlorine clearly in your
       equation.
   c) What is the oxidation number or oxidation state of
       the halogen in:
       i) F_2 ii) HCl iii) BrO_3^- iv) IO^- v) Cl_2O_7?

6 Fluorine (F_2) is a powerful oxidising agent.
   a) What is an oxidising agent?
   b) Write a half equation to show a fluorine molecule
       (F_2) acting as an oxidising agent.
   c) Explain why fluorine is the most powerful oxidising
       agent in Group 7.
   Lithium (Li) is a reducing agent.
   d) What is a reducing agent?
   e) Write a half equation to show lithium acting as a
       reducing agent.
   Lithium and fluorine react vigorously together.
   f) What do we call this type of reaction?
   g) Add up the half equations from parts b) and e) to
       get the full equation for the reaction between
       lithium and fluorine.

11 d-block elements

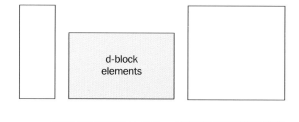

Most of the metals we use in our everyday lives
are from this part of the Periodic Table.

Think of all the metal objects that you have used directly
or indirectly today:
If you have switched on a light, then you have used
a pure d-block element – copper. It is used in electrical wiring.

We often use these metals as alloys (mixtures of metals).
This changes their properties to match particular uses.
(See page 84).
The most common alloy of all is steel. This can vary
in its composition, but is over 95 per cent iron, which is another
d-block element.

▶ Physical properties

You could call the d-block elements 'typical' metals.
Can you recall the general properties of metals?
They:
- have high melting and boiling points
- conduct electricity and heat
- are hard and dense
- can be hammered into shapes (they are malleable)
- can be drawn out into wires (they are ductile).

Look at the graph below:
It shows the melting points of the elements in order of atomic number:
The d-block elements are shown in green.

Iron, used mainly as steel, has many uses

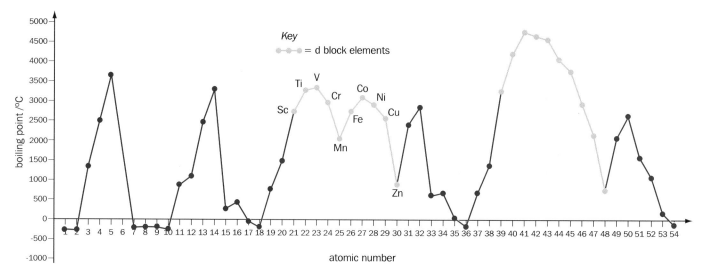

- What patterns can you see?
- Would you predict a similar pattern if density was plotted
  against atomic number?

▶ Electronic structures

We have looked at the electronic structures of the d-block elements before on page 92.
Look at the first row of d-block elements shown below:
Notice the arrangement of electrons in chromium and copper.

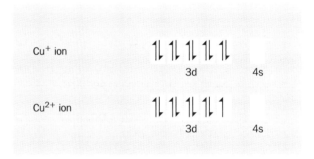

Cu atom   3d   4s

Scandium	Sc	$1s^2 2s^2 2p^6 3s^2 3p^6\, 3d^1 4s^2$
Titanium	Ti	$1s^2 2s^2 2p^6 3s^2 3p^6\, 3d^2 4s^2$
Vanadium	V	$1s^2 2s^2 2p^6 3s^2 3p^6\, 3d^3 4s^2$
Chromium	Cr	$1s^2 2s^2 2p^6 3s^2 3p^6\, 3d^5 4s^1$ (remember the stability of the half-filled sub-shell, discussed on page 15)
Manganese	Mn	$1s^2 2s^2 2p^6 3s^2 3p^6\, 3d^5 4s^2$
Iron	Fe	$1s^2 2s^2 2p^6 3s^2 3p^6\, 3d^6 4s^2$
Cobalt	Co	$1s^2 2s^2 2p^6 3s^2 3p^6\, 3d^7 4s^2$
Nickel	Ni	$1s^2 2s^2 2p^6 3s^2 3p^6\, 3d^8 4s^2$
Copper	Cu	$1s^2 2s^2 2p^6 3s^2 3p^6\, 3d^{10} 4s^1$ (this arrangement enables copper atoms to have a full 3d sub-shell)
Zinc	Zn	$1s^2 2s^2 2p^6 3s^2 3p^6\, 3d^{10} 4s^2$

Forming ions

Would you expect the d-block elements to form positive ions or negative ions?
Like all metals, they lose electrons forming cations (positive ions).
They lose electrons from their outer s sub-shell and/or d sub-shell.
Many d-block elements form more than one type of ion.
For example, copper forms Cu^+ and Cu^{2+} ions.
So their **oxidation number can vary**.
This is discussed further on the next page.

Cu^+ ion   3d   4s

Cu^{2+} ion   3d   4s

Let's take iron as an example:
The electronic structure of the Fe^{2+} ion is:
$1s^2 2s^2 2p^6 3s^2 3p^6\, 3d^6$
Look at the electronic structure of an Fe atom in the table above:
- Which electrons have been lost when it forms Fe^{2+}?
- Can you write the electronic structure of the Fe^{3+} ion?
- Why are Fe^{3+} ions particularly stable?

Now consider titanium:
- Which electrons would be 'lost' when titanium is in its $+4$ oxidation state?
- Why wouldn't you expect to find Ti with an oxidation number of $+5$?

Some d-block elements are called **transition metals**.
These can be defined as elements that form at least one ion with a **partially filled d sub-shell**.

This definition excludes scandium and zinc from the list of transition metals.
Scandium forms only one ion, Sc^{3+}.
- How many electrons does the Sc atom lose to form the Sc^{3+} ion?
- What is the electronic structure of the Sc^{3+} ion?

Zinc also forms only one ion, unlike many d-block elements.
Its formula is Zn^{2+}.
- What is the electronic structure of the Zn^{2+} ion?
- Why don't we call scandium and zinc transition metals?

133

▷ Variable oxidation number

If you were asked the formula of copper chloride, what would you write?
Without more information, you could not answer for sure. Remember in the last chapter we included Roman numerals in the names of some halogen compounds. Can you recall why we had to do this?

In order to write the correct formula of copper chloride, you need to know if it refers to copper(I) chloride or copper(II) chloride. Then you could write CuCl or $CuCl_2$. Many other d-block elements can also have more than one oxidation state in their compounds.

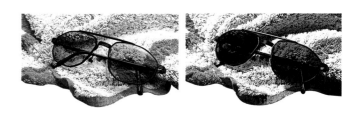

Photochromic glass contains tiny crystals of silver and copper halides
$Cu^+(s) + Ag^+(s) \rightleftharpoons Cu^{2+}(s) + Ag(s)$
Clusters of silver atoms cause glass to darken in light

The oxidation numbers of the first row of d-block elements are shown below:
The most important ones are in red. Those in brackets are rare.

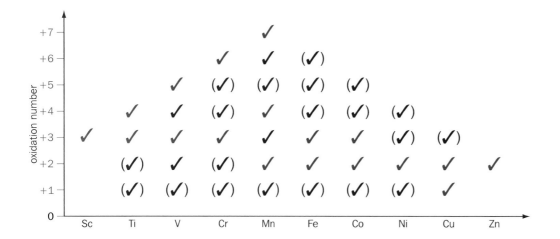

- Which element can have the highest oxidation number?
  Which electrons are involved when it exists in this oxidation state?
- Can you see a pattern?

Look at the first ten ionisation enthalpies of vanadium and chromium:

	1st	2nd	3rd	4th	5th	6th	7th	8th	9th	10th
Ionisation enthalpy (kJ mol^{-1}) for V	650	1414	2828	4507	6294	12 362	14 490	16 760	19 860	22 240
Ionisation enthalpy (kJ mol^{-1}) for Cr	653	1592	2987	4740	6686	8738	15 540	17 822	20 200	23 580

Argon core

- Where is there a large jump in the values for a) vanadium and b) chromium?
- How does this help to explain the maximum oxidation numbers of V and Cr?

The maximum oxidation numbers of the elements up to manganese involve all the 3d and 4s electrons. To use any more would mean breaking into a full shell. This would take a lot more energy.

134

Notice that the oxidation numbers don't simply keep rising as we go across the row.
After manganese, the attraction of the increasing positive charge on the nucleus for the nearer 3d electrons gets stronger.
Therefore the common oxidation numbers tend to involve only the outermost 4s electrons.
Examples are +2 for Fe, Co and Ni, and the +1 oxidation state for Cu.

On page 131 you looked at the electronic structure of the Fe^{3+} ion.
Why was it particularly stable?
The same principle applies to the Mn^{2+} ion.
The loss of the two 4s electrons, leaves 5 electrons in the 3d sub-shell.
This ion has the stability associated with a half-filled sub-shell.

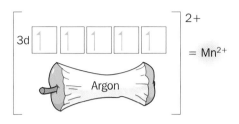

The higher oxidation numbers are usually found in **complex ions** or in compounds with oxygen or fluorine. (See table opposite.)
Why do you think that we find the highest oxidation numbers when transition metals are combined with the most electronegative elements?

Oxide	Oxidation state
TiO_2	+4
V_2O_5	+5
CrO_3	+6
Mn_2O_7	+7
Fe_2O_3	+3
Co_2O_3	+3
NiO	+2
CuO	+2

You never find Mn^{7+} or Cr^{6+} as individual ions in ionic compounds.
These ions would possess a very **high charge density**. (See page 72.)
It would also take a lot of energy to actually remove 4, 5, 6 or 7 electrons.
However, you have probably met MnO_4^- ions in experiments using potassium manganate(VII). Can you recall their colour?

The formation of complex ions involves dative bonding. (See page 59.)
We will discuss this in more detail on the next page.

The bonding in compounds such as CrO_3 is also covalent in character. Look at the examples opposite:

We can observe some of these various oxidation numbers during redox reactions.
The ions of transition metals are **coloured**.
This makes it possible to tell which ion is present in a solution.
We can see a sequence of oxidation states using vanadium.
Look at the diagrams below:

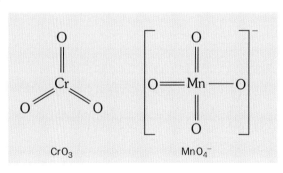

CrO_3 MnO_4^-

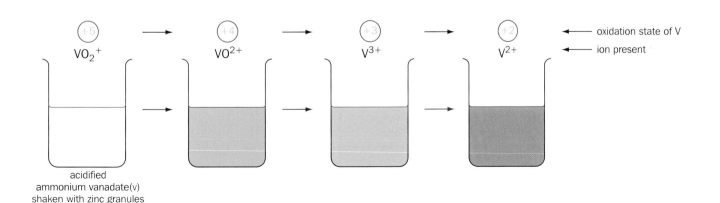

acidified ammonium vanadate(V) shaken with zinc granules

135

▶ Complex ions

Have you ever tested for water using cobalt chloride paper?
Can you remember what happens if water is present?
The blue colour in 'cobalt chloride' paper is caused by $[CoCl_4]^{2-}$ ions.
When we add water, it turns pink. The blue $[CoCl_4]^{2-}$ ions change into
$[Co(H_2O)_6]^{2+}$ ions which are pink.

Both $[CoCl_4]^{2-}$ and $[Co(H_2O)_6]^{2+}$ are called **complex ions**.
These are formed when a central metal ion is surrounded
by negative ions or molecules containing atoms with
lone pairs of electrons.

*The test for water – 'blue cobalt chloride paper
turns pink'*

> **The surrounding ions or molecules are called ligands.**

In $[CoCl_4]^{2-}$, the central Co^{2+} ion is surrounded by four Cl^- ions.
The overall charge on the complex ion is worked out
by adding together the charges on any ions present.
In this case,

$$\underset{\text{(from } Co^{2+})}{+2} \quad + \quad \underset{\text{(from four } Cl^- \text{ ions)}}{(-1)\times 4} \quad = \quad \underset{\text{(The overall charge on } [CoCl_4]^{2-})}{-2}$$

In $[Co(H_2O)_6]^{2+}$ each water molecule is neutral. So the overall charge on the
complex equals the charge on the central Co^{2+} ion.

● Can you name the ligands in each complex ion above?

The ligands bond to the central metal ion by dative bonds,
sometimes called coordinate bonds. (See page 59.)
Can you see why ligands must contain atoms with at least
one lone pair of electrons?

Look at the diagram of the complex ions below:

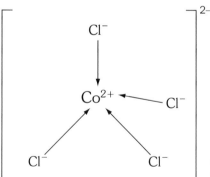

*Six water ligands form
dative bonds with Co^{2+}*

*Four chloride ligands
surround Co^{2+} in this
complex ion*

Can you recall what the arrow-head on each bond tells us?
Each ligand donates a lone pair of electrons into
empty orbitals on the metal ion.

> **The number of lone pairs donated to the metal ion
> is called the coordination number of the ion.**

Therefore the Co^{2+} ion has a coordination number of 4
in $[CoCl_4]^{2-}$.
● What is the coordination number of the cobalt ion in $[Co(H_2O)_6]^{2+}$?

136

▶ Shapes of complex ions

Do you remember how we work out the shapes of molecules?
On page 60 we saw how the bonding pairs of electrons repel
each other. They get as far apart as possible.
We can use this to explain the shapes of complexes.

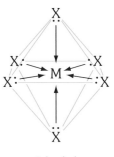

The most common coordination number is 6, followed by 4,
and occasionally 2.

coordination number 2

$$X : \longrightarrow M \longleftarrow : X$$

linear

coordination number 4

tetrahedral

coordination number 6

octahedral

Some complexes in which the metal ion has a coordination number of 4
seem to go against the rules. They adopt a square planar shape:
Look at the complex opposite:

However, these are really special cases of 6 coordinated complexes.
Look at the octahedral shape shown above.
In square planar complexes the ligands at the top and bottom
of the octahedron are further from the central metal ion.
These are not counted as 'nearest neighbours',
making the coordination number 4, and not 6.
The four nearest ligands form the square from the octahedron.

The arrangement of ligands in octahedral and square planar
complexes makes **stereoisomerism** possible.

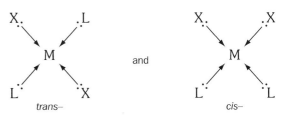

square planar

The four cyanide ligands are arranged
in a square around the central nickel(II) ion

> **Isomers are molecules (or complexes) with the same
> formula but different arrangements of atoms (or ions).**

In stereoisomers, the atoms (or ions) form the same bonds,
but cannot be superimposed. They have different
arrangements in space.
Look at the examples below and opposite:

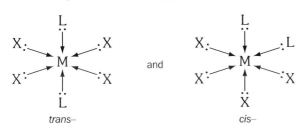

trans–   and   *cis–*

Stereo-isomers in the square planar arrangement.
cis-isomers have common ligands on the same side
trans-isomers have the same ligands on opposite
sides

> **Small ligands, like water,
> tend to form octahedral
> complexes.
> Larger ligands, like Cl⁻,
> tend to form tetrahedral
> complexes.**

● Why can't $[CoCl_2Br_2]^{2-}$, which is tetrahedral, form stereoisomers?

▶ Coloured compounds

One of the striking features of transition metal compounds
is their variety of **colours**.
Many gemstones take their characteristic colours from
traces of transition metal ions.
Look at the photo and table opposite:

Cobalt(II) oxide is used to make stained glass, and chromium compounds are
used in dyeing. The colours of some common transition metal ions are shown
below:

Emeralds contain Cr^{3+} ions

Gemstone	Ion	Colour
jade or emerald	Cr^{3+}	green
topaz	Fe^{3+}	yellow
turquoise	Cu^{2+}	blue/green

Titanium	Vanadium	Chromium	Manganese	Iron	Cobalt	Nickel	Copper
Ti^{3+}(aq) purple	V^{3+}(aq) green	Cr^{3+}(aq) violet	Mn^{2+}(aq) pale pink	Fe^{2+}(aq) pale green	Co^{2+}(aq) pink	Ni^{2+}(aq) green	Cu^{2+}(aq) blue
		CrO_4^{2-}(aq) yellow	MnO_4^{-}(aq) purple	Fe^{3+}(aq) yellow			
		$Cr_2O_7^{2-}$(aq) orange					

The ions above all absorb particular colours of the spectrum.
For example, Ti^{3+}(aq) absorbs green light. Red and blue light
pass through, so the solution looks purple.
The light is absorbed by electrons jumping to slightly higher,
empty orbitals. (See page 142.)

The ions above are more accurately shown as complex ions.
What is the ligand that surrounds the central metal ion in solutions?
Let's look at the structure of the Fe^{3+}(aq) ion:

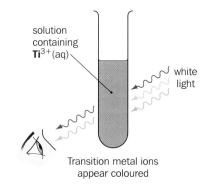

solution
containing
Ti^{3+}(aq)

white
light

Transition metal ions
appear coloured

Transition metal ions appear coloured

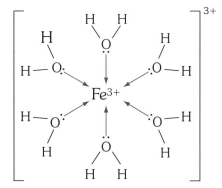

The colour of this complex ion is pale purple.
Does this agree with the table above?
Like many hydrated metal ions with high charge densities,
the water ligands tend to break down:

$$[Fe(H_2O)_6]^{3+}(aq) + H_2O(l) \overset{\text{hydrolysis}}{\rightleftharpoons} [Fe(H_2O)_5OH]^{2+}(aq) + H_3O^{+}(aq)$$
pale purple   yellow

Can you see why the charge on the complex ion changes from 3+ to 2+?
As an H^{+} ion is removed from $[Fe(H_2O)_6]^{3+}$, it leaves an OH^{-} ion
bonded to the iron. If you add up the charges on the ions, we get:

     3+ (from Fe^{3+}) + (−1) (from OH^{-}) = 2+.

We say that the $[Fe(H_2O)_6]^{3+}$(aq) ion has been **hydrolysed.** (See page 107.)
The H_3O^{+}(aq) ions formed make solutions of iron(III) salts acidic.

Iron(III) chloride is used in etching

138

Reactions in solution

If we add alkali (hydroxide ions) to hydrated transition metal ions, we see precipitates forming.
Look at the examples below:

Chromium(III)

$[Cr(H_2O)_6]^{3+}$(aq) forms a pale green precipitate
of hydrated chromium (III) oxide, Cr_2O_3, with alkali.
This will then dissolve if you add more alkali:

$$[Cr(H_2O)_6]^{3+}(aq) + 6\,OH^-(aq) \longrightarrow [Cr(OH)_6]^{3-}(aq) + 6\,H_2O$$
excess alkali   deep green solution

Iron(II)

When we add sodium hydroxide solution to an iron(II) salt,
we see a dirty green precipitate form:

$$[Fe(H_2O)_6]^{2+}(aq) + 2\,OH^-(aq) \longrightarrow Fe(OH)_2(s) + 6\,H_2O(l)$$
mucky green

Iron(III)

With salts of iron(III) we get a red-brown precipitate:

$$[Fe(H_2O)_6]^{3+}(aq) + 3\,OH^-(aq) \longrightarrow Fe(OH)_3(s) + 6\,H_2O(l)$$
rusty brown

We can use these reactions to distinguish between iron(II) and iron(III) salts.

Cobalt(II)

Adding the weak alkali, ammonia (NH_3) solution, gives us a blue precipitate:

$$[Co(H_2O)_6]^{2+}(aq) + 2\,OH^-(aq) \longrightarrow Co(OH)_2(H_2O)_4(s) + 2\,H_2O(l)$$
blue

This dissolves in excess ammonia:

$$Co(OH)_2(H_2O)_4(s) + 6\,NH_3(aq) \longrightarrow [Co(NH_3)_6]^{2+}(aq) + 4\,H_2O(l) + 2\,OH^-(aq)$$
pale yellow solution

The $[Co(NH_3)_6]^{2+}$(aq) ion is oxidised in air to form $[Co(NH_3)_6]^{3+}$(aq).

Nickel(II)

A similar reaction is seen with nickel(II) salts as with cobalt(II) above
when ammonia solution is added.
The hydrated nickel(II) hydroxide is a green gelatinous (jelly-like) solid.
It also dissolves in excess ammonia solution as $[Ni(NH_3)_6]^{2+}$(aq) forms.
(However, Ni^{2+} is not oxidised in air.)

Copper(II)

If we add sodium hydroxide or ammonia to copper(II) salts,
we see a pale blue gelatinous solid form. This is hydrated copper(II) hydroxide:

$$[Cu(H_2O)_6]^{2+}(aq) + 2\,OH^-(aq) \longrightarrow Cu(OH)_2(H_2O)_4(s) + 2\,H_2O(l)$$
pale blue

In excess ammonia, the precipitate dissolves to give
a beautiful, deep blue solution:

$$Cu(OH)_2(H_2O)_4(s) + 4\,NH_3(aq) \longrightarrow [Cu(NH_3)_4(H_2O)_2]^{2+}(aq) + 2\,OH^-(aq) + 2\,H_2O(l)$$
deep blue solution

139

▶ More about ligands

How many examples of ligands have we met so far
in this chapter? They are listed opposite, together with
some other common ligands:
What do the ligands all have in common?
Can you remember how the ligands use their lone pairs
of electrons when bonding to the metal ion?

Ligand	Name
H_2O	aqua
NH_3	ammine
NO	nitrosyl
CO	carbonyl
Cl^-	chloro
OH^-	hydroxo
CN^-	cyano
SCN^-	thiocyanato

No wonder they're called **complex** ions!

Naming complex ions

The names of complex ions are long and look rather complex!
It is often easier to visualise the complex from its formula.
However, you might come across the written names
and need to translate these into a formula.

Rules

1. We start with the name(s) of the ligands, in alphabetical order.
   (See the table at the top of this page).
   The number of ligands present can be shown by putting mono,
   di, tri, tetra, penta or hexa in front of its name.

2. We end with the name of the metal, with its oxidation number
   in brackets.
   If the complex ion has a positive charge, we use
   the metal's English name.
   For example, the hexaaquacopper(II) ion, i.e. $[Cu(H_2O)_6]^{2+}$.
   If the complex ion has a negative charge, we use
   a shortened version of the metal's English or Latin name,
   finishing off with **-ate**.
   For example, the tetrachlorocuprate(II) ion, i.e. $[CuCl_4]^{2-}$.

   The other Latin version of a transition metal's name that
   you need to know is ferrate, for negative iron complexes.

$[FeOH(H_2O)_5]^{2+}$
= pentaaquahydroxoiron(III) ion

$[Fe(CN)_6]^{4-}$
= hexacyanoferrate(II) ion

Now look at the examples in the green boxes which illustrate the rules:

Multidentate (or polydentate) ligands

The ligands listed at the top of the page are all called **unidentate
(or monodentate)**.
This means that each molecule or ion only forms
one dative (or coordinate) bond to the central metal ion.

However, some ligands can form 2 bonds to the metal.
These are called **bidentate** ligands.
Look at the top diagram of the ligands opposite:

Where do you think the word 'dentate' comes from?
Can you imagine each ligand 'biting' hold of the metal ion?
A **bi**dentate ligand has two 'bites'!

Some molecules can donate even more lone pairs
of electrons into the central metal ion.
We call these ligands **multidentate (or polydentate)**.

Can you see how the multidentate ligand $EDTA^{4-}$ forms its bonds?

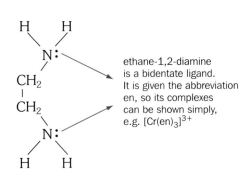

ethane-1,2-diamine
is a bidentate ligand.
It is given the abbreviation
en, so its complexes
can be shown simply,
e.g. $[Cr(en)_3]^{3+}$

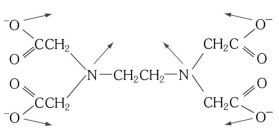

$EDTA^{4-}$ (a hexadentate ligand)

140

Substitution of ligands

On page 139 we looked at reactions of transition metal ions in solution. For example, we can summarise what happens when we add excess ammonia to copper(II) ions in solution:

$$[Cu(H_2O)_6]^{2+}(aq) + 4\,NH_3(aq) \longrightarrow [Cu(NH_3)_4(H_2O)_2]^{2+}(aq) + 4\,H_2O(l)$$

blue   deep, royal blue solution

This is called a **substitution** reaction.
Four water ligands have been replaced by four ammonia ligands.

Another example is when we add concentrated hydrochloric acid to aqueous copper(II) ions:

$$[Cu(H_2O)_6]^{2+}(aq) + 4\,Cl^-(aq) \rightleftharpoons [CuCl_4]^{2-}(aq) + 6\,H_2O(l)$$

blue   yellow

Under these conditions, chloride ions replace water molecules around the copper ion.
However, if we then add more water, the solution turns green, and eventually blue. Why do you think this happens?
Notice the equilibrium sign above:
The addition of water moves the position of the equilibrium left.
From previous work, can you explain why?
You can read more about equilibria in Chapters 29 and 30.

Not only the energetic stability of the complex formed determines whether or not one ligand replaces another.
When we look at reactions with multidentate ligands, we find that they readily replace unidentate ligands.
For example:

$$[Ni(H_2O)_6]^{2+}(aq) + EDTA^{4-}(aq) \longrightarrow [Ni(EDTA)]^{2-}(aq) + 6\,H_2O(l)$$

Chemical reactions are favoured if the products can be arranged in a more 'disorderly' way than the reactants.
We call this an increase in **entropy**.
How many individual ions or molecules are found on each side of the equation above?
The 6 water molecules released result in more disorder.
So EDTA replaces the water ligands.
We will look in more detail at entropy in Chapter 26.

Nickel also forms a stable complex with butanedione dioxime.
The complex forms as a red precipitate. It can be used to detect the presence of nickel(II) ions.
The precipitate can also be collected to work out *how much* nickel is in a sample.
Look at the structure of the complex opposite:

- How many dative bonds does each ligand form with nickel? Which word describes this type of ligand?

The ligands form a ring structure in this complex.
We call this **chelation**.
Butanedione dioxime is said to be a **chelating** ligand.
The complex formed is a **chelate** compound.

- Can you see how ethane-1,2-diamine (en) forms chelates?

A solution containing $[Cu(NH_3)_4(H_2O)_2]^{2+}$ ions

The equilibrium mixture above appears green as both $[Cu(H_2O)_6]^{2+}$ (blue) and $[CuCl_4]^{2-}$ (yellow) are present

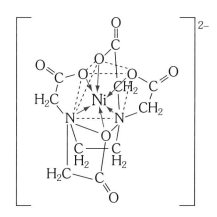

$[Ni(EDTA)]^{2-}$ complex ion

The ring structure makes this a chelate compound

141

▶ Chemistry at work: Transition metal complexes

Copper: Complex colours

Monastral blue pigment provides us with very intense
blue and green shades. It was widely used by
the Impressionist artists.
You can see an example opposite:

The pigment is a complex of copper ions with a multidentate ligand.
Look at its structure below:

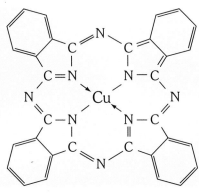

*This painting by Renoir also includes
cobalt blue, ($CoO.Al_2O_3$), green
viridian ($Cr_2O_3.2H_2O$) and
chrome yellow ($PbCrO_4$)*

We saw how transition metal compounds absorb
part of the visible spectrum of light on page 138.
- Which part of the spectrum do you think monastral blue absorbs?

To explain why transition metal ions absorb energy we need
to look closer at their energy levels in complexes.
The presence of ligands around the central ion causes
the d-orbitals to split.
How many electrons will a Cu^{2+} ion have in its 3d sub-shell?
(The atomic number of copper is 29.)
Look at the diagram below:

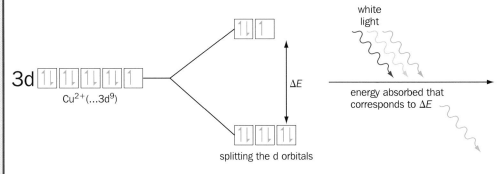

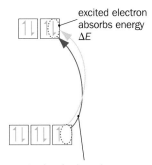

The gap between the d-orbitals is different for each transition metal ion.
So each one has its characteristic colour. Notice how these change
depending on the oxidation state of the ion.
You saw the range of colours for vanadium ions on page 135.

The energy absorbed can be
worked out by the equation:

$$\Delta E = h\nu$$

where ν is the frequency
of light absorbed and
h is Planck's constant

We also find that different ligands have an effect on the colour
of the central metal ion in different complexes. For example,
$[Cu(H_2O)_6]^{2+}$ is blue, whereas $[Cu(NH_3)_4(H_2O)_2]^{2+}$ is a deep royal blue,
and $[CuCl_4]^{2-}$ is yellow.
- Why do you think this happens?

A more recent use of a pigment is in double yellow lines!
These contain the pigment lead chromate ($PbCrO_4$).

Iron: Complex transporter

We all rely on a transition metal complex to carry oxygen around our bodies. It is haemoglobin – a complex made from protein, a haem molecule and an iron(II) ion.
Look at part of its structure opposite:

* How many bonds does the haem form to Fe^{2+}?

Oxygen molecules also have lone pairs of electrons that bond to the Fe^{2+} ion, and then get carried along in our blood. The bond breaks when the oxygen gets to the cell where it is needed for respiration.

You probably know about the dangers of carbon monoxide poisoning. People die every year, many on holiday, from the effects of faulty gas heaters. If a flue is blocked, carbon monoxide builds up. The victim becomes drowsy and will die without fresh air. This is because carbon monoxide bonds to haemoglobin just as oxygen does. However, its dative bonds to the Fe^{2+} ion are not easily broken. Soon many of the Fe^{2+} sites are occupied by carbon monoxide molecules. They are no longer available to transport oxygen. So the cells become starved of oxygen and death will follow. Carbon monoxide is one of the gases given out by cars. However, a catalytic converter can turn most of it to carbon dioxide (although this is a 'greenhouse' gas!). (See also page 169.)

The red colour of blood comes from oxyhaemoglobin

Silver: Complex solutions

Many silver compounds are insoluble in water.
But its common complex ions, $[Ag(NH_3)_2]^+$, $[Ag(S_2O_3)_2]^{3-}$ and $[Ag(CN)_2]^-$ are all soluble. This has led to these uses:

a) Chemical tests

Do you remember the test for halide ions with silver nitrate solution, followed by adding ammonia solution? (See page 124.)
When silver chloride dissolves in dilute ammonia solution, it forms the complex ion $[Ag(NH_3)_2]^+$.
This ion is also in Tollens' reagent, used to test for aldehydes (see page 222). The Ag^+ ion is reduced to silver, which coats the inside of a test tube.

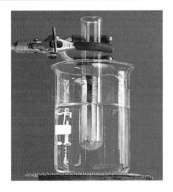

Results of the 'silver mirror' test for aldehydes

b) Silver plating and the extraction of silver

We can silver-plate metal objects by using them as an anode when we electrolyse a solution containing silver ions.
The solution used is one containing $[Ag(CN)_2]^-$ ions.

Silver is extracted from its ore, containing insoluble silver sulphide, by first dissolving it in a cyanide solution of CN^- ions.
The silver is then displaced by powdered zinc.

c) Photography

Do you remember from page 124 how silver bromide is used in photographic film?
When a photograph is developed, it is washed with thiosulphate solution.
This removes any unreacted silver bromide from the film as soluble $[Ag(S_2O_3)_2]^{3-}$ is formed.
What would happen if the film was not washed with 'thio'?

Developing a film

▶ Redox reactions of transition metal compounds

We have already seen how the transition metals can
exist in a variety of oxidation states.
Changing from one oxidation state to another will involve
the transfer of electrons.

- If the metal's oxidation number decreases in a reaction,
  is it being reduced or oxidised?
  Is it acting as a reducing agent or an oxidising agent?

There is a quick way to remember:
If an element's **oxidation number is reduced** (gets lower),
then it **has been reduced**.
It has gained electrons, so it is acting as an oxidising agent.

Common oxidising agents are chromate(VI) ions, CrO_4^{2-},
dichromate(VI) ions, $Cr_2O_7^{2-}$, and
manganate(VII) ions, MnO_4^-.
Let's look at half equations that show how they gain electrons.
Notice how they all need acidic conditions:

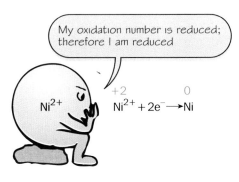

Nickel(II) ion gets philosophical!

$$CrO_4^{2-}(aq) + 8\,H^+(aq) + 3\,e^- \longrightarrow Cr^{3+}(aq) + 4\,H_2O(l)$$
$$Cr_2O_7^{2-}(aq) + 14\,H^+(aq) + 6\,e^- \longrightarrow 2\,Cr^{3+}(aq) + 7\,H_2O(l)$$
$$MnO_4^-(aq) + 8\,H^+(aq) + 5\,e^- \longrightarrow Mn^{2+}(aq) + 4\,H_2O(l)$$

Oxidising agents in action
(Notice how their oxidation
numbers are reduced in the
process of gaining electrons).

We have already looked at half equations in the last chapter.
But you can now see the steps for balancing more difficult
half equations involving polyatomic ions in the box below:

Half equations with polyatomic ions

1. Work out the oxidation numbers of the transition metal
   on either side of the half equation. For example,

   $$\overset{+6}{CrO_4^{2-}} \longrightarrow \overset{+3}{Cr^{3+}}$$

2. Use these to put in the electrons involved.

   $$CrO_4^{2-} + 3\,e^- \longrightarrow Cr^{3+}$$

3. Balance excess oxygen atoms by adding H_2O molecules
   to the other side of the half equation.

   $$\overset{+6}{CrO_4^{2-}} + 3\,e^- \longrightarrow \overset{+3}{Cr^{3+}} + 4\,H_2O$$

4. The new H atoms, introduced by adding H_2O's,
   can be balanced by adding H^+ ions to the other side:

   $$CrO_4^{2-} + 8\,H^+ + 3\,e^- \longrightarrow Cr^{3+} + 4\,H_2O$$

5. Add in state symbols if required:

   $$CrO_4^{2-}(aq) + 8\,H^+(aq) + 3\,e^- \longrightarrow Cr^{3+}(aq) + 4\,H_2O(l)$$

Notice that the total charge on either side of the half equation
is the same, and so is the number of atoms.
In Chapter 33 you can find out about the data we can use
to predict whether or not redox reactions are feasible.

Example

You can use manganate(VII) ions to estimate the concentration of iron(II) ions in a solution. For example, you might want to find out the amount of iron in a health tablet.
Look at the titration opposite:

Do you remember from page 121 how to add up half equations?
The two half equations here are:

$$MnO_4^-(aq) + 8\,H^+(aq) + 5\,e^- \longrightarrow Mn^{2+}(aq) + 4\,H_2O(l) \text{ and}$$
$$Fe^{2+}(aq) \longrightarrow Fe^{3+}(aq) + e^-$$

but the numbers of electrons in each half equation must cancel out.
So we multiply everything in the bottom one by 5, giving:

$$MnO_4^-(aq) + 8\,H^+(aq) + \cancel{5\,e^-} \longrightarrow Mn^{2+}(aq) + 4\,H_2O(l)$$
$$+ \qquad\qquad 5\,Fe^{2+}(aq) \longrightarrow 5\,Fe^{3+}(aq) + \cancel{5\,e^-}$$
$$\overline{MnO_4^-(aq) + 5\,Fe^{2+}(aq) + 8\,H^+(aq) \longrightarrow Mn^{2+}(aq) + 5\,Fe^{3+}(aq) + 4\,H_2O(l)}$$

We can judge the end point by noting the first permanent purple colour.
This is when the $MnO_4^-(aq)$ has just reacted with all the $Fe^{2+}(aq)$ ions present.

You can try a calculation for this titration on page 151.

We can get a more accurate result for Fe^{2+} ions if we use dichromate ions to oxidise it. This is because compounds such as potassium dichromate(VI) can be prepared to a higher degree of purity than potassium manganate(VII). An indicator is needed that will change colour as it gets oxidised by the first excess dichromate(VI) ions.

Let's look at this redox reaction:
The two half equations are:

$$Cr_2O_7^{2-}(aq) + 14\,H^+(aq) + 6\,e^- \longrightarrow 2\,Cr^{3+}(aq) + 7\,H_2O(l) \text{ and}$$
$$Fe^{2+}(aq) \longrightarrow Fe^{3+}(aq) + e^-$$

- Can you see why there are 6 electrons in the top half equation?
  (Remember there are 2 Cr's, each changing oxidation number.)
- What do we have to do so that the electrons on each side cancel out?

Adding up the half equations we get:

$$Cr_2O_7^{2-}(aq) + 14\,H^+(aq) + \cancel{6\,e^-} \longrightarrow 2\,Cr^{3+}(aq) + 7\,H_2O(l)$$
$$+ \qquad\qquad 6\,Fe^{2+}(aq) \longrightarrow 6\,Fe^{3+}(aq) + \cancel{6\,e^-}$$
$$\overline{Cr_2O_7^{2-}(aq) + 6\,Fe^{2+}(aq) + 14\,H^+(aq) \longrightarrow 2\,Cr^{3+}(aq) + 6\,Fe^{3+}(aq) + 7\,H_2O(l)}$$

- Check the total charge and number of atoms on either side of the equation.
  Do they balance?

We can show which ions are reduced and which are oxidised.
Remember that if the oxidation number gets reduced in the change, then that substance is also reduced. The opposite applies when deciding whether something gets oxidised.
Look at the equations opposite:

Titrating $Fe^{2+}(aq)$ ions against $MnO_4^-(aq)$ ions

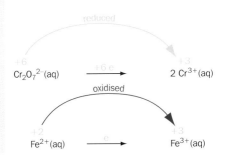

145

▶ Catalysis and the transition metals

Another useful property of the transition metals and their compounds
is their ability to act as catalysts.
You will know from previous work that catalysts speed up reactions.
At the end of the reaction they remain chemically unchanged.
Catalysts are very important in making new substances
on a large scale in industry.

Can you recall any catalysts used in industry?
You might remember that iron is a catalyst used in the Haber process.
Look at the table below:

*This gauze is made from platinum and rhodium.
The gauze has a large surface area and is used
when making nitric acid*

Manufacture of...	Transition metal or its compound used as catalyst at some stage in the process
Poly(ethene)	$TiCl_4$
Sulphuric acid	V_2O_5
Ammonia	Fe or Fe_2O_3
Margarine	Ni
Ethanal	Cu or CuO
Nitric acid	Pt (platinum) and Rh (rhodium)

Transition metals are also needed in trace amounts
in plants and animals. They are often involved in
enzyme reactions.
The table below shows some of the transition metals we have
in different organs of our body (measured in parts per million):

Organ	Copper	Cobalt	Manganese
Brain	17.5	–	0.34
Liver	24.9	0.18	1.68
Kidney	17.3	0.23	0.93

> There are two types of catalysis: **homogeneous** and **heterogeneous**

1. Homogeneous catalysis

In this the reactants and catalyst are ***in the same state (or phase)***.
For example, when a reaction takes place in solution
and the catalyst is a hydrated transition metal ion also in solution.
This is illustrated in the reaction between hydrogen peroxide
and 2,3-dihydroxybutanedioate (tartrate) ions.
It is a very slow reaction until you add cobalt(II) ions.
Look at the diagrams below:

Very slow reaction

catalyst

① Co^{2+}

Add cobalt(II) chloride
catalyst

②

The pink Co^{2+} turns to green Co^{3+}
as an intermediate is formed

③

The Co^{2+} remains at
the end of the reaction

You can show the stages in the reaction on an enthalpy level diagram, sometimes called a reaction profile:
(These diagrams are looked at in detail in Chapter 24.
Catalysts are discussed in Chapter 27.)

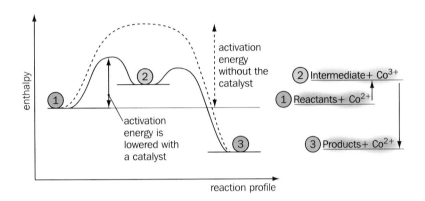

The ability to change oxidation states makes transition metal ions good catalysts for redox reactions.
They provide reactions with an easier route to the products by lowering the activation energy. (See page 332.)

2. Heterogeneous catalysis

In this the reactants and catalyst are in a ***different state (or phase)***.
For example, in reactions between gases catalysed on the surface of a solid transition metal.
Catalytic converters in car exhausts are actual examples.
The pollutant gases react on the surface of precious metals, such as rhodium and platinum, inside the converter. (See page 169.)

Transition metals have empty orbitals in the metal atoms available for bonding. The gas molecules can form weak, temporary bonds with the atoms on the metal's surface.
This weakens the original bonds between atoms in the gas molecules.
When they break, new bonds form between nearby reactant molecules, and the temporary bonds to the metal's surface break.
The new products of gas are then free to move away.
This leaves the metal unchanged, although it did play a part in the reaction.

In the Haber process, sites on the surface of the iron catalyst can be 'blocked' by impurities of sulphur. So eventually the 'poisoned' catalyst has to be replaced.

Heterogeneous catalysis is shown in the diagrams below:

The rhodium and platinum in this catalytic converter are held on a ceramic honeycomb support. This maximises the surface area of metals available to catalyse reactions and you don't have to use so much of the precious metals. Heterogeneous catalysts can be **'poisoned'** *by impurities on their surface. For example, lead atoms* **reduce the efficiency** *of catalytic converters. In 1999 leaded petrol was finally banned in the UK.*

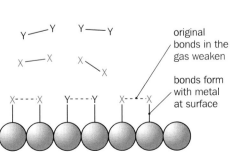

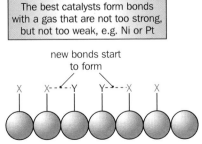

▶ Autocatalysis

What does 'auto' refer to in the word *auto*biography?
What do you think the word 'autocatalysis' means?

In some reactions, we find that one of the products turns out
to be a catalyst for that particular reaction.
This is called **autocatalysis**.
In effect, the reaction catalyses itself.
We don't need to add a catalyst ourselves.

A common example is in the redox reaction between
ethanedioate ions ($C_2O_4^{2-}$) and manganate(VII) ions.
You can find out the concentration of the toxic ethanedioate
by titration with manganate(VII). The purple colour of MnO_4^-(aq)
is removed as the reaction proceeds.

Rhubarb leaves contain ethanedioic acid

- How can we tell the end point of the titration?

Like any redox reaction, we can construct two half equations:

$$\overset{+3}{C_2O_4^{2-}}(aq) \longrightarrow \overset{+4}{2\,CO_2}(g) + 2\,e^-$$

$$\overset{+7}{MnO_4^-}(aq) + 8\,H^+(aq) + 5\,e^- \longrightarrow \overset{+2}{Mn^{2+}}(aq) + 4\,H_2O(l)$$

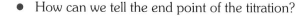

the ethanedioate
ion ($C_2O_4^{2-}$)

- Which substance is being oxidised and which is reduced?

Remember that we now have to make the electrons cancel out
before we can add up the two half equations.
We can do this by multiplying the top half equation by 5,
and the bottom one by 2.
Then we get:

$$5\,C_2O_4^{2-}(aq) \longrightarrow 10\,CO_2(g) + 10\,e^-$$
$$+ \quad 2\,MnO_4^-(aq) + 16\,H^+(aq) + 10\,e^- \longrightarrow 2\,Mn^{2+}(aq) + 8\,H_2O(l)$$
$$\overline{5\,C_2O_4^{2-}(aq) + 2\,MnO_4^-(aq) + 16\,H^+(aq) \longrightarrow 10\,CO_2(g) + 2\,Mn^{2+}(aq) + 8\,H_2O(l)}$$

- Which ion do you think acts as the catalyst for the reaction?

The ability of manganese to adopt different oxidation states
helps the reaction to proceed via intermediates with
a lower activation energy.
This is an example of homogeneous catalysis because the Mn^{2+} ions
are dissolved in the solution, as are the reactants we start with.

How do you think the rate of an autocatalysed reaction will change
as the reaction happens?
Look at the graph opposite:

Can you see how the reaction will start off slowly.
But as the catalyst is formed we will see the reaction
speed up.

You can find out more about catalysts and rates of reaction
in Chapters 27 and 28.

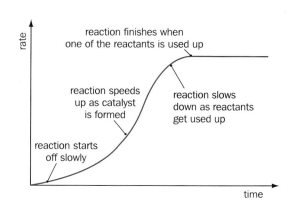

148

▶ Chemistry at work: Copper and platinum

Copper has been used for over 5000 years.
Its beautiful colour meant it was used for jewellery,
as well as various pots and pans.
Today, we value copper so much that we mine deposits
with as little as 0.5 per cent of the metal present.
When we extract the metal, over 99 tonnes of waste, crushed rock
are left over after we get less than one tonne of copper.

Malachite

Chalcopyrite

Peacock ore

A copper mine in Australia

Have you ever noticed any roofs made from a 'green' metal?
Copper is not a very reactive metal. It resists corrosion,
and so is used as protective sheeting. When exposed to the air
it slowly turns green (as a patina of basic copper carbonate forms).
Look at the photo opposite:

You are already familiar with the main use of copper in electrical wiring.
Since it doesn't react with hot water, we also have copper
water pipes and hot water cylinders in our homes.

Copper alloys are very common.
Bronze (copper and tin) and brass (copper and zinc) are examples.
The coins we all use every day are copper alloys.
Even 'silver' coins contain mainly copper.
Look at the table opposite:

Copper and its compounds do add beauty to our lives.
In stained glass windows, the blues and greens result
from adding copper(II) oxide. If mixed with a strong
reducing agent, we get a very intense red colour.

Copper forms a green patina when used outdoors

Coin	Metals in alloy
1p, 2p	copper (97%), zinc (2.5%), tin (0.5%)
5p, 10p, 50p	copper (75%), nickel (25%)
20p	copper (84%), nickel (16%)
£1	copper (70%), zinc (24.5%), nickel (5.5%)

Platinum is a very expensive metal.
Complexes of platinum are now used to fight the growth of
tumours. In the 1960s it was discovered, by accident, that a
platinum complex could inhibit cells dividing.
The complex has been given the name **cisplatin**.
Its formula is *cis*-$[PtCl_2(NH_3)_2]$.

● Can you draw this square planar complex?

Its toxicity is a drawback to its use as an anti-cancer drug.

*Platinum is a precious metal.
How is it used to reduce pollution?*

Summary

Transition metals:
- are hard and dense
- have high melting points
- are less reactive than Group 1 or Group 2 metals
- form coloured compounds
- have variable oxidation states, so they can form compounds with more than one formula.
  For example, iron(II) oxide, FeO, and iron(III) oxide, Fe_2O_3.
- form complexes with ligands
- are important catalysts in industry (heterogeneous catalysis), and in our bodies (homogeneous catalysis).

▶ Questions

1 Copy and complete:
The metals in the d-block of the Periodic table are not as .... as the metals in Groups 1 or 2.
Transition metals form .... compounds, and can adopt a variety of .... states.
.... ions are formed when .... donate a pair of electrons to the central transition metal ion.
Transition metals and their compounds are frequently used in industry as .... to speed up reactions.

2 Name four transition metals and what they are used for. Say why each metal is chosen for that particular use.

3 a) Give the electronic configuration of:

   i)   vanadium (atomic number 23)
   ii) cobalt (atomic number 27)
   iii) zinc (atomic number 30).

   b) Why are vanadium and cobalt called transition metals, whereas zinc is not.
   c) What could you refer to zinc as?

4 What is the electronic structure of:

   a) chromium (atomic number 24)
   b) copper (atomic number 29)?
   c) Explain the arrangement of the electrons in a) and b).

5 Using electrons in boxes, show the outer electrons in the following ions:

   a) Fe^{2+} and Fe^{3+}
   b) Cu^+ and Cu^{2+}
   c) Mn^{2+} and Mn^{4+}
   d) Explain which of each pair of ions in a) and b) has the more stable electronic structure.

6 a) Explain why the highest oxidation state of chromium is +6.
   b) Why do we never get Cr^{6+} ions formed?
   c) Name the two common ions that contain chromium in the +6 oxidation state.

7 This question refers to the first row of the d-block:

Sc	Ti	V	Cr	Mn	Fe	Co	Ni	Cu	Zn

   a) Which element can form the highest oxidation number? What is this number?
   b) Which element can only form 2+ ions?
   c) Which element is used as a catalyst in the Haber process?
   d) Which two elements have atoms with half-filled 3d sub-shells?
   e) Which element is used for electrical wires?
   f) Which element has +1 and +2 as its main oxidation states?
   g) Which element forms a 2+ ion that is violet in solution?
   h) Which element forms two ions that are strong oxidising agents with formulae XO_4^{2-} and $X_2O_7^{2-}$?
   i) Which element forms a chloride that can be used to test for water?
   j) Which element forms a dirty green hydroxide that is oxidised in air to form a rusty brown precipitate?
   k) Which element's aqueous ions form a deep blue solution in concentrated ammonia solution?
   l) Which element is used as a catalyst in the manufacture of margarine?

8 a) Describe how ligands bond to transition metal ions.
   b) What is the coordination number of the Co^{2+} ions in the complex ion $[CoCl_4]^{2-}$?
   c) What is the shape of the $[CoCl_4]^{2-}$ ion?
   d) Why is $[CoCl_4]^{2-}$ called an anionic complex?
   e) Draw a complex ion of Co^{2+} that has an octahedral shape. Is your complex anionic or cationic?
   f) What do you think is the shape of the complex ion $[Ag(NH_3)_2]^+$?
   g) Why is the $[Ag(NH_3)_2]^+$ ion important in the test for halide ions? (Look back to the table on page 124).
   h) Explain why we describe the shape of some complex ions as square planar.
   h) What is the charge on the central metal ion, X, in each of these complexes:
   i) $[XCl_6]^{3-}$ ii) $[X(H_2O)_6]^{2+}$ iii) $[XCl_3(NH_3)_3]$

9 a) Why do we describe water as a *unidentate* (or *monodentate*) ligand?

b) Draw a bidentate ligand and show how it bonds to a central metal ion.

c) Look at the ion, EDTA^{4-} (an abbreviation of the molecule's old name – ethylenediaminetetracetic acid):

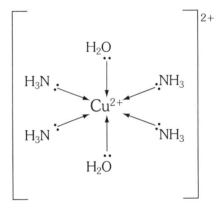

EDTA^{4-}

i) How many dative bonds does this ligand form with a Ni^{2+} ion?

ii) Using your answer from part i), how do we classify this multidentate (or polydentate) ligand?

iii) What is the charge on the complex ion formed in part i)?

10 Write half equations for the changes shown below:

a) $Fe \longrightarrow Fe^{3+}$

b) $Cu^{2+} \longrightarrow Cu^+$

c) $V^{2+} \longrightarrow V^{3+}$

d) $VO^{2+} \longrightarrow V^{3+}$

e) $VO_2^+ \longrightarrow V^{2+}$

f) $Mn^{2+} \longrightarrow MnO_2$

g) $CrO_3 \longrightarrow Cr^{2+}$

h) $MnO_3 \longrightarrow MnO_4^-$

i) $Mn_2O_7 \longrightarrow Mn^{2+}$

j) Say which of the changes above are reduction reactions. Explain how you decided.

k) Which substances above are acting as reducing agents. Explain your answer.

l) Add the half equations from parts c) and d) to get a full balanced equation.

m) Now do the same with the half equations from parts b) and f).

11 a) Explain the following terms:
homogeneous and heterogeneous catalysis.

b) Give an example of each type of catalysis.

c) How can a transition metal ion's changing oxidation state catalyse a reaction. Draw an enthalpy level diagram to help explain.

d) Give four examples of the use of transition metals or their compounds as catalysts in industry.

12 A student has 250 cm^3 of a solution containing iron(II) sulphate.
She wants to find the concentration of the solution.
She decides to titrate the solution against 0.02 mol dm^{-3} potassium manganate(VII) solution.

Having taken a 25.0 cm^3 portion of the original solution of iron(II) sulphate, she finds the end point when she has added 15.0 cm^3 of the manganate(VII) solution.

a) Write the half equation for the change:
$Fe^{2+} \longrightarrow Fe^{3+}$

b) Write the half equation for the change:
$MnO_4^- \longrightarrow Mn^{2+}$

c) Add the two half equations to get the balanced equation.

d) Use the equation to find the ratio of the number of moles of manganate(VII) ions and iron(II) ions that react together.

e) How did the student find the end point in the titration?

f) How many moles of manganate(VII) ions were used up in the titration?

g) How many moles of iron(II) ions must have been in the 25 cm^3 portion of iron(II) sulphate solution?

h) Work out the concentration of the iron(II) sulphate solution in mol dm^{-3}.

i) Sometimes concentrations are shown in grams per 100 cm^3 of water.
What is the concentration of the iron(II) sulphate expressed in these units?
(A_r values: Fe = 56, S = 32, O = 16)

13 Look at the complex ion below:

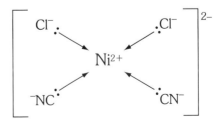

a) Write the formula of this ion.

b) What is the name of the ion?

c) Draw an isomer of the complex.

d) What do we call this type of isomerism?

Look at the ion below:

e) What do we call the shape of this complex?

f) Name the complex.

g) Draw an isomer of this complex ion.

▶ The Periodic Table

1 The diagram below shows the trend in electronegativity of the elements in Period 3.

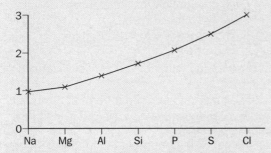

a) Define the term *electronegativity*. [2]

b) Explain briefly the trend in electronegativity across Period 3. [2]

c) State and explain the trend in electronegativity down Group 1. [2]

d) Give the type of bonding between phosphorus and oxygen in P_4O_{10}. Explain how the type of bonding in P_4O_{10} can be predicted from electronegativity values. The electronegativity of oxygen is 3.5. [3]

(AQA)

2 The table below contains electronegativity values for the elements of Period 3, except for that of chlorine.

Element	Na	Mg	Al	Si	P	S	Cl	Ar
Electro-negativity	0.9	1.2	1.5	1.8	2.1	2.5		no value

a) Predict values for the electronegativities of
i) chlorine and ii) lithium. [2]

b) State why argon has no electronegativity value. [1]

(AQA)

3 Ionisation energies in $kJ\,mol^{-1}$ of three elements **R**, **S** and **T** which are consecutive in atomic number are

	1st	2nd	3rd	4th	5th	6th	7th
R	1251	2297	3822	5158	6542	9362	11 018
S	1521	2666	3931	5771	7238	8781	11 996
T	419	3051	4412	5877	7975	9649	11 343

a) In which group of the Periodic Table would **T** be found? Justify your answer. [2]

b) Estimate the 8th ionisation energy of the element **S** to 2 significant figures. [2]

c) What type of electron (s, p, etc.) is removed when an atom of **R** is ionised by the removal of one electron? [1]

d) Write an equation with state symbols to represent the reaction accompanied by the second ionisation energy of **T** (use **T** as the symbol for the element). [2]

e) The sketch graph shows the first ionisation energies of **R**, **S** and **T**. Continue the sketch so as to show the pattern of the first ionisation energies of the next three elements of the Periodic Table, **U**, **V** and **W**, assuming that transition elements are not involved.

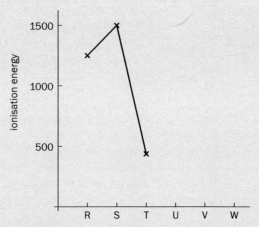

f) The first six ionisation energies of another element **M** are

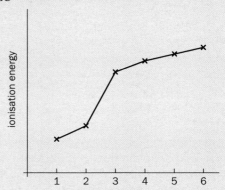

Explain why **M** cannot have an atomic number less than 12. [3]

▶ Periodicity and chemical properties

4 The atomic radii (in pm) of four elements are listed below:

   64;   77;   152;   227.

Assign the correct atomic radius to each of the following elements:

carbon;   fluorine;   lithium;   potassium. [$1\frac{1}{2}$]

(WJEC)

5 a) Copy the table on the next page and complete it to show some of the properties of some of the elements in the third period of the Periodic Table.

Further questions on the Periodic Table

	Compound of sodium and oxygen	Compound of phosphorus and chlorine	Compound of sulphur and oxygen
Formula of compound			
Physical state at 298 K and 1.0 atm			
Nature of bonding			
Type of structure			

b) For the compound containing sodium, and for the compound containing sulphur, give:
   i)   an equation for the reaction with water
   ii) the approximate pH of the solution formed. [3]

c) Describe what you would observe when the compound containing phosphorus is added to water and write an equation for the reaction.   [3]

(AQA)

6 a) There is a trend in the methods used for the preparation of the chlorides of the third period elements Na – S. Write equations, including state symbols, for the preparation of
   i)   sodium chloride by neutralisation and
   ii) silicon tetrachloride by direct combination. [4]

b) Suggest, with a brief explanation, two reasons why silicon tetrachloride could not be made by a similar method to sodium chloride.   [4]

c) Anhydrous samples of magnesium chloride, $MgCl_2$ and phosphorus(III) chloride, PCl_3, were added separately to water and the solutions stirred. In each case, describe what you would observe, give the names or formulae of the products and comment on the pH of any resulting solution.   [8]

(AQA)

7 a) Complete the following table with answers i) to vii).

	Compound of sodium and chlorine	Compound of aluminium and chlorine	Compound of silicon and chlorine	Compound of phosphorus and chlorine
Formula of compound	NaCl	i)	$SiCl_4$	PCl_5
Physical state at room temperature and atmospheric pressure	Solid	Solid	ii)	Solid
Effect of water	Dissolves forms neutral soln	iii)	iv)	v)
Type of structure at room temperature and atmospheric pressure	Ionic lattice	Simple molecular	vi)	vii)

[7]

b) i) Describe one observation that could be made when silicon tetrachloride is exposed to moist air.   [1]
   ii) Write an equation for the reaction between silicon tetrachloride and water.   [2]

(AQA)

8 a) How can electronegativity values be used to predict whether a given chloride is likely to be ionic or covalent?   [2]

b) i)   State the type of bonding in aluminium chloride.
   ii) Write an equation to show what happens when aluminium chloride dissolves in water.
   iii) Suggest a value for the pH of aluminium chloride solution and give one reason why some H^+ ions are released into this solution. [4]

c) State the type of bonding in sodium oxide.   [1]

d) Write an equation for the reaction of sodium oxide with water and suggest a value for the pH of the resulting solution.   [2]

(AQA)

9 a) This part of the question concerns the following oxides;

Na_2O; MgO; Al_2O_3; SiO_2; P_4O_{10}; SO_2.

   i) Identify **X** by eliminating oxides, in turn, from the above list, on the basis of the following statements.

   I   *Statement*: **X** is a solid with a giant lattice structure.
       X is **Not** …

   II *Statement*: **X** is a basic and has ionic bonding.
       X is **Not** …

   III *Statement*: **X** is very soluble in water.
       X is **Not** …

   Therefore the formula of oxide **X** is …
   [3]

   ii) Write a balanced equation for the reaction of the oxide you believe to be **X** with water.   [$\frac{1}{2}$]

   iii) Select the formula of **one** oxide, **from the above list**, which has acidic properties and **one** which has both acidic and basic properties (amphoteric).   [1]

b) Calculate the volume of a $0.100\ mol\ dm^{-3}$ solution of aqueous silver nitrate required for a complete reaction with the chloride ion liberated when 0.30 g of Al_2Cl_6 is completely hydrolysed. (A_r values: Al = 27, Cl = 35.5)

   $[Ag^+(aq) + Cl^-(aq) \longrightarrow AgCl(s)]$ [3]

(WJEC)

153

Further questions on the Periodic Table

10 From the oxides with formulae

Na_2O	MgO	Al_2O_3	SiO_2	P_4O_{10}	SO_2

choose
a) a solid with a simple molecular structure;
b) a giant covalent structure;
c) an oxide which is readily soluble in water to give an alkaline solution. [3]

(WJEC)

11 a) Complete the following table.

	Na	Mg	Al	Si	P	S	Cl
Formula of chloride					■		
Bonding in each chloride							

[3]

b) A chloride of phosphorus, **A**, contains 22.5% P by mass. Reaction of this compound with more chlorine gives another chloride, **B**, containing 14.9% P.

i) Calculate the empirical formula of the two chlorides. (A_r values: P = 31, Cl = 35.5) [3]

ii) Write an equation for the reaction of **A** with chlorine to give **B**. [1]

(EDEXCEL)

▶ Group 2 elements (s-block)

12 a) Give the essential experimental details for performing a flame test on an unknown solid. [3]

b) The following tests were carried out to identify an unknown salt, A.

● The white salt, A, gave an apple green flame test.

● An aqueous solution of A produced a white precipitate of compound B when treated with dilute sulphuric acid.

● A second aqueous solution of A, when treated with aqueous sodium carbonate, gave a solution of compound C and a white precipitate of compound D.

● The precipitate of D was removed by filtration. Solid D, when treated with dilute hydrochloric acid, produced a gas which gave a white precipitate when bubbled through limewater.

● A portion of the filtrate, containing C, was treated with dilute nitric acid followed by aqueous silver nitrate. An off-white precipitate of compound E was formed. The precipitate of E dissolved easily when concentrated aqueous ammonia was added but only partially with dilute aqueous ammonia.

● When chlorine water was added to the remainder of the filtrate, containing C, a yellow/orange solution of substance F was formed.

i) Identify the cation present in A [1]
ii) Identify by name or formula the substances B to F, and A. [6]
iii) Write an equation for the reaction between A and aqueous sodium carbonate. [1]
iv) Identify, by name or formula, the gas evolved when solid D is treated with dilute hydrochloric acid.
v) When chlorine water is added to an aqueous solution of C, a yellow/orange solution is formed. Write an equation for this reaction and give the name of this type of reaction. [2]

(AQA)

13 Metal nitrates decompose on heating.
What is the trend in the thermal stability of nitrates in Group 2 metals?
Write the equation for one such decomposition. [2]

(EDEXCEL)

14 a) i) A Group II metal **X** does **not** react with cold water but reacts rapidly with steam. Identify **X** and give a balanced equation for its reaction with steam. [1]

ii) A second Group II metal **Y** does react with cold water and, upon heating in excess oxygen, forms a basic oxide **Z**. Give a balanced equation for the reaction of **Y** with water and the formula of oxide **Z**. [1]

b) Describe a simple test which could be used to distinguish between compounds of calcium, strontium and barium and what observations you would expect for the compounds of one specific element. [1]

(WJEC)

▶ Group 7 elements

15 a) Concentrated sulphuric acid is added to separate unlabelled solid samples of sodium chloride, sodium bromide and sodium iodide.

i) Write an equation to represent the reaction between sulphuric acid and sodium chloride.

ii) Describe one *different* observation you could make in each case that would enable you to identify the halide ion present in the sample.

iii) Account for the different behaviours of the halide ions in their reactions with concentrated sulphuric acid.

b) Describe, giving details of the observations you could make in each case, how you would use aqueous solutions of ammonia and silver nitrate to confirm the identities of the halide ions in aqueous solutions of the unlabelled samples in (a).

(AQA)

Further questions on the Periodic Table

16 Consider the information in the table about the halogens and hydrogen halides and answer the questions which follow.

	Fluorine	Chlorine	Bromine	Iodine
Electronegativity of halogen	4.0	3.0	2.8	2.5
Boiling point of hydrogen halide / K	293	188	206	238

a) Define the term *electronegativity*. [2]

b) Briefly explain the steady increase in the boiling points of the hydrogen halides from HCl to HI. [2]

c) Explain why the boiling point of hydrogen fluoride is higher than that of any of the other hydrogen halides. [4]

(AQA)

17 In a titration to determine the concentration of iodine in an aqueous solution, 25.00 cm^3 of the iodine solution were titrated with 0.02000 mol dm^{-3} aqueous sodium thiosulphate. The end point was reached when 23.35 cm^3 of the sodium thiosulphate had been added.

a) Which indicator is used in this titration? [1]

b) Write a balanced ionic equation to show how iodine and thiosulphate ions react. [2]

c) What is the oxidation number of the iodine when the reaction is complete? [1]

d) Calculate the concentration, in mol dm^{-3}, of the iodine solution. [2]

(AQA)

18 Write down the oxidation states (numbers) of the elements in the following species:

I as I^-; Mn in MnO_4^-; O in H_2O; I as I_2; Mn in MnO_2.

(WJEC)

19 When chlorine gas is bubbled through potassium iodide solution a redox reaction occurs.

a) What is meant by a **redox reaction**? [2]

b) Write an ionic equation for the reaction. [2]

c) What is observed in this reaction? [2]

(NICCEA)

20 a) Iodine reacts with hot concentrated sodium hydroxide solution according to the equation:

$$3 I_2(aq) + 6 NaOH(aq) \longrightarrow 5 NaI(aq) + NaIO_3(aq) + 3 H_2O(l)$$

   i) What is the oxidation number of iodine in I_2; NaI; $NaIO_3$? [2]

   ii) What is the name given to this type of redox reaction? [1]

b) An experiment was carried out to determine the purity of a sample of sodium iodate, $NaIO_3$, made by the reaction described in a).

0.060 g of the sample was dissolved in pure water to make 100 cm^3 of solution.

A 10.0 cm^3 portion of this solution was taken and added to an excess of acidified potassium iodide solution. The iodine liberated was titrated with 0.0100 M sodium thiosulphate solution.

   i) What piece of apparatus would you use to measure out the 10.0 cm^3 sample? [1]

   ii) Name a suitable indicator to use for this titration and give the colour change expected.

   iii) The volume of sodium thiosulphate solution required in the titration was 16.7 cm^3. Calculate the number of moles of sodium thiosulphate used.

   iv) The equation for the reaction between iodine, I_2, and thiosulphate ions, $S_2O_3^{2-}$, is

$$I_2(aq) + 2 S_2O_3^{2-}(aq) \longrightarrow 2 I^-(aq) + S_4O_6^{2-}(aq)$$

Calculate the number of moles of iodine molecules, I_2, which reacted with the sodium thiosulphate solution. [1]

   v) The equation for the reaction between sodium iodide and sodium iodate, $NaIO_3$, is

$$NaIO_3(aq) + 5 NaI(aq) + 3 H_2SO_4(aq) \longrightarrow 3 I_2(aq) + 3 H_2O(l) + 3 Na_2SO_4(aq)$$

Calculate the number of moles of sodium iodate, $NaIO_3$, in the **original sample.** [1]

   vi) Calculate the mass of sodium iodate, $NaIO_3$, in the original sample and hence calculate the percentage purity of the sample to 2 significant figures.

(Molar mass of $NaIO_3$ = 198 g mol^{-1}) [2]

(EDEXCEL)

▶ Transition elements (d-block elements)

21 a) Transition metals and their compounds can act as heterogeneous catalysts. Explain what is meant by the terms *heterogeneous* and *catalyst*.

b) State one feature of transition metals which makes them able to act as catalysts.

c) Write an equation for a reaction which is heterogeneously catalysed by a transition metal or one of its compounds. State the catalyst used.

(AQA)

22 a) i) State what is meant by the term *ligand*.

   ii) Describe briefly how the bond is formed between a metal ion and a ligand in a complex ion.

b) Explain what is meant by the term *bidentate* as applied to a ligand.

Further questions on the Periodic Table

c) The bidentate ligand, 1,2-diaminoethane, $NH_2CH_2CH_2NH_2$, reacts with an aqueous solution of copper(II) sulphate to give a deep blue solution containing the ion $[Cu(NH_2CH_2CH_2NH_2)_2(H_2O)_2]^{2+}$.
   i) What is the oxidation state of copper in this ion?
   ii) What is the co-ordination number of copper in this ion?
   iii) What causes the colour to change in this reaction?
   iv) Write an equation for this reaction. (You may use "en" for $NH_2CH_2CH_2NH_2$).

23 Silver has the electronic configuration $[Kr]4d^{10}5s^1$.

Give two characteristics of silver and its compounds which support the view that silver should not be classified as a transition element.

(AQA)

24 a) You are provided with an aqueous solution of copper(II) sulphate, E, and with four other aqueous solutions labelled F, G, H and I.

F to I are aqueous solutions of the following compounds **but not in the order given below**: ammonia; barium chloride; potassium iodide; silver nitrate.

Four tests were carried out, in which each of the solutions F to I was added to separate 2 cm^3 samples of solution E. The observations are given in the table below.

TEST	OBSERVATION
Addition of 6 drops of F	No change
Addition of 6 drops of G	A heavy dark precipitate appears and the solution loses its blue colour
Addition of H dropwise until there is no further change	A light precipitate appears which quickly dissolves to give a dark blue solution
Addition of 6 drops of I	A white precipitate is formed.

Deduce the identity of each of the solutions F to I and write ionic equations for any reactions which take place.

(AQA)

25 a) When concentrated hydrochloric acid is added to aqueous copper(II) sulphate until in excess, a yellow solution containing the complex ion, **P**, is formed. Give the formula of the complex ion, **P**. [1]

b) The addition of a slight excess of iron filings to aqueous copper(II) sulphate produces a solution of **Q** and a solid which is then removed by filtration.
   i) Write the ionic equation for this reaction. [1]
   ii) Give two observations that could be made. [2]
   iii) In aqueous solution, **Q** exists as a complex ion. Give the formula of this complex ion. [1]

c) Describe the charge and shape of each of the ions **P** and **Q**, using words from the following list: anionic; cationic; neutral; octahedral; planar; tetrahedral. [2]

d) The addition of aqueous sodium hydroxide to the solution containing **Q** produces a precipitate of iron(II) hydroxide which, when filtered, slowly turns into a brown solid, **R**, on the filter paper.
   i) State the colour of iron(II) hydroxide. [1]
   ii) Give the formula of **R**. [1]
   iii) With what does iron(II) hydroxide react to produce **R**? [1]
   iv) What type of reaction occurs in the formation of both **Q** and **R**? [1]

(AQA)

26 Use the Periodic Table to complete the electronic configurations of the following atoms: Ge, Cr, Cu. You may use the notation [Ar] to represent the inner configuration of each atom.

27 When 0.140 g of impure iron was dissolved in dilute sulphuric acid, the resulting solution reacted with 20.0 cm^3 of 0.0200 mol dm^{-3} $K_2Cr_2O_7$ solution. The half equation for the reduction of $Cr_2O_7^{2-}$ ions is

$$Cr_2O_7^{2-} + 14\,H^+ + 6e^- \longrightarrow 2\,Cr^{3+} + 7\,H_2O$$

a) Write a balanced ionic equation for the reaction between Fe^{2+} ions and $Cr_2O_7^{2-}$ ions.
b) Calculate the percentage of iron, by mass, in the impure sample. (A_r of Fe = 56) [6]

(AQA)

28 Four species of the transition elements of the 3d series are given below.

$$VO_3^-; \quad Cu[(NH_3)_4(H_2O)_2]^{2+}; \quad MnO_2; \quad Fe_2O_3$$

Complete the table by writing the formula of the species which contains the transition element in the given oxidation state.

Oxidation state	Formula of species
+5	
+2	

[2]

(WJEC)

Further questions on the Periodic Table

29 This question is about vanadium.
  a) Give the electron structures of

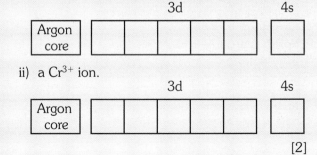

  [2]

  b) Aqueous solutions of vanadium(III) contain the ion $[V(H_2O)_6]^{3+}$.
    i) Name the ion. [1]
    ii) State its colour. [1]
    iii) State the shape of this ion. [1]
    iv) Name the type of bond between the ligands and the V^{3+} ion. [1]

  c) Vanadium exists in several oxidation states which are quite easily interconverted.
    i) What is the oxidation state of vanadium in the VO_2^+ ion? [1]
    ii) VO_2^+ can be reduced to VO^{2+} using an acidic aqueous solution of sulphite ions. The half equation for the oxidation of sulphite ions is:
$$SO_3^{2-}(aq) + H_2O(l) \longrightarrow SO_4^{2-}(aq) + 2 H^+(aq) + 2e^-$$
      A. Write the half equation for the reduction of VO_2^+ in acidic solution. [1]
      B. Hence deduce the equation for the reaction between VO_2^+ and SO_3^{2-} ions in aqueous solution. [2]
    iii) Name the reagent used to convert a solution of VO_2^+ ions to vanadium(II). How would you know when the reaction was complete? [2]
      (WJEC)

30 a) List **three *chemical*** characteristics of the transition elements. [3]
  b) Give **one** example, of your own choice, of the ***chemical*** use of a named transition metal of the 3d series **or** one of its compounds in a major industrial process. State the chemical property on which the use depends. [1]
  c) Complete the boxes below by inserting arrows to show the ground state electronic configuration of
    i) a chromium atom;

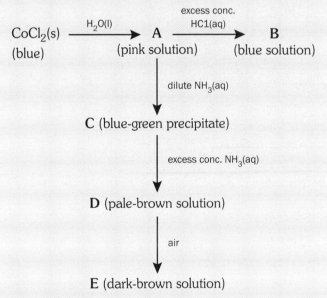

    ii) a Cr^{3+} ion.

  [2]

  d) In acidic aqueous solution the dichromate(VI) ion, $Cr_2O_7^{2-}$, is a powerful oxidising agent. The oxidation of iron(II) ions by dichromate(VI) ions may be represented by
$$Cr_2O_7^{2-}(aq) + 14 H^+(aq) + 6 Fe^{2+}(aq) \longrightarrow$$
$$2 Cr^{3+}(aq) + 6 Fe^{3+}(aq) + 7 H_2O(l)$$
    i) Deduce the change in the oxidation state of chromium in this reaction. [1]
    ii) Calculate the number of moles of $Fe^{2+}(aq)$ in 25.00 cm^3 of acidic aqueous iron(II) sulphate containing 12.15 g dm^{-3} of iron(II) sulphate, $FeSO_4$, ($M_r = 151.91$). [2]
    iii) Calculate the volume of aqueous potassium dichromate(VI) of concentration $0.0200 \text{ mol dm}^{-3}$ that will completely oxidise the number of moles of $Fe^{2+}(aq)$ in d) ii). [2]
      (WJEC)

31 Using the example given for zinc, complete in the diagram below the other two electronic configurations.

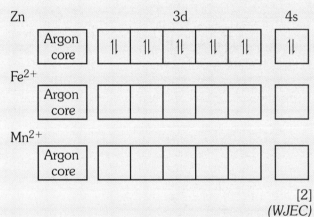

  [2]
  (WJEC)

32 Examine the reaction scheme below

CoCl₂(s) (blue) → [H₂O(l)] → A (pink solution) → [excess conc. HCl(aq)] → B (blue solution)

A → [dilute NH₃(aq)] → C (blue-green precipitate) → [excess conc. NH₃(aq)] → D (pale-brown solution) → [air] → E (dark-brown solution)

Identify, by formula, each of the cobalt species in the products **A** to **E**. [5]
  (AQA)

12 Introduction to organic chemistry

The great variety of life on Earth is built on the foundations
of organic chemistry.
All **organic** compounds contain carbon atoms, although its oxides,
carbonates and hydrogencarbonates are not classed
as organic compounds.
The molecules that form the basis of all living things
are based on carbon compounds.
Carbon atoms form the 'backbone' of these molecules –
from the proteins that make up the muscles and enzymes in your body
to the DNA that determines your characteristics.

*Organic carbon-based molecules form
the basis of all life*

▷ Functional groups

This section of the book looks at some groups of organic compounds.
Each chapter deals with a class of compounds with similar structures.
Particular groupings of atoms cause molecules to behave
in certain ways.
These groupings are called **functional groups**.
Look at the examples of functional groups below:

Class of compounds	Functional group
alcohols	$R - O - H$
aldehydes	$R - C {\displaystyle {}^{O}_{H}}$
ketones	$R \atop R$ $> C = O$
carboxylic acids	$R - C {\displaystyle {}^{O}_{O-H}}$
esters	$R - C {\displaystyle {}^{O}_{O-R}}$
halogenoalkanes (haloalkanes)	$R - X$
amines	$R - N {\displaystyle {}^{H}_{H}}$
amides	$R - C {\displaystyle {}^{O}_{NH_2}}$
amino acids	$R - \overset{\overset{\displaystyle NH_2}{|}}{C} - C {\displaystyle {}^{O}_{O-H}}$
nitriles	$R - C \equiv N$

where **R** is an **alkyl group**, or a
hydrogen atom.
An alkyl group has the formula
C_nH_{2n+1},
i.e. when $n = 1$ we get CH_3,
$\quad\quad\quad n = 2$ we get C_2H_5,
$\quad\quad\quad n = 3$ we get C_3H_7,
$\quad\quad\quad$ etc.

> **Notice that:**
> **each carbon atom must have**
> **4 covalent bonds; each hydrogen**
> **1 bond; each oxygen**
> **2 bonds; and each nitrogen**
> **3 bonds.**

● Can you explain the number of bonds that each
of the atoms above can form?

▷ Homologous series

A 'family' of compounds that have a common functional group is called a **homologous series**.
The simplest series of compounds is the **alkanes**.
We will look in detail at these compounds in the next chapter.
They are made from carbon atoms bonded to each other and to hydrogen atoms with single covalent bonds.
Look at the first ten alkanes below:

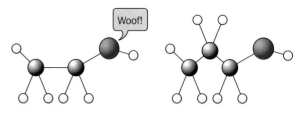

Members of the alcohol 'family'

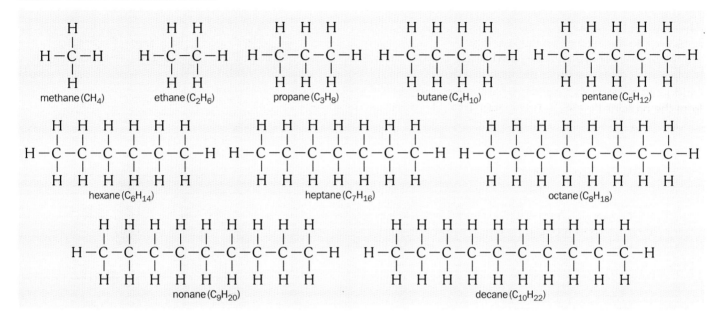

If you replace one of the H atoms with a functional group, you get a new homologous series.
The functional group brings with it new physical properties and chemical reactions.
Look at the examples below:

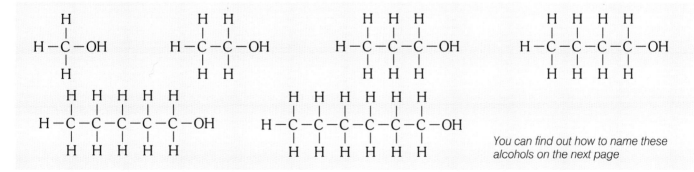

You can find out how to name these alcohols on the next page

This is the start of the homologous series of alcohols.

Structural formula

Look at all the molecules drawn on this page:
You can see each atom's position in the molecule and the bonds between them.
Can you see any other ways of arranging the atoms in the examples above?
This way of showing a molecule is called its
structural (or displayed) formula.
Can you recall the difference between an empirical and a molecular formula?
Look at the example in the box opposite:
Notice how we can abbreviate a structural formula.

Example
Butane ($M_r = 58$)
Empirical formula = C_2H_5
Molecular formula = C_4H_{10}
Structural formula =
$CH_3CH_2CH_2CH_3$

159

▷ Naming organic compounds

There are millions of organic compounds.
New ones are constantly being made in research labs
all over the world.
So chemists need a system of naming organic compounds
that can be applied consistently. A name should tell us
as much as possible about the molecules it describes.

We can tell the number of carbon atoms from the alkane
referred to in the name.
Look back to the alkanes on the last page:
Sometimes the alkane's name is used in full.
In other molecules, we use a shortened version:

I.U.P.A.C. (the International Union of Pure and Applied Chemistry) devised the systematic way of naming organic molecules.

Number of carbon atoms	Abbreviation used
1	meth-
2	eth-
3	prop-
4	but-
5	pent-
6	hex-
7	hept-
8	oct-
9	non-
10	dec-

There are now well over 10 million compounds known on Earth

Do you recall the table of functional groups on page 158?
You need to recognise the way their compounds are named.
Look at the table below:

Class of compounds	Functional group	Recognised in name by	Examples
alcohols	—OH	-(an)**ol**	ethanol, butan-1-ol
aldehydes	—CHO	-(an)**al**	methanal, propanal
ketones	—CO—	-(an)**one**	butanone, hexan-2-one
carboxylic acids	—COOH	-(an)**oic acid**	octanoic acid, decanoic acid
esters	—COOR where R = alkyl group, e.g. CH_3 or C_2H_5	-(an)**oate**	methyl ethanoate, propyl hexanoate
halogenoalkanes (haloalkanes)	—CH_2X where X = halogen atom	**fluoro-, chloro-, bromo-, iodo-**	3-bromopentane, 1,2-dichloroethane
amines	—NH_2	-(yl)**amine**	ethylamine, butylamine
amides	—$CONH_2$	-(an)**amide**	pentanamide, heptanamide
amino acids	NH_2CR_2COOH where R = alkyl group or H atom	**amino-** -(an)**oic acid**	2-aminopropanoic acid, 2-aminobutanoic acid
nitrile	—CN	-**nitrile**	ethanenitrile, pentanenitrile

Notice the shorthand used to represent the functional groups.
- Can you relate these to the structural formulae in the table on page 158?
- Why do you think that some of the examples from the table have numbers in their names?

The system for naming compounds has to have some way of telling us the position of the functional group in the molecule.
So we number the carbon atoms from the end nearest the functional group.
Look at the example opposite:
Can you see how each molecule is the same?
Remember that the structural (or displayed) formula is a 2D representation of a 3D molecule.
- How are four bonding pairs of electrons distributed around a central atom? (See page 60.)
Look at the 3D drawing of chloroethane below:

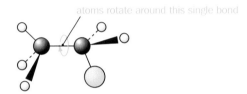

Atoms can rotate around the single bonds from each carbon atom.
Therefore the displayed formulae shown below are all the same molecule:

$$
\begin{array}{c}
\text{H} \quad \text{H} \\
| \quad | \\
\text{H}-\text{C}-\text{C}-\text{H} \\
| \quad | \\
\text{H} \quad \text{Cl}
\end{array}
\quad
\begin{array}{c}
\text{is the} \\
\text{same as}
\end{array}
\quad
\begin{array}{c}
\text{H} \quad \text{H} \\
| \quad | \\
\text{H}-\text{C}-\text{C}-\text{Cl} \\
| \quad | \\
\text{H} \quad \text{H}
\end{array}
\quad
\begin{array}{c}
\text{is the} \\
\text{same as}
\end{array}
\quad
\begin{array}{c}
\text{H} \quad \text{Cl} \\
| \quad | \\
\text{H}-\text{C}-\text{C}-\text{H} \\
| \quad | \\
\text{H} \quad \text{H}
\end{array}
\quad
\begin{array}{c}
\text{and by flipping} \\
\text{the molecule over}
\end{array}
\quad
\begin{array}{c}
\text{is the} \\
\text{same as}
\end{array}
\quad
\begin{array}{c}
\text{H} \quad \text{H} \\
| \quad | \\
\text{Cl}-\text{C}-\text{C}-\text{H} \\
| \quad | \\
\text{H} \quad \text{H}
\end{array}
$$

- *What are the 2 other equivalent structures?*

Here are the structural formulae of some examples from the last page:

Structural formula	Name	Structural formula	Name
$CH_3CH_2CH_2OH$	butan-1-ol	$\begin{array}{c} Cl \quad Cl \\ \| \quad \| \\ CH_2CH_2 \end{array}$	1,2-dichloroethane
$CH_3CH_2C{\small\begin{array}{c}\nearrow O \\ \searrow H\end{array}}$	propanal	$CH_3CH_2CH_2CH_2NH_2$	butylamine
$\begin{array}{c} O \\ \| \| \\ CH_3CCH_2CH_2CH_2CH_3 \end{array}$	hexan-2-one	$CH_3CH_2CH_2CH_2C{\small\begin{array}{c}\nearrow O \\ \searrow NH_2\end{array}}$	pentanamide
$CH_3CH_2CH_2CH_2CH_2CH_2CH_2C{\small\begin{array}{c}\nearrow O \\ \searrow OH\end{array}}$	octanoic acid	$\begin{array}{c} NH_2 \\ \| \\ CH_3CHC{\small\begin{array}{c}\nearrow O \\ \searrow OH\end{array}} \end{array}$	2-aminopropanoic acid
$CH_3C{\small\begin{array}{c}\nearrow O \\ \searrow OCH_3\end{array}}$	methyl ethanoate	$CH_3C{\equiv}N$	ethanenitrile

- Can you draw the other examples from the last page that are not shown above?

$$
\begin{array}{c}
Br \\
| \\
CH_3CHCH_2CH_3 \\
①\quad②\quad③\quad④
\end{array}
$$

$$
\begin{array}{c}
Br \\
| \\
CH_3CH_2CHCH_3 \\
④\quad③\quad②\quad①
\end{array}
$$

Both these molecules are 2-bromobutane.

▷ Structural isomers

On the last page we looked at some different ways
of drawing the same molecule.
However, given a molecular formula, we can sometimes draw
different structures.
Look at the examples below:

Molecular formula = C_3H_7Br

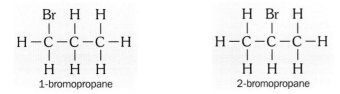

1-bromopropane   2-bromopropane

The different structural (or displayed) formulae show molecules
that can't be superimposed on each other. They have different structures.
The two different molecules are called **isomers**.

Isomers are molecules with the *same molecular formula* but *different structural formulae*.

In other words, isomers have the same number and type of atoms,
but these are arranged differently within each molecule.

Example
Given the molecular formula $C_3H_6Br_2$, how many isomers exist?

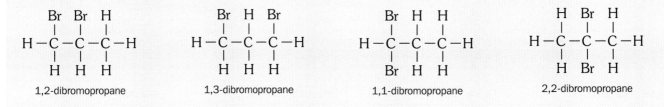

1,2-dibromopropane   1,3-dibromopropane   1,1-dibromopropane   2,2-dibromopropane

So there are four possible isomers. This is called **position isomerism**.

Notice that structures such as those shown below
do not represent new isomers. They are repeats
of the first isomer shown in the example above.
You need to remember that groups can rotate
around the C—C bonds when drawing isomers!

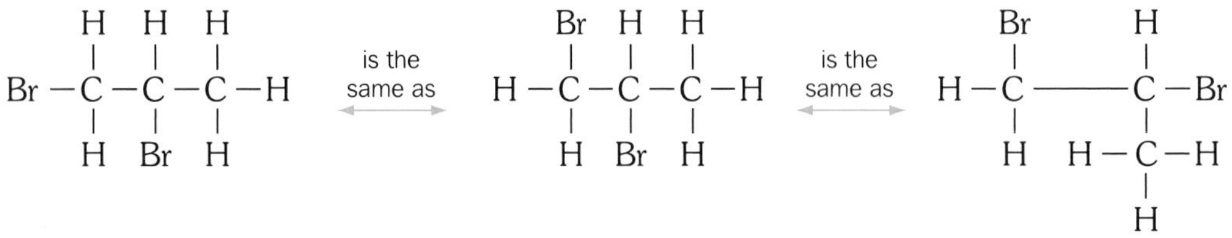

All these are different representations of the same isomer, i.e. 1,2-dibromopropane.

Now let's consider the isomers with the formula C_3H_8O:

propan-1-ol

propan-2-ol

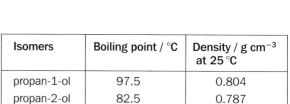

Look, quickly! She's building isomers already!

This is another example of position isomerism.
The two isomers are different molecules, but they are both alcohols.
Therefore, they will undergo similar reactions, although there will be differences.
For example, the rate of a particular reaction may well differ.
Their physical properties will also be different.
Look at the table opposite:

But can the atoms in C_3H_8O be arranged to make a molecule
that is not an alcohol?
Look at the isomer below:

Isomers	Boiling point / °C	Density / g cm^{-3} at 25 °C
propan-1-ol	97.5	0.804
propan-2-ol	82.5	0.787

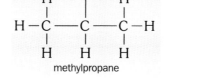

methoxyethane (an ether)

The properties of ethers are very different from those of the alcohols.
This is an example of **functional group isomerism**.
- Will the ether above be able to form hydrogen bonds between its molecules?
  (See page 70.)
- What effect will this have on its boiling point compared with
  its isomers in the alcohol family?
- Why would you expect their chemical properties to be very different?

The last type of structural isomerism is sometimes called **chain isomerism**.
Chain isomers differ in the way the carbon 'backbones' of the molecules
are arranged.
For example:

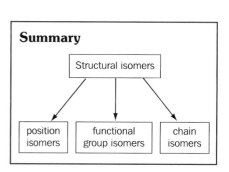

Summary

Structural isomers

position isomers

functional group isomers

chain isomers

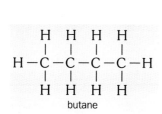

butane

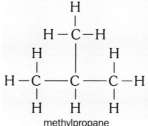

methylpropane

Remember that simply 'bending' the carbon chain does not produce a different
molecule. So the isomers shown above are the only ones possible for C_4H_{10}.

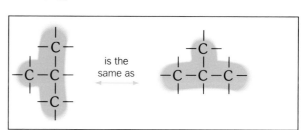

is the same as

is the same as

You can see another example on the next page.
You can also read about the differing physical properties
of chain isomers on page 167.

163

Example
A sample of a hydrocarbon contained 14.4 g of carbon and 2.8 g of hydrogen.
Its relative molecular mass is 86.
a) What is the compound's empirical formula?
b) What is its molecular formula?
c) Draw the structures of the different possible isomers.
(Relative atomic masses: C = 12, H = 1)

a) Ratio of moles C : H

Number of moles of carbon $= \dfrac{14.4}{12} = 1.2$ moles   Number of moles of hydrogen $= \dfrac{2.8}{1} = 2.8$ moles

$$
\begin{array}{ccc}
C & : & H \\
1.2 & : & 2.8
\end{array}
$$

(to get the simplest whole-number ratio, divide both sides by 0.4)

$$
\begin{array}{ccc}
3 & : & 7
\end{array}
$$

Therefore the empirical formula is **C_3H_7**

b) The relative molecular mass of the compound is 86.
The relative molecular mass of C_3H_7 is $(12 \times 3) + (1 \times 7) = 43$

$\dfrac{86}{43} = 2$ so there are 2 units of C_3H_7 in this compound

i.e. its molecular formula is $(C_3H_7) \times 2 =$ **C_6H_{14}**

c) The structures of the possible isomers are:

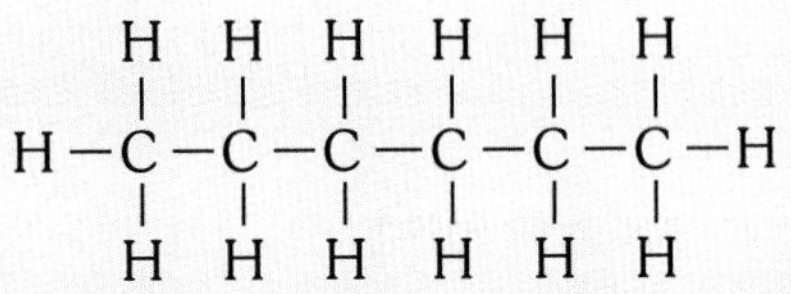

or $CH_3CH_2CH_2CH_2CH_2CH_3$
hexane

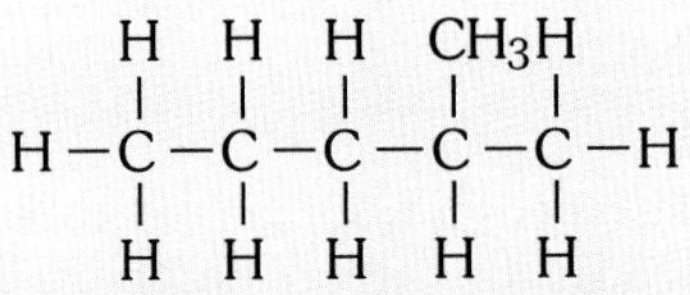

or $CH_3CH_2CH_2CH(CH_3)CH_3$
2-methylpentane

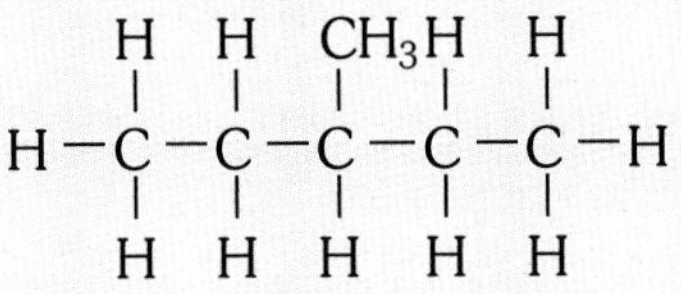

or $CH_3CH_2CH(CH_3)CH_2CH_3$
3-methylpentane

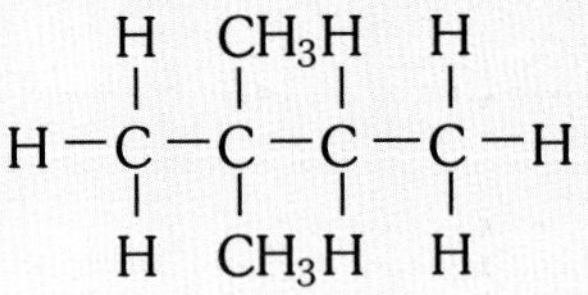

or $CH_3C(CH_3)_2CH_2CH_3$
dimethylbutane

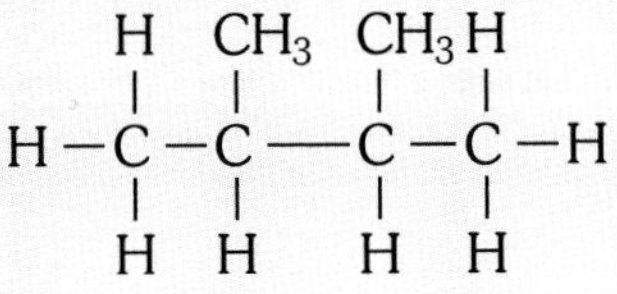

or $CH_3CH(CH_3)CH(CH_3)CH_3$
2,3-dimethylbutane

Summary

- Organic chemistry is the study of carbon-based molecules.
- Organic compounds can contain one or more **functional groups**.
- The functional groups determine a compound's reactions.
- We can represent an organic compound by its molecular formula, *e.g.* C_2H_6O, but its structural formula gives more information, *e.g.* CH_3CH_2OH.
- **Isomers** are molecules with the same molecular formula, but different structural formulae.
- There are three types of structural isomers:
  i) position isomers,
  ii) functional group isomers, and
  iii) chain isomers.
  (Stereoisomers are dealt with later in the book. See pages 177 and 247.)

▷ Questions

1 Name the following functional groups:

a) $\begin{array}{c} R \\ R \end{array}\!\!>\!\!C{=}O$

b) $R - C\!\!\underset{O-H}{\overset{O}{\lessgtr}}$

c) $R - C\!\!\underset{O-R}{\overset{O}{\lessgtr}}$

d) $R - O - H$

2 Give the structural formula (or displayed formula) of the second member of the homologous series for each of these functional groups:
For example, the alcohol will be:

CH_3CH_2OH or

$$H - \underset{\underset{H}{|}}{\overset{\overset{H}{|}}{C}} - \underset{\underset{H}{|}}{\overset{\overset{H}{|}}{C}} - O - H$$

a) amine   c) aldehyde   e) amide
b) nitrile   d) chloroalkane f) carboxylic acid

3 A hydrocarbon has the empirical formula CH_2.
Its relative molecular mass is 42.
What is its molecular formula?

4 Look at the formulae of the first ten alkanes shown on page 159:
a) Work out a general formula for the alkanes shown.
b) Give the molecular formula and structural formula of the next alkane in the homologous series.

5 Give the structural formula of each of these compounds:
a) propan-1-ol   f) octanenitrile
b) butanal   g) ethyl butanoate
c) pentan-2-one   h) 1,3-dichlorobutan-1-ol
d) hexylamine   i) 2-aminopentanoic acid
e) 2,3-dibromoheptane   j) 1,1,2-trifluoroethane

6 Name these molecules:

a) $\underset{\underset{Cl}{|}}{CH_3CHCH_3}$

b) $CH_3CH_2C\!\!\underset{H}{\overset{O}{\lessgtr}}$

c) $H - C\!\!\underset{OH}{\overset{O}{\lessgtr}}$

d) $CH_3CH - CH_2 - \underset{\underset{F}{|}}{\overset{\overset{F}{|}}{C}} - CH_3$
(with Cl below the first CH)

(Hint: If we have more than one group in the name we write them in alphabetical order.)

7 Draw the structural isomers of:
a) pentane
b 1-chlorobutane
c) 1,1-dibromobutane.

8 A hydrocarbon was analysed and found to contain 2.4 g of carbon and 0.5 g of hydrogen.
Its relative molecular mass is 58.
a) Work out its empirical formula.
b) Work out its molecular formula.
c) Draw and name each structural isomer of this molecule.

9 A forensic scientist was asked to analyse a colourless liquid found at the scene of a crime.
Her analysis showed that the compound contained 6.0 g of carbon, 1.5 g of hydrogen and 4.0 g of oxygen.
Further analysis showed its relative molecular mass was 46.
a) What is the empirical formula of the liquid?
b) What is its molecular formula?
c) Draw two possible isomers.
d) Chemical tests showed that the compound was an alcohol.
Name the colourless liquid.

13 The alkanes

Our world would be a very different place without **alkanes**.
Imagine life without the products of crude oil and natural gas.
We would have no alkane-based fuels such as petrol, diesel and kerosine.
The plastics industry is also fed with raw materials from crude oil.

So what are alkanes?
We have already met the first ten members of the alkane family on page 159.
Look at the model of octane below and the way we show this in 2D:
Notice the tetrahedral arrangement around each carbon atom.

Alkanes are important fuels

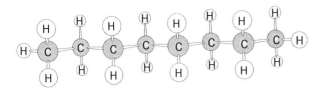

3D model of octane (bond angles = 109.5°)

How many elements make up an alkane?
The alkanes are examples of **hydrocarbons**.

$$H-\underset{\underset{H}{|}}{\overset{\overset{H}{|}}{C}}-\underset{\underset{H}{|}}{\overset{\overset{H}{|}}{C}}-\underset{\underset{H}{|}}{\overset{\overset{H}{|}}{C}}-\underset{\underset{H}{|}}{\overset{\overset{H}{|}}{C}}-\underset{\underset{H}{|}}{\overset{\overset{H}{|}}{C}}-\underset{\underset{H}{|}}{\overset{\overset{H}{|}}{C}}-\underset{\underset{H}{|}}{\overset{\overset{H}{|}}{C}}-\underset{\underset{H}{|}}{\overset{\overset{H}{|}}{C}}-H$$

The full structural (or displayed) formula of octane

A hydrocarbon is a compound containing *hydrogen and carbon only*.

You can see that there are only single, covalent bonds in an alkane molecule.
Therefore, the alkanes with straight or branched chains of carbon atoms contain the maximum number of hydrogen atoms possible.
We call them **saturated** molecules.
So we can say that:

alkanes are *saturated hydrocarbons*.

Look at their formulae on page 159:
● Can you see a pattern?
The general formula of an alkane is:

C_nH_{2n+2}

e.g. when $n = 3$, we get C_3H_8

The only exceptions to this rule are the **cycloalkanes**.
Can you imagine the ends of a carbon chain joining together?
Look at cyclopentane opposite:

You can imagine the carbon atom at each end of the chain in pentane losing a hydrogen atom in order to bond to each other.
● Can you draw a molecule of cyclohexane?
● What is its formula?
● What is the general formula for a cycloalkane?
These compounds form an important part of petrol.

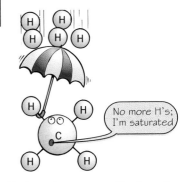

Methane is a saturated hydrocarbon

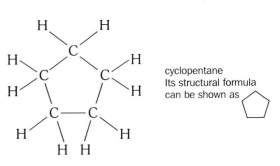

cyclopentane
Its structural formula can be shown as

● *Why will the C—C bonds in smaller cycloalkanes, such as cyclopropane, be under strain?*

▷ Physical properties of the alkanes

Do you remember much from your previous work on oil?
Crude oil is a **mixture** of compounds, mainly alkanes.
The mixture varies depending on where the oil
was drilled from the ground.
For example, oil from the North Sea is richer in the lighter alkanes
than oil from Saudi Arabia. It is lighter in colour and evaporates
more easily. We say it is more **volatile**.

- What happens to the boiling point of the alkanes
  as their molecules increase in size?
- How is the difference in their boiling points used to
  separate groups of alkanes from crude oil?

Look at the diagram of the fractionating column
opposite and the graph below:

An oil refinery at night

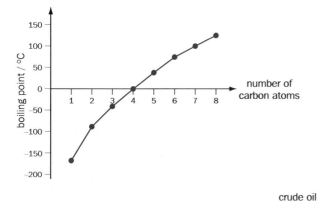

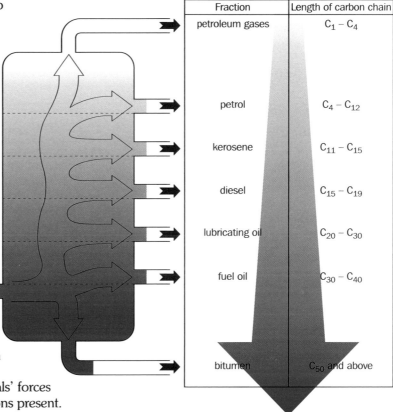

Fraction	Length of carbon chain
petroleum gases	$C_1 - C_4$
petrol	$C_4 - C_{12}$
kerosene	$C_{11} - C_{15}$
diesel	$C_{15} - C_{19}$
lubricating oil	$C_{20} - C_{30}$
fuel oil	$C_{30} - C_{40}$
bitumen	C_{50} and above

crude oil vapour

Notice the patterns in physical properties
as molecular mass increases.
The higher boiling points, densities and viscosities
can be explained by increasing intermolecular forces.
Can you recall your work on van der Waals' forces on
page 67?
The larger the molecule, the stronger the van der Waals' forces
between them. This is because there are more electrons present.
Remember that these electrons move within the molecules.
So the more electrons, the greater the number of temporary
dipoles set up and induced in neighbouring molecules.

You might then expect isomers of a compound to have
the same boiling points. But look at the boiling points
of the isomers of pentane below:
If we study the shapes of the isomers, then we can
explain the differences. Look at the models below:

As the molecular mass of alkanes increases:
- their boiling points increase
  (they get less volatile)
- they are harder to ignite
- they get more dense
- they become more viscous (thicker)

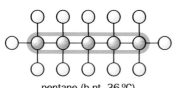

pentane (b.pt. 36 °C)

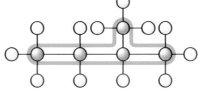

2-methylbutane (b.pt. 28 °C)

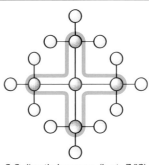

2,2-dimethylpropane (b.pt. 7 °C)

Pentane's long, thin molecules can come into closer contact
than the more spherical 2,2-dimethlypropane molecules.
This gives rise to more induced dipoles on neighbouring molecules,
(i.e. stronger van der Waals' forces) resulting in pentane's higher boiling point.

167

▷ Reactions of the alkanes

Combustion

As you know, alkanes are often used as fuels.
They provide most of us with energy to heat our homes
and to transport us around. There is a good chance that
the electricity you use has been generated in
oil- or gas-fired power stations.

This plane burns kerosene – a mixture of alkanes containing molecules mainly with 11 or 12 carbon atoms

In all these uses, we burn the alkanes to release
some of the chemical energy stored in their molecules.
They react with the oxygen in the air to form mostly
carbon dioxide and water.
We call this a **combustion** reaction.
The general equation for any hydrocarbon, such as an alkane
burning in oxygen is:

This is called ***complete*** combustion.
All the carbon atoms are converted to carbon dioxide.
You can identify the products of combustion using
the apparatus below:

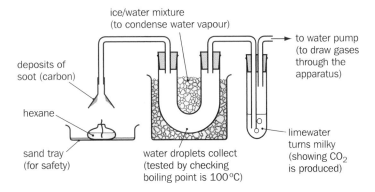

The equation for this reaction is:

$$\text{hexane} + \text{oxygen} \longrightarrow \text{carbon dioxide} + \text{water}$$
$$2\,C_6H_{14}(l) + 19\,O_2(g) \longrightarrow 12\,CO_2(g) + 14\,H_2O(g)$$

Why don't we see any water being formed when we burn
methane on a gas cooker? What do you notice about
the windows in the lab on a cold day when lots of Bunsen burners
are being used?

In the experiment above, you can see some soot forming
inside the funnel above the flame. This is carbon.
Where do you think this comes from?

Not all the carbon in the hexane turns into carbon dioxide.
The hexane is not completely oxidised when burned in air.
We call this ***incomplete*** combustion.
What evidence do you see around cities of carbon deposits?

The buildings in a city are blackened by deposits of carbon (produced from the incomplete combustion of fuels)

▷ Pollution from combustion

Another product of incomplete combustion is **carbon monoxide**.
This is a toxic gas. Its formula is CO.
It forms when we ignite petrol or diesel in a car engine.
Inside the cylinders of the engine, there is not enough oxygen
to oxidise the fuel completely. This produces carbon monoxide
which is released into the air through the car's exhaust.

Carbon monoxide is so harmful because it reduces our body's
ability to carry oxygen in the blood. It also has no smell.
Why do you think this makes it dangerous?
Normally, oxygen is carried by the haemoglobin in our red blood cells.
A bond is made between the haemoglobin molecule
and the oxygen molecule. The bond breaks when the oxygen
is needed for respiration in a cell.

However, carbon monoxide forms a bond with haemoglobin
that can't be broken. So the blood cells have less haemoglobin
available for carrying oxygen. The lack of oxygen getting
to the brain will eventually cause death.
This happens in enclosed spaces. For example, you might have read
in newspapers about faulty gas boilers or fires blamed
for tragic accidents in the home.

The amount of carbon monoxide given off from cars
can be reduced by catalytic converters. (See page 147.)
These are used in the car's exhaust system.
The gases given off from the combustion of fuel in the engine
pass through a honeycomb containing precious metal catalysts.
Look at the diagram below:

*Oxygen is available in 'oxygen bars' to
fight the effects of pollution from cars in
Tokyo streets.
Ozone (O_3) is a pollutant produced at
street-level from cars. It can be formed by
complex reactions of nitrogen oxides with
oxygen in the air*

A catalytic converter

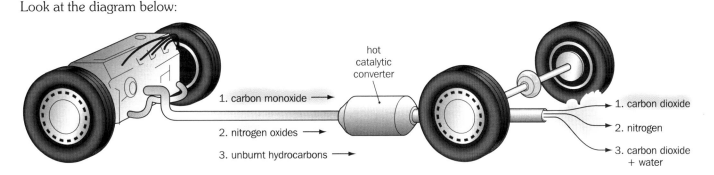

1. carbon monoxide →
2. nitrogen oxides →
3. unburnt hydrocarbons →

hot catalytic converter

1. carbon dioxide
2. nitrogen
3. carbon dioxide + water

Can you see what the carbon monoxide is turned into?
The use of catalytic converters cannot solve another problem
associated with the burning of hydrocarbons.
You will have heard about the **greenhouse effect**.
Look at the diagram opposite:

Gases, such as carbon dioxide and water vapour,
absorb some of the heat waves given off as the Earth cools down.
We are lucky to have these natural 'greenhouse gases'.
Without them, the Earth would be about 30 °C colder!

But whenever we burn a hydrocarbon, even if a catalytic converter
is used, we give off more carbon dioxide into our atmosphere.
We are disturbing the natural balance of carbon dioxide.
More carbon dioxide, plus other 'greenhouse gases', such as
methane from cattle and rice fields, are causing **global warming**.

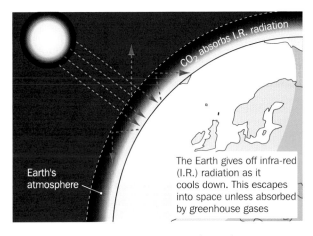

CO_2 absorbs I.R. radiation

Earth's atmosphere

The Earth gives off infra-red
(I.R.) radiation as it
cools down. This escapes
into space unless absorbed
by greenhouse gases

*Carbon dioxide and water vapour are the main
'greenhouse gases'*

▷ Substitution reactions of the alkanes

The alkanes are not a very reactive group of hydrocarbons.
What do we have to do to start off a reaction between
an alkane and oxygen?
Besides reacting with oxygen during combustion,
the alkanes will also react with halogens.
As in combustion, the reaction only starts after an input of energy.
In this case, the reactions happen in sunlight.
We can show this by adding bromine to hexane.
Look at the experiment below:

*Butane needs the energy from the match
to start off its reaction with oxygen*

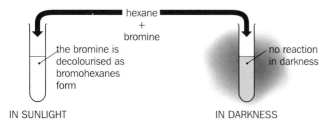

hexane
+
bromine

the bromine is
decolourised as
bromohexanes
form

no reaction
in darkness

IN SUNLIGHT   IN DARKNESS

*Substitution in the alkane!
H is replaced by Cl*

Methane reacts more vigorously with halogens than hexane.
Look at the equation below:

$$\text{methane} + \text{chlorine} \xrightarrow{\text{sunlight}} \text{chloromethane} + \text{hydrogen chloride}$$
$$CH_4 + Cl_2 \longrightarrow CH_3Cl + HCl$$

This is called a **substitution** reaction.
As the name suggests, a hydrogen atom is substituted by a chlorine atom.
The reaction shown above is explosive in bright sunlight.

> **The smaller the alkane, the faster the reaction.**
> **Substitution occurs most readily with F_2, followed by Cl_2, then Br_2. It is slowest with I_2.**

Can you work out the products when methane reacts with bromine?

Now let's see if we can explain how the reaction shown above happens.
We call this the **mechanism** of a reaction.
You will need to understand the mechanisms of most organic reactions
we deal with in this section of the book.

Initiation step

The sunlight needed to start the reaction provides ultraviolet light.
This breaks the Cl—Cl bond:

$$Cl_2 \xrightarrow{\text{uv light}} \bullet Cl + \bullet Cl$$
two chlorine free radicals

As the single covalent bond breaks, each chlorine atom leaves
with one of the shared pair of electrons.
This is called **homolytic fission** of the bond.
Each chlorine atom produced has a single unpaired electron.
This makes it very reactive.
We call these chlorine atoms **free radicals**. (The dot on each
chlorine free radical represents an unpaired electron.)

> An **initiation** step produces free radicals
> from the molecules we start with.

Curly arrows in mechanisms
We show the movement of
a single electron like this:

whereas a pair of electrons
moving is shown by:

They must be drawn accurately.

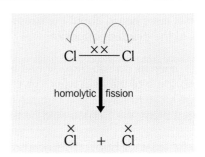

Cl ×× Cl

homolytic fission

×   ×
Cl   +   Cl

> Alkanes undergo *free radical*
> *substitution* with halogens.

Propagation steps

Now the free radicals attack the methane molecules:

$$CH_4 + \bullet Cl \longrightarrow \bullet CH_3 + HCl$$

This can be shown more fully:

$$H_3C \overset{\frown}{-} H \quad \bullet Cl \longrightarrow H_3C\bullet + H - Cl$$

The $\bullet CH_3$ radical produced can then attack a chlorine molecule:

$$\bullet CH_3 + Cl_2 \longrightarrow CH_3Cl + \bullet Cl$$

Again this can be shown as:

$$H_3C\bullet + Cl \overset{\frown}{-} Cl \longrightarrow H_3CCl + \bullet Cl$$

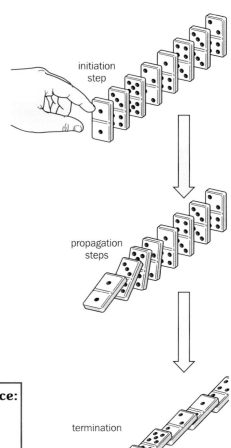

initiation
step

propagation
steps

termination

Thus a chlorine free radical is regenerated which can attack another methane molecule. So the reaction continues.
Can you see why these are called **propagation** steps?

> **In propagation steps, a free radical reacts with a molecule to produce:**
> **a) a new molecule, and**
> **b) a new free radical.**
> **The new free radical can then carry on the sequence of reactions.**

Termination steps

Whenever two free radicals meet, they react to form a molecule:

$$\bullet Cl + \bullet C \longrightarrow Cl_2$$
$$\bullet Cl + \bullet CH_3 \longrightarrow CH_3Cl$$
$$\bullet CH_3 + \bullet CH_3 \longrightarrow C_2H_6$$

Can you see why these are called termination steps?
These reactions 'mop up' free radicals, preventing further reaction.

> **A termination step removes free radicals.**
> **Eventually the reactions will stop.**

As you can see from the last equation, a small amount of ethane will be produced.
This in turn can be attacked by any free radicals it collides with.
What products could possibly be formed?

Similarly, the chloromethane may also be attacked by free radicals.
What would this produce?

Therefore a variety of products will be made.
The exact amounts depend on the proportions of methane and chlorine that we start with. The more chlorine, the higher the proportions of CH_2Cl_2, $CHCl_3$ and CCl_4 formed.

unpaired
electron

Free radicals will attack anything.
They are very reactive.

171

▷ Chemistry at work: Petrol

On page 167 we saw how the mixture of compounds in crude oil
is separated into fractions. But fractional distillation is not the only
process that takes place in a modern oil refinery.
Cracking turns larger, less useful alkanes into smaller,
more useful ones. We also get other useful hydrocarbons called alkenes
in the process. You can read more about this on page 184.
Reforming converts straight-chain alkanes into compounds that
burn more effectively in engines.
You can read about this on the next page.
Before you do, you need to know more about petrol.

Octane numbers: Don't knock them!

In petrol engines, the petrol and air is mixed in a carburettor.
This fuel mixture is then fed into a cylinder in the engine,
where it is compressed, then ignited by the spark plugs.
However, as the piston compresses the mixture it can ignite too soon.
This causes a metallic rattling noise, known as **'knocking'** in the engine.

Chemists have found out that the more branched an alkane chain,
the less likely it is to cause 'knocking'.
A scale was invented to compare the performance of different fuels.
The fuels are given an **'octane number'**.
On this scale, heptane was given the value of 0 (zero) whilst
2,2,4-trimethylpentane, a branched alkane, was given 100.
Look at their structures below:

OCTANE NUMBER   0   100

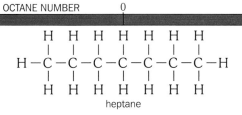

heptane

2,2,4-trimethylpentane

So a good modern petrol mixture should have a high octane number,
showing little tendency to 'knock'. The petrol fraction from crude oil
contains mainly straight-chain alkanes with low octane numbers (around 70).
So to raise the octane number, more branched alkanes and other hydrocarbons called arenes are blended in.
Until recently, lead compounds were also added to petrol to boost its octane number.
However, growing concern about lead pollution has resulted in its removal from petrol.
Lead is particularly dangerous for children. It slows down a child's brain development and reduces intelligence.

A petrol for every season

It is important for the smooth running of an engine
that the petrol vapour mixes with air in the right proportions
in the carburettor. In cold weather, less petrol will vaporise
than in warm weather. In very hot weather too much might vaporise.
So petrol companies supply a different blend of compounds
for each season of the year.
● What type of alkane would you add to make petrol more volatile?

The petrol mixture in winter needs to be more volatile

Reforming alkanes

So where do the oil companies get their hydrocarbons
with high octane numbers from?

It makes economic sense to use some of their lower octane
compounds from the fractional distillation of oil.

These straight-chain alkanes undergo a chemical change to turn them into
new, smoother-burning compounds. The new compounds can be
branched alkanes, ring (cyclical) alkanes or arenes (aromatic compounds).
You can find out more about arenes in Chapter 17.

The process is called **reforming**.

Look at the type of changes we get by reforming alkanes:

A catalytic reformer unit and furnaces in an oil refinery

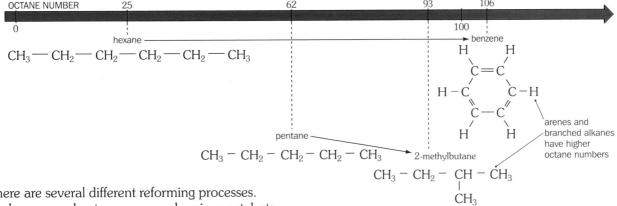

There are several different reforming processes.
Each one uses heat, pressure and various catalysts.
The catalyst is often the very precious metal, platinum.
The Platinum-Reforming process is called **'Platforming'**.
Can you see why it is called this?

When blended into the petrol, the higher octane number products
suffer from less 'knocking' in the engine.
They produce a more efficient, smoother-burning fuel.

Platinum / rhenium catalyst used in oil refinery's reformer

Oil and global stability

Oil supplies have had a big impact on world peace and stability
over the last century.

An American ban on oil exports to Japan was partly responsible
for Japan's attack on Pearl Harbour in 1941. Also in World War Two,
Germany invaded Russia to capture its oilfields.

Nearer to the present was the Gulf War in 1991.
Iraq invaded her neighbour Kuwait, the world's fourth-largest
oil-supplying nation. Control of Kuwait's oil supplies could possibly
have given Iraq unwanted economic and political influence
over the nations in the Western world.
So the USA and her allies came to Kuwait's aid and forced
the Iraqis back inside their own borders.

To understand why oil supply and pricing have such an effect on
world economy and peace, we must appreciate that two-thirds
of the entire world's energy comes from oil and natural gas.
As a raw material, oil provides us with about 30 000 different chemicals.
The Middle East has 65 per cent of the world's oil reserves,
so it is very important in world politics and stability.

Many of Kuwait's oil wells were set alight in the Gulf War

▷ Chemistry at work: Getting rid of waste

Did you know that many plastics are alkanes?
Plastics, such as poly(ethene) and poly(propene) are alkanes with very long chains.
One of the advantages of using these large alkanes is their lack of chemical reactivity. As in all alkanes, the bonds are not polar. (The electronegativity of carbon and hydrogen is almost the same.)
So they resist attack by air, water, acids or alkalis.

However, their stability becomes a disadvantage when we try to dispose of them. Most of our household waste goes to **landfill sites**. In other words, it is dumped in large holes in the ground. When the hole is full, the rubbish is covered with soil. Many plastics will remain unchanged, although new plastics are increasingly likely to be biodegradable. (See page 259.)

In this chapter we have looked at the two main reactions of the alkanes. One is their substitution reaction with chlorine in sunlight. Some plastics that are used now are decomposed in sunlight if left long enough. These are photochemical reactions. The other main reaction is combustion.
So can this be used to help solve our waste problem?

Some countries are using their waste plastics as fuels to generate electricity. For example, Switzerland uses almost three-quarters of its domestic plastic waste in this way. Look at the energy contents of the fuels opposite:

This is a way of getting at the energy 'locked up' in oil because the raw material for making plastic is crude oil. It also helps to reduce the sheer volume of rubbish dumped. We are simply running out of space for new landfill sites.

However, when waste is **burned in incinerators** there is a risk of pollution. If combustion is incomplete, we get carbon monoxide given off. As you have seen on page 169, this is toxic. Many plastics are substituted alkanes. The other atoms present, such as chlorine, mean that toxins, such as **dioxins**, are produced. A very high temperature is needed in the incinerator to make sure they are broken down before they are released into our air. You can see the structure of a dioxin below:

a dioxin

Any sulphur present in the waste will make **sulphur dioxide** gas. This, together with **nitrogen oxides**, will cause acid rain. Chimneys can be fitted with 'scrubbers' to stop these gases escaping. A base, such as calcium carbonate, neutralises the acidic gases.

Micro-organisms in landfill sites can also produce harmful products, but they make **methane** gas as well. At first this was seen as a disadvantage because houses near tips were at risk of exploding. But it is now being piped off and used as a fuel.

Poor people in Manila, Phillipines, scavenge in a landfill tip

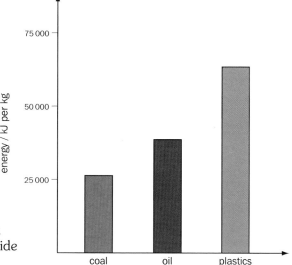

energy / kJ per kg — 75 000, 50 000, 25 000 — coal, oil, plastics

The people and land around Seveso in Italy were poisoned by dioxins following an accident in 1976

Have you seen symbols like this on plastics? They help with recycling. This stands for High Density Poly(ethene).

Summary

- The **alkanes** are saturated hydrocarbons.
- Their general formula is C_nH_{2n+2}
- **Crude oil** is a mixture of compounds, containing mainly alkanes. Crude oil is separated into fractions (compounds with boiling points within certain ranges). This is done by **fractional distillation**.
- As their molecular masses increase, their boiling points increase, they get more dense, more viscous, less volatile, and are harder to ignite.
- The alkanes are unreactive owing to their non-polar bonds, but they do burn in oxygen to form carbon dioxide and water. However, in air, **combustion** is often *incomplete*. Then, as well as CO_2 and H_2O, we get carbon particles (soot) and toxic carbon monoxide too. When we burn petrol in engines we get sulphur dioxide, nitrogen oxides and unburnt hydrocarbons as pollutants. Using catalytic converters in car exhausts helps to cut down on these pollutants.
- The alkanes undergo **substitution** reactions with halogens in sunlight. This photochemical reaction has a **free radical** mechanism.

Crude oil contains a mixture of alkanes

▷ Questions

1 Copy and complete:
.... hydrocarbons are called alkanes. Examples include ethane, whose formula is .... , and ...., whose formula is C_6H_{14}.

They are largely unreactive compounds. Their main reactions are:
a) .... – in which they react with oxygen to form carbon dioxide and ....
b) substitution – in which .... atoms are replaced by halogen atoms in the presence of .....

The alkanes are important fuels, but in cars their combustion is ...., and particles of .... (soot) and carbon .... (a toxic gas) are formed as well as the usual products. Petrol engines also give off .... dioxide and oxides of .... which contribute to .... rain.

2 a) What is the general formula of an alkane?
b) What is the formula of dodecane, with 12 carbon atoms?
c) Some alkanes are cyclical (have a ring-type structure). Draw a molecule of cyclobutane.
d) Do cyclical alkanes obey the general formula for alkanes? What is their general formula?
e) Why is cyclobutane less stable than butane?

3 a) Name the process whereby crude oil is separated into its fractions.
b) List the main fractions we get from crude oil.
c) Explain why large alkanes have higher boiling points than small alkanes.

4 a) Draw the apparatus you could use to show that carbon dioxide and water are produced when octane burns.
b) How can you test for each product?
c) During incomplete combustion, carbon monoxide is one of the products. Explain its effects on the body.
d) List the pollutants given out by cars burning petrol.
e) How does a catalytic converter help to reduce pollution from cars.
f) Do catalytic converters help us solve the problem of global warming? Explain your answer.
g) What causes the problem of 'knocking' in a car's engine?
h) How do oil companies improve the octane number of their petrols?

5 Ethane reacts with bromine in bright sunlight.
a) What do we call this type of reaction?
b) Write an equation to show the reaction between an ethane molecule and a bromine molecule.
c) What happens to start the reaction off?
d) What do we call this first step in the mechanism?
e) Give an equation to show one of the propagation steps in the reaction.
f) Explain what happens in a termination step.
g) Give three examples of possible termination steps for the reaction between ethane and bromine.
h) If we have excess bromine present, give the structural formula of the other halogenoalkanes made.

6 Draw a table showing the advantages and disadvantages of using a) landfill sites, and b) incineration, to get rid of waste.

14 The alkenes

Whenever you eat a banana, you can thank an alkene
for keeping it fresh.
Look at the photo opposite:
The bananas are green when they are picked and transported
to this country. We store them until they are needed.
Then ethene gas is passed over the fruit which speeds up
the ripening process before they are sold.

Ethene is the most important of the alkene family.
It is used to make a wide range of products. (See page 185.)

How can you tell the number of carbon atoms in ethene?
Its formula is C_2H_4.
How does this differ from ethane, which is one of the alkanes
that we looked at in the last chapter?
Look at the displayed and structural formulae of ethene below:

*Bananas are ripened by ethene. You can
read about more uses of the alkenes on
page 185*

$$H \diagdown \quad \diagup H$$
$$C = C \qquad CH_2 = CH_2 \qquad ethene$$
$$H \diagup \quad \diagdown H$$

As you can see, there is a **double bond** between the two carbon atoms.
Is each carbon bonded to its maximum number of hydrogen atoms?
The alkenes are called **unsaturated** hydrocarbons.
You might have heard margarines advertised as 'high in polyunsaturates'.
The hydrocarbon chains in the molecules of oils in the margarine
contain carbon–carbon double bonds.

Alkene	Formula
ethene	C_2H_4
propene	C_3H_6
butene	C_4H_8
pentene	C_5H_{10}

*The position of the double bond is shown
by inserting a number.
Can you draw pent-2-ene?*

Look at the table opposite:
Can you see a pattern in the formulae?
The general formula of an alkene (containing one double bond) is:

$$\boxed{C_nH_{2n}}$$

As with the alkanes, it is also possible to get cycloalkenes.
You can represent the structural formula of cyclohexene as:

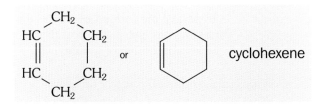

cyclohexene

We obtain the alkenes by **cracking** the higher fractions from crude oil.
Can you recall from previous work what 'cracking' means?

In an oil refinery, larger alkanes are broken down ('cracked')
into smaller, more useful alkanes.
The by-products are alkenes (mainly ethene).
For example,

$$nonane \xrightarrow[\text{catalyst}]{\text{heat}} heptane + ethene$$

$$C_9H_{20} \longrightarrow C_7H_{16} + C_2H_4$$

You can crack a hydrocarbon in the lab as shown opposite:
You can read more about cracking on page 184.

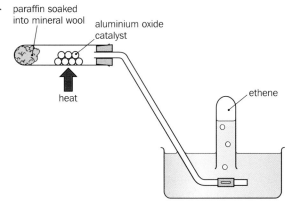

▷ Stereoisomers

As well as the structural isomers we saw on page 162, we can also have **stereoisomers**.

The molecules of stereoisomers have atoms that are each bonded to the same neighbouring atoms. However, the resulting molecules **cannot be superimposed**.

Everyday examples to help you imagine this could be a pair of gloves or shoes, or a left-hand and right-hand drive car. You can't lay one shoe on top of the other, with both soles facing downwards, and get an identical match!

A left-hand and right-hand drive car cannot be superimposed – no matter how hard you try!

▷ Geometric isomerism in alkenes

One form of stereoisomerism is **geometric isomerism**. Look at the example below:

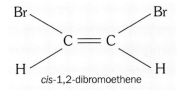

cis-1,2-dibromoethene   *trans*-1,2-dibromoethene

Unlike a single bond, the **atoms cannot rotate around a double bond**. So the Br atoms in the first example are stuck on the same side of the molecule. When a pair of identical atoms, or groups of atoms, is on the same side of the double bond, we call it the **cis-** isomer. When the pair is on opposite sides, it is called the **trans-** isomer.

(The prefix *trans-* means 'across'. Can you think of a word that starts with *trans-*? What is a *trans*-atlantic flight?) This gives us a way of distinguishing the two geometric isomers when naming them.

No matter how you try, these two molecules cannot be placed directly on top of each other to give the same structure.

You can best see this if you make models of the isomers yourself. Then try to superimpose them.
● Can you draw the structural formulae of but-2-ene?
Look at the *cis*- and *trans*- isomers of this alkene below:

CH₃ \ / CH₃   CH₃ \ / H
 C = C   C = C
H / \ H   H / \ CH₃
  cis-but-2-ene   *trans*-but-2-ene

We can have geometric isomers whenever we have structures such as

A \ / B   A \ / A   A \ / A
 C = C   or   C = C   or   C = C
E / \ D   B / \ D   B / \ B

● Can you work out the number of isomers in each case?

Stereoisomers

geometric isomers (organic molecule contains carbon–carbon double bond) | optical isomers (see page 247)

You can also see this form of isomerism in inorganic compounds. Page 137 shows stereoisomers of transition metal complexes.

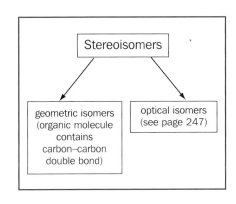

▷ Reactions of the alkenes

The alkenes themselves have relatively few uses.
However, they are reactive because of their carbon–carbon double bonds.
This makes them very important starting material in making
many useful compounds. For example, many of the plastics
that we use every day are derived from ethene originally.
You can read more about making plastics in Chapter 21.

Carrier bags are made from poly(ethene)
(commonly called polythene)

We can compare the reactions of different hydrocarbons by looking at:
hexane (an alkane) C_6H_{14},
hexene (an alkene), C_6H_{12}, and
cyclohexene (a cycloalkene) C_6H_{10}.
Can you draw their structural or displayed formulae?

Look at the results of the tests below:

a) Combustion

Hexane burning

Hexene burning

Cyclohexene burning

We met the general equation for the complete combustion of a hydrocarbon
on page 168. Can you remember the products?
Carbon dioxide and water will be formed, but there are other products too.
You can see from the flames above that the hydrocarbons
are not completely oxidised when we burn them on mineral wool.
Which one of the three produces the most black smoke?
The black smoke is mainly unburned carbon.

> **We find that the higher the ratio of carbon to hydrogen in
> the hydrocarbon, the dirtier the flame.**

Look at the formulae of the three compounds above.
Is the pattern above consistent with their formulae?

b) Mixing with bromine water (ethanol is added to aid mixing)

hexane
+
bromine

no reaction

hexene
+
bromine

yellow bromine water
turns colourless

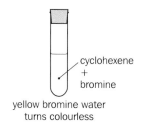

cyclohexene
+
bromine

yellow bromine water
turns colourless

> **This can be used to test for unsaturated hydrocarbons: they decolourise bromine water.**

The equation for the reaction of hexene with bromine is:

$$C_6H_{12} + Br_2 \longrightarrow C_6H_{12}Br_2$$

This is called an **addition** reaction.
It is typical of most alkene reactions.
The carbon–carbon double bond in the alkene 'opens up'
and a bromine atom is 'added' on to both carbon atoms.
You can see the mechanism for this reaction on the page 181.

c) **Mixing with acidified potassium manganate(VII)**
Again, we add ethanol to help the liquids mix.

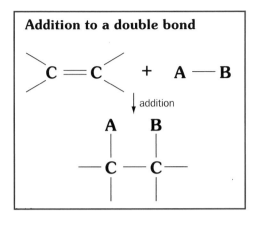

Addition to a double bond

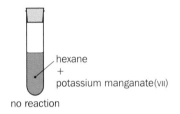

hexane
+
potassium manganate(VII)

no reaction

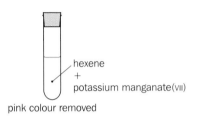

hexene
+
potassium manganate(VII)

pink colour removed

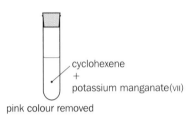

cyclohexene
+
potassium manganate(VII)

pink colour removed

This can also be used to test for an unsaturated compound.
The reaction is complex. Two —OH (alcohol) groups are added
across the double bond in a redox reaction.
In the case of ethene, this will give ethane-1,2-diol (HO—CH_2CH_2—OH).

Addition of hydrogen to alkenes

This is an important reaction in the manufacture of margarine.
The oils from which we make margarine are unsaturated.
They are too runny to spread on to bread. By adding hydrogen,
we can increase the molecular mass of the oils and straighten their chains.
This has the effect of thickening the oil. The amount of hydrogen
added can be varied to get just the right consistency,
i.e. a soft solid that will spread straight from the fridge.
The addition reaction only occurs with a catalyst, usually nickel,
at 140 °C. The catalyst is finely divided to increase its surface area.
So an alkene, such as ethene, can be changed into an alkane:

$$C_2H_4 + H_2 \xrightarrow{\text{Ni}} C_2H_6$$
$$\text{ethane}$$

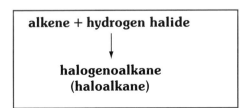

Hydrogen is added to edible oils to turn them into margarine

alkene + hydrogen $\xrightarrow[\text{catalyst}]{\text{Ni}}$ alkane

Addition of a hydrogen halide to alkenes

This is a similar reaction to the addition of a halogen to an alkene.
In this case, we get a halogenoalkane containing just one halogen atom.
For example, when concentrated hydrogen bromide solution is added to
ethene:

$$C_2H_4 + HBr \longrightarrow C_2H_5Br$$
$$\text{bromoethane}$$

You can look at this reaction in more detail on page 182.

alkene + hydrogen halide

↓

halogenoalkane
(haloalkane)

▷ The mechanism of addition

Can you remember what we mean by the 'mechanism' of a reaction? (See page 170.)

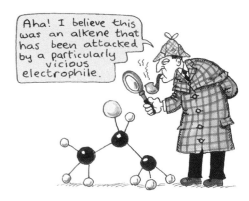

Working out the steps in the mechanism is like a detective reconstructing events at the scene of a crime. We can use our knowledge of the reactant molecules involved to propose a likely chain of events.
This leads us logically to the new product molecules formed at the end of the reaction.

The last reaction we looked at was the addition of a hydrogen halide to an alkene.
Now let's see if we can explain how this addition reaction takes place:

The mechanism explains how a reaction takes place

First of all we need to look more closely at the double bond in an alkene.
Look at the 'dot and cross' diagram of ethene opposite:
Can you see how many electrons are involved in a double bond?
Scientists believe that two electrons spend most of their time in between the carbon atoms, as in a normal covalent bond.
The other 2 electrons in the double bond are most likely to be found in two sausage-shaped areas above and below the two carbon atoms.
You can see this below:

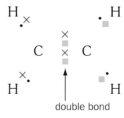

double bond

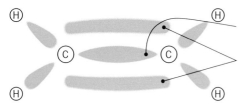

This is a 'normal' single bond, called a sigma (σ) bond (containing 2 electrons).

The two areas, above and below the plane of the ethene molecule, are called a pi (π) bond. This is where the other 2 electrons in the double bond are found.

So there is a relatively high concentration of electrons in the double bond.
We say that it is an area **'rich in electrons'**.
Therefore this part of the alkene is slightly negatively charged compared with the rest of the molecule. It has a higher electron density.
So do you think a double bond is more likely to be attacked by a positive or a negative species? (Remember that opposite charges attract.)

Alkenes are attacked by parts of molecules that are short of electrons.
These areas of the attacking molecule carry a slight positive charge.
We say they are **'electron-deficient'** and we call them **electrophiles**.
The word 'electrophile' means 'electron-loving' or 'electron-seeking'.

> **Electrophiles** are electron-deficient species.
> They attack electron-rich parts of other molecules.

Now let's consider the molecule of a hydrogen halide.
Look at the molecule of hydrogen bromide opposite:
H—Br is a polar molecule.
It acts as an electrophile because of the partial positive charge on the hydrogen atom.

$$\overset{\delta+}{H} \longrightarrow \overset{\delta-}{Br}$$

Bromine is more electronegative than hydrogen, so the pair of electrons in the bond are found, on average, nearer the bromine atom. (See page 68)

Now we can show the mechanism of the addition reaction.
Notice where the curly arrows start and finish:
They show the movement of a pair of electrons.

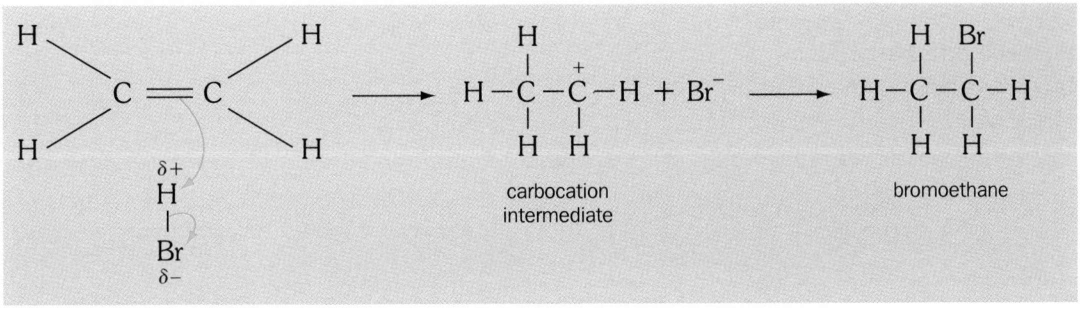

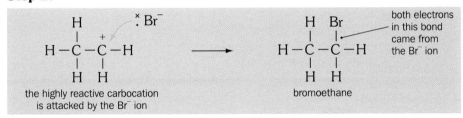

carbocation
intermediate

bromoethane

This is called **electrophilic addition.**

Let's look at the mechanism above in more detail:

Step 1:

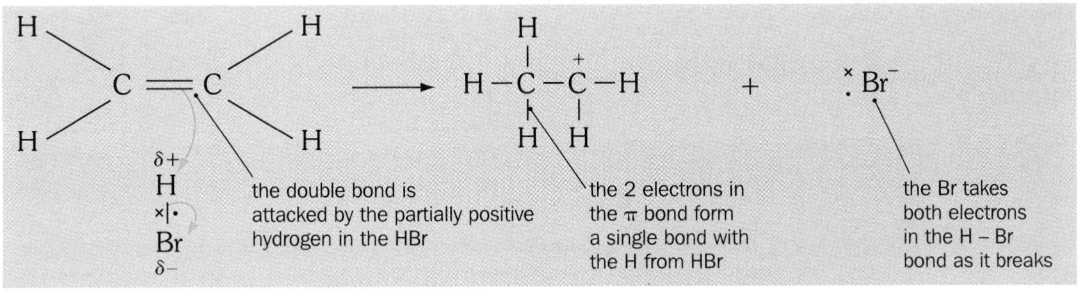

the double bond is
attacked by the partially positive
hydrogen in the HBr

the 2 electrons in
the π bond form
a single bond with
the H from HBr

the Br takes
both electrons
in the H – Br
bond as it breaks

What happens to the pair of electrons in the H—Br bond?
Compare this with the homolytic fission of a covalent bond on page 170:
In the case of HBr, both electrons from the bond go on to
the Br atom as the bond breaks. So a Br⁻ ion is formed.

> **The 'unequal' breaking of a covalent bond is called heterolytic fission.**

Step 2:

both electrons
in this bond
came from
the Br⁻ ion

the highly reactive carbocation
is attacked by the Br⁻ ion

bromoethane

The **carbocation** is present only for an instant before it is attacked by
the Br⁻ ion.
Carbocations are highly reactive intermediates formed in reactions.

> **A carbocation is a positive ion with the charge centred on a carbon atom.**

They exist for only a fraction of a second before being attacked.
Notice that the carbon atom carrying the positive charge has only three bonds.
It is electron-deficient. So it is open to attack by electron-rich species,
such as the Br⁻ ion.
Bromoethane is formed instantaneously.

> **The alkenes undergo electrophilic attack in their addition reactions.**
> **The reactions are called electrophilic addition.**

▷ Predicting products of addition

The addition reaction on the last page involved ethene.
But what product would be formed if we react
but-1-ene, CH_2=$CHCH_2CH_3$, with hydrogen bromide?
Can you see that we could get two possible products?
The isomers 1-bromobutane or 2-bromobutane could be formed.

Look at the equation below:

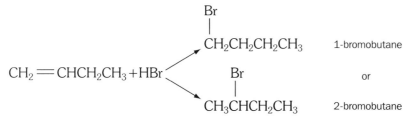

Experiments show that 2-bromobutane is the major product.
Just a small amount of 1-bromobutane is formed.
So why is this? The answer lies in the mechanism.

On the last page we saw that in Step 1 a carbocation is made.
Look at the two possible structures of the ions:

1. 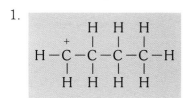   2.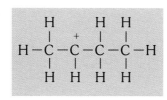

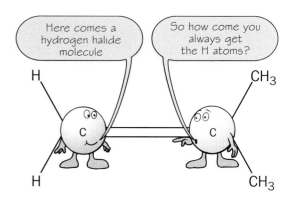

The first carbocation shown above is called a **primary** carbocation.
It has only one alkyl group attached to the carbon carrying the charge.

The second carbocation is called a **secondary** carbocation.
It has two alkyl groups attached to the carbon carrying the charge.

If the major product is 2-bromobutane, which carbocation do you think
is more likely to be formed?
The secondary ion is more stable than the primary one.

This is because alkyl groups tend to donate electrons
to the carbon atom they are attached to.
In this case, it has the effect of reducing the charge density
on the positively charged carbon atom in the carbocation.
In the secondary carbocation the positively charged carbon
is stabilised by two alkyl groups, each donating electrons –
whereas in the primary cation there is only one alkyl group.

So the formation of the secondary carbocation, in preference to
the primary ion, results in more 2-bromobutane being formed.
We can predict the major product formed using **Markovnikov's Rule**.
It states that:

> **When we add an HX molecule to an alkene, the H atom
> will join on to the carbon that already has more H atoms.**

You can check this by looking at the reaction of but-1-ene above:
However, you should now be able to **explain** why we get
much more of one product than another.

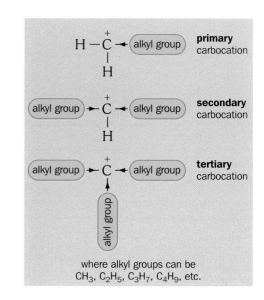

where alkyl groups can be
CH_3, C_2H_5, C_3H_7, C_4H_9, etc.

If we react 2-methylpropene with a hydrogen halide, we can get a **tertiary** carbocation formed:

- Do you think tertiary carbocations are more stable than primary or secondary ones?
- So what will be the major product in this case?

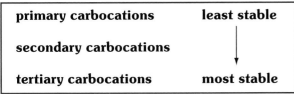

2-methylpropene   2-chloro-2-methylpropane

primary carbocations	least stable
secondary carbocations	
tertiary carbocations	most stable

- Why don't we need to worry about Markovnikov's Rule in reactions with ethene or but-2-ene?

▷ Mechanism of addition with halogens

We have said that the mechanism for reactions of the type:

$$\text{C=C} + A-B \longrightarrow -\overset{A}{\underset{}{C}}-\overset{B}{\underset{}{C}}-$$

can be described as electrophilic addition.
But what if atoms A and B are the same, as in the case of the halogens, e.g. Cl_2 or Br_2?

These are still electrophilic additions, but where does the electrophile come from?

As the non-polar halogen molecule approaches the double bond, a dipole is induced in the halogen. The molecule is polarised. The electrons in the halogen molecule are repelled by the concentrated negative charge in the double bond. This makes the end of the halogen molecule that is nearest to the alkene slightly positive compared with the other end. This creates the electrophile to add to the double bond:

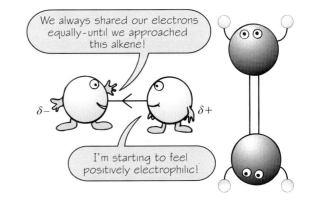

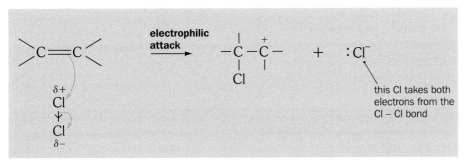

Heterolytic fission of the halogen–halogen bond takes place, and the halide ion attacks the carbocation:

1,2-Dichloroethane is used to make chloroethane from which we make PVC plastics

183

▷ Chemistry at work: Cracking

We saw on page 176 how large alkanes can be broken down by heating them as they pass over a catalyst.
This is how we make alkenes in the petrochemical industry.
The reaction is called **cracking**.

Oil companies can vary the conditions to get different products from cracking. They use the process to get a better match between the supply of fractions from their crude oil and the demand for products in society.
Can you guess which fraction will be in most demand?

Look at the table below:

Heavier fractions are cracked in these steel reactors

Fractions	North Sea oil (approx. %)	Demand (approx. %)
gas	2	2
petrol	24	29
kerosine	12	8
diesel and gas oil	19	22
fuel oil and bitumen	43	29

(Up to 10% may be used as fuel in the refinery itself and there are losses in the processing.)

There are two main types of cracking in oil refineries:

1. Thermal cracking

Here the reaction is carried out at high temperatures (often between 500 °C and 700 °C) and at high pressures.
At these high temperatures C—C bonds in the alkanes break and free radicals form.
Look at the example below:

$$CH_3(CH_2)_7CH_2 \text{———} CH_3 \longrightarrow CH_3(CH_2)_7\overset{\bullet}{C}H_2 + \overset{\bullet}{C}H_3$$

reactive free radicals

Initiation step in thermal cracking

This is homolytic fission of the C—C bond. Do you remember what this means? (See page 170.) The forming of the free radicals is the initiation step in the mechanism of cracking.
The free radicals produce a variety of alkenes as they break down.
Smaller alkanes are formed in some of the termination steps.

free radicals

alkenes   shorter chain alkanes

2. Catalytic cracking

In this process a lower temperature is used, but it is still between 400 °C and 500 °C.
The alkanes are mixed with a zeolite catalyst under slight pressure.
The acidic oxides in the catalyst help to break C—H bonds, forming carbocations.
The carbocation can then lose an H^+ ion to form an alkene.
The reactive carbocations can also react with other alkanes to form new branched alkanes.
These compounds have higher octane numbers. (See page 172.)
They are used to improve the quality of the mixture in petrol.

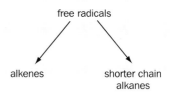

$$R - CH_2 - \overset{+}{C}H - R$$
carbocation

breaks down   reacts with other alkanes

alkenes   branched alkanes (higher octane numbers)

▷ Chemistry at work: Uses of ethene and epoxyethane

Ethene is the smallest and most useful of all the alkenes.
Whereas the alkanes are unreactive, we can use ethene
as a starting material for many new products.
What makes ethene more reactive than an alkane?

Look at the spider diagram below:
It shows some of the major products from ethene.
For example, antifreeze can be made because of the reactivity
of ethene's double bond. It is made in a two-stage process:

$$2\ CH_2{=}CH_2 + O_2 \xrightarrow[\text{silver catalyst}]{300\,^\circ C} 2\ CH_2 - CH_2$$

| ethene | oxygen in air | **epoxyethane** |

The ethene also reacts with the oxygen, producing CO_2 and H_2O.
The reaction gives out a lot of energy, so the temperature
must be carefully controlled in the reactor.
The epoxyethane is very reactive because of the strain in the ring formed.
The bond angles in the ring average 60°, much smaller than
carbon's preferred 109.5° in its tetrahedral arrangement.
So the ring is ready to split open.
Care is needed when using this unstable intermediate in industry.
It reacts with water to form ethane-1,2-diol, used in antifreeze:

$$CH_2 - CH_2 + H_2O \longrightarrow CH_2 - CH_2$$

| epoxyethane | water | ethane-1,2-diol |

*Ethane-1,2-diol is a very effective
antifreeze for cars. You can read more
about it on page 201*

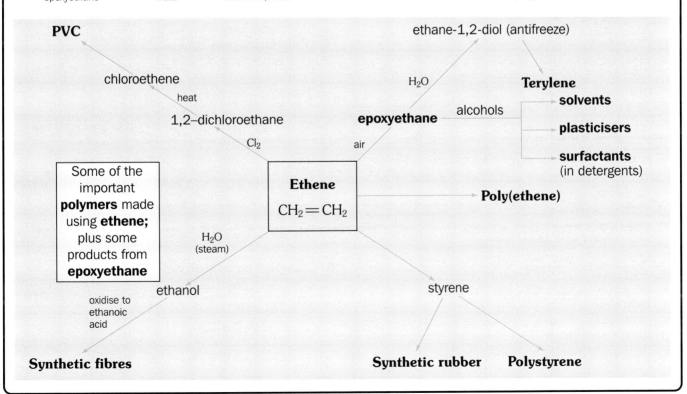

PVC

ethane-1,2-diol (antifreeze)

chloroethene

Terylene

heat

H_2O

1,2–dichloroethane

alcohols → solvents

epoxyethane

plasticisers

Cl_2

air

surfactants
(in detergents)

Some of the
important
polymers made
using **ethene;**
plus some
products from
epoxyethane

Ethene
$CH_2 = CH_2$

Poly(ethene)

H_2O
(steam)

ethanol

styrene

oxidise to
ethanoic
acid

Synthetic fibres

Synthetic rubber **Polystyrene**

Summary

- The **alkenes** are ***unsaturated*** hydrocarbons.
- They contain at least one C = C double bond.
- They show geometric isomerism as there is no rotation around the double bond. This results in *cis-* and *trans-* isomers.
- Alkenes decolourise bromine water.
  This can be used as a test for an unsaturated compound.
- The alkenes are ***attacked by electrophiles*** (electron-deficient species).
  These are attracted by the high electron density around the C=C double bond.
- The alkenes undergo **electrophilic addition** reactions.
  For example when they react with bromine:

$$\begin{array}{c} \diagup \\ \diagdown \end{array} C = C \begin{array}{c} \diagdown \\ \diagup \end{array} + Br_2 \longrightarrow \begin{array}{cc} Br & Br \\ | & | \\ -C-C- \\ | & | \end{array}$$

You can see a summary of the reactions of alkenes on page 266.

▷ Questions

1 Copy and complete:
The alkenes all contain at least one carbon–carbon .... bond. This makes them much more .... than the alkanes.
The .... electron density around their .... bond makes them open to attack by .....
Their reactions are called .... addition.
.... water is used to test for an unsaturated compound. It turns from yellow to .... as a result of an .... reaction.

2 There are two isomers of 1,2-dichloroethene.

a) Draw the two isomers.
b) What do we call this type of isomerism?
c) Explain why these isomers arise but there is only one possible structure for 1,2-dichloroethane.
d) Draw the isomers of 1,2-dichloro-1-fluoroethene.

3 You are given three hydrocarbons to compare:

heptane, hept-1-ene and cycloheptene.

Describe and explain any similarities and differences you would see when each one is:
a) burned in air,
b) shaken with a mixture of potassium manganate(VII), dilute sulphuric acid and ethanol.

4 a) Complete this equation:

$$C_{10}H_{22} \xrightarrow{\text{heat, } Al_2O_3 \text{ catalyst}} C_8H_{18} + ...$$

b) Name each reactant and product.
c) What do we call this type of reaction?
d) Why is it important in the oil industry?

5 a) Complete this equation:

$$CH_3CH{=}CH_2 + H_2 \longrightarrow ....$$

b) Name the reactants and product.
c) Which catalyst is used in the reaction?
d) How is the catalyst made as effective as possible?
e) What is the temperature used in the reaction?
f) Explain why this type of reaction is important in the manufacture of margarine.

6 Explain each of these terms:
a) an electrophile
b) a carbocation
c) a primary carbocation
d) a tertiary carbocation
e) heterolytic fission
f) electrophilic addition.

7 a) Put the carbocations below in order of stability (most stable first):

$$CH_3\overset{+}{C}H_2 \qquad CH_3\overset{+}{C}HCH_3 \qquad CH_3-\overset{+}{\underset{\underset{CH_3}{|}}{C}}-CH_3$$

b) Explain your answer to part a).

8 Complete these equations:
a) $C_2H_4 + Br_2 \longrightarrow ....$
b) $C_2H_4 + HCl \longrightarrow ....$
c) $CH_2{=}CHCH{=}CH_2 + 2F_2 \longrightarrow ....$
d) $CH_3CH_2CH{=}CH_2 + HBr \longrightarrow ....$

15 The halogenoalkanes (haloalkanes)

Have you ever had to have an anaesthetic?
If you have, then you will have been put to sleep
by a **halogenoalkane** (also known as a haloalkane).
The earliest anaesthetic was called chloroform.
Its modern name is trichloromethane. Can you draw
its structure? It is no longer used because it can damage
your liver. Nowadays you are more likely to be given
a gas known as 'halothane':

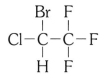

We can think of halogenoalkanes as alkanes with one or more
of their hydrogen atoms replaced by halogen atoms.
The simplest will have the general formula:

$$C_nH_{2n+1}X$$ where X = F, Cl, Br, or I

They are rarely found naturally but their compounds are important
in the chemical industry. They are used to make other useful substances,
as well as having many uses themselves. For example, they are used
as flame retardants. The halogen atom greatly reduces
the flammability of the corresponding alkane.
You can read more about some of these uses on pages 192 and 193.

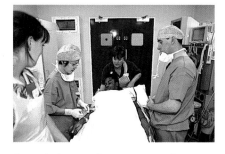

Some halogenoalkanes are used as anaesthetics

- Can you give the systematic name of 'halothane' (shown opposite)?

The fabric on all soft furniture must now be treated with a flame retardant (which is often a halogenoalkane)

▷ Bond strengths

The reactions of the halogenoalkanes usually involve substitution
of the halogen atom. It is replaced by another atom or group of atoms.
Look at the table below:

Bond	Bond length / nm	Bond enthalpy / kJ mol^{-1}
C—F	0.138	467
C—Cl	0.177	346
C—Br	0.194	290
C—I	0.214	228

The C—F bond is the strongest, and C—I is the weakest.

In a substitution reaction the carbon–halogen bond is broken.
This means that the most reactive halogenoalkanes
are the compounds of iodine.

- Can you see the pattern between the length of a bond and the energy needed to break it?

fluoroalkanes	**least reactive**
chloroalkanes	↓
bromoalkanes	
iodoalkanes	**most reactive**

▷ Reactions of the halogenoalkanes

Substitution reactions

When we add an aqueous solution of sodium hydroxide
to a halogenoalkane, we get a substitution reaction:

$$CH_3CH_2CH_2Br + OH^-(aq) \xrightarrow{\text{hydrolysis}} CH_3CH_2CH_2OH + Br^-(aq)$$

1-bromopropane   alkali   propan-1-ol

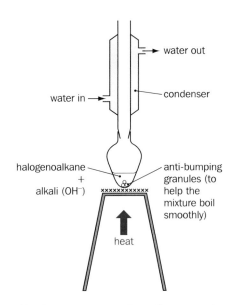

Heating reactants **under reflux** stops the
liquids evaporating off

The product is an alcohol.
The rate of the reaction depends on the halogen atom present.
As we saw on the last page, we would expect iodopropane
to react faster than bromopropane.
How quickly do you think chloropropane reacts with alkali?

For slow reactions, we can heat the mixture under **reflux**.
Look at the apparatus opposite:

This enables us to boil up reacting mixtures containing
volatile liquids, without the liquids evaporating off.
The attack on the halogenoalkane is made by the OH⁻ ion.
The negative ion is an **'electron-rich'** species
(the opposite of the electrophiles in the last chapter).
The OH⁻ ion acts as a **nucleophile**.

> **A nucleophile is an 'elecron-rich' species.**
> **It has a lone pair of electrons available to attack**
> **an 'electron-deficient' carbon atom.**

In the case of a halogenoalkane, the 'electron-deficient' carbon
is the one bonded to the halogen. Can you think why?

Look at the table opposite:

Element	Electronegativity
carbon	2.5
fluorine	4.0
chlorine	3.0
bromine	2.8
iodine	2.5

As you can see, most of the halogens are more electronegative
than carbon. This results in the shared electrons in
carbon–halogen bonds being, on average, nearer to the halogen atom.
The bond is polarised, with the halogen carrying a partial negative charge.
This leaves the carbon atom with a slight positive charge.
In other words, the carbon atom is 'electron-deficient'.
As such, this carbon is open to attack by a nucleophile.
Therefore:

> **Halogenoalkanes undergo nucleophilic substitution.**

- Which bond is most highly polarised:
  C—F, C—Cl, C—Br or C—I?
- Which will be attacked most readily by a nucleophile?
- Does this agree with the rates of reaction on the last page?
- So which is more important in deciding the rate of reaction:
  the strength of the carbon–halogen bond or the polarity of the bond?

We will consider the mechanism shown opposite in more detail on page 190:

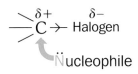

Halogenoalkanes are attacked
by nucleophiles.
They undergo nucleophilic
substitution.

188

▷ Other nucleophilic substitution reactions

With cyanide ions

The halogenoalkane is boiled under reflux with potassium cyanide dissolved in ethanol.
For example,

$$CH_3CH_2CH_2Br + CN^- \longrightarrow CH_3CH_2CH_2CN + Br^-$$

1-bromopropane   cyanide ion   butanenitrile

Notice that this reaction has **_added an extra carbon atom to the chain_**.
It is an important reaction when considering how to make new compounds from natural organic raw materials. (See page 264.)
The nitrile group can be reduced (have H atoms added).
It then forms a primary amine. Or it can be hydrolysed to a carboxylic acid. (See page 245.)

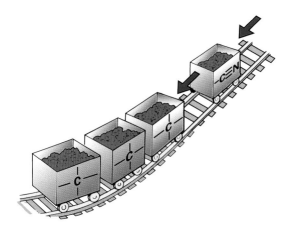

A carbon chain is extended by adding a nitrile (—C≡N) group

With ammonia (NH₃)

Although ammonia is a neutral molecule, the nitrogen atom carries a partial negative charge and has a lone pair of electrons.
This makes it a potential nucleophile.
The initial attack on a halogenoalkane forms an amine:

$$CH_3CH_2CH_2Br + NH_3 \longrightarrow CH_3CH_2CH_2NH_2 + HBr$$

1-bromopropane   ammonia   propylamine
(a primary amine)

> $\ddot{N}H_3$ **is the nucleophile**

The amine formed is also a nucleophile.
It will attack any unreacted bromopropane in the mixture:

$$CH_3CH_2CH_2Br + CH_3CH_2CH_2NH_2 \longrightarrow (CH_3CH_2CH_2)_2NH + HBr$$

dipropylamine
(a secondary amine)

> $C_3H_7\ddot{N}H_2$ **is the nucleophile**

The secondary amine formed can also act as a nucleophile.

$$CH_3CH_2CH_2Br + (CH_3CH_2CH_2)_2NH \longrightarrow (CH_3CH_2CH_2)_3N + HBr$$

tripropylamine
(a tertiary amine)

> $$C_3H_7 - \overset{\displaystyle ..}{\underset{\displaystyle H}{N}} - C_3H_7 \text{ is the nucleophile}$$

If any unreacted bromopropane still remains, the tertiary amine can attack it:

$$CH_3CH_2CH_2Br + (CH_3CH_2CH_2)_3N \longrightarrow (CH_3CH_2CH_2)_4N^+Br^-$$

tetrapropylammonium bromide
(a quaternary ammonium ion)

> $$C_3H_7 - \overset{\displaystyle ..}{\underset{\displaystyle C_3H_7}{N}} - C_3H_7 \text{ is the nucleophile}$$

So the reaction of a halogenoalkane with ammonia yields a mixture of products.
The amount of primary amine will be increased if you start with excess ammonia. Can you see why?

- Which atom in ammonia and in the amines enables them to act as nucleophiles?
- How many lone pairs of electrons does this atom have?
- Can you suggest a mechanism for the reaction of bromopropane a) with ammonia, and b) with a primary amine?

189

▷ **Mechanism of nucleophilic substitution**

The reactions on the last two pages are typical of halogenoalkanes.
The halogen atom is replaced by another atom or group of atoms.
In other words, the halogen is substituted.

On page 188 we saw why the attack on a halogenoalkane
is by a nucleophile. Can you remember why?

There are two possible mechanisms for this attack:

1. First the bond between the carbon and halogen atoms breaks.
   This forms a carbocation.
   The carbocation is then immediately attacked by the nucleophile.
Look at the mechanism below:

(a)

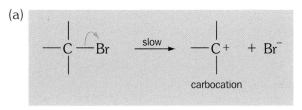

Then:

(b)   **S_N1 mechanism**

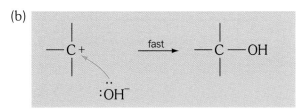

- Can you recall which type of carbocation is most stable?
  Is it a primary, secondary or tertiary carbocation?
- So which type of halogenoalkane is more likely to be attacked
  as described by this mechanism?

2. As the nucleophile forms a bond with the carbon next to the halogen atom,
   the bond between the carbon and halogen atoms breaks.
Look at the mechanism below:

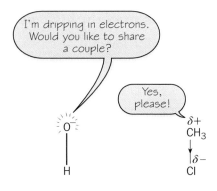

OH⁻ is a nucleophile!

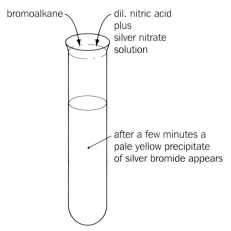

Can you explain these observations?
(Hint: the nucleophile is the H_2O molecule
from $AgNO_3(aq)$)
This can be used to test for
halogenoalkanes.

- What would you see with a
  chloroalkane? (See page 124)

S_N2 mechanism
(You can read more about
these mechanisms on page
347.
It explains what S_N1 and
S_N2 stand for.)

(Notice the heterolytic fission of the C—Br bond.)

We can do experiments to gain evidence of the method of attack.
This is covered in detail on page 347.
The first mechanism shows how tertiary halogenoalkanes
undergo substitution.
We find that primary halogenoalkanes are attacked as shown
in the second mechanism.
The picture is not really clear with secondary compounds.

190

▷ Elimination reactions of halogenoalkanes

Nucleophilic substitution is not the only type of reaction
that halogenoalkanes are involved in.
On page 188 we looked at their reaction with alkali,
e.g. with aqueous sodium hydroxide. This is a typical reaction
in which the nucleophile displaces the halogen.

However, if the sodium hydroxide is dissolved in ethanol
instead of water, we get a different reaction:

$$
\underset{\substack{\text{bromoethane}}}{
\begin{array}{c}
\text{H} \quad \text{Br} \\
| \quad\quad | \\
\text{H} - \text{C} - \text{C} - \text{H} \\
| \quad\quad | \\
\text{H} \quad \text{H}
\end{array}}
+ \underset{\substack{\text{ethanolic} \\ \text{hydroxide ions} \\ \text{(ions are dissolved in ethanol)}}}{\text{OH}^- \text{(ethanol)}}
\longrightarrow
\underset{\substack{\text{ethene}}}{
\begin{array}{c}
\text{H} \qquad \text{H} \\
\diagdown \qquad \diagup \\
\text{C} = \text{C} \\
\diagup \qquad \diagdown \\
\text{H} \qquad \text{H}
\end{array}}
+ \underset{\substack{\text{water}}}{\text{H}_2\text{O}}
+ \underset{\substack{\text{bromide ions}}}{\text{Br}^-}
$$

In this case we get an alkene formed.
We don't get the alcohol as in a nucleophilic substitution.
● What has happened to the bromoethane molecule in order to
change it into an ethene molecule? Which atoms has it lost?

In effect the bromoethane has lost an H atom and a Br atom.
In other words, HBr has been **eliminated** from the original molecule.

> An **elimination reaction** involves the *loss of a small molecule*, such as water
> or a hydrogen halide, from the original molecule.

Mechanism of elimination

In the ethanol, the OH⁻ ions act as a *base* rather than
a nucleophile.
You probably already know that an acid donates H⁺ ions.
Bases, being the 'opposites' of acids, accept H⁺ ions.
So the OH⁻ ion takes an H⁺ ion from the carbon atom
next to the one bonded to the halogen.
As this happens, the carbon–halogen bond breaks.
The halogen takes both electrons in the bond,
forming the halide ion:

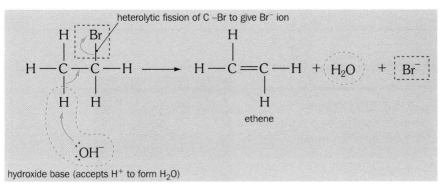

This shows how important the conditions are in organic reactions.

> In water OH⁻ ions act as **nucleophiles** in **substitution** reactions with halogenoalkanes.
> However, when dissolved in ethanol, OH⁻ ions act as **bases** in **elimination** reactions

191

▷ Chemistry at work: Uses of halogenoalkanes

CFCs

The initials CFC are given to a group of compounds called chlorofluorocarbons. They contain carbon, fluorine and chlorine atoms. CFCs are all **very unreactive**. They are not flammable and are not toxic. Different CFCs have different boiling points which make them suitable for different uses.

The first CFC made in 1930 by Thomas Midgley was dichlorodifluoromethane, CCl_2F_2. It was developed as a **refrigerant** to replace ammonia which was dangerous if it leaked out because it is toxic. Midgley demonstrated that his replacement substance was not toxic and was not flammable at a meeting of the American Chemical Society. He inhaled a lungful of it and used it to blow out a candle! The halogenoalkanes have since found uses as **flame retardants**, making flammable materials safer to use.

Dichlorodifluoromethane was later used as an **aerosol propellant**. Other CFCs were developed for other applications. Trichlorofluoromethane, CCl_3F, was used as a **blowing agent** for making expanded foam plastics. 1,1,2-trichloro-1,2,2-trifluoroethane was used as a **solvent for degreasing** electronic circuits.

Can you draw a molecule of this compound?

Unfortunately the very stability of CFCs has lead to a serious environmental problem. They can persist in the atmosphere for about 100 years. This allows them to be carried to the upper atmosphere, the stratosphere, where they meet high energy ultraviolet radiation coming from the Sun. The CFCs break down releasing chlorine atoms (free radicals). For example

$$CCl_3F \xrightarrow{\text{light}} CCl_2F\bullet + Cl\bullet$$

These atoms react rapidly with **ozone** (O_3) molecules which protect us from damaging ultraviolet radiation from the Sun.

The reaction is complex, but in the first step the chlorine free radical destroys an ozone molecule.

It has been calculated that one chlorine atom can remove a million ozone molecules.

CFCs from old refrigerators can contribute to damage to the ozone layer

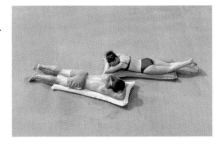

Scientists have predicted that if just 1% of the ozone layer is destroyed there could be 70 000 new cases of skin cancer around the world each year

Replacing CFCs

When it was realised that CFCs were ***depleting the ozone layer*** their use began to be phased out. Some of the important replacements developed are HFCs, hydrofluorocarbons, which break down more quickly in the atmosphere and do not release chlorine atoms. For example 1,1,1,2-tetrafluoroethane, CF_3CH_2F, is now used as a refrigerant.

This aerosol contains no CFCs

Lava lamps

Lava lamps were first sold in the 1960s by Haggerty Enterprises of Chicago, USA. Originally they were marketed as a soft light for people who enjoyed watching late night television. They have remained popular as a novelty feature, particularly with students.

Lava lamps rely on the principle that non-polar alkanes and polar water molecules don't mix. Alkanes, however, are less dense than water and would simply float on top. Chlorinated alkanes mix well with alkanes but are more dense because they contain heavier chlorine atoms. A mixture of alkanes and chlorinated alkanes is used in a lava lamp which is just denser than water. A bright dye to colour the organic layer and a polymer to make the water layer more viscous complete the mixture in the lamp.

A lava lamp has an ordinary light bulb at its base. When switched on it warms the solid alkane/chlorinated alkane mixture above it. A heat transfer coil helps speed up the melting process. The organic liquid expands as it melts, becomes less dense than the water and slowly floats upwards. As it reaches the top of the glass container it cools, contracts, becomes more dense than water and sinks.

Lava lamps contain chloroalkanes

'Halogeno-plastics'

Many plastics contain halogen atoms. The most common is PVC (polyvinyl chloride). It has many uses, from waterproof clothing to replacement windows.

One problem with disposing of the plastic by incineration (see page 174) is that acidic hydrogen chloride gas is given off. This can be removed by 'scrubbing' the gases leaving the chimney with a basic slurry.

Another common plastic is formed from tetrafluoroethene. It is used to make non-stick linings for pans.

'Teflon' was originally developed by rocket scientists!

Other uses of halogenoalkanes

The compound 2-bromo-2-chloro-1,1,1-trifluoroethane, $CF_3CHBrCl$, is known by the name Halothane. It has been developed as an **anaesthetic** for use in hospitals.

Chloralkanes are very good solvents. Dichloromethane is used as a **paint stripper** because it can even dissolve dried paint. It has largely replaced trichloromethane and tetrachlomethane because it is much less toxic.

Halogenoalkanes are also used by **dry cleaners**.

Halogenoalkanes are good at dissolving grease

Summary

- If we replace one or more hydrogen atoms in an alkane by halogen atoms, we get a halogenoalkane (haloalkane).
- The **iodoalkanes are the most reactive** because the C—I bond is weaker than C—Br, C—Cl and C—F. The C—F bond is strongest.
- **Halogenoalkanes** are attacked by nucleophiles (electron-rich species) because the carbon next to the halogen carries a partial positive charge. They undergo **nucleophilic substitution**.
- Suitable nucleophiles include alkali, OH^-(aq), cyanide, CN^-(aq), ammonia, NH_3, and amines. Water will also attack them.
- Their reaction with cyanide means that halogenoalkanes are important intermediates in making new compounds in industry.
- Halogenoalkanes also undergo **elimination** reactions with hydroxide ions dissolved in ethanol.

You can read about their many uses on the previous pages and see a summary of their reactions on page 266.

▷ Questions

1 Copy and complete:

The halogenoalkanes are attacked by ...., undergoing .... reactions. The attacking species all have a .... pair of .... which form a bond with the .... atom next to the halogen.

The reaction with OH^-(aq) will give an ...., whereas OH^- dissolved in ethanol will yield an ..... This is an example of an .... reaction.

Ammonia gives an .... , and cyanide produces a ..... Fluoroethane will be .... reactive than iodoethane because the C—F bond is much .... than the C—I bond.

2 Draw these molecules:
   a) iodomethane
   b) 1,2-dibromopentane
   c) 1,1,1-trichloropropane
   d) 2,3-dibromo-1,1-difluorobutane

3 Complete these equations, and name all the organic compounds involved:

   a) $CH_3CH_2CH_2CH_2Cl + CN^-$(aq) $\longrightarrow$ .... + ...

   b) $(CH_3)_2CHBr + OH^-$(aq) $\longrightarrow$ .... + ...

   c) $CH_3CH_2Cl + OH^-$(ethanol) $\longrightarrow$ .... + ... + ...

   d) $CH_3I + CN^-$(aq) $\longrightarrow$ .... + ...

   e) $CH_3CH_2Br + NH_3 \longrightarrow$ .... + ...
   (in excess)

   f) $CH_3CH_2CH_2Br + (CH_3CH_2CH_2)_3N \longrightarrow$ ....

4 Look at the apparatus below:

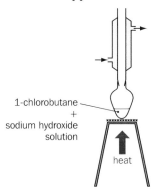

1-chlorobutane + sodium hydroxide solution

heat

   a) What do we call this method of heating?
   b) Why do we need to use it in the reaction above?
   c) What else would you add to the flask to make sure the reaction mixture boils smoothly?
   d) Write an equation for the reaction in the flask.
   e) Explain its mechanism.
   f) How would the mechanism differ if we had used a tertiary halogenoalkane?

5 Look at the table of boiling points below:

Halogenoalkane	Boiling point/°C
dichloromethane	40.1
trichloromethane	61.8
tetrachloromethane	76.6
dibromomethane	97.1

How does the boiling point vary with the relative formula mass in these compounds? Explain the trend.

6 Show the uses of halogenoalkanes on a spider diagram.

Most people are familiar with the word 'alcohol'.
It is used in *everyday* life to describe a variety of drinks
from 'alcopops' to whisky.
But how many people know the actual compound responsible
for the intoxicating effect of these drinks? Do you?

The alcohol referred to in 'alcoholic' drinks is **ethanol**.
The alcohols are the family of compounds in which
one (or more) ––OH group replaces an H atom in an alkane.
You will now be able to tell the structure of ethanol from its name:

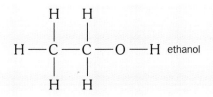 ethanol

This molecule has been used to make wine, beer and spirits
long before people knew about its chemistry.
Ethanol can be formed by the action of yeast on sugar.
The first alcoholic drink was probably made by crushing grapes,
then leaving the mixture in a warm place. The white coating
you see on the skins of grapes is a natural yeast.
The reaction can be shown as:

$$C_6H_{12}O_6 \xrightarrow[\text{yeast}]{\text{fermentation}} 2\,C_2H_5OH + 2\,CO_2$$

glucose   **ethanol**   **carbon dioxide**

You can read more about how we make ethanol and its uses
on page 200.

Alcoholic drinks contain ethanol

Grapes are fermented to make wine

▷ Physical properties

The boiling points of the alcohols are relatively high
when compared with those of the corresponding alkane.
For example, ehanol boils at 78 °C whereas ethane boils at −88.5 °C.
The smaller alcohols also mix well (are **miscible**) with water,
unlike alkanes.

Obviously the —OH group has a big effect on the properties of an alcohol.
What type of forces do you think operate between their molecules?
Larger van der Waals' forces can't account for the higher than expected
boiling points.
Do you recall the name of the particularly strong dipole–dipole
intermolecular forces? They exist when molecules contain
a hydrogen atom bonded to a very electronegative atom.
Do we have this situation in an alcohol?

Look at the diagram opposite:

There is hydrogen bonding between the molecules in an alcohol.

hydrogen bonds

▷ Reactions of the alcohols

Oxidation

We have already seen compounds with primary, secondary and tertiary structures.
Look at the alcohols below:

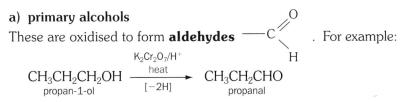

a primary alcohol   a secondary alcohol   a tertiary alcohol

In most organic reactions the functional group determines the product formed with a particular reagent. For example, you learn that halogenoalkanes react with aqueous sodium hydroxide and that an alcohol is formed. You then know that this applies to any halogenoalkane. The actual structure of the compound may affect the rate of the reaction, but not the type of product formed.

However, with the alcohols, although they all contain the —OH group, the position of the group is sometimes important.
This is true when we oxidise an alcohol.
We can use potassium dichromate(VI) solution, $K_2Cr_2O_7$, acidified with dilute sulphuric acid.

> In organic reactions it is useful to think of oxidation and reduction as:

a) primary alcohols

These are oxidised to form **aldehydes** $-C\overset{\displaystyle O}{\underset{\displaystyle H}{\diagup}}$. For example:

$$CH_3CH_2CH_2OH \xrightarrow[\text{[−2H]}]{\overset{K_2Cr_2O_7/H^+}{\text{heat}}} CH_3CH_2CHO$$
propan-1-ol   propanal

> **Oxidation is the addition of oxygen atoms or the removal of hydrogen atoms.**
> **Reduction is the removal of oxygen atoms or the addition of hydrogen atoms.**

● Can you see what has happened to the $CH_3CH_2CH_2OH$ molecule? How many H atoms does it lose?

If the oxidising agent is in excess, the aldehyde is then oxidised.

The **carboxylic acid** is formed $-C\overset{\displaystyle O}{\underset{\displaystyle OH}{\diagup}}$:

$$CH_3CH_2CHO \xrightarrow[\text{[+O]}]{\overset{K_2Cr_2O_7/H^+}{}} CH_3CH_2COOH$$
propanal   propanoic acid

● Can you see what has happened to the CH_3CH_2CHO molecule? How many oxygen atoms has it gained?

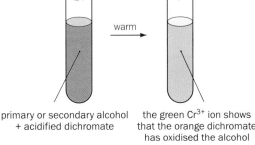

primary or secondary alcohol + acidified dichromate → (warm) the green Cr^{3+} ion shows that the orange dichromate has oxidised the alcohol

We can also oxidise the alcohols using alkaline potassium manganate(VII) solution.
In industry alcohols are oxidised using air and a catalyst such as silver.

b) secondary alcohols

If you start with a secondary alcohol, the oxidation will give a **ketone** $\diagdown C\!=\!O$:

$$\underset{\text{propan-2-ol}}{CH_3\overset{\displaystyle OH}{\underset{\displaystyle |}{C}}HCH_3} \xrightarrow[\text{heat}]{K_2Cr_2O_7/H^+} \underset{\text{propanone}}{CH_3\overset{\displaystyle O}{\underset{\displaystyle \|}{C}}CH_3}$$

> **In industry:**
>
> $$CH_3OH + O_2$$
> methanol   air
>
> $$\xrightarrow{\text{Ag} \mid 500\ °C}$$
>
> $HC\overset{\displaystyle O}{\underset{\displaystyle H}{\diagup}} + 2\,H_2O$
> methanal

● Can you see why we can't get an aldehyde formed from a secondary alcohol?
Can you ever get a hydrogen bonded to the same carbon that forms the C=O bond?
Remember that there are two alkyl groups attached to that carbon!
● Why is it very hard to oxidise the ketone formed to a carboxylic acid?

It is also impossible to oxidise a tertiary alcohol without breaking a C—C bond.
● Why can't we get a C=O bond forming in this case?

> ● *Why is this method, rather than a chemical oxidising agent, chosen in industry?*

▷ Breaking the O—H bond

Reaction with sodium

Can you remember what happens when sodium metal reacts with water?
Which gas is given off?

The reaction with an alcohol is similar, though not as vigorous. It is sometimes used to get rid of small amounts of sodium left over after experiments.
Why would it be an unsuitable way to dispose of large quantities of sodium?
Here is the equation for a typical reaction:

$$2\,CH_3CH_2OH + 2\,Na \longrightarrow 2\,CH_3CH_2O^-Na^+ + H_2$$

ethanol   sodium   sodium ethoxide   hydrogen gas

Sodium reacts with ethanol, giving off hydrogen gas

The balanced equation can also be written:

$$CH_3CH_2OH + Na \longrightarrow CH_3CH_2O^-Na^+ + \tfrac{1}{2}H_2$$

You might recall from previous work that:
an acid + metal $\longrightarrow$ a salt + hydrogen
In this reaction the alcohol is acting as an acid.
It loses an H^+ from the hydroxyl, —OH, group
and a salt is made (sodium ethoxide in the example above).

Reaction with carboxylic acids

The alcohols react slowly with carboxylic acids.
H^+ ions from a strong acid catalyse the reaction.
An equilibrium mixture is produced. The ester and water
made react together to re-form the reactants.

The general equation is:

> **alcohol + carboxylic acid $\overset{acid}{\rightleftharpoons}$ ester + water**

Some esters can be used as additives for foods.
Many have pleasant smells. (See page 236.)

The characteristic smells of fruits are often the result of esters. Artificial flavourings use synthetic esters to imitate nature

An example of a typical reaction is:

$$CH_3CH_2CH_2OH + CH_3COOH \longrightarrow CH_3COOCH_2CH_2CH_3 + H_2O$$

propan-1-ol   ethanoic acid   propyl ethanoate   water

If you consider the mechanism of this reaction there are two alternatives:
a) The C—O bond breaks in the alcohol, i.e.

$$CH_3CH_2CH_2{-}OH + \underset{H-O}{\overset{O}{\diagdown}}CCH_3 \longrightarrow \overset{O}{\diagdown}CCH_3 + H_2O \quad ✗$$

$$CH_3CH_2CH_2-O$$

b) The O—H bond breaks in the alcohol, i.e.

$$CH_3CH_2CH_2-O{+}H + \underset{HO}{\overset{O}{\diagdown}}CCH_3 \longrightarrow \overset{O}{\diagdown}CCH_3 + H_2O \quad ✓$$

$$CH_3CH_2CH_2-O$$

Experiments have been carried out using alcohol with ^{18}O atoms.
These 'labelled' atoms can be detected by their extra mass.
They show that the ^{18}O atoms are found in the ester after the reaction.
This provides us with evidence that mechanism b) is correct.
● Can you see why? Where would the ^{18}O atoms end up if a) was correct?

▷ Nucleophilic substitution in alcohols

Breaking the C—O bond

In the last chapter we saw the bond between a carbon and a halogen atom was polarised.
Can you recall which was more electronegative – the carbon or the halogen?
A similar situation exists with the alcohols.

Let's look at the nature of the C—O bond in an alcohol.
The electronegativity of carbon is 2.5, whereas oxygen's is 3.5.
So which atom has the greater 'pull' on the electrons in the C—O bond?
The carbon atom will be deficient in electrons compared with the oxygen atom.
So the carbon will carry a partial positive charge.
Therefore it will be open to attack from nucleophiles.
(Remember that these are electron-rich species.)
Let's look at an example of attack by a nucleophile below.

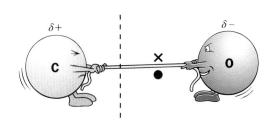

Oxygen has a greater attraction for the electrons in the C—O bond

Halogenation

We can replace the hydroxyl group (—OH) with a halogen atom.
The reactants are the alcohol plus the hydrogen halide.
The nucleophile will be a halide ion.

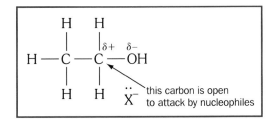

Alcohols undergo nucleophilic substitution

a) Substitution by chlorine

The reaction with dry hydrogen chloride gas is catalysed by zinc chloride.
The alcohol is boiled under reflux as the gas is bubbled through.

$$CH_3CH_2OH + HCl \longrightarrow CH_3CH_2Cl + H_2O$$
ethanol   chloroethane

Mechanism

Step 1:

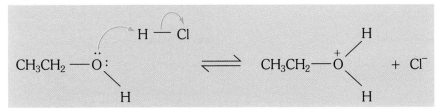

This is called **protonation** of the alcohol.

The zinc chloride catalyst (or a strong acid providing H^+ ions) speeds up the protonation step.

Step 2:

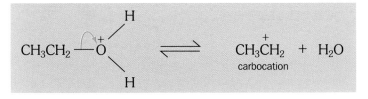

Protonation makes it easier for the alcohol to lose water.

Step 3:

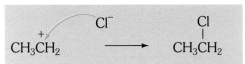

Steps 2 and 3 can happen simultaneously.

We can also use **phosphorus(v) chloride** to make a chloroalkane.
This reaction happens rapidly at room temperature:

$$CH_3CH_2OH + PCl_5 \longrightarrow CH_3CH_2Cl + POCl_3 + HCl$$

The fumes of HCl given off can be used as **a test for the —OH group**.

b) Substitution by bromine or iodine

The hydrogen halide for this reaction, or for chlorination, can be produced **in situ**.
This means that the reagents to make the hydrogen halide are mixed with the alcohol. For example, HBr is made by reacting potassium bromide with concentrated sulphuric acid:

$$KBr + H_2SO_4 \longrightarrow KHSO_4 + HBr$$

The HBr then reacts with the alcohol also present in the mixture.
For example:

$$\underset{\text{propan-1-ol}}{CH_3CH_2CH_2OH} + HBr \longrightarrow \underset{\text{1-bromopropane}}{CH_3CH_2CH_2Br} + H_2O$$

Alternatively, we can use phosphorus(III) bromide or iodide (PBr_3 or PI_3).
These can also be made *in situ* by refluxing bromine or iodine with red phosphorus and the alcohol. For example:

$$\underset{\text{ethanol}}{3\,CH_3CH_2OH} + PI_3 \longrightarrow \underset{\text{iodoethane}}{3\,CH_3CH_2I} + H_3PO_3$$

▷ Dehydration reaction

The last type of reaction that alcohols undergo is **dehydration**.

> **Dehydration is the removal of a water molecule from a reactant, i.e. $-H_2O$**

This happens when we heat the alcohol with concentrated sulphuric acid:

$$CH_3CH_2OH \xrightarrow[\text{heat}]{\text{c. } H_2SO_4} CH_2{=}CH_2 + H_2O$$

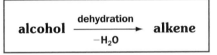

We can think of the mechanism as shown below:

Step 1: Protonation:

$$CH_3CH_2 - \underset{H}{O} + H^+ \rightleftharpoons CH_3CH_2 - \overset{+}{O}\underset{H}{\overset{H}{<}}$$
from H_2SO_4

Step 2: Loss of water:

$$CH_3CH_2 - \overset{+}{O}\underset{H}{\overset{H}{<}} \rightleftharpoons CH_3\overset{+}{C}H_2 + H_2O$$

Step 3: Loss of H^+:

$$CH_3 - \overset{+}{C}H_2 + HSO_4^- \rightleftharpoons CH_2{=}CH_2 + H_2SO_4$$

In reality the second two steps may both happen at once.
In excess alcohol, the carbocation formed in Step 2 can be attacked by the nucleophilic oxygen atom in an alcohol molecule.
This produces some ether in the products:

$$CH_3 - \overset{+}{C}H_2 \quad \overset{..}{:}O - CH_2CH_3 \longrightarrow \underset{\text{ethoxyethane}}{CH_3CH_2 - O - CH_2CH_3} + H^+$$

Excess acid limits the amount of ether formed.
Dehydration can also occur if we pass hot alcohol vapour over an aluminium oxide catalyst.

Q *What reaction do camels never undergo?*

A *Dehydration!*

▷ Chemistry at work: Ethanol

Drink to the fuel of the future?

People are becoming increasingly interested in using ethanol as a fuel.
It is already used here on a small scale in heaters as methylated spirits.
This is mainly industrially produced ethanol, with the more toxic alcohol
methanol added. This makes it cheaper, as no tax is paid because
you can't drink it. ('Meths drinkers' risk blindness and death!)

The industrial production uses ethene as a raw material.
We get ethene by the cracking of fractions from crude oil.
This is reacted with steam, using a catalyst of phosphoric(V) acid
at 350 °C and 60 atmospheres pressure:

$$CH_2{=}CH_2(g) + H_2O(g) \xrightarrow{\text{H}_3\text{PO}_4 \text{ catalyst}} CH_3CH_2OH(g)$$

ethene   steam   ethanol

*Ethanol burns with a 'clean' flame.
It produces less carbon monoxide and
carbon particles (soot) than hydrocarbons*

This is a relatively cheap process, especially for countries with
their own oil fields. But it is still more expensive than petrol,
and to make it this way still uses up our dwindling oil reserves.

Brazil has started making ethanol on a large scale, but not from ethene.
It does not have its own supply of crude oil and is trying to import less.
Brazil has the right climate to grow plenty of sugar cane.
The sugar is fermented with yeast to produce ethanol, not for drinking,
but as fuel for cars. The equation for fermentation is:

$$C_6H_{12}O_6 \xrightarrow{\text{fermentation}} 2\,C_2H_5OH + 2\,CO_2$$

*Brazil manufactures ethanol
on a large scale*

The ethanol cannot form more than 15% of the fermenting mixture.
In higher concentrations, the ethanol poisons the yeast (which is a fungus).
So to get the ethanol you have to distil the mixture.
This heating, of course, requires energy and therefore costs money
and uses up more precious resources. But more sugar cane can be grown
each year. It is a renewable source of energy, unlike fossil fuels.
The ethanol itself can be used in cars with adapted engines
or in normal cars as a mixture with petrol. The mixture is called 'gasohol'.

But it is the environment that could really benefit if we start using
ethanol as fuel. As you know, the huge volumes of carbon dioxide
given off when we burn fossil fuels are causing the 'greenhouse effect'.
(See page 169.) The carbon that has been 'locked away' for millions of years
in coal, oil and natural gas is being released.
But ethanol also gives off carbon dioxide when it is made and when it burns:

$$C_2H_5OH(l) + 3\,O_2(g) \xrightarrow{\text{combustion}} 2\,CO_2(g) + 3\,H_2O(g)$$

However, the carbon dioxide released into the atmosphere is balanced by
the carbon dioxide absorbed during photosynthesis as the sugar cane grew:

$$6\,CO_2(g) + 6\,H_2O(l) \xrightarrow{\text{photosynthesis}} C_6H_{12}O_6(aq) + 6\,O_2(g)$$

*Like all green plants, sugar cane removes
carbon dioxide from the air during
photosynthesis*

● Try making a balance sheet for CO_2 taken in and given out
  per mole of ethanol produced, then burned.

▷ Chemistry at work: Other alcohols

The 'baby' of the family

Methanol is becoming more important in industry.
On the last page we saw how it is added to industrial alcohol.
A purple dye is also added to make methylated spirits.
On page 172 we looked at the need for oil companies to change
their petrol mixtures depending on the season.
Methanol is sometimes one of the ingredients used in blending petrol.
Its octane number is 114. (See page 172.)
It is also cheap and, like ethanol, burns with a cleaner flame
than the hydrocarbons used in petrol. It produces less carbon monoxide.

However, volume for volume, it produces less energy, so
you would need bigger fuel tanks on cars or more frequent visits
to fill up with fuel. It also absorbs water vapour from the air
(it is said to be hygroscopic). This corrodes parts of the engine.

Methanol is also being used more often as a starting material
for making new compounds in industry.

*Some cars in Germany and the U.S.A.
run on methanol*

Anti-freeze – a co-ol alcohol

Ice has a much more open structure than liquid water. When water
freezes its volume expands by 10 per cent. Antifreeze is added to car
radiators during winter to prevent the water from freezing, expanding
and cracking the engine.

A common antifreeze is ethane-1,2-diol, CH_2OHCH_2OH, often known
under the name ethylene glycol. Mixing equal parts of this liquid with
water lowers the freezing point to $-37\,°C$. Since the temperature outside
rarely falls this low, the coolant remains liquid and the engine is
protected.

Ethane-1,2-diol also protects engines against corrosion (unlike methanol
above!). And because it has 2 hydroxyl (OH) groups it mixes very well
with water in the cooling system. Can you explain why?
(Think about hydrogen bonding.)

However, the toxic nature of the compound is a concern at airports.
Aircraft are routinely sprayed with antifreeze before they take off in cold
weather. The de-icing of a single Boeing 737 uses about $1500\,dm^3$ of
the fluid. Modern airports recycle it to prevent it getting into
water courses.

A non-toxic replacement antifreeze has been developed. It contains
propane-1,2-diol. Far from being toxic this alcohol is an approved
component of cosmetics and snack foods.

Can you draw a molecule of the compound?

*This plane is being de-iced with
ethane-1,2-diol*

Summary

- Alcohols contain at least one —OH group (sometimes called a hydroxyl group).
- They have higher boiling points than expected because of hydrogen bonding between their molecules.
- Primary alcohols are oxidised to aldehydes, then to carboxylic acids.
  Secondary alcohols are oxidised to ketones.
  Tertiary alcohols cannot be oxidised easily.
- The O—H bond breaks when the alcohol reacts with:
  i) sodium to form an alkoxide + hydrogen,
  ii) a carboxylic acid to form an ester + water.
- The C—O bond breaks when the alcohol reacts with a nucleophile, such as a halide ion. The —OH is replaced by the halogen.
  This is an example of **nucleophilic substitution**.
- Alcohols also undergo **dehydration** (removal of H_2O) when heated with concentrated sulphuric acid.
  An alkene is produced.

  You can see a summary of the alcohols' reactions on page 266.

▷ Questions

1 Copy and complete:
The smallest member of the alcohols is .... whose formula is CH_3OH. Like other alcohols, its boiling point is .... than expected for a molecule of its mass. This is because of .... bonding between its molecules. It reacts with sodium, giving off .... gas and forming .... methoxide. It will also react with a carboxylic acid to form an .... and water. A little concentrated sulphuric acid is added to .... this reaction.

When you oxidise a primary alcohol, an .... is formed. On further oxidation, this turns into a .... acid. On the other hand, secondary alcohols form .... when they are oxidised.

Alcohols undergo .... substitution with hydrogen chloride, in the presence of a strong acid or zinc chloride .....
When heated with concentrated sulphuric acid they undergo a .... reaction, forming an .... plus water.

2 a) Draw the following molecules:

  i)   ethanol
  ii) propan-2-ol
  iii) propane-1,2-diol

b) Predict the order of the boiling points of the three alcohols in part a).
   Explain your answer.

c) Do you think the three molecules will be miscible (mix well) with water?
   Explain your answer.

3 Look at the change shown below:

$$CH_3CH_2OH \longrightarrow CH_3CHO \longrightarrow CH_3COOH$$

a) What do we call these types of reaction?
b) What reagents and conditions are needed for the reactions to take place?
c) Name the products formed in each reaction.
d) Name the product if we had started with propan-2-ol.

4 Complete these equations:

a) $CH_3CH_2CH_2OH + Na \longrightarrow$ .... + ...

b) $CH_3OH + PCl_5 \longrightarrow$ ... + $POCl_3$ + ...

c) $CH_3CHOHCH_3 + HCl \longrightarrow$ .... + ...

d) $CH_3CH_2OH + PI_3 \longrightarrow$ .... + H_3PO_3

5 a) Name the products when propan-2-ol is heated with concentrated sulphuric acid.
b) What do we call this type of reaction?
c) What type of compound can also be produced if we have excess propan-2-ol present?

6 Ethanol is produced when glucose solution, $C_6H_{12}O_6$, is mixed with yeast in warm conditions.

a) What do we call this type of reaction?
b) Write an equation to show the reaction to form ethanol.
c) How is ethanol made from ethene? Give an equation and the conditions used.
d) Discuss the advantages and disadvantages of producing ethanol by each method above for use as a fuel in cars.

▷ Introduction to organic chemistry

1 Draw the structure of 2-chloro-3-methylbutane. [1]
(WJEC)

2 Analysis of an organic compound, which contains carbon, hydrogen and oxygen only, gave 54.5% by mass of carbon and 9.1% by mass of hydrogen. Its relative molecular mass was found to be 88. Calculate the empirical and molecular formula of the compound.

3 A compound, **X**, has a molar mass of $58.08 \, \text{g mol}^{-1}$ and the following composition by mass.

C 62.04%; H 10.41%; O 27.55%.

Calculate the molecular formula of **X**. [2]
(WJEC)

▷ The alkanes

4 Petrol is a mixture which includes alkanes of chain length C_5 to C_{10}. It burns explosively in a car engine to provide energy.
a) Write an equation for the complete combustion of octane, C_8H_{18}. [2]
b) Name **two** other products formed by the incomplete combustion of petrol. [2]
c) Draw and name one branched-chain isomer of hexane, C_6H_{14}. [2]
(NICCEA)

5 A great variety of hydrocarbons with chain and ring structures can form because carbon atoms have the ability to form strong and stable bonds with other carbon atoms and with hydrogen atoms. Structural isomerism is possible, so that different compounds can exist which have the same molecular formula. In unsaturated hydrocarbons, different compounds can sometimes exist which have the same structural formula.
a) Explain the meaning of the term *saturated*, giving the structural formula of a saturated hydrocarbon.
b) i) Explain the meaning of the term *structural isomerism*.
   ii) Draw the three structural isomers of molecular formula C_4H_8.
(AQA)

6 The alkane heptane, C_7H_{16}, is found in one of the fractions obtained in the fractional distillation of petroleum.
a) What property of the fractions allows them to be separated in this way?
   Name a fraction in which heptane occurs. [2]
b) Write an equation for the complete combustion of heptane. [1]
(AQA)

7 In diffused light methane combines readily with chlorine in a photochemical substitution reaction forming chloromethane as the initial organic product. Further chlorination produces a mixture of chlorinated hydrocarbons.
a) Explain the term **photochemical substitution**. [2]
b) Write equations to represent the following steps in the reaction:
   i) The initial step [1]
   ii) Two propagation steps [2]
   iii) A termination step. [1]
(NICCEA)

8 a) When excess methane reacts with chlorine, the main product is chloromethane.
   i) Under what conditions does this reaction occur? [1]
   ii) Give the mechanism for this reaction. [4]
b) Heptane and octane are liquids at room temperature with boiling points of 98 °C and 126 °C respectively. What type of intermolecular forces of attraction are present in such liquids? [1]
c) Liquid alkanes such as heptane and octane occur in petrol used as fuel to drive cars.
   i) Give two reasons why liquid fuels are generally preferred to gaseous ones. [2]
   ii) The combustion characteristics of fuels for internal combustion engines in cars can be considerably improved by adding branched chain alkanes, cycloalkanes, aromatic hydrocarbons or tetraethyllead(IV) (lead tetraethyl). Two of these are now considered to be hazardous to health. Select these two and identify the health hazard with which each is associated. [2]
(EDEXCEL)

9 Butane reacts with chlorine, in a free radical chain reaction, to form 1-chlorobutane as one of the products. The reaction takes place in a number of steps:

Step 1

$$\text{Cl}-\text{Cl} \longrightarrow \text{Cl} \cdot + \text{Cl} \cdot \qquad \text{Initiation}$$

Step 2

$$\text{Cl} \cdot + \text{CH}_3\text{CH}_2\text{CH}_2\text{CH}_3 \longrightarrow \text{CH}_3\text{CH}_2\text{CH}_2\dot{\text{C}}\text{H}_2 + \text{HCl}$$

Step 3

$$\text{CH}_3\text{CH}_2\text{CH}_2\dot{\text{C}}\text{H}_2 + \text{Cl}_2 \longrightarrow \text{CH}_3\text{CH}_2\text{CH}_2\text{CH}_2\text{Cl} + \text{Cl} \cdot$$

Step 4

$$\text{CH}_3\text{CH}_2\text{CH}_2\dot{\text{C}}\text{H}_2 + \text{Cl} \cdot \longrightarrow \text{CH}_3\text{CH}_2\text{CH}_2\text{CH}_2\text{Cl} \qquad \text{Termination}$$

a) What condition is needed to promote **Step 1**? [1]
b) What type of bond breaking occurs in **Step 1**? [1]
c) Classify the type of reaction step occurring in **Steps 2** and **3**. [1]
d) Suggest an equation for another possible chain termination step. [1]

e) Give one other example of a reaction with a free radical chain mechanism. [1]

(EDEXCEL)

10 a) Name and give the molecular formula of the following hydrocarbon, **X**, which is a constituent of the fuel used in road vehicles

$$H_3C - \underset{\underset{\displaystyle CH_3}{|}}{\overset{\overset{\displaystyle CH_3}{|}}{C}} - CH_2 - \underset{\underset{\displaystyle CH_3}{|}}{CH} - CH_3$$

b) Using the molecular formula, write an equation for the complete combustion of **X**.

(AQA)

▷ The alkenes

11 Draw the full structural (graphic) formula of but-1-ene. [1]

(WJEC)

12 a) Explain how it is possible for two unsaturated molecules with the same structural formula to be different. [1]

b) Draw the structures of the two molecules with molecular formula C_4H_8 to illustrate your answer to a). [2]

c) What term is used to refer to this type of isomerism?

(AQA)

13 a) Heptane is cracked to form ethene and one other product. Name the type of mechanism involved in thermal cracking and write an equation for the reaction. [2]

(AQA)

14 Define the following terms and illustrate them by drawing displayed formulae in each case.

a) *Structural isomerism* showing appropriate isomers of C_4H_{10}. [4]

b) *Geometrical isomerism*, showing the appropriate isomers of C_4H_8. [4]

15 Which one of the following compounds exhibits *cis-trans* isomerism?

A $CH_3CH=CHCH_3$
B $(CH_3)_2C=CHCH_3$
C $(CH_3)_2C=CH_2$
D $CH_2=CHCH_2CH_3$

(NICCEA)

16 The structures of some organic compounds are given below:

$CHCl=CHCl$ $(CH_3)_2C=C(CH_3)_2$
     A   **B**

$(CH_3)_2CHCH(CH_3)Br$ $(CH_3)_2C=C(CH_3)Br$
     C   **D**

State which **one** of the compounds will exhibit geometrical isomerism. [1]

(WJEC)

17 Explain carefully why alkenes undergo electrophilic addition reactions. Outline the mechanism of the reaction between but-2-ene and bromine and name the product. [10]

(AQA)

18 Write a balanced equation to illustrate the cracking of decane, $C_{10}H_{22}$, to form ethene. [1]

(WJEC)

19 Propene can be used to make a number of important chemical products. The processes involved can be summarised in the diagram:

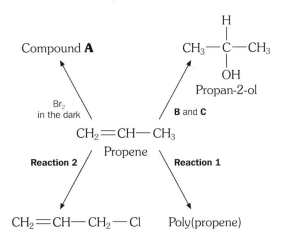

a) Give the **displayed** formula and name of compound **A**. [2]

b) State the type of reaction occurring and the type of reagent used in the formation of compound **A**. [2]

c) Give the formulae of compounds **B** and **C**. [2]

d) Write a **balanced** equation for the formation of poly(propene) from propene in **Reaction 1**. [2]

e) Suggest a reagent and condition for **Reaction 2**. [2]

f) State the type of mechanism in the substitution in **Reaction 2**. [1]

g) Give the systematic name for $CH_2=CH-CH_2-Cl$. [1]

(WJEC)

20 The structural formula of an alkene is given below:

$$\underset{\displaystyle H}{\overset{\displaystyle CH_3}{\diagdown}} C = C \underset{\displaystyle \underset{\underset{\displaystyle CH_3}{|}}{CHCH_3}}{\overset{\displaystyle H}{\diagup}}$$

Give the full systematic name of the alkene.

(WJEC)

21 a) i) Show the mechanism for the reaction of bromine with ethene. [2]

ii) Classify the mechanism of the reaction in (a) i). [1]

iii) State how alkenes are manufactured on a large scale. [1]

iv) Write a balanced equation for the direct hydration of ethene. [1]

b) Alkenes and substituted alkenes are the source of a large number of important polymers.
Name **one** polymer manufactured from a **substitute alkene**, show the structure of the repeating unit of the polymer chain and state a large scale use for the polymer. [2]

(WJEC)

22 a) There are both cyclic and non-cyclic isomers of hydrocarbons with a given molecular formula. [1]

i) Draw full structural formulae for cyclopropane, **A**, and cyclopropene, **B**. [2]

ii) Draw **two** non-cyclic structural isomers of **A** and **B**; state the class of compound to which each belongs. [2]

iii) A common polymer has the same empirical formula as **A**. Give the empirical formula, and the name of the polymer. [1]

b) 0.54 g of a hydrocarbon, **C**, were burnt in excess oxygen. The water produced was absorbed by passing through calcium chloride tubes, which gained 0.54 g in mass. The carbon dioxide was absorbed by potassium hydroxide, which gained 1.76 g.

i) Show that the empirical formula of **C** is C_2H_3. [2]

ii) Given that 0.01 mole of **C** was used, derive the molecular formula of **C**. Show your working. [2]

(OCR)

23 Myrcene, $C_{10}H_{16}$, is a naturally occurring oil present in bay leaves. The structure of myrcene is shown below.

a) Reaction of a 0.100 mol sample of myrcene with hydrogen at room temperature and pressure (r.t.p.) produced a saturated alkane, **A**.

i) Explain what is meant by the term *saturated alkane*.

ii) Determine the molecular formula of the saturated alkane, **A**.

iii) Construct a balanced equation for the reaction of myrcene with hydrogen.

iv) Calculate the volume of hydrogen that reacted with the sample of myrcene.
[1 mole of gas molecules occupy $24.0\,dm^3$ at r.t.p.] [5]

b) Squalene is a naturally occurring oil present in shark-liver oil. A 0.100 mol sample of squalene reacted with $14.4\,dm^3$ of hydrogen at r.t.p. to form a saturated hydrocarbon $C_{30}H_{62}$.

i) Calculate how many double bonds there are in each molecule of squalene.

ii) Suggest the molecular formula of squalene. [3]

(OCR)

24 Formation of epoxyethane by the partial oxidation of ethene by air, in the presence of a catalyst, is an exothermic process ($\Delta H = -210\,kJ\,mol^{-1}$).

a) Write an equation for the reaction, name the catalyst and suggest a hazard associated with the process. [4]

b) i) Write an equation for the reaction between one mole of epoxyethane and one mole of water. [2]

ii) Give the structure of the compound formed when the product in part b) i) undergoes a further reaction with two more moles of epoxyethane. [3]

(AQA)

25 a) Write an equation for the formation of epoxyethane from ethene and explain briefly why the product is highly reactive. [4]

b) Predict the major organic product of the reaction between but-1-ene and hydrogen bromide. Explain the basis of your prediction. [4]

(AQA)

▷ The halogenoalkanes (haloalkanes)

26 a) Give the structure of 2-bromo-2,3-dimethyl-butane. [1]

b) Name the *type* of reaction which could be used to convert this compound into 2,3-dimethylbutan-2-ol. Suggest a suitable reagent and the conditions for the reaction. [3]

(AQA)

27 a) Compound A ($M_r = 215.8$) contains 22.24% carbon, 3.71% hydrogen and 74.05% bromine by mass. Show that the molecular formula of A is $C_4H_8Br_2$. [3]

b) There are nine structural isomers of molecular formula $C_4H_8Br_2$, three of which have branched carbon chains. Give the names and draw the graphical formulae of any two of the branched chain isomers of $C_4H_8Br_2$. [4]

c) 2-bromopropane, $CH_3CH(Br)CH_3$, reacts with KOH to form two different products. One product is formed by an elimination reaction, while the other is formed by a substitution reaction. For each type of reaction, suggest the condition(s) most likely to lead to that type of reaction and draw the structure of the organic product. [4]

d) For the reaction between 2-bromopropane and potassium cyanide: [1]
   i) give the name or formula of the attacking species involved; [1]
   ii) give the name of the mechanism involved; [1]
   iii) write an equation for the reaction; [1]
   iv) draw the graphical (displayed) formula for the organic product. [1]
(AQA)

28 On heating, the compound 1-bromobutane, $CH_3CH_2CH_2CH_2Br$, undergoes reactions, as shown in the scheme below.

$$CH_3CH_2CH_2CH_2OH \xleftarrow{\textbf{I}} CH_3CH_2CH_2CH_2Br \xrightarrow{\textbf{II}} CH_3CH_2CH_2CH_2CN$$
$$\downarrow \textbf{III}$$
$$CH_3CH_2CH{=}CH_2$$

a) For each of the reactions shown, name the reagent and the solvent used. [6]

b) If 1-chlorobutane was used in the reaction **I** in place of 1-bromobutane, what difference (if any) would you expect in the rate of reaction? Explain your answer. [2]

c) If 2-bromo-2-methylpropane was used in reaction **I** in place of 1-bromobutane, what difference (if any) would you expect in the rate of reaction? Explain your answer. [2]
(OCR)

29 a) Name the type of reaction taking place when 2-bromopropane is converted into propene in the presence of a strong base. Outline a mechanism for this reaction. [5]

b) Give the structural formula of 2-bromo-2-methylbutane. [1]

c) Give the structural formulae of the two alkenes obtained when 2-bromo-2-methylbutane reacts with ethanolic potassium hydroxide.
Deduce the names of these two products. [4]
(AQA)

30 a) i) State the conditions under which chlorine and methane react. [1]
   ii) Name the classification which is given to the mechanism of this reaction. [1]

b) Give the systematic names **OR** formulae of the organic compounds, **A**, **B**, **C** and **D**, derived from 1-bromobutane in the reaction scheme below.

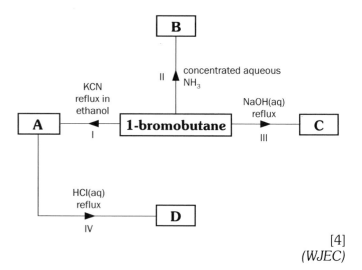

[4]
(WJEC)

31 For each of the following reactions, give the name of the type of mechanism involved and the formula of the attacking species.

a) $CH_3CH_2CH_2Br + NaOH \longrightarrow$
$$CH_3CH_2CH_2OH + NaBr$$

b) $C_2H_4 + HBr \longrightarrow CH_3CH_2Br$ [4]

32 a) A student attempted to analyse a sample of bromobutane for purity. One method was to hydrolyse the bromobutane with an excess of sodium hydroxide and to calculate the amount of alkali left by titration with hydrochloric acid.

$$C_4H_9Br + OH^- \longrightarrow C_4H_9OH + Br^-$$

Calculate the purity of the bromobutane from the following data:
mass of impure bromobutane $= 3.5\,g$
volume of 0.5 M sodium hydroxide $= 50.0\,cm^3$
volume of 0.1 M sodium hydroxide $= 10.0\,cm^3$
(A_r of C $= 12$, H $= 1$, Br $= 80$) [4]

b) Compare the ease of hydrolysis of 1-bromobutane with that of 1-iodobutane and 1-chlorobutane related to bond enthalpy and bond polarity.
(Up to 2 marks may be obtained for the quality of language in this part.) [7]
(NICCEA)

▷ **The alcohols**

33 Using structural formulae, complete and balance the equation for the fermentation of glucose:

$$C_6H_{12}O_6(aq) \longrightarrow \ldots\ldots + \ldots\ldots$$ [2]
(EDEXCEL)

34 Propene, C_3H_6, can be made by the dehydration of propan-1-ol.
a) Draw a displayed formula for propene. [1]
b) Propan-1-ol can be dehydrated by passing its vapour over a heated catalyst or by heating it with a dehydrating agent.
   Name
   i) a suitable catalyst and
   ii) a suitable dehydrating agent. [2]
c) i) Give the name of, and draw a displayed formula for, a secondary alcohol which is an isomer of propan-1-ol. [2]
   ii) If your laboratory had no propan-1-ol, would your isomer in c) i) be equally suitable for making propene?
   Justify your answer. [2]
   (AQA)

35 Two isomeric products of molecular formula C_6H_{12} are formed when 2,3-dimethylbutan-2-ol reacts with concentrated sulphuric acid.
a) Name the type of reaction taking place and give the structure of the carbonium ion intermediate formed.
b) Explain briefly why two products are formed and give the structures of these isomers. [6]
   (AQA)

36 There are four structurally isomeric alcohols of formula $C_4H_{10}O$. Graphical formulae of these isomers, labelled, A, B, C and D are shown below:

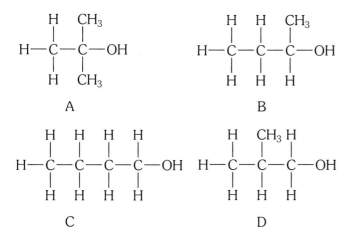

a) Identify the type of alcohol represented
   i) by A and
   i) by B. [2]
b) Give the name of alcohol A. [1]
c) Select one of the alcohols A, B, C or D which will, on oxidation, produce an aldehyde.
   i) Give the structural formula of the aldehyde produced in this reaction.
   ii) State the reagents and conditions required for the aldehyde to be the main product of the oxidation reaction. [3]

d) Alcohols A, B, C and D are readily dehydrated.
   i) What is meant by the term *dehydration*? [1]
   ii) State the type of compound formed by dehydration of alcohols. [1]
   iii) Suggest suitable reagent(s) and conditions for the dehydration of alcohols. [1]
   iv) Select one of the alcohols A, B, C or D which gives a single product on dehydration. Draw the structural formula of the product.
   v) Select one of the alcohols A, B, C or D which, on dehydration, would give two products which are structurally isomeric. Draw structural formulae for these isomers and explain why the formation of two structural isomers is possible in this case. [4]
   (AQA)

37 Some reactions of butan-2-ol are illustrated on the following reaction scheme.

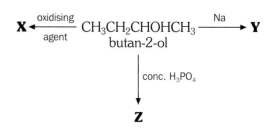

a) Write the name and structural formula for the organic product **X**. [2]
b) Name a suitable oxidizing agent for obtaining **X** and name a suitable acid to use with it. [2]
c) Give a formula for the ionic product **Y** showing clearly its ionic charges. [2]
d) **Z** is a mixture of isomeric products. Give structural formulae for two of them. [2]
e) What type of organic reaction is the production of **Z** from butan-2-ol? [1]
   (OCR)

38 a) i) Give the structure of 3-methylbutan-2-ol.
   ii) Name and outline the mechanism for the reaction taking place when 3-methylbutan-2-ol is converted into 2-methylbut-2-ene in the presence of a strong acid.
   iii) Explain why 3-methylbut-1-ene is also formed in this reaction. [8]
b) Give the structure of the product obtained when 3-methylbutan-2-ol is treated with acidified potassium dichromate(VI). [1]
   (AQA)

Further questions on organic chemistry 1

39 This question is about the preparation of ethyl ethanoate from ethanol and ethanoic acid by the following reaction

$$C_2H_5OH + CH_3CO_2H \rightleftharpoons CH_3CO_2C_2H_5 + H_2O$$

A student prepared ethyl ethanoate as follows:

- A mixture of ethanol, ethanoic acid and concentrated sulphuric acid was placed in a distillation flask fitted with a reflux condenser, the flask being immersed in a cold water bath.
- The water in the bath was then heated to boiling and the flask contents boiled under reflux for approximately 20 minutes.
- The flask was then allowed to cool and set up for distillation; ethyl ethanoate was distilled off.
- The ethyl ethanoate was shaken with aqueous sodium carbonate and the lower aqueous layer discarded. The upper ethyl ethanoate layer was shaken with aqueous calcium chloride to remove unused ethanol, the lower layer being discarded. The ethyl ethanoate was then placed in a flask with anhydrous calcium chloride and allowed to stand for half an hour.
- Finally, the liquid was filtered and re-distilled.

a) What is meant by the term **reflux** and why is it necessary in this preparation? [3]

b) Why was the ethyl ethanoate shaken with aqueous sodium carbonate? [2]

c) Why was the ethyl ethanoate allowed to stand in contact with anhydrous calcium chloride? [1]

d) The student reacted 21 g of pure ethanoic acid with the exactly calculated amount of ethanol and a small quantity of concentrated sulphuric acid. 20 g of ethyl ethanoate was obtained. What was the percentage yield? Suggest why a higher yield was not obtained. [5]

e) Identify the products of reaction if ethyl ethanoate is boiled with aqueous sodium hydroxide. [2]

(EDEXCEL)

What do you think the word **'aromatic'** means?
You've probably come across it in shops that sell aromatic oils,
or perhaps candles that give off aromatic fumes as they burn.
The word aromatic is used to describe a variety of pleasant-smelling
'aromatherapy' products.

The source of the odours is often an **aromatic compound**.
Their molecules contain one, or more, **benzene rings**.
The study of aromatic compounds makes up a large part
of chemical research.
Many of the products used in medicine and farming
are based on compounds containing benzene rings.

*Aromatherapy treatments
are becoming increasingly
popular*

▶ The structure of benzene

Benzene is a colourless, volatile liquid.
It has been used by chemists since the 1800s.
It is a good solvent for other organic compounds,
but is immiscible (does not mix) with water.
At one time, chemists used it with few precautions.
However, we know now that it is highly toxic,
and is said to be a carcinogen (a cancer-causing agent).
It can even be absorbed through the skin.

Early studies showed that the formula of benzene was C_6H_6.
But the chemists working around 1860 struggled to work out
its structure. Can you suggest a straight-chain structure for C_6H_6,
with each carbon forming four bonds and each hydrogen one bond?
It was then that a German chemist, called Friedrich August Kekulé,
had a strange dream. Pondering the problem, he dozed off
and dreamed that the benzene molecules were snakes!
One of the snakes bit its own tail, forming a circle.
When Kekulé woke up, he claimed that his dream inspired him
to propose the structure below:

*F.A. Kekulé proposed a structure for
benzene in 1865*

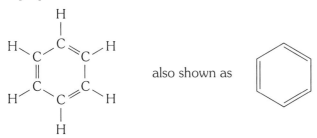

also shown as

But one thing still puzzled chemists. If Kekulé's structure was correct,
there should be two isomers of compounds like those opposite:
However, only one could be found.
This led Kekulé to suggest that benzene rapidly switched
between two equivalent structures. This is shown below:

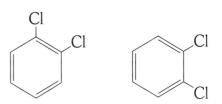

Evidence of isomers like these could not be found

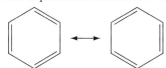

The equivalent structures are an example of **resonance**.

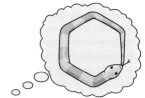

**The structure of benzene
can be summarised as:**

▷ The nature of the benzene ring

Building on Kekulé's ideas about the structure of benzene,
we now have experimental evidence to support our model.

X-ray diffraction studies provide us with the bond lengths and angles:

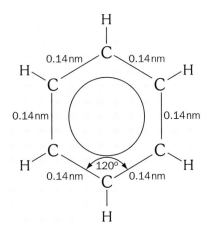

*This is an electron density map.
It shows the contours of charge density
(areas with lots of lines close together are
the places where you are most likely
to find electrons)*

What do you notice about the carbon–carbon bond lengths?
The carbons in the benzene ring form a symmetrical hexagon,
with all the atoms in the same plane. It is a flat (planar) molecule.

We can compare the bond lengths in benzene with the average values
found in single and double bonds.
Look at the table below:

Bond	Bond length / nm
C—C in cyclohexane	0.15
C┄┄C in benzene	**0.14**
C=C in cyclohexene	0.13

As you can see, the length of the carbon–carbon bonds in benzene
lies between the length of a single and double bond.
We can think of the bonds as a **hybrid** between a single and double bond.
Because all the bonds are equivalent, it is best to represent
benzene as shown below:

Do you recall the bonding in ethene? On page 174 we looked at
the nature of a double bond.
Look back to the diagram in the centre of page 174:

The bonding in benzene can be thought of as a basic framework
of single (sigma) σ bonds.
A p orbital from each carbon atom overlaps, above and below
the plane of the ring.
The p orbitals form two continuous loops, with each carbon donating
one electron into this π (pi) bond.
The electrons in the π bond are not then associated with
any particular carbon atom. They become **delocalised** electrons.
This is shown in the 'space-filling' model opposite:

The electron density map at the top of the page provides evidence
for this model.

However, the Kekulé structure is
still used at times.
For example, it is sometimes
useful when explaining
mechanisms.

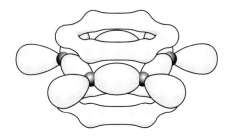

*You can see the delocalised rings of
electrons above and below the plane of
the atoms in this model*

▶ Attack on the benzene ring

Another difficulty with the Kekulé structure is the nature
of benzene's chemical reactions.
Imagine that benzene did actually contain three double bonds
within its ring of carbon atoms.
What reactions would you expect it to undergo?
(Think back to the alkenes in Chapter 14.)

In fact benzene does not easily take part in addition reactions.
Look at the results of the test opposite:
This is further proof that 'normal' double bonds
don't exist in benzene.

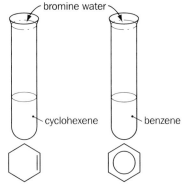

What does this test show?

However, like the alkenes, ***benzene is open to attack from electrophiles***.
Why do you think this is the case?
(Remember that electrophiles are 'electron-deficient'.)
Which part of the benzene molecule has a high electron density?
(Look at the electron density map on the last page.)

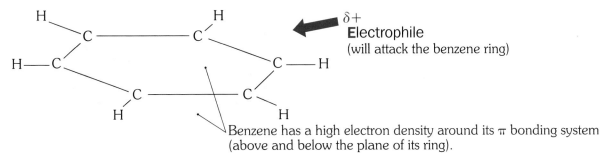

$\delta+$
Electrophile
(will attack the benzene ring)

Benzene has a high electron density around its π bonding system
(above and below the plane of its ring).

When an alkene reacts there is addition across its double bond.
This produces a molecule with only single bonds.
For example:

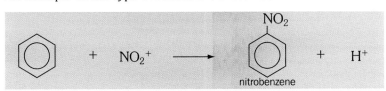

In benzene, this would disrupt its complete delocalised ring
of electrons. The product formed would be much less stable
than benzene itself. Therefore it is not likely to form.

However, benzene will react if it can keep its delocalised ring.
It does this by **substitution** of one, or more, of its hydrogen atoms
by a new atom or group of atoms.
Therefore:

I'll swap one of my H's
for an electrophile

Benzene undergoes electrophilic substitution reactions.

An example of this type of reaction is shown below:

$$\text{benzene} + NO_2^+ \longrightarrow \text{nitrobenzene}(NO_2) + H^+$$

nitrobenzene

Notice that the delocalised ring of electrons is still intact.
There is more evidence for the stability of benzene in question 3 on page 220.

▷ Electrophilic substitution in benzene

Nitration

Many of the dyes used to colour fabrics are derived from benzene.
We make benzene itself from the products of crude oil.
The benzene is then converted into nitrobenzene.
This reaction is called **nitration**.
The nitrobenzene is used to make the reactants to manufacture dyes.
Nitration is also important when making explosives, such as TNT
(**tri**nitro**tol**uene).

Nitrobenzene is used to make phenylamine – an important compound in the manufacture of dyes. (See page 218)

> **Nitration is the introduction of the —NO₂ group into a molecule.**

Conditions

Benzene is nitrated by *a mixture of concentrated nitric and sulphuric acids*.
The reactants are refluxed between 55 °C and 60 °C.

The mixture of acids react, forming the **NO₂⁺ electrophile**:

$$HNO_3 + 2\,H_2SO_4 \longrightarrow NO_2^+ + 2\,HSO_4^- + H_3O^+$$

nitryl cation
(or nitronium ion)

The powerful electrophile then attacks the benzene:

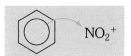

The nitrobenzene is a pale yellow oil that smells of almonds.
The overall equation can be summarised as:

benzene   nitrobenzene

The overall equation shown:

benzene $+ HNO_3 \xrightarrow[\text{55-60°C}]{\text{conc. } H_2SO_4}$ nitrobenzene $+ H_2O$

Mechanism

Let's see if we can explain how this reaction takes place.
Once the NO₂⁺ electrophile has been made, it is attracted
to the electron-rich ring of benzene:

NO₂⁺   (Remember that the curly arrow shows the movement of a pair of electrons.)

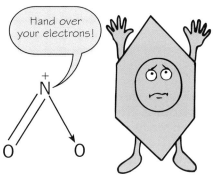

Hand over your electrons!

Electrophilic attack on the electron-rich benzene

The NO₂⁺ accepts a pair of electrons from the π bonding in the ring.
This forms an intermediate cation:

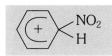

Notice that the highly stable delocalised ring of electrons has been disrupted.
To re-establish the delocalised ring, an H⁺ ion is released:

The intermediate cation could also lose the NO₂⁺ ion at this stage, forming benzene again.
Why do you think we have to heat the reacting mixture under reflux
to get a reasonable yield of nitrobenzene?

Sulphonation

> **Sulphonation is the introduction of the —SO₃H group into a molecule.**

Benzene is sulphonated by heating with concentrated sulphuric acid under reflux for several hours.
The reaction happens more quickly with 'fuming' sulphuric acid.
This contains sulphur trioxide (SO_3) in the acid.
The SO_3 is believed to be the electrophile.
Look at the molecule opposite:

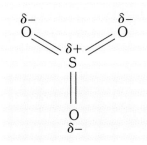

Which is more electronegative sulphur or oxygen?

* Which part of the SO_3 molecule will attack the benzene ring?
The equation is shown below:

benzenesulphonic acid

The product is used to make phenol (C_6H_5OH, ⬡—OH).
Phenol is used to make plastics and dyes.
It is also used to kill bacteria in products such as TCP
(**tri**chloro**p**henol).
Look at the molecule opposite:

OH
Cl—⬡—Cl
2,4,6-trichlorophenol
Cl

TCP contains a benzene ring substituted with one —OH group and three Cl atoms

Halogenation

As the name suggests, this reaction introduces a halogen atom into a molecule.
Bromine and chlorine react with benzene in the presence of a catalyst.
The catalyst can be iron(III) bromide or aluminum chloride.
Alternatively iron can be used, and the halide catalyst will be made
in situ (in the reaction flask).
In the reaction below, a bromine atom substitutes a hydrogen atom:

$$\text{⬡} + Br_2 \xrightarrow{FeBr_3} \text{⬡}-Br + HBr$$

bromobenzene

But where does the electrophile come from?
The answer to this lies with the catalyst.
The catalyst induces an imbalance of charge on the non-polar halogen molecule:

$$\overset{\delta+}{Br} \longrightarrow \overset{\delta-}{Br:} \longrightarrow FeBr_3$$

In this case, one of the Br atoms forms a dative bond
with the Fe^{3+} ion in $FeBr_3$. This draws electrons from the Br—Br bond,
leaving one Br atom slightly deficient in electrons. So this Br atom
carries a partial positive charge and it acts as the electrophile:

catalyst is regenerated

$$\text{⬡} \overset{\delta+}{Br}-\overset{\delta-}{Br} \rightarrow FeBr_3 \longrightarrow \text{⬡}\langle \overset{Br}{\underset{H}{}} + [FeBr_4]^- \longrightarrow \text{⬡}-Br + HBr + FeBr_3$$

bromobenzene

Chlorobenzene made by this reaction is also used to make phenol.

Friedel–Crafts reactions

Sometimes chemists need to modify an arene in order to make
new products to sell. Examples include detergents or the reactants needed
to make plastics, such as poly(phenylethene) – commonly called polystyrene.
To form these products they often have to substitute an alkyl group
(or an acyl group) for a hydrogen in the benzene ring.
Examples of alkyl and acyl groupings are shown below:

*Synthetic detergents often contain
derivatives of benzene with long alkyl
chains*

> **Friedel–Crafts** reactions result in *the introduction of a
> side-chain* into a benzene ring.
> They are called **alkylation** or **acylation** reactions.

You can see an example below:

$$\text{benzene} + CH_3CH_2Cl \xrightarrow[\text{catalyst}]{AlCl_3} \text{ethylbenzene} (CH_2CH_3) + HCl$$

The reactions are named after the chemists who first discovered them.
They involve attack on the benzene ring by an *electrophile*
carrying a positive charge on a carbon atom, i.e. a carbocation.

The electrophile is often formed by adding an aluminium chloride catalyst
to a halogenoalkane.
As we saw on the last page with iron(III) bromide, this induces a charge
on the reactant. It creates the electrophile:

$$CH_3-\underset{\underset{H}{|}}{\overset{\overset{H}{|}}{C}}-Cl \to AlCl_3 \longrightarrow CH_3\overset{+}{C}H_2 + \left[AlCl_4\right]^-$$
$$\text{carbocation}$$

The carbocation electrophile then attacks the benzene ring:

$$\overset{+}{C}H_3CH_2 \quad \left[AlCl_4\right]^- \longrightarrow$$

The aluminium chloride catalyst is regenerated in the final step:

$$\longrightarrow + HCl + AlCl_3$$

Friedel–Crafts reactions are another example of **electrophilic substitution**
into the benzene ring.

▷ Addition reactions of benzene

Most reactions of benzene are electrophilic substitutions.
Remember that these reactions leave the benzene ring intact.
The ring of delocalised electrons is not disrupted.
However, **under severe conditions benzene does undergo addition**.

Addition of hydrogen

The most widely used reaction is the addition of hydrogen.
This is used to make cyclohexane, needed in the manufacture
of nylon.
The reaction is similar to the hydrogenation of alkenes
but harsher conditions are needed.
Temperatures up to 300 °C and pressures of 30 atmospheres are used.
A catalyst of Raney nickel (a finely divided form of nickel)
speeds up the reaction:

benzene $+$ $3H_2$ $\xrightarrow[\substack{300\,°C\\30\ atm}]{\substack{Ni\\catalyst}}$ cyclohexane

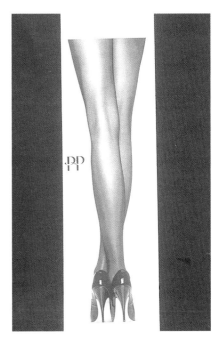

Cyclohexane is used to make the reactants needed to manufacture nylon

This can be represented as shown below:

benzene $+$ $3H_2$ $\xrightarrow[\substack{300\,°C\\30\ atm}]{Ni}$ cyclohexane

Addition of chlorine

Another addition reaction happens with benzene and chlorine in sunlight.
Can you recall another reaction that only occurs between
a hydrocarbon and chlorine if sunlight is present?
On page 166 we looked at the reaction of alkanes with chlorine.
The initiation step was the formation of chlorine free radicals.
The fact that sunlight is needed with benzene suggests that
the mechanism also involves free radicals.

Look at the reaction below:

benzene $+$ $3Cl_2$ $\xrightarrow{\text{sunlight}}$ 1,2,3,4,5,6-hexachlorocyclohexane

1,2,3,4,5,6-hexachlorocyclohexane has been used as an insecticide

▶ Reactions of substituted benzene rings

Phenol

We can now look at the effect that other groups in the benzene ring have on the reactions of aromatic compounds.

The phenols are compounds with one or more —OH groups in the benzene ring. Look at the simplest, phenol, below:

OH

phenol

Phenol is a solid made up of crystals.
Its melting point is low (43 °C), but higher than that of benzene (6 °C).
Hydrogen bonding accounts for the difference (see page 76).

It is slightly acidic and will react with a strong alkali:

OH + NaOH ⟶ O⁻Na⁺ + H₂O

phenol   sodium hydroxide   sodium phenoxide

Phenol was first extracted in 1834. It was originally named carbolic acid. It is now considered too corrosive to use as a disinfectant

This shows that it is more acidic than simple alcohols.
For example, ethanol (C₂H₅—OH) does not react with sodium hydroxide.
This is because the negative charge on the phenoxide ion is spread around the whole ion. So this ion is more stable than the ethoxide ion formed when ethanol loses an H⁺ ion.
Look at the ions opposite:

We can also compare the reactions of phenol with those of benzene.
Experiments show us that ***phenol undergoes substitution much more readily than benzene.***

- Can you recall the mechanism of attack on a benzene ring?
- Why are electrophiles likely to attack the ring?
- Will the attack happen more quickly if there is an even higher density of electrons in the ring?

The oxygen atom in phenol has two lone pairs of electrons that are not involved in bonding.
These are drawn towards the delocalised system around the benzene ring.
So the ***—OH in phenol is an electron-donating group.***
This also helps to explain why phenol can lose an H⁺ ion.
The O—H bond is slightly weakened as electrons are drawn away from that end of the molecule.
Look at the reaction below:

$CH_3CH_2 \rightarrow O^-$
ethoxide ion
(with charge concentrated on O atom)

phenoxide ion
(with charge spread around the whole ion)

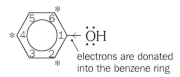

electrons are donated into the benzene ring

✳ These positions are activated in phenol

OH

Br   OH   Br

+ 3 Br₂ ⟶   + 3 HBr

bromine
water

Br

2,4,6-tribromophenol
(a white precipitate)

The product when bromine water and phenol are mixed

Remember that benzene needed a catalyst and pure bromine for this reaction to happen.
Notice that the electrophile substitutes into the ring at positions 2, 4 and 6.
We can say that:

Electron-donating groups cause attack on the benzene ring in the **2, 4 and 6 positions.**

Nitrobenzene

Unlike the —OH group in phenol, the —**NO₂** group in nitrobenzene *withdraws electrons from the delocalised ring.*

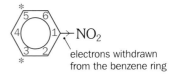

electrons withdrawn
from the benzene ring

* These positions are activated in nitrobenzene

- What effect do you think this will have on its rate of reaction with electrophiles compared to benzene?
- Will electrophiles find a richer source of electrons in nitrobenzene's ring or in benzene itself?

Not surprisingly, we find that **nitrobenzene reacts more slowly than benzene** in this type of reaction.
Look at the reaction below:

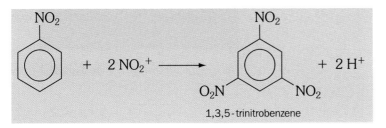

1,3,5-trinitrobenzene

Notice that now the 3 and 5 positions in the ring are attacked.
We find that:

> **Electron-withdrawing groups** activate the **3 and 5 positions** in the benzene ring.

TNT stands for trinitrotoluene (toluene is the old name for methylbenzene)

▷ Reactions in side-chains

Sometimes the reactions of substituted arenes do not involve the benzene ring.
We have already seen one example on the last page with phenol.
When mixed with sodium hydroxide, the –OH group reacts.
The benzene ring is not attacked at all.
You can see another example on the next page. It shows how nitrobenzene can be turned into aniline.
Again the reaction involves the substsituted group rather than the benzene ring.

In general, the functional groups present in a side-chain will undergo many of their usual reactions.
For example:

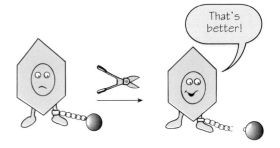

Sometimes the stable benzene ring is not affected in reactions if a side-chain is present!

a typical reaction of a
halogenoalkane
i.e. nucleophilic substitution

However, they can be affected by the benzene ring in the molecule.
The main example of this *effect* is seen in aromatic alkyl compounds.
The benzene ring can induce reactions in the alkyl side-chain which do not normally occur.
For example, methylbenzene is oxidised by potassium manganate(VII) in an alkaline solution:

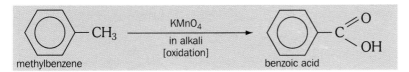

a reaction that is
not typical of an alkane
i.e. oxidation by manganate(VII) ions

Normally, an alkane would not react with potassium manganate(VII).

▷ Chemistry at work: Dyes

We find benzene rings in the molecules of most dyes.
The dyeing industry is based on aromatic compounds containing nitrogen.

Phenylamine is the starting material for many dyes.
It is made by reducing nitrobenzene.
We can get nitrobenzene by nitrating benzene from crude oil.
(See page 212.)
It can be **reduced** by tin (Sn) and concentrated hydrochloric acid in the lab.
In industry iron and the acid is used:

Many of the synthetic dyes used in these clothes are derived from phenylamine

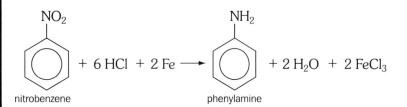

The phenylamine goes on to make **azo dyes**.
These dyes link benzene rings through the —N=N— (azo) grouping.
The dyes absorb light from the visible spectrum, so they appear coloured.
Look at the structures of some azo dyes below:

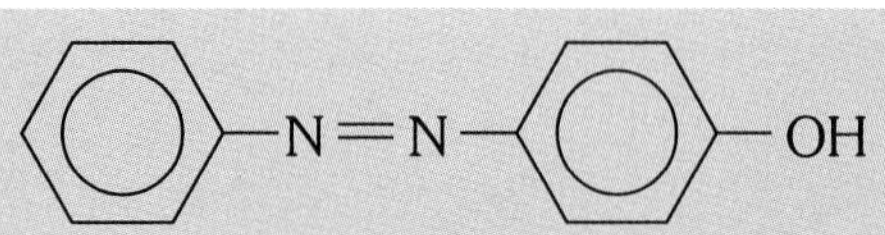

orange azo dye

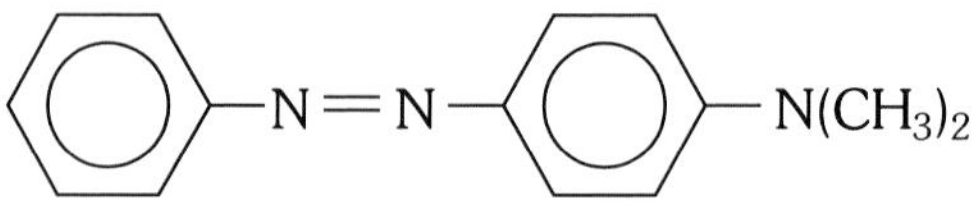

yellow azo dye

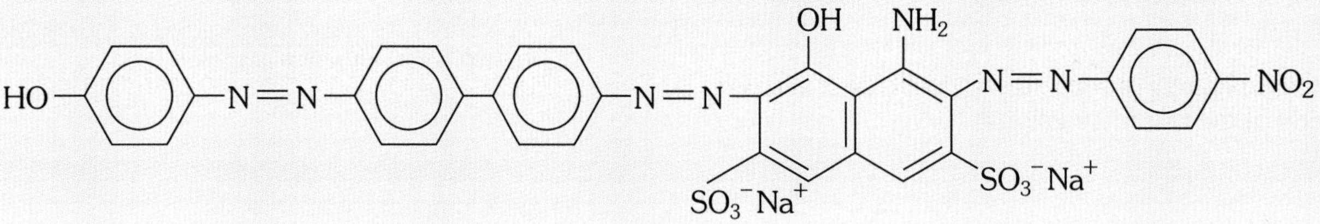

green azo dye

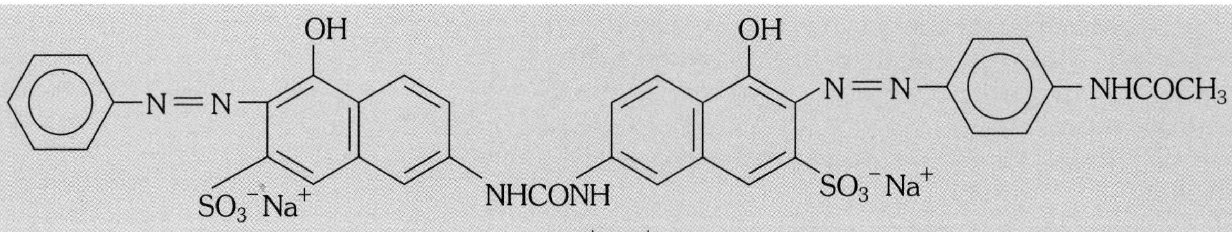

red azo dye

You can read more about the reactions to make dyes on page 243.

▷ Chemistry at work: Controlling pests

The agrochemical industry research and manufacture various forms of chemical pesticides.
Many of these are based on arenes.
There are three main areas of interest in this industry:
- Herbicides for the control of weeds and unwanted plants
- Insecticides to control insects
- Fungicides to control the growth of fungi.

Herbicides

The main point in crop farming is to remove unwanted, competitive plants, and to replace them with the desired single species of plant. This might involve the removal of wild flowers and grasses from a field in which only wheat is to be grown. When competition for root space, nutrients and sunlight is removed, the crop will grow more efficiently.

Cl—⟨○⟩—OCH_2COOH
Cl

2,4-dichlorophenoxyethanoic acid
2,4-D

We can do this by the selective use of particular herbicides, many of which are quite complex arene-based compounds.
One of these is 2, 4-dichlorophenoxyethanoic acid (2,4-D).
This is used for the selective control of broad-leaved weeds.
Another is 2,4,5-trichlorophenoxyethanoic acid (2,4,5-T),
which is banned in the USA, but is presently being used in the UK.

Insecticides

CCl_3
Cl—⟨○⟩—CH—⟨○⟩—Cl

dichloro**d**iphenyl**t**richloroethane
DDT

Dichlorodiphenyltrichloroethane is one of the best-known and most effective of the early insecticides. It is commonly known as DDT. This pesticide was widely used to kill fleas and body lice amongst the troops during the Second World War. Through continual use, many insects developed a resistance to DDT. Increasing concentrations were required to bring about the desired effects. This resulted in large amounts being found higher up the food chain.
In the 1960s the use of DDT declined rapidly and it was finally banned in the UK in 1984.

Another effective insecticide, which is easily and cheaply made, is the phosphorus-based arene compound known as Parathion®. This pesticide is still in use in developing countries because it is cheap, but it is also very dangerous. It is responsible for more deaths among agricultural workers who do not wear protective clothing than any other pesticide!

Fungicides

⟨○⟩
   N
   $||$
   C—$NHCOOCH_3$
   N
   $|$
$CH_3CH_2CH_2CH_2$—NH—CO
benomyl

These are used to control fungi which are harmful to plants. Although about 100 000 species are known, only 200 or so are known to cause significant plant disease. One of the most serious plant diseases was the 'potato blight' which virtually wiped out the potato crop in Ireland between 1845 and 1847. It caused a famine in which over a million people died. It was not until 1885 that an effective fungicide against potato blight was devised.

Of the modern aromatic fungicides, one called benomyl is widely used for protection against fungal attack on fruit, vines and a variety of other crops.

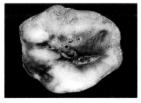

A potato affected by potato blight

Summary

- The formula of benzene is C_6H_6.
- Its molecules are flat, with the 6 carbon atoms arranged in a hexagon:

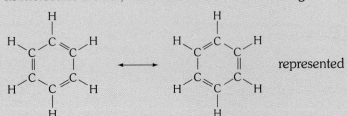

represented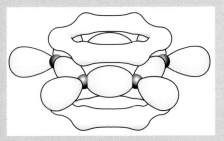

This shows the π bonding system above and below the ring of carbon atoms

- The strength of the bond between each pair of carbon atoms is the same.
- A **ring of delocalised electrons** lies above and below the plane of the molecule.
- This π (pi) bonding makes the benzene ring stable.
- However, it is attacked by **electrophiles** (attracted by the electrons in the ring system).
- It then undergoes **substitution** reactions.

▷ Questions

1 Copy and complete:
Aromatic compounds contain .... rings.
The six carbon atoms form a .... shape, with a ring of .... electrons above and below the .... of the molecule.
This .... bonding system makes the benzene ring stable.
Benzene undergoes .... substitution reactions.

2 Benzene is a hydrocarbon.
   a) What will be formed if it undergoes complete combustion?
   b) Write an equation for the complete combustion of benzene.
   c) Look back to page 178 and predict the type of flame you would see when benzene burns in air.

3 a) Draw the Kekulé structure of benzene.
   b) Explain the actual bonding in a benzene molecule.

The delocalised ring of electrons confers stability to a benzene molecule. This can be shown by working through the questions below.
Look at the enthalpy change obtained by experiment when hydrogen is added to benzene:

$$C_6H_6 + 3\,H_2 \longrightarrow C_6H_{12} \qquad \Delta H = -208\,kJ\,mol^{-1}$$
benzene

   c) Draw an enthalpy level diagram showing this reaction. (See page 296.)

This can be compared with the enthalpy change calculated assuming benzene contained three double bonds.
Look at the reaction below:

$$C_6H_{10} + H_2 \longrightarrow C_6H_{12} \qquad \Delta H = -120\,kJ\,mol^{-1}$$
cyclohexene

   d) Multiply ΔH for this reaction by 3 to find the enthalpy change for the hydrogenation of Kekulé's model of a benzene molecule.

   e) Draw the enthalpy change from part d) on your enthalpy level diagram from part c).
   (Remember that the product, C_6H_{12}, will end up at the same enthalpy level in both reactions).
   f) Does the Kekulé structure have a higher or lower enthalpy content than an actual benzene molecule?
   g) The difference in enthalpies is called the **stabilisation enthalpy** of benzene.
   What is its value?

4 a) Complete the equation for the reaction that occurs when benzene reacts with a mixture of concentrated nitric acid and sulphuric acid:

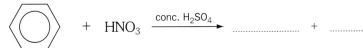

   b) Complete this sentence:
   The reaction shown above is called the .... of benzene.
   c) What are the name and formula of the electrophile in the reaction? What conditions are used?
   d) Write an equation to show how the electrophile is made.

5 a) Complete this equation:

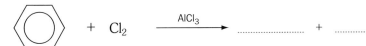

   b) Explain how the aluminium chloride catalyses this reaction.

6 Ethylbenzene is important in the manufacture of polystyrene.
   a) Give the structural formula of ethylbenzene.
   b) It is made by reacting benzene, ethene, HCl and $AlCl_3$.
   Suggest a mechanism for the reaction, which includes a Friedel–Crafts reaction.

18 Aldehydes and ketones

Have you ever smelled nail varnish remover?
The solvent used to get rid of the nail varnish is propanone.
It is widely used in industry and laboratories to dissolve things.

Propanone is an example of a **carbonyl compound**.
These compounds all contain the C=O group (carbonyl group).
Propanone is one of a family of organic compounds called **ketones**.
The ketones are closely related to another group of carbonyl compounds
called **aldehydes**.
Let's look at the differences between aldehydes and ketones:

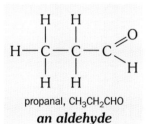

propanal, CH_3CH_2CHO
an aldehyde

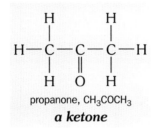

propanone, CH_3COCH_3
a ketone

Propanone (a ketone) is a useful solvent

As you can see from above:

> An **aldehyde** has a hydrogen atom bonded to the carbonyl
> group, whereas a **ketone** has two carbon atoms bonded to the
> carbonyl group.

Their general structures are:

aldehydes

ketones

where R = alkyl or aryl group
(with a benzene ring)

*Specimens are preserved in formalin,
which is a solution of methanal (an
aldehyde) in water*

The presence of the oxygen atom has a big influence on the properties
of aldehydes and ketones.
Oxygen is much more electronegative than carbon.
The oxygen atom attracts the electrons in the C=O bond more strongly
than the carbon atom. On average, the electrons are found nearer
the oxygen atom, making it rich in electrons. So the carbonyl group is polar.
The oxygen carries a slight negative charge, and the electron-deficient carbon
carries a partial positive charge.
This uneven distribution of electrons makes the whole molecule polar.
So would you expect aldehydes and ketones to have higher boiling points
than non-polar molecules of a similar mass?

Look at the table opposite:
* Put the molecules in order of boiling point.
In aldehydes and ketones there are no hydrogen atoms bonded directly to oxygen.
* Do you think that the molecules of an aldehyde or a ketone can form
  hydrogen bonds between themselves?
* Which compounds in the table do form hydrogen bonds?

The smaller aldehydes and ketones are soluble in water.
This is because they can form hydrogen bonds with water molecules.

$\delta+ \quad \delta-$ the polar
C=O carbonyl group

Compound	M_r	Boiling point / °C
butanal	72	76
butanone	72	80
pentane	72	36
butan-1-ol	74	118
propanoic acid	74	141

* *Can you explain these boiling points?*
*Aldehydes and ketones have
permanent dipole–dipole forces
between molecules*

221

▷ Reactions of aldehydes and ketones

There are **two main differences** between the reactions of aldehydes and ketones:

> 1. **Aldehydes can be oxidised easily, whereas to oxidise a ketone you have to break a C—C bond, and**
> 2. **Aldehydes react more readily with nucleophiles.**

We can look at these reactions in more detail below.

Oxidation

Can you remember your work on oxidising alcohols? (See page 196.)
When you oxidise a primary alcohol, an aldehyde is formed.
What happens if you have an excess of the oxidising agent present?
Look at the reaction below:

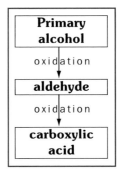

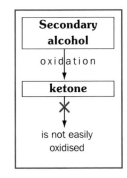

$$CH_3C\overset{O}{\underset{H}{\diagup}} \ + \ [O] \ \xrightarrow[heat]{K_2Cr_2O_7/H_2SO_4} \ CH_3C\overset{O}{\underset{OH}{\diagup}}$$

ethanal   ethanoic acid

In general we can say:

> aldehyde $\xrightarrow{oxidation}$ **carboxylic acid**

The aldehydes are oxidised even in mild conditions.
For example, a cold, neutral solution of potassium manganate(VII) will work.
Even silver ions (Ag^+) will oxidise an aldehyde.
This reaction is used to distinguish aldehydes from ketones.
The silver ions are present in **Tollens' reagent**.
It contains the complex ion of silver and ammonia, $Ag(NH_3)_2^+$.
Look at its reaction with an aldehyde below:

$$CH_3CHO \ + \ 2\,Ag(NH_3)_2^+ + 3\,OH^- \xrightarrow{heat} CH_3COO^- + 2\,Ag \ + \ 4\,NH_3 + 2\,H_2O$$

colourless   silver
solution   mirror

The test forms a **silver mirror** on the inside of the test tube.
Look at the photo opposite:

Most aldehydes, except aromatic ones, also give a positive test with **Fehling's solution**. This contains copper(II) ions (Cu^{2+}) which act as a weak oxidising agent.
They oxidise the aldehyde to the corresponding carboxylic acid.
In the process Cu^{2+} ions themselves get reduced to Cu^+ ions.
The Cu^+ ions form a **red/orange precipitate** (Cu_2O) in a positive test.

On the other hand, ketones are only oxidised under extreme conditions.
The ketone molecule must be broken up. It then gives a mixture of carboxylic acids.
● Why don't ketones react with Tollens' reagent or Fehling's solution?

A silver mirror forms when Tollens' reagent is heated with an aldehyde (but not a ketone)

A red/orange precipitate forms when Fehling's solution is warmed with an aldehyde (but not a ketone)

Iodoform reaction

Ketones that contain the methyl group (—CH₃) undergo a distinctive reaction with an alkaline solution of iodine.

The aldehyde ethanal also reacts in a similar way.

This oxidation reaction gives a yellow precipitate of triiodomethane (CHI_3).

The reaction is still known by the old name of this compound, iodoform.

You have probably heard of chloroform.

- What was it used for?
- Can you guess its modern (IUPAC) name and its formula?

The iodoform reaction is used to detect the following structures:

As well as oxidation, the reaction involves halogenation and the cleavage of C—C bonds.

Look at the sequence below:

$$R-\underset{\underset{O}{\parallel}}{C}-CH_3 + 3NaIO \longrightarrow R-\underset{\underset{O}{\parallel}}{C}-CI_3 + 3NaOH$$

(formed from I₂ + NaOH)

halogenation

$$R-\underset{\underset{O}{\parallel}}{C}-CI_3 + NaOH \longrightarrow R-C\underset{O^-Na^+}{\overset{O}{<}} + CHI_3$$

triiodomethane (iodoform)

oxidation and cleavage of C—C bond

The yellow precipitate can be identified as CHI_3 by its melting point (119 °C).

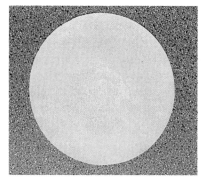

Triiodomethane (CHI_3)
(old name iodoform)

Reduction

- Can you recall which type of alcohols we oxidise to make aldehydes? What about making ketones?
- What do you think will happen if we **reduce** the aldehydes and ketones?

We can reduce aldehydes and ketones using either:

a) hydrogen with a nickel catalyst:

$$CH_3-\underset{\underset{O}{\parallel}}{C}-CH_3 + H_2 \xrightarrow[\text{catalyst}]{\text{Ni}} CH_3-\underset{\underset{OH}{|}}{CH}-CH_3$$

Aldehyde
reduction ↓
primary alcohol

Ketone
reduction ↓
secondary alcohol

b) chemical reducing agents, such as lithium tetrahydridoaluminate(III), $LiAlH_4$, (in dry ether). Or we can use the milder sodium tetrahydridoborate(III), $NaBH_4$, (in aqueous solution):

$$CH_3CH_2C\overset{O}{\underset{H}{<}} + 2[H] \xrightarrow{NaBH_4/H_2O} CH_3CH_2CH_2OH$$

Mechanism:

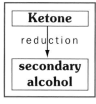

H^- is the nucleophile.

We can think of this as a **nucleophilic addition** reaction. (See next page.)

▷ Nucleophilic addition to aldehydes and ketones

We have already seen on page 211 that the carbonyl group
is polar. The carbon atom is deficient in electrons
compared with the more electronegative oxygen atom.
This makes the carbon atom open to attack by nucleophiles.
Remember that nucleophiles are rich in electrons.
They can donate a pair of electrons to an atom that is short of electrons.

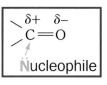

Both aldehydes and ketones are attacked by cyanide ions (CN^-).
Look at the reaction below:

1.
$$\underset{\delta+}{\diagdown}C\underset{\delta-}{=}O \ +:CN^- \longrightarrow \diagdown C \diagup \overset{\cdot\cdot}{\underset{CN}{O^-}}$$
nucleophilic attack by CN⁻

We then add a strong acid, providing H^+ ions:

2.
$$\diagdown C \diagup \overset{\cdot\cdot}{\underset{CN}{O^-}} \ + \ H^+ \longrightarrow \diagdown C \diagup \overset{OH}{\underset{CN}{}}$$
protonation (adding H^+)

Overall the reaction can be summarised as:

$$\diagdown C = O \ + \ HCN \longrightarrow \diagdown C \diagup \overset{OH}{\underset{CN}{}}$$
The product is a 2-hydroxynitrile (or cyanohydrin)

We call this type of reaction **nucleophilic addition.**
- Can you see why it is classed as an addition reaction?

The 2-hydroxynitrile compounds (or cyanohydrins) can then
be used to make new substances by hydrolysing or reducing the —CN group.
This is discussed in more detail on page 245.

Look at the reactions of propanal and propanone with HCN below:

$$CH_3CH_2CHO + HCN \xrightarrow{NaCN} \underset{H}{\overset{CH_3CH_2}{\diagdown}} C \diagup \overset{OH}{\underset{CN}{}}$$

$$\underset{CH_3}{\overset{CH_3}{\diagdown}} C = O \ + \ HCN \xrightarrow{NaCN} \underset{CH_3}{\overset{CH_3}{\diagdown}} C \diagup \overset{OH}{\underset{CN}{}}$$

The product of propanone and HCN is used in the manufacture of perspex

- But which of the two reactions do you think would occur more readily?

To answer this we must look at the strength of the partial positive charge
on the carbonyl carbon in each compound.

Let's consider the number of alkyl groups attached to the carbon in each case:

propanal $\underset{H}{\overset{CH_3CH_2}{\diagdown}}\underset{\delta+}{}C\underset{\delta-}{=}O$ propanone $\underset{CH_3}{\overset{CH_3}{\diagdown}}\underset{\delta+}{}C\underset{\delta-}{=}O$

- Which carbon atom has the larger $\delta+$ charge?
- Which is more readily attacked by a nucleophile?

Remember that alkyl groups tend to donate electrons. They will tend
to reduce the positive charge on an electron-deficient carbon atom.
As you can see above, the propanone has two alkyl groups bonded to
the carbonyl carbon atom.
On the other hand, propanal has only one alkyl group donating electrons
to reduce the charge on the carbonyl carbon. So its $\delta+$ charge is larger.

Aldehydes undergo nucleophilic addition more readily than ketones.

▷ Condensation reactions of aldehydes and ketones

On the last page we saw how aldehydes and ketones
undergo addition reactions.
Sometimes addition is followed by the the loss
of a small molecule, H_2O, in an elimination reaction.
The overall reaction is called **condensation**.

***Addition* followed by *elimination* is called a condensation reaction.**

Ammonia (NH_3) and its related compounds react in this way
with aldehydes and ketones.
Look at the compounds derived from ammonia below:

NH_2OH NH_2NH_2

hydroxylamine   hydrazine

$$NH_2NH-\underset{NO_2}{\overset{NO_2}{\bigcirc}}-NO_2$$

2,4-dinitrophenylhydrazine

If we represent these as NH_2X, the general reaction can be shown:

1. Addition:

$$\underset{/}{\overset{\diagdown}{C}}=O \; + \; NH_2-X \longrightarrow \underset{/}{\overset{\diagdown}{C}}\underset{NH-X}{\overset{OH}{\diagup}}$$

2. Elimination:

$$\underset{/}{\overset{\diagdown}{C}}\underset{NH-X}{\overset{OH}{\diagup}} \xrightarrow{-H_2O} \underset{/}{\overset{\diagdown}{C}}=N\diagdown X$$

The reaction with **2,4-dinitrophenylhydrazine** (also known as
Brady's reagent) is important.
It is used to ***identify specific aldehydes and ketones.***
The derivatives formed are yellow or orange crystalline compounds.
The crystals have very sharp melting points.
You measure their melting points, then look them up in a table of data.
This identifies the derivative made, and therefore the actual aldehyde or
ketone that you started with.
An example of the reaction is shown below:

*Crystals of a product formed from
2,4-dinitrophenylhydrazine and
a carbonyl compound*

1. Addition:

$$\underset{CH_3}{\overset{CH_3}{\diagdown}}C=O + NH_2NH-\underset{}{\overset{NO_2}{\bigcirc}}-NO_2 \longrightarrow \underset{CH_3}{\overset{CH_3}{\diagdown}}C\underset{NHNH-\bigcirc-NO_2}{\overset{OH \quad NO_2}{\diagup}}$$

2. Elimination:

$$\underset{CH_3}{\overset{CH_3}{\diagdown}}C\underset{NHNH-\bigcirc-NO_2}{\overset{OH \quad NO_2}{\diagup}} \longrightarrow \underset{CH_3}{\overset{CH_3}{\diagdown}}C=N\underset{NH-\bigcirc-NO_2}{\overset{NO_2}{\diagdown}} \; + H_2O$$

orange crystals of the
2,4-dinitrophenylhydrazone derivative

*Students determining the melting point of
a Brady's reagent derivative*

▷ Chemistry at work: Aldehydes and ketones

From fingernails to false teeth!

Propanone is a very effective solvent.
It is widely used as nail varnish remover.

Some propanone is converted into another ketone, 4-methylpentan-2-one.
This substance is more commonly known by the initials MIBK.
These come from its older name of methyl isobutyl ketone.
It is an important solvent for plastics such as PVC
and for adhesives such as Evostick.

Propanone is an important raw material in the manufacture of perspex,
poly(methyl 2-methylpropenoate). This polymer has a very wide range
of uses including car light assemblies and false teeth.

$$CH_3\diagdown$$
$$C=O \quad \text{propanone}$$
$$CH_3\diagup$$

Propanone is used as a solvent in some glues

The smallest aldehyde

Methanal is very toxic. It attacks the retina of the eye. A 40% solution
of methanal in water is known as formalin. It has been used to preserve
biological specimens.

Methanal is the starting point for making a number of different
polymers. Poly(methanal) is a particularly strong plastic from which
machine parts such as gear wheels are made.

The reaction between methanal and urea produces a polymer
which is an excellent electrical insulator. It is used for plugs and sockets.

The polymer which is obtained from methanal and phenol
is heat resistant. It has been used on rocket nose cones
and heat shields.

$$H\diagdown$$
$$C=O \quad \text{methanal}$$
$$H\diagup$$

Methanal is used to make the plastic in plug sockets

Sleepy compound

Ethanal forms simple polymers. The trimer, $(CH_3CHO)_3$, is used as
a sleep-inducing drug.

The tetramer, $(CH_3CHO)_4$, is commonly called metaldehyde.
It is sold as slug poison pellets or as a solid fuel for camping stoves.

$$CH_3\diagdown$$
$$C=O \quad \text{ethanal}$$
$$H\diagup$$

Four ethanal molecules link to make a fuel used in camping stoves

Sweet compounds

Some sugars have properties which are typical of aldehydes or ketones. Glucose and fructose are monosaccharide sugars with the formula $C_6H_{12}O_6$.

Glucose behaves chemically like an aldehyde and is sometimes called an aldose. It behaves like this because about 1% of glucose molecules exist as an open chain structure which contains an aldehyde group.

Fructose behaves chemically like a ketone and is known as a ketose. Its open chain structure contains a ketone group.

aldehyde ⇌ glucose

ketone ⇌ fructose

Sucrose, the sugar commonly used at home, is made from one glucose and one fructose molecule joined together. Its formula is $C_{12}H_{22}O_{11}$

Fast forward!

During the manufacture of 'chrome' videotape, the ketone called butanone is *especially* useful.

The videotape itself is actually a very long strip of strong, electrically resistant polyester, upon which is deposited the magnetic recording surface. This recording surface is mainly composed of about 50% lubricants and polyurethane binders and 50% chromium(IV) oxide (CrO_2). This mixture is 'dissolved' in the solvent butanone and then evenly coated over very long polyester sheets. After the butanone solvent is evaporated and the tape is 'cured', it is split into long narrow strips to fit the video cassette cases.

The butanone solvent used is fairly cheap and it is a satisfactory solvent for the polyurethane binder. Since butanone is also quite volatile, it evaporates readily from the freshly coated 'magnetic' surface mixture, to leave a uniform coating. Butanone is therefore an adequate, cost-effective solvent for use in the videotape industry.

CH_3CH_2 \
CH_3 $C=O$ butanone

Butanone is used in the manufacture of videotapes

Summary

- Aldehydes and ketones are examples of **carbonyl compounds**.

  The carbonyl group is 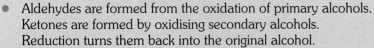 .

- Aldehydes are formed from the oxidation of primary alcohols.
  Ketones are formed by oxidising secondary alcohols.
  Reduction turns them back into the original alcohol.

- Aldehydes can be readily oxidised to form carboxylic acids.
  This is used to distinguish between aldehydes and ketones in tests by
  heating with **Fehling's solution or Tollens' reagent** (the 'silver mirror' test).
  Aldehydes are oxidised and give positive tests. (See page 222.)

- Aldehydes and ketones undergo two main types of reaction:
  a) **nucleophilic addition**, and
  b) **condensation** (addition followed by elimination).

- We can use **2,4-dinitrophenylhydrazine** (Brady's reagent) to identify
  specific aldehydes or ketones.
  You can see a summary of their reactions on page 267.

▶ **Questions**

1 Copy and complete:
   Aldehydes and ketones both contain the .... group.
   Aldehydes are easily ...., for example by warming with
   potassium dichromate(VI) and dilute sulphuric acid,
   unlike the ketones.
   We can tell an aldehyde from a ketone by heating
   with .... solution. An ..../red precipitate of
   copper(I) oxide forms with the aldehyde as it gets .....

   We can use sodium .... dissolved in .... to reduce
   aldehydes and ketones. The aldehydes give ....
   alcohols, whereas the ketones yield .... alcohols.
   Their reaction with HCN is another example of ....
   addition.

   We can identify a particular aldehyde or ketone by
   reacting it with Brady's reagent (2,4-....). Crystals are
   produced that we can identify from their .... point.
   This is an example of a .... reaction.

2 Draw the structural formula of:
   a) methanal   b) hexan-2-one   c) pentanal

3 Explain the relative boiling points of the compounds
   in the table below:

Compound	M_r	Boiling point / °C
propanal	58	50
propanone	58	56
ethanoic acid	60	118
propan-1-ol	60	97.5
butane	58	−0.5

4 a) Descibe how you would test and distinguish
      between an aldehyde and ketone using Tollens'
      reagent.
   b) Explain how the test works.
   c) Describe how you would identify a specific
      carbonyl compound using Brady's reagent.
   d) Show with equations the reaction that would take
      place if the compound tested in part c) was
      propanal.

5 Give the structural formula of the organic product
   formed in each reaction below:
   a) Propanal is heated with potassium dichromate(VI)
      and dilute sulphuric acid.
   b) Propanone is reacted with hydrogen in the
      presence of a nickel catalyst.
   c) Pentan-3-one reacts with HCN in the presence of
      sodium cyanide and dilute hydrochloric acid.
   d) Butanal reacts with hydroxylamine (NH_2OH).

6 a) Name two reducing agents that will react with
      propanone.
   b) What will the product be?
   c) Write an equation to show the reaction with one of
      the reducing agents.
   d) Explain the mechanism of attack on the
      propanone molecule.

7 a) Write an equation to show the reaction between
      butanone and HCN.
   b) Explain the mechanism of the reaction.
   c) Which would you expect to react faster with HCN:
      butanone or butanal. Explain your answer.

19 Carboxylic acids and related compounds

Whenever you put vinegar on your fish and chips, you are using a carboxylic acid. Although less than 10 per cent of the solution, ethanoic acid gives vinegar its sharp taste and smell.
The formula of ethanoic acid is CH_3COOH.
Its displayed or structural formula is shown below:

ethanoic acid

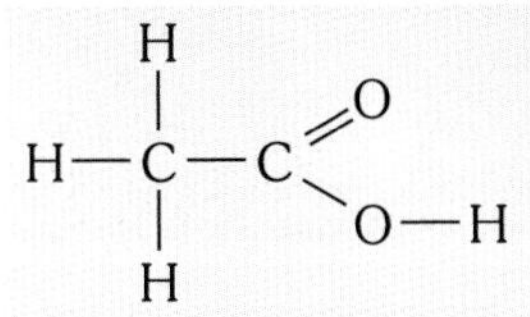

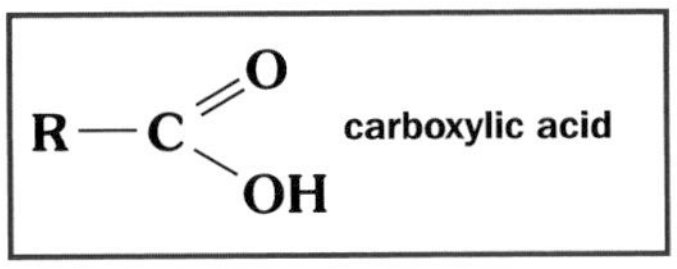

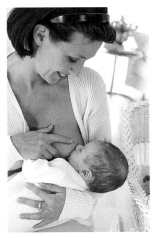

Human breast milk contains a substituted carboxylic acid (2-hydroxypropanoic acid)

In fact the first food you ever had might well have contained a common substituted carboxylic acid. Human breast milk, and cow's milk, both contain 2-hydroxypropanoic acid (sometimes called lactic acid). Can you draw its structure? Can you write a rule for naming simple carboxylic acids?

Related compounds

In this chapter we will also meet some derivatives of carboxylic acids. These are shown below:

acid chlorides (or acyl chlorides)

acid anhydrides

esters

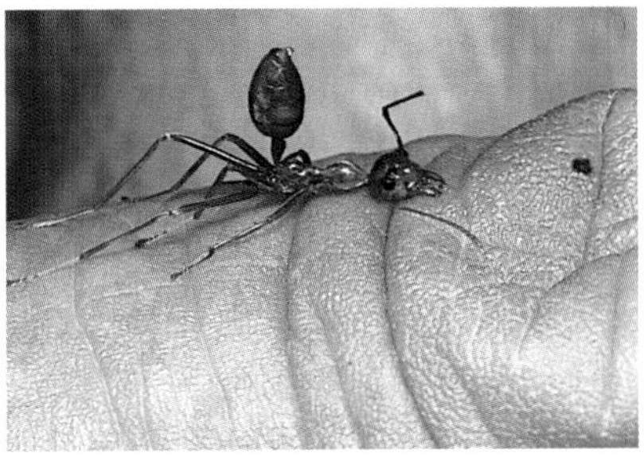

Methanoic acid provides the sting from biting ants and nettles

Physical properties of carboxylic acids

Can you recall the forces of attraction between the molecules of carboxylic acids? We looked at them on page 77.
The intermolecular forces are strong.
Look at the table opposite:

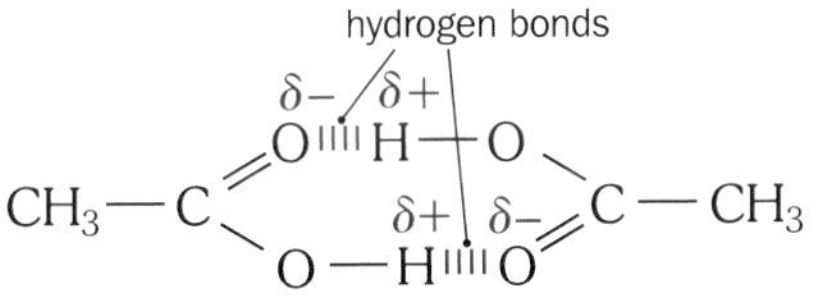

Compound	Relative molecular mass	Boiling point / °C
butan-1-ol	74	118
propanoic acid	74	141

Why is it fairer to compare the boiling point of propanoic acid with butan-1-ol rather than propan-1-ol?

We know that ***hydrogen bonds*** exist in alcohols.
They also form in carboxylic acids, but are even stronger.
Their molecules 'pair up', forming **dimers**:

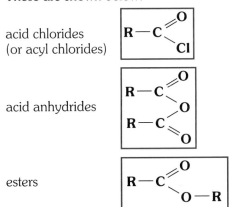

a dimer of ethanoic acid

The ability to form hydrogen bonds also explains the high solubility of the smaller carboxylic acids in water.
As the non-polar hydrocarbon chain gets longer, it starts to have a greater effect, and the acids get less soluble.

▷ Reactions of carboxylic acids

Reacting as acids (breaking the O—H bond)

The carboxylic acids are weak acids.
For example, only a tiny fraction of ethanoic acid's molecules split up (or **dissociate**) in water:

$$CH_3COOH + H_2O \rightleftharpoons CH_3COO^- + H_3O^+$$
ethanoic acid ethanoate ion

The equilibrium lies well over to the left-hand side.
The extent of this can be shown by the dissociation constant K_a.
The larger the value of K_a, the stronger the acid.
So whereas the value of K_a for a strong acid such as nitric acid is about $40 \, mol \, dm^{-3}$, K_a for ethanoic acid is only $1.7 \times 10^{-5} \, mol \, dm^{-3}$.
You can find out more about dissociation constants on page 385.

Vinegar is a solution containing about 7 per cent ethanoic acid

However, the carboxylic acids are stronger acids than alcohols.
This is due to:

1. weakening of the O—H bond in the acid by the presence of the adjacent carbonyl group:

electrons in the C–O bond drawn towards double bond
electrons are drawn away from O–H bond

$$R - C \underset{O \leftarrow H}{\overset{O}{\nearrow}}$$

2. the stability of the anion formed when the H^+ ion leaves.

Look at the bond lengths opposite:

$$H - C \overset{0.123 \, nm \quad O}{\underset{0.136 \, nm \quad O - H}{}} \rightleftharpoons H - C \overset{0.127 \, nm \quad O}{\underset{0.127 \, nm \quad O^-}{}} + H^+$$
methanoic acid methanoate ion

The carbon–oxygen bonds are equivalent in the methanoate ion. (See below):

As you can see, the carbon–oxygen bonds in the methanoate ion are the same length. The negative charge is not concentrated on one oxygen atom but is spread over the whole —COO^- group:

$$H - C \overset{O}{\underset{O}{\diagdown}} -$$
the methanoate ion is a 'resonance hybrid' of the structures opposite

$$H - C \overset{O}{\underset{O^-}{\diagup}} \longleftrightarrow H - C \overset{O^-}{\underset{O}{\diagup}}$$

This delocalisation of electrons stabilises the ion.
It is not as open to attack by H^+ ions, and therefore is less likely to re-form the original acid molecule again.

You can see how other atoms substituted into carboxylic acids affect its acidity on page 385. Do you think that electron-withdrawing groups would make them stronger or weaker acids? Why?

The carboxylic acids undergo the usual reactions of acids.
However, they will be slower than strong acids of equal concentration because fewer $H^+(aq)$ ions will be present.

Sodium benzoate (⬡—COO^-Na^+), a salt of benzoic acid, is used as a food preservative

	acid	+	alkali	→	a salt	+	water
	CH_3COOH	+	$NaOH$	→	$CH_3COO^-Na^+$	+	H_2O
	ethanoic acid		sodium hydroxide		sodium ethanoate	+	water

	acid	+	a metal	→	a salt	+	hydrogen
2	CH_3COOH	+	Mg	→	$(CH_3COO^-)_2Mg$	+	H_2
	ethanoic acid		+ magnesium	→	magnesium ethanoate	+	hydrogen

	acid	+	a carbonate (or hydrogencarbonate)	→	a salt	+	water	+	carbon dioxide
2	CH_3COOH	+	K_2CO_3	→	$2\,CH_3COO^-K^+$	+	H_2O	+	CO_2
	ethanoic acid	+	potassium carbonate	→	potassium ethanoate	+	water	+	carbon dioxide

Reduction

We have already met the carboxylic acids when we looked at the oxidation of alcohols (page 190) and aldehydes (page 212). As you know, oxidation is the 'chemical opposite' of reduction. So what do you think we might get if we reduce a carboxylic acid? Look at the reaction below:

$$CH_3CH_2C \overset{O}{\underset{O-H}{\Big<}} \quad \xrightarrow[\text{then } H_2O]{\text{LiAlH}_4 \text{ (in dry ether)}} \quad CH_3CH_2CH_2OH$$

propanoic acid   propan-1-ol

The reducing agent is the powerful lithium tetrahydridoaluminate(III). The reduction product is the primary alcohol. It is not possible to prepare an aldehyde by reducing a carboxylic acid.

Esterification (breaking the C—O bond)

Again, this is not a new reaction to us. On page 191 we saw how carboxylic acids react with alcohols to form esters. A strong acid, usually sulphuric acid, is used as a catalyst. Heating under reflux will also speed up the reaction. Remember that the reaction does not go to completion. An equilibrium mixture is formed as shown below:

$$\underset{\text{ethanoic acid}}{CH_3COOH} + \underset{\text{propan-1-ol}}{CH_3CH_2CH_2OH} \overset{\text{acid}}{\rightleftharpoons} \underset{\text{propyl ethanoate}}{CH_3COOCH_2CH_2CH_3} + \underset{\text{water}}{H_2O}$$

The general equation is:

$$\boxed{\textbf{acid} + \textbf{alcohol} \overset{H^+}{\rightleftharpoons} \textbf{ester} + \textbf{water}} \quad \textbf{esterification}$$

What does the evidence shown on page 191 suggest about the mechanism of attack?
It appears that the alcohol acts as a nucleophile. Its oxygen atom attacks the electron-deficient carbon in the carboxyl group:

$$\begin{array}{c} H \\ \ddot{\underset{}{O}} - C_3H_7 \\ \overset{\delta+}{\underset{H_3C - C}{}} \overset{O}{\underset{O-H}{\Big<}} \end{array}$$

Halogenation

The electron-deficient carbon is also open to attack from nucleophiles containing halogen atoms. Reagents such as PCl_5, SCl_2O or PBr_3 can be used. Which bond is broken in the carboxylic acid below?

$$\underset{\text{ethanoic acid}}{CH_3C\overset{O}{\underset{OH}{\Big<}}} + PCl_5 \longrightarrow \underset{\text{ethanoyl chloride}}{CH_3C\overset{O}{\underset{Cl}{\Big<}}} + POCl_3 + HCl$$

The product formed is a type of compound called an **acid chloride**. We will look at these in more detail on the next page.

In the reaction above the acid chloride formed is a liquid, as is the compound of phosphorus. So the two have to be separated. What is the advantage in using the reaction below?

$$CH_3C\overset{O}{\underset{OH}{\Big<}} + SCl_2O \xrightarrow[\text{reflux}]{\text{heat} \atop \text{under}} CH_3C\overset{O}{\underset{Cl}{\Big<}} + SO_2 + HCl$$

- What happens to the number of oxygen and hydrogen atoms as propanoic acid is reduced to propan-1-ol?
- Does this agree with our definition of reduction on page 190?

Carboxylic acids (except methanoic acid) can't be oxidised.

Esters are used to manufacture synthetic fibres (polyester). They are often mixed with natural fibres to make them more hard-wearing

▷ Acid chlorides

Acid chlorides (or carbonyl chlorides) have many reactions
in common with carboxylic acids.
The exceptions are the typical reactions of acids.
Why do you think that acid chlorides don't react with metals?
Can they release H^+ ions when a molecule dissociates?

The acid chlorides are more reactive than carboxylic acids.

These liquids start giving off fumes if exposed to air.
They react with the water vapour in the air. We see white fumes
as hydrogen chloride gas is given off.
Look at the photo opposite and the equation below:

Acid chlorides react vigorously with water

$$CH_3CH_2-C\underset{Cl}{\overset{O}{<}} + H_2O \longrightarrow CH_3CH_2-C\underset{OH}{\overset{O}{<}} + HCl$$
propanoyl chloride   propanoic acid

The acid chlorides are so reactive because the carbonyl carbon
is very short of electrons. Both oxygen and chlorine attract electrons
towards themselves. This leaves the carbon bonded to them
very open to attack from any nucleophile.
In the carboxylic acid, there is a smaller partial positive charge
on the carbonyl carbon. Electrons are drawn into
the C=O double bond from the C—O bond.
Look at the diagrams below:

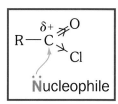

$$R-\overset{\delta+}{C}\underset{O\leftarrow H}{\overset{O}{<}} \qquad R-\overset{\delta+}{C}\underset{Cl}{\overset{O}{<}}$$

- Which carbonyl carbon has the
  larger positive charge?

In general, the reactions of acid chlorides can be summarised as:

$$R-C\underset{Cl}{\overset{O}{<}} + HZ \longrightarrow R-C\underset{Z}{\overset{O}{<}} + HCl$$

If the nucleophile is a molecule containing hydrogen, then HCl gas
is likely to be given off in the reaction.
Look at the reaction of ethanoyl chloride with water below:

With water

$$CH_3C\underset{Cl}{\overset{O}{<}} + H_2O \longrightarrow CH_3C\underset{OH}{\overset{O}{<}} + HCl$$
ethanoyl chloride   ethanoic acid

Mechanism:

$$\begin{array}{c}
H \\
\underset{\cdot\cdot}{O}-H \\
\end{array}
\quad
CH_3C\underset{Cl}{\overset{\delta+O}{<}}
\longrightarrow
CH_3-\underset{O^-}{\overset{\overset{+O{<}^H_H}{|}}{C}}-Cl
\longrightarrow
CH_3-C\underset{O}{\overset{O-H}{<}} + HCl$$

With an alcohol

$$CH_3C(=O)Cl + CH_3CH_2CH_2OH \longrightarrow CH_3C(=O)OCH_2CH_2CH_3 + HCl$$

ethanoyl chloride   propan-1-ol   propyl ethanoate
(an ester)

This reaction is used to prepare esters.

Why is it better than using the alcohol plus a carboxylic acid?

With ammonia

$$C_6H_5C(=O)Cl + NH_3 \longrightarrow C_6H_5C(=O)NH_2 + HCl$$

benzoyl chloride   benzamide
(an amide)

With an amine

$$CH_3C(=O)Cl + CH_3NH_2 \longrightarrow CH_3C(=O)NHCH_3 + HCl$$

ethanoyl chloride   N-methylethanamide
(a substituted amide)

You can read more about amides in the next chapter.

▶ Acid anhydrides

Acid chlorides are used to prepare another group of carboxylic acid derivatives called **acid anhydrides.**

Look at the reaction below:

$$R-C(=O)Cl + R'-C(=O)O^-Na^+ \longrightarrow R-C(=O)-O-C(=O)-R' + NaCl$$

acid chloride   salt of a   an acid anhydride
carboxylic acid

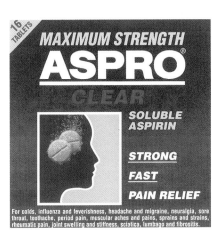

*Ethanoic anhydride is used in the manufacture of aspirin.
(See page 271)*

The acid anhydrides undergo all the reactions of acid chlorides, but not as vigorously. For example:

$$CH_3C(=O)-O-C(=O)C_2H_5 + H_2O \longrightarrow CH_3C(=O)OH + C_2H_5C(=O)OH$$

ethanoic propanoic anhydride   ethanoic acid   propanoic acid

$$CH_3C(=O)-O-C(=O)CH_3 + C_2H_5OH \longrightarrow CH_3C(=O)OC_2H_5 + CH_3C(=O)OH$$

ethanoic anhydride   ethanol   ethyl ethanoate   ethanoic acid
(an ester)

▷ Esters

Esters are responsible for the sweet smells we get from many fruits.
They are more volatile than carboxylic acids.
Can you think why?

We have already seen how they can be formed from
alcohols reacting with a carboxylic acid (pages 191 and 221).
Or we can use an acid chloride or an acid anhydride (both on page 223).
But now let's consider breaking down esters.

Most 'fruity' smells are mixtures of esters

Hydrolysis of esters

As you know, the reaction between an alcohol and a carboxylic acid
is reversible. The ester formed is attacked by the other product, water.
This splits the ester back into the original alcohol and carboxylic acid.

> **The breakdown of a molecule by water is called hydrolysis.**

The reaction to form the ester is catalysed by a strong acid.
As an equilibrium mixture is produced, the reverse reaction
is also speeded up by the acid. So the hydrolysis of an ester
is catalysed by concentrated sulphuric or hydrochloric acid:

> $$\text{ester + water} \underset{}{\overset{\text{acid}}{\rightleftharpoons}} \text{alcohol + carboxylic acid}$$ **acid hydrolysis**

Can you remember what else we can do to speed up the reaction?

The hydrolysis is more effective if we use alkali instead of acid.
In this case the attack is by the nucleophilic OH^- ion.
It is attracted to the carbonyl carbon in the ester:

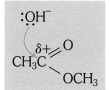

nucleophilic attack
on an ester by OH^-

Hydrolysis of an ester is speeded up by heating under reflux

The **salt of the carboxylic acid** is produced in the hydrolysis.
(We can't have an alkali and an acid in the same solution).

> **ester + alkali $\longrightarrow$ alcohol + salt of carboxylic acid**

Notice that this reaction is not reversible.

sodium ethanoate

If we want the original carboxylic acid, we can add a strong acid.
Then the carboxylate ion gains an H^+ ion to give the acid molecule:

$$CH_3COO^- + H^+ \longrightarrow CH_3COOH$$
$\quad\quad$ excess acid $\quad\quad\quad\quad$ ethanoic acid

With larger carboxylic acids, the undissociated molecule
will be only slightly soluble.
So it can be precipitated out of solution by the strong acid:

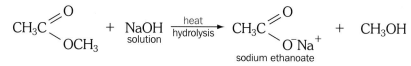

soluble benzoate ion $\quad\quad\quad\quad\quad\quad$ insoluble benzoic acid

Making soap

People have been making some form of soap since Roman times.
It is made from the natural esters we find in oils and fats.

The esters are hydrolysed using alkali in a reaction
called **saponification**.

The esters in oils and fats are called glycerides.
They are based on the propane-1,2,3-triol molecule.
(Its old name was glycerol.)
Look at the example below:

$$CH_2 - O - CO + CH_2 \frac{}{16} CH_3$$
$$CH - O - CO + CH_2 \frac{}{16} CH_3$$
$$CH_2 - O - CO + CH_2 \frac{}{16} CH_3$$

You can see that there are long hydrocarbon chains in the ester.
These dominate the properties of fats and oils, making them
insoluble in water.

In industry the oils or fats are boiled up with sodium hydroxide solution.
The esters are hydrolysed as shown below:

$$CH_2 - O - CO + CH_2 \frac{}{16} CH_3$$
$$CH - O - CO + CH_2 \frac{}{16} CH_3 \ + \ 3\,NaOH \ \xrightarrow{heat} \ 3\,CH_3 + CH_2 \frac{}{16} COO^- Na^+ \ + $$
$$CH_2 - O - CO + CH_2 \frac{}{16} CH_3$$

sodium stearate

$$CH_2 - OH$$
$$CH - OH$$
$$CH_2 - OH$$
propane-1,2,3-triol
(glycerol)

oil/fat   +   alkali   ⟶   soap   +   alcohol

> **Soap molecules are the sodium salts of long-chain fatty acids.**

The soap is precipitated from the reaction mixture by adding salt
(sodium chloride).

Soaps will contain a mixture of salts from the different fatty acids found
in the oil or fat you started with.
Look at the photo opposite:

We use soap because it is good at getting rid of grease,
otherwise water alone would do.
Look at the diagrams below that show how soap works:

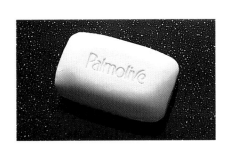

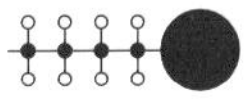

- *Which two oils are used to make this soap?*
- *Can you explain how the soap molecules remove grease? (See the diagrams below)*

$$\text{≬●} \ = \ CH_3 + CH_2 \frac{}{n} COO^-$$

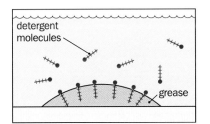
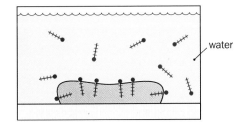
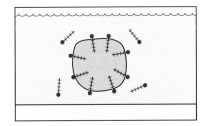

▷ Chemistry at work: Esters and carboxylic acids

Sweet-smelling esters

Esters are largely responsible for the sweet smells of fruits.
They form part of the complex mixture of compounds
that give a fruit its characteristic smell and taste.
For example, 280 compounds have been identified in
the aroma of strawberries.
Scientists are trying to understand more about how these
volatile substances are made in plants. Then they hope
to improve the quality of fruit produced.

Although it would be too expensive to recreate the smell and taste
of natural fruits exactly, simpler mixtures of esters and
carboxylic acids are added to imitate nature.
They appear on packaging as **flavourings**.

Another use of esters is in **perfumes**.
It can take years of research to produce a new perfume
with just the right mixture of compounds.
As well as an instantly recognisable smell, cosmetic scientists
also aim for a certain volatility. Too volatile, and the esters
will evaporate off quickly so the perfume would have
to be reapplied too often.
What would be the problem if the mixture was not volatile enough?

Some esters smell fruity

Perfumes contain esters

Keep edible longer!

Look at the list of ingredients from a fruit drink below:
The carboxylic acids, their salts and esters are highlighted.

> Fruit juices (apple, blackcurrant),
> sugar, water, citric acid ,
> colour (anthocyanins), flavourings ,
> preservatives (potassium sorbate ,
> sodium metabisulphite, sodium benzoate),
> antioxidant (ascorbic acid)

This squash contains esters and carboxylic acids

Notice that sodium or potassium salts of carboxylic acids are used.
For example benzoic acid is good at stopping the growth of bacteria.
However, it is insoluble in water, so it would be difficult
to mix in many food products, such as the squash above.
Can you think why the sodium salt of benzoic acid does dissolve in water?
Sodium benzoate is used in many foods as a **preservative**.
You can see its structure opposite:

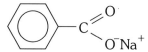

Sticky ester?

Esters can also be used as **solvents** in glues.
For example, polystrene cement has polystyrene (poly(phenylethene))
dissolved in ethyl ethanoate.
When you use the glue, the ethyl ethanoate evaporates off.
The polystyrene is left behind to harden and stick
the surfaces together.

Softer plastics

Polyesters are a common synthetic material.
But esters are also used to modify the properties of other plastics.
They are used with PVC (polyvinyl chloride) to make it more flexible.
The plastic used to make window frames is hard and rigid.
It is called uPVC. The u stands for unplasticised.

The PVC used to wrap foods contains esters as **plasticisers**.
These are molecules that get between the long chains
of the plastic molecules and stop
them binding together so strongly.
The structure of a plasticiser is
shown here:

$$CH_3(CH_2)_3\overset{\overset{\displaystyle CH_2CH_3}{|}}{C}HCH_2-O-C\overset{\displaystyle O}{<}$$
$$CH_3(CH_2)_3\underset{\underset{\displaystyle CH_2CH_3}{|}}{C}HCH_2-O-C\underset{\displaystyle O}{<}(CH_2)_4$$

Esters are used as plasticisers in PVC wrapping. There are now some health concerns over compounds from such wrappings being absorbed into foods

Put a plant in your tank!

Have you seen bright yellow rape growing in fields in spring
and early summer?
Biodiesel is a renewable fuel produced from oil extracted from plants
such as rape and sunflower.
It is designed to replace or be added to the diesel we get from crude oil.
British Biodiesel Ltd uses rapeseed oil to make biodiesel
because rape grows well in the UK climate.
Diesel engines don't have to be changed to run on biodiesel
and it reduces pollution from exhaust fumes.
It will be best used where cleaner running is needed quickly.
It can help improve air quality in cities. When used by boats
on canals and rivers, it breaks down quickly if it gets spilt.

The oils from the rapeseed are mixed with methanol in the presence
of potassium hydroxide:

Rapeseed is used to make biodiesel

$$\text{rapeseed oil + methanol} \xrightarrow{\text{KOH}} \text{propane-1,2,3-triol + methyl ester}$$
$$\text{(biodiesel)}$$

This reaction is used elsewhere in the chemical industry to make
pure fatty acids.
The propane-1,2,3-triol (glycerol) can be used in the manufacture of paints.
It is also used to make nitroglycerine explosive.

Pure fatty acids

The hydrolysis of natural oils or fats gives us a mixture of fatty acids.
The methyl esters produced in the reaction above
can be separated by fractional distillation, then hydrolysed
to give pure carboxylic acids.
These are useful starting materials for making longer chain molecules.
For example, the lithium salt of linolenic acid is used to treat cancer
of the pancreas.

Summary

- **Carboxylic acids** all contain the grouping:

- Their melting points are higher than expected because of hydrogen bonding.
- The carboxylic acids are **weak acids**:

    $$CH_3COOH + H_2O \rightleftharpoons CH_3COO^- + H_3O^+$$

    The position of equilibrium above lies well over to the left.
    They undergo the same reactions as other acids.
    For example, with an alkali they form a salt plus water.
    They give off CO_2 with carbonates.

- They react with alcohols, in the presence of a strong acid, to give an **ester** and water (in a reversible reaction).

- **Esters** are hydrolysed in the reverse reaction above.
    Soap can be made by hydrolysing the esters in oils or fats using an alkali.

- **Acid chlorides and acid anhydrides** also react with alcohols, but much more readily than carboxylic acids.
    They also react with water, ammonia and amines.
    Acid chlorides are more reactive than acid anhydrides.

    There is a summary of the main reactions on page 268.

▶ # Questions

1 Copy and complete:

Carboxylic acids are .... acids, so a solution will contain a .... proportion of undissociated acid .....
Ethanoic acid has .... bonding between its molecules, forming a .... with a .... melting point than expected.

Carboxylic acids show the usual reactions of acids. They form a .... and water when they react with an alkali. Carbon dioxide gas is given off when a .... is added to the acid.

Esters can be made by reacting the carboxylic acid with an .... The reaction is slow and reversible even when we have a .... acid present as a catalyst.
Esters can be hydrolysed by boiling with a strong alkali, such as sodium ..... This reaction is used to make .... in industry.

Acid chlorides and acid .... are more reactive than carboxylic acids. You can convert them into their 'parent' carboxylic acids by reacting them with .....

2 a) Give the structural formula of propanoic acid.
  b) Show with an equation what happens when it is added to water.
  c) Draw a diagram to show the intermolecular bonds between two propanoic acid molecules.
  d) Explain the difference in acidity between propanoic acid and propan-1-ol.

3 a) How would you convert ethanoic acid into ethanol?
  b) What do we call this type of reaction?
  c) Describe one way to make methyl propanoate.
  d) What do we call this type of reaction?
  e) Name the nucleophile in the reaction in part c).

4 a) Write an equation to show how to make butanoyl chloride.
  Give the equations for the reactions between:
  b) propanoyl chloride and water
  c) ethanoyl chloride and methanol
  d) ethanoyl chloride and ammonia
  e) benzoyl chloride and ethylamine

5 a) Write an equation to show how to make ethanoic anhydride.
  Give the equations for the reactions between ethanoic anhydride and:
  b) water
  c) methanol
  d) ammonia
  e) propylamine.

6 a) Write an equation to show the hydrolysis of ethyl ethanoate by heating with sodium hydroxide solution.
  b) Give an equation that shows the saponification of an ester found in a natural oil. You can represent the alkyl groups by the letter R.
  c) Draw a spider diagram showing some uses of esters.

20 Organic nitrogen compounds

In this chapter we will look at amines, amino acids, amides and nitriles.

▶ Amines

Have you ever visited a fish market or a shop that sells fresh fish? If you have, you will know the characteristic smell of **amines**. Amines are an important class of organic nitrogen compound. They are used in the manufacture of many dyes, drugs and plastics. There are three classes of amine. These are primary, secondary and tertiary amines. Look at their structures below:

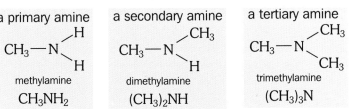

a primary amine

$$CH_3-N\begin{smallmatrix}H\\\\H\end{smallmatrix}$$

methylamine

CH_3NH_2

a secondary amine

$$CH_3-N\begin{smallmatrix}CH_3\\\\H\end{smallmatrix}$$

dimethylamine

$(CH_3)_2NH$

a tertiary amine

$$CH_3-N\begin{smallmatrix}CH_3\\\\CH_3\end{smallmatrix}$$

trimethylamine

$(CH_3)_3N$

- How many alkyl (or aryl) groups are attached to the nitrogen atom in each class of amine?

As you can see from the compounds shown above, amines can be thought of as substituted ammonia (NH_3) molecules.

In a primary amine, one of ammonia's hydrogens has been replaced:

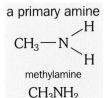

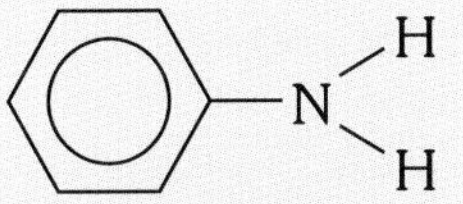

$$\bigcirc\!-N\begin{smallmatrix}H\\\\H\end{smallmatrix}$$ a primary aryl amine

phenylamine

$C_6H_5NH_2$

All three hydrogens are replaced in a tertiary amine. Amines can also form quaternary cations. These are equivalent to the ammonium ion, NH_4^+. For example:

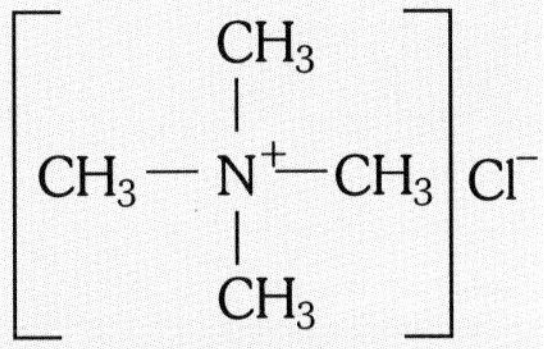

$$\left[CH_3-\underset{\underset{CH_3}{|}}{\overset{\overset{CH_3}{|}}{N^+}}-CH_3\right]Cl^-$$

tetramethylammonium chloride

$(CH_3)_4N^+Cl^-$

These salts are white crystalline solids that are soluble in water.

Primary and secondary amines form hydrogen bonds between their molecules. Why can't tertiary amines?
These are not as strong as those formed between alcohols or carboxylic acids. Can you think why not?
Smaller amines of all three classes are soluble in water. Hydrogen bonds form between the amine and water molecules.

Fish oil contains amines such as trimethylamine

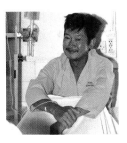

Amines and their derivatives are used as drugs to treat many diseases such as malaria and 'sleeping sickness'

Quaternary ammonium salts are used in detergents to help remove stains. They are called cationic surfactants

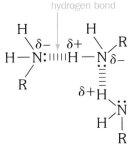

Amines form hydrogen bonds between their molecules

239

▷ Amines as bases

As you might expect of compounds related to ammonia, amines are weak bases.
In water the following equilibrium is established:

$$CH_3CH_2NH_2 + H_2O \rightleftharpoons CH_3CH_2NH_3^+ + OH^-$$

The hydroxide ions (OH^-) formed cause the solution to be alkaline.
So an amine solution will turn red litmus blue.

Like all bases, they react with acids to form salts:

$$CH_3CH_2NH_2 + HCl \longrightarrow CH_3CH_2N^+H_3\ Cl^-$$
ethylammonium chloride

$$(CH_3CH_2)_2NH + HCl \longrightarrow (CH_3CH_2)_2N^+H_2\ Cl^-$$
diethylammonium chloride

$$(CH_3CH_2)_3N + HCl \longrightarrow (CH_3CH_2)_3N^+H\ Cl^-$$
triethylammonium chloride

In these reactions the amine accepts an H^+ ion from the acid.
The lone pair of electrons on the nitrogen atom in the amine forms a dative bond with the H^+ ion.
(The dative bond was discussed on page 67.)
This is shown below:

Red litmus turns blue in a solution of an amine

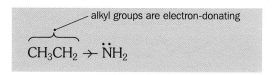

or

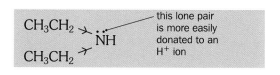

a 'dot and cross' diagram showing nitrogen donating its lone pair to H^+

The strength of an amine as a base depends on three things:
1. the availablity of nitrogen's lone pair to bond with H^+
2. the stability of the positive ion formed, and
3. the solubility of the amine

Remember that alkyl groups tend to donate electrons.
So how will this affect the first two factors listed above?
Let's consider ethylamine and diethylamine:

Ethylamine is a primary amine. It has one alkyl group which donates electrons towards the nitrogen atom.
On the other hand, diethylamine is a secondary amine.
It has two alkyl groups, each feeding electrons to nitrogen.
This makes the nitrogen's lone pair more accessible in diethylamine than in ethylamine.
The **two** ethyl groups also reduce the density of charge on the positive ion produced to a greater extent.

What would you predict about the strength of triethylamine as a base? This is where the solubility factors noted above become important. The tertiary amine is less soluble in water.
Read on and use the table on the next page to answer the question.

alkyl groups are electron-donating

$$CH_3CH_2 \rightarrow \ddot{N}H_2$$

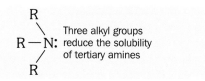
this lone pair is more easily donated to an H^+ ion

Three alkyl groups reduce the solubility of tertiary amines

Do you recall K_a, the dissociation constant that we used to indicate the strength of a carboxylic acid in the last chapter? We can also use K_b, a constant that tells us the strength of a base. As with K_a, **the larger the value of K_b, the stronger the base**. You can learn more about equilibrium constants in Chapter 30.

Look at the table opposite:
Do these values agree with the examples we looked at on the last page?
What can you say about the relative strength of phenylamine as a base?

Amine	K_b / mol dm^{-3}
ethylamine	5.1×10^{-4}
diethylamine	10.0×10^{-4}
triethylamine	5.6×10^{-4}
phenylamine	4.2×10^{-10}

K_b for ammonia is 1.8×10^{-5} mol dm^{-3}.
What does this tell you about the strength of ammonia as a base compared with a) alkylamines and b) phenylamine

> **Phenylamine is a weaker base than the alkylamines or ammonia.**

In phenylamine nitrogen's lone pair of electrons is drawn into the benzene ring to extend the delocalised system:

the nitrogen donates electrons into the delocalised system, making its lone pair less available for bonding to an H$^+$ ion

This makes nitrogen's lone pair less available for bonding with H$^+$ ions. The resulting positive ion has a high charge density on the nitrogen as electrons are pulled into the benzene ring. This destabilises the ion, making it less likely to form or to exist for any length of time.

Preparation of amines

We can make amines in a number of different ways. Ammonia can be added to a halogenoalkane (haloalkane). We use a concentrated solution of ammonia in ethanol:

$$CH_3CH_2Cl + NH_3 \xrightarrow{100\,°C} CH_3CH_2NH_2 + HCl$$
chloroethane   ammonia   ethylamine

As we saw on page 183, the primary amine formed will in turn attack the halogenoalkane. This produces the secondary amine:

$$CH_3CH_2Cl + CH_3CH_2NH_2 \longrightarrow (CH_3CH_2)_2NH + HCl$$
diethylamine

Can you write the equation for the secondary amine reacting with the halogenoalkane? What about the formation of tetraethylammonium chloride? As you can see, a mixture of amines is produced. Therefore, this is not a good method for preparing a specific amine.

A better way is the reduction of a nitro-compound or a nitrile:

$$\left\{ CH_3CH_2NO_2 \xrightarrow[\text{then } H_2O]{\text{LiAlH}_4 \text{ (in dry ether)}} CH_3CH_2NH_2 \right.$$
$$\text{or } CH_3C{\equiv}N$$

Alternatively, vapour of the nitrile or nitro compound and hydrogen are passed over a nickel catalyst. To prepare an aromatic amine, the nitrobenzene is reduced by tin and concentrated hydrochloric acid (see page 218):

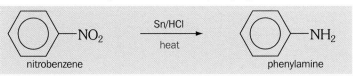

nitrobenzene — NO_2 $\xrightarrow[\text{heat}]{\text{Sn/HCl}}$ — NH_2 phenylamine

Our levels of an enzyme called monoamineoxidase control our risk-taking tendencies!

Phenylamine is important in the dyeing industry

▷ Reactions of amines

We have already seen on page 240 how amines react as **bases**. They accept H^+ ions to form salts.

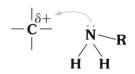

Amines can attack electron-deficient carbon atoms. They can act as nucleophiles

Alkylation

On the last page we also recalled the chain of reactions that occur when we mix ammonia with a halogenoalkane. These reactions between the amines and the halogenoalkanes are called **alkylation**.
Can you see why?
Like ammonia, the amines formed **act as nucleophiles** and they also attack the halogenoalkane.

Acylation

Amines can also act as nucleophiles when they react with acid chlorides and acid anhydrides.
It is not surprising that amines attack acid chlorides.
Remember that acid chlorides contain a strongly electron deficient carbon atom. This will attract the lone pair on an amine's nitrogen atom, initiating nucleophilic attack:

$$CH_3C \overset{O}{\underset{Cl}{\diagup}} \qquad \text{nucleophilic attack}$$
$$\ddot{N}H_2CH_2CH_3$$

The product is a **substituted amide**:

N-ethylethanamide $\quad CH_3C \overset{O}{\underset{NHCH_2CH_3}{\diagup}} \qquad (+HCl)$

In effect, we have removed one of the amine's hydrogen atoms from the —NH_2 group and replaced it by an acyl group (R—CO—) Hence, we call this type of reaction **acylation**.

Fumes of HCl are given off when an amine reacts with an acid chloride

With transition metal ions

Do you remember how transition metals form complex ions?
In chapter 11 we met complex ions formed with ammonia.
Amines react in a similar way. They use the lone pair of electrons on their nitrogen atom to form a dative bond with the central transition metal ion.
Look at the complex below:

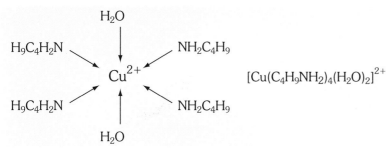

$[Cu(C_4H_9NH_2)_4(H_2O)_2]^{2+}$

Can you recall the name we give to molecules that donate a pair of electrons to the central ion?

If you look back to page 138, you will see how a ligand with two amine groups combines with a transition metal ion. What do we call such a ligand?

This deep blue complex is formed between Cu^{2+} ions and butylamine

With nitric(III) acid (or nitrous acid), HNO₂

This is a very important reaction in the manufacture of dyes.
The starting material is an aromatic amine, such as phenylamine.
The nitric(III) acid (or nitrous acid) is produced in situ.
We add sodium nitate(III), $NaNO_2$, to a solution
of the aromatic amine in concentrated hydrochloric acid:

$$NaNO_2 + HCl \longrightarrow HNO_2 + NaCl$$
nitric(III) acid
(nitrous acid)

The nitric(III) acid produced then reacts with the aromatic amine:

benzenediazonium chloride

The reaction is called **diazotisation**.
The reacting mixture is kept cool, below 5 °C,
because the diazonium ion is so reactive.
It reacts with water above 5 °C, giving off nitrogen gas (N_2).
In industry it is used to react with other benzene compounds,
forming brightly coloured **azo dyes**. (See page 218.)
An example is shown below:

phenoxide ion
(produced from phenol
reacting with alkali)

an azo dye
(an orange precipitate)

Coupling!

This is known as a **coupling reaction**. Can you see why?
The compound of benzene added, in this case phenol,
is called a **coupling agent**.

Look at the photo opposite:
Although the solution containing the diazonium ion is ice-cold,
the reaction with the coupling agent happens immediately.
Can you recall what type of reagent attacks a benzene ring?
On page 199 we saw how the electron-rich ring is open to attack
from electrophiles.
Look at the structure of a diazonium ion above:
Can you see which part of it acts as the electrophile?

The azo dyes are very stable, unlike diazonium ions.
The benzene rings on either side of the —N=N— group,
or azo group, become linked. The delocalised system of electrons
extends through the —N=N— group, which acts like a bridge.
This extended delocalisation makes the azo dyes stable.
Why do you think that this is so important for a good dye?

When nitric(III) acid (or nitrous acid) is added to an alkyl amine,
we get a different reaction. A mixture of products is formed.
The intermediate diazonium ion made, $[R—N\equiv N]^+$, is so unstable
that it can't be isolated and it decomposes immediately.
It breaks down into a mixture of alcohols and alkenes, plus nitrogen gas (N_2).

What happens to a poor dye in bright sunshine?

▷ Amides

Amides are important compounds in plants and animals.
If you look on the side of a cereal box, you may well see that niacin is listed in the ingredients. This is an example of a carboxylic acid that is a B vitamin. It gets converted into an amide in one of its reactions as it is used by our bodies.

> The amides contain the $-C\underset{NH_2}{\overset{O}{\diagdown}}$ group.

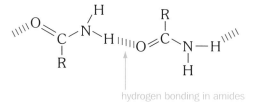

Nicotinamide is found in liver, leafy green vegetables and milk

Physical properties

The amides have higher boiling points than expected for molecules of a similar mass.
Methanamide is a liquid at room temperature.
From ethanamide onwards they are solids.
Can you think why? Why do other 'families' of compounds, such as alcohols, carboxylic acids and amines, have relatively high boiling points?
Look at the diagram opposite:

The smaller amides are soluble in water. Why?

hydrogen bonding in amides

Preparing amides

They can be made by:

1. heating an ammonium salt of a carboxylic acid:

$$CH_3C\underset{O^-NH_4^+}{\overset{O}{\diagdown}} \xrightarrow{\text{heat}} CH_3C\underset{NH_2}{\overset{O}{\diagdown}} + H_2O$$

ethanamide

or

2. adding concentrated ammonia solution to an acid chloride:

$$CH_3C\underset{Cl}{\overset{O}{\diagdown}} + NH_3 \longrightarrow CH_3C\underset{NH_2}{\overset{O}{\diagdown}} + HCl$$

Reactions of amides

Hydrolysis

Amides react with both acids and bases.
The reactions involve nucleophilic attack on the carbonyl carbon.
This results in substitution of the —NH$_2$ group:
Look at the reactions opposite:

$$R-C\underset{NH_2}{\overset{O}{\diagdown}} + H_2O \xrightarrow{\text{hydrolysis}} \begin{cases} \xrightarrow[\text{acid}]{H^+} R-C\underset{OH}{\overset{O}{\diagdown}} + NH_4^+ \\ \xrightarrow[\text{alkali}]{OH^-} R-C\underset{O^-}{\overset{O}{\diagdown}} + NH_3 \end{cases}$$

amide

carboxylic acid

salt of carboxylic acid

Hofmann degradation

This is a useful reaction in organic synthesis.
In effect, it **removes one carbon** atom from the original chain.
We add bromine and an alkali to the amide:

$$R-C\underset{NH_2}{\overset{O}{\diagdown}} \xrightarrow{Br_2/\text{conc. NaOH}} R-NH_2 \;(+ CO_3^{2-})$$

The amine formed has one less carbon than the amide that we started with.

Dehydration

We can *remove* H_2O from an amide by heating it with phosphorus(V) oxide (P_2O_5 or P_4O_{10}):

$$R-C\underset{NH_2}{\overset{O}{\big<}} \xrightarrow[\text{heat}]{P_2O_5} \underset{\text{nitrile}}{R-C\equiv N} + H_2O$$

You can read more about nitriles below.

▷ Nitriles

Chemists find nitriles so important because *adding a nitrile group (—CN) to a molecule increases the length of the chain by one carbon atom.*
This is useful if the starting material to make a new compound does not have enough carbon atoms to begin with.
Starting materials are often taken from the petrochemical industry. Sometimes they are oils and fats extracted from plants or animals.

The nitriles are named by counting the number of carbon atoms and adding the ending -nitrile to the appropriate alkane.
For example, $CH_3CH_2CH_2C\equiv N$ is called butanenitrile.

We have seen on page 183 how nitriles can be made from halogenoalkanes:

$$\underset{\text{chloromethane}}{CH_3Cl} + K^+CN^- \xrightarrow[\text{in ethanol}]{\text{heat under reflux}} CH_3C\equiv N + K^+Cl^-$$

Once the carbon chain has been lengthened, you can either:
1. **hydrolyse the nitrile**
The nitrile can be boiled with acid:

$$RCN + HCl + 2\,H_2O \longrightarrow RCOOH + NH_4Cl$$

$$\underset{\text{nitrile}}{R-C\equiv N} \xrightarrow[\textbf{by HCl/H}_2\textbf{O}]{\textbf{hydrolysis}} \underset{\text{carboxylic acid}}{R-C\underset{OH}{\overset{O}{\big<}}}$$

The carboxylic acid formed can then be converted into a range of other products.
Look back to page 227 to see what functional groups can be introduced via a carboxylic acid:
2. **reduce the nitrile**
Again, lithium tetrahydridoaluminate(III) can be used as the reducing agent, followed by adding water:

$$R-C\equiv N + 4\,[H] \xrightarrow[\substack{\textbf{by LiAlH}_4 \textbf{ in dry ether} \\ \textbf{(followed by H}_2\textbf{O)}}]{\textbf{reduction}} R-CH_2-NH_2$$

The amine formed can also act as the intermediate in 'multi-step' synthesis routes to new compounds.
You can find out more about the synthesis of organic compounds in Chapter 22.

Nitriles are important chemicals when devising ways of preparing new compounds

The refining of crude oil provides the starting materials for many compounds in industry

Which 'chain store' would you visit to remove a carbon atom?

▷ Amino acids

This group of compounds contains two functional groups: an amino group (—NH_2) and a carboxylic acid (—COOH). They are one of the most vital sets of compounds found in all living things.
Amino acids are the 'building blocks' of proteins. Proteins are present in our muscles, hair, skin, blood, nerves and tendons. They form enzymes, antibodies and many hormones.
So you can see just how important amino acids are!

We will find out how they combine to make proteins in Chapter 21, which looks at polymers.

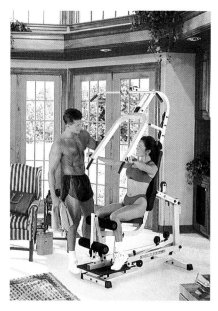
Amino acids make up the protein found in muscle

Chemical properties

The amino acids will undergo the usual reactions of amines and carboxylic acids.
However, they also react within each molecule.
This is because they contain an acidic and a basic group.
Look at the reaction below:

$$H_2N - \underset{\underset{R}{|}}{CH} - C\underset{OH}{\overset{O}{<}} \rightleftharpoons \overset{+}{H_3N} - \underset{\underset{R}{|}}{CH} - C\underset{O^-}{\overset{O}{<}}$$

a zwitterion (from the German *zwei* meaning two)

The ion is called a **zwitterion**. It has a positive and a negative part.
This ionic nature makes amino acids crystalline solids, soluble in water.

Solutions of amino acids will resist changes in pH when we add acid or alkali to them:

Add acid:

$$\overset{+}{H_3N} - \underset{\underset{R}{|}}{CH} - C\underset{O^-}{\overset{O}{<}} + H^+ \rightarrow \overset{+}{H_3N} - \underset{\underset{R}{|}}{CH} - C\underset{OH}{\overset{O}{<}}$$

Solutions that do this are called **buffer solutions**.
You can learn more about them on page 392.

Add alkali:

$$OH^- + \overset{+}{H_3N} - \underset{\underset{R}{|}}{CH} - C\underset{O^-}{\overset{O}{<}} \rightarrow H_2N - \underset{\underset{R}{|}}{CH} - C\underset{O^-}{\overset{O}{<}} + H_2O$$

Naturally occurring amino acids

The proteins that are found in our bodies are made up from twenty-odd different amino acids.
However, they are all 2-amino-carboxylic acids.
Look at the simplest example below:

$$H_2N - \underset{\underset{H}{|}}{\overset{\overset{H}{|}}{C}} - COOH$$

glycine (aminoethanoic acid)

Glycine is neutral, but other amino acids can be acidic or basic depending on the groups attached to their side-chains.
Biochemists still refer to the amino acids by their common names.
They abbreviate these to three letters when recording the sequence of amino acids in a protein. So glycine becomes Gly.

The following is the amino acid sequence of a hormone found in sheep:
Ser.Tyr.Ser.Met.Glu.His.Phe.Arg.Try.Gly.Lys.Pro. Val.Gly.Lys.Lys.Arg.Arg.Pro.Val.Lys.Val.Tyr.Pro. Ala.Gly.Glu.Asp.Asp.Glu.Ala.Ser.Glu.Ala.Pro.Leu. Glu.Phe

Optical isomerism

The naturally occurring amino acids also have another
structural feature in common.
They form the same type of **optical isomers**.

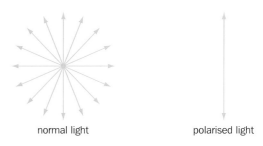

normal light   polarised light

| **Optical isomers rotate the plane of polarised light.** |

Normal light is not polarised. It is made up from
electromagnetic radiation, with electric and magnetic fields
vibrating at right angles to each other in *every possible direction*.
Light that has passed through polarised glass only vibrates
in one direction. Look at the diagram opposite:

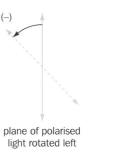

plane of polarised light rotated left   ...or right

If a molecule contains a carbon atom bonded to four different groups
then it exhibits optical isomerism.
There are two ways to arrange the groups around the carbon atom
that cannot be superimposed.
The two optical isomers are ***mirror-images*** of each other.
They are said to be ***asymmetric*** molecules.
(Remember that isomers are molecules with the same atoms
but different arrangements in space.)
Look at the diagram below:

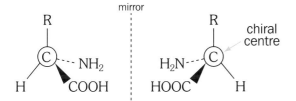

| **The two optical isomers are called enantiomers.** |

Make a model of two optical isomers. Try to place one on top
of the other so that all the atoms correspond. Can you do it?

| **The carbon attached to four different atoms or groups is called the chiral centre.** |

The two molecules that are mirror images will rotate
the plane of polarised light in different directions.
One will rotate it left by the same amount that the other rotates it right.
A mixture containing equal amounts of the two enantiomers
is called a **racemic mixture** or **racemate**.
The racemate has no effect on the plane of polarised light.

To distiguish the two enantiomers, the sign $(+)$ or $(-)$ is put in front of the name.
$(+)$ enantiomers rotate the plane of polarised light clockwise,
whereas $(-)$ ones rotate it anticlockwise. An example is $(+)$-alanine.

Enzymes in our bodies are sensitive to the structure of optical isomers.
They will only work with one of the pair.
All other properties and reactions of optical isomers will be the same.

All naturally occurring amino acids are optically active, except one.
Why isn't glycine optically active? Look at its structure on the last page?
Is it an asymmetric molecule? Has it got a chiral carbon atom?

*Diagram of a simple polarimeter.
Can you explain how it works?*

247

▷ Chemistry at work: Proteins

On page 246 we saw how important proteins are.
These vital compounds are made up from amino acids.
You can read how their long molecules (polymers) are formed
in the next chapter.

Our bodies can make proteins from amino acids.
We need to include eight amino acids in our diet which our bodies
cannot make themselves.
We take them into our bodies as animal or plant protein.
The proteins are broken down in the digestive system into amino acids
which can then be reassembled into new proteins.

Proteins are broken down by hydrolysis.

There are enzymes, given the general name proteases,
in the small intestine which catalyse the hydrolysis.
They help to break the **peptide links** that join the amino
acids together.

Look at the diagram opposite:

Sources of protein include meat, fish, cheese, milk, nuts and soya

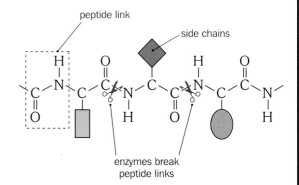

peptide link

side chains

enzymes break peptide links

Structure of proteins

Proteins are thought of as having four levels of structure.
The **primary structure** describes the sequence of amino acids
in the protein chain.
From a small number of amino acids we can produce millions
of different proteins.

The protein chain is usually folded or twisted in one of two
arrangements. Either it forms a coiled helix or it forms a pleated sheet.
This is known as the **secondary structure**. Interactions between
different parts of the protein chain hold it in shape.

The coiled helix or pleated sheet chain is folded upon itself in a
complex manner and is again held like this by interactions between
different parts of the chain.
This is the **tertiary structure** of the protein.
The shape taken up by the protein is particularly important for molecules
which act as enzymes. They must have a very precise shape
in order to interact with a specific substrate molecule. The part of the
protein molecule involved in this interaction is called the active site.

In some proteins a number of molecules are attracted to each other and
form a larger structure. This is the **quaternary structure**.

The hormone insulin is a protein. It controls the uptake of glucose
by our bodies.
People who can't produce this hormone suffer from diabetes.
Insulin forms a hexamer containing six monomer molecules.

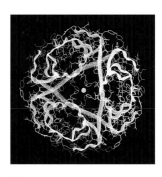

This represents the tertiary structure of insulin

People suffering from diabetes need regular injections of insulin

Summary

- **Amines** are weak bases.
  They react with acids to form salts.
- They act as nucleophiles in reactions with halogenoalkanes to produce
  a range of substituted amines (see page 241).
- Amines can be prepared by reduction of nitriles.
  The reduction of nitro-compounds is the best way to prepare aromatic amines.
- Aromatic amines react with nitric(III) acid (or nitrous acid) to form diazonium salts.
  These are important intermediates in the dyeing industry.
- **Amides** and **nitriles** are also important in chemical synthesis of new compounds.
  You can see a summary of the reactions of amines, amides and nitriles on page 269.
- **Amino acids** show both acidic and basic properties because they have
  amine and carboxylic acid groupings in the same molecule.
- Amino acids join together to make proteins (through peptide links).
- Proteins are broken down by hydrolysis of the peptide links.

▷ Questions

1 Copy and complete:

Amines are bases. They react with .... to form salts, such as tetramethyl.... chloride. They have higher boiling points than expected because of .... bonding between molecules.

They can be prepared by reacting .... with a halogenoalkane, although this produces a variety of amines.
A better way is the .... of a nitrile by lithium tetrahydridoaluminate(III) in dry ether. Aromatic amines are prepared by .... nitro-compounds using .... and concentrated hydrochloric acid.

.... salts are important in making dyes. They are made by reacting an aromatic amine with nitric(III) acid (or .... acid) at a temperature between .... and .... °C.

Proteins are made up of long sequences of .... acids, joined together by .... links. These links are broken down in a .... reaction.

2 a) Look at the three molecules below:

$$\overset{..}{N}$$ with H, H, H

$$CH_3CH_2\overset{..}{N}H_2$$

(benzene ring)$-\overset{..}{N}H_2$

Put ammonia, ethylamine and phenylamine in order of their strength as bases (strongest base first).
b) Explain how you arrived at this order.

3 Complete this equation:
  a) $CH_3CH_2CH_2Br + NH_3 \longrightarrow$ .... + ...
  b) Give the conditions needed for the reaction in part a).
  c) **Explain** why this is not a good method to prepare the amine in part a).
  d) Suggest a better way to prepare the amine in part a).
  e) Name the reagents and conditions you would use to prepare a sample of phenylamine.
  f) Describe how you would convert the phenylamine into an azo dye. Give equations and conditions for each step.

4 Complete these equations:

  a) $CH_3COO^-NH_4^+ \xrightarrow{\text{heat}}$ .... + ...
  b) $CH_3COCl + NH_3 \longrightarrow$ .... + ...
  c) Name the organic product if you react butanamide with:
      i) bromine and conc. sodium hydroxide solution
      ii) phosphorus(V) oxide.

5 a) How would you prepare propanenitrile from chloroethane?
  b) Name the organic product when you:
      i)   hydrolyse propanenitrile
      ii) reduce propanenitrile.
  c) Give the reagents and conditions needed for the reactions in part b).

6 a) Draw the other enantiomer of alanine shown here:
  b) Label its chiral centre.
  c) What do we call a mixture containing equal amounts of each enantiomer?

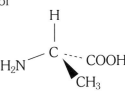

21 Polymers

▷ Plastics

Introduction

Think of the many things made from plastics that we use in our lives:
From your toothbrush to the keyboard on your computer, plastics are everywhere. It's hard for us to imagine a world without plastics.

Plastics are examples of synthetic **polymers**.
Polymers are very large molecules made up of many repeating units.
A polymer is made by joining together hundreds or thousands of small, reactive molecules called **monomers**.

In the 1930s chemists worked out how to make long-chain molecules.
However, the discovery of the most common plastic was made by accident. Poly(ethene), or polythene, was first made in a high-pressure vessel that was being used to investigate the reaction of ethene with an aldehyde.
There was a slight leak in the vessel and some oxygen entered.
When the vessel was opened, researchers found a waxy solid.
The first poly(ethene) had been made.

Fortunately, they didn't just throw away the result of their mishap.
They found its empirical formula was CH_2.
Its relative molecular mass was very high, and they realised the potential of their discovery. But further development was hindered by the difficulty in repeating the experiment.

A few years later, it was realised that the amount of oxygen present was a vital factor, as well as the temperature and pressure.
The reaction did not involve the aldehyde:

Poly(ethene) made like this is called **low-density polythene**.
Its large molecules are branched, not straight.
This makes it impossible for the chains to pack neatly together and accounts for its low density.

However, in the 1950s a chemist called Karl Ziegler discovered a catalyst that helped produce poly(ethene) with straight chains.
Once again, the discovery was rather lucky as an essential ingredient for the catalyst to work was an impurity left in his reaction vessel.
This new type of poly(ethene) had different properties.
Its chains could pack closely together and formed high-density poly(ethene).
This is a much stronger plastic and has a higher melting temperature.
So it can be used to make water pipes and containers that can be sterilised.

This shows how the forces between the polymer chains are very important when considering its properties.

Which things in this photo are made from synthetic polymers?

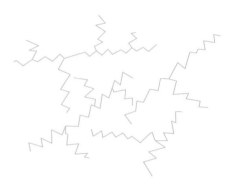

The branched chains in low density poly(ethene) can't pack in regular patterns

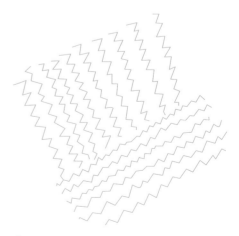

Chains in high density poly(ethene) line up and form crystalline areas in the plastic

▶ Properties of plastics

We have just seen how the shape of a polymer chain
can affect its density.
We also saw that high-density poly(ethene) melts at
a higher temperature than low-density poly(ethene).
Can you think why?
What type of attraction will be holding neighbouring chains together
in poly(ethene)? Remember that each chain is made from
non-polar molecules (see page 73).

Straight chains can approach each other more closely
than branched chains.
There will be more contact between their molecules.
So there will be stronger van der Waals forces between chains.

Polymers with straight chains are also stronger for the same reasons.
Where the chains are packed together in regular patterns,
we get crystalline regions in the plastic.

Some plastics can be drawn out into fibres.
Poly(propene) is one example. It is the plastic used for milk crates.
But when it is made into fibres, it is used in carpets.
Look at the diagram below:

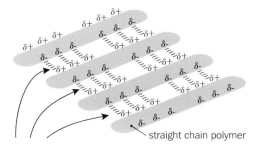

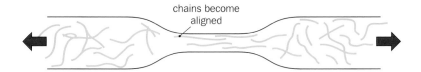

*Van der Waals forces (forces of attraction
between instantaneous dipoles) act along the
length of the polymer chain. This results in
polymers with higher melting points and greater
tensile strength than those with randomly
branched chains*

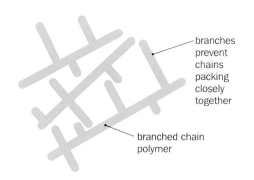

branches
prevent
chains
packing
closely
together

branched chain
polymer

chains become
aligned

The presence of polar groups along the length of the polymer
will also increase its strength.
In polymers such as nylon there are strong intermolecular forces
between chains. Nylon is a polyamide. We met amides
in the last chapter (see page 244). Can you guess
what type of forces exist between nylon's molecules?

The strongest types of forces between chains are covalent bonds.
Imagine a polymer chain actually covalently bonded
to its neighbouring chains. This is how rubber tyres
are made more durable. Sulphur atoms make **'cross-links'**
between the rubber chains. The process is called **vulcanisation**.

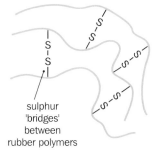

sulphur
'bridges'
between
rubber polymers

*Rubber is vulcanised to
make it harder wearing*

Thermosets and thermoplastics

Plastics like poly(ethene) soften when we heat them.
They can be remoulded to make new shapes.
These are called **thermoplastics**.
It is relatively easy to separate the chains, although
the longer the chain the higher the melting point.
Can you think why?

Other polymers can be made up from giant networks of atoms.
These thermosetting plastics, or **thermosets,** cannot be melted.
Chains can't be separated because there are covalent bonds
between them. If heated strongly enough, these hard, rigid plastics
eventually char and burn. At this point, covalent bonds
are being broken in the thermoset.

Thermoplastic

Thermoset

▷ Addition polymers

Can you remember how alkenes, such as ethene, react?
What happens to their double bond? (See page 181.)

> **Poly(ethene) is formed from ethene in an addition polymerisation reaction.**

In addition reactions we can think of the double bond
between carbon atoms as 'opening up'.
Then new single bonds are formed with other atoms.
In the case of polymerisation, the new bonds are formed
between molecules of the monomer.
Look at the reaction below:

Low-density poly(ethene) was used to make this bag

We can represent the reaction like this:

$$n \, C_2H_4 \xrightarrow{\text{addition polymerisation}} \text{(C}_2H_4\text{)}_n$$

ethene → poly(ethene)   where n = a large number

By replacing one or more of the hydrogen atoms in ethene
we can get a variety of other addition polymers.
Examples are shown in the tables below:

Monomer	Polymer and some uses
chloroethene	poly(chloroethene) used for: gutters, records, windows, doors, insulation for wires
tetrafluoroethene	poly(tetrafluoroethene) used for: non-stick lining for pans, electrical insulation
phenylethene	poly(phenylethene) used for: expanded form is used for heat insulation, packaging, cups; non-expanded form is used for yoghurt pots, toys

Example – Poly(propene)

propene monomer

Poly(propene) is another addition polymer.
It can have 3 different structures, depending on
the conditions used to make it:

1. **isotactic** – all the methyl groups are on the **same side** of the chain:

2. **syndiotactic** – the methyl groups **alternate regularly** from side to side:

3. **atactic** – the methyl groups are **arranged randomly** along the chain.
   This is a soft, rubbery plastic because its chains can't pack
   together in a regular pattern, unlike the other 2 forms
   of poly(propene).

▷ Mechanism of addition polymerisation

At the start of the chapter we looked at two types of poly(ethene).
One has a high density and the other a low density.
We can explain how each type is formed by looking at
the mechanism of polymerisation.

This toy is made from high-density poly(ethene)

Low-density poly(ethene) is made up of branched polymer chains.
A molecule that starts off the reaction is needed.
This is called an **initiator**.
Look back to page 250:
What was the initiator when poly(ethene) was discovered?
Can you recall the type of mechanism that starts with
an initiation step? (See page 170.)

The initiator produces a free radical. Peroxides are often used:

$$\text{Peroxide} \xrightarrow[\text{electron}]{\text{loses an}} \text{Rad·} \quad \textbf{Initiation step}$$
$$\text{(initiator)} \qquad\qquad \text{(free radical)}$$

Remember that a free radical is very reactive.
This then reacts with an ethene molecule:

$$\text{Rad·} + CH_2 = CH_2 \longrightarrow Rad - CH_2 - \overset{\bullet}{C}H_2$$

> **This is homolytic fission of the double bond. (See page 170.)**

The free radical produced can then attack another ethene.

$$Rad - CH_2 - \overset{\bullet}{C}H_2 + CH_2 = CH_2 \longrightarrow Rad - CH_2 - CH_2 - CH_2 - \overset{\bullet}{C}H_2$$

And so on:

$$Rad - CH_2 - CH_2 - CH_2 - \overset{\bullet}{C}H_2 + CH_2 = CH_2 \longrightarrow Rad - CH_2 - CH_2 - CH_2 - CH_2 - CH_2 - \overset{\bullet}{C}H_2$$

These are the **propagation steps** (see page 171).

Sometimes a branched chain will result from a polymer free radical
where the spare electron is not at the end of the chain:

$$\sim\sim\sim CH_2 - \overset{\overset{\displaystyle H}{|}}{C}H - CH_2 \sim\sim\sim + Rad - \sim\sim\sim CH_2 - \overset{\bullet}{C}H_2 \longrightarrow Rad - \sim\sim\sim CH_2 - CH_2 + \sim\sim\sim CH_2 - \overset{\overset{\displaystyle H}{|}}{\overset{\bullet}{C}}H - CH_2 \sim\sim\sim$$

$$+ CH_2 = CH_2$$

$$\overset{\bullet}{C}H_2$$
$$|$$
$$CH_2$$
$$|$$
$$\sim\sim\sim CH_2 - CH - CH_2 - \sim\sim\sim$$

branched chain starts like this

How will the polymerisation reaction stop?
Look back to page 171 and find out about **termination steps**.

On the other hand, high-density polyethene is only made from
straight chains.
Ziegler catalysts ensure that ethene molecules can only join
end to end:

$$M - CH_2 - CH_3 \longrightarrow M - CH_2 - CH_2 - CH_2 - CH_3 \longrightarrow M - CH_2 - CH_2 - CH_2 - CH_2 - CH_2 - CH_3$$
$$\text{Ziegler catalyst}$$
$$CH_2 = CH_2 \qquad\qquad CH_2 = CH_2$$

linear chain is produced with a Ziegler catalyst

The catalyst is an organo-metallic compound, in which M is the metal.

▷ Condensation polymerisation

Not all polymers are formed by addition reactions.
Some are produced as a result of a **condensation** reaction.
We met this type of reaction on page 225.
Can you remember what happens?

Examples of polymers formed like this are nylon, polyester,
and one of the first plastics manufactured called Bakelite.
Bakelite is a hard, brittle thermoset, seen in the brown plugs
on very old electrical equipment.
One of the latest polymers to be successfully developed,
called Kevlar, is also made in a condensation reaction.

Kevlar has found a wide variety of uses,
including strong, lightweight tennis
rackets reinforced by its fibres

Nylon

Nylon was invented just before the Second World War.
It was used to make parachutes in place of silk.
Silk is an example of a natural protein. Can you recall
from the last chapter which monomers combine in proteins?

Chemists in the 1930s were trying to copy the natural protein
structures of wool and silk. They are made from amino acids,
joined by **peptide links**. Look at the structure below:

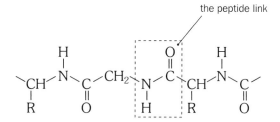

Part of a silk protein chain

Silk chains pack together to form
pleated sheets

An American chemist called Wallace Carothers worked out that
he could get the same structure by reacting amines with carboxylic acids.
The trick was to use monomers with an amine group ($-NH_2$)
or acid group ($-COOH$) at each end.
Look at the reaction below:

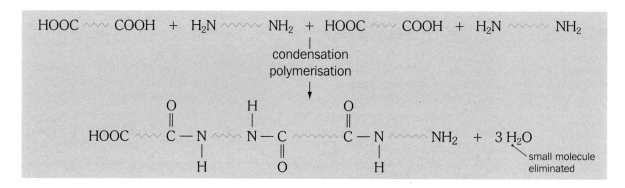

Remember that *a condensation reaction is defined as an addition reaction
followed by an elimination reaction*. So a small molecule is always given off
in condensation reactions.
● How does this differ from addition polymerisation?

In industry we use acid chlorides instead of carboxylic acids to make nylon.
● Why do you think this is the case? Which is the more reactive grouping?
● Which small molecule will be eliminated when we use an acid chloride?

Different types of nylon can be made depending on the length
of the carbon chains in the monomers.
Can you see why the most common nylon, shown below,
is called nylon-6,6?

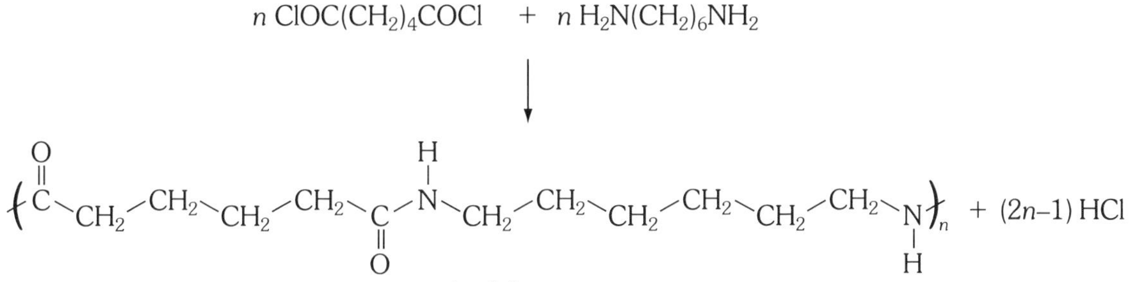

$$n \ ClOC(CH_2)_4COCl \quad + \quad n \ H_2N(CH_2)_6NH_2$$

nylon-6,6

+ $(2n-1)$ HCl

● Can you draw part of a nylon-6,10 polymer chain?

The nylons are called **polyamides**. Kevlar is also a polyamide
which you can read more about on the next page.

Polyamide chains are held to each other by *hydrogen bonds*.
Remember that these are strong intermolecular forces.
The chains are 'cold drawn' to align them in the same direction.
This maximises the hydrogen bonding and increases the strength
of the fibre formed.
Look at the diagram below:

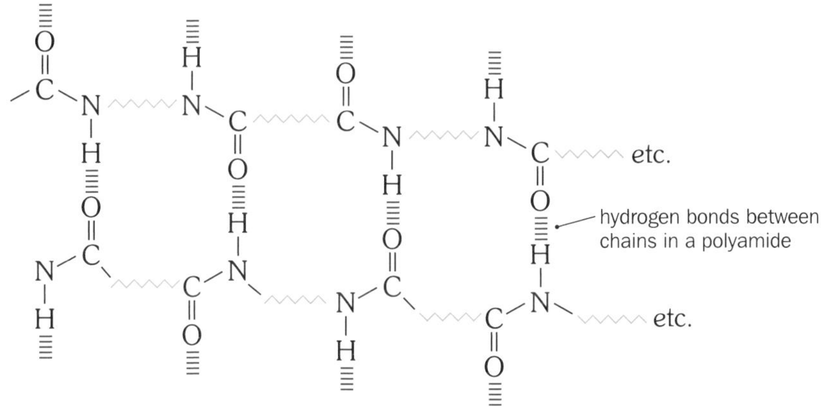

Nylon being cold drawn into fibres

etc.

hydrogen bonds between
chains in a polyamide

etc.

Polyesters

Can you remember how to make an ester? (See pages 197 and 233.)
How could we adapt the reaction to make a *poly*-ester?
Look at the reaction below:

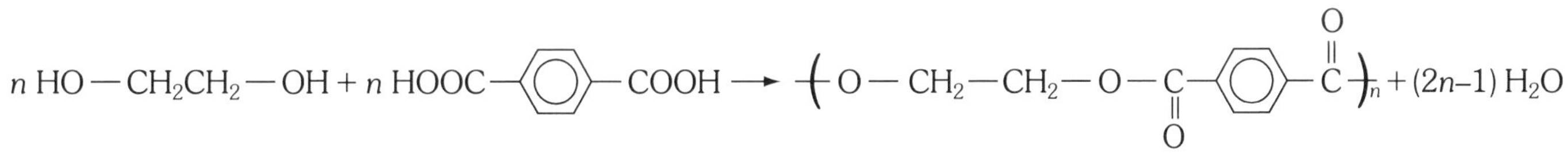

$$n \ HO-CH_2CH_2-OH + n \ HOOC-\bigcirc-COOH \longrightarrow$$

+ $(2n-1)$ H$_2$O

poly(ethene-1,4-benzoate) – also known as Terylene

---

a di-ol + a di-carboxylic acid ⟶ a polyester

▷ Chemistry at work: New developments in polymers

Kevlar: a versatile plastic

Kevlar is a polyamide, containing benzene rings. It is very strong, but flexible. It is also resistant to fire and abrasion.
It has these properties because of its structure. Its long, flat polymer chains can line up next to each other in a regular pattern. There is extensive hydrogen bonding between the chains.
Look at part of its structure opposite:

These properties have led to Kevlar being used to make bullet-proof vests, ropes, fire-protective clothing (as used by Formula 1 racing drivers) and modern 'leathers' worn by motorcycle riders. It is also used to reinforce other materials, such as the rubber in tyres. The latest tennis rackets also contain Kevlar, where its low density and strength are important. The wings of fighter jets can also be made of Kevlar.

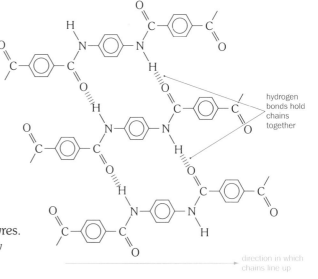

hydrogen bonds hold chains together

direction in which chains line up

These police officers have Kevlar in their bullet-proof vests

Kevlar protects racing drivers against fire

Tencel – fibre of the future?

Tencel is a new fibre made from the wood pulp of specially grown trees. The trees are replanted faster than they are used. It is a cellulose fibre produced without chemical reactions, using a non-toxic solvent.

The production process

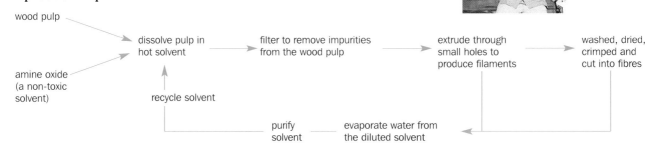

99 per cent of the solvent is recycled, giving a production process with little pollution. The properties of Tencel compare very well with other natural and synthetic fibres, and discarded Tencel is biodegradable. Courtaulds now have a specially built plant in Grimsby producing Tencel. Look for the label on the clothes you buy.

Recycled PETs?

PET are the initials used for the polymer poly(ethylene terephthalate); modern name poly(ethene-1,4-benzoate). It is a polyester (see page 255).

PET was first used as a textile fibre under the names of Terylene and Crimplene. Materials made from the new fibres were popular because they were crease-resistant.

In recent years PET has been used to make bottles for fizzy drinks. After use the bottles can be recycled. They are melted down and then used to make products including carpets, anoraks, felt for tennis balls and even the sails for tall ships.

The polyester bottle can be recycled

Five two-litre PET lemonade bottles can be recycled and turned into one T-shirt.

Five two-litre PET lemonade bottles can be recycled into a T-shirt.

Polyurethane – not just a foam!

Polyurethane is a polymer probably best known as a spongy foam used to pack cushions or as a rigid foam used to insulate fridges and cavity walls in houses.

It can also be produced as a rubbery material. In this form it is used to make Wellington boots, the soles for training shoes and extra-strong condoms.

In the sporting arena, polyurethane is marketed as the stretch fabric Lycra. It is used to coat footballs so that they can travel faster. It is also the adhesive which binds together bits of shredded old tyres to form a material used for the surface of athletics tracks and children's playgrounds.

Polyurethane is used to make Lycra swimwear

New glue?

Scientist are currently working on a new type of polymer that can glue living tissue in place.

The liquid glue is injected inside the body. It could be used to repair damaged cartilage, a common sporting injury. The liquid glue fixes the cartilage in place. It is set by irradiating the joint with ultraviolet light for a couple of minutes. This triggers the liquid monomer molecules to join together. New tissue can then grow in the matrix formed by the polymer. Eventually the polymer dissolves, leaving the new cartilage in place.

A new polymer is being developed to help repair damaged cartilage

▷ Chemistry at work: New developments in polymers

Conducting polymers

Most polymers are electrical insulators which make them very useful for making plugs, sockets and light switches.

A group of polymers have been developed, however, which conduct electricity. One of the first was a polymer based on poly(ethyne).

Conducting polymers have a number of advantages over metals which they can replace. They don't corrode and they are much less dense. They are likely to be used in situations such as space craft where saving weight is important.

Alarming suits!

Conducting polymers can be used to make protective clothing. They can actually warn the wearer if the safety suit gets torn. This can save lives in particularly hazardous environments. Total protection is needed where there is a danger of biological or chemical weapons being used and in medical research. Can you think of any other situations?

Look at the diagram below:

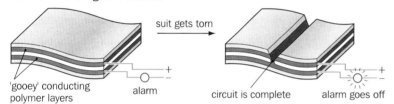

Warning of a tear in this suit could save this worker's life

The two layers of conducting polymer will come into contact if the suit is punctured. This completes a circuit which is linked to an alarm, such as a buzzer, in the face mask.

TV on a T-Shirt?

Some conducting polymers give out light when a voltage is applied. The efficiency of transferring electrical energy into light energy in these plastics is being improved all the time by researchers. At present they can be used to make panels for low-energy background lighting. By changing the structure of the polymers we can make plastics that give out different colours. Eventually scientists hope to develop flexible TV screens that can be folded or rolled up. Clothes could have moving displays of colour or even have TV screens as a fashion item.

Smart polymers

You've read about memory metals on page 78, but we also have memory polymers.
Smart polymers can be moulded into a particular shape, then irradiated with high-energy electrons (beta radiation). It is heated, reshaped and cooled. It does, however, 'remember' the shape it had when irradiated. The plastic returns to this shape when it is reheated. It is called a heat-shrinking polymer. They are used where awkward shapes are needed.

▷ Chemistry at work: Biodegradable plastics

Biodegradable plastics

All the household plastic waste that we put out as refuse simply goes into waste landfill sites. This is both wasteful on natural resources and damaging to the environment since most of the plastic waste is non-biodegradable. This means that it is not broken down naturally by the microbes in the soil.
So, what can we do to help solve some of these problems?

Well, apart from recycling which is often not cost effective, or incineration which produces toxic gases, chemists have developed plastics which will actually biodegrade naturally! Four such biodegradable plastics include starch-filled plastic, bacterial thermoplastic, photodegradable plastic and soluble plastic.

Starch-filled plastic

Thermoplastics, when buried for many years, eventually become brittle. They fracture and break down into smaller pieces which may then be decomposed naturally. If the surface area of the plastic being buried could be increased, then the decomposition process would be much quicker. Scientists have now developed plastics which contain small amounts of starch granules. The bacteria and fungi present in moist soil use the starch as 'food'. As the starch is used up, the plastic is broken into smaller pieces, producing a larger surface area. With an oxidant added, these plastics may be biologically decomposed even faster!

Bacterial thermoplastic

ICI have developed a bacterial synthesised plastic called poly(3-hydroxybutyrate) or PHB. When fed on sugars or alcohol, or carbon dioxide and hydrogen, the bacteria produce granules of PHB. The plastic made from these granules is totally biodegradable. The action of bacteria, fungi or algae, which may be found in the soil, rivers, lakes and oceans, cause it to decompose naturally in about 9 months.

However, despite the advantage to the environment, the cost of PHB is about 15 times more than poly(ethene) – so environmental friendliness comes at a price!

Bottles made from biodegradable plastic, in various stages of degradation

Photodegradable plastic

Polymer chains can be designed to include carbonyl groups (C=O) which absorb energy from the near ultraviolet region of the electromagnetic spectrum. Because of the carbonyl group, the polymer chain 'traps' this energy, which causes the bonds in the region of the carbonyl group to break down. As the polymer breaks into smaller fragments, the plastic will biodegrade much more quickly.

Water-soluble plastics

A plastic called poly(ethenol) has been developed, which is made from the reaction between a polymer called poly(ethenyl ethanoate) and methanol. This plastic can be tailored to be either insoluble or soluble to varying degrees, in hot, cold or warm water. The degree of solubility then allows the plastic to have differing uses.

Preparing water-soluble laundry bags in a hospital

Soiled hospital laundry may be collected into bags made from the relevant, soluble poly(ethenol). It is then placed in the wash where the bag dissolves and the laundry is let out, reducing the risk of spreading disease by handling.

Summary

- **Polymers** are very large molecules made from small, reactive molecules called **monomers**.
- There are two types of reaction to form polymers:
  a) **addition** polymerisation (in which monomers contain C=C double bonds), and
  b) **condensation** polymerisation (in which two different monomers react together, and each monomer has reactive groupings at both ends of the molecule).
  The polymer is the only product in addition polymerisation.
  In condensation polymerisation a small molecule is also given off in the reaction.
  Poly(ethene) is an example of an addition polymer.
  Nylon is an example of a condensation polymer.

- Plastics that can be softened when heated are called **thermoplastics**.
- **Thermosets,** or thermosetting plastics, have covalent bonds between their chains.
  This 'cross-linking' means they cannot be melted. At high temperatures, they will char and decompose.
- Many of the plastics we use today can be recycled or are biodegradable to help with disposal.

▶ **Questions**

1 Copy and complete:

Plastics are made from long-chain molecules called.....
These large molecules are formed when lots of small, reactive molecules, called .... , combine. For example, ethene molecules react with each other to form .....

There are two types of polymerisation reaction:
i) .... and ii) .....
In i) there is only one product formed, for example ..... In ii) a small molecule is also eliminated, for example when a polymer such as .... is made.

.... can be softened when heated and remoulded, whereas .... can only be moulded once when the object is manufactured.

Plastic waste can be a pollution problem. Nowadays plastics have been developed which are .... and break down in a variety of ways. Others can be re-used or .....

2 a) How was poly(ethene) first discovered?
   b) Why did the first poly(ethene) produced have a low density?
   c) How does the structure of high-density poly(ethene), HDPE, differ from the low-density form (LDPE) of the plastic?
   d) What are the advantages of HDPE over LDPE?
   e) Why was the discovery of HDPE rather lucky?
   f) Give two uses of LDPE and two uses of HDPE.

3 Look at the parts of three polymers shown below:

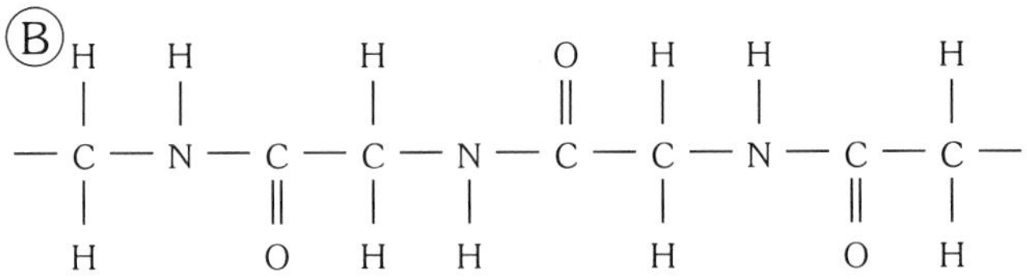

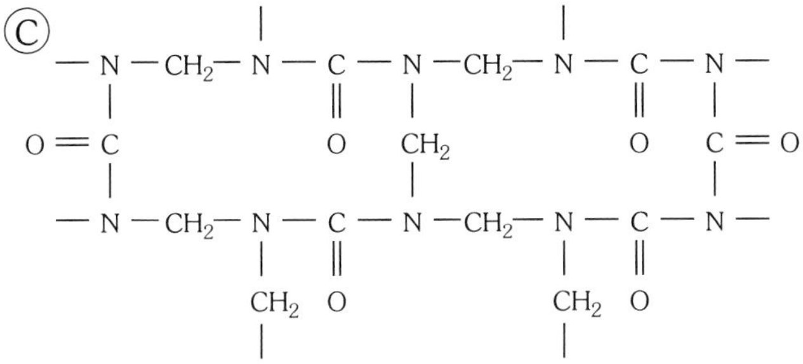

a) What type of intermolecular forces hold neighbouring chains together in A? Explain how these forces arise.
b) What type of intermolecular forces hold neighbouring chains together in B?
c) Draw two chains of B next to each other, showing how the molecules line up.
d) What do we call the covalent bonds between chains in C?
e) Which of the three polymers will be most resistant to heat?
f) Explain any other differences you might expect between A, B and C.

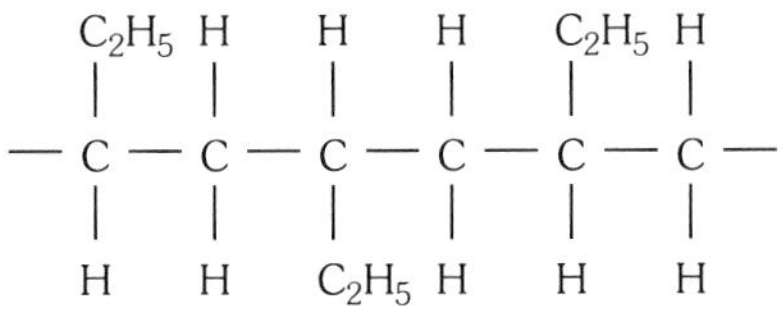

4 a) Complete this equation showing the formation of poly(ethene):

$$n\,C_2H_4 \longrightarrow \ldots.$$

b) What do we call the type of reaction shown in part a)?

c) We can show the reaction in part a) using structural formulae. Complete this equation:

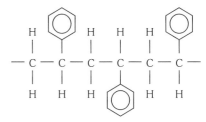

?

d) Look at the polymer below:

```
      CH₃   H   CH₃   H   CH₃   H   CH₃   H
       |    |    |    |    |    |    |    |
   —   C  — C  — C  — C  — C  — C  — C  — C  —
       |    |    |    |    |    |    |    |
       H    H    H    H    H    H    H    H
```

Name this polymer. Why is it called isotactic?

e) Give the structural formula of the monomer that made the polymer shown in part d).

f) List two uses of the polymer shown in part d).

5 a) Describe the free radical mechanism of addition when low-density poly(ethene) is made.

b) Show how a Ziegler catalyst can be used to make high-density poly(ethene).

6 a) Draw part of the polymer chain of nylon-6,6.

b) Give the structural formula of the two monomers that make nylon-6,6?

c) Name the small molecule given off when the two monomers in part b) react together.

d) What do we call the type of reaction used to make nylon-6,6?

e) What do we call the —CO—NH— grouping that is repeated along the nylon polymer?

f) In which natural polymers do we find the grouping shown in part e)?

7 Nylons are named by giving numbers after the word nylon. The first number indicates the number of carbon atoms in the diamine monomer. The second number shows the number of carbon atoms in the dicarboxylic acid or acid chloride.
Nylon-6,10 is becoming more popular because it uses castor oil as the source of raw materials rather than crude oil.

a) Give the structural formulae of the two monomers that make up nylon-6,10.

b) Draw part of the polymer chain of nylon-6,10.

c) Can you think of a way of making nylon from a single monomer? Try to draw its structural formula.

8 Terylene is a polyester.
It is made from the monomers ethane-1,2-diol and benzene-1,4-dicarboxylic acid.

a) Give the structural formulae of the two monomers.

b) Terylene is formed by condensation polymerisation. Name the small molecule eliminated in the reaction.

c) Draw the repeating unit in the Terylene polymer.

d) Look at your answer to part c):
What intermolecular forces operate between neighbouring chains?

e) Polyesters are common synthetic fibres.
How could you align the polymer chains in the manufacturing process? Why is this important?

f) What type of plastic might result if we use propane-1,2,3-triol instead of ethane-1,2-diol as one of the monomers to make a polyester? Can you see how chains could become cross-linked?

g) How would you expect the properties of the polyester produced in part f) to differ from Terylene?

9 Look at the part of a polymer chain shown below:

```
       H   ⬡       H   H   H   ⬡
       |   |       |   |   |   |
   —   C — C   —   C — C — C — C  —
       |   |       |   |   |   |
       H   H   ⬡       H   H
```

a) Can you draw the structure of the monomer that produced this plastic? (Hint: It contains a C=C bond.)

b) What do we call this plastic?

c) In which type of polymerisation reaction does this plastic form?

d) How might the position of the benzene rings affect the strength and density of the plastic?
(Hint: Think how the chains can pack together.)

10 Kevlar is a polyamide.

a) Name another synthetic polyamide.

b) Why is Kevlar such a strong plastic?

c) List four uses of Kevlar.

d) Give one way in which synthetic polyamides differ from protein polymers.

e) Give one way in which synthetic polyamides are the same as protein polymers.

11 The lack of chemical reactivity is a major advantage in many uses of plastics. However, this becomes a disadvantage when we come to dispose of them.

Discuss the various ways in which chemists have worked to overcome the problems of plastic pollution. (You might also refer to page 174 for some other information.)

Making new and useful organic compounds is the job of many research chemists. How many organic compounds have you used getting ready to leave home today? Look at the label from a shampoo opposite:

For example, soaps, cosmetics, aerosols and plastics may well be essential to your daily routine.
Some of the organic compounds used occur naturally and just need to be extracted. Some will have been synthesised especially to mimic natural substances, such as perfumed products. Can you think of any? Others, like the plastics in your toothbrush, will be designed to have a particular set of properties.

PLEASE RETURN PACKAGING TO
THE BODY SHOP FOR RECYCLING

INGREDIENTS: Aqua, Sodium Laureth Sulfate, Cocamidopropyl Betaine, Dimethicone, Steareth-2, Acrylates/C10-30 Alkyl Acrylate Crosspolymer, Phenoxyethanol, Parfum, Bertholletia excelsa, Glycol Stearate, Benzyl Alcohol, Sodium Benzoate, Sodium Hydroxide, Polyquaternium-10, Laureth-23, Laureth-2, Steareth-10, Benzophenone-4, Benzophenone-3, Methylparaben, Butylparaben, Ethylparaben, Propylparaben, CI 19140, CI 17200, CI 42090.

© THE BODY SHOP, BN17 6LS, UK

This is part of the label from Brazil Nut Rich shampoo. Which of the substances listed above are organic compounds?

▶ Synthetic routes

In order to make new compounds we need to know the typical reactions of functional groups.
Then, given an available starting material, we can plan a series of reactions that end up with the desired product.
Often we get the raw materials from crude oil, fats or vegetable oils. Let's look at an example:

How can we make an azo-dye using crude oil as the main raw material?

We can get benzene from oil refineries. This is a product from a process called catalytic reforming. So starting with benzene:

a synthetic route

Step 1:

Step 2:

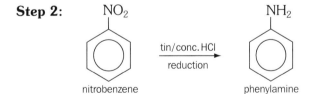

Step 3:

Step 4:

▶ Calculating yields

In each step along a synthetic route you will lose some of your product.
This could be as a result of losses by evaporation or in solvents
used to extract products along the way. Many organic reactions do not
go to completion, yielding less than 100% of pure product.

We can calculate the yield by working out how much we could get in theory,
assuming all our starting compound could be converted into product.
This figure is then compared to the actual amount obtained practically.
Put as an equation:

$$\text{percentage yield} = \frac{\text{actual mass obtained practically}}{\text{mass of product assuming 100\% conversion}} \times 100$$

We get losses in the purification necessary at each stage (handling losses)

Example
A research chemist worked out a way to convert ethanol into ethanoyl chloride.
She started with 92.0 g of ethanol and managed to prepare 68.0 g of ethanoyl chloride.
What was her yield?

First of all, we need to work out the mass of ethanoyl chloride assuming 100% conversion:
From the equation 1 mole of ethanol gives 1 mole of ethanoyl chloride.

$$C_2H_5OH \longrightarrow C_2H_5COCl$$
ethanol　　　　ethanoyl chloride

1. Work out the relative molecular mass of ethanol and ethanoyl chloride:

ethanol	ethanoyl chloride
$(2 \times C) = 2 \times 12 = 24$	$(2 \times C) = 2 \times 12 = 24$
$(6 \times H) = 6 \times 1 = 6$	$(5 \times H) = 5 \times 1 = 5$
$+ (1 \times O) = 1 \times 16 = 16$	$(1 \times O) = 1 \times 16 = 16$
$\overline{46}$	$+ (1 \times Cl) = 1 \times 35.5 = 35.5$
	$\overline{80.5}$

2. Calculate how much ethanoyl chloride could be made (assuming 100% conversion):
   From the relative molecular masses we see that:

   46 g of ethanol could give 80.5 g of ethanoyl chloride.

   The question tells us that the chemist started with 92 g of ethanol.

   Therefore,

   92 g of ethanol could give **161 g of ethanoyl chloride (assuming 100% conversion).**
   (i.e. (46×2) g of ethanol could yield (80.5×2) g of ethanoyl chloride.)

   Now we can work out the percentage yield:

   The question tells us that the actual yield was 68 g of ethanoyl chloride.
   Remember that:

   $$\text{percentage yield} = \frac{\text{actual mass obtained practically}}{\text{mass of product assuming 100\% conversion}} \times 100$$

   Therefore,

   The yield was $\dfrac{68}{161} \times 100 = \textbf{42.2\%}$

▷ 'Stepping up' a homologous series

Sometimes we find that our desired product contains more carbon atoms than our starting compound. Do you recall a reaction that adds a carbon atom to a compound?
On page 189 we saw how a halogenoalkane is converted into a nitrile:
For example:

$$CH_3Cl \xrightarrow[\substack{KCN\ dissolved \\ in\ ethanol}]{\substack{heat\ under \\ reflux\ with}} CH_3CN$$

chloromethane   ethanenitrile

This is a useful reaction to 'step up' a homologous series.

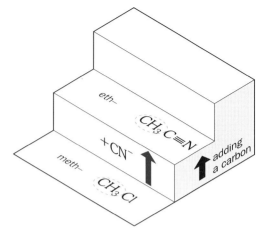

'Stepping up' by reacting with a cyanide (CN⁻) ion

Example
How can we convert ethanol (C_2H_5OH) into propanal (C_2H_5CHO)?

To add a carbon atom to the chain, we first need a halogenoalkane:

Step 1:

$$C_2H_5OH \xrightarrow[\substack{NaBr\ and \\ conc\ H_2SO_4}]{HBr\ made\ from} C_2H_5Br$$

ethanol   bromoethane

We can now add the extra carbon atom:

Step 2:

$$C_2H_5Br \xrightarrow[\substack{KCN\ in\ ethanol}]{\substack{Heat\ under \\ reflux\ with}} C_2H_5C{\equiv}N$$

bromoethane   propanenitrile

Ethanol can be obtained by fermenting sugar. It can also be made by hydration of ethene (which is produced by cracking products from crude oil)

The nitrile is often converted to an amine:

Step 3:

$$C_2H_5C{\equiv}N \xrightarrow[\substack{(in\ dry\ ether) \\ followed\ by\ H_2O}]{LiAlH_4} C_2H_5CH_2NH_2$$

propanenitrile   propylamine

We know that we can oxidise primary alcohols into aldeydes. So the —NH_2 group can be replaced:

Step 4:

$$C_2H_5CH_2NH_2 \xrightarrow[\text{above 10 °C}]{HCl\ /\ NaNO_2} C_2H_5CH_2OH$$

propylamine   propan-1-ol

And finally oxidise the alcohol:

Step 5:

$$C_2H_5CH_2OH \xrightarrow[\text{dilute sulphuric acid and distil}]{\text{aqueous potassium dichromate}} C_2H_5C\!\!\begin{array}{c} \nearrow O \\ \searrow H \end{array}$$

propanal

- What happens to the yield of propanal if there is excess potassium dichromate present? Why?

▷ 'Stepping down' a homologous series

We met another way to change the length of the carbon chain on page 244. It is called the **Hofmann degradation reaction**. Unlike conversion to a nitrile, this reaction *removes a carbon atom*. It involves removing the —C=O group from an amide:

$$C_2H_5C\overset{O}{\underset{NH_2}{<}} \xrightarrow{Br_2/NaOH(aq)} C_2H_5NH_2$$

propanamide   ethylamine

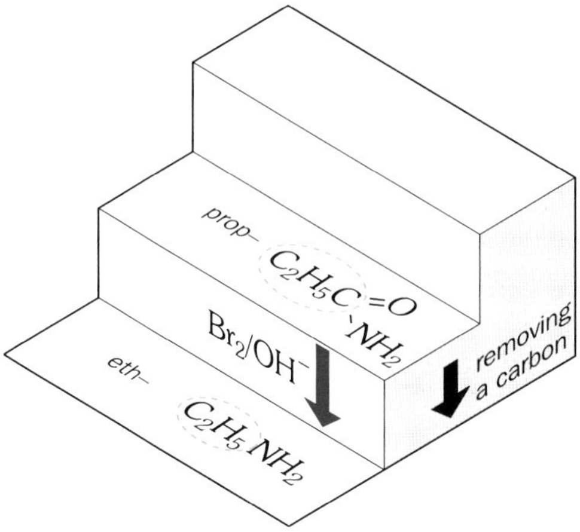

'Stepping down' – Hofmann degradation to remove a carbon atom

Let's look at an example of how this reaction might be used:

Example
How can we convert octanoic acid (obtained from the hydrolysis of vegetable oils) into heptylamine?

In this problem we have to reduce the number of carbon atoms from 8 to 7. So we need to decide a route to make an amide.
This can be done in two steps:

Step 1:

$$C_7H_{15}C\overset{O}{\underset{OH}{<}} \xrightarrow{PCl_5} C_7H_{15}C\overset{O}{\underset{Cl}{<}}$$

octanoic acid   octanoyl chloride

Step 2:

$$C_7H_{15}C\overset{O}{\underset{Cl}{<}} \xrightarrow{conc.\ NH_3} C_7H_{15}C\overset{O}{\underset{NH_2}{<}}$$

octanoyl chloride   octanamide

Then we can use the Hofmann degradation to remove a carbon atom:

Step 3:

$$C_7H_{15}C\overset{O}{\underset{NH_2}{<}} \xrightarrow{Br_2/NaOH} C_7H_{15}NH_2$$

octanamide   heptylamine

Natural oils, such as that extracted from sunflowers, provide carboxylic acids with even numbers of carbon atoms

▷ Adding a carbon chain to benzene

Can you remember how we can join a carbon chain on to a benzene ring? This is another useful reaction in the synthesis of new compounds. Benzene can be obtained from crude oil as we saw in the example on page 262. It can have a carbon chain added via a **Friedel–Crafts reaction**.
We looked at these reactions on page 214:

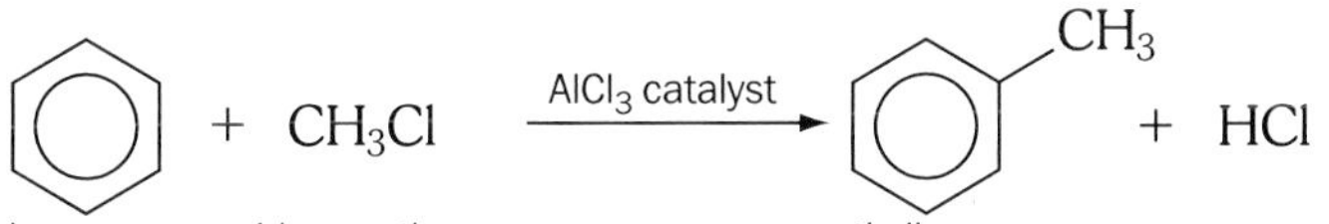

benzene   +   CH₃Cl $\xrightarrow{AlCl_3\ catalyst}$ methylbenzene   +   HCl

▷ Summary of organic reactions

When planning synthetic routes it is useful to have the reactions
of the main classes of organic compounds in one place to refer to.
(It also helps with your revision!)
Some useful reactions for synthesis are summarised here:

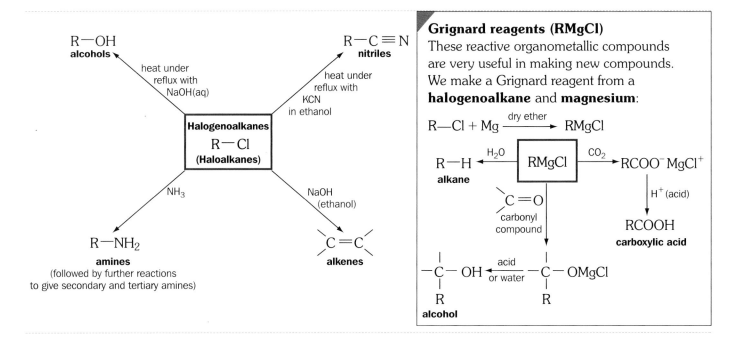

Grignard reagents (RMgCl)

These reactive organometallic compounds
are very useful in making new compounds.
We make a Grignard reagent from a
halogenoalkane and **magnesium**:

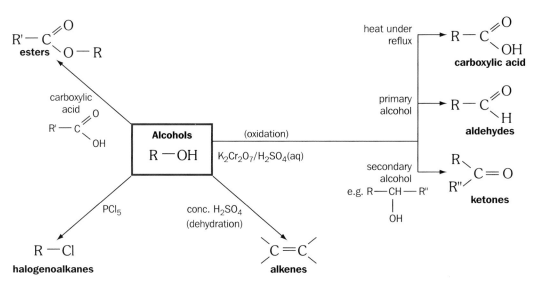

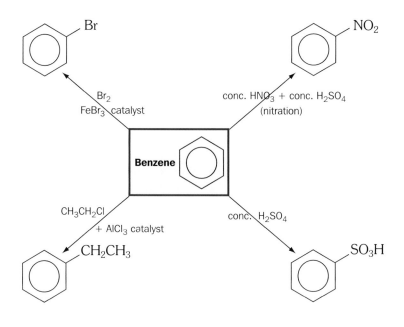

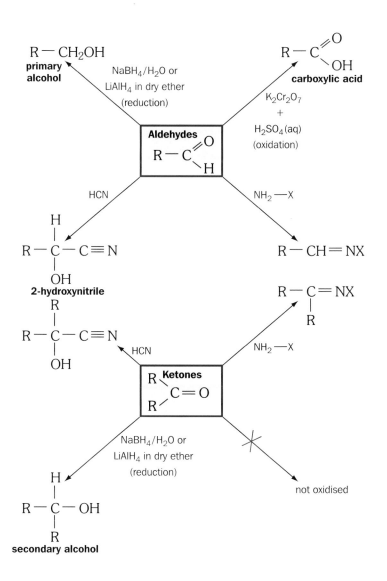

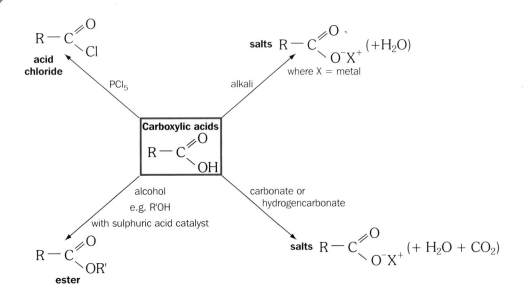

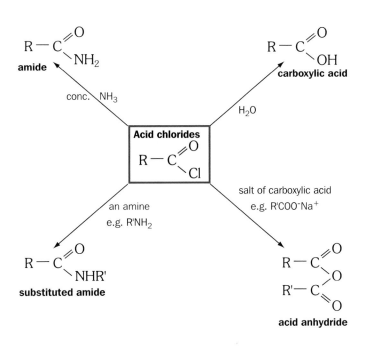

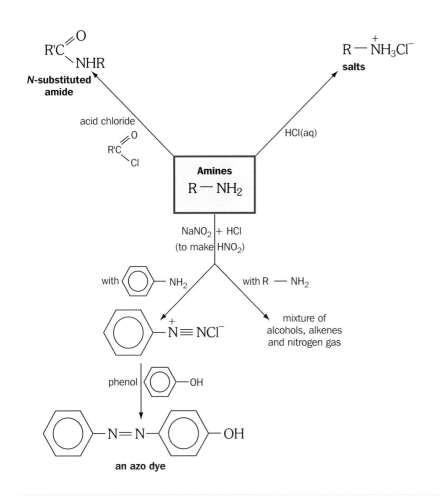

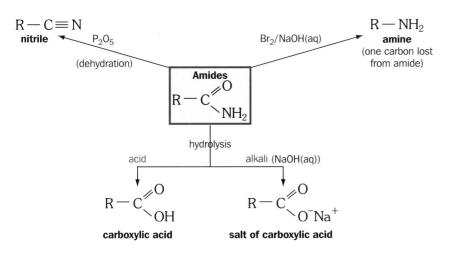

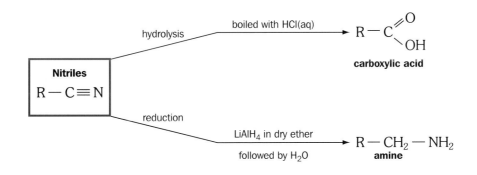

▷ Chemistry at work: Pharmaceutical drugs

The pharmaceutical industry employs many chemists
in their research and development sections.
These chemists try to develop new drugs to treat diseases.
They often work from the active ingredients of herbal remedies,
seeking to modify and improve molecules isolated from natural products.

For example, penicillin kills disease-causing bacteria. It is an **antibiotic**.
It was discovered in 1928 by Alexander Fleming.
However, nowadays we are finding more bacterial infections that are resistant
to the drug. The new strains of bacteria have enzymes that can
break down the antibiotic before it can act. So chemists are producing
similar molecules, but with new side chains.
The modified antibiotic will not fit into the active site in the enzyme molecule
and can attack the bacteria effectively.

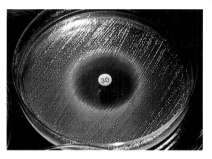

Penicillin moulds produce antibiotic compounds

Aspirin

Have you ever taken a tablet to get rid of a headache?
The development of **analgesics**, drugs that relieve pain, is an example
of some early work of chemists in the pharmaceutical industry.

The bark of the willow tree has been used for over 2000 years
to relieve pain and to treat fevers (**antipyretic**).
Chemists in the 1800s managed to identify the active ingredient in the bark
and in 1870 worked out that it was changed to salicylic acid in the body.
(The Latin word for willow is *salix*.)
The modern name for salicylic acid is 2-hydroxybenzoic acid.
Look at its structure below:

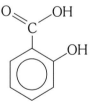

2-hydroxybenzoic acid (salicylic acid)

The bark of the willow tree was used in ancient times to treat fevers

However, patients treated with the acid suffered irritation in the mouth
and stomach, although it was effective at treating their fevers.
The sodium salt of salicylic acid caused less irritation, but tasted horrible.

Eventually in the 1890s, Felix Hofmann, a German chemist,
found that an ester of salicylic acid worked well.
It had reduced side effects and tasted all right too!
The ester is show below:

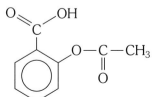

2-ethanoyloxybenzenecarboxylic acid
(aspirin!)

Aspirin is an analgesic and antipyretic. What does this mean?

The ester was given the trade name Aspirin and the process to make it was patented by the German chemical company, Bayer.

salicylic acid   ethanoic anhydride   aspirin   ethanoic acid

Notice that ethanoic anhydride is used rather than ethanoyl chloride to make the ester. Can you think why?
(Remember how vigorously acid chlorides react. The anhydride is also cheaper to make.)
Aspirin is now also used to reduce the risk of heart disease.
It can be made more soluble in water by converting it to its sodium salt.

- Can you draw the structural formula of this sodium salt?
- Why do you think the ionic grouping helps its solubility.
- Why is it desirable for a drug to be more soluble?
- If chemists want a drug that dissolves into fatty tissue, they often build on a hydrocarbon side chain. Why does this work?

The sodium salt of aspirin is more soluble

Other analgesics

Do you know the names of any other pain-relief medicines besides aspirin?
You've probably heard of **paracetamol**.
It was first sold in the 1950s.
This analgesic and antipyretic drug can be taken by children and is better than aspirin for people with ulcers.
You might have younger brothers and sisters or you might even remember taking a liquid medicine called Calpol yourself.
This can be given in small doses from an early age and contains paracetamol.
However, too much paracetamol causes damage to your liver.
Here is the structure of paracetamol:

paracetamol
(or *N*-(4-hydroxyphenyl)ethanamide)

Very small doses of paracetamol are safe for children

In the 1960s chemists at Boots developed **ibuprofen** as an alternative to aspirin.
You can now buy it 'over the counter'.
Look at its structure below:

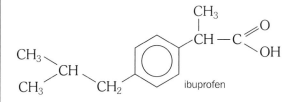

ibuprofen

- Ibuprofen is an optically active compound. Can you find its chiral centre?

Many drugs with a chiral centre have only one enantiomer which is biologically active.
By only producing the active form, we can cut doses by half.
This reduces any side-effects of the drug.

Ibuprofen is called an OTC ('over the counter') drug

▷ Chemistry at work: Other drugs

We can think of drugs as compounds that affect the way our bodies function in some way. A medicine is a drug which has benefits for a person with a disease. Strong analgesics work by blocking sites in the brain that receive impulses from nerves indicating pain.

Alcoholics are addicted to the legalised drug ethanol

On the other hand, a poison is a drug that has a bad effect on some part of our body. We have seen on page 143 how carbon monoxide gas affects haemoglobin in our blood. The gas is a poison to your body.

The relationship between a drug's use as a medicine or a poison is interesting.
Ethanol is a legalised drug, but in large amounts it is a poison. Alcoholic drinks can relax us and in small amounts may well help to reduce stress.

However, heavy drinking over time will cause liver damage. A sudden large quantity can also cause alcoholic poisoning which can kill you.
More deaths are actually caused by car accidents as a result of drinking and driving.

Cannabis is an illegal drug, but is finding uses in medicine. For example, it helps people with cancer. The drugs they take to treat the cancer can make them vomit, but cannabis has been found to reduce their nausea.

Cocaine is a much abused drug. It is so dangerous because it is addictive.
But it was the first local anaesthetic to be used at the end of the 1800s. Chemists have since made new molecules, closely related to cocaine, that are not addictive.

'Hard' drugs, like heroin, are very addictive

Morphine is used to treat people in serious pain. It is also addictive and is closely related to the most commonly used 'hard' drug, heroin. Heroin has a slightly different structure, which enables it to dissolve in the fatty tissue around the brain much more quickly.

Morphine can be extracted from poppies and is the basis of **opium**. Chemists altered the structure of morphine to make a less addictive analgesic called **codeine**.
Look at their structures below:

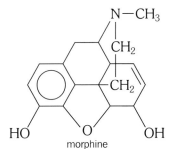

morphine

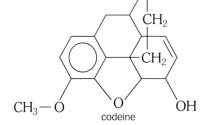

codeine

- How does the molecule of codeine differ from that of morphine?

▷ Questions

1 We can obtain ethene from cracking the products of crude oil.
Devise a way of changing ethene into the following compounds, stating the reagents and conditions needed:
a) bromoethane
b) ethylamine
c) ethanal
d) ethanamide
e) ethanoyl chloride
f) propan-1-ol
g) methylamine

2 a) Identify the compounds labelled A to F in the reaction sequence below. Give their name and structural formula in each case.

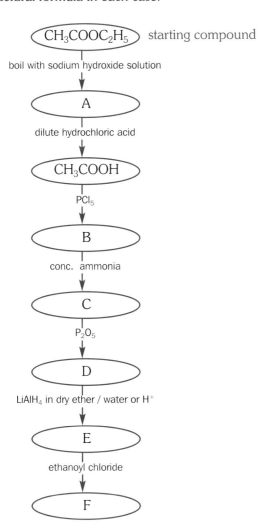

b) Name the starting compound.
c) What do we call the type of reaction when the starting compound is converted to compound A?
d) What type of reaction converts:
   i) C to D
   ii) D to E?

3 Two students were asked to prepare a sample of aspirin in the lab.
In the first stage they converted methyl 2-hydroxybenzoate (from oil of wintergreen) into 2-hydroxybenzoic acid.
This was done in the two steps shown below:

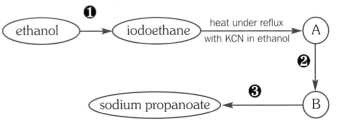

They started with 2.0 g of methyl 2-hydroxybenzoate. After drying, they had managed to collect 1.6 g of the 2-hydroxybenzoic acid.
a) Work out the relative molecular mass of methyl 2-hydroxybenzoate.
   (A_r values: C = 12, H = 1, O = 16)
b) Work out the relative molecular mass of 2-hydroxybenzoic acid.
c) Using the equations above, how many moles of 2-hydroxybenzoic acid should we get from one mole of methyl 2-hydroxybenzoate?
d) Calculate the students' percentage yield.

In the second stage of the preparation, they performed the following reaction with their 1.6 g of 2-hydroxybenzoic acid:

e) Assuming the students could get a 100% yield of aspirin, what mass of aspirin would they produce?
f) The students collected 1.4 g of crude product.
If this had been pure aspirin, what would be the percentage yield for this second stage?
g) Assuming 1.4 g of pure aspirin was made, what is the overall percentage yield having started with 2.0 g of methyl 2-hydroxybenzoate?

4 Name the reagents and conditions labelled by numbers in the synthetic route below.
Also identify the products labelled by letters:

ethanol ❶→ iodoethane heat under reflux with KCN in ethanol → A

❷

sodium propanoate ←❸ B

273

Can you think of some jobs that require people to find out which substances are present in a sample? Or perhaps find out the amounts of substances present in a sample?
Such work will involve analysis by chemical and/or physical means.

People working in forensics, medicine, food production, pharmaceuticals or environmental health will all need to analyse samples. They often use a combination of techniques to solve a problem.

In this chapter we will look at the analysis of organic compounds.

This environmental scientist is testing the quality of water

▷ Chemical analysis

Much of the analysis done in labs nowadays is done in machines. However, we still need to understand how to interpret the results of a chemical analysis.
One technique involves burning the organic compound in pure oxygen.

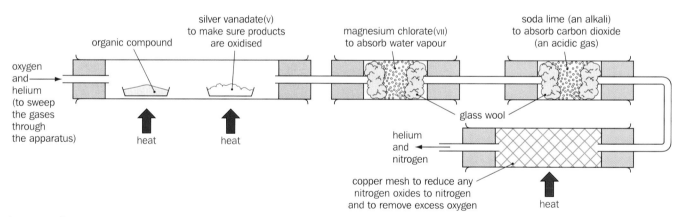

Apparatus for the chemical analysis of an organic compound

We can then analyse the products formed and work out the quantity of carbon, hydrogen, and nitrogen in the original sample.

We will look at an example on the next page.

For example, carbon dioxide produced is absorbed by soda lime. Any water vapour is absorbed by magnesium chlorate(VII).
Therefore weighing these before and after the gases have passed over will tell us the masses of CO_2 and H_2O produced.

Modern machines measure the thermal conductivity of the gases before they enter one of the absorption tubes. They measure it again as the gases leave the tubes. The machine is calibrated to convert that into the mass of CO_2 or H_2O absorbed.
Similar readings tell us the mass, if any, of nitrogen that is left mixed with the helium carrier gas at the end.

Example

0.225 g of a volatile organic compound is burned in pure oxygen.
Analysis in the apparatus on the last page shows that
0.440 g of carbon dioxide, 0.315 g of water and 0.070 g of nitrogen
are produced.
What is the empirical formula?
(Remember that this is the simplest ratio of the number of moles
of each element in the compound. You can see a calculation on page 40.
An organic example is also shown on page 164.)

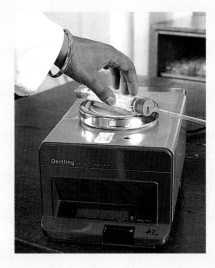

(Relative atomic masses: C = 12, H = 1, N = 14, O = 16)

First of all we must find the ***mass of carbon and hydrogen*** in the compound.

So how much carbon is there in 0.440 g of CO_2?
The relative molecular mass of CO_2 is $12 + (2 \times 16) = 44$
One mole of CO_2 has a mass of 44 g of which 12 g is carbon.

Therefore any sample of CO_2 will contain $\frac{12}{44} \times$ (total mass of CO_2) g of carbon.

So in this question there is $\frac{12}{44} \times 0.440$ g of carbon present.

= 0.120 g of carbon

Now we do the same for the hydrogen in water.
How much hydrogen is there in 0.315 g of H_2O?
The relative molecular mass of H_2O is $(2 \times 1) + 16 = 18$
One mole of H_2O has a mass of 18 g of which 2 g is hydrogen.

Therefore any sample of H_2O will contain $\frac{2}{18} \times$ (total mass of H_2O) g of hydrogen.

So in this question there is $\frac{2}{18} \times 0.315$ g of hydrogen present.

= 0.035 g of hydrogen.

We also have **0.070 g of nitrogen** formed in the experiment.

At this point we should check that the masses of carbon, hydrogen and nitrogen
add up to the mass of compound we started with. This will show us if any other
elements were in the original compound.

$0.120 + 0.035 + 0.070 = 0.225$

So no other elements are present.
(If the masses don't add up to the mass of the sample, the difference is likely to
be made up by oxygen present in the original compound.)

If we convert these masses into moles, we can work out the empirical formula:

C	:	H	:	N
$\frac{0.120}{12}$		$\frac{0.035}{1}$		$\frac{0.070}{14}$
0.010	:	0.035	:	0.005
10	:	35	:	5
2	:	7	:	1

So the empirical formula is **C_2H_7N**.

Empirical Formula!
Call this the
simplest ratio?!!

▷ Analysis using a mass spectrometer

On the last page we used chemical analysis to work out
the empirical formula of an organic compound.
What other information would you need before you could
work out its molecular formula?

We looked at a mass spectrometer on page 22.
Turn back and remind yourself how it works:
This instrument is often used to find the **relative molecular mass**
(or relative formula mass) of organic compounds.

We saw on page 25 how an electron can be knocked from a molecule.
The positive ion formed is called the **parent ion** (or **molecular ion**).
It is the peak on the spectrum with the highest mass/charge ratio.
This ratio gives us the relative mass because the charge equals 1
if only one electron has been removed.

Other peaks produced come from fragments of the original molecule.
The bombarding electrons used to ionise the sample
also break up the molecule at the same time.

Look at the simplified mass spectrum below:
It is taken from the unknown compound in the example on the last page.

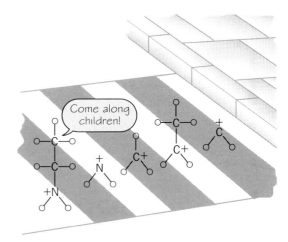

$C_2H_7N^+$ is the parent ion in our unknown sample from the last page. It is also called the molecular ion

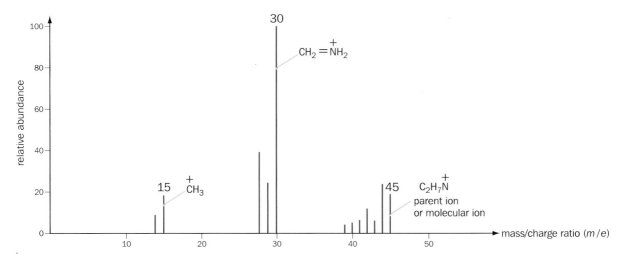

What is the relative mass of the parent ion (molecular ion)?
This means that the relative molecular mass is 45.
Its empirical formula is C_2H_7N.
Adding the relative atomic masses gives us:

$$(2 \times 12) + (7 \times 1) + 14 = 45$$

So in this case the empirical formula is the same as the molecular formula.

High resolution mass spectrometers

These more sensitive spectrometers can find the mass of a molecule
very accurately. One of these instruments could determine
the relative molecular mass of our C_2H_7N sample to be 45.057845.
Using a normal low resolution machine the parent ion peak at 45
could have been formed by other molecules. For example,
CH_3NO also has a relative molecular mass of 45.
However, a high resolution spectrum of this compound would show
a parent ion of mass 45.021461.
So the actual molecular formula can be stated with some certainty.

Some accurate relative atomic
masses:
C-12 = 12.0000000 (by definition)
H-1 = 1.0078246
N-14 = 14.0030738
O-16 = 15.9949141

Why would you see some very small
peaks at a higher mass than the
parent ion? (Hint: Think isotopes!)

Fragmentation

As mentioned previously, molecules are broken up into smaller fragments in a mass spectrometer. The bombarding electrons break bonds, forming molecular species that would not normally exist. It is the ions formed by these fragments that give compounds a characteristic mass spectrum. So interpretation of the mass spectrum on the last page would also help to reveal whether the parent ion of mass 45 was $C_2H_7N^+$ or CH_3NO^+.

We can use a data bank of known spectra on a computer to match against the one taken from an unknown sample. If the same conditions are used to ionise the sample as quoted in the reference tables, compounds can be positively identified. We call this '**fingerprinting**'.

The formation of ions depends to some extent on the stability of the ion produced in fragmentation. Do you remember your work on carbocations? Can you recall why the tertiary ions are the most stable?

Mass spectra can be used to identify unknown compounds by 'fingerprinting'

Look at the mass spectra below for the two isomers of C_2H_6O, showing some of the main peaks:

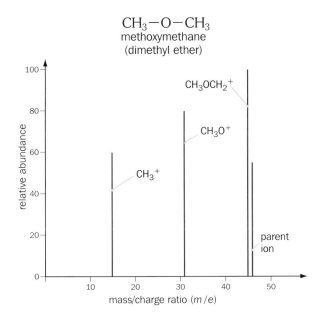

$CH_3{-}O{-}CH_3$
methoxymethane
(dimethyl ether)

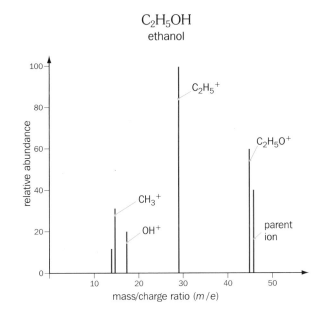

C_2H_5OH
ethanol

Can you see how evidence from the fragments can help us work out the structure of a molecule?

Look at the fragments formed from C_2H_7N on the last page:

- Where are the major peaks?
- Which fragments caused these peaks? (The major peak is $CH_2{=}\overset{+}{N}H_2$ at 30.)
- How would you expect this mass spectrum to differ from that of CH_3NO?
- Can you draw the structural or displayed formula of C_2H_7N?

▷ Spectrometry

You have now seen how mass spectrometry can be used
by organic chemists.
We can also use other physical techniques to find out
the structure of organic compounds.
These rely on their molecules absorbing certain energies.

We provide energy in the form of electromagnetic radiation.
Look at the low energy part of the electromagnetic spectrum below:

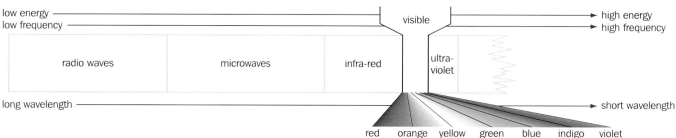

The sample is exposed to a range of frequencies (or energies).
The range depends on the exact technique being used.
Over the next few pages we will look at the use of
ultraviolet, visible, infra-red and radio waves.
Then we observe which frequencies have been absorbed or emitted.
This is called **spectrometry**.

Wavelengths are sometimes used instead of frequencies in analysis.
You need to know that the higher the frequency, the higher the energy.
But the higher the wavelength, the lower the energy of the radiation.

▷ Ultraviolet and visible spectrometry

This method looks at absorption of light in the visible
and ultraviolet range.

As you know, some compounds are coloured. But why?
The azo dyes on page 218 contain the —N＝N— linkage
between benzene rings.
The benzene ring is called a **chromophore**.
It absorbs in the ultraviolet range.
Look at its absorption spectrum below:

An ultraviolet spectrophotometer

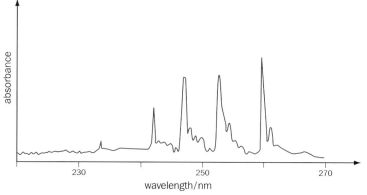

Absorption spectrum of benzene

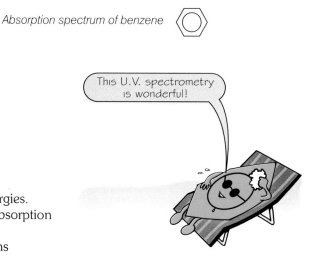

This U.V. spectrometry is wonderful!

It is benzene's π bonds that enable it to absorb these particular energies.
We find that the more double bonds in a molecule, the greater its absorption
in the ultraviolet range.
Molecules containing atoms with non-bonding lone pairs of electrons
also tend to absorb in this range.

Benzene absorbing some u.v. rays!

278

The energy is absorbed as electrons in the molecule
jump into higher energy levels. These are **molecular** energy levels.
They are produced whenever atomic orbitals combine to form covalent bonds.
Look at the diagrams below:

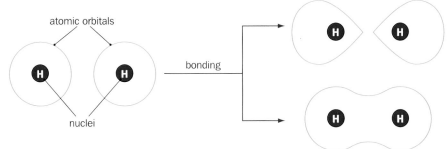

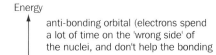

Energy

anti-bonding orbital (electrons spend
a lot of time on the 'wrong side' of
the nuclei, and don't help the bonding

bonding orbital (where electrons are
found mostly between the two nuclei,
bonding them together)

The main molecular energy levels would produce sharp lines
in a spectrum, like the atomic spectrum on page 11.
However, the picture is complicated by other energy levels
associated with vibrational and rotational energy states.
This results in broad **bands** rather than lines in a spectrum.
So the spectra produced in the u.v. or visible range are not
usually used to identify compounds by 'fingerprinting'.
But they can show us where double bonds are present,
and are useful for spotting compounds containing benzene rings.

Absorption in the visible range

Benzene appears colourless because it absorbs u.v. radiation,
not visible radiation. However, its absorption is shifted
to the visible range by the —N=N— link in azo dyes.
This link is called an **auxochrome**.

For example, the dye opposite absorbs light
in the higher energy part of the visible spectrum.
So the green and blue light is removed, leaving orange
and red to enter your eye.
You can see this in the diagram below:

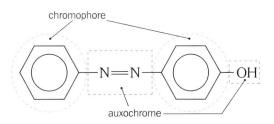

The structure of the orange azo dye,
4-hydroxyazobenzene

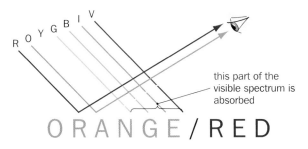

this part of the
visible spectrum is
absorbed

Beta-carotene is an interesting example that you can
think of next time you eat a carrot.
It gives carrots their orange colour.
The molecule has 11 double bonds:

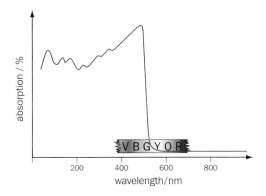

The visible / u.v. spectrum of β-carotene

• Which part of the visible spectrum does it absorb?

▷ Infra-red spectrometry

This technique is used more widely than visible or u.v.
spectrometry. This is because all organic molecules
absorb in the infra-red range of wavelengths.
The absorption bands are also narrower and easier to interpret.

The lower energy absorbed corresponds to changes in the vibration
of the bonds between atoms.
It helps if we think of the bonds as springs, with the atoms as balls
at each end. The bonds have a natural frequency at which they vibrate.
If we provide energy that corresponds to this frequency,
it stimulates larger vibrations and energy is absorbed.
This is called the **resonance frequency** of that vibration.
What do you think will affect its value?

H_2O could have the vibrations shown below

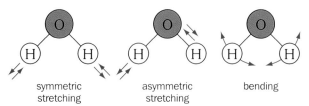

symmetric stretching   asymmetric stretching   bending

We can use our example from earlier in the chapter
to see how bonds can vibrate in different ways.
Look at the diagrams opposite:

As well as the vibrations like those for H_2O;
ethylamine's —NH_2 group can vibrate as shown:

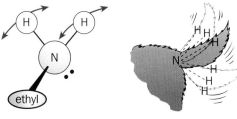

by 'wagging'

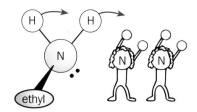

by 'rocking'

Each type of vibration will absorb characteristic frequencies.
These are often expressed as wavenumbers (measured in cm^{-1}).
However, we cannot be too specific when quoting
the characteristic absorption frequency of a bond.
The nature of the rest of the molecule shifts the energy absorbed
in each particular molecule. But we can say that the amine group
(—NH_2) will absorb in the range 3350 to 3500 cm^{-1}.
So we can identify functional groups from an infra-red spectrum.
Look at the i.r. spectrum of ethylamine below:

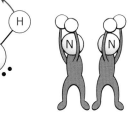

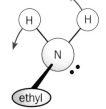

by 'twisting'

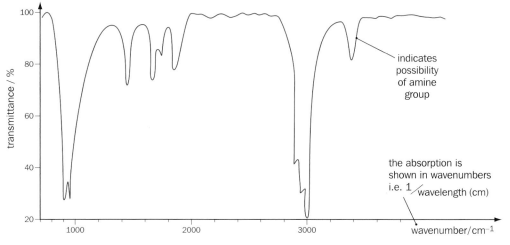

indicates possibility of amine group

the absorption is shown in wavenumbers i.e. $\frac{1}{\text{wavelength (cm)}}$

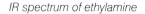

Notice that the 'peaks' are recorded as 'troughs'. The machine (called a spectrophotometer) detects the infra-red radiation that passes through the sample.

IR spectrum of ethylamine

You also get many peaks which we can use to 'fingerprint'
an unknown compound from its i.r. spectrum.

Characteristic absorption frequencies

Look at the chart below:
It shows us where some different bonds absorb in the i.r. range:

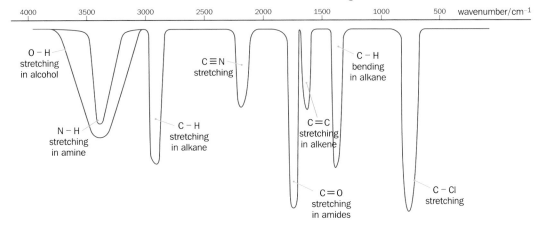

These values will always be given to you in a question.
Look at the values in the table opposite:
You can see that absorption bands overlap considerably.
That is why we **need to use a variety of techniques** to
work out the structure of a new compound.

Now let's see if we can interpret an i.r. spectrum using the data above:

Groups	Wave number range/cm^{-1}
amines	3500–3350
amides	3500–3140
alcohols (hydrogen bonded)	3750–3200
carboxylic acids (hydrogen bonded)	3300–2500

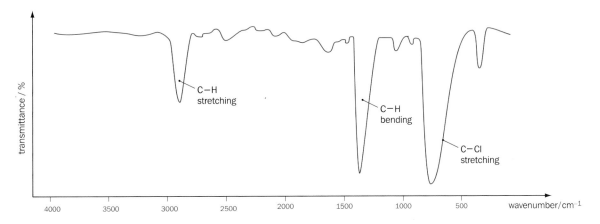

As you can see, analysis is not an exact science!
There are often peaks that we can't identify, but we can certainly
get clues about which groups are present.
The example above is actually chloromethane.

The i.r. spectrum of oct-1-ene is shown below:

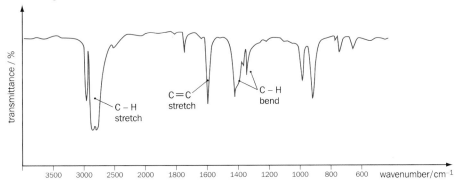

▷ Nuclear magnetic resonance (n.m.r.)

Like infra-red spectrometry, this final technique is widely used.
It is based on the fact that the nucleus of a hydrogen atom
acts as a tiny magnet. The nucleus, in this case a proton,
can spin, just as electrons spin. It is this movement
of electrical charge that produces a small magnetic effect.

In nuclear magnetic resonance we put the sample in a magnetic field.
The hydrogen nuclei can either line up with the field,
or by spinning in the opposite direction, line up against it.
Look at the diagram below:

*This scientist is examining the n.m.r.
spectrum of an unknown compound*

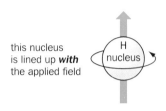

this nucleus
is lined up **with**
the applied field

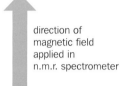

direction of
magnetic field
applied in
n.m.r. spectrometer

this nucleus
is lined up **against**
the applied field

The difference in energy between the two energy levels is small.
It corresponds to the energy carried by radiation in the radio wave range.
In n.m.r. the nuclei flip between one level and the other.

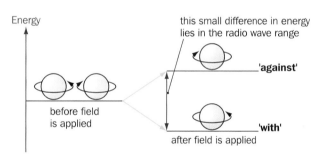

*Samples for n.m.r. analysis are
placed in a narrow tube*

The size of the gap between these nuclear energy levels
varies slightly. It depends on the atoms in the rest of the molecule.
Therefore it can be used to identify hydrogen atoms
in particular parts of a molecule.
Lets consider methanol, CH_3OH. The energy absorbed
as nuclei of the H atoms in the —CH_3 group flip between
levels is different from that of the H nucleus in the —OH group.

In practice we vary the magnetic field applied. This is
easier than changing the radio waves and then detecting
which wavelengths have been absorbed.
As we change the magnetic field, the different H nuclei flip
between levels at different field strengths.

The differences are measured relative to a standard compound.
The standard chosen is tetramethylsilane (TMS), $Si(CH_3)_4$.
All its H atoms are equivalent, so it only produces one line
on an n.m.r. spectrum. So all other compounds are compared
by quoting the shift away from the standard TMS line.
This is called the **chemical shift** (δ). Its units are parts per million (ppm).

We use solvents such as CCl_4 when preparing
samples for n.m.r. Can you think why?
How many H atoms are there in this solvent?
We can also use solvents which contain deuterium
(^2H or D) in place of the usual ^1H atoms if the
solvent is a compound of hydrogen. This is
because n.m.r. only works in this range with nuclei
that have an odd mass number, e.g. ^1H or ^{13}C.

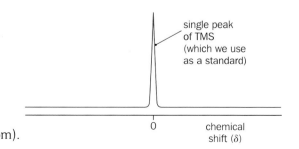

single peak
of TMS
(which we use
as a standard)

0   chemical
shift (δ)

Low resolution n.m.r.

Look at the low resolution n.m.r. spectrum from CH_3OH below:

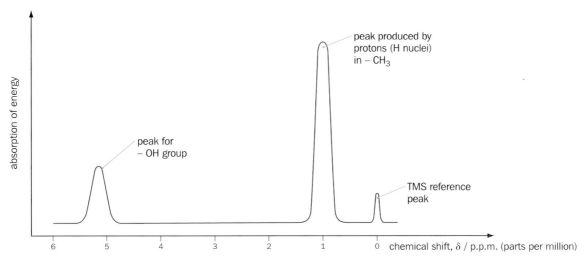

The n.m.r. spectrum will give us the relative numbers of each type of H atom in the molecule.

The area under each peak is proportional to the number of H atoms of that particular type. These areas are calculated by the machine which traces steps at each peak. The height of each step is proportional to number of H atoms recorded at that peak:
Look at the n.m.r. spectrum of ethanol (CH_3CH_2OH) below which includes its **integration trace**:

We can identify the peak from an —OH group by using ^2H_2O (or D_2O) as a solvent. The H in the alcohol group is replaced by the deuterium and the peak disappears.

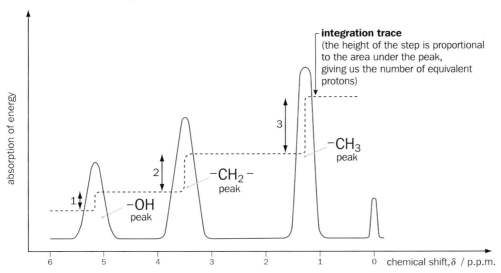

The steps are in the ratio 3 : 2 : 1 for CH_3 : CH_2 : OH.
This matches the number of H atoms in each part of the molecule.

The chemical shift for H atoms bonded to the same atom does vary in different molecules.
For example, R—CH_3 has an average chemical shift of 0.9 (where R = alkyl group), whereas Cl—CH_3 has a shift of 3.0.

Tables also show much overlap, with shifts quoted over ranges, just as in the infra-red data on page 281.
So once again this stresses the need for combined techniques to discover the structure of new or unknown compounds.

▷ High resolution n.m.r.

The peaks shown in the n.m.r. spectra so far are really
clusters of peaks.
These become apparent using high resolution n.m.r. spectrometry.

Look at the n.m.r. spectrum of bromoethane (CH_3CH_2Br) below:

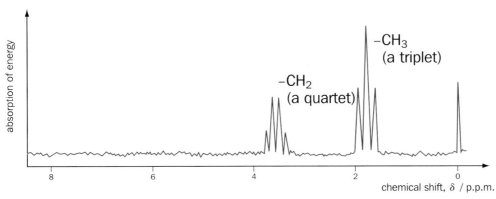

> **$n + 1$ rule:**
> A set of n protons
> (H atoms) will split the
> n.m.r. signal of its
> adjacent (non-
> equivalent) protons
> into $n + 1$ peaks.

The 'mini-peaks' arise from the effects of small magnetic fields
produced by the other H atoms nearby in the molecule.
The greater the number of adjacent H atoms, the more peaks seen.
This is because we have more possible combinations of H nuclei
lining up with or against each 'mini' magnetic field.

Therefore high resolution n.m.r. can give us more information
about the numbers of neighbouring H atoms.

We can predict the number of mini-peaks using the **$n+1$ rule**.
If n = the number of H atoms adjacent, then the main peak will be split
into $n+1$ mini-peaks. These more detailed peaks are called
doublets, triplets, quartets, etc.

We can look at the n.m.r. spectrum above to show how the rule works:
The CH_3 peak is split into a triplet (3 mini-peaks).
This is because there are 2 H atoms adjacent in the CH_2 grouping.
So $n = 2$, making $n+1 = 3$, which tells us the degree of splitting.

The peak that corresponds to CH_2 is split into a quartet (4 mini-peaks).
It has 3 H atoms 'next-door' in the CH_3 grouping.
So in this case $n = 3$, and $n+1 = 4$.

Look at the examples of this 'spin–spin' splitting effect below:

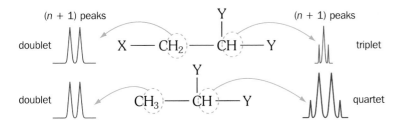

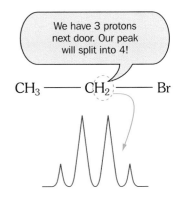

> We have 3 protons
> next door. Our peak
> will split into 4!

> We have two
> H's next door, so our
> peak will split into 3!

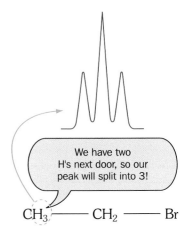

We only get this splitting effect if adjacent H atoms are not equivalent.
That's why our standard, TMS, has only one sharp peak.
All of the H atoms in $Si(CH_3)_4$ are equivalent.
We say that they are in the same molecular environment.

Applying the n + 1 rule

▷ Chemistry at work: Instrumental analysis

'Hardly any' mass spectra!

High resolution mass spectrometers are useful when we need to identify very small amounts of substance.

Since 1995 labs have used this technique to test urine samples from athletes. This has resulted in more athletes being banned for using drugs. However, some athletes argue that, with the increased sensitivity, innocently taken legal food supplements are producing positive dope tests.

Forensic scientists also use mass spectra to identify traces of drugs.

In the food industry, it can detect contaminants, such as pesticides left on fruit or vegetables.
Combined with other techniques, it can also be used to monitor pollution.

You can read more about the uses of mass spectrometry on page 26.

Linford Christie was accused of taking the banned anabolic steroid nandrolone. He strongly denied the charge and was later cleared by British track authorities

"Blow in here, sIR"

A driver who has failed a roadside breath test for alcohol is then taken to the police station. He or she is asked to provide a sample of breath for infra-red analysis. (Alternatively a sample of blood is taken and analysed using gas chromatography.)

Ethanol (C_2H_5OH) is the alcohol in wine, beer and spirits. The —OH group absorbs i.r. radiation at $3340 \, cm^{-1}$. However, absorption by H_2O molecules in the breath affects the signal. So the C—H absorption at $2950 \, cm^{-1}$ is used to determine the concentration of ethanol present. If this value is multiplied by 2300, it gives the concentration of ethanol in the blood. This should not be above 80 mg of ethanol per $100 \, cm^3$ of blood. This evidence is then presented in a court of law.

Infra-red spectrometry has also helped to discover art forgeries. One example was a painting claimed to have been painted by Bissiet between 1956 and 1958. Infra-red analysis of the paint showed that it contained a polymer only recently made for household emulsions!

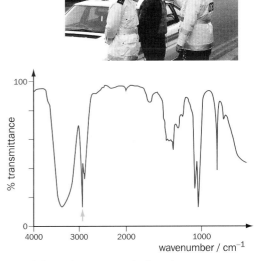

Infra-red spectrum of ethanol

Putting the organ in organic chemistry

An application of nuclear magnetic resonance (n.m.r.) is used in hospitals. Magnetic Resonance Imaging (MRI) can view the organs inside your body. The patient is placed inside a machine called a body scanner. It contains a powerful magnet. A computer analyses the radio waves absorbed by the hydrogen atoms in different organs, building up a picture of your insides.
Unlike high energy X-rays, MRI is harmless to the patient. So there can be frequent tests, for example to monitor the success of treating tumours.
It is particularly useful for studying the brain.

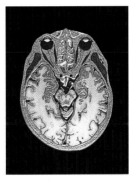

MRI can view internal organs. Which organ is this?

Summary

We can find out the structure of an unknown compound in various ways. We can use:

a) chemical analysis
- tests for various functional groups
- analysis to reveal the empirical formula of the compound and/or

b) instrumental analysis
- mass spectrometry
- visible and ultraviolet spectrometry
- infra-red spectrometry
- nuclear magnetic resonance spectrometry.

A combination of these techniques will be needed to work out the structure of a new compound.
An unknown compound can often be identified by 'fingerprinting'.
For example, matching the i.r. spectrum against a computer database of known compounds.

▶ Questions

1 Copy and complete:

We have to find the structural formula of compound X. We can find the simplest ratio of elements in X, called its .... formula, by chemical analysis.
Using .... spectrometry can tell us the .... molecular mass of the compound from the peak given by the .... ion. From this information, we can work out the .... formula of X.
To find its structure we can analyse the fragments in its .... spectrum and look at the absorption of electromagnetic .... (usually either ultraviolet, ..., infra-red or radio waves). This will give us information on the functional groups present. The infra-red spectrum is often .... against a .... of spectra from known compounds on a computer. This is called .....

2 A compound contains 75% carbon and 25% hydrogen by mass.
Work out the empirical formula.
(Hint: Imagine you start with 100 g of the compound.)

3 An unknown sample of a hydrocarbon was analysed by combustion.
On complete combustion, 3.02 g of the compound gave 8.86 g of carbon dioxide and 5.43 g of water.
a) Work out how many moles of carbon there are in 8.86 g of carbon dioxide.
b) Work out how many moles of hydrogen there are in 5.43 g of water.
c) Work out the empirical formula.

4 Look at the mass spectrum for butanone below:

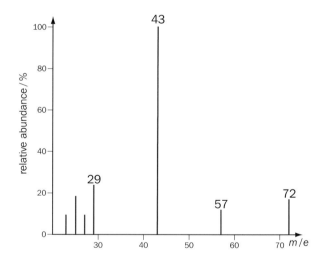

a) Give the structural formula of butanone.
b) Write the formula of the parent or molecular ion.
c) Why is the parent or molecular ion important if we only have the empirical formula of an unknown compound?
d) Other compounds also have a relative molecular mass of 72 (for example, $CH_2 = CHCOOH$). How would a high resolution mass spectrometer help to distinguish between the possibilities?
e) Look at the mass spectrum above:
Identify the fragments that have caused the peaks at the mass/charge ratios of:
i) 43 ii) 57 iii) 29.
f) Sketch what the mass spectrum of $CH_2 = CHCOOH$ might look like.

5 Look at the mass spectrum of a straight-chain alkane below:

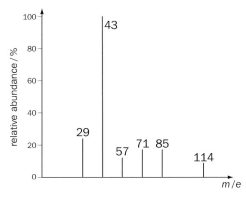

a) What is the general formula of an alkane?
b) What is the relative molecular mass of the alkane whose mass spectrum is shown above?
c) Can you work out its molecular formula and explain the regular peaks in the spectrum?

6 Compound C has a number of double bonds in its structure. Look at its absorption spectrum in the ultraviolet/visible range of the electromagnetic spectrum:

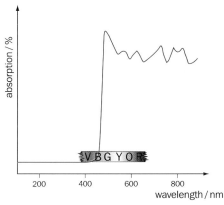

a) What will be the colour of compound C? Explain your answer.
b) Why don't we use ultraviolet or visible spectrometry very often to identify unknown compounds by 'finger-printing'?

7 a) Why is infra-red spectrometry a more useful technique for organic chemists than ultraviolet or visible spectrometry?
b) Explain how molecules absorb infra-red radiation.

Look at the infra-red spectrum of butan-2-ol below:

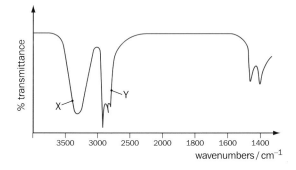

c) Using the data on page 281, identify the peaks marked X and Y on the i.r. spectrum.
d) Why would it be difficult to determine the exact structure of a new compound discovered using only one technique, such as i.r. spectrometry?

8 This question is about two isomers, A and B, of C_2H_6O.
Look at the low resolution mass spectra and n.m.r. spectra of the isomers below:

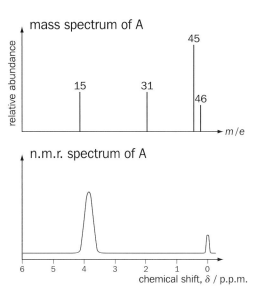

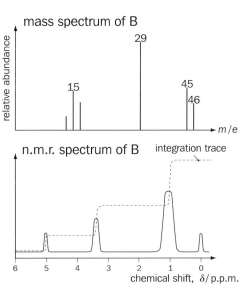

a) Give the structural formulae of A and B.
b) Explain the fragmentation patterns in their mass spectra.
c) Why does the low resolution n.m.r. spectrum of B have three peaks whereas that of A only has one?
d) What does the integration trace on the n.m.r. spectrum of B tell us?
e) If we had used high resolution n.m.r., apply the $n+1$ rule to predict the splitting patterns for each peak on the n.m.r. spectrum of B.

Further questions on organic chemistry 2

▶ Aromatic compounds

1 Benzene is amongst the most important aromatic compounds in industrial use. Two reactions of benzene are shown below:
a) Name the substances A to E. [5]

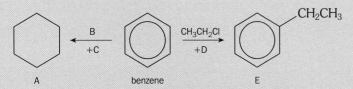

b) Benzene undergoes addition reactions and electrophilic substitution reactions. Look at the reactions to form A and B, classify each of them as addition or electrophilic substitution and explain carefully how you arrived at your answer. [2]

2 When the compound with the formula shown below reacts with aqueous sodium hydroxide, one of the chlorine atoms is replaced.

CH_2Cl

Cl

a) Draw a displayed formula for the product of the reaction. [1]
b) Explain the difference in the reactivities of the two chlorine atoms. [2]

3 Some important reactions of benzene can be summarised in a flow sheet:

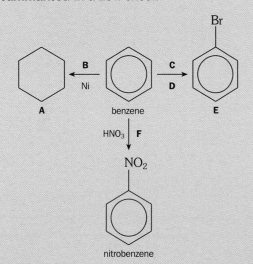

a) Name substances **A** to **F**. [6]
b) i) The reactions to form **E** and nitrobenzene are electrophilic substitutions. Give the formula and charge of the electrophile in each reaction. [2]

ii) In the reaction to form nitrobenzene it is important to keep the temperature below 55 °C. Suggest a reason for this. [1]
iii) Suggest **one** use for compounds formed by the nitration of arenes. [1]
c) i) State the conditions for the reaction to form **A** from benzene. [2]
ii) Benzene reacts with chlorine to form 1,2,3,4,5,6-hexachlorocyclohexane, an important insecticide.
Write a **balanced** equation for this reaction. [1]
(EDEXCEL)

4 a) Draw the structures of the organic products of the reaction of propene and benzene with bromine **and** classify these reactions. [2]
b) Name the catalyst used in the bromination of benzene. [½]
c) Explain why there is a difference in the reactions undergone by propene and benzene with bromine. [2]
(WJEC)

5 Below is a reaction scheme for some aromatic compounds.

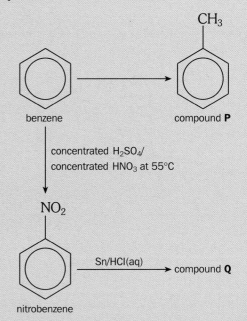

a) i) Give the reagents and conditions for the conversion of benzene into compound **P**.
ii) Give the name of the mechanism of this reaction. [2]
b) Draw the graphical formulae of the possible organic products when excess chlorine is passed through boiling compound **P** in strong sunlight. [3]
c) i) Classify the type of reaction occurring when nitrobenzene is converted into compound Q. [1]
ii) Draw the graphical formula of compound Q. [2]
(AQA)

6 A hydrocarbon is known to contain a benzene ring. It has a relative molecular mass of 106 and has the following composition by mass: C, 90.56%; H, 9.44%.
   a) i) Use the data above to show that the empirical formula is C_4H_5.
      ii) Deduce the molecular formula.
      iii) Draw structures for all possible isomers of this hydrocarbon that contain a benzene ring. [7]
   b) In the presence of a catalyst (such as aluminium chloride), one of these isomers, **A**, reacts with chlorine to give only **one** monochloro-product **B**.
      i) Deduce which of the isomers in a) iii) is **A**.
      ii) Draw the structure of **B**. [2]
   c) In the presence of ultraviolet light, **A** reacted differently with chlorine to give another monochloro-product **C** as well as several polychloro-products.
      i) State the type of reaction involved in the conversion of **A** into **C**.
      ii) Suggest why several other polychloro-products were formed in this reaction. [2]
                                                        (OCR)

7 a) Cyclohexane, C_6H_{10}, contains one C=C double bone in its molecule, of the type found in ethene. It reacts with hydrogen to form cyclohexane, C_6H_{12}, as follows:

   $$C_6H_{10} + H_2 \longrightarrow C_6H_{12}$$

   Calculate ΔH for this reaction, given that the enthalpies of formation of cyclohexene and cyclohexane are $-36\,kJ\,mol^{-1}$ and $-156\,kJ\,mol^{-1}$ respectively. [2]
   b) Benzene undergoes a similar reaction with hydrogen to form cyclohexane:

   $$C_6H_6 + 3\,H_2 \longrightarrow C_6H_{12}$$

   Predict the value of ΔH for this reaction, assuming that benzene contains three C=C double bonds of the type found in ethene. [1]
   c) The actual value of ΔH for the reaction in c) is $-207\,kJ\,mol^{-1}$. What can you deduce from this about the stability of the benzene ring? Use an enthalpy diagram to illustrate your answer.

                                                        [3]
   d) Give the reagents and conditions necessary for the conversion of benzene to nitrobenzene. [2]
   e) Write a mechanism for this reaction. [4]
                                                        (EDEXCEL)

▶ **Aldehydes and ketones**

8 a) Copy the following table and complete the blank spaces to show some of the reactions of propanal.

Reactant	Reagent	Organic product	
		Name	Displayed formula
CH_3CH_2CHO	Fehling's solution		
CH_3CH_2CHO	$NaBH_4$		
CH_3CH_2CHO		2-hydroxybutanenitrile	

                                                        [6]
   b) Describe and explain what you would see in the reaction of propanal with Fehling's solution. [3]
   c) Give another example of this type of reaction with propanal. [2]
                                                        (AQA)

9 a) Propanal can be converted into three different organic compounds as shown by the reaction sequence below. Give the structures of the new compounds **X**, **Y** and **Z**. [3]

   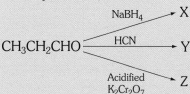

   b) Outline a mechanism for the formation of Y. [4]
                                                        (AQA)

10 a) Give a chemical test by which you could distinguish between ethanal and propanone. State the reagent(s) and conditions for the test, describe what you would observe, and give the name or formula of the organic product. [4]
   b) Consider the following series of reactions involving ethanal, and then answer the questions which follow.

   $$S \xleftarrow{HCN} CH_3CHO \xrightarrow{2,4\text{-dinitrophenylhydrazine}} T$$
   $$\downarrow NaBH_4$$
   $$U$$

      i) Draw displayed formulae to show the structures of compounds **S**, **T**, and **U**. [3]
      ii) Give the name of **T** and describe its appearance [2]
   c) Give the name and an outline of a mechanism for the reaction of ethanal with HCN to produce compound **S**. [4]
                                                        (AQA)

11 Butan-1-ol can be oxidised by acidified potassium dichromate(VI) using two different methods.
   a) In the first method, butan-1-ol is added dropwise to acidified potassium dichromate(VI) and the product distilled off immediately.

i) Using the symbol [O] for the oxidising agent, write an equation for this oxidation of butan-1-ol, showing clearly the structure of the product. State what colour change you would observe. [3]

ii) Butan-1-ol and butan-2-ol give different products on oxidation by this first method. By stating a reagent and the observation with each compound, give a simple test to distinguish between these two oxidation products. [3]

b) In a second method, the mixture of butan-1-ol and acidified dichromate(VI) is heated under reflux. Identify the product which is obtained. [1]

c) Give the structures and names of two branched chain alcohols which are both isomers of butan-1-ol. Explain why only one of these is oxidised when warmed with acidified potassium dichromate(VI). [4]

(AQA)

12 a) CH_3CHO reacts with a particular reagent to form ethanol.
i) What type of reaction is involved? [1]
ii) Use this example to explain the nature of this type of reaction. [2]

b) When ethanol is warmed under reflux with excess acidified potassium dichromate solution, ethanal reforms but further reaction then occurs forming Y, $C_2H_4O_2$.

Identify compound Y by giving its name and structural formula. [2]

(WJEC)

13 Classify the types of reaction and draw the graphical formulae of the organic products of the reaction of propanal with:
a) sodium tetrahydridoborate(III), $NaBH_4$; [2]
b) Fehling's solution; [2]
c) hydrogen cyanide [2]

(AQA)

▶ Carboxylic acids and related compounds

14 Write balanced equations for the following hydrolysis reactions.
a) i) ethanoyl chloride and water;
ii) ethanoic anhydride and water. [4]
b) What difference is there in the conditions needed for the hydrolyses shown in a) i) and a) ii) above? [1]
c) Give the formulae of two organic compounds which react together to give a product having the formula CH_3COOCH_3. [2]

(AQA)

15 Some data relating to propane, ethanol and methanoic acid are given in the table.

Compound	Relative molecular mass	Boiling point / °C
Propane	44	−42.2
Ethanol	46	78.5
Methanoic acid	46	101.0

a) i) State what is meant by the term *polar bond* and explain how one can arise within a molecule. [2]
ii) Draw the graphical formula for each of the compounds in the table and clearly show the polarity of any polar bonds present. [4]

b) i) State the type of intermolecular force present in propane and explain why it has a low boiling point. [2]
ii) State the main type of intermolecular force present in both pure ethanol and pure methanoic acid. Draw diagrams to show clearly this force in each of the compounds. Suggest a reason for the higher boiling point of methanoic acid.

(AQA)

16 a) Name the functional group present in **F**. [4]

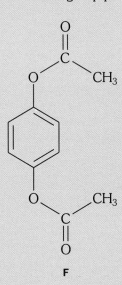

F

b) When **F** is treated with hot dilute aqueous sodium hydroxide, followed by acidification, two organic compounds **G**, $C_2H_4O_2$, and **H**, $C_6H_6O_2$, are formed.
i) Draw the structural formulae of **G** and **H**. [2]
ii) Write a balanced chemical equation for the reaction that has taken place. [2]

c) From the reaction of 19.4 g of **F** used in the reaction, 10.0 g of **G** and 10.0 g of **H** were isolated. Calculate:
i) the yield of **H** obtained in the reaction; [2]
ii) the yield of **G** obtained in the reaction. [2]

d) i) What is meant by the saponification of fats? [1]
   ii) What product of industrial importance is formed in the process? [1]
   (OCR)

17 An ester **A**, is used as a raspberry flavouring in some foods.
   a) Give **one** common use of esters other than as food flavourings.
   b) Ester A has a molecular formula, $C_6H_{12}O_2$ and can be formed in the presence of a homogeneous catalyst, by the reaction of acid **B** with alcohol **C** shown below:

   $$CH_3 \!-\! CH \!-\! CH_2OH$$
   $$\mid$$
   $$CH_3$$
   c

   i) Name alcohol **C**.
   ii) Identify acid **B** and draw the structure of ester **A**.
   iii) Give a suitable homogeneous catalyst for the formation of ester **A** and explain the term *homogeneous*.
   iv) Alcohols **D** and **E** are isomers of alcohol **C**. Alcohol **D** exhibits optical isomerism, and alcohol **E** is unaffected by acidified potassium dichromate(VI) solution. Draw the structures of alcohols **D** and **E**.
   (AQA)

▶ Organic nitrogen compounds

18 a) Give the systematic names of the following compounds.
   i) $CH_3CH_2CH(NH_2)COOH$
   ii) $CH_3CH_2CH_2NH_2$ [2]
   b) Write down the structural formula of the organic product formed when $CH_3CH_2CH(NH_2)COOH$ reacts with (i) sodium hydroxide and (ii) concentrated hydrochloric acid. [2]
   (AQA)

19 a) Write balanced equations for the following hydrolysis reactions:
   i) ethanamide and aqueous sodium hydroxide
   ii) propanenitrile and aqueous hydrochloric acid [4]
   b) Give the formulae of two organic compounds which react together to give a product of formula $CH_3CH_2NHCOCH_3$ [2]
   (AQA)

20 a) Explain why phenylamine is a weaker base than (phenylmethyl)amine, $C_6H_5CH_2NH_2$. [2]
   b) Write an equation for the formation of (phenylmethyl)amine from benzenecarbonitrile, C_6H_5CN, and name the type of reaction involved. [2]

c) The compound, $(C_6H_5CH_2)NH(CH_2)_{11}CH_3$, which is a secondary amine, can be converted into a cationic fabric-softening product by reaction with excess chloromethane. Name the type of product formed and give the structural formula of this compound. [3]
   (AQA)

21 This question is about two nitrogen compounds.
   a) To which class of organic compound does each of the following compounds belong?
   $C_2H_5NH_2$; CH_3CONH_2 [2]
   b) $C_2H_5NH_2$ is a gas with a distinctive odour at room temperature. The odour associated with the compound disappears when the gas is shaken with dilute hydrochloric acid, but returns when excess aqueous sodium hydroxide is added. Explain these observations. [4]
   c) CH_3CONH_2 has a powerful odour. When the compound is heated with aqueous sodium hydroxide a new gas with a different odour is slowly released. Identify the gas evolved and explain with the aid of an equation what is happening in this reaction [2]
   (WJEC)

22 State which **one** of the following will show optical isomerism.
   A $CH_2(NH_2)COOH$
   B $CH_3CH(NH_2)COOH$
   C $(CH_3)_2C\!=\!CHCl$
   D CH_3CH_2COOH [1]
   (WJEC)

▶ Polymers

23 Poly(phenylethene) is formed from phenylethene in the following reaction.

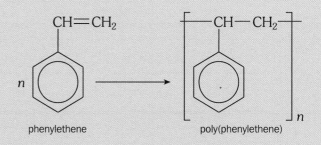

phenylethene   poly(phenylethene)

Classify the type of polymerisation reaction occurring in the formation of poly(phenylethene) and state the reagents necessary to bring about the reaction. [3]

24 a) Explain the term *polymerisation*. [1]
   b) Polymers found in natural materials can be formed by the reaction between amino acids.

i) Draw a displayed formula for the product formed when two molecules of alanine, $CH_3CH(NH_2)COOH$, react. [1]

ii) Give the name of the important linkage formed and draw a ring round it on the formula drawn in (b)(i). [2]

iii) Give the name of the type of naturally-occurring polymer containing this linkage. [1]

c) Polyethene is an example of a synthetic polymer. It is manufactured in two main forms, low density poly(ethene) and high density poly(ethene).

i) Write an equation to represent the polymerisation of ethene. [1]

ii) What is the main structural difference between the polymer chains in the two main forms of poly(ethene)? Explain how this difference affects the densities of the polymers. [3]

iii) Give one further physical property that is affected by the structural difference given in c) ii). [1]

iv) Low density poy(ethene) is manufactured *via* a free radical mechanism. Draw a graphical formula to represent the free radical formed between a free radical, **R•**, and a molecule of ethene in the reaction. [1]

v) What type of catalyst is used in the manufacture of high density poy(ethene)? [1]

d) Poly(ethene) is a non-biodegradable plastic.

i) Explain the term *non-biodegradable*. [1]

ii) Give one environmental benefit of using biodegradable plastics. [1]

(AQA)

25 The polymer *perspex* which is poly(methyl 2-methylpropenoate) is made from the monomer shown below.

$$H_2C=C\begin{array}{c} CH_3 \\ \diagup \\ \diagdown \\ COOCH_3 \end{array}$$

Draw the repeating unit of perspex. [1]

26 Addition polymerisation is used to produce a range of plastics and construction materials. The table below shows several polymers, and the monomers from which they are made.

Polymer	Monomer
Polystyrene	$CH_2=CHC_6H_5$
Orlon	$CH_2=CHCN$
Perspex	$CH_2=C(CH_3)COOCH_3$
Poly(propenoic acid)	$CH_2=CHCOOH$

a) Glass poly(alkenoate) cements are formed by reaction of a glass powder with an acidic polymer. They are used as fillings for teeth. Poly(propenoic acid) is one such acidic polymer. Write a balanced equation to show its formation from its monomer. [2]

b) Discuss the different types of attractive forces that exist between polymer molecules, using at least **three** of the polymers above to illustrate your answer. You should comment on the relative strengths of the forces and explain their nature, preferably by use of diagrams. [3]

c) Increasing use of plastics makes landfill site management difficult, because they decompose very slowly. Incineration is one alternative which greatly decreases the bulk of solid waste.

i) Suggest possible problems associated with incineration of a polymer such as Orlon. [2]

ii) State **one** alternative means of disposal of plastics. [1]

(OCR)

27 Nylon 6,6 has the formula

$$—(CH_2)_4—CONH—(CH_2)_6—NHCO—(CH_2)_4$$
$$—CONH—(CH_2)_6—NHCO—$$

a) Give the formulae of the two monomers which combine to make nylon 6,6. [2]

b) What is the name of the other product in this polymerisation? [1]

c) Suggest, including an equation, what will happen if nylon 6,6 is boiled with dilute acid. [4]

(NICCEA)

28 a) Polymers may be naturally occurring or synthetic. Name

i) a synthetic polyalkene [1]

ii) a synthetic polyamide [1]

iii) a natural polyamide [1]

iv) a synthetic polymer containing no hydrogen [1]

b) Terylene is a polymer made from ethane-1,2-diol and benzene-1,4-dicarboxylic acid. It is a condensation polymer.

i) Draw the structural formulae of the two compounds which are used to make Terylene. [2]

ii) Give a structural formula of the polymer. [2]

iii) Explain the meaning of the term **condensation** in this context. [1]

iv) Suggest why polyesters are not suitable for use under strongly alkaline conditions. [1]

c) Suggest why polymers such as Terylene soften over a range of temperatures rather than having a sharp melting point. [1]

▶ Organic synthesis

29 3-Amino-4-methylbenzenesulphonic acid can be obtained from benzene in three steps.

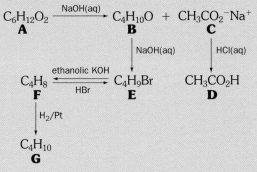

a) For steps 1 and 3, name the type of reaction taking place and suggest a suitable reagent or combination of reagents. [4]

b) Identify the reactive inorganic species present in step 2 and outline a mechanism for this reaction. [5]

(AQA)

30 Consider the following reaction scheme and answer the questions which follow.

$$CH_3CH_2CH_2OH \rightarrow B \rightarrow CH_3CH_2COOH \rightarrow D$$

A beneath first; C beneath CH$_3$CH$_2$COOH; F to the side of D

A →Na(s)→ G

D →F→ CH$_3$CH$_2$CONHCH$_3$ (E)

a) Give the reagent(s) and condition(s) required for the direct conversion of compound A into compound C. [3]

b) The conversion of A into C proceeds via compound B. Give the structure of B and describe how the conditions you have described in (a) could be modified to give B, rather than C, as the major product. [2]

c) Compound D may be prepared by the reaction of compound C with PCl$_5$ under anhydrous conditions. Write an equation for the reaction, state what is meant by the term *anhydrous conditions* and explain why such conditions are necessary. [4]

d) Identify, by name or formula, the reagent F, and draw the displayed formula of compound E.

e) Which gas is given off when sodium is added to compound A? Give the name of compound G. [2]

(AQA)

31 Consider the following series of reactions and answer the questions which follow.

$$C_6H_{12}O_2 \xrightarrow{\text{NaOH(aq)}} C_4H_{10}O + CH_3CO_2^-Na^+$$
$$\textbf{A} \qquad\qquad \textbf{B} \qquad\qquad \textbf{C}$$

B →NaOH(aq)→ , C →HCl(aq)→

$$C_4H_8 \underset{\text{HBr}}{\overset{\text{ethanolic KOH}}{\rightleftarrows}} C_4H_9Br \qquad CH_3CO_2H$$
$$\textbf{F} \qquad\qquad\qquad \textbf{E} \qquad\qquad \textbf{D}$$

F →H$_2$/Pt→ C$_4$H$_{10}$ **G**

a) i) What type of reaction is represented by the conversion **E** to **F**? [1]

ii) The product **F** exists in two stereoisomeric forms. Draw them, and state the feature of the molecule which makes this isomerism possible. [3]

iii) Give a simple chemical test, stating what you would see, for the functional group present in **F**. [2]

iv) **F** is more reactive than **G**. Suggest in terms of the bonding of these compounds why this is so. [2]

b) Compound **E** displays optical isomerism.
i) State what this means. [1]
ii) Sketch the optical isomers of **E**. [2]

c) The reaction of **E** to give **B** is a nucleophilic substitution.
i) What is meant by the term **nucleophile**? [1]
ii) Give the structural formula for **B**. [1]
iii) Give a simple chemical test for the functional group in **B**, and say what you would see. [2]

d) The type of reaction exemplified by A ⟶ B + C is important in the manufacture of soap.
i) What type of reaction is this? [1]
ii) **A** could be reacted with aqueous acid to give **B** and **D**. If the same quantity of **A** was treated with aqueous acid, instead of aqueous alkali, how would the yield of **B** differ? Explain your answer. [1]

e) Consider the reaction **C** ⟶ **D**.
i) Name **D** [1]
ii) Identify the acid–base conjugate pair in this reaction. [1]
iii) Explain why this reaction occurs. [2]

(EDEXCEL)

▶ Organic analysis

32 a) The structure of 2,4-dimethylpentane, is shown below:

$$H_3C-CH-CH_2-CH-CH_3$$
$$\qquad\; | \qquad\qquad\quad |$$
$$\qquad CH_3 \qquad\qquad CH_3$$

Explain why the low resolution n.m.r. spectrum of of 2,4-dimethylpentane shows three peaks with relative areas $6:1:1$. [3]

b) An isomer of 2,4-dimethylpentane has the structure shown below:

$$\qquad\qquad CH_3\; CH_3$$
$$\qquad\qquad\; | \qquad |$$
$$H_3C-C-C-CH_3$$
$$\qquad\qquad\; | \qquad |$$
$$\qquad\qquad CH_3\; H$$

How many peaks will there be in its low resolution n.m.r. spectrum? [1]

Further questions on organic chemistry 2

33 The percentage by mass of an organic compound, X, is C = 54.5%; H = 9.10%; O = 36.4%.

a) Find the empirical formula of X. [2]

b) Combustion of one mole of X produces 88 g of carbon dioxide. Use this information to find the molecular formula of compound X. [2]

(WJEC)

34 Benzocaine is a local anaesthetic, often used in ointments which soothe the effects of sunburn. It can be made by the route shown:

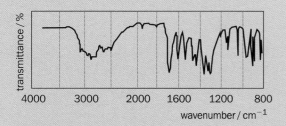

$M_r = 167$ $M_r = 195$

a) Name two functional groups present in benzocaine. [2]

b) i) Suggest the substances you would reflux with compound A to carry out step 1 in the laboratory. [2]

ii) Draw a labelled diagram of the apparatus you would use to carry out step 1. [3]

iii) There is a compound C which contains an acyl chloride group and will react much more quickly than compound A to give compound B. Write the structural formula of compound C. [2]

c) The mass spectrum of an impure sample of benzocaine, made by step 2, includes peaks with m/e ratios of 165, 195 and 120. Account for each of these peaks. [5]

d) The infra-red spectrum shown below is that of either A or B. Use the spectrum to identify which it is, using data given in chapter 23 page 281. Explain how you arrive at your answer. [2]

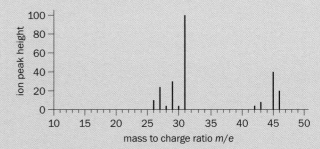

(WJEC)

35 a) An organic compound **A** has a molar mass of $46\ \mathrm{g\ mol^{-1}}$ and the following elemental composition by mass:

     C 52.13%;   H 13.15%;   O 34.72%

Determine the molecular formula of **A**. [2]

b) The organic compound **A** has an infrared spectrum which shows the following features:

Absorption at $2900\ \mathrm{cm^{-1}}$ C—H stretching frequency
Absorption at $3300\ \mathrm{cm^{-1}}$ O—H stretching frequency
Absorption at $1050\ \mathrm{cm^{-1}}$ C—O stretching frequency
Absorption at $1400\ \mathrm{cm^{-1}}$ C—H bending frequency

The shape and position of the —OH peak indicates substantial hydrogen bonding.

i) Explain, briefly, what is meant by the term ***hydrogen bonding***. [1]

ii) By reference to the infrared spectrum and your answer to a) deduce the structure of **A**. Give **three** reasons in support of your answer. [4]

c) The mass spectrum of **A** is given below.

Using the structural formula of **A** deduced above, suggest formulae for the positive ions responsible for m/e peaks at 45, 31 and 29. [3]

d) i) When **A** is treated with ethanoyl chloride a compound **B** is formed containing 4 carbon atoms.
Give the name and structure of **B** and state to which class of organic compounds it belongs. [3]

ii) State how you would carry out the addition of ethanoyl chloride to the compound, **A**, paying particular attention to safety. [2]

(WJEC)

Think of the last time you used the energy produced
by a chemical reaction:
You might have used the energy from burning natural gas
to cook a meal or to heat your home. Or what about
any transport you've been on? Even if you have used
a bicycle or walked, the energy has been released from
chemical reactions in your body's cells.
In fact we all use this energy from our cells constantly
just to stay alive. It helps us maintain our body temperature
and enables our vital organs to function.

In this chapter we will look at the energy changes
from reactions and how we can work them out.

*The energy given out when gas burns is
used to cook food*

▷ Enthalpy changes (ΔH)

We often use the term 'energy change' to describe what happens
in a reaction.
However, for most reactions we do, we really should say
'enthalpy change' (ΔH).
Enthalpy change refers to energy changes in reactions that take place
at a ***constant pressure***.
It is the change in heat content between products and reactants,
in an open system.
The reactions that we normally carry out in the lab are done
at atmospheric pressure. Our test tubes, beakers and flasks
are not sealed. We make no attempt to keep the volume constant,
especially when gases are given off. The work done by any gases
pushing against atmospheric pressure is accounted for
in these 'open systems'.
***So these energy changes, at constant pressure, are strictly
enthalpy changes.***

Think of a reaction that produces a gas:
What would happen to the pressure in a sealed vessel (i.e. a closed
system) in this reaction?
What might happen if the vessel was made of glass?

Such reactions, done at a constant volume, can be carried out in
strong vessels such as a bomb calorimeter.
Look at the diagram opposite:

In this case, the energy change is called the **internal energy change (ΔU).**
Any gases made can't do any work as there is no change in the volume
of the system.

In reactions involving only solids or liquids,

$$\Delta H = \Delta U \text{ (approximately)}$$

even in open systems, as no work is done by gases.

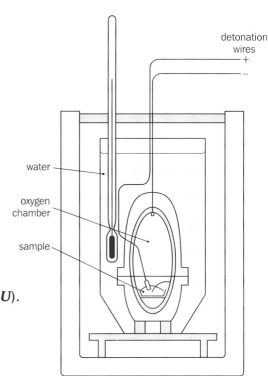

*A bomb calorimeter is used to determine the
total energy content of foods*

▷ Enthalpy level diagrams

You will have met examples of exothermic and endothermic reactions in your previous work.
Can you recall which gives out and which takes in heat?
Look at the picture opposite:
It might help you to remember.

We can show the enthalpy changes in reactions on an **enthalpy level diagram.**

These show us the enthalpy (or 'heat content') stored in the reactants compared with the enthalpy stored in the products.
Look at the examples below:

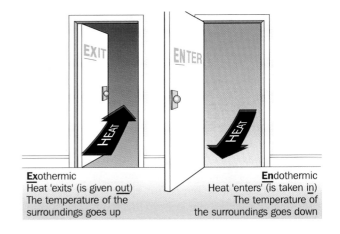

Exothermic
Heat 'exits' (is given out)
The temperature of the surroundings goes up

Endothermic
Heat 'enters' (is taken in)
The temperature of the surroundings goes down

Exothermic enthalpy level diagram

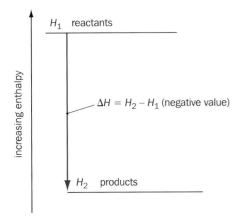

Note that we can't measure the actual enthalpy (or heat content) of reactants or products. We can measure ΔH, the change in enthalpy

ΔH (we say 'delta H') is the symbol for the 'change in enthalpy' in a reaction.
Look at the enthalpy level diagram opposite:
It is for an exothermic reaction.
Notice that the products have less enthalpy than the reactants.
Try subtracting the enthalpy of the reactants from the enthalpy of the products.
Do you get a negative number?
$\Delta H = H(\text{products}) - H(\text{reactants})$
Therefore,

> **ΔH values for exothermic reactions are given a negative sign.**

The difference in the enthalpy of the chemicals is given out as heat.
So the temperature of the reacting mixture and its surroundings rises as the reaction happens.

Example

$HNO_3(aq) + NaOH(aq) \longrightarrow NaNO_3(aq) + H_2O(l)$ $\Delta H = -57.6 \text{ kJ mol}^{-1}$

● Can you draw an enthalpy level diagram to show this change?

Endothermic enthalpy level diagram

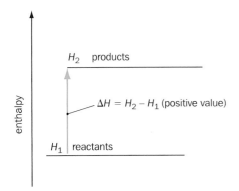

In endothermic reactions, the products have more enthalpy than the reactants.
So $H(\text{products}) - H(\text{reactants})$ is a positive number.

> **ΔH values for endothermic reactions are given a positive sign.**

The extra energy needed to form the products is taken in from the surroundings. The surroundings include the thermometer, the reaction vessel, the air around the vessel, any water present in solutions and your hand if you touch the vessel!
Therefore the temperature falls as the reaction happens.

▷ Working out enthalpy changes in solutions

We can calculate the enthalpy change in a reaction by measuring the temperature change. We can use a thermometer or a temperature probe linked to a data-logger.

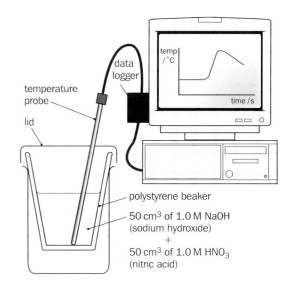

Example: Finding out the enthalpy of neutralisation
Look at the apparatus opposite:

Why do you think that the beaker is made from polystyrene?
Here are the results from the experiment:

Starting temperature of solutions $= 19.0\,°C$
Maximum temperature reached $= 25.1\,°C$
Change in temperature $= 6.1\,°C$

We can now use the results to calculate the enthalpy change. The equation below allows us to work out the heat absorbed by the solution:

Heat =	**mass of solution ×**	**specific heat capacity ×**	**change in temp.**
(J)	**(g)**	**(J K^{-1} g^{-1})**	**(K or °C)**

The solution is made up mainly from water. So we can use water's data i.e. $1\,cm^3$ has a mass of $1\,g$, and its specific heat capacity is $4.2\,J\,K^{-1}\,g^{-1}$. In other words, it takes $4.2\,J$ of energy to raise the temperature of $1\,g$ (which equals $1\,cm^3$) of water by $1\,K$ (which is the same as $1\,°C$).

Now we can put the figures from our experiment into the equation above:

Heat (absorbed by solution) $= 100 \times 4.2 \times 6.1\,J$
$= 2562\,J$

This is the enthalpy change in our beaker. It will be given a negative sign because it is an exothermic reaction. Heat energy is given out to the surroundings.
But normally ΔH refers to the number of moles reacting as shown in the balanced equation:

$$HNO_3(aq) + NaOH(aq) \longrightarrow NaNO_3(aq) + H_2O(l)$$

We didn't start with 1 mole of reactants.
We had $50\,cm^3$ of $1.0\,M$ solutions. These contain:

$$\text{number of moles} = \frac{50 \times 1.0}{1000} = 0.05 \text{ moles}$$

(See page 38 if you need to practise this type of calculation.)
Therefore if 1 mole of HNO_3 and $NaOH$ react, the enthalpy change (or heat given out) will be:

$$\Delta H_{neut} = -\left(2562 \times \frac{1.0}{0.05}\right) J\,mol^{-1} = -51\,240\,J\,mol^{-1} = -51.2\,kJ\,mol^{-1}$$

Notice that this is lower than the value given on page 296.
Can you think why? Where might heat be lost in the experiment?

We can reduce the error in measuring temperature changes as shown on the graph:

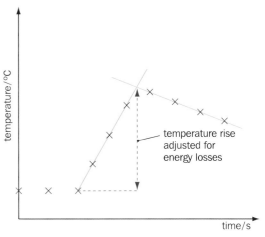

This method for adjusting temperature change is especially useful for slow reactions. Can you think why?

▷ Standard conditions

If you measure the enthalpy change in the same reaction
at different temperatures and pressures, you get different answers.
ΔH also depends on the amount of substances reacting.
So in order to compare and use data, we need a standard set of conditions.

The **standard conditions** have been agreed as:

Temperature:	**298 K** (which is 25 °C)
Pressure:	**1 atmosphere** (which is $1.01 \times 10^5 \, N \, m^{-2}$ or 101 kPa, where $1 \, N \, m^{-2} = 1$ pascal)
Solutions:	**$1 \, mol \, dm^{-3}$**

The amount of substance is included in the definitions
for the variety of enthalpy changes we need to know.
The amount is expressed in **moles**.

Enthalpy changes that take place under standard conditions
are given the symbol:

$$\Delta H^{\ominus}_{298}$$

Notice from the last page that its units are **$kJ \, mol^{-1}$**.
From now on we will leave out the 298 to keep things concise.
Now let's look at some enthalpy changes we need to know about.

Standard enthalpy of reaction ($\Delta H^{\ominus}$)

Notice that we can leave out the word 'change' after enthalpy.
This is the enthalpy change that occurs in any reaction
under standard conditions. It refers to the amounts of substance
shown in the balanced chemical equation.
So we must be careful to state the equation or mistakes can be made.
For example,

$$2 \, H_2(g) + O_2(g) \longrightarrow 2 \, H_2O(l) \qquad \Delta H^{\ominus} = -571.6 \, kJ \, mol^{-1}$$

This is the enthalpy change when 2 moles of hydrogen react with
1 mole of oxygen to make 2 moles of water.
On the other hand:

$$H_2(g) + \tfrac{1}{2} O_2(g) \longrightarrow H_2O(l) \qquad \Delta H^{\ominus} = -285.8 \, kJ \, mol^{-1}$$

- Can you see the relationship between the two values of ΔH?
- Why is the second one only half the first?

Also notice the state symbol next to H_2O:
Remember that the reaction is at 298 K (25 °C). At this temperature
H_2O is a liquid, although in the heat of the reaction
it is produced as a gas.

$$H_2(g) + \tfrac{1}{2} O_2(g) \longrightarrow H_2O(g) \qquad \Delta H^{\ominus} = -241.8 \, kJ \, mol^{-1}$$

- Can you explain why this value of ΔH is not $-285.8 \, kJ \, mol^{-1}$?
  (Hint: Look at the enthalpy level diagram opposite.)

Converting °C to K (Kelvin):

$$\boxed{K = °C + 273}$$

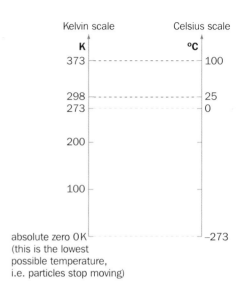

absolute zero 0 K
(this is the lowest
possible temperature,
i.e. particles stop moving)

*Lord Kelvin proposed the idea of absolute
zero in 1848*

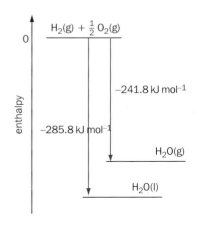

298

Standard enthalpy of formation ($\Delta H_f^\ominus$)

We define the enthalpy of formation as:

> $\Delta H_f^\ominus$ = the enthalpy change when 1 mole of a compound is made from its elements in their standard states, under standard conditions.

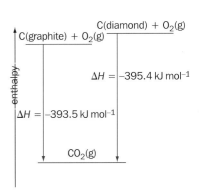

Examples

The standard enthalpy of formation of carbon dioxide, refers to this reaction:

$$C(graphite, s) + O_2(g) \longrightarrow CO_2(g) \qquad \Delta H_f^\ominus[CO_2(g)] = -393.5 \, kJ \, mol^{-1}$$

Notice that carbon is in the form of graphite.
Where an element exists as allotropes (see page 63),
we always use the most stable form.
The enthalpy level diagram opposite gives us evidence that
graphite is energetically more stable than diamond.

This shows that graphite is 1.9 kJ mol⁻¹ energetically more stable than diamond

Another example is the enthalpy of formation of ethanol, C_2H_5OH:

$$2\,C(graphite, s) + 3\,H_2(g) + \tfrac{1}{2}O_2(g) \longrightarrow C_2H_5OH(l) \qquad \Delta H_f^\ominus[C_2H_5OH(l)] = -277.1 \, kJ \, mol^{-1}$$

Of course, we could never make ethanol by combining the elements directly
as shown in the equation above. But you will see how we can calculate
enthalpies of formation indirectly on the next page.

Standard enthalpy of combustion ($\Delta H_c^\ominus$)

We define this as:

> $\Delta H_c^\ominus$ = the enthalpy change when 1 mole of the substance burns completely in oxygen under standard conditions

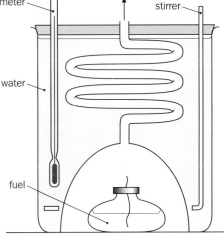

A combustion calorimeter

Examples

The standard enthalpy of combustion of hydrogen is shown by this equation:

$$H_2(g) + \tfrac{1}{2}O_2(g) \longrightarrow H_2O(l) \qquad \Delta H_c^\ominus[H_2(g)] = -285.8 \, kJ \, mol^{-1}$$

Can you see why the enthalpy of formation of carbon dioxide above
has the same value as the enthalpy of combustion of graphite?

We can use the apparatus opposite to measure enthalpies of combustion:
For example, the enthalpy of combustion of heptane is shown by:

$$C_7H_{16}(l) + 11\,O_2(g) \longrightarrow 7\,CO_2(g) + 8\,H_2O(l) \qquad \Delta H_c^\ominus[C_7H_{16}(l)] = -4816.9 \, kJ \, mol^{-1}$$

Standard enthalpy of atomisation of an element ($\Delta H_{at}^\ominus$)

This is defined as:

> $\Delta H_{at}^\ominus$ = the enthalpy change when 1 mole of gaseous atoms is made from the element in its standard state, under standard conditions.

Examples

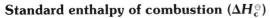

$$Na(s) \longrightarrow Na(g) \qquad \Delta H_{at}^\ominus[Na(s)] = +107.3 \, kJ \, mol^{-1}$$
$$\tfrac{1}{2}H_2(g) \longrightarrow H(g) \qquad \Delta H_{at}^\ominus[\tfrac{1}{2}H_2(g)] = +218.0 \, kJ \, mol^{-1}$$
$$S(rhombic, s) \longrightarrow S(g) \qquad \Delta H_{at}^\ominus[S(rhombic, s)] = +278.8 \, kJ \, mol^{-1}$$

Notice the $\tfrac{1}{2}H_2$ here – from the definition we only want 1 mole of H atoms formed!

▷ Using enthalpy cycles

We mentioned on the last page that *some enthalpy changes can't be measured directly*.
The example quoted was the enthalpy of formation of ethanol.
There are also many other compounds that cannot be made directly from their elements.
But values for $\Delta H_f^\ominus$ can be worked out using other enthalpy changes that we can find from experiments.
The enthalpy of formation of a compound is a useful way of judging the compound's **energetic stability**.
Let's remind ourselves of its definition from the last page:

$\Delta H_f^\ominus$ = the enthalpy change when 1 mole of a compound is made from its elements in their standard states, under standard conditions.

From this it follows that the enthalpy of formation of any element (in its most stable form under standard conditions) must be zero.
It has also been decided that *the enthalpy of an element is zero.*
(Remember that absolute values for the enthalpy of a substance can't be measured, only changes in enthalpy.)
This then provides us with a reference line against which we can measure a compound's energetic stability.

> The more exothermic the enthalpy of formation, the more energetically stable a compound is.

So if we can work out a value of $\Delta H_f^\ominus$ for a theoretical new compound, we can see if it is likely to form. This won't give us the whole picture, but if you find a large endothermic value it is most unlikely that the new compound could *ever* be formed.

We can work out these values by applying **Hess's Law**.

> Hess's Law states that the enthalpy change in turning any reactants into a set of products is the same no matter what route we take.

The diagram opposite helps to explain this:

Now we can try an example of an enthalpy cycle.
We will use it to see how $\Delta H_f^\ominus$ of ethanol is worked out.
The cycle relies on the fact that we can work out enthalpies of combustion experimentally. (See the apparatus on the last page.)

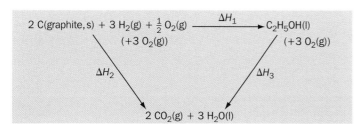

(The 3 O_2's cancel each other out in ΔH_1, so we can leave them out of the cycle.)
Using Hess's Law we can say that:

$$\Delta H_1 = \Delta H_2 - \Delta H_3$$

where ΔH_1 is $\Delta H_f^\ominus [C_2H_5OH(l)]$, the value we want to work out.

The lower the enthalpy of a substance, the more stable it is

Enthalpy cycle:
Look at the diagram below: a, b, c, d and e represent enthalpy changes for each of the reactions:

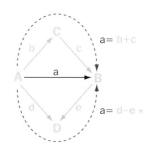

So there are 3 routes from A to B.

$$a = b + c = d - e$$

It doesn't matter what route we take, as long as we start with A and finish with B.

* Notice that if we go against the direction of the arrow, the sign of the enthalpy change is reversed.

We know the values for the enthalpies of combustion from tables of data.
These values come from very accurate experiments using
the bomb calorimeter (see page 295).
The values we need are:

$$\Delta H_c^{\ominus}[\text{C, graphite(s)}] = -393.5 \, \text{kJ mol}^{-1}$$

$$\Delta H_c^{\ominus}[\text{H}_2(\text{g})] = -285.8 \, \text{kJ mol}^{-1}$$

$$\Delta H_c^{\ominus}[\text{C}_2\text{H}_5\text{OH(l)}] = -1367.3 \, \text{kJ mol}^{-1}$$

We can now work out a value for ΔH_2:

$$\begin{aligned}
\Delta H_2 &= (2 \times \Delta H_c^{\ominus}[\text{CO}_2(\text{g})]) + (3 \times \Delta H_c^{\ominus}[\text{H}_2(\text{g})]) \\
&= (2 \times -393.5) + (3 \times -285.8) \\
&= -787.0 - 857.4 \\
&= -1644.4 \, \text{kJ mol}^{-1}
\end{aligned}$$

And we know from the data given above that:

$$\Delta H_3 = \Delta H_c^{\ominus}[\text{C}_2\text{H}_5\text{OH(l)}] = -1367.3 \, \text{kJ mol}^{-1}$$

Now we substitute our values into the 'enthalpy cycle' equation:

$$\begin{aligned}
\Delta H_1 &= \Delta H_2 - \Delta H_3 \\
\Delta H_1 &= (-1644.4) - (-1367.3) \\
&= -1644.4 + 1367.3 \\
&= -277.1 \, \text{kJ mol}^{-1}
\end{aligned}$$

So the **enthalpy of formation** of ethanol is calculated as **$-277.1 \, \text{kJ mol}^{-1}$**.

The enthalpy cycle can also be shown on an enthalpy level diagram:

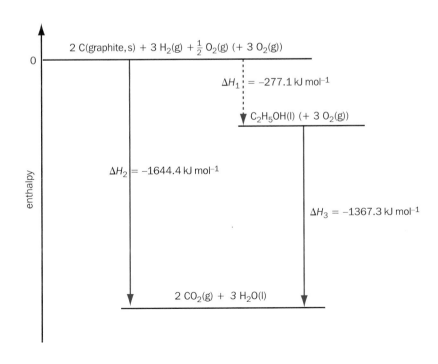

▷ Using enthalpies of formation

On the last page we used enthalpies of combustion to calculate the enthalpy change in a reaction. In our example the reaction was the formation of ethanol from its elements.
We can also use known enthalpies of formation to work out $\Delta H^\ominus$ of any reaction using an enthalpy cycle.

Hess's cycle!

Example

What is the standard enthalpy of reaction for this change:

$$C_2H_4(g) + HBr(g) \longrightarrow C_2H_5Br(l)$$
$$\text{ethene} + \text{hydrogen bromide} \quad \text{bromoethane}$$

You are given this data:

$\Delta H_f^\ominus[C_2H_4(g)] = +52.2 \text{ kJ mol}^{-1}$

$\Delta H_f^\ominus[HBr(g)] = -36.4 \text{ kJ mol}^{-1}$

$\Delta H_f^\ominus[C_2H_5Br(l)] = -90.5 \text{ kJ mol}^{-1}$

First of all, let's use this information to build an enthalpy cycle. We know the enthalpies of formation, so we need the elements in their standard states in our cycle:

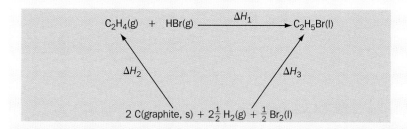

where $\Delta H_2 = \Delta H_f$ of both reactants
and $\Delta H_3 = \Delta H_f$ of the product

From the enthalpy cycle we can say that:

$$\Delta H_1 = -\Delta H_2 + \Delta H_3 \text{ or } \Delta H_1 = \Delta H_3 - \Delta H_2$$

We know from the data given above that:

$$\Delta H_3 = \Delta H_f^\ominus[C_2H_5Br(l)] = -90.5 \text{ kJ mol}^{-1}$$

Now we need to work out ΔH_2:

$$\begin{aligned}\Delta H_2 &= \Delta H_f^\ominus[C_2H_4(g)] + \Delta H_f^\ominus[HBr(g)] \\ &= \quad +52.2 \quad + \quad (-36.4) \\ &= +15.8 \text{ kJ mol}^{-1}\end{aligned}$$

We now substitute our values for ΔH_3 and ΔH_2 into the enthalpy cycle equation:

$$\begin{aligned}\Delta H_1 &= \Delta H_3 - \Delta H_2 \\ &= (-90.5) - (+15.8) \\ &= -90.5 - 15.8 \\ &= \mathbf{-106.3 \text{ kJ mol}^{-1}}\end{aligned}$$

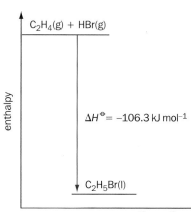

● Having worked out $\Delta H^\ominus$, do you think the reaction might be possible? Try to explain why. (Think about energetic stability.)

The examples that we have looked at so far in this chapter have all involved organic compounds.
However, we also have data referring to the complete range of chemical compounds.
The next example shows this:

Example
Use the following data to calculate the enthalpy change when 1 mole of ammonium sulphate dissolves in water.

$$\Delta H_f^{\ominus}[NH_4^+(aq)] = -132.5 \, kJ \, mol^{-1}$$
$$\Delta H_f^{\ominus}[SO_4^{2-}(aq)] = -909.3 \, kJ \, mol^{-1}$$
$$\Delta H_f^{\ominus}[(NH_4)_2SO_4(s)] = -1180.9 \, kJ \, mol^{-1}$$

The enthalpy cycle will be:

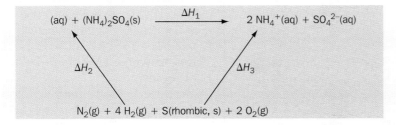

From the enthalpy cycle:

$$\Delta H_1 = \Delta H_3 - \Delta H_2$$

We are given ΔH_2 as $\Delta H_f^{\ominus}[(NH_4)_2SO_4(s)] = -1180.9 \, kJ \, mol^{-1}$

But we'll have to work out ΔH_3:
Notice that we have 2 moles of $NH_4^+(aq)$ ions formed in the balanced equation:
Therefore we will have to multiply $\Delta H_f^{\ominus}[NH_4^+(aq)]$ by 2:

$$\begin{aligned}
\Delta H_3 &= (2 \times \Delta H_f^{\ominus}[NH_4^+(aq)]) + \Delta H_f^{\ominus}[SO_4^{2-}(aq)] \\
&= \quad (2 \times -132.5) \quad + \quad (-909.3) \\
&= \quad \quad (-265.0) \quad \quad + \quad (-909.3) \\
&= -1174.3 \, kJ \, mol^{-1}
\end{aligned}$$

Now substitute our values into the enthalpy cycle:

$$\begin{aligned}
\Delta H_1 &= \Delta H_3 - \Delta H_2 \\
&= (-1174.3) - (-1180.9) \\
&= (-1174.3) + 1180.9 \\
&= \mathbf{+6.6 \, kJ \, mol^{-1}}
\end{aligned}$$

Notice that this is an endothermic change.
- Would you expect ammonium sulphate to dissolve in water?

In fact, ammonium sulphate is soluble in water.
Energetic stability isn't the only factor that determines whether reactions happen or not.
We look at this in more detail in Chapter 26.

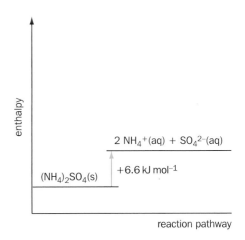

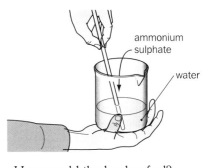

- How would the beaker feel?
- What happens to the temperature?

▷ Average bond enthalpies

In previous chapters we have looked at the strength of covalent bonds by quoting bond energies. This term is often used, although **bond enthalpies** is a more accurate description. They tell us the amount of energy needed to break a bond. Look at the table opposite:

Bond	Average bond enthalpy / kJ mol^{-1}
C—H	+413
C—Cl	+346
C—C	+347
C=C	+612

The values given in data books are actually *average* bond enthalpies. This is shown in the example below. It gives the enthalpy changes as each bond is broken in methane (CH_4):

The first bond dissociation enthalpy is:

$$CH_4 \longrightarrow CH_3 + H \qquad \Delta H^{\ominus}_{d1} = +425 \, kJ \, mol^{-1}$$

the second bond dissociation enthalpy is:

$$CH_3 \longrightarrow CH_2 + H \qquad \Delta H^{\ominus}_{d2} = +470 \, kJ \, mol^{-1}$$

the third bond dissociation enthalpy is:

$$CH_2 \longrightarrow CH + H \qquad \Delta H^{\ominus}_{d3} = +416 \, kJ \, mol^{-1}$$

the fourth bond dissociation enthalpy is:

$$CH \longrightarrow C + H \qquad \Delta H^{\ominus}_{d4} = +335 \, kJ \, mol^{-1}$$

As you can see, each requires a different amount of energy. The average value for the C—H bond in methane is:

$$\frac{+425+470+416+335}{4} = +412 \, kJ \, mol^{-1}$$

This is very close to the average value quoted in data books which is $+413 \, kJ \, mol^{-1}$.

Some bond dissociation enthalpies can be found experimentally. Others can be calculated from known data and an enthalpy cycle.

These bond dissociations can be summarised as:

$$CH_4(g) \xrightarrow{\Delta H^{\ominus}_{at}} C(g) + 4 \, H(g)$$

This is called the **enthalpy of atomisation** of methane. It can be calculated using an enthalpy cycle. (See the example of NH_3 below.) Its value is $+1662 \, kJ \, mol^{-1}$. This is the equivalent of four C—H bonds. So the average C—H bond enthalpy from an enthalpy cycle is:

$$\frac{+1662}{4} = +415.5 \, kJ \, mol^{-1}$$

Example
What is the average bond enthalpy of the N—H bonds in ammonia (NH_3)? You are given:

$$\Delta H^{\ominus}_{at}[\tfrac{1}{2}N_2(g)] = +472.7 \, kJ \, mol^{-1}$$
$$\Delta H^{\ominus}_{at}[\tfrac{1}{2}H_2(g)] = +218.0 \, kJ \, mol^{-1}$$
$$\Delta H^{\ominus}_{f}[NH_3(g)] = -46.1 \, kJ \, mol^{-1}$$

Firstly, construct the cycle that uses the data given to us:

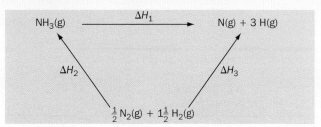

If we can find ΔH_1 (sometimes called the **dissociation enthalpy** of ammonia), we know the enthalpy change on breaking the three N—H bonds in NH_3.

From the cycle:

$$\Delta H_1 = \Delta H_3 - \Delta H_2$$

We know that $\Delta H_2 = \Delta H_f^\ominus[NH_3(g)] = -46.1 \text{ kJ mol}^{-1}$

To work out ΔH_3 we need to remind ourselves of the definition of standard enthalpy of atomisation from page 289:
It refers to the formation of **1 mole of gaseous atoms.**
In our enthalpy cycle we have **3 moles of H(g)** atoms formed.
Therefore:

$$\Delta H_3 = (\Delta H_{at}^\ominus[\tfrac{1}{2}N_2(g)]) + (3 \times \Delta H_{at}^\ominus[\tfrac{1}{2}H_2(g)])$$
$$= \quad +472.7 \quad + \quad (3 \times +218.0)$$
$$= +1126.7 \text{ kJ mol}^{-1}$$

Now we substitute into the enthalpy cycle equation:

$$\Delta H_1 = \Delta H_3 - \Delta H_2$$
$$= (+1126.7) - (-46.1)$$
$$= (+1126.7) + 46.1$$
$$= +1172.8 \text{ kJ mol}^{-1}$$

Remember that this represents the enthalpy change as 3 moles of N—H bonds are broken.
Therefore the average bond enthalpy of N—H in ammonia is:

$$\frac{+1172.8}{3} = \textbf{+390.9 kJ mol}^{-1}$$

Using average bond enthalpies to work out $\Delta H^\ominus$

We can use bond enthalpies to calculate a rough value for $\Delta H^\ominus$ for any reaction. Why is the value only rough? Let's look at the reaction between hydrogen and chlorine. Remember that:

> **Breaking bonds requires energy. It is endothermic.**
> **Making new bonds gives out energy. It is exothermic.**

$$H_2(g) + Cl_2(g) \longrightarrow 2HCl(g)$$

We can show these changes in an enthalpy cycle or on an enthalpy level diagram. Look opposite:

From the enthalpy cycle:

$$\Delta H_1 = \Delta H_2 - \Delta H_3$$
$$\Delta H_2 = [1 \times (H—H)] + [1 \times (Cl—Cl)]$$
$$= \quad +436 \quad + \quad +242$$
$$= +678 \text{ kJ/mol}$$

$$\Delta H_3 = 2 \times (H—Cl)$$
$$= 2 \times (+431)$$
$$= +862 \text{ kJ mol}^{-1}$$

So $\Delta H_1 = \Delta H_2 - \Delta H_3 = (+678) - (+862) = \textbf{-184 kJ mol}^{-1}$

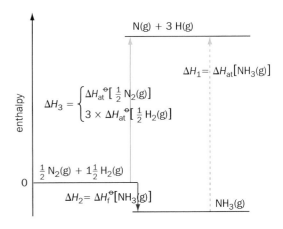

An enthalpy level diagram to show $\Delta H_{at}^\ominus[NH_3(g)]$

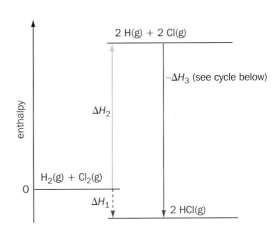

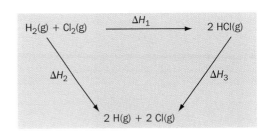

Bond	Average bond enthalpy / kJ mol^{-1}
H—H	+436
Cl—Cl	+242
H—Cl	+431

▷ Chemistry at work: Enthalpy changes

Fireworks

Have you ever wondered how we get
the stunning effects you see at a firework display?
There are plenty of combustion reactions, mainly
involving gunpowder.

A giant firework display in the Nevada Desert

Gunpowder was discovered about a thousand years ago
by the Chinese. Firecrackers were used in
religious festivals.
To get the fierce, exothermic reaction, you need a fuel
and a rapid supply of oxygen. The oxygen is provided
by an oxidising agent, such as potassium nitrate (KNO_3).

fuel + oxidising agent $\longrightarrow$ gas products + heat

Look at the diagram of the rocket:

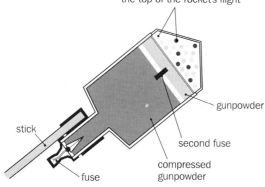

metals and their compounds
produce stars and sparks at
the top of the rocket's flight

gunpowder

stick

second fuse

compressed
gunpowder

fuse

Can you explain how it works?

Don't try this at home!

Look at the photos opposite:
These were taken at a firework party in the Nevada desert.
150 specially invited enthusiasts met to set off an incredible display
of pyrotechnics.
One event, called 'Desert Fusion', used about 1000 kg of magnesium
to create a flash similar to a nuclear bomb!

Celebrations for the millennium in Paris

Keep your hands warm!

Have you ever used 'hand-warmers', perhaps when
watching sport or out walking in the winter?
Look at the photo opposite:

Hand-warmers are a practical use of an **exothermic** process.
A tough plastic packet contains a supersaturated solution
of sodium ethanoate. It gets crystallised when we bend
a small metal disc in the packet. As the solution crystallises,
bonds are formed between particles and energy is given out.

If you boil the packet for a few minutes, the crystals will redissolve
and so the packet can be used many times.

...or cold!

A 'cold pack' can be used on minor strains and sprains.
It consists of a thin, inner plastic bag containing water,
inside a stronger bag containing ammonium nitrate powder.

When you shake the bags strongly, the inner bag breaks.
The ammonium nitrate then dissolves in the water
in an **endothermic** reaction.
This causes the temperature to fall sharply.

Rocket science

Scientists in the U.S.A. have been working on ways to make
new, more powerful rocket fuels.
At present it takes 5 tonnes of fuel to send 1 tonne of equipment
into space. So the search is on for low-density fuels that give out
lots of energy when they react.

The team of 15 scientists, working for the U.S. Air Force, have succeeded
in making a highly unstable form of nitrogen.
Known as nitrogen-5, it has 5 nitrogen atoms forming a positively charged ion.
It was prepared in a compound with fluorine and arsenic as a few crystals.

Normal nitrogen, N_2 gas, makes up almost 80 per cent of our atmosphere.
As you know, it is an unreactive gas. Its molecules are very energetically stable.
However, the new form of nitrogen exists in a much higher energy state,
and it just can't wait to turn back into its stable form.
When it does, not surprisingly, it explodes producing gas and giving out heat –
ideal for a rocket propellant.

The new form of nitrogen, which many believed impossible to make,
has only been made on a small scale (less than a gram).
It has to be stored at $-80\,°C$ in ampoules made of Teflon.
Now the scientists have to find a way to make larger amounts safely.
Then nitrogen-5 could really make a bang in the world of rocket science!

Summary

- ΔH refers to the **enthalpy change** in a reaction.
  It is the energy change measured at a constant pressure.

- ΔH is always measured from the point of view of the chemicals involved.
  If the products have less enthalpy than the reactants, ΔH is negative
  and the surroundings get hotter. The reaction is **exothermic**.
  On the other hand, if the reactants have less enthalpy than the products,
  ΔH is positive. The reaction is **endothermic**.

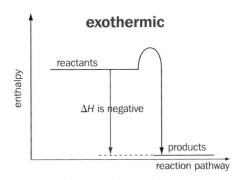

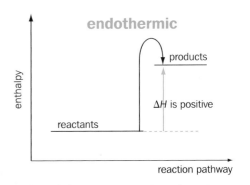

- We can work out the energy transferred in a solution using the equation:

  energy change = mass × specific heat × change in temperature

  This can then be used to get a value for ΔH, the enthalpy change when
  the quantities shown in the balanced equation react together.

- **Standard conditions** are chosen to be **298 K and 101 kPa** (1 atm),
  with any solutions having a concentration of **1.0 mol dm^{-3}** (1 M).

- Here are some definitions of enthalpy changes that you need to know:
  The standard enthalpy of formation ($\Delta H_f^\ominus$) is defined as:
  the enthalpy change when 1 mole of a compound is made from its
  elements in their standard states, under standard conditions.
  (The enthalpy of the most stable form of an element, under standard
  conditions, is taken to be zero.)

  The standard enthalpy of combustion ($\Delta H_c^\ominus$) is defined as:
  the enthalpy change when 1 mole of the substance burns completely in
  oxygen under standard conditions

  The standard enthalpy of atomisation of an element ($\Delta H_{at}^\ominus$)
  is defined as:
  the enthalpy change when 1 mole of gaseous atoms is made
  from the element in its standard state, under standard conditions.

- **Hess's Law** states that the enthalpy change in turning reactants into
  products is the same no matter what route we take.
  Some enthalpy changes are difficult to measure experimentally.
  But we can use an **enthalpy cycle** to calculate enthalpy changes indirectly.

  Bond enthalpies tell us the amount of energy needed to break a bond.
  They are average (mean) values.

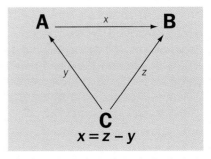

Hess' cycle (an enthalpy cycle)

▷ Questions

1   Copy and complete:
In an .... reaction, heat is given out and the temperature of the surroundings ..... The reactants have .... enthalpy than the products.
Reactions which take in energy from the surroundings are called .... resulting in a .... in the temperature. The enthalpy change for this type of reaction is given a .... sign.

Standard enthalpy changes are quoted at .... K and .... kPa. For example, the standard enthalpy of .... is the enthalpy .... when 1 mole of the substance burns completely in oxygen, under .... conditions.

2   A student added $100 \, cm^3$ of a $2.0 \, mol \, dm^{-3}$ solution of hydrochloric acid to $100 \, cm^3$ of $2.0 \, mol \, dm^{-3}$ sodium hydroxide solution.
He recorded the temperature rise as $11.5 \, °C$.
a) Write the equation for the reaction.
b) Calculate the heat given out in the reaction.
    (Assume the specific heat capacity of the reaction mixture to be $4.2 \, J \, K^{-1} \, g^{-1}$ and its density to be $1 \, g \, cm^{-3}$.)
c) Work out how many moles there are in $100 \, cm^3$ of the $2.0 \, mol \, dm^{-3}$ solutions of acid and alkali.
d) From the answers above, what is the enthalpy of neutralisation for the reaction between hydrochloric acid and sodium hydroxide solutions?
e) Draw the apparatus the student could have used to perform the experiment.
f) Consider the sources of experimental error and the effect they would have on the student's value for the enthalpy of neutralisation.

3   Another student measured the enthalpy of combustion of ethanol, C_2H_5OH, by using a calorimeter.
The calorimeter contained $200 \, cm^3$ of water and its temperature rose by $6.2 \, °C$.
a) Draw the apparatus used in the experiment.
b) Work out how much heat was given out by the burning ethanol.
    (The specific heat capacity of water is $4.2 \, J \, K^{-1} \, g^{-1}$ and its density is $1 \, g \, cm^{-3}$.)
c) The ethanol was weighed before and after the experiment. Its mass decreased by $0.19 \, g$.
    How many moles of ethanol were burned in the experiment?
    (A_r values: C = 12, O = 16, H = 1.)
d) Using the answers above, calculate the enthalpy of combustion of ethanol.
e) The value given for the enthalpy of combustion of ethanol in a data book is $-1367.3 \, kJ \, mol^{-1}$.
    Can you think of any reasons for the difference between this and the value obtained in the student's experiment?

4   What do we call these enthalpy changes:
a) $\frac{1}{2} N_2(g) \longrightarrow N(g)$
b) $C_3H_8(g) + 5 \, O_2(g) \longrightarrow 3 \, CO_2(g) + 4 \, H_2O(l)$
c) $3 \, C(graphite, \, s) + 4 \, H_2(g) \longrightarrow C_3H_8(g)$

5   a) Using the data below, work out the enthalpy change for the reaction shown in question 4 c):

    $\Delta H_c^{\ominus}[C(graphite, \, s)] = -393.5 \, kJ \, mol^{-1}$
    $\Delta H_c^{\ominus}[H_2(g)] = -285.8 \, kJ \, mol^{-1}$
    $\Delta H_c^{\ominus}[C_3H_8(g)] = -2219.2 \, kJ \, mol^{-1}$

    b) Draw an enthalpy level diagram to show the reactions you used to answer part a).

6   a) Using the data below:

    $\Delta H_c^{\ominus}[C(graphite, \, s)] = -393.5 \, kJ \, mol^{-1}$
    $\Delta H_c^{\ominus}[C(diamond, \, s)] = -395.4 \, kJ \, mol^{-1}$

    calculate the enthalpy change for the reaction:

    $C(graphite) \longrightarrow C(diamond)$

    b) Draw these enthalpy changes from your cycle in part a) on an enthalpy level diagram.
    c) Use your answer to part b) to explain why carbon in the form of graphite has an enthalpy value of zero.

7   Use the data below:

    $\Delta H_f^{\ominus}[C_2H_4(g)] = +52.2 \, kJ \, mol^{-1}$
    $\Delta H_f^{\ominus}[C_2H_6(g)] = -84.7 \, kJ \, mol^{-1}$

    to calculate the standard enthalpy of reaction for:

    $C_2H_4(g) + H_2(g) \longrightarrow C_2H_6(g)$

8   Look at the reaction below:
    $B_2H_6(g) + 3 \, O_2(g) \longrightarrow B_2O_3(s) + 3 \, H_2O(l)$
    $\Delta H^{\ominus}$ for the reaction as shown is $-2157.0 \, kJ \, mol^{-1}$.
    Use this information and the data below to calculate the enthalpy of formation of $B_2H_6(g)$:

    $\Delta H_f^{\ominus}[B_2O_3(s)] = -1264.0 \, kJ \, mol^{-1}$
    $\Delta H_f^{\ominus}[H_2O(l)] = -285.8 \, kJ \, mol^{-1}$

9   a) Use the bond enthalpies below to calculate the enthalpy of formation of hydrazine, $N_2H_4(l)$.

Bond	Bond enthalpy / kJ mol^{-1}
N—N	158
N—H	391
N≡N	945
H—H	436

    b) Explain why your answer to part a) does not give us an accurate value.

25 Lattice enthalpy

In the last chapter we saw how bond enthalpies can be used to measure the strength of a covalent bond.
In ionic compounds we use the standard **lattice enthalpy** (or lattice energy) to judge the strength of attraction between ions.
This is defined as:

> $\Delta H_{lattice}^{\ominus}$ = the enthalpy change when 1 mole of the ionic lattice is formed from its ions in the gaseous state under standard conditions.

This can be summarised in an equation:

> $X^+(g) + Y^-(g) \longrightarrow X^+Y^-(s) \qquad \Delta H_{lattice}^{\ominus} = \text{lattice enthalpy}$

Lattice enthalpies are always exothermic, as new bonds are made.
They have a negative sign.
On the other hand, bond enthalpies are always endothermic.
Can you think why?
(See page 305.)

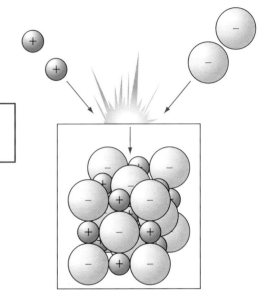

Energy is given out when oppositely charged ions come together to form a giant lattice

▷ Calculating lattice enthalpies

We cannot measure lattice enthalpies directly by experiment.
It is very difficult to isolate gaseous ions of opposite charge, then bring them together to react, whilst measuring the energy given out!
As in the last chapter, the answer is to construct an enthalpy cycle.
This particular type, used to calculate lattice enthalpies, is called a **Born–Haber cycle**.

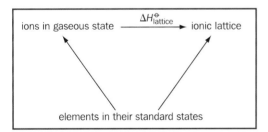

Born–Haber cycle

Look at the example below for sodium chloride:

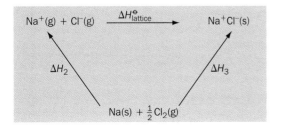

We can work out the lattice enthalpy of sodium chloride

310

We can find values for all the enthalpy changes involved in the Born–Haber cycle by experiment, except the lattice enthalpy. This is worked out from the cycle.

We need all the following data to carry out the calculation:

$\Delta H_f^\ominus[NaCl(s)] = -411.2\,kJ\,mol^{-1}$, i.e. $Na(s) + \frac{1}{2}Cl_2(g) \longrightarrow NaCl(s)$

$\Delta H_{at}^\ominus[Na(s)] = +107.3\,kJ\,mol^{-1}$, i.e. $Na(s) \longrightarrow Na(g)$

$\Delta H_{at}^\ominus[\frac{1}{2}Cl_2(g)] = +121.7\,kJ\,mol^{-1}$, i.e. $\frac{1}{2}Cl_2(g) \longrightarrow Cl(g)$

1st ionisation enthalpy of $Na(g) = +496\,kJ\,mol^{-1}$
This is the enthalpy change when 1 mole of electrons is removed from 1 mole of gaseous atoms, under standard conditions.

    i.e. **Na(g) $\longrightarrow$ Na$^+$(g) + e$^-$**

1st electron affinity of $Cl(g) = -348.8\,kJ\,mol^{-1}$
This is the enthalpy change when 1 mole of electrons is added to 1 mole of gaseous atoms, under standard conditions.

    i.e. **Cl(g) + e$^-$ $\longrightarrow$ Cl$^-$(g)**

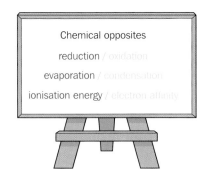

Can you think of any others?

From the Born–Haber cycle:

$\Delta H_{lattice}^\ominus = \Delta H_3 - \Delta H_2$

ΔH_3 is given in the data above:

$\Delta H_3 = \Delta H_f^\ominus[NaCl(s)] = -411.2\,kJ\,mol^{-1}$

However, ΔH_2 is more complicated!
There are four enthalpy changes involved in ΔH_2:

Let's look at the sodium first of all:

1. We need to change 1 mole of solid Na into separate gaseous atoms ($\Delta H_{at}^\ominus[Na(s)]$).
2. We then need to remove 1 mole of electrons from the gaseous atoms (first ionisation energy of Na(g)).

Then if we consider the chlorine:

3. We break half a mole of Cl—Cl bonds to get 1 mole of Cl(g) atoms ($\Delta H_{at}^\ominus[\frac{1}{2}Cl_2(g)]$).
4. Then we add 1 mole of electrons to the Cl(g) atoms (first electron affinity of Cl(g)).

So ΔH_2 equals the enthalpy changes in steps $1 + 2 + 3 + 4$.

                $\left.\begin{array}{c} \\ \\ \\ \\ \\ \end{array}\right\} \Delta H_2$

Using the data above we get:

$\Delta H_2 = (+107.3) + (+496) + (+121.7) + (-348.8)$

    $= +376.2\,kJ\,mol^{-1}$

Now we can substitute our values into the Born–Haber cycle:

$\Delta H_{lattice}^\ominus = \Delta H_3 - \Delta H_2$

    $= (-411.2) - (+376.2)$

    $= -411.2 - 376.2$

    $= \mathbf{-787\,kJ\,mol^{-1}}$

So the standard lattice enthalpy of sodium chloride is $-787\,kJ\,mol^{-1}$.

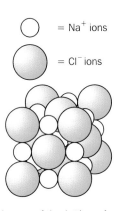

    $\bigcirc$ = Na$^+$ ions

    $\bigcirc$ = Cl$^-$ ions

This is part of the lattice of sodium choride

▷ Born–Haber enthalpy level diagram

We can also show the enthalpy changes in the Born–Haber cycle
on an enthalpy level diagram:

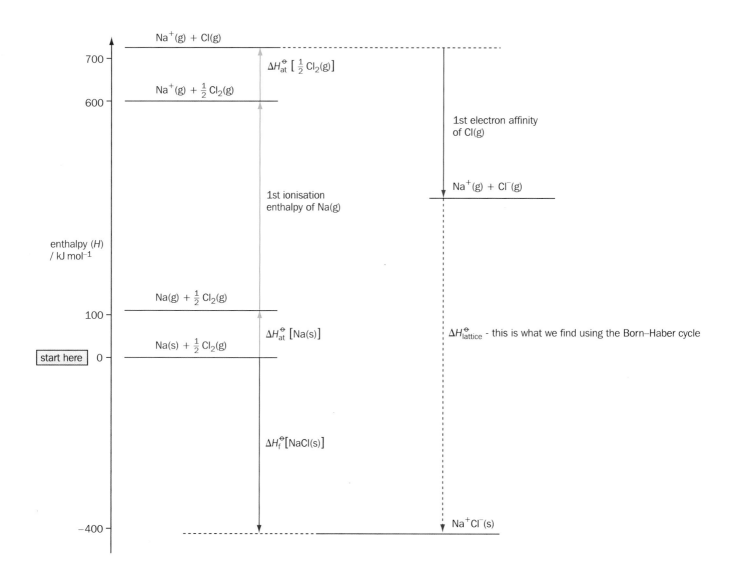

Notice the largest positive (energetically unfavourable) change
is the ionisation enthalpy.
The largest negative (energetically favourable) change is the lattice enthalpy.
There is a balance between the energy put in to remove electrons from the
metal atoms and the energy released when the lattice is formed.
If the ionisation enthalpy is too large to be regained by the lattice enthalpy,
the compound is unlikely to form.

▷ Theoretical values of $\Delta H^{\ominus}_{lattice}$ compared with actual values

Scientists can calculate lattice enthalpies using equations that describe the electrostatic forces between ions. They know the arrangement of ions in a lattice from X-ray diffraction studies. They then assume the ions are points of charge, approaching each other from infinity. By applying their electrostatics equations, a theoretical value for the standard lattice enthalpy can be worked out.

The model used in calculating theoretical values is based on perfect ionic bonding. A purely ionic compound would be made from perfectly spherical ions. Their charge would be distributed evenly around the sphere. In the lattice, the ions would be just touching, with no overlap of electron clouds. Look at the values for theoretical lattice enthalpies and the values based on the experimental data used in a Born–Haber cycle:

Compound	Lattice enthalpies / kJ mol^{-1}	
	Actual value (based on Born–Haber cycle)	Theoretical value
NaF	−918	−912
NaCl	−787	−770
NaBr	−742	−735
NaI	−705	−687
AgF	−958	−920
AgCl	−905	−833
AgBr	−891	−816
AgI	−889	−778

Compare the values of the sodium halides with the silver halides:
● Which values differ more from the theoretical values?
● So which set of halides is more like the perfect ionic model?
Remember that the lattice enthalpy is a measure of the strength of the bonding between the ions.
Compare the values of sodium fluoride with silver fluoride:
● Which has the stronger bonding between ions?
Do the same for other pairs:
● Is there a consistent pattern?
Now look at the trends going down each set of halides:
● What is the pattern?

Ionic compounds between alkali metals and halogens show close agreement between theoretical and actual values. This shows that their bonding is a good match to the model of perfect ionic bonding.
In general we find that the greater the difference between electronegativities the closer the agreement to the ideal model.
Silver halides have stronger bonding than their matching sodium halides.
This is because there is a **degree of covalency in the bonding** between ions in silver compounds (see page 72).
The electron clouds of oppositely charged ions overlap slightly. This also explains the difference between their theoretical and actual lattice enthalpies. Their bonding is **not purely ionic**.

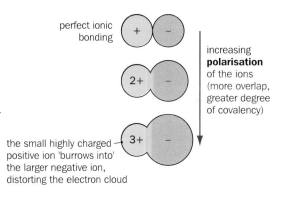

perfect ionic bonding

increasing **polarisation** of the ions (more overlap, greater degree of covalency)

the small highly charged positive ion 'burrows into' the larger negative ion, distorting the electron cloud

▷ Calculating other lattice enthalpies

We have seen how to work out the standard lattice enthalpy of sodium chloride.
We can now apply the same method to **magnesium oxide**.
What factors do you think will have the biggest effect on its lattice enthalpy?

We will need the following data:

$\Delta H_f^{\ominus}[MgO(s)] = -601.7 \, kJ \, mol^{-1}$

$\Delta H_{at}^{\ominus}[Mg(s)] = +147.7 \, kJ \, mol^{-1}$

1st ionisation enthalpy of magnesium $= +738 \, kJ \, mol^{-1}$ i.e. $Mg(g) \longrightarrow Mg^{+}(g) + e^{-}$
2nd ionisation enthalpy of magnesium $= +1451 \, kJ \, mol^{-1}$ i.e. $Mg^{+}(g) \longrightarrow Mg^{2+}(g) + e^{-}$

$\Delta H_{at}^{\ominus}[\frac{1}{2}O_2(g)] = +249.2 \, kJ \, mol^{-1}$

1st electron affinity of oxygen $= -141 \, kJ \, mol^{-1}$ i.e. $O(g) + e^{-} \longrightarrow O^{-}(g)$
2nd electron affinity of oxygen $= +798 \, kJ \, mol^{-1}$ i.e. $O^{-}(g) + e^{-} \longrightarrow O^{2-}(g)$

(Notice that the 2nd electron affinity of oxygen is positive, i.e. endothermic.
This is true of all values of electron affinity after the first electron
has been added. Subsequent electrons will tend to be repelled
by the negative ions, and we have to put in energy to overcome this.)

The Born–Haber cycle is:

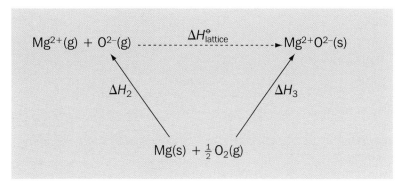

Magnesium oxide's high lattice enthalpy makes it ideal for lining kilns

From the cycle:

$\Delta H_{lattice}^{\ominus} = \Delta H_3 - \Delta H_2$

ΔH_3 is given in the data above:

$\Delta H_3 = \Delta H_f^{\ominus}[MgO(s)] = -601.7 \, kJ \, mol^{-1}$

Now we have to calculate ΔH_2:

Let's look at magnesium first:
We need these enthalpy changes:

$$Mg(s) \xrightarrow{\Delta H_{at}^{\ominus}} Mg(g) \xrightarrow{\text{1st I.E.}} Mg^{+}(g) \xrightarrow{\text{2nd I.E.}} Mg^{2+}(g)$$

When we add these up we get:

$(+147.7) + (+738) + (+1451)$

$= +2336.7 \, kJ \, mol^{-1}$

The other part of ΔH_2 deals with oxygen's enthalpy changes:

$$\tfrac{1}{2} O_2(g) \xrightarrow{\Delta H_{at}} O(g) \xrightarrow{\text{1st E.A.}} O^-(g) \xrightarrow{\text{2nd E.A.}} O^{2-}(g)$$

When we add these up we get:

$(+249.2) + (-141) + (+798)$

$= +906.2 \, \text{kJ mol}^{-1}$

Therefore,

$\Delta H_2 = (+2336.7) + (+906.2)$

$= +3242.9 \, \text{kJ mol}^{-1}$

Now we can substitute our values into the Born–Haber cycle:

$\Delta H^{\ominus}_{\text{lattice}} = \Delta H_3 - \Delta H_2$

$= (-601.7) - (+3242.9)$

$= -601.7 - 3242.9$

$= \mathbf{-3845 \, kJ \, mol^{-1}}$

So the standard lattice enthalpy of magnesium oxide is $-3845 \, \text{kJ mol}^{-1}$.

- How does this value compare with the lattice enthalpy of sodium chloride? (Look back to page 311.)
- Why do you think magnesium oxide's lattice enthalpy is so large?

The lattice enthalpy indicates the strength of the bonding between ions.
The ions in magnesium oxide, Mg^{2+} and O^{2-} ions, are both relatively small and carry quite a large charge.
This gives them both a very high charge density.
Therefore the electrostatic force of attraction between ions is very strong.
This also explains the very high melting point (3125 K).

We are strongly attracted to each other

Mg^{2+} O^{2-}

...........almost inseparable!

MgO has a large lattice enthalpy.

Other hints

Here are some things to remember if you have to calculate the lattice enthalpy of a compound with a formula such as M_2X or MX_2.
Examples could be sodium oxide, Na_2O, or calcium bromide, $CaBr_2$.
Watch out for these points:

Na₂O

a) 2 moles of Na(g) atoms are needed, so your Born–Haber cycle will include:

$\mathbf{2} \times \Delta H_{at}[\text{Na(s)}]$

b) You will then need to remove 1 mole of electrons from each of your 2 moles of Na(g) atoms. So make sure your cycle includes:

$\mathbf{2} \times$ 1st ionisation enthalpy of Na(g)

CaBr₂

a) 2 moles of Br(g) atoms are needed, so your Born–Haber cycle will include:

$\mathbf{2} \times \Delta H_{at}[\tfrac{1}{2} Br_2(l)]$

b) You will then need to add 1 mole of electrons to each of the 2 moles of Br(g) atoms. So make sure your cycle includes:

$\mathbf{2} \times$ 1st electron affinity of Br(g)

▷ Lattice enthalpy and dissolving

When an ionic compound dissolves its lattice breaks down.

$$X^+Y^-(s) \xrightarrow{\Delta H^\ominus_{\text{solution}}} X^+(aq) + Y^-(aq)$$

You might think that with such high lattice enthalpies,
ionic compounds would have no chance of dissolving.
We know that this is not true.

We also need to consider the new bonds made as a solid dissolves.
The polar water molecules form bonds with the ions.
On page 52 we saw how they attract each other:
The ions in solution become surrounded by water molecules.
They are now called **hydrated ions**.

The strength of these bonds is indicated by the **hydration enthalpy**:

$$X^+(g) + Y^-(g) \xrightarrow{\Delta H^\ominus_{\text{hydration}}} X^+(aq) + Y^-(aq)$$

If this energy is similar in size to the lattice enthalpy,
then there is a chance that the compound will dissolve.
Look at the enthalpy level diagram for sodium chloride below:

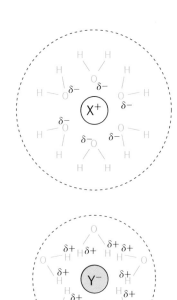

Hydrated ions. The attraction extends to other water molecules further away from the ions.

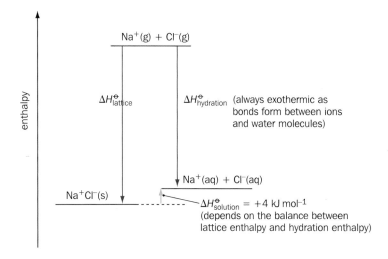

As you know, sodium chloride is soluble in water.
But why does it dissolve when our diagram above shows
that its hydrated ions are 4 kJ mol^{-1} less energetically stable
than solid sodium chloride?
To answer this, we must also consider the disorder resulting
from the dissolving of a solid. Changes are favoured by
an increase in disorder.

● Which has a more disorderly arrangement of ions–
   the ions in the solid lattice or the ions in solution?

The amount of disorder is called **entropy**.
In the case of sodium chloride, the increase in disorder
outweighs the unfavourable enthalpy change.
We will look at entropy in more detail in the next chapter.

Summary

- The standard **lattice enthalpy** ($\Delta H_{lattice}^{\ominus}$) of an ionic compound is defined as: the enthalpy change when 1 mole of the ionic lattice is formed from its ions in the gaseous state under standard conditions.
  It is the enthalpy change we get when:

$$K^+(g) + Y^-(g) \longrightarrow X^+Y^-(s)$$

- We can't measure the lattice enthalpy directly by experiment. However, we can construct a Born–Haber cycle (an enthalpy cycle we get by applying Hess's Law; *see page 300*).
  For example:

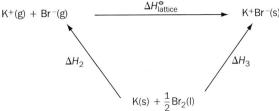

So $\Delta H_{lattice}^{\ominus} = \Delta H_3 - \Delta H_2$
where all the values in ΔH_2 and ΔH_3 can be determined by experiments.

- There are differences between lattice enthalpies worked out from the experimental data in a Born–Haber cycle and the theoretical values calculated by looking at electrostatic forces.
  Any differences arise because of a degree of covalency in the bonding between some ions.

- The standard **hydration enthalpy** is shown below:

$$X^+(g) + Y^-(g) \xrightarrow{\Delta H_{hydration}^{\ominus}} X^+(aq) + Y^-(aq)$$

The enthalpy change when an ionic compounds dissolves ($\Delta H_{solution}^{\ominus}$) is a balance between $\Delta H_{lattice}^{\ominus}$ and $\Delta H_{hydration}^{\ominus}$.

▷ Questions

1 Copy and complete:

The standard lattice enthalpy is the enthalpy .... when .... mole of ionic lattice is formed from its ions in the .... state under standard conditions.
Lattice enthalpies give us an indication of the strength of .... bonds. They always have a .... sign.
We can work out lattice enthalpies using a Born–.... cycle.
To work out the .... lattice enthalpy of sodium chloride, we use this cycle:

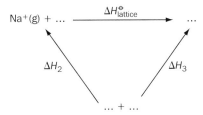

From the cycle, we can say:

$\Delta H_{lattice}^{\ominus} = ... - ....$

We call ΔH_3 the standard enthalpy of .... of sodium chloride. ΔH_2 consists of the standard enthalpy of .... of sodium, its first .... enthalpy, plus chlorine's enthalpy of .... and its first electron .... .

2 a) Write an equation to show the change that we describe as the lattice enthalpy of lithium fluoride.
   b) Draw an enthalpy cycle you can use to work out the lattice enthalpy of lithium fluoride.
   c) Make a list of all the data you need to calculate the lattice energy of lithium fluoride. Look up the values in the data pages at the back of the book.
   e) Calculate the lattice enthalpy of lithium fluoride.

3 a) Use the data in the back of the book to work out the lattice enthalpy of i) beryllium iodide, BeI_2, and ii) strontium iodide, SrI_2. (1st I.E. of Sr = 550 kJ mol^{-1}; 2nd I.E. of Sr = 550 kJ mol^{-1})
   b) The theoretical value calculated for the lattice enthalpy of beryllium iodide is -2653 kJ mol^{-1}. The theoretical value calculated for the lattice enthalpy of strontium iodide is -1937 kJ mol^{-1}. Compare these theoretical values with your answers in a).
     i) How can you explain the differences?
     ii) Explain why the difference between the values for beryllium iodide is larger than that for strontium iodide?

4 a) Use the data at the back of the book to work out the lattice enthalpy of sodium oxide, Na_2O.
   b) The theoretical value calculated for the lattice enthalpy of sodium oxide is -2481 kJ mol^{-1}. What does this information and your answer from part a) tell you about the bonding in sodium oxide?

317

26 Entropy and free energy

In this chapter we will look at how we can predict
whether or not reactions are feasible.
This could save a chemist's valuable time.
It is not worth doing research on a reaction
that could never happen!
In order to understand this we will need to think more deeply
about the changes that occur in chemical reactions.

*Is this chemist wasting his time?
Entropy can help to find the answer*

▷ Entropy

We have now seen that there is a difference in the energy content
between reactants and products in chemical reactions.
If products have a lower energy content (enthalpy) than reactants,
then the reaction is exothermic. We can say that the reactants
are energetically unstable with respect to the products.

However, this is no guarantee that the reaction will occur.
The reactants may well be kinetically stable with respect
to the products. Remember that the activation energy
must be overcome before a reaction can occur.
If this activation energy is large, then the reaction
will not start at room temperature, no matter how exothermic it is,
unless we provide a large amount of energy initially.
This explains why some exothermic reactions
do not happen spontaneously.

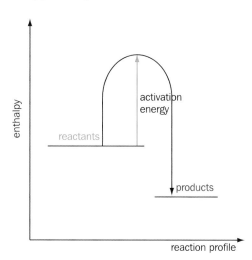

*Although these products are energetically more
stable than the reactants, the large activation
energy makes the reactants kinetically stable*

But what about endothermic reactions?
Surely they should never occur spontaneously.
After all, the products are energetically unstable
with respect to the reactants. But, as you know, some do!
So how can we explain this?

The answer lies in the **change in entropy**, given the symbol ΔS.

Entropy (S) is a measure of disorder in a system

What happens if you drop a pile of your notes on the floor?
What are the chances of them landing in a neat pile?
Things naturally tend to be disordered, and that includes chemicals.

But what does disorder look like in chemistry?
Which has the more orderly arrangement: a solid or a liquid?
A liquid or a gas? A solid or its solution in water?

The more disorder that results from a reaction,
the more likely it is to happen.

So changes that result in more moles of gas being produced are more likely to happen spontaneously.
Gases have the most disorderly arrangement of particles, and different ways of spreading about their energy.
As well as molecules vibrating, they can also rotate and move around at different speeds.

Liquids and solutions also have many ways of arranging their particles and distributing their energy.
But the disorder in solids is limited to different ways their energy can be shared between its vibrating particles.

Chemists have tables of entropy values to use.
Look at the table below:

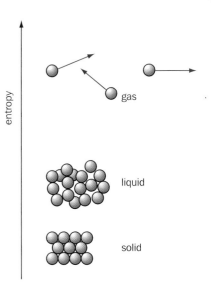

Substance	Standard entropy (S) / $J\,mol^{-1}\,K^{-1}$
helium, He(g)	126.0
fluorine, F_2(g)	158.6
water, H_2O(l)	69.9
carbon (diamond), C(s)	2.4
carbon (graphite), C(s)	5.7
magnesium, Mg(s)	32.7

Do the values in the table agree with the ideas above?

Total entropy changes, ΔS_{total}

So far we have looked at the entropy changes in the substances involved in a physical or chemical change.
We call the entropy changes in the system, ΔS_{system}.
But we must also think about the entropy of the surroundings.
This helps to explain why there are many more spontaneous exothermic reactions compared with endothermic ones.
When a change gives out heat, this energy increases the disorder of the particles in the surroundings. For example, air molecules will move around more quickly.

Let's think about an exothermic reaction that we do in a test tube.
The glass absorbs some of the energy given out,
so its particles have more energy and can distribute it in more ways.
The gas molecules in the air will also increase their entropy.
This is called the entropy change in the surroundings, $\Delta S_{surroundings}$.

So when we consider entropy changes we must think about changes in both the system (internal) and the surroundings (external).
We can show this in an equation:

$$\Delta S_{total} = \Delta S_{system} + \Delta S_{surroundings}$$

So for any spontaneous change, we can say that ΔS_{total} must be positive.

If the *total* amount of disorder decreases in a change, then it will not happen.

There is an increase in entropy when solids dissolve.
(ΔS_{system} is positive – favourable.)
But if the enthalpy change is endothermic then the entropy in the surroundings decreases.
($\Delta S_{surroundings}$ is negative – unfavourable.)
ΔS_{total} is the balance of these two factors.

▷ Calculating entropy changes

Chemists can use tables of entropy values to calculate the entropy change in a reaction.
The standard molar entropies are listed for elements and compounds at 298 K. Look at the example below:

Example
Do you know the test for hydrogen gas?
The 'pop' we hear is the reaction between hydrogen and oxygen in the air. H_2O is made in the reaction:

$$2\,H_2(g) + O_2(g) \longrightarrow 2\,H_2O(l)$$

What is the entropy change in the reaction above?

We can look up in tables the standard molar entropies:

	$S^\ominus$/ J mol^{-1} K^{-1}
H_2(g)	65.3
O_2(g)	102.5
H_2O(l)	69.9

Then we use these to work out $\Delta S^\ominus_{system}$:

$$\Delta S^\ominus_{system} = S^\ominus_{products} - S^\ominus_{reactants}$$

$$S^\ominus_{products} = 2 \times S^\ominus[H_2O(l)]$$

$$= 2 \times 69.9 = 139.8\,\text{J mol}^{-1}\text{K}^{-1}$$

$$S^\ominus_{reactants} = (2 \times S^\ominus[H_2(g)]) + S^\ominus[O_2(g)]$$

$$= (2 \times 65.3) + 102.5 = 233.1\,\text{J mol}^{-1}\text{K}^{-1}$$

We now put these values into the equation $\Delta S^\ominus_{system} = S^\ominus_{products} - S^\ominus_{reactants}$ to get:

$$\Delta S^\ominus_{system} = 139.8 - 233.1$$

$$= -93.3\,\text{J mol}^{-1}\text{K}^{-1}$$

So the negative value tells us that the products in this reaction are less disordered.
There is a decrease in entropy in the system. Can you think why?

This indicates that the reaction is not favoured in terms of entropy. But what other aspect of entropy should we consider before we can say that this reaction cannot occur spontaneously? Remember from the last page we said that for any spontaneous change, ΔS_{total} must be positive.
We also know that:

$$\Delta S_{total} = \Delta S_{system} + \Delta S_{surroundings}$$

So now we should look at the entropy change in the surroundings.

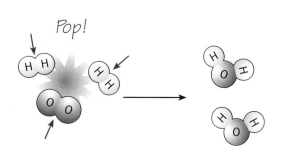

Pop!

ΔS_{system} decreases in this reaction under standard conditions.
We have gases turning to a liquid and fewer moles of molecules after the reaction

Is the reaction to test for hydrogen exothermic?
You can feel the heat given off in the hot glass
at the mouth of the test tube following the test.
As we learned on the last page, this will increase the entropy
of the surroundings.

The actual value is given by the equation:

$$\Delta S_{surroundings} = \frac{-\Delta H}{T}$$

Notice the negative sign in the equation:
When we enter the negative value of ΔH for any exothermic reaction,
the two negatives make a positive. In other words,
the entropy increases, as we would expect.

The value for ΔH for this reaction can be looked up
or worked out from an enthalpy cycle.

$$\Delta H^{\ominus}_{reaction} = -571.6 \, \text{kJ mol}^{-1}$$

(Notice ΔH is quoted in **kJ mol**$^{-1}$, not **J mol**$^{-1}$.)

So we now work out the entropy change in the surroundings

by substituting into the equation $\Delta S_{surroundings} = \dfrac{-\Delta H}{T}$

(where $T = 298 \, \text{K}$ because all values are given under standard conditions
and the value for $\Delta H^{\ominus}_{reaction}$ is converted from kJ to J).

$$\Delta S_{surroundings} = -\frac{(-571\,600)}{298}$$

$$= +1918.1 \, \text{J mol}^{-1} \text{K}^{-1}$$

Now we can work out the total entropy change from:

$$\Delta S_{total} = \Delta S_{system} + \Delta S_{surroundings}$$

$$= -93.3 + 1918.1$$

$$= +1824.8 \, \text{J mol}^{-1} \text{K}^{-1}$$

Therefore the reaction can happen spontaneously.
Notice how important the entropy change in the surroundings
is for highly exothermic reactions.

But what do we have to do before we get hydrogen to 'pop'?
Remember at the start of the chapter we talked about
the effect of activation energy on a reaction.

Although the total entropy change tells us that the reaction
can occur spontaneously, it tells us nothing about the rate.
The hydrogen and oxygen are 'kinetically' stable.
They don't react until we apply a lighted splint.
Then the reaction that our calculations show should 'go'
will proceed in a flash!

*Explosions happen spontaneously once
energy has been supplied. The explosive
is a solid or liquid that reacts to give
gaseous products.*

● *What can you say about the entropy
change in an explosion?*

Now that's
what I call
disorder
in the
surroundings!

▷ Free energy

We have now seen how entropy and enthalpy changes
are both important factors that 'drive' reactions.
A positive entropy change is the deciding factor when
predicting if a change might be spontaneous at room temperature.

Can you now see how spontaneous endothermic reactions can occur?
Although the enthalpy suggests these reactions should not happen
at room temperature, there must be a large increase in entropy.
This then overrides the unfavourable enthalpy change.

Chemists combine the effects of entropy and enthalpy
in one quantity called the **Gibbs free energy**.
(J. Willard Gibbs was an American scientist working in the second half
of the nineteenth century.)

The change in Gibbs free energy, or free energy, is given by:

J. Willard Gibbs

| $\Delta G = \Delta H - T\Delta S_{system}$ |

where T = the temperature in K

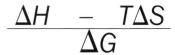

The balance between enthalpy and entropy!

This appeals to chemists because they don't have to think about
the surroundings when they calculate free energy.

Can you can see how we can use ΔG for deciding whether reactions
will 'go' spontaneously?
Try putting a 'favourable' value for ΔH and ΔS
into the equation above:
What sign does ΔG turn out to have in your example?

| **Spontaneous changes always have a negative ΔG.** |

Can you use the equation to explain why some endothermic reactions
happen spontaneously?
Using the equation helps you to see how the feasibility of a reaction
is a balance between entropy and enthalpy.

You already know about some reactions that do not go to completion.
They produce an equilibrium mixture.
For these reactions the value of ΔG is ± 60 kJ mol^{-1}.
Slight negative values favour the products.
The diagram below shows us the possibilities:

The other factor in the equation is the temperature.
Notice that ΔS is multiplied by the temperature in the equation above.
So reactions that cannot happen at room temperature (298 K)
may be made possible by raising the temperature.

Calculating changes in free energy

We can work out free energy changes using tables of data.
Do you remember using enthalpy cycles to calculate enthalpy changes?
We can use the same cycles with free energy because we have
standard free energies of formation for compounds.
(The standard free energy of formation of any element is taken as zero,
as with enthalpy values.)
The cycle can be shown as:

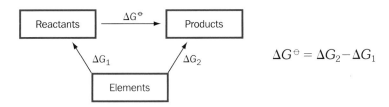

$$\Delta G^{\ominus} = \Delta G_2 - \Delta G_1$$

Let's look at the decomposition of calcium carbonate, $CaCO_3$:

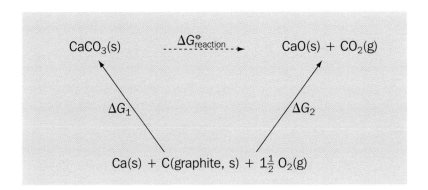

From tables of data:

$\Delta G_f^{\ominus}[CaCO_3(s)] = -1128.8\,kJ\,mol^{-1}$

$\Delta G_f^{\ominus}[CaO(s)] = -604.0\,kJ\,mol^{-1}$

$\Delta G_f^{\ominus}[CO_2(g)] = -394.4\,kJ\,mol^{-1}$

Using the cycle we can say that:

$$\Delta G_{reaction}^{\ominus} = \Delta G_2 - \Delta G_1$$
$$\Delta G_1 = \Delta G_f^{\ominus}[CaCO_3(s)]$$
$$= -1128.8\,kJ\,mol^{-1}$$

and

$$\Delta G_2 = \Delta G_f^{\ominus}[CaO(s)] + \Delta G_f^{\ominus}[CO_2(g)]$$
$$= -604.0 + (-394.4)$$
$$= -998.4\,kJ\,mol^{-1}$$

Putting these values into the free energy cycle equation

$$\Delta G_{reaction}^{\ominus} = \Delta G_2 - \Delta G_1$$
$$= -998.4 - (-1128.8)$$
$$= -998.4 + 1128.8$$
$$= +130.4\,kJ\,mol^{-1}$$

The value of **ΔG is positive**.
This tells us that the reaction is **_not spontaneous at 298 K_**.
However, at high temperatures, the reaction
can be made to happen.

*Calcium carbonate is decomposed to make
this lime, but the temperature inside
a lime kiln is about 1500 °C!
The lorries are spreading lime on to soil. The
lime was made by roasting calcium carbonate in
a lime kiln at temperatures around 1500 °C*

Summary

- **Entropy (S)** is a measure of the **disorder** in a system. We can think of chemical disorder increasing as we move from solids to liquids to gases. The number of ways particles can be arranged and the number of ways in which their energy can be distributed increases.

- Reactions are favoured when the resulting change in entropy is positive.

$$\Delta S_{total} = \Delta S_{system} + \Delta S_{surroundings}$$

- For any spontaneous change, the **total change in entropy must be positive**.

- Exothermic reactions will increase the entropy in the surroundings.

- We can see if a reaction is possible or not using a term called the **Gibbs free energy (ΔG)**. This combines the effect of enthalpy and entropy in the equation:

$$\Delta G = \Delta H - T\Delta S_{system}$$

- For a reaction to be spontaneous, **ΔG must have a negative value**. Reactions that don't happen at room temperature can be made to happen by raising the temperature. This increases the size of the $-T\Delta S$ term for reactions with a positive entropy change, making ΔG more negative. Therefore the reaction is more likely to happen.

Entropy is molecular anarchy!

▷ Questions

1 Copy and complete:

The entropy of a system is a measure of the .....

$$\Delta S_{total} = \Delta S.... + \Delta S....$$

For a chemical reaction to be spontaneous, ΔS_{total} must be ..... An exothermic reaction will .... the entropy of the surroundings.

The .... free energy can also be used to predict the feasibility of reactions. It is given by the equation:

$$\Delta G = \Delta H - ....\Delta S$$

In a spontaneous reaction, ΔG will be .....

2 Look at the standard entropy values below:

Substance	Standard entropy / $J\,mol^{-1}\,K^{-1}$
nitrogen	95.8
neon	146.2
steam	188.7
water	69.9
aluminium	28.3
silicon	18.8

Can you explain the differences in entropy values in the table?

3 a) Work out the entropy change in the molecules for the reaction:

$$N_2(g) + 2\,O_2(g) \longrightarrow 2\,NO_2(g)$$

You will need the standard entropy values below:

	Standard entropy / $J\,mol^{-1}\,K^{-1}$
N_2(g)	95.8
O_2(g)	102.5
NO_2(g)	240.0

b) Using your answer to part a), what can you say about ΔS_{system} in the reaction between nitrogen and oxygen under standard conditions?

c) $\Delta H^{\ominus}$ for the reaction above is $+33.2\,kJ\,mol^{-1}$. Use this to work out the change in entropy in the surroundings. (Take care with the units!)

d) Use your answers to parts a) and c) to work out the total change in entropy for the reaction.

e) Is the reaction between nitrogen and oxygen feasible under standard conditions?

f) Work out the change in the Gibbs free energy (ΔG) for the reaction. (Remember to use ΔS_{system} in the equation.)

g) Explain why some NO_2(g) is formed in thunderstorms and inside car engines, but not in air under standard conditions

27 Kinetics – rates of reaction

In this chapter we will look at **reaction kinetics**.
Have you come across the word 'kinetic' before?
You probably know about kinetic energy from your previous work.
This is the energy associated with an object's mass and speed.
The faster something moves the greater its kinetic energy.
In chemistry, 'kinetics' is the study of *rates of reaction*.
The rate of a reaction tells us *how quickly* it happens.
How do you think a molecule's kinetic energy affects
its rate of reaction?

Some reactions are fast, and others are slow.
Can you think of a reaction which happens very quickly?
Fast reactions, like dynamite exploding, start and finish
within a fraction of a second.
Slow reactions, like concrete setting, may take days,
weeks, or even years to finish.
Can you think of any other slow reactions?

It is important for scientists in industry to know
how fast a reaction goes. They have to find out
exactly how much of their product they can make
each hour, day or week.

We can't work out the rate of a reaction from its chemical equation.
Equations can only tell us how much product we can get.
They don't say how quickly it is made.

Enthalpy changes don't tell us the rate of a reaction either.
They can give us a clue as to whether or not reactions might happen.
For example, a highly endothermic reaction is unlikely
to occur spontaneously (without a large energy input).
But even a highly exothermic reaction, in which the products formed
are far more energetically stable than the reactants, is not necessarily
a fast reaction. Can you think why?
Look at the enthalpy level diagram opposite:

Chemical reactions have an **activation energy**.
This is the energy needed to start off the reaction.
Some reactions have large activation energies.
In this case, we say that the reactants are *kinetically stable*
with respect to the products. They won't start reacting
unless we provide the initial energy to start the reaction.
If the overall reaction is highly exothermic, we say that
the reactants are kinetically stable, but energetically unstable
with respect to the products.
Can you think of any reactions like this?
Why do these reactions carry on once we have started them off?
Can you think of any reactions with a very small activation energy?

An example of a fast reaction

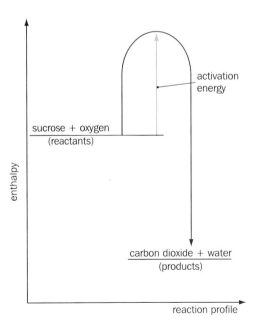

An example of a slow reaction

Why doesn't the sucrose in your sugar bowl burst into flames?

325

▷ Investigating rates of reaction

We have just seen that chemical equations and enthalpy changes
cannot tell us the rate of a reaction. In fact:
we can only find the rate by actually doing experiments.

During a reaction, we could measure how much reactant
is being used up as the reaction proceeds.
On the other hand, we might choose to measure how much product
is being formed over time.
The method we choose depends on the reaction we are looking at.
Here are some of the techniques that can be used:

Students measuring rates of reaction

In reactions that **give off a gas**:

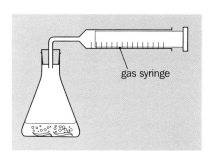

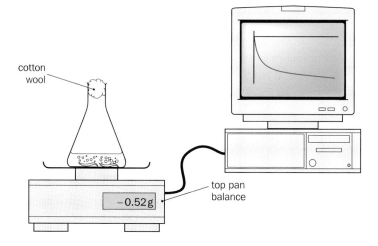

In reactions that involve solutions **changing colour**:

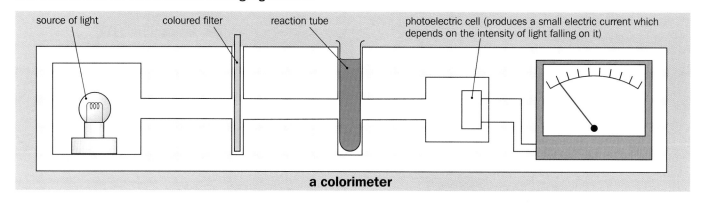

a colorimeter

In reactions that involve a **change in conductivity of solutions**
(i.e. the number of ions in solution change):

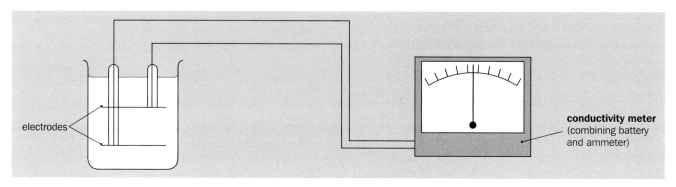

326

In reactions where the concentration of a reactant or a product can be found **by titration:**

Sampling and quenching; a small sample of the reacting solution is taken. The reaction is stopped or quenched as quickly as possible. Then the sample is titrated to find the concentration of the target reactant or product.

- Can you think how we might quench a reaction in which acid was a reactant?

Alternatively, the same reaction can be done several times but quenched after different times. Then we do the titration.

Other methods can be used that follow changes in any physical property of the reacting mixture.

- When could you use a pH probe and data logger?

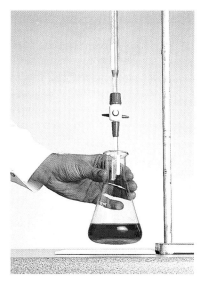
Titration

▷ Graphs and rates of reaction

We can then plot the results gained from experiments on a graph.

Look at the graph opposite:

It shows us how the concentration of a product increases as the reaction proceeds.
We can use this type of graph to measure the rate of a reaction at any given time.
The slope of the line tells us how quickly the reaction was going at that time.
So **the units we use to express the rate of a reaction are** $\mathbf{mol\,dm^{-3}\,s^{-1}}$.
We find that:

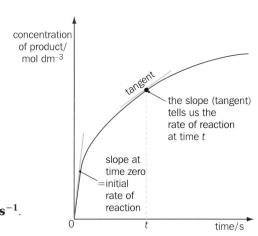

The steeper the slope, the faster the reaction.

- When is the reaction fastest?
- How can you tell that the reaction is slowing down as time passes?
- How do you know when the reaction has stopped?

We could also plot the decrease in concentration of a reactant over time.
Look at the graph opposite:

- Can you see how this relates to the first graph?
- Can you answer the same questions about it?

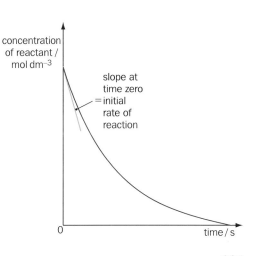

327

▷ Collision theory

As you know, all substances are made up of particles.
These particles might be atoms, molecules or ions.
Before we can get a chemical reaction, the particles
of the reactants must crash together. They must collide.
This is called the **collision theory**.

A gentle collision produces no reaction

> **The more collisions between particles in a given time,
> the faster the reaction.**

Do you think that **all** collisions between reactant particles
will result in a reaction?
In other words, will the particles collide with enough energy
to start a reaction? Will they have enough energy to overcome
the activation energy?

*However, a harder collision may well
produce a reaction!*

To answer these questions, we need to know more about
the way energy is distributed between particles.
Look at the graph below:

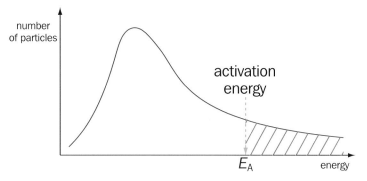

The distribution of energies
at temperature T.
It is called the **Maxwell–Boltzmann
distribution**.

As you can see, at any given temperature, the energy is spread
between the particles. A few have a small amount of energy.
A few have a lot of energy, but most lie in between.
Only a certain number of molecules in the sample will have
enough energy to react. They will have energy greater than
the activation energy needed to start a reaction.
Other particles may collide but will just bounce off each other.

> **The *higher the energy* of the colliding particles,
> the *greater the chances of effective collisions*,
> i.e. ones that result in a reaction.**

On page 305 we saw how we can think of a reaction
in terms of bond breaking and bond making.
The idea that all the old bonds break, then the new ones form,
is a simple model. In actual reactions, these two events happen
at the same time. But it is sometimes a useful model to apply.
Can you relate the collision theory to the bond breaking/
bond making model?
We can think of the ineffective collisions as those in which
there is not enough energy to start the bond breaking process.

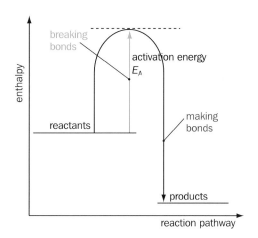

Collisions can also be ineffective if the particles hit each other at the wrong angle.
Particles must collide *'in the correct orientation'* to produce a reaction.

▷ Factors affecting rates of reaction

You will have studied rates of reaction in previous work.
Can you remember all the ways we can speed up
a reaction?
Any ways of increasing the number of *effective collisions*
in a given time will increase the rate of a reaction.

> **The factors affecting rates of reaction include:**
>
> **surface area** (of solid reactants)
>
> **concentration** (of reactants in solution)
>
> **pressure** (of gaseous reactants)
>
> **temperature**
>
> **catalysis**

Some reactions are also speeded up by **light**.
Can you remember the reaction between methane and chlorine
from page 170? How does light start off the reaction?
These are called **photochemical reactions**.
We will now look at each of the factors in turn.

▷ Effect of surface area

Have you ever tried to light a bonfire or a camp fire?
Which burns more quickly: a block of wood
or a pile of wood shavings?
We find that small pieces of solids, especially powders,
react faster than large pieces.

Surface area is a measure of how much surface is exposed.
So for the same mass of wood, the shavings have a larger surface area
than the block of wood.

Powders have a very large surface area.
There are lots of particles exposed at their many surfaces.
We can compare heating an iron nail with heating iron filings.
The oxygen molecules in the air can attack the iron atoms
in the powdered filings more readily.
So with iron filings, there are lots more collisions
in a given time. The reaction is very fast.
The iron nail has a much smaller surface area. It only reacts slowly.

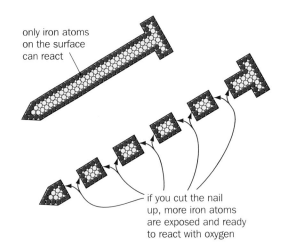

only iron atoms
on the surface
can react

if you cut the nail
up, more iron atoms
are exposed and ready
to react with oxygen

> **As we increase the surface area, we increase the rate**
> **of reaction.**

When a solid lump is cut into pieces,
Its rate of reaction always increases.
In the lump, most particles are locked up inside,
In order to react, they have to collide!
But powders have lots of particles exposed,
If cut fine enough, they might even explode!

▷ Effect of concentration

Have you ever seen the reaction between marble chips
and dilute hydrochloric acid? Carbon dioxide is given off.
What happens to the rate at which carbon dioxide is given off
if we use more concentrated acid?
Look back to the methods we can use to measure
the rate of a reaction on page 326.
Which could we use to follow this reaction?
We find that:

> **As we increase the concentration, the rate of reaction
> usually increases.**

We can use the collision theory to explain why
more concentrated solutions react more quickly.
The H^+ ions from the acid can only react with the marble chips
when they collide.
Look at these diagrams:

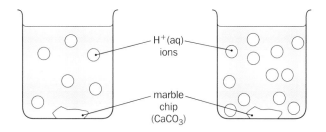

The H^+ ions move randomly through the water.
As you increase the concentration of the acid, there are
more H^+ ions in the same volume.
Therefore there is a greater chance of H^+ ions
colliding, and reacting, with carbonate ions on the surface of
the marble. You increase the rate of the reaction.

It's a bit like dancing at a club. When a popular track
is played, lots more people crowd on to the dance-floor.
The concentration of people on the dance-floor increases.
There is now a lot greater chance of bumping into someone else!

▷ Effect of pressure

Look at the syringes of gas opposite:
If the end is sealed, how can you increase the pressure
inside the syringe?
By pressing the plunger in, you now have the
same number of gas particles in a smaller volume.
In other words, you have increased the concentration of the gas.
Therefore:

> **In reactions which involve gaseous reactants,
> increasing the pressure usually increases the rate of reaction.**

The reaction between acid and marble chips
(calcium carbonate) can be summarised by
an ionic equation:

$$2H^+(aq) + CO_3{}^{2-}(s) \longrightarrow CO_2(g) + H_2O(l)$$
carbonate ions

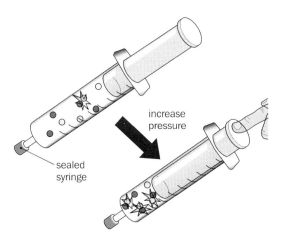

There are more collisions in a given time when you
increase the pressure of a gas

▷ Effect of temperature

Why do we keep our food in a fridge?
Some of the substances in food react with oxygen in the air.
Have you ever tasted milk that has gone off?
If you have, you will know the sour taste of acids!
Oils and fats in many foods turn 'rancid' when left in air.
They react and turn into carboxylic acids.
The **low temperature** in your fridge **slows down**
the reactions that make food go off.

As we increase the temperature, we increase the rate of reaction.

What happens to the way particles move when you heat them up?
The particles have more energy. They move around more quickly.
As they travel faster, there are more collisions in a certain time.
Therefore, reactions get faster as we raise the temperature.
However, the increased frequency of collisions
can't be the only factor at work.

Temperature has a dramatic effect on rates of reaction.
If you raise the temperature by 10 °C, you roughly **double** the rate
of many reactions! Yet calculations can show us that a 10 °C rise
will only increase the number of collisions in a given time by 6%.

Remember on page 328 we said that not all collisions
resulted in a reaction. Not all collisions are **effective**.
Some colliding particles just bounce off each other.
They don't collide with enough energy to start a reaction.
They don't have enough energy to overcome the activation energy
for that particular reaction.
However, the higher the temperature, the more particles
have energies that match or exceed the activation energy.
Look at the graph below:

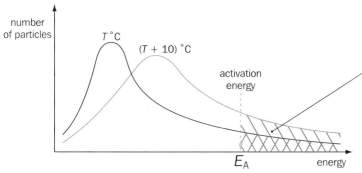

The shaded area under the curve gives us the number of particles
with an energy greater than the activation energy.
What can you say about this number as the temperature
is increased by 10 °C?

In summary, raising the temperature:
1. **makes particles collide more often (producing a small increase in rate), and**
2. **makes it more likely that collisions result in a reaction (producing a large increase in rate).**

331

▷ Effect of a catalyst

Have you ever seen a car with a repair like the one
shown in the photo? A dent or hole has been mended with filler.
Car repair kits use a **catalyst** to harden the filler quickly.
We have already met catalysts in our previous work.
Can you remember which type of metals (and their compounds)
make good catalysts?

> **A catalyst is a substance which speeds up a chemical reaction.
> At the end of the reaction, the catalyst remains chemically
> unchanged.**

Let's look at an example:
Hydrogen peroxide (H_2O_2) breaks down slowly at room temperature.
Small bubbles of oxygen gas appear on the sides of a beaker
containing its solution.
However, as soon as you add manganese(IV) oxide, the oxygen
is given off rapidly.
The manganese(IV) oxide is a catalyst for the reaction:

*A catalyst added to the filler causes it to
set quickly. It can then be sanded down*

hydrogen peroxide $\xrightarrow{\text{manganese(IV) oxide}}$ water + oxygen

$2\,H_2O_2(aq) \xrightarrow{\text{MnO}_2(s)} 2\,H_2O(l) + O_2(g)$

We say that the manganese(IV) oxide **catalyses** the reaction.
Notice that the catalyst does not actually appear in the equation.
We can write it above the arrow, showing it is there during the reaction.

So how do catalysts work?
Look at the enthalpy level diagram opposite:
It shows us the energy changes when substances react.
You will remember that the energy needed to start a reaction
is called its **activation energy.**

> **A catalyst lowers the activation energy.**

Catalysts do this by providing an alternative route for the reaction
or by weakening the bonds in reactant molecules. (See page 147.)
Look at the graph below:

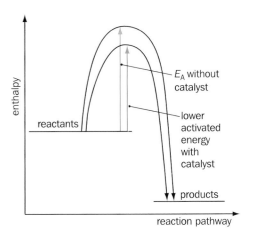

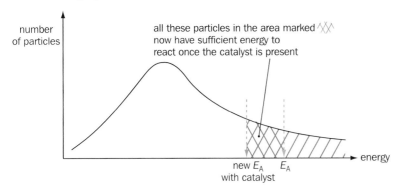

A catalyst makes it easier for particles to react.
You can think of it as being like a high-jump competition.
If you lower the bar, a lot more people can jump over it.
With a catalyst, a lot more particles have enough energy to react.

Catalysts in industry

Industrial chemists have always recognised the importance of catalysts. A good catalyst can increase your profits. How do you think catalysts could save money?

Just a twist
Of your catalyst
And reactions will shoot
Through an easier route!

Look at the list of some of the catalysts used in industry:

Manufacture of...	Catalyst used at some stage in the process
ethene by cracking large hydrocarbons	Al_2O_3
poly(ethene)	$TiCl_4$
ethanal	Cu or CuO
esters	H^+ ions from acid
sulphuric acid	V_2O_5
nitric acid	Pt (platinum) and Rh (rhodium)
ammonia	Fe or Fe_2O_3
margarine	Ni

You can read more about the manufacture of ammonia on page 362.
Nitric acid is covered on page 364, sulphuric acid on page 361,
esters on page 197 and cracking ethene on page 184.
You can read about making margarine at the bottom of this page.

> **There are two types of catalysis:**
>
> 1. **homogeneous** – in which the reactants and catalyst are in the same state.
>   For example, if the reaction takes place in solution and the catalyst is a metal ion dissolved in water. (See page 146.)
>
> 2. **heterogeneous** – in which the reactants and catalyst are in a different state.
>   For example, in reactions between gases catalysed on the surface of a solid metal. (See page 147.)

Catalytic converters

You may have read about the use of catalytic converters in cars on page 169. The exhaust gases are passed over a **honeycomb coated with precious metals**, such as platinum. This reduces pollutants such as carbon monoxide, nitrogen oxides and unburnt hydrocarbons.

- Which type of catalysis do you find inside a car's catalytic converter?
- Why do you think the catalyst is coated on to a honeycomb structure?

Inside a catalytic converter

Making margarine

Margarines are made from unsaturated vegetable oils, containing C=C bonds. The oils are liquids which are too runny to spread on bread. The problem has been solved by adding hydrogen to the natural oil molecules. This straightens the molecules so that they can pack together more closely. The forces between molecules get stronger, resulting in a higher melting point.
A ***nickel catalyst*** is used to speed up the reaction.
Chemists have to work out just the right amount of hydrogen to add. If they add too much, the margarine will be too hard to spread when it comes out of the fridge. If they don't add enough, the margarine will be too soft and runny if left out of the fridge!

Just the right consistency!

▷ Effect of enzymes

Do you use 'biological' washing powders at home?
These contain **enzymes** which break down stains.

An enzyme called amylase breaks down starch

> **An enzyme is a *biological catalyst*.**
> **They are large, soluble protein molecules.**

Enzymes help reactions to take place at the relatively low temperatures
inside living things.
The reactions are examples of homogeneous catalysis.

All plants and animals, including ourselves, depend on enzymes to stay alive.
Each enzyme catalyses a particular chemical reaction.
For example, an enzyme called amylase is in our saliva.
It starts to break down starchy foods in our mouths.

On page 332 we saw the breakdown of hydrogen peroxide
using a catalyst. Hydrogen peroxide is a poison.
It can build up inside living things.
However, we have an enzyme in many of our cells
which can break down the poison.

Catalase breaking down hydrogen peroxide

An enzyme in the liver can break down hydrogen peroxide
very quickly. Like all enzymes, it is very efficient.
Each enzyme molecule can deal with thousands of
reacting molecules every second!

$$\text{hydrogen peroxide} \xrightarrow{\text{enzyme in liver called catalase}} \text{water} + \text{oxygen}$$

How enzymes work

Enzymes are large protein molecules.
Each different enzyme has its own *special shape*.
The reactants fit into the enzyme, like a lock and key.
The reactant slots into the enzyme at its **active site**.
Look at the diagram below:

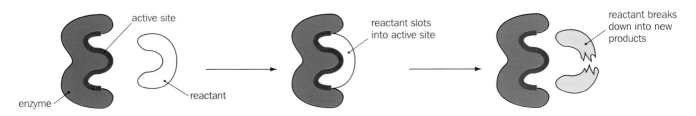

Other enzymes can build up big molecules from small ones.

Effect of temperature on enzymes

The enzymes in biological powder don't work if you use
water that is too hot.
Look at the graph opposite:

- What do we call the temperature at which
  an enzyme works best?
- What is your body temperature? Why do you think that
  most enzymes work best at around 40 °C?

As the temperature rises, what do you think happens
to the way an enzyme molecule vibrates?
If the enzyme gets too hot, it changes shape.
So the reactants will no longer fit snugly into
the enzyme's active site. It can't catalyse the reaction.
We say that the enzyme is **denatured.**
Changes in pH can also denature an enzyme.

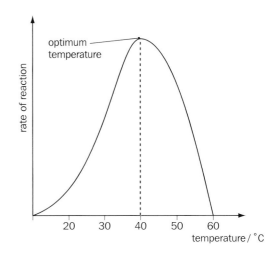

Fermentation

People have used enzymes to make new products
for thousands of years. Alcoholic drinks and bread
are both made using the enzymes in **yeast**.

Yeast is a type of fungus. Like all living things,
it contains enzymes. Yeast feeds on sugars,
turning them into alcohol.
The reaction is called **fermentation**.

The enzymes in yeast break down the sugar, **glucose**, into
ethanol (which we know as alcohol).
Carbon dioxide is also given off:

$$\text{glucose} \xrightarrow{\text{fermentation}} \text{ethanol} + \text{carbon dioxide}$$
$$\text{(sugar)} \qquad\qquad\qquad \text{(alcohol)}$$

$$C_6H_{12}O_6 \xrightarrow[\text{yeast}]{\text{enzymes in}} 2\,C_2H_5OH + 2\,CO_2$$

The amount of ethanol in the fermenting mixture
cannot rise above about 18 per cent. At this level,
the ethanol poisons the yeast.
We have to *distil* the mixture to get purer ethanol.

Alcoholic drinks

Look at the table below:

Drink	% ethanol	How the drink is made
beer	3.5	fermenting hops
wine	11.5	fermenting grapes
sherry	20	fermenting grapes, then adding ethanol
whisky	35	fermenting malt, then distilling

- Why must we add ethanol to 'fortify' wines, like port or sherry?
- Yeast grows naturally on the skins of grapes. How does this
  help to explain why wine has been known for thousands of years?
- Why is drinking alcohol before driving so dangerous?

There was an unfortunate beast.
Who fermented some sugar with yeast.
When he swallowed the brew
His stomach, it grew
'Til BANG! CO₂ was released!

335

▷ Chemistry at work: Immobilised enzymes

As you know, enzymes are incredibly efficient catalysts.
This makes them very attractive catalysts for use in industry.
This has fostered many new biotechnology companies.

However, a problem had to be solved before enzymes
could be used to make very pure compounds, such as drugs.
Enzyme reactions are examples of homogeneous catalysis.
The reactions happen in solution. So this leaves you with
the task of separating the product formed from the enzymes.
As well as sometimes requiring very pure substances,
you also want the enzymes back to use again to catalyse more reactions.

The answer was to bind the enzymes chemically
to an unreactive substance, such as a plastic.
Then the reactants are passed through a column
containing the enzymes fixed in position.
The enzymes are said to be **immobilised**.

The products pass out of the bottom of the column
with no enzyme impurities.
The column can be used continuously.
Look at the example showing some uses of whey:

For every kilogram of cheese we make, we get
9 litres of liquid whey. This has its uses:

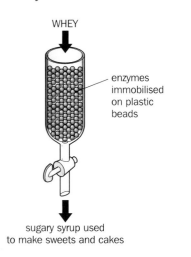

Summary

Chemical reactions are speeded up by increasing:
- **surface area**
- **concentration (or pressure if gases are reacting)**
- **temperature.**
  Light speeds up **photochemical** reactions.
- The **collision theory** explains why these factors affect the rate or speed of a reaction. When particles collide more often in a certain time, reactions speed up. With higher temperatures, the collisions are also more energetic. More particles have an energy greater than the activation energy. This means that a higher proportion of collisions result in a reaction.
- Some reactions are also speeded up by a **catalyst.** The catalyst itself is not chemically changed at the end of the reaction. Catalysts lower the activation energy needed for a particular reaction. So more particles have enough energy for effective collisions.

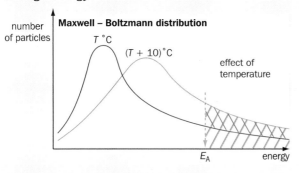 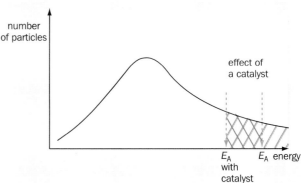

- **Enzymes** are *biological catalysts*.
- They are large protein molecules which catalyse specific reactions.
- Their molecules have special shapes, which include an **active site**. Reacting molecules slot into these active sites. Then the reaction takes place very quickly, at a relatively low temperature.
- Enzymes change their shape if you heat them too strongly. They no longer work, and we say that they are **denatured.** Changing the pH also denatures enzymes by changing their shape.

▷ Questions

1 Copy and complete:

The following factors affect rates of reactions:
...., ... (or .... if the reactants include gases), ..., and sometimes .... (in photochemical reactions).

We can use the .... theory to explain why these factors affect rates of reaction. For example, if we increase the .... of a solution, there are more particles in a given ..... Therefore there will be .... collisions in a given time and the rate of reaction .....

Changing the temperature has a .... effect on rates. Not only is the frequency of .... increased, but more importantly, they are more energetic and more likely to .... a reaction. In other words, there are more .... collisions in a given time.

.... catalysts are called enzymes. These large, soluble .... molecules have .... sites where reactions take place. They are .... by heating and changes in .....

2 Look at the reactions below and suggest how we could follow the rate of reaction by experiment. Explain your choice of method in each case:

a) $MgCO_3(s) + 2 HCl(aq) \longrightarrow MgCl_2(aq) + H_2O(l) + CO_2(g)$

b) $2 I^-(aq) + H_2O_2(aq) + 2 H^+(aq) \longrightarrow I_2(aq) + 2 H_2O(l)$

3 A student did two experiments with calcium carbonate chips and dilute hydrochloric acid at $20\,°C$.
In experiment 1, she used $20\,cm^3$ of the dilute acid.
In experiment 2, she used $10\,cm^3$ of the same acid mixed with $10\,cm^3$ of water.
Here are her results:

Time / min	Total mass of CO_2 evolved / g	
	Expt. 1	Expt. 2
0	0	0
2	0.55	0.27
4	0.71	0.35
6	0.78	0.38
8	0.80	0.40
10	0.80	0.40

a) Give the equation for the reaction.
b) Does the answer to part a) tell us anything about the rate of the reaction?
c) Draw one graph displaying both sets of results. Label your lines Expt. 1 and Expt. 2.
d) Do you think the dilute hydrochloric acid or the calcium carbonate was in excess? Explain your answer.
e) Experiment 1 was repeated at $30\,°C$. Sketch the line you would expect on your graph. Label this line Expt. 3.

4 a) 'A 10 degree rise in temperature often will roughly double the rate of reaction.' Why does temperature have such a dramatic effect on rate of reaction? Use the concept of activation energy and a sketch graph of the distribution of energy in a sample of molecules to help your explanation.
b) Use a similar graph to explain the effect of a catalyst on the rate of a reaction.
c) Explain the terms homogeneous and heterogeneous catalysis and give an example of each type of reaction.

5 Two students got the results opposite when they added a piece of magnesium ribbon to excess dilute sulphuric acid:

Time/s	Volume of gas / cm³
0	0
30	27
60	48
90	62
120	69
150	75
180	80
210	80

a) Draw the apparatus the students could have used.
b) Which gas was given off? How would you test for it?
c) Write an equation for the reaction.
d) Draw a graph to show their results.
e) The students did their experiment again, but this time they cut the same mass of magnesium ribbon into small pieces. Sketch the line you would expect for this experiment on your graph from part d).
f) Explain your answer to part e).
g) List three ways in which the students could slow down the rate of their reaction.
h) Use your graph to work out the initial rate of the original reaction (in cm³/s). Hint: Draw a tangent to the line at 0,0 and work out its slope (see page 339).

6 a) List three catalysts used in industry and say what they are used to make.
b) Why is catalysis important in the manufacture of margarine?
c) How do catalytic converters work in a car's exhaust?
d) Carbon dioxide is called a greenhouse gas. Why will catalytic converters not help us to solve the problem of global warming?

7 a) What are enzymes?
b) Give an example of an enzyme reaction in your body.
c) Explain why enzymes don't work when they are denatured.
d) Enzymes in yeast break down glucose. What do we call this reaction?
e) Write an equation to show the reaction in part d).
f) Why do people making homemade beer leave their reacting mixtures in the airing cupboard?

28 Rate equations

In the last chapter we looked at the factors that affect
rates of reaction. Can you remember them?
You can look back to the list on page 329 to check.

We also looked at different ways of measuring rates by experiments.
Remember that the rate or kinetics of a reaction
can only be found out through practical work.

You might think reactions that are highly exothermic
will be fast reactions because the products formed
are so much more energetically stable than the reactants.
However, on page 325 we saw that reactants may be
energetically unstable, but kinetically stable, with respect to
their products.
Can you explain why?

*Why doesn't the box of matches burst into
flames spontaneously?*

▷ Results from rate experiments

Imagine we have a reaction:

$$X(aq) + Y(aq) + Z(aq) \longrightarrow A(aq) + B(aq)$$
coloured substance

We could use one of the techniques shown on pages 326 and 327
to measure the rate of the reaction.
We can show the results as we vary the concentration of each reactant
on graphs.

First of all let's see what happens when we vary the concentration of X,
keeping everything else the same.
We might choose to follow the rate by measuring the absorption of colour
as the concentration of B builds up.
What instrument would you use?
The readings can then be changed into concentrations of B as time passes.
Look at the results of four experiments below:

> **Abbreviation:**
> **[X] = concentration of X**

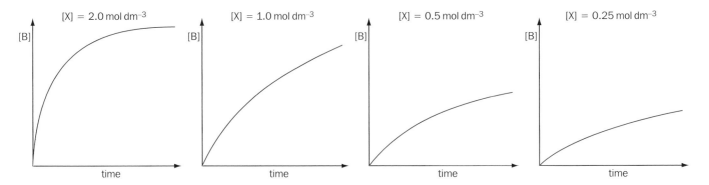

We know the concentration of X that we start with
and we can work out the initial rate from the slope of each graph
as the reaction starts off. (See the graph opposite.)
This will show us the rate at different initial concentrations of X.
You can see some sample results below:

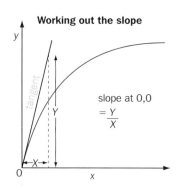

Working out the slope

slope at 0,0
$= \dfrac{Y}{X}$

Concentration of X / mol dm^{-3}	Initial rate of reaction / mol dm^{-3} s^{-1}
2.0	0.01
1.0	0.005
0.5	0.0025
0.25	0.00125

We also know that the rate is zero when we have no X present.
This gives us enough points to plot on a graph to show
how the rate depends on the concentration of X:

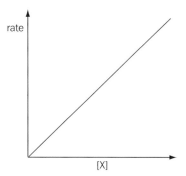

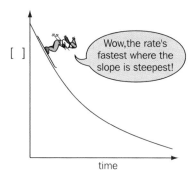

Wow, the rate's fastest where the slope is steepest!

This graph shows us that the rate is directly proportional
to the concentration of X. In other words:

    if we double the concentration of X, we double the rate of the reaction.

We can write this mathematically as:

    rate $\propto$ **[X]**   (rate is proportional to the concentration of X)

Look at the results of similar experiments varying only Y:

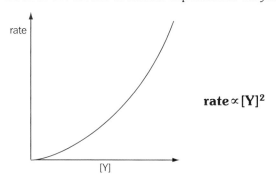

rate $\propto$ **[Y]^2**

Then varying only Z:

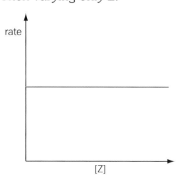

This shows that the **rate does not depend on [Z]**.

▷ Rate equations

On the last page we saw how to work out the effect of varying
the concentration of reactants on the rate of the reaction:

$$X(aq) + Y(aq) + Z(aq) \longrightarrow A(aq) + B(aq)$$

We looked at the graphs below:

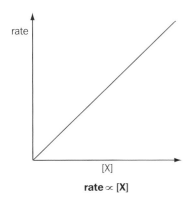

rate ∝ [X]

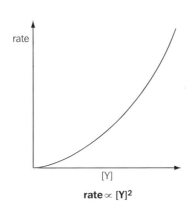

rate ∝ [Y]²

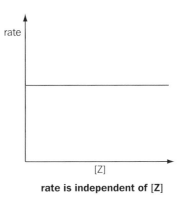

rate is independent of [Z]

We can show these relationships as equations:

$$\boxed{\textbf{rate} = \textbf{\textit{k}}' \times \textbf{[X]}}$$

$$\boxed{\textbf{rate} = \textbf{\textit{k}}'' \times \textbf{[Y]}^2}$$

$$\boxed{\textbf{rate} = \textbf{\textit{k}}''' \times \textbf{[Z]}^0}$$

(any number raised to the
power 0 is 1)

We can combine all the equations into one equation that
describes the effects of changing the concentrations of X, Y and Z.

The overall equation is:

$$\text{rate} = k \times [X] \times [Y]^2 \times [Z]^0$$

We don't usually show the '×' signs and we know that $[Z]^0 = 1$.
So we can rewrite the equation as:

$$\boxed{\textbf{rate} = \textit{k}\textbf{[X][Y]}^2}$$

This is called an overall **rate equation**,
where k is called the **rate constant** for the reaction
(at that particular temperature).

As you can see from the equation, the larger the value of k,
the faster the rate of the reaction will be.

- What do you think will happen to the value of k
  if we raise the temperature of the reactants?
- What will happen to k if we add a catalyst to the reaction?

Notice that the rate equation for a reaction is not related
to the balanced chemical equation at all.
In our example above, Z does not even appear in the rate equation
although it is one of the reactants.
We will explain how this can happen on page 346.

> **The rate equation cannot be
> worked out from the balanced
> chemical equation. It has to
> be found by experiments.**

▷ Order of a reaction

Chemists don't usually talk about rates of reaction as being 'proportional to the concentration of reactant Y squared'. They talk about the order of a reaction with respect to Y.

> **The order of a reaction with respect to a particular reactant is the power to which that reactant is raised in the rate equation.**

In our example, the reaction is **first order** with respect to X,

second order with respect to Y, and

zero order with respect to Z.

> **The overall order of a reaction is the sum of all the powers to which reactants are raised in the overall rate equation.**

So in our example, the overall order for the reaction is $1 + 2 = 3$. (1 from [X] and 2 from $[Y]^2$).

We say that the overall order for the reaction is 3, or that this is a third order reaction.

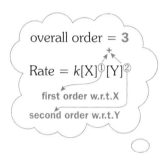

overall order = **3**

Rate = $k[X]^{①}[Y]^{②}$

first order w.r.t. X

second order w.r.t. Y

Units of the rate constant, k

We need to know how to work out the units of the rate constant, k. Its units will vary depending on the order of the reaction. We work out the units of k by putting in the units for the rate (often $mol\,dm^{-3}\,s^{-1}$) and the concentrations ($mol\,dm^{-3}$) into the rate equation.
Then we rearrange the equation to find the units of k.

Let's look at the various cases you might meet:

1st order	2nd order	3rd order
rate = $k[X]$	rate = $k[X][Y]$	rate = $k[X][Y]^2$
$mol\,dm^{-3}\,s^{-1} = k \times mol\,dm^{-3}$	$mol\,dm^{-3}\,s^{-1} = k \times (mol\,dm^{-3})^2$	$mol\,dm^{-3}\,s^{-1} = k \times (mol\,dm^{-3})^3$
$\dfrac{mol\,dm^{-3}\,s^{-1}}{mol\,dm^{-3}} = k$	$\dfrac{mol\,dm^{-3}\,s^{-1}}{(mol\,dm^{-3})^2} = k$	$\dfrac{mol\,dm^{-3}\,s^{-1}}{(mol\,dm^{-3})^3} = k$
$s^{-1} = k$	$mol^{-1}\,dm^3\,s^{-1} = k$	$mol^{-2}\,dm^6\,s^{-1} = k$

When stating the units, remember that the power (or index) has its sign reversed if it's on the bottom line of an equation. For example:

$$\frac{1}{10} = 10^{-1} \quad \text{or} \quad \frac{1}{10^{-6}} = 10^6$$

so

$$\frac{1}{mol} = mol^{-1} \quad \text{or} \quad \frac{1}{dm^{-6}} = dm^6$$

▷ Finding out rate equations

We have now met several new ideas about rates of reaction.
Let's see if we can use these on some actual reactions
to find out their rate equations.

Example 1

Nitrogen(V) oxide decomposes as shown below:

$$2\,N_2O_5(g) \longrightarrow 4\,NO_2(g) + O_2(g)$$

Look at the results calculated from experiments done at different
initial concentrations of N_2O_5:

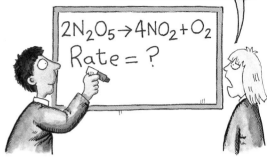

Initial $[N_2O_5]$ / 10^{-3} mol dm^{-3}	Initial rate of reaction / 10^{-5} mol dm^{-3} min^{-1}
1	2.5
2	5.0
4	10.0
8	20.0

(Notice the units in the headings in the table above:
The 10^{-3} means that all the concentrations of N_2O_5 are multiplied
by 10^{-3}. The same applies to 10^{-5} in the rate column.
Also note that the rate has been measured per minute, not per second).

● What happens to the rate when we double the concentration of N_2O_5?
● Can you express this relationship mathematically?

From these results we can see that the rate is directly proportional
to the concentration of N_2O_5.
Therefore:

rate $= k[N_2O_5]$

So the reaction is first order.

Another way to find out whether a reaction is first order
is by looking at a rate curve like the one below:
You check the times it takes for the concentration of a reactant
to fall to half the original value taken. This is called its **half-life ($t_{1/2}$)**.

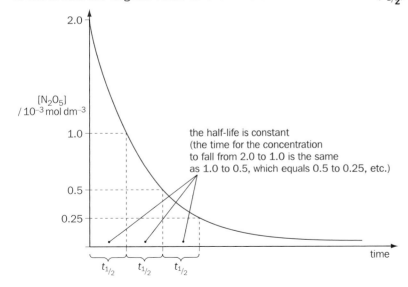

the half-life is constant
(the time for the concentration
to fall from 2.0 to 1.0 is the same
as 1.0 to 0.5, which equals 0.5 to 0.25, etc.)

A reaction is first order with respect to a reactant if its half-life is constant.

Example 2

Hydrogen iodide gas decomposes when we heat it:

$$2\,HI(g) \longrightarrow H_2(g) + I_2(g)$$

Look at the results of work done to find how the rate varies
with different starting concentrations of HI at 650 K.

Initial [HI] / 10^{-3} mol dm^{-3}	Rate of reaction / 10^{-10} mol dm^{-3} s^{-1}
1	1
2	4
4	16
8	64

- What happens to the rate when we double the concentration of HI?

In this reaction, if we double the concentration, the rate goes up four times.
Find two tests from the table where the concentration goes up
by a factor of 4 (is quadrupled): What happens to the rate?

We can say that the rate is proportional to the concentration of HI squared.
So the rate equation is:

rate $= k[\text{HI}]^2$

Let's see what the rate curve looks like for this second order reaction:

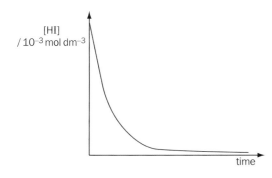

As you can see, the rate changes much more quickly than in
a first order graph.

Working out the value of a rate constant

We can calculate the value of a rate constant
from experimental results once we know the rate equation.
We simply put in our values for a particular concentration
and its rate of reaction into the rate equation.
Let's look at the last two examples:
Choose any pair of values from the results tables. Try some yourself too!

Example 1

rate $= k[\text{N}_2\text{O}_5]$

$5.0 \times 10^{-5} = k \times 2 \times 10^{-3}$

$\dfrac{5.0 \times 10^{-5}}{2 \times 10^{-3}}\,\text{min}^{-1} = k$

$\mathbf{2.5 \times 10^{-2}\,min^{-1} = k}$

Example 2

rate $= k[\text{HI}]^2$

$16 \times 10^{-10} = k \times (4 \times 10^{-3})^2$

$\dfrac{16 \times 10^{-10}}{(4 \times 10^{-3})^2}\,\text{mol}^{-1}\,\text{dm}^3\,\text{s}^{-1} = k$

$\mathbf{1.0 \times 10^{-4}\,mol^{-1}\,dm^3\,s^{-1} = k}$

▷ Third order reactions

So far the examples of actual reactions that we have studied
have involved one reactant decomposing.
But many reactions involve two or more reactants.
The same methods apply, but you have to analyse results
more carefully to see the effect of changing concentrations.
Let's look at an example:

Example

Look at the reaction below:

$$H_2O_2(aq) + 2\,H^+(aq) + 2\,I^-(aq) \longrightarrow 2\,H_2O(l) + I_2(aq)$$

We can judge the initial rate of reaction by timing
how long it takes for iodine to first appear in the solution.
The rate is easily worked out from timings:

$$\boxed{\textbf{rate} \propto \frac{1}{\textbf{time}}}$$

We say that rate is inversely proportional to time.
So the longer the time it takes for iodine to appear,
the slower the rate of reaction.

Here are the results of a series of experiments:

Experiment number	Initial concentrations / mol dm^{-3}			Initial rate / 10^{-6} mol dm^{-3} s^{-1}
	$[H_2O_2]$	$[H^+]$	$[I^-]$	
1	0.01	0.1	0.01	2.0
2	0.02	0.1	0.01	4.0
3	0.02	0.2	0.01	8.0
4	0.01	0.1	0.02	4.0

- Which experiments would you compare to see the effect
  of $[H_2O_2]$ on the rate? Why?
- What is the effect of doubling the concentration of H_2O_2
  on the rate of the reaction?
- Now try the same steps to judge the effect of H^+ and I^- ions.
  (Hint: Did you choose Experiments 1 and 4 to look at
  the effect of I^- ions?)

As you have probably worked out:

rate $= k[H_2O_2][H^+][I^-]$

Notice again that the rate equation has nothing to do with
the balanced chemical equation. Although there are $2\,H^+$ ions
in the balanced equation, the reaction is first order
with respect to $[H^+]$. The same applies to I^- ions.

- What is the overall order of the reaction?
- What would the graph look like if you plotted the concentration
  of H_2O_2 against time?

344

▷ Chemistry at work: Rates of reaction

Chemical reactions which save lives

Your life could one day be saved by a car air bag.

When a car fitted with an air bag is in a crash, a sensor at the front of the car detects the sudden slowing down and triggers the ignition of a mixture of chemicals. The chemicals react together to release a large volume of nitrogen gas. The nitrogen inflates a nylon bag located in the steering wheel. Your head hits the bag not the wheel.
Some of the gas escapes through small holes in the bag. This further softens the impact.
All of this happens in less than a second.

The gas generating chemicals are a mixture of sodium azide (NaN_3), potassium nitrate(V) (KNO_3) and silicon dioxide (SiO_2). When ignited the sodium azide decomposes to produce nitrogen gas and sodium metal.

$$2\,NaN_3(s) \longrightarrow 2\,Na(s) + 3\,N_2(g)$$

The sodium reacts with the potassium nitrate to release more nitrogen.

$$10\,Na(s) + 2\,KNO_3(s) \longrightarrow K_2O(s) + 5\,Na_2O(s) + N_2(g)$$

Both reactions are so exothermic that the heat produced melts the remaining solids together with the silicon dioxide.
This forms a safe type of glass.

$$K_2O(s) + Na_2O(s) + SiO_2(s) \longrightarrow \text{glass}$$

Bombs away!

The South American bombardier beetle has an unusual way of defending itself against predators. It sprays them with a hot, corrosive liquid from a gland on the tip of its abdomen which rotates a bit like a gun turret.

The gland has two separate chambers.
One contains a mixture of hydroquinone and hydrogen peroxide and the other contains two enzymes, catalase and peroxidase.
When the beetle feels threatened it mixes the contents of the two chambers.
The enzymes catalyse the decomposition of the hydroquinone and hydrogen peroxide in rapid and highly exothermic reactions.
The oxygen produced from the decomposition of the hydrogen peroxide builds up pressure which propels the hot spray with great accuracy towards the attacker.

▷ Mechanisms and kinetics

Do you remember some of the mechanisms you have studied
in organic chemistry?
One of the ways that we can get evidence to support
our ideas about the route a reaction takes is kinetic studies.
We can deduce steps by looking at the rate equation
derived from experiments.

At the start of the chapter we looked at an imaginary reaction:

$$X(aq) + Y(aq) + Z(aq) \longrightarrow A(aq) + B(aq)$$

Its rate equation was found to be:

$$\text{rate} = k[X][Y]^2$$

Notice that reactant Z does not appear in the rate equation.
The rate is affected only by the slower steps in the mechanism.
These relatively slow steps are called **rate determining steps**.
So we can deduce that any steps involving Z are fast.
They happen immediately and so don't affect the rate.

The rate determining step (or steps) can be thought of as
a 'bottle-neck' in the route to the products.
Once past any 'bottle-necks', the reaction speeds to its destination!

Let's use the rate equation for our imaginary reaction
to propose two possible mechanisms:

The reaction is first order with respect to X
and second order with respect to Y.
This means that X will appear in one rate determining step,
but Y will feature twice. This could be in two different steps
or two Y's might appear in one step.

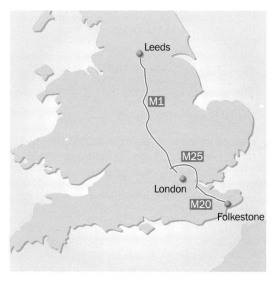

The rate determining step in this route could well be the M25!

Mechanism 1

Step 1 $X + Y \xrightarrow{\text{SLOW}}$ intermediate D

Step 2   intermediate $D + Y \xrightarrow{\text{SLOW}}$ intermediate E

Step 3   intermediate $E + Z \xrightarrow{\text{FAST}} A + B$

Mechanism 2

Step 1 $Y + Y \xrightarrow{\text{SLOW}}$ intermediate F

Step 2   intermediate $F + X \xrightarrow{\text{SLOW}}$ intermediate G

Step 3   intermediate $G + Z \xrightarrow{\text{FAST}} A + B$

Steps 1 and 2 are the rate determining steps in each proposed mechanism.

▷ Hydrolysis of bromoalkanes

We can use rates of reaction to help us find out
the mechanism when bromoalkanes are hydrolysed.
You may recall from page 190 that halogenoalkanes
are attacked by nucleophiles. H_2O will attack them,
but hydroxide ions, OH^-, are more effective.
The reaction below shows the hydrolysis:

$$C_4H_9Br + OH^- \longrightarrow C_4H_9OH + Br^-$$

There are two possible mechanisms for the reaction:

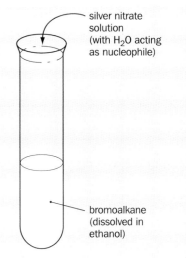

1. S_N1 mechanism

The S stands for substitution,
the N for nucleophilic,
the 1 indicates that the reaction is first order.

Tertiary bromoalkanes are hydrolysed via the S_N1 mechanism.
The rate determining step is the formation of the carbocation:

$$CH_3 - \overset{\overset{\displaystyle Br}{|}}{\underset{\underset{\displaystyle CH_3}{|}}{C}} - CH_3 \xrightarrow{\text{slow}} CH_3 - \overset{+}{\underset{\underset{\displaystyle CH_3}{|}}{C}} - CH_3 + Br^-$$

Followed by immediate attack by any OH^- ions present:

$$CH_3 - \overset{+}{\underset{\underset{\displaystyle CH_3}{|}}{C}} - CH_3 + OH^- \xrightarrow{\text{fast}} CH_3 - \overset{\overset{\displaystyle OH}{|}}{\underset{\underset{\displaystyle CH_3}{|}}{C}} - CH_3$$

The rate equation is found experimentally to be:

rate = k[bromoalkane]

The silver nitrate can identify when
the Br^-(aq) ion has been made i.e.
when the hydrolysis has happened.
Experiments show that the rate of
formation of cream AgBr precipitate
depends on:
a) the concentration of bromoalkane
   only with tertiary compounds
   (S_N1 mechanism).
b) the concentration of both
   bromoalkane and water with
   primary compounds
   (S_N2 mechanism).

2. S_N2 mechanism

We find that ***primary*** bromoalkanes follow this mechanism.
The 2 indicates a second order reaction.
This suggests that there must be two molecules or ions
involved in the rate determining step.

The mechanism that supports this is shown below:

$$CH_3 - CH_2 - \overset{\delta+}{C}H_2 \rightarrow \overset{\delta-}{Br} \xrightarrow{\text{slow}} CH_3 - CH_2 - CH_2 \overset{\cdots Br}{\underset{\cdots OH}{}} \xrightarrow{\text{fast}} CH_3 - CH_2 - CH_2 - OH + Br^-$$

$$:OH^-$$

intermediate forms as C—Br
breaks and C—OH forms

The rate equation in this case is found by experiments to be:

rate = k[bromoalkane][OH^-]

- Can you see how these two rate equations relate to the suggested mechanisms?
- Why do you think tertiary carbocations are more likely to form
  as intermediates than primary carbocations? (See page 182.)

Secondary bromoalkanes seem to follow a mixture of S_N1 and S_N2 mechanisms.

Summary

- We can show the rate of a reaction mathematically by its **rate equation**.
- This rate equation can only be found by experiment. For example, in the reaction $X + Y \longrightarrow Z$, the rate equation could be:

    rate $= k[Y][X]^2$

  where the reaction is first order with respect to Y, second order with respect to X, and third order overall.
- k is called the **rate constant** for the reaction at that particular temperature. Its value increases as we raise the temperature or use a catalyst. The units of k vary depending on the order of a reaction.
- Rates of reaction give us valuable evidence for proposing mechanisms for reactions. The slow steps will involve the reactants that appear in the rate equation. These are called **rate determining steps**.

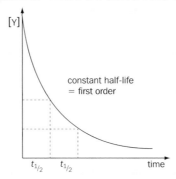

constant half-life
= first order

▷ Questions

1   Copy and complete:

A rate equation tells us how the rate of a reaction is affected by the .... of reactants. We can only work it out by doing ..... The rate equation always includes a .... constant, given the symbol ..... The size of this constant .... with temperature. It will be .... at higher temperatures. Its value will .... if we use a catalyst.

The order of a reaction is the sum of the .... to which the concentrations are raised in the rate equation. For example, if the rate equation is:

    rate $= k[A][B]$

then the overall order for the reaction is .....
This reaction would be .... order with respect to A, and .... order with respect to B.
If the rate of a reaction does not depend on a reactant, then it is said to be .... order with respect to that reactant.

Rate equations give us valuable information about the .... of a reaction, i.e. the route by which reactants turn to products. The .... steps are called the rate .... steps. Reactants in the rate .... steps will appear in the rate .... for the reaction.

2   Look at this rate equation:

    rate $= k[Y][Z]^2$

a) What do we call k? What are its units in this case?
b) What is the order of the reaction with respect to Y?
c) What is the order of the reaction with respect to Z?
d) What is the overall order of the reaction?
e) Sketch graphs that show how the rate varies with
   i) [Y], and ii) [Z].

3   The decomposition of N_2O_5 is shown below:

    $2 N_2O_5(g) \longrightarrow 4 NO_2(g) + O_2(g)$

The initial rate of reaction was determined at different starting concentrations of N_2O_5 at 328 K:

Concentration of N_2O_5/ mol dm^{-3}	Initial rate of reaction/ mol dm^{-3} s^{-1}
1.0×10^{-4}	1.5×10^{-8}
2.0×10^{-4}	3.0×10^{-8}
3.0×10^{-4}	4.5×10^{-8}
4.0×10^{-4}	6.0×10^{-8}
5.0×10^{-4}	7.5×10^{-8}

a) Draw a graph to show these results.
b) How is the rate of the reaction affected by the concentration of N_2O_5?
c) What is the order of the reaction?
d) Write the rate equation for the reaction.
e) Explain how you could work out the rate equation directly from the table of results given above.
f) Work out the value of the rate constant at 328 K. (Don't forget the units!)
g) The reaction was repeated at 298 K.
   At this temperature the initial rate of reaction was found to be 3.5×10^{-9} mol dm^{-3} s^{-1} when you start with a concentration of 1.0×10^{-4} mol dm^{-3} N_2O_5.
   Calculate the rate constant at 298 K.
h) Sketch the graph you would expect to see if the concentration of N_2O_5 had been monitored continuously in one of the experiments using data logging equipment.
i) How does the graph in part h) support your expression for the rate equation in part d)?

4   A group of students investigated the rate of reaction between iodine and propanone:

$$CH_3COCH_3(aq) + I_2(aq) \xrightarrow{H^+(aq)} CH_3COCH_2I(aq) + H^+(aq) + I^-(aq)$$

They followed the rate of reaction using a colorimeter.
a) Why is a colorimeter suitable for monitoring this reaction?

They set up the following experiments:

Expt. no.	Vol. of 4M propanone/ cm³	Vol. of 4M HCl/ cm³	Vol. of 0.0125M iodine/ cm³	Vol. of water/ cm³
1	4	4	4	0
2	2	4	4	2
3	1	4	4	3
4	4	2	4	2
5	4	1	4	3
6	4	4	2	2
7	4	4	1	3

b) Which experiments would you look at to see the effect of the concentration of:
   i)   propanone
   ii) iodine
   iii) hydrochloric acid
   on the rate of reaction?

The students converted their readings on the colorimeter into concentrations of iodine and plotted these against time. Look at their graph for experiments 1, 2, 3, 6 and 7:

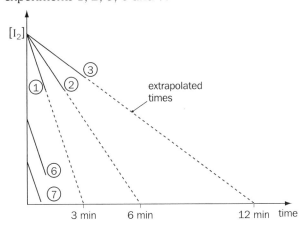

c) What does the graph tell you about the order of the reaction with respect to propanone?
d) What does the graph tell you about the effect iodine has on the rate of the reaction? Therefore, what is the order of the reaction with respect to iodine?
e) The reaction is first order with respect to H⁺(aq). Write the overall rate equation for the reaction of propanone and iodine.
f) Do you think that iodine will be a reactant in a rate determining step. Why?
g) What are the units of the rate constant in part e)?

5   The nitration of benzene can be followed using a dilatometer because there is a slight decrease in the volume of liquid as the reaction proceeds.

a) Look at the diagram below and explain how the dilatometer works:

b) The reaction is zero order with respect to benzene and first order with respect to nitric acid. Write the rate equation for the reaction above.

6   Look at the results of the reaction between bromate(V) ions and bromide ions in acidic conditions:

$$BrO_3^-(aq) + 5\,Br^-(aq) + 6\,H^+(aq) \longrightarrow 3\,Br_2(aq) + 3\,H_2O(l)$$

Expt. no.	Conc. of bromate(V)/ mol dm⁻³	Conc. of bromide/ mol dm⁻³	Conc. of H⁺(aq)/ mol dm⁻³	Relative initial rate
1	0.5	0.5	0.5	1
2	0.5	1.0	0.5	2
3	0.25	0.5	0.5	0.5
4	0.25	0.5	1.0	2

a) What is the order of reaction with respect to
   i)   bromate(V) ions
   ii) bromide ions
   iii) H⁺(aq) ions
b) Write a rate equation for the reaction above.
c) Suggest three ways in which we could follow the rate of this reaction. Explain each choice.

7   There are two possible mechanism for the hydrolysis of a bromomalkane:

$$RBr + OH^- \longrightarrow ROH + Br^-$$

a) Explain the S_N1 mechanism.
b) Explain the S_N2 mechanism.
c) Let's look at the hydrolysis of 1-bromopropane: Experiments show that if we double the concentration of OH⁻ ions the rate of hydrolysis is doubled. Doubling the concentration of 1-bromopropane also doubles the rate. Write the rate equation and say which mechanism it provides evidence for.
d) How would you expect the rate to be affected by the concentration of each reactant if we hydrolysed 2-methyl-2-bromopropane with OH⁻ ions? Explain your answer.

Further questions on energy and rates

▷ Enthalpy change

1 The standard enthalpy change of atomisation of methane is 1662 kJ mol^{-1} and of ethane is 2924 kJ mol^{-1}.
   a) The atomisation of methane may be written as
   $$CH_4(g) \longrightarrow C(g) + 4H(g)$$
   Write an equation to show the atomisation of ethane. [1]
   b) Use the data to calculate the average bond energy of i) a C—H bond; and ii) a C—C bond. [3]
   c) The standard enthalpy change of formation of methane, $\Delta H_f^\ominus[CH_4(g)]$, $C(s) + 2H_2(g) \longrightarrow CH_4(g)$ cannot be measured directly. Suggest what enthalpy changes need to be known in order to calculate $\Delta H_f^\ominus[CH_4(g)]$. [2]

   (OCR)

2 1.308 g of zinc was added to an excess of copper(II) sulphate. The heat energy transferred was measured and found to be 4.40 kJ.

   Calculate the standard enthalpy change for the reaction, giving its correct sign and units.

   (A_r of Zn = 65.5) [3]

   (AQA)

3 A student was using yeast to ferment glucose and wished to work out whether there would be a significant temperature change during the process. 18.0 g (0.100 mole) of glucose were dissolved in 250 g of water and yeast added. The reaction is:
   $$C_6H_{12}O_6(aq) \longrightarrow 2C_2H_5OH(aq) + 2CO_2(g)$$
   $$\Delta H^\ominus = -97.9 \text{ kJ mol}^{-1}$$
   a) i) How much heat energy was produced in the experiment? [1]
   ii) Use the expression

   Energy produced (in joules) =
   Mass of water × 4.18 × Rise in temperature

   to calculate the rise in temperature. Ignore the masses of glucose and yeast for this purpose. [2]
   b) i) Would this temperature prove to be a serious problem in the laboratory-scale process? Justify your answer. [2]
   ii) Suggest whether the exothermic nature of the reaction would be a problem in the large-scale brewing of beer in batches of 50 000 litres. Justify your answer. [2]

   (AQA)

4 This question is about sulphur dioxide, SO_2. Sulphur dioxide is used in the production of sulphuric acid, H_2SO_4, by the contact process. In this process sulphur dioxide is catalytically oxidised to sulphur trioxide, SO_3, according to the following gaseous equilibrium:
   $$2SO_2(g) + O_2(g) \rightleftharpoons 2SO_3(g)$$

Standard enthalpies of formation are as follows:

	$O_2(g)$	$SO_2(g)$	$SO_3(g)$
$\Delta H_f^\ominus(298K)/kJ \text{ mol}^{-1}$	0	−297	−395

   a) Calculate the standard enthalpy change for the reaction at 298 K. [2]
   b) Why is $\Delta H_f^\ominus$ for oxygen equal to zero? [1]

   (OCR)

5 Use Hess's law and the data given to calculate the standard enthalpy change for the following reaction:
   $$Li_2CO_3(s) \longrightarrow Li_2O(s) + CO_2(g)$$

Compound	$Li_2CO_3(s)$	$Li_2O(s)$	$CO_2(g)$
$\Delta H_f^\ominus/kJ \text{ mol}^{-1}$	−1216	−596	−394

   [3]

   (AQA)

6 Use the Hess cycle and the data, at 298 K, to calculate the standard enthalpy change of formation of cyanogen, including its sign and unit.

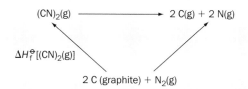

   [3]

   (EDEXCEL)

7 The cracking of propane also produces propene.
   $$C_3H_8 \longrightarrow C_3H_6(g) + H_2(g)$$

   Calculate the standard enthalpy change for this reaction. Use the data, at 298 K.

   $\Delta H_f^\ominus[C_3H_8(g)] = -104.5 \text{ kJ mol}^{-1}$

   $\Delta H_f^\ominus[C_3H_6(g)] = +20.2 \text{ kJ mol}^{-1}$

   Your answer should include a sign and units. [2]

   (EDEXCEL)

8 Ammonia is a covalent molecule.
   a) Describe what is meant by a covalent bond. [1]
   b) Explain the meaning of *bond enthalpy*. [1]
   c) Calculate the bond enthalpy of the N—H bond in NH_3 using the data given below. Show your method of working clearly. [3]
   $$N_2(g) + 3H_2(g) \longrightarrow 2NH_3(g)$$
   $$\Delta H^\ominus{}_{(298K)} = -92 \text{ kJ mol}^{-1}$$

Bond	Bond enthalpy / kJ mol^{-1}
N≡N	946
H—H	436

d) The enthalpy of formation of

$$\begin{array}{ccc} H & & H \\ \diagdown & & \diagup \\ N & \!\!-\!\! & N \\ \diagup & & \diagdown \\ H & & H \end{array}$$

(g) is

94 kJ mol^{-1}.

Using the N—H bond enthalpy derived in c), calculate the bond enthalpy of the N—N bond. (If you have not derived the N—H bond enthalpy in c), use the value 400 kJ mol^{-1}.) [2]
(OCR)

9 a) State the meaning of the term **standard enthalpy change of formation**, $\Delta H_f^{\ominus}(298\,K)$.
b) Butane gas is sometimes used for heating and cooking. The combustion of butane, C_4H_{10}, which is represented by the equation below is a highly exothermic process:

$$C_4H_{10}(g) + \tfrac{13}{2}O_2(g) \longrightarrow 4\,CO_2(g) + 5\,H_2O(g);$$
$$\Delta H_c^{\ominus} = -2877\ \text{kJ mol}^{-1}$$

i) Show a relationship between the enthalpy change for this reaction, $\Delta H_c^{\ominus}$, and the standard enthalpy changes of formation, $\Delta H_f^{\ominus}$, of the reactants and products. [1]

ii) Using the data below calculate the standard enthalpy change of formation of butane.

Substance	$O_2(g)$	$CO_2(g)$	$H_2O(g)$
Standard enthalpy change of formation. $[\Delta H_f^{\ominus}(298\,K)/\text{kJ mol}^{-1}]$	0	−394.0	−286.0

[2]
(WJEC)

▷ **Lattice enthalpy**

10 The following data have been collected together to use in a Born–Haber cycle for copper(II) bromide, $CuBr_2$.

Atomisation energy of bromine, $\Delta H_{at}^{\ominus}\,[\tfrac{1}{2}Br_2(l)]$
    $= +111.9$ kJ mol^{-1}
Atomisation energy of copper, $\Delta H_{at}^{\ominus}\,[Cu(s)]$
    $= +338.3$ kJ mol^{-1}
First ionisation energy of copper $= +746.0$ kJ mol^{-1}
Second ionisation energy of copper
    $= +1958.0$ kJ mol^{-1}
Electron affinity of bromine, $E_{aff}[Br(g)]$
    $= -324.6$ kJ mol^{-1}
Enthalpy change of formation of $CuBr_2(s)$,
    $\Delta H_f^{\ominus}[CuBr_2(s)] = -141.8$ kJ mol^{-1}

a) Copy the following outline of the Born–Haber cycle and complete the empty boxes by putting in the formula and state symbols for the appropriate species.

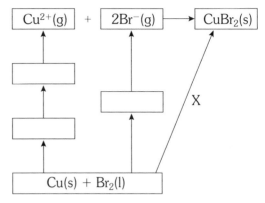

b) Give the name of the enthalpy change for the change taking place at X.
c) Calculate the standard lattice enthalpy of $CuBr_2(s)$.
[4]
(AQA)

11 Some people define the term *lattice energy* as a measure of the energy needed to dissociate a crystal of an ionic compound so that the ions are an infinite distance apart.

For example:

$$Na^+Cl^-(s) \rightleftharpoons Na^+(g) + Cl^-(g)$$

The value of the lattice energy depends on the charge densities of the two ions and structure of the crystal. Consider the data below:

Compound	Lattice enthalpy /kJ mol^{-1}	Compound	Lattice energy /kJ mol^{-1}
LiF	1022	MgF_2	2913
LiCl	846	CaF_2	2611
LiBr	800	SrF_2	2476
LiI	744	BaF_2	2341
NaF	902	RaF_2	2284
KF	801	TlF_3	5493
RbF	767	PbF_2	2460
CsF	716	PbF_4	9467

a) i) Quote data from the table above to illustrate the trend in lattice energy as groups in the s-block are descended. [1]
ii) Quote date from the table to illustrate the trend in lattice energy as Group 7 is descended. [1]
iii) State the trend in lattice energy in the halides of metals as *any* group in the Periodic Table is descended. [1]
iv) Suggest why the lattice energy changes in the way you have stated in iii). [3]
(OCR)

Further questions on energy and rates

12 a) Explain, in qualitative terms, the effect of ionic charge and of ionic radius on the numerical magnitude of a lattice energy.

b) The lattice energy of copper(II) oxide can be found using a Born–Haber cycle.
Write equations, including state symbols, which correspond to

- the enthalpy change of formation of copper(II) oxide
- the lattice energy of copper(II) oxide
- the first ionisation energy of copper

c) Use the data below to construct a Born–Haber cycle and hence calculate a value for the lattice energy of copper(II) oxide.

Enthalpy change	/kJ mol^{-1}
Atomisation of copper	339
First ionisation energy of copper	745
Second ionisation energy of copper	1960
Atomisation of oxygen: $\frac{1}{2}O_2(g) \longrightarrow O(g)$	248
First electron affinity of oxygen	−141
Second electron affinity of oxygen	791
Formation of copper(II) oxide	−155

[15]
(OCR)

13 a) The diagram below shows an enthalpy cycle for the formation of aqueous magnesium chloride. (The diagram is not drawn to scale)

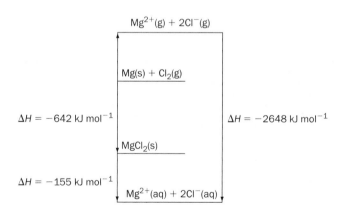

Mg^{2+}(g) + 2Cl$^-$(g)

Mg(s) + Cl$_2$(g)

$\Delta H = -642$ kJ mol^{-1}

$\Delta H = -2648$ kJ mol^{-1}

MgCl$_2$(s)

$\Delta H = -155$ kJ mol^{-1}

Mg^{2+}(aq) + 2Cl$^-$(aq)

i) Give the equation which represents the *lattice enthalpy* of MgCl$_2$(s). [1]

ii) Calculate the value of the lattice enthalpy of MgCl$_2$(s). [1]

b) Explain the meaning of the following: [3]
i) the *enthalpy of atomisation* of chlorine is 122 kJ mol^{-1}. [1]
ii) the *electron affinity* of chlorine is −364 kJ mol^{-1}. [1]

c) i) The enthalpy of atomisation of magnesium is 148 kJ mol^{-1}.

Using all the data in this question, calculate the enthalpy change of the reaction:
$$Mg(g) \longrightarrow Mg^{2+}(g) + 2e^-.$$ [3]

ii) Explain why the second ionisation enthalpy of magnesium is greater than its first ionisation enthalpy [1]
(OCR)

▷ Entropy and free energy

14 Phosphorus pentachloride, PCl$_5$, is prepared by passing chlorine gas through phosphorus trichloride, PCl$_3$.

$$PCl_3(l) + Cl_2(g) \rightleftharpoons PCl_5(s)$$

a) Use the following data to calculate the enthalpy change at 298 K for the production of 1 mole of phosphorus pentachloride from the trichloride. Your answer should include a sign and units.

Compound	$\Delta H_f^{\ominus}$/kJ mol^{-1}
PCl$_3$	−319.7
PCl$_5$	−443.5

[2]

b) Use your answer from a) to calculate the entropy change in the surroundings at 298 K. Your answer should include a sign and units. [3]

c) The standard entropy change of the system for this reaction is −215.6 J mol^{-1} K^{-1}.
i) Suggest **two** reasons why $\Delta S^{\ominus}_{\text{system}}$ has a negative value. [2]
ii) Calculate the total entropy change, $\Delta S^{\ominus}_{\text{total}}$, for the reaction. [1]
iii) Will the reaction proceed spontaneously at 298 K? Explain your answer. [1]

d) The apparatus used in this reaction is ice-cooled. How does the yield of phosphorus pentachloride change when the temperature is allowed to rise? [2]
(EDEXCEL)

15 a) In the following equation, T represents temperature.

$$\Delta G = \Delta H - T\Delta S$$

Give the names of the other terms. [3]

b) i) Calculate the value, stating units, of ΔS for the following reaction at 25 °C.

$$CaO(s) + H_2O(l) \longrightarrow Ca(OH)_2(s)$$

($\Delta G = -55.2$ kJ mol^{-1}, $\Delta H = -65.2$ kJ mol^{-1}) [3]

ii) Explain the significance of the signs of the values for each of the following terms in the above reaction:

ΔG, ΔH, ΔS. [3]
(AQA)

▷ Kinetics – rates of reaction

16 a) State the effect, if any, of each of the following changes on the overall value of the activation energy for a chemical reaction: i) increase in temperature, and ii) use of a catalyst. [2]

b) Give one reason why an increase in temperature and the presence of a catalyst both speed up the rate of a chemical reaction. [1]

17 a) i) Copy the axes below and sketch a graph to show the Maxwell–Boltzmann distribution curve for molecular energies in a gas at a fixed temperature.
E_a is the activation energy for a chemical reaction in this gas.

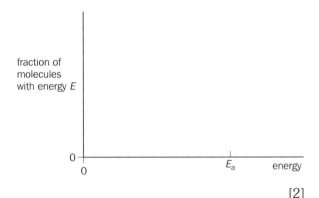

[2]

ii) Indicate on your graph the proportion of molecules which can react. [2]

iii) A catalyst which increases the rate of reaction is added to the gas. What effect does this have on the Maxwell–Botzmann distribution curve and on the proportion of molecules which can react? [2]

b) The catalyst is a heterogeneous catalyst. Explain the term *heterogeneous*.
Give an example of heterogeneous catalysis and name a process in which it is used. [3]

18 Excess calcium carbonate as small pieces was allowed to react with 100 cm^3 of 0.1 mol dm^{-3} hydrochloric acid. A total of 120 cm^3 of carbon dioxide was formed.

a) Sketch a graph to show how the volume of CO_2 evolved changed with time until the reaction ceased.

b) On the same axes, sketch curves labelled A, B and C for the following experiments, carried out at the same temperature.

A 50 cm^3 0.2 mol dm^{-3} hydrochloric acid with excess small pieces of calcium carbonate.

B 50 cm^3 0.1 mol dm^{-3} hydrochloric acid with excess small pieces of calcium carbonate.

C 50 cm^3 0.1 mol dm^{-3} hydrochloric acid with excess powdered calcium carbonate. [6]

(c) Define the term *activation energy* and explain the role of a catalyst in increasing the rate of a reaction. [3]
(AQA)

19 Describe the different modes of action of heterogeneous and homogeneous catalysts, giving one example of each type. [6]
(OCR)

20 a) What is meant by the term *heterogeneous* as applied to a catalyst? [1]

b) Name the three essential steps in the process of heterogeneous catalysis. [3]

c) State two reasons, other than catalyst poisoning, why a chosen substance might prove to be a poor heterogeneous catalyst. In each case, state which of the steps in part b) is affected. [4]
(AQA)

21 a) Explain why, at a given temperature, hydrochloric acid reacts faster with powdered calcium carbonate than it does with lumps of calcium carbonate. [2]

b) The collision theory states that reactions can only occur when particles collide. Give a reason why collisions between particles do not always lead to a reaction. [1]
(AQA)

22 The graph below represents the Maxwell–Boltzman distribution of molecular energies at a temperature $T_1 \text{ K}$.

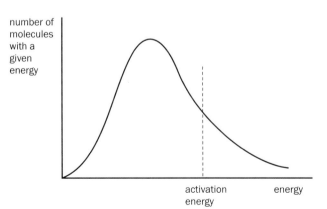

a) Sketch on the same axes, the curve which shows the distribution of molecular energies at a higher temperature $T_2 \text{ K}$.
T_2 is approximately 20 K greater than T_1. [2]

b) Use the graphs to explain how the rate of a gas phase reaction changes with increasing temperature. [4]
(EDEXCEL)

▷ Rate equations

23 The table shows data obtained for the reaction between nitrogen monoxide and hydrogen in the gaseous phase at 750 °C.

$$2\,NO(g) + 2\,H_2(g) \longrightarrow N_2(g) + 2\,H_2O(g)$$

Experiment	Initial conc. of H_2/mol dm^{-3}	Initial conc. of NO/mol dm^{-3}	Initial rate /mol dm^{-3} min^{-1}
1	0.012	0.002	1.20
2	0.012	0.004	2.40
3	0.024	0.002	4.80

a) What is the order of this reaction with respect to hydrogen? [1]

b) Write an expression for the rate of the reaction. [1]

c) Calculate the value of the rate constant and give its units. [3]

d) Explain why the rate of a reaction increases when the temperature increases. [3]

e) If the temperature is raised above 750 °C, what will happen to the value of the rate constant of the reaction? [1]

(AQA)

24 The decomposition of dinitrogen pentoxide, N_2O_5, has been studied in solution. When tetrachloro-methane is used as a solvent, one product (nitrogen dioxide) is retained in solution, whilst oxygen is given off as the other product. The equation for the overall process is as follows:

$$N_2O_5(CCl_4) \longrightarrow 2\,NO_2(CCl_4) + \tfrac{1}{2}O_2(g)$$

a) Draw a diagram of the apparatus you would use to follow the rate of this reaction. [2]

b) The rate equation for the reaction is:

rate $= k[N_2O_5]$

A suggested mechanism for the reaction is

1st step	$N_2O_5 \longrightarrow NO_2 + NO_3$
2nd step	$NO_2 + NO_3 \longrightarrow NO + \tfrac{1}{2}O_2 + NO_3$
3rd step	$NO + NO_3 \longrightarrow 2\,NO_2$

i) What is the order of reaction with respect to N_2O_5? [1]

ii) What are the units of the rate constant k? [1]

iii) Suggest which is the rate determining step, and explain your reasoning. [3]

(AQA)

25 a) Persulphate ions, $S_2O_8^{2-}$, react with iodide ions in aqueous solution to form iodine and sulphate ions, SO_4^{2-}. The effect of persulphate ions on the rate of this reaction can be measured as follows:

Some starch and a small measured quantity of sodium thiosulphate solution are added to potassium persulphate solution. Potassium iodide solution is added and the time measured for the solution to change colour. This occurs when all the sodium thiosulphate is used up and the starch reacts with the iodine. The reaction is repeated using different concentrations of potassium persulphate.

i) What is the final colour of the reaction mixture? [1]

ii) Why is the concentration of iodide ions constant until the reaction mixture changes colour? [1]

b) The rate of reaction is measured by taking the reciprocal of the time for the colour of the reaction mixture to change.

Typical results are shown in the table below:

$[S_2O_8^{2-}]$(aq)/mol dm^{-3}	Time/s	1/time/s^{-1}
0.0100	480	2.08×10^{-3}
0.0090	533	1.88×10^{-3}
0.0075	640	1.56×10^{-3}
0.0060	800	1.25×10^{-3}

i) Plot a graph of 1/time on the vertical axis against concentration of persulphate ions on the horizontal axis. [3]

ii) Use your graph to deduce the order of the reaction with respect to persulphate ions. Justify your answer. [2]

c) i) The reaction is first order with respect to iodide ions. Use this information and your answer to c) ii) to write the overall rate equation for the reaction. [1]

ii) What are the units for the rate constant? [1]

(AQA)

26 A and B react together to give Z.

$$A + B \longrightarrow Z$$

Experiments were carried out to investigate the order of reaction with respect to each reagent. In experiment 1, the concentration of A was kept constant but that of B was varied. In experiment 2, the concentration of B was kept constant but that of A was varied.

The results were plotted on a graph:

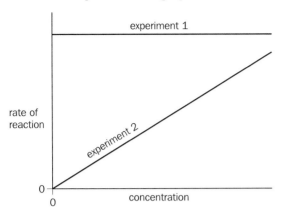

a) From the graph, deduce the order of reaction:
   i) with respect to A;
   ii) with respect to B. [2]
b) Write the rate equation for the reaction between A and B. [1]
c) Using 0.40 mol dm^{-3} A and 0.20 mol dm^{-3} B, the initial rate of reaction in mol dm^{-3} s^{-1} was 6.0 × 10^{-3}. Calculate the value of the rate constant for this reaction and state its units. [2]
d) A student considered three possible mechanisms for the reaction.

   Mechanism 1: $A + B \longrightarrow P$
   $P + B \longrightarrow Z$
   Mechanism 2: $B + Q \longrightarrow R$
   $R + B \longrightarrow S$
   $S + A \longrightarrow Z$
   Mechanism 3: $A + A \longrightarrow T$
   $T + B \longrightarrow A + Z$

   i) State what is meant by the term *rate determining step*. [1]
   ii) For each mechanism, explain whether or not it is consistent with the rate equation in (b). Hence, identify the rate determining step. [4]
   (OCR)

27 a) 2-Bromo-2-methylpropane, $(CH_3)_3CBr$, and sodium hydroxide react according to the following equation:

   $$(CH_3)_3CBr + OH^- \longrightarrow (CH_3)_3COH + Br^-$$

   The following data give the results of three experiments used to determine the rate equation for the reaction at 25 °C:

Expt	Initial [(CH$_3$)$_3$CBr] /mol dm^{-3}	Initial [OH$^-$] /mol dm^{-3}	Initial rate of reaction /mol dm^{-3} s^{-1}
1	1.0 × 10^{-3}	2.0 × 10^{-1}	3.0 × 10^{-3}
2	2.0 × 10^{-3}	2.0 × 10^{-1}	6.0 × 10^{-3}
3	3.0 × 10^{-3}	4.0 × 10^{-1}	6.0 × 10^{-3}

From these results it can be deduced that the rate equation is

$$\text{Rate} = k\,[(CH_3)_3CBr]$$

i) Show how the data can be used to deduce that the reaction is first order with respect to $(CH_3)_3CBr$, and zero order with respect to OH^-.
ii) Calculate a value for the rate constant at this temperature and state its units.
iii) Calculate the initial rate of reaction when the initial concentration of $(CH_3)_3CBr$ is 4.0 × 10^{-3} mol dm^{-3} and that of OH^- is 1.0 × 10^{-1} mol dm^{-3}. [6]
b) Name and outline a mechanism for the reaction of the primary haloalkane, CH_3CH_2Br, with aqueous sodium hydroxide. [4]
c) Give a simple test to distinguish between the organic products of the reactions in part (a) and part (b) by stating the reagent used and what you would see with each compound. [3]
(AQA)

28 a) The rate of reaction between compounds C and D was studied at a fixed temperature and some results obtained are shown in the table below.

Experiment	Initial conc. of C/mol dm^{-3}	Initial conc. of D/mol dm^{-3}	Initial rate, r/mol dm^{-3} s^{-1}
1	0.010	0.010	1.0 × 10^{-6}
2	0.020	0.010	4.0 × 10^{-6}
3	0.030	0.020	9.0 × 10^{-6}
4	0.040	0.020	to be calculated

Use the data in the table to deduce the order of reaction with respect to compound C and the order of reaction with respect to compound D. Hence calculate the initial rate of reaction in experiment 4. [3]
b) Methyl ethanoate is hydrolysed by sodium hydroxide. In a series of experiments at a given temperature, the reaction was found to be first order with respect to this ester and also first order with respect to hydroxide ions. In one of these experiments, when the initial concentration of both reagents was 0.020 mol dm^{-3}, the initial rate of reaction was found to be 8.8 × 10^{-5} mol dm^{-3} s^{-1}.
i) Write an equation for the reaction between methyl ethanoate and hydroxide ions.
ii) Write the rate equation for the reaction and calculate the value of the rate constant, with its units, at this temperature.
iii) In a further experiment at the same temperature, the initial concentration of hydroxide ions was 2.0 mol dm^{-3}. Under these conditions the reaction appears to be zero order with respect to hydroxide ions. Suggest why this is so. [8]
(AQA)

29 Equilibrium mixtures

Have you ever seen a plastic that changes colour as you hold it?
The plastic contains substances which change colour
as they get warm.
They go back to their original colour when they cool down again.
They are used to make children's toothbrushes and toys.

while brushing

after brushing

> **Changes which can go forwards or backwards
> are called reversible.**

The most common reversible changes we come across
are changes of state. Ice melting in our drinks, boiling water
in a kettle and the condensation on windows are examples.

But some chemical reactions are also reversible.
The products can react to give us back the reactants
that we started with.
Let's look at an example :

Example
If we gently heat some blue (hydrated) copper sulphate crystals,
we get a white powder formed.
Look at the diagram opposite:
At the mouth of the test-tube, we see condensation forming.

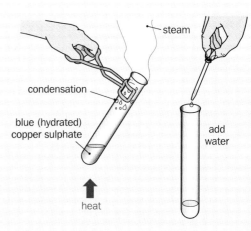

steam

condensation

blue (hydrated)
copper sulphate

add
water

heat

When blue (hydrated) copper sulphate is heated, it loses the water
which is bound up in its crystals.
You get a white powder called anhydrous copper sulphate:

$$CuSO_4.5H_2O \longrightarrow CuSO_4 + 5H_2O$$

hydrated copper sulphate   anhydrous copper sulphate   water
(blue crystals)   (white powder)

If we now add a few drops of water to the anhydrous copper sulphate,
it turns blue again. The hydrated copper sulphate has been re-formed.
You can use this reaction to test for water.

$$CuSO_4 + 5H_2O \longrightarrow CuSO_4.5H_2O$$

So the reaction is reversible.
Reversible reactions can be shown by arrows pointing in both directions:

$$CuSO_4.5H_2O \rightleftharpoons CuSO_4 + 5H_2O$$

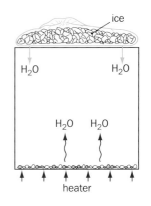

ice

H_2O H_2O

H_2O H_2O

heater

But imagine if we did the experiment in a box from which no substances
could escape.
Look at the diagram opposite:
The water that leaves the blue crystals as a gas condenses on the cooler sides
and top of the box. It drips back on to the white powder.
If the heating is kept the same, eventually the two reversible reactions
will be happening continuously, at the same rate.
● What can you say about the amount of each substance in the box now?

▷ Closed systems and equilibrium

The box we talked about in the copper sulphate reaction
is sometimes called a **closed system**.
In a truly closed system there are no substances and no energy
exchanged with the surroundings.
When we have a closed system, reversible changes will reach
a **state of equilibrium**.

For example, when ammonia and hydrogen chloride gases meet
they react. They form a white cloud of ammonium chloride powder.
You can reverse this reaction by heating the ammonium chloride.
Ammonium chloride solid is broken down by heat, forming
ammonia and hydrogen chloride gases again.

In a closed system, at a suitable temperature, both reactions will happen
at once. Eventually both the forward and backward reactions
will be going *at the same rate.*

$$NH_3 \quad + \quad HCl \quad \rightleftharpoons \quad NH_4Cl$$
ammonia + hydrogen chloride ⠀⠀ ammonium chloride

*This is a 'smoke' of ammonium chloride
formed from HCl(g) and NH$_3$(g). The
ammonium chloride decomposes on
heating to re-form the gases*

This is called **dynamic equilibrium**.
Do you know what the word 'dynamic' means?
You might have read about dynamic footballers,
or dynamic pop-stars. People who have lots of energy
and are always on the move!

'Dynamic' refers to movement.
In dynamic equilibrium there is constant movement.
Reactants are changing to products. Products are changing
to reactants. At the point of equilibrium, the *rates* of the
forward and backward reactions are the same.
What do you think happens to the amounts of reactants and
products at that point?

> **When equilibrium** is reached, the amount of each
> substance *stays the same*.
> There *appears* to be no change.

*Both back and forth, and to and fro,
The equilibrium does go.
Forwards and backwards, at the same rate,
The system reaches a steady state*

The position of equilibrium

Dynamic equilibrium is not like a balancing see-saw.
There need not be equal amounts of reactants and
products in the equilibrium mixture.

Look at the cartoon opposite :
The man can appear to be still near the bottom or near the top.
He doesn't have to be half-way up the escalator.
As long as he is climbing at the same rate as the steps are going down,
he is in dynamic equilibrium.

Therefore, the position of an equilibrium can lie
in favour of the reactants or the products.
It can lie to the left or to the right, as you look at the equation.

▷ Affecting the position of equilibrium

We can change the position of an equilibrium by altering conditions.
For example, we can change **concentrations** of reactants or products.
Temperature also affects the equilibrium mixture.
If the reaction involves gases, then changing the
pressure might affect the equilibrium as well.

As you know from Chapter 27, these factors affect rates of reaction.
But it is important to note that:

> **A catalyst does not affect the position of equilibrium.**

This is because both forward and backward reactions are speeded up.
So the time it takes for a state of equilibrium to be reached will be quicker,
but the amounts of reactants and products present won't change.

The French chemist Le Châtelier did much of the early work
on reactions at equilibrium. His ideas can still be applied to most reactions
at conditions we will meet.
Le Châtelier's Principle can be summarised as:

> **The position of equilibrium shifts to try to cancel out
> any changes you introduce.**

Henri Le Châtelier (1850—1936)

'Which way will the balance lie?'
Le Châtelier did cry.
'It will move to cancel out
Whichever change you bring about.'

▷ Changing concentrations

For example, you might increase the concentration of a reactant.
This will make the forward reaction go faster for a while.
But then, as a result of this, the products increase in concentration.
So the backward reaction speeds up until we reach equilibrium again.
However, the new position of equilibrium will lie further over
to the products.

Look at the diagram opposite:

In effect, we have added more to the left-hand side,
so the equilibrium shifts to the right, as if to remove it.
Let's look at an example:

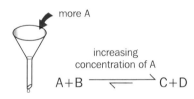

*equilibrium moves to right
to reduce the concentration of A*

Example
You might remember that bromine water is used to test
for unsaturated hydrocarbons (see page 178).
The strength of its yellow colour tells us
how many bromine molecules (Br_2) are in the solution.
If we add a little sodium hydroxide solution (alkali) to bromine water,
the solution turns colourless.

If we now add dilute hydrochloric acid, the yellow colour returns.

● What do these results tell you about the concentration
of bromine molecules?

Let's see if we can explain these observations:

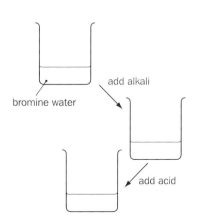

Bromine water is an equilibrium mixture:

$$Br_2(aq) + H_2O(l) \rightleftharpoons Br^-(aq) + OBr^-(aq) + 2\,H^+(aq)$$
yellow   colourless

When you add alkali (OH⁻), H⁺ ions are removed.
The acidic $H^+(aq)$ ions are neutralised by the $OH^-(aq)$ ions:

$$H^+(aq) + OH^-(aq) \longrightarrow H_2O(l)$$

Acid plus alkali gives a salt and water, H^+ ions are led to the slaughter!

The equilibrium moves to the right to try to replace the $H^+(aq)$ ions.
This means that more bromine molecules, Br_2, and H_2O must react
to form more $H^+(aq)$ ions to replace those removed from solution.
So the yellow colour fades as bromine molecules are used up.

When you add acid, $H^+(aq)$ ions are added to the mixture.
The equilibrium shifts to the left to get rid of them.
This makes more Br_2 molecules, and the yellow colour
gets deeper again.

▷ Changing pressure

Changing the pressure can also affect a mixture at equilibrium.
However, there must be different numbers
of gas molecules on either side of the equation.

Look at the diagram opposite:
If you increase the pressure, the equilibrium shifts to
try to reduce it again.
Moving to the side with the least number of gas molecules
will lower the pressure.
● Why would the position of equilibrium in a reaction with
  equal numbers of gas molecules on either side of the equation
  be unaffected by pressure?

Let's look at an example where pressure does affect
the equilibrium mixture:

You might have seen brown nitrogen dioxide (NO_2) gas when studying
the breakdown of nitrates.
In a closed system, the nitrogen dioxide forms an equilibrium mixture
with dinitrogen tetroxide (N_2O_4). This is a pale yellow gas:

$$2\,NO_2(g) \rightleftharpoons N_2O_4(g)$$
brown gas   pale yellow gas

If we take some NO_2 gas in a sealed syringe, we can look at
the effects of changing the pressure.
When we press the plunger down, the pressure is increased.
● What do you think will happen?
At first the brown colour gets deeper as the concentration of NO_2 increases.
But then if you look carefully, you can see that the colour of the brown gas
gets paler.
The position of equilibrium shifts to try to decrease the pressure.
It moves to the right, to the side with the fewest molecules of gas.

● Explain what would happen if you pulled the plunger outwards.

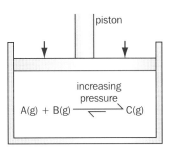

piston

increasing pressure

$$A(g) + B(g) \rightleftharpoons C(g)$$

equilibrium moves to the side with
the least number of gas molecules
to reduce the pressure.

(Remember that the pressure
of a gas is related to the number
of molecules present.)

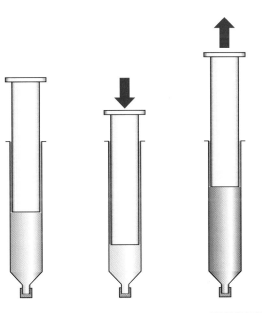

▶ Changing temperature and equilibrium

Look back to Le Châtelier's Principle on page 358:

Can you say what will happen if you increase the temperature
of an equilibrium mixture?
The position of the equilibrium shifts to reduce the temperature.
But how can it do that?

Let's use the example of nitrogen dioxide from the last page:

When NO_2 reacts to form N_2O_4 the reaction is exothermic.
The temperature rises in the reaction.
On the other hand, when N_2O_4 breaks down to NO_2 it is endothermic.
The temperature falls.

Look at the enthalpy level diagram opposite:

If we take a sealed vessel of the equilibrium mixture,
then cool it down, what do you think will happen?
How can the equilibrium shift in order to increase
the temperature again?
In other words, how can it shift to oppose the change
that you have introduced?

Look at the diagrams below:

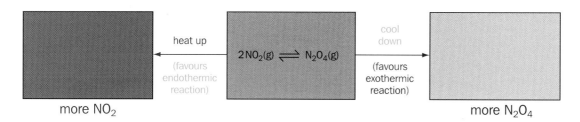

We can generalise and say that in an equilibrium mixture:

> **Increasing** the temperature favours the endothermic reaction.
> **Decreasing** the temperature favours the exothermic reaction.

exothermic

$$2NO_2(g) \rightleftharpoons N_2O_4(g)$$

endothermic

Can you see the different activation energies for the forward and backward reactions?

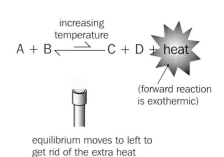

equilibrium moves to left to
get rid of the extra heat
and reduce the temperature

Look at the reaction below:
It is used in industry to make ammonia (NH_3) in the Haber process.
(See pages 362 and 363.)

$$N_2(g) + 3\,H_2(g) \rightleftharpoons 2\,NH_3(g) \qquad \Delta H = -92 \text{ kJ mol}^{-1}$$

By convention the enthalpy change for the forward reaction
is always quoted. Of course, the equation must be shown
because reactants could be called products if it was written in reverse!

In this case, the forward reaction is exothermic, giving out heat,
Therefore, the backward reaction is endothermic. It takes in heat.
So if you increase the temperature the backward reaction
is favoured, as this will lower the temperature.
Therefore, at high temperatures, the equilibrium mixture
will have more N_2 and H_2 than before.

You can read more about this process on page 363.

▷ Equilibrium in action

Many of the important reactions in industry are reversible.
This is a challenge for industrial chemists.
They have to choose conditions that will produce as much product as possible in the shortest possible time, bearing in mind safety!
You can read about some of this work in the next few pages.

▷ The Contact process

Sulphuric acid is made in the Contact process.
It is one of the most important manufactured chemicals (see page 365).
The raw materials are sulphur, air and water.

Stage 1:

Sulphur is turned into **sulphur dioxide**.
We can import the sulphur on ships from Poland or the U.S.A.
It can also be extracted from impurities in crude oil or natural gas.
However North Sea gas contains very little sulphur, so it can't be used.
The sulphur burns in air:

$$S(l) + O_2(g) \longrightarrow SO_2(g)$$
sulphur   oxygen   sulphur dioxide

Stage 2:

This is the important step because the reaction is reversible.
The sulphur dioxide is turned into **sulphur trioxide**.

$$2\,SO_2(g) + O_2(g) \rightleftharpoons 2\,SO_3(g) \qquad \Delta H = -197\,kJ\,mol^{-1}$$
sulphur dioxide   oxygen   sulphur trioxide

Chemists want as much SO_3 as they can, as quickly as possible.
Notice that the reaction is exothermic.
A low temperature would favour the forward reaction. But if it's too low, the rate of reaction will be too slow. A compromise of 450 °C is chosen.
You still get a good yield (97%) of SO_3 at this temperature, and at a reasonable rate.

So what about the pressure chosen? Count the molecules of gas on either side of the equation. How could you get more SO_3?
Increased pressure would also favour more SO_3, but with a 97% yield anyway, it's not worth spending much money compressing the gases.
They are compressed slightly to push them through the pipes and reaction vessels.
The pressure is only just above 1 atmosphere or 100 kPa.

A catalyst, vanadium(V) oxide, is used to speed up the rate at which equilibrium is reached.
● Why do you think there are 4 layers of catalyst?

Stage 3:

In the final stage sulphur trioxide is converted into **sulphuric acid.** The sulphur trioxide gets absorbed into a mixture of 98% sulphuric acid and 2% water. In effect, the sulphur trioxide reacts with the water:

$$SO_3(g) + H_2O(l) \longrightarrow H_2SO_4(l)$$
sulphur trioxide   water   sulphuric acid

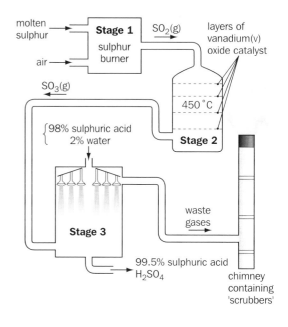

Economic and environmental aspects

● 99.5% of the sulphur dioxide in stage 2 gets converted into sulphur trioxide. Sulphur dioxide causes acid rain, so there are strict controls on the waste gases. Scrubbers use calcium carbonate (a base) to react with acidic gases in the chimney.

● The reactions in each stage give out heat. This energy is not wasted, but used to heat gases.

● If you use water to absorb the sulphur trioxide in stage 3, a fine mist of sulphuric acid is formed. This can't be condensed and would pollute the air.

361

▷ The Haber process

Ammonia is another very important chemical.
The Haber process is used in industry to make ammonia.
It is the raw material for many fertilisers, such as ammonium nitrate.
Ammonia is also used to make nitric acid, which is used
to make explosives.

These uses meant that it was important to discover
how to make ammonia on a large scale.

It was just before the First World War in Germany.
In their preparation for war, the Germans realised
that they would need to make their own
fertilisers and explosives.
Both were made from nitrogen compounds imported
from South America.
The supplies of nitrogen compounds – from bird droppings
in Peru and sodium nitrate from Chile – had nearly
run out. When war started, they wouldn't be able to
ship them back to Germany anyway.

So scientists raced to find a way to turn nitrogen gas in the air
into useful nitrogen compounds.

Fritz Haber was a lecturer in a technical college in Germany.
In 1909 he managed to make an equilibrium mixture
containing nitrogen, hydrogen and ammonia.

$$N_2(g) + 3\,H_2(g) \rightleftharpoons 2\,NH_3(g)$$

Haber's apparatus is shown opposite:

He had shown that it was possible to turn nitrogen into ammonia.
But with this equipment, he could only make about 100 g of ammonia!

Then BASF, a German chemical company, invested over a million pounds
to 'scale up' the process. The process needed high pressures.
The first reaction vessel blew up under the strain!

It was a chemical engineer called Carl Bosch who solved the problem.
He devised a double-walled steel vessel which could work safely
at 300 times atmospheric pressure.

Over 6500 experiments were carried out to find the best catalyst.
An **iron catalyst** worked well.
It was improved further by adding traces of other metal oxides.

In 1913, the first ammonia factory was making about 30 tonnes a day.
Without this supply, the First World War might have ended much sooner.

However, the Haber process is still used today to make
millions of tonnes of ammonia. About 85 per cent of this ammonia
goes on to make fertilisers to help feed the world!
This shows us both the good and bad effects of the chemical industry.

Fritz Haber (1868–1934) got the Nobel Prize for Chemistry in 1918 for making ammonia from nitrogen and hydrogen

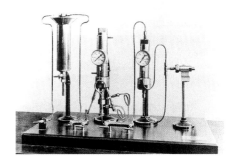

Haber's apparatus

Carl Bosch (1874–1940) was awarded the Nobel Prize for Chemistry in 1931 for his work on high-pressure reactions

Conditions chosen for the Haber Process

Look at the reaction below:

$$N_2(g) + 3\,H_2(g) \;\rightleftharpoons\; 2\,NH_3(g) \qquad \Delta H = -92\,kJ\,mol^{-1}$$

People running the process must choose conditions carefully.
They want to make as much ammonia as possible, as quickly as possible.

Look at the graphs opposite:

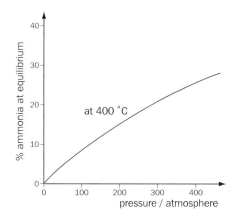

- What happens to the amount of ammonia in the
  equilibrium mixture when you
  – raise the pressure?
  – raise the temperature?

You can get high yields of ammonia by using high pressure
and a low temperature.
The conditions chosen for the Haber process are:

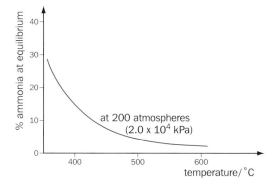

> - **a pressure between 150 and 300 atmospheres**
>   **(i.e. between $1.5 \times 10^4\,kPa$ and $3.0 \times 10^4\,kPa$)**
> - **a temperature of about 400 °C – 450 °C**
> - **an iron catalyst**

- Why do you think that we don't use even higher pressures?
  What about the costs involved?

Think about the safety problems that Bosch faced.
Higher pressures need ever thicker pipes and reaction vessels.
This adds to the initial costs of building the plant (called capital costs).
Also, compressing gases takes energy and therefore costs money.

- Why aren't lower temperatures than 400 °C used?

Think about your work on rates of reaction.
It's no use getting a very high yield if you have to wait days to get it!
Remember that the iron catalyst will speed up the rate
at which equilibrium is reached, but won't affect its position.
The equilibrium mixture would contain only about 15% ammonia.
However, equilibrium is never actually reached as ammonia
is constantly drawn off by cooling it down into a liquid.

> **Raw materials for the Haber process**
> Air (for nitrogen)
> Natural gas (to make hydrogen)
> Steam (to make hydrogen and to
> generate high pressures)

Costs are reduced by:
- recycling unused nitrogen and hydrogen, and
- using the energy given off in the reaction to heat up the in-coming gases.

You can see a flow chart for the Haber process below:

The Haber Process

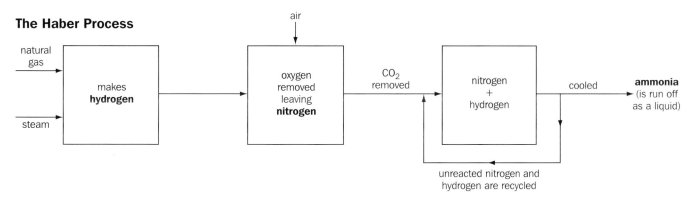

▷ Making nitric acid in industry

Have you ever seen a farmer or a gardener spreading fertiliser
on the soil?
Farmers add millions of tonnes of fertilisers to the soil each year.

Most fertilisers contain **nitrogen**, for example, ammonium nitrate.
Its chemical formula is NH_4NO_3.
Plants need nitrogen to grow. They use it to make proteins
and other essential compounds.

Ammonium nitrate is made by reacting ammonia, from the Haber process,
with nitric acid.
Ammonia is also the starting material for making the nitric acid itself.
Let's look at its manufacture in industry:

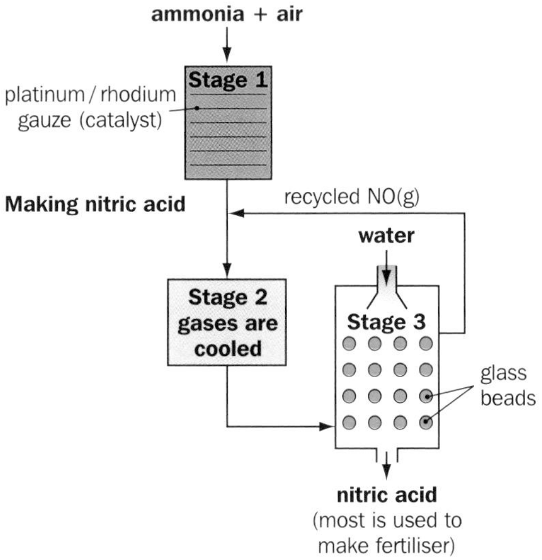

*Ammonia and nitric acid make ammonium
nitrate fertiliser*

Stage 1:

In the first stage ammonia reacts with oxygen.
The ammonia is *oxidised* in a reversible reaction.
This reaction will not happen without a catalyst.
A platinum, mixed with rhodium, gauze is used:

$$\underset{\text{ammonia}}{4\,NH_3(g)} + \underset{\text{oxygen}}{5\,O_2(g)} \overset{\text{platinum/rhodium}}{\rightleftharpoons} \underset{\text{nitrogen monoxide}}{4\,NO(g)} + \underset{\text{water}}{6\,H_2O(g)} \qquad \Delta H = -910\,\text{kJ mol}^{-1}$$

● What conditions would favour making more nitrogen monoxide (NO)?
In fact, the temperature at the surface of the gauze is about 900 °C.
● Can you see why? (Look at the enthalpy change of the reaction.)
The reaction gives out enough energy to heat up the reacting gases itself.

A pressure of 7 atmospheres (7.0×10^2 kPa) is used.
● Why do you think this relatively low pressure for industry is chosen?
Look at the gas molecules on either side of the equation. Is there much difference?
Will it be worth spending a lot compressing the gases to a very high pressure?
This slightly increased pressure is used to move the gases around the system.

Stage 2:

Then the nitrogen monoxide is mixed with air.
It changes into nitrogen dioxide:

$$\underset{\text{nitrogen monoxide}}{2\,NO(g)} + \underset{\text{oxygen}}{O_2(g)} \rightleftharpoons \underset{\text{nitrogen dioxide}}{2\,NO_2(g)} \qquad \Delta H = -115\,\text{kJ mol}^{-1}$$

● Why do you think that the gases are cooled at this stage?

Stage 3:

Finally, the nitrogen dioxide reacts with water
to make **nitric acid, HNO_3**.

$$\underset{\text{nitrogen dioxide}}{3\,NO_2(g)} + \underset{\text{water}}{H_2O(l)} \longrightarrow \underset{\text{nitric acid}}{2\,HNO_3(aq)} + \underset{\text{nitrogen monoxide}}{NO(g)}$$

Most of this nitric acid is used to make fertilisers with ammonia.
The siting of a fertiliser factory is discussed on page 366.

ammonia + air

platinum / rhodium
gauze (catalyst)

Stage 1

Making nitric acid

recycled NO(g)

water

**Stage 2
gases are
cooled**

Stage 3

glass
beads

nitric acid
(most is used to
make fertiliser)

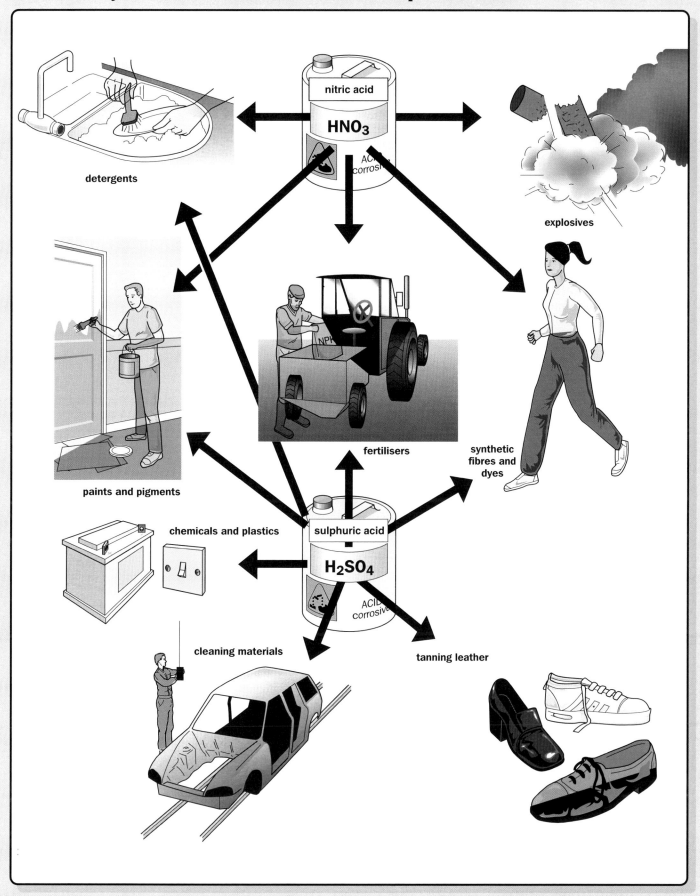

detergents

nitric acid

HNO₃

ACID corrosive

explosives

paints and pigments

fertilisers

synthetic fibres and dyes

chemicals and plastics

sulphuric acid

H₂SO₄

ACID corrosive

cleaning materials

tanning leather

▶ Chemistry at work: Building a chemical plant

As you can see from the previous page, both nitric acid
and sulphuric acid are used to make fertilisers.
There is a large fertiliser factory at Billingham on Teesside.
We can see why this site was chosen to build the plant on this page.

The factory can make its own ammonia and nitric acid.
These react with each other to make **ammonium nitrate,** NH_4NO_3.
Which essential element does this supply to plants?

There is also a sulphuric acid plant on the site.
The sulphuric acid is used to make phosphoric acid from
phosphate rock.
The phosphoric acid reacts with more ammonia to make
ammonium phosphate fertiliser, $(NH_4)_3PO_4$.
Look at the formula of ammonium phosphate above:
Which **two** essential elements does it provide?

Potassium is put into fertilisers as **potassium chloride,** KCl,
or **potassium nitrate,** KNO_3.
Which potassium compound provides **two** essential elements?
Look at the map below:

This is the ICI site at Billingham

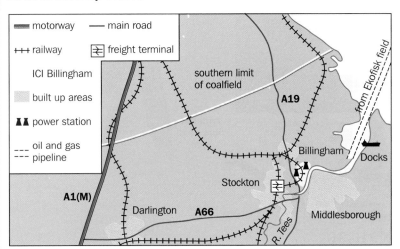

So why build the factory at Billingham?
It is near the North Sea. This is important for a supply of natural gas (methane, CH_4).
Remember that natural gas is a raw material for the Haber process.
(See page 363.)

*   What else would you need methane for in the factory?

*   Which river is nearby? Plenty of water is needed to make steam.
*   What is steam used for when making ammonia?
    Can you remember the **pressure** used in the Haber process?

*   Is the factory near a port to bring in phosphate rock and sulphur
    (needed to make sulphuric acid) from other countries?
The company can also export its fertilisers from a port.

*   Why are good road and rail links important?
*   What would be your concerns if a large fertiliser factory
    was built near your home?

You need good transport to distribute your product

Summary

- Many reactions are 'one-way' only.
  Reactants form products. The products formed cannot turn back into the reactants again.

- Some reactions are **reversible**.
  Reactants form products, but the products can also react together to form the reactants again.

- In a closed system, where nothing is allowed to escape, a reversible reaction can reach a position of **equilibrium**.
  The amounts of reactants and products stay the same.
- At this point, the reaction is in **dynamic** equilibrium.
  The forward reaction and the backward reaction are going ***at the same rate***.

- The position of the equilibrium can be altered by changing conditions.
  The equilibrium always shifts to try to cancel out the change introduced.
  For example, increasing the temperature favours the endothermic reaction.

  If gases are involved, increasing the pressure will shift the position of equilibrium
  towards the side with fewer molecules of gas.

  Adding a catalyst does not affect the composition of an equilibrium mixture.
  However, it does speed up the rate at which equilibrium is reached.

▶ Questions

1 Copy and complete:

If we have a .... reaction in a closed system, then the reactants and .... will reach a position of .....
In this situation, the amounts of reactant and .... are .... because the rate of the .... reaction is the same as the rate of the .... reaction. We call this .... equilibrium.

If we change the conditions, the .... of equilibrium shifts in the direction that will counteract the .....

A .... will speed up the rate at which equilibrium is ...., but will not affect the .... of equilibrium.

2 Look at the reaction below:

$$H_2O(g) + C(s) \rightleftharpoons CO(g) + H_2(g) \qquad \Delta H = +130 \, kJ \, mol^{-1}$$

Explain what happens to the position of equilibrium if we:

a) increase the pressure
b) increase the concentration of hydrogen gas
c) increase the temperature
d) add a catalyst?

3 Dichromate(VI) ions ($Cr_2O_7^{2-}$) are orange and chromate(VI) ions (CrO_4^{2-}) are yellow:

$$2 \, CrO_4^{2-}(aq) + 2 \, H^+(aq) \rightleftharpoons Cr_2O_7^{2-}(aq) + H_2O(l)$$

What will happen to the colour of the equilibrium mixture if we add:
a) acid (H^+(aq) ions)?
   Explain your answer.
b) alkali (OH^-(aq) ions)?
   Explain your answer.

4 Look at the reaction below:
$$PCl_5(s) \rightleftharpoons PCl_3(l) + Cl_2(g)$$

a) What happens to the amount of solid present in the equilibrium mixture if we increase the pressure?
b) When we increase the temperature the amount of solid decreases. What does this tell you about the enthalpy change of the forward reaction?

5 What will be the effect of decreasing the pressure on each of the equilibrium mixtures below?

a) $2 \, NO_2(g) \rightleftharpoons N_2O_4(g)$

b) $2 \, H_2(g) + CO(g) \rightleftharpoons CH_3OH(g)$

c) $CaCO_3(s) \rightleftharpoons CaO(s) + CO_2(g)$

d) $Br_2(l) \rightleftharpoons Br_2(g)$

e) $H_2(g) + I_2(g) \rightleftharpoons 2 \, HI(g)$

f) $ICl(l) + Cl_2(g) \rightleftharpoons ICl_3(s)$

6 Ammonia is made in industry by the Haber process.
a) Write the word and symbol equation for making ammonia.
b) What are the raw materials for the nitrogen and hydrogen used in the process?
c) What is the catalyst used?
d) What temperature and pressure are chosen for the process?
e) Explain why the conditions in d) are used.

7 Describe how we make sulphuric acid and nitric acid in industry. Include a flow diagram of each process and explain the conditions used wherever reversible reactions are involved.

30 Equilibrium constants

In the last chapter we saw how reversible reactions, in a closed system, can form mixtures in dynamic equilibrium.

Chemists have studied many of these equilibrium mixtures in detail. Their experiments show us that there is a relationship between the concentrations of reactants and products.
We call this the **Equilibrium Law**.
Unlike the rate equations in Chapter 28, this relationship is related to the balanced chemical equation.

Let's look at the equilibrium mixture below:

$$2\,HI(g) \;\rightleftharpoons\; H_2(g) + I_2(g)$$

Experiments show us that at equlilibrium:

$$\frac{[H_2(g)]_{eq} \times [I_2(g)]_{eq}}{[HI(g)]^2_{eq}} = K_c \text{ (a constant at any given temperature)}$$

K_c is called the **equilibrium constant**.
(The 'c' in K_c refers to concentrations.)

- Can you see how the balanced equation relates to the equilibrium expression?

We can generalise this **Equilibrium Law** as shown below:

For the equilibrium mixture:

$$m\,A + n\,B \;\rightleftharpoons\; y\,C + z\,D$$

the equilibrium constant is given by the expression:

$$K_c = \frac{[C]^y_{eq}[D]^z_{eq}}{[A]^m_{eq}[B]^n_{eq}}$$

So the products from the forward reaction come on the top line of the expression.
The reactants appear on the bottom line.

You can see why it is essential to write the chemical equation you are referring to. For example, if we had written:

$$H_2(g) + I_2(g) \;\rightleftharpoons\; 2\,HI(g)$$

then the equilibrium constant would be worked out from:

$$K_c' = \frac{[HI(g)]^2_{eq}}{[H_2(g)]_{eq} \times [I_2(g)]_{eq}} \left(\text{which equals } \frac{1}{K_c}\right)$$

Example

Let's look at the first equation again:

$$2\,HI(g) \;\rightleftharpoons\; H_2(g) + I_2(g)$$

We can find out the actual concentrations of HI(g), H_2(g) and I_2(g) in an equilibrium mixture by experiment.
We can use titration or a colorimeter in this case.
What would we have to do before titration could be used?
(Hint: Look at the state symbols in the equation.)

Here are some results below, taken at 827 °C:

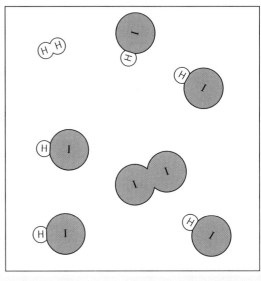

	Concentration at equilibrium / mol dm^{-3}
HI(g)	0.05
H$_2$(g)	0.01
I$_2$(g)	0.01

To find the value of K_c we put the results from the table into the equilibrium expression:

$$K_c = \frac{[H_2(g)]_{eq} \times [I_2(g)]_{eq}}{[HI(g)]^2_{eq}}$$

So this becomes:

$$K_c = \frac{0.01 \times 0.01}{(0.05)^2}$$

$$K_c = \mathbf{0.04}$$

(K_c has no units in this case.)

An equilibrium mixture of HI(g), H$_2$(g) and I$_2$(g) at 827 °C. The intensity of violet colour can be used to work out the concentration of I$_2$(g)

Units of K_c

Notice that K_c has no units in the example above.
You can see why below:
We work out the units by entering all the concentration units into the equilibrium expression.
Then, as with the rate equations in Chapter 28, we cancel them out to arrive at the units for K_c.

Let's look at another reaction we've seen in the last chapter:

$$2\,NO_2(g) \;\rightleftharpoons\; N_2O_4(g)$$

$$K_c = \frac{[N_2O_4(g)]_{eq}}{[NO_2(g)]^2_{eq}}$$

Substituting in the units of concentration, we get:

$$K_c = \frac{mol\,dm^{-3}}{(mol\,dm^{-3})^2} = \frac{\cancel{mol\,dm^{-3}}}{\cancel{mol\,dm^{-3}} \times mol\,dm^{-3}} = \frac{1}{mol\,dm^{-3}} = \mathbf{mol^{-1}\,dm^3}$$

If there are the same number of moles on each side of the balanced equation, K_c will have no units

The value of K_c for this reaction is found by experiment to be 8.7 at 298 K.
So K_c should be written as 8.7 mol^{-1} dm^3.

● Can you see why the earlier example had no units?
(Remember to say if there are no units when answering exam questions.)

▷ Values of K_c

On the last page we looked at the equilibrium constants for two reactions.

For the reaction, at 827 °C, $2\,HI(g) \rightleftharpoons H_2(g) + I_2(g)$, K_c is 0.04.

In the other reaction at 25 °C, $2\,NO_2(g) \rightleftharpoons N_2O_4(g)$, K_c is $8.7\,mol^{-1}\,dm^3$.

But what do these values of K_c tell us about the equilibrium mixtures
in the two reactions?
Are there more reactants or products in the equations as written?

Remember that products appear on the top line of the equilibrium expression.
Reactants are on the bottom.
So what can you say about the value of K_c if we have a lot more products
than reactants?

I see a large K_c — you will be rich in products.

**For large values of K_c, the position of the equilibrium lies well
over to the right.
Products predominate in the equilibrium mixture.**

For values of K_c near 1, there is a fairly equal balance of reactants and products
in the equilibrium mixture.

**For small values of K_c, the position of the equilibrium lies well
over to the left.
Reactants predominate in the equilibrium mixture.**

All chemical reactions can be thought of as reversible reactions
to some extent. But **if K_c is very large**, e.g. 10^{10},
we can say that the reaction has **gone to completion**.

On the other hand, **if K_c is very small**, e.g. 10^{-10},
then there is **effectively no reaction**.

So what can we say about our two examples above?
In the first one:

$$\frac{[H_2(g)]_{eq} \times [I_2(g)]_{eq}}{[HI(g)]^2_{eq}} = 0.04$$

This tells us that the number on the bottom line must be bigger
than the number on the top line of the equilibrium expression.
$(0.04 = 4/100.)$
In fact, the value of $[HI(g)]^2$ must be 25 times greater than
the value of $[H_2(g)] \times [I_2(g)]$. So if we start with pure HI,
then at 827 °C, the position of equilibrium must lie to the left.
There is more HI present in the mixture than H_2 and I_2.
In the second example:

$$\frac{[N_2O_4(g)]_{eq}}{[NO_2(g)]^2_{eq}} = 8.7\,mol^{-1}\,dm^3$$

● Which number is bigger: the value of $[N_2O_4(g)]$ or $[NO_2(g)]^2$?
The position of equilibrium lies over to the right,
in favour of the product, N_2O_4, at 25 °C.

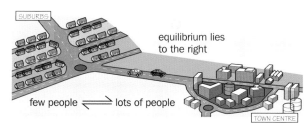

*Just after rush hour there are more people in the town
centre than in the suburbs. Some people go home early
but these are replaced in the town centre by shoppers.
K_c will be large*

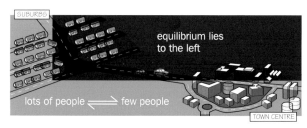

*At night, most people have gone home. Some night-time
workers arrive in the town centre, but these are replaced in
the suburbs by people leaving work late.
K_c will be small*

▶ Finding K_c by experiment

Now we'll look at an equilibrium mixture made up from solutions.
We will see how to calculate its equilibrium constant in an experiment.

Ammonia dissolves in water and in organic solvents.
In this experiment the two solutions must be immiscible (do not mix)
so that two layers form.
We want to find the equilibrium constant when the two solutions
are in contact.

$$NH_3(aq) \rightleftharpoons NH_3(\text{organic solvent})$$

If we start with a solution of ammonia in water and shake this
with an equal volume of the organic solvent, some of the ammonia
will dissolve in the organic layer.
Eventually dynamic equilibrium will be set up.
At this point, the rate at which ammonia leaves the water layer
will be the same as the rate at which it enters from the organic layer.
Look at the diagram opposite:

Can you think how we could find the concentration of ammonia
in each layer?
Ammonia is alkaline. So we can titrate it against acid
that we know the concentration of.
Look at the results below:

We start with a 0.100 mol dm^{-3} solution of ammonia in water at 20 °C.
Once equilibrium has been reached, we run off a 20.0 cm^3 portion
of the aqueous (water) layer.
We titrate this against 0.100 mol dm^{-3} hydrochloric acid, using methyl red indicator.
The end point is reached when 18.8 cm^3 of acid have been added.

We can find the concentration of ammonia in the aqueous layer:

$$NH_3(aq) + HCl(aq) \longrightarrow NH_4Cl(aq)$$

This shows us that 1 mole of hydrochloric acid reacts with 1 mole of ammonia.
In the titration we used:

$\dfrac{18.8 \times 0.100}{1000}$ moles of hydrochloric acid, which reacted with the same number of moles of ammonia.

$= 1.88 \times 10^{-3}$ moles

So we have 1.88×10^{-3} moles of ammonia in 20 cm^3.
Now we can find its concentration by working out
the number of moles in 1000 cm^3 (1 dm^3):

concentration of ammonia dissolved in water $= 1.88 \times 10^{-3} \times \dfrac{1000}{20}$ mol dm^{-3}

$$= 0.094 \text{ mol dm}^{-3}$$

Knowing this, we must have $(0.100 - 0.094) = 0.006$ moles of ammonia
in 1 dm^3 of the organic layer.
We can use this to calculate K_c at 20 °C.

$$K_c = \frac{[NH_3(\text{organic solvent})]_{eq}}{[NH_3(aq)]_{eq}}$$

$$= \frac{0.006}{0.094} = \mathbf{6.38 \times 10^{-2}} \quad (K_c \text{ has no units in this case})$$

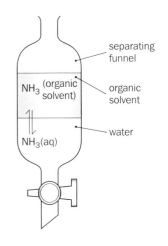

Student using a separating funnel to separate two liquids

separating funnel

NH_3 (organic solvent)

organic solvent

water

$NH_3(aq)$

Titration using methyl red

▷ Gases at equilibrium (K_p)

Partial pressures

Most of the equilibrium mixtures we have looked at so far
have involved gases. To find their equilibrium constants
we have used concentrations.
But we often use measurements of pressure to indicate how much gas
is in a space. The higher the pressure, the more gas in the space,
and the higher its concentration.

So equilibrium constants for reactions involving gases
are often quoted in terms of **partial pressures** of gas.
The equilibrium constant is then given the symbol K_p. (See next page.)

The partial pressure of a gas in a mixture is the pressure due to that particular gas.

For example, say that you have a box containing half hydrogen
and half oxygen gas.
The total pressure in the box is 100 kPa.

The partial pressure of hydrogen, given the symbol p_{H_2}, is 50 kPa.
The partial pressure of oxygen, p_{O_2}, in the mixture is also 50 kPa.

We can say this because the pressure caused by equal amounts
of any gas, at a certain temperature and volume, is the same.
1 mole of hydrogen gas will be at the same pressure as 1 mole of oxygen
under the same conditions.
Look at the diagram below:

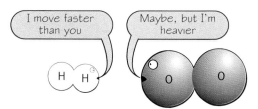

$$\frac{\text{pressure}}{\text{of a gas}} \propto \text{its concentration}$$

The more gas in a given volume, the higher the pressure

The same number of moles of any gas will exert the same force per unit area as they bash against the walls of their container

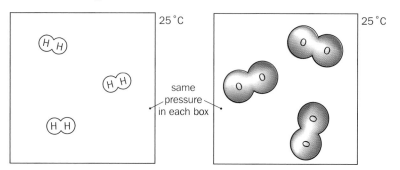

(The units of pressure are Pascals, where $1\,\text{Pa} = 1\,\text{N m}^{-2}$.
Standard pressure is taken as 101 000 Pa or 101 kPa,
sometimes rounded off to 100 kPa).

In this example it was easy to work out the partial pressures
because we had a 50 : 50 mixture.
In more difficult examples, we work out the fraction of each gas
in the mixture from the number of moles of each gas present.
This is called the **mole fraction** of the gas.

> **mole fraction of gas X** $= \dfrac{\textbf{number of moles of X}}{\textbf{total number of moles of gas}}$

In our example above, the mole fraction of hydrogen is 0.5.
What is the mole fraction of oxygen?
So we can say that:

> **the partial pressure of a gas = its mole fraction × total pressure**

In the example above, the partial pressure of oxygen $= 0.5 \times 100\,\text{kPa} = 50\,\text{kPa}$.

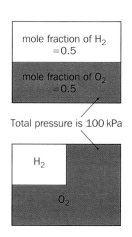

What are the partial pressures of H_2 and O_2 in this box?

Example
An equilibrium mixture contains 0.20 moles of steam (H_2O), 0.50 moles of carbon monoxide (CO), 0.80 moles of hydrogen (H_2) and 0.25 moles of carbon dioxide (CO_2) at 560 °C.
The total pressure is 125 kPa.
What is the partial pressure of each gas?

1. First of all work out the total number of moles of gas in the mixture:

   total moles of gas = 0.2 + 0.5 + 0.8 + 0.25 = 1.75 moles

2. Now work out the mole fraction of each gas:

$$\text{mole fraction} = \frac{\text{number of moles}}{\text{total number of moles}}$$

mole fraction of $H_2O(g) = \dfrac{0.20}{1.75} = 0.11$ mole fraction of $CO(g) = \dfrac{0.50}{1.75} = 0.29$

mole fraction of $H_2(g) = \dfrac{0.80}{1.75} = 0.46$ mole fraction of $CO_2(g) = \dfrac{0.25}{1.75} = 0.14$

   When you add up all the mole fractions, they should equal 1.
   Can you see why?
   Do the values above (0.11 + 0.29 + 0.46 + 0.14) add up to 1.00?

3. We can finish off by calculating the partial pressures for each gas:

   partial pressure = mole fraction x total pressure

Therefore:

$p_{H_2O} = 0.11 \times 125 = \textbf{13.75 kPa}$ $p_{CO} = 0.29 \times 125 = \textbf{36.25 kPa}$

$p_{H_2} = 0.46 \times 125 = \textbf{57.5 kPa}$ $p_{CO_2} = 0.14 \times 125 = \textbf{17.5 kPa}$

(Remember that adding up the partial pressures should give the total pressure
– check the answers above.)

▶ Working out K_p

The expression for K_p is derived from the balanced equation,
just like K_c. Instead of concentrations we use partial pressures.
In the example above, the reaction is:

$$H_2(g) + CO_2(g) \rightleftharpoons H_2O(g) + CO(g)$$

So the expression for K_p is:

$$K_p = \frac{p_{(H_2O)_{eq}} \times p_{(CO)_{eq}}}{p_{(H_2)_{eq}} \times p_{(CO_2)_{eq}}}$$

At 560 °C we can put in the values we worked out above:

$$K_p = \frac{13.75 \times 36.25}{57.5} \times 17.5 = \textbf{0.50} \text{ (no units)}$$

Notice that there are no units. As with K_c, they cancel out completely
if we have the same number of moles on either side of the balanced equation.

Look at the equilibrium expression opposite:
The units for K_p for the reaction $2\,SO_2(g) + O_2(g) \rightleftharpoons 2\,SO_3(g)$
will be kPa^{-1}. Can you work out why?

$$K_p = \frac{p^2_{(SO_3)_{eq}}}{p^2_{(SO_2)_{eq}} \times p_{(O_2)_{eq}}}$$

▶ The effect of changing conditions on K_c and K_p

In the last chapter we looked at what happened to the position of equilibrium when we altered conditions.
Can you remember how to apply Le Châtelier's Principle?
If we introduce a change to an equilibrium mixture, the position of equilibrium re-adjusts to reduce the effects of the change.
Let's see how changing conditions affects an equilibrium constant:

Effect of changing concentration on K_c

What happens if we increase the concentration of reactants
in an equilibrium mixture?
This will make the forward reaction go faster for a while.
But then, as the products increase in concentration,
the backward reaction speeds up until we reach equilibrium again.
However, the new position of equilibrium will lie further to the right.
The equilibrium mixture will contain more of the products.

> **But the actual value of K_c will *not* be
> changed by altering concentrations.**

At first sight, this seems strange. If we have more products,
then won't the value of K_c increase?
Experiments have shown that this does not happen.
Not all the new reactants added are converted into products.
Although we get more products, we also have more reactants,
so the value of K_c does not change.
K_c stays the same, at any given temperature, no matter how we alter
the concentrations of reactants or products.

We can show this by looking at an example.
We can use the reaction of an alcohol and a carboxylic acid:

$$CH_3CH_2OH(l) + CH_3COOH(l) \underset{}{\overset{acid}{\rightleftharpoons}} CH_3COOCH_2CH_3(l) + H_2O(l)$$

ethanol   ethanoic acid   ethyl ethanoate   water

concentrations at
equilibrium / mol dm^{-3} 0.075   0.075   0.200   0.100
(at 25 °C)

$$K_c = \frac{[CH_3COOCH_2CH_3(l)]_{eq}[H_2O(l)]_{eq}}{[CH_3CH_2OH(l)]_{eq}[CH_3COOH(l)]_{eq}}$$

When we enter the equilibrium concentration into the expression above,
we get $K_c = 3.56$ (no units).
If we suddenly double the concentration of ethanol to 0.150 mol dm^{-3},
experiments show that once equilibrium has been re-established we have:

$[CH_3CH_2OH(l)]_{eq} = 0.131$ mol dm^{-3} and $[CH_3COOH(l)]_{eq} = 0.056$ mol dm^{-3}

$[CH_3COOCH_2CH_3(l)]_{eq} = 0.219$ mol dm^{-3} and $[H_2O(l)]_{eq} = 0.119$ mol dm^{-3}

- Put these new values into the expression for K_c.
Did you find that K_c is roughly the same, bearing in mind some experimental error?

So by increasing the concentration of one of the reactants,
we do get more products, without changing the value of K_c.

> **Altering concentrations
> will affect the position
> of equilibrium, but will
> not change the value
> of K_c.**

Effect of changing pressure on K_p

The pressure of a gas is proportional to its concentration.
So as with concentration on the last page:

K_p is unaffected by changes in pressure.

As we increase the pressure, the position of equilibrium
will shift to the side with fewer molecules of gas.
This has the effect of reducing the pressure again.
But when equilibrium is re-established, the value of K_p
will be the same as before.

The effect of temperature on K_c and K_p

Have you noticed the way that we always give the temperature
when quoting a value for an equilibrium constant?
We have to do this because:

The value of an equilibrium constant changes with temperature. (It is the **only** change that alters the value of K_c or K_p.)

Look at the reaction below:

$$H_2(g) + CO_2(g) \rightleftharpoons H_2O(g) + CO(g) \qquad \Delta H = +41 \text{ kJ mol}^{-1}$$

$$K_c = \frac{[H_2O(g)]_{eq}[CO(g)]_{eq}}{[H_2(g)]_{eq}[CO_2(g)]_{eq}}$$

The table below shows the values of K_c at different temperatures:

Temperature/ °C	K_c (no units in this case)
25	1.00×10^{-5}
427	0.12
627	0.60
827	1.45
1027	2.82

- What happens to the size of K_c as we increase the temperature?
- What does this tell us about the shift in the position of equilibrium?

Look back to Le Châtelier's Principle on page 358:
Now apply it to the reaction above.
- Would you expect more products as we raise the temperature?

The forward reaction is endothermic.
As we increase the temperature, the position of equilibrium
will shift to the right, thereby reducing the temperature.
The new equilibrium mixture will contain more of the products,
and less reactants, than the original mixture.

In this example, if you want more product as quickly as possible,
you would do the reaction at a high temperature.
Not only will more product form, but the rate at which we reach
the point of equilibrium will also be speeded up.
- How does this differ from the Haber process? (See page 363.)

Altering pressure can affect the position of equilibrium, but will not change the value of K_p.

When will altering the pressure not affect the position of equilibrium? For example, count the number of gas molecules on either side of the equation shown lower down this page.

Altering the temperature will affect the position of equilibrium, and change the value of K_c or K_p.

▷ Chemistry at work: Equilibria and growing crops

Equilibrium in a flash?

As you know, the air is mainly a mixture of two gases, oxygen and nitrogen.
At the temperatures and pressures we normally find, the two gases don't react with each other.
But at high temperatures the gases can be made to react.
This is a very important reaction in the nitrogen cycle.

During a thunderstorm, lightning enables some nitrogen oxides to be made. These dissolve in rain and so nitrogen, which is vital for plants to grow well, gets into the soil.
Remember that most plants can't use nitrogen gas directly from the air.
Look at the reaction below for nitrogen reacting with oxygen:

$$N_2(g) + O_2(g) \rightleftharpoons 2NO(g)$$

Values for K_p at different temperatures are in the table opposite:

- What can you say about the position of equilibrium at all of the temperatures shown? Why doesn't this surprise you?
- Is the forward reaction exothermic or endothermic? How can you work this out?
- So what do you think happens in a lightning flash?

The same reaction is responsible for some of the pollution from cars.
In the high temperatures in a car engine, even unreactive nitrogen reacts.

- Can you remember how we are reducing pollution from nitrogen oxides given off by cars? (See page 169.)

What happens to the equilibrium at the high temperatures generated by a flash of lightning?

Temperature/°C	K_p (no units in this case)
25	4×10^{-31}
427	5×10^{-13}
827	4×10^{-8}
1227	1×10^{-5}

Wot! NO gas? And no units!

Striking a balance

We looked at the Haber process on page 363. It is used to make ammonia:

$$N_2(g) + 3H_2(g) \rightleftharpoons 2NH_3(g) \qquad \Delta H = -92\,\text{kJ mol}^{-1}$$

Most of the ammonia goes on to make fertilisers. So this is an artificial way of getting nitrogen from the air into the soil.
Look at the values for K_p at different temperatures:

Temperature / °C	K_p / kPa^{-2}
25	6.76×10^{1}
127	4.07×10^{-5}
227	3.55×10^{-6}
327	1.66×10^{-7}
427	7.76×10^{-9}
527	6.92×10^{-10}

- Can you see why the units of K_p are kPa^{-2}?
- What would the units be if the pressure were measured in atmospheres (atm) instead of kPa?

Crops are harvested. They don't have a chance to replace the nitrogen they have taken from the soil by decaying naturally. So farmers have to add fertilisers to their fields

- Which temperature gives the best yield of ammonia?
- Can you remember the conditions chosen for the process?
Remember that a compromise is reached between the position of equilibrium and the rate of reaction.
- Why is the iron catalyst important in the process?

Pest control

Chemists play an important role in feeding the world.
Not only do they produce the fertilisers to increase crop yields,
but they also protect the crops from pests.

Pesticide molecules, such as the pyrethroids, kill insects
by attacking the nervous system.
They have to get into the insect's nerve-cell membranes to work.
A particular pesticide's activity (or effectiveness) is often
related to its ability to do this. Effective pesticides
move rapidly out of aqueous solution into the fatty tissue
of the cell membrane.

So how is equilibrium involved?
You might remember from page 371 how ammonia dissolves
in two immiscible solvents, namely water and a non-polar organic solvent.
Pesticides will also distribute or partition themselves between two solvents.
They enter the insect in solution, then get absorbed into
the fatty tissue.

The equilibrium expression for the distribution of a solute
between two solvents is sometimes called a **partition coefficient**.
The expression for solute X in solvents A and B is given by:

$$X(\text{solvent A}) \rightleftharpoons X(\text{solvent B})$$

$$K_c \text{ (partition coefficient)} = \frac{[X(\text{solvent B})]_{eq}}{[X(\text{solvent A})]_{eq}}$$

The ratio is constant at a given temperature.

For pesticides, a partition coefficient is calculated where:

$$K_c \text{ (partition coefficient)} = \frac{[\text{pesticide}(\text{octan-1-ol})]_{eq}}{[\text{pesticide}(\text{aq})]_{eq}}$$

Can you draw the structural formula of octan-1-ol?
It is fairly similar to the fatty tissue in insects.
So the larger the value of K_c, the more effective a pesticide
is likely to be.
Chemists look for values between 10^5 and 10^7.

This, of course, tells us nothing about the rate at which the equilibrium
is reached. So other experiments have to be done to check
the speed of absorption.

Genetic engineering has now developed crops that can produce
their own pesticides in their cells.
However, there is much controversy over the long-term effects
of such crops on the environment and on health.
Many crops in the U.S.A. are now genetically modified in some way.

- What are your views on the issue?

Here are two types of pesticide molecule:

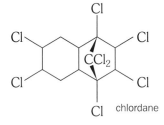

permethrin

*Insects can destroy a crop.
Swarms of locusts can plague farmers
in Africa and the Middle East*

*These protesters are destroying the
genetically modified crops in this test site
in Norfolk*

chlordane

Summary

We can generalise the **Equilibrium Law** as shown below:

For the equilibrium mixture:

$$m\,A + n\,B \rightleftharpoons y\,C + z\,D$$

the **equilibrium constant (K_c)** is given by the expression:

$$K_c = \frac{[C]^y_{eq}[D]^z_{eq}}{[A]^m_{eq}[B]^n_{eq}}$$

For reactions involving gases we can write an equilibrium constant (K_p) in terms of the partial pressures (p) of each gas. For example:

$$2\,HI(g) \rightleftharpoons H_2(g) + I_2(g)$$

$$K_p = \frac{p_{(H_2)eq}\, p_{(I_2)eq}}{p^2_{(HI)eq}}$$

The **units of K_c and K_p** vary depending on the balanced equation it refers to.
To work out the units of K_c, insert the units of concentration ($mol\,dm^{-3}$) into the equilibrium expression, then cancel out as necessary.
For K_p insert the units of pressure (mostly kPa).
If there is the same number of moles on either side of the equation then the equilibrium constant has no units.

The larger the value of K_c or K_p, the further to the right the position of equilibrium lies i.e. the more products are present in the equilibrium mixture.

Here is a summary of the effects of different conditions on equilibrium mixtures:

Alter this factor	Does it affect the position of equilibrium?	Does it affect the value of K_c or K_p?
concentration	yes	no
pressure	yes (if there are different numbers of gas molecules on either side of the equation)	no
catalyst	no	no
temperature	yes	yes

For an **exothermic** reaction, the value of the equilibrium constant **decreases as we raise the temperature**.
For an **endothermic** reaction, the value of the equilibrium constant **increases as we raise the temperature**.

Catalysts speed up the rate at which equilibrium is reached. However, they don't affect the composition of the equilibrium mixture.

▶ Questions

1 Copy and complete:

For the equilibrium mixture:

$$a\,E + b\,F \rightleftharpoons c\,G + d\,H$$

we can find K_c (the equilibrium ....) from this expression:

$$K_c = \frac{.... [H]^d_{eq}}{.... ....}$$

If we have .... in the equilibrium mixture, then we use partial .... to work out K_p. For example:

$$s\,T(g) \rightleftharpoons y\,Z(g)$$

$$K_p = \frac{....}{....}$$

If the value of K_c or K_p is large, then we have more of the .... in the .... mixture.

Changing concentrations will affect the .... of equilibrium, but will not change the value of ..... Temperature affects both the .... of equilibrium and the value of .... or ..... For example, when the forward reaction is exothermic, then the value of the equilibrium .... will .... if we raise the temperature. A .... will not affect the composition of the equilibrium mixture, although the equilibrium is established more quickly. So the value of the equilibrium .... is .....

2 a) Write the equilibrium expression used to find K_c for the reaction below:

$$Fe^{3+}(aq) + SCN^-(aq) \rightleftharpoons [Fe(SCN)]^{2-}(aq)$$

b) What will be the units of K_c for the reaction shown in a)?

c) The numerical value of K_c at 298 K is about 1000 for the reaction above.
What does this tell you about the position of the equilibrium at 298 K?

3 Write down the expressions for K_p in the following reactions:

a) $N_2(g) + O_2(g) \rightleftharpoons 2\,NO(g)$

b) $N_2O_4(g) \rightleftharpoons 2\,NO_2(g)$

c) $H_2(g) + Br_2(g) \rightleftharpoons 2\,HBr(g)$

d) In which of the reactions above will K_p have units?
If the partial pressures of the gases are measured in kPa, what are the units of K_p in this case?

4 Ammonia is made in the Haber process by the reaction:

$$N_2(g) + 3\,H_2(g) \rightleftharpoons 2\,NH_3(g)$$

a) Write down the equilibrium expression for K_p.

The partial pressures of the gases in an equilibrium mixture at 723 K (450 °C) are shown below:

	$N_2(g)$	$H_2(g)$	$NH_3(g)$
Partial pressure / 10^2 kPa	48.5	145	106.5

b) What is the total pressure in the example above? (Don't forget to multiply the numbers in the table by 10^2 (100).)

c) Calculate the value of K_p. (Don't forget the units!)

d) What does the value for K_p tell you about the position of the equilibrium in the Haber process under the conditions quoted above?

e) The value of K_p at 298 K (25 °C) is 67.6 kPa^{-2}. Compare this with your answer in part c) and say why the Haber process does not operate at 298 K.

5 We have looked at the equilibrium established between hydrogen iodide, hydrogen and iodine gases at the start of this chapter:

$$2\,HI(g) \rightleftharpoons H_2(g) + I_2(g)$$

At 700 K the value of K_c is 0.02.

a) Write the expression for K_c.

b) Why does K_c have no units in this example?

We start with a 1 dm^3 vessel containing pure hydrogen iodide and leave it to reach equilibrium. At equilibrium, the contents are analysed and we find that there we have 4.8×10^{-4} moles of iodine.

c) How many moles of hydrogen must be present?

d) How many moles of hydrogen iodide are left in the vessel at equilibrium?

(Your answers to parts a) and c) will help you to work this out).

6 We can use equilibrium constants to predict the relative stability of complexes formed by metal ions (see page 141).
For example:

$$[Ag(H_2O)_2]^+(aq) + 2\,NH_3(aq) \rightleftharpoons [Ag(NH_3)_2]^+(aq) + 2\,H_2O(l)$$

The equilibrium constant (called the **stability constant**) for this reaction at 298 K is over 1×10^7 mol^{-2} dm^6.
Which is the more stable of the two silver complex ions? Explain your reasoning.

31 Acid/base equilibria

Most people think of acids as fuming, corrosive liquids
which are very dangerous.
However, not all acids are like this.
Most of us enjoy a little acid on our fish and chips!
Do you know which acid vinegar contains? (See page 230.)

Vinegar has the sharp, sour taste of acids.
(The Latin word for sour is *acidus*.)
Citric acid gives oranges and lemons their sharp taste.
These fruits also contain ascorbic acid, better known as vitamin C!
These are examples of **weak acids**.

Orange juice contains citric acid

You will also have used acids in your science lessons.
The three common acids found in schools and colleges are:

hydrochloric acid	**HCl**
sulphuric acid	**H$_2$SO$_4$**
nitric acid	**HNO$_3$**

These are **strong acids**.

Do you know which one of these strong acids is found
in our stomachs?
Hydrochloric acid is used to help enzymes break down large molecules
in our food into smaller molecules. It also kills bacteria taken in with food.

Fizzy drinks are acidic

***Whether we call an acid strong or weak depends on its equilibrium
mixture when it is added to water.***
We will look at this in more detail on page 384.

From your previous work with acids, you should know that they:

- turn blue litmus red
- have a pH less than 7 (at 25 °C)
- react with a base or an alkali (a soluble base) to give a salt and water only.
    $$HCl(aq) + NaOH(aq) \longrightarrow NaCl(aq) + H_2O(l)$$
    $$H_2SO_4(aq) + CuO(s) \longrightarrow CuSO_4(aq) + H_2O(l)$$
- react with a carbonate to give a salt, carbon dioxide and water:
    $$2\,HCl(aq) + CaCO_3(s) \longrightarrow CaCl_2(s) + CO_2(g) + H_2O(l)$$
- react with metals to give a salt and hydrogen:
    $$2\,HNO_3(aq) + Mg(s) \longrightarrow Mg(NO_3)_2(aq) + H_2(g)$$
    (The metal must be above copper in the Reactivity Series.)

HCl is a strong acid!

Salts are compounds made when we replace the hydrogen in an acid by a metal.

Hydrochloric acid (HCl) makes salts called chlorides.
Sulphuric acid (H$_2$SO$_4$) gives sulphates and hydrogensulphates.
Nitric acid (HNO$_3$) gives nitrates.

▷ Neutralisation

Have you seen adverts for indigestion remedies on TV?
Indigestion feels like a 'burning' sensation in your stomach.
It is caused by too much hydrochloric acid.
You can cure the pain quickly by taking a tablet.
The tablet contains an **alkali** which gets rid of the excess acid.
The reaction between an acid and an alkali is called **neutralisation.**

These tablets neutralise excess acid in the stomach

If you ever get stung by a bee, you'll be grateful for this reaction!
A bee's sting is acidic. It can be neutralised by
treating it with bicarbonate of soda
(sodium hydrogencarbonate, $NaHCO_3$).
- Why shouldn't you use sodium hydroxide on the sting?
- Do you know how to ease the pain from a wasp sting?

Look at the formulae of the strong acids on the last page:
Which element do they all contain?
In fact, **all acids contain hydrogen.**

Bee stings are acidic. Wasp stings are alkaline

You will have noticed that most acids we use are aqueous solutions.
The acid molecules are dissolved in water.
Acids need water before they can show the acidic properties
listed on the previous page.
Let's look at citric acid (the acid in oranges) as an example:

Test	Results for pure citric acid	Results for citric acid solution
blue litmus paper	remains blue	turns red
sodium carbonate	no reaction	fizzes, giving off carbon dioxide
magnesium ribbon	no reaction	fizzes, giving off hydrogen
does it conduct electricity?	no, as no free ions present	yes, as free ions are present in solution

- How does water affect the properties of citric acid?
- Can you think of another test to show if a substance is acidic?

Without water, substances do not show their acidic properties.

Let's see what difference the water makes:
In water, the acid molecules ionise (split up).
We can look at hydrogen chloride gas, $HCl(g)$, as an example:
It only shows its acidic properties when we dissolve it in water.
We call the solution formed hydrochloric acid:

$$HCl(g) \xrightarrow{\text{dissolve in water}} H^+(aq) + Cl^-(aq)$$

Remember that all acids contain hydrogen.
When dissolved in water, the hydrogen enters the solution as $H^+(aq)$ **ions**.

> **It is $H^+(aq)$ ions that make a solution acidic.**

When we neutralise an acid, the $H^+(aq)$ ions are removed from the solution.
Alkaline solutions contain hydroxide ions, $OH^-(aq)$:

> **$H^+(aq) + OH^-(aq) \xrightarrow{\text{neutralisation}} H_2O(l)$**

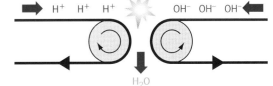

We can think of the H^+ and OH^- ions as 'cancelling each other out'.

▶ The Brønsted–Lowry theory of acids and bases

On the last page we saw how acidic solutions are formed
when $H^+(aq)$ ions are produced.
Can you write the electronic structure of an H^+ ion?
This would be tricky because it has no electrons.
When a hydrogen atom loses its one electron, all we are left with
is a proton.

A proton cannot exist by itself except under extreme conditions.
Its incredibly small size means it has a very high charge density
and will react with any molecules around.
So another way of showing the reaction of HCl with water is:

$$HCl(aq) + H_2O(l) \longrightarrow H_3O^+(aq) + Cl^-(aq)$$

The $H_3O^+(aq)$ ion can be thought of as a water molecule bonded to
an H^+ ion. For convenience we often write $H^+(aq)$ instead.
The Brønsted–Lowry theory says that:

Acids are proton (H^+) donors.
Bases are proton (H^+) acceptors.

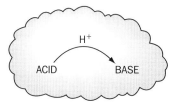

Let's apply the theory to the equation above.
We can think of any acidic molecules dissolving in water
as a reversible reaction:

$$HCl(aq) \; + \; H_2O(l) \; \rightleftharpoons \; H_3O^+(aq) \; + \; Cl^-(aq)$$

donates an H^+ accepts an H^+ donates H^+ ions   accepts H^+ ions

So HCl is an acid, and H_2O is a base.
Each acid has an associated base called its conjugate base.
In our example here, Cl^- is the conjugate base of HCl.
They form an acid–base pair called a **conjugate pair**.
In the example above we have:

$$\underbrace{(HCl(aq)) + (H_2O(l))}_{} \rightleftharpoons (H_3O^+(aq)) + (Cl^-(aq))$$

conjugate pair

Can you see the acid–base conjugate pairs?

Let's look at another example:

$$NH_3(aq) \; + \; H_2O(l) \; \rightleftharpoons \; NH_4^+(aq) \; + \; OH^-(aq)$$

accepts H^+ ion   donates H^+ ion   donates H^+ ion   accepts H^+ ion
base 1   **acid 2**   **acid 1**   **base 2**

● Can you name the acid–base conjugate pairs?
Notice that in this case, water acts as an acid,
unlike the first example above.
So applying the Brønsted–Lowry theory means that water
can behave as an acid or a base depending on the reaction.

H^+ ion = a proton

*A base, like NH_3, always has a lone pair of
electrons available for bonding.
Lone pair donors are sometimes called
Lewis bases.
The acceptor of the lone pair is called a
Lewis acid.*

▷ pH values

You are familiar with the pH scale from your previous work.
What is the name of the indicator we use in a pH test?

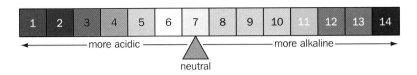

more acidic — neutral — more alkaline

A pH meter gives a more accurate value for the pH of a solution than U.I. paper

We get the range of colours because universal indicator is a mixture.
of different indicators.

But the pH value of a solution can tell a chemist a lot more
than whether a solution is strongly acidic or alkaline.
Which ions make a solution acidic? (See page 381.)
The letters pH come from a German word, *Potenz*, meaning 'power',
and H is from $[H^+]$. Can you remember what square brackets mean?

So a pH value tells us the concentration of $H^+(aq)$ ions in a solution.
But how is a concentration turned into a pH value?
What can you say about the pH of a strongly acidic solution?
The equation linking pH to the concentration of $H^+(aq)$ ions is:

$$pH = -lg\,[H^+(aq)]$$

where lg stands for logarithm (log) to the base 10
e.g. $lg\,10^{-1} = -1$, $lg\,10^{-5} = -5$ (Can you see why *Potenz* is included in **pH**?)

Let's look at some examples to see how this works:

Example
We have a solution of $0.1\ mol\,dm^{-3}$ hydrochloric acid.
What is its pH value?

$pH = -lg\,[H^+]$

In this example the concentration of H^+ ions is
$0.1\ mol\,dm^{-3}$ as HCl almost completely dissociates in water
(see next page). Putting this into the equation we get:

$pH = -lg\,0.1$ (on your calculator, press 0.1,
then log. It should say -1)

$= -(-1)$

$= +1$

So a solution of $0.1\ mol\,dm^{-3}$ HCl(aq) has a pH value of 1.

We can also find out the concentration of $H^+(aq)$ ions when told the pH of a solution:

Example
A solution has a pH of 4.
What is the concentration of hydrogen ions in solution?

$4 = -lg\,[H^+]$

$-4 = lg\,[H^+]$ (on your calculator find the antilog of -4.
Make sure you know how to do this calculation!)

$10^{-4}\ mol\,dm^{-3} = [H^+]$

▶ Strong and weak acids

Would you rather have vinegar or hydrochloric acid
on your fish and chips?
At the start of the chapter, we looked at some examples of
strong and weak acids.
There are weak acids, such as the ethanoic acid in vinegar.
Other acids, like the sulphuric acid in a car battery, are strong acids

Strong acids are better at producing $H^+(aq)$ ions when added to water.
Imagine we have the same number of molecules of a strong and a weak acid,
in the same volume of water.
The strong acid will produce more $H^+(aq)$ ions than the weak acid.
So for the same initial concentration of acid, a solution of a strong acid
contains a greater concentration of $H^+(aq)$ ions.

*Do you enjoy a little ethanoic acid on your
chips? Ethanoic acid is a weak acid*

Let's use hydrochloric acid as an example of a strong acid,
and ethanoic acid as a weak acid.

Strong acids dissociate (split up) almost completely in water.
For hydrochloric acid:

$$HCl(aq) \rightleftharpoons H^+(aq) + Cl^-(aq)$$

the position of equilibrium lies far over to the right.

In weak acids the acid molecules split up, just as in a strong acid.
But at the same time, the H^+ ions and negative ions in solution
join up again. They form the original undissociated acid molecules.
For ethanoic acid:

*A car battery contains sulphuric acid
– a strong acid*

$$\underset{\text{ethanoic acid}}{CH_3COOH(aq)} \rightleftharpoons \underset{\text{ethanoate ion}}{CH_3COO^-(aq)} + H^+(aq)$$

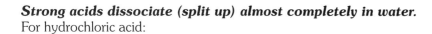

Look back to the acid–base conjugate pairs on page 382.
What is the conjugate base of ethanoic acid?
We can think of the ethanoate ion as being a stronger base than
ethanoic acid is an acid.
In other words, ethanoate ions are better at accepting H^+ ions than
ethanoic acid is at donating H^+ ions.
So the position of equilibrium lies well over to the left.

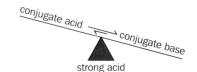

A strong acid has a weak conjugate base

The weaker the acid, the further the equilibrium lies to the left.
There will be more undissociated molecules in the solution,
and fewer $H^+(aq)$ ions – the ions that cause acidic properties.

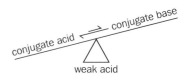

A weak acid has a strong conjugate base

You must take care when using the terms strong, weak,
dilute and concentrated.
Strong and weak refer to an acid's ability to dissociate in water.
Strong acids are effective donators of H^+ ions to water molecules.
They are mostly dissociated in solution.
But you can have a very dilute solution of a strong acid.
The strong acid will still be almost completely dissociated,
but there will be a low concentration of $H^+(aq)$ ions.

▶ Dissociation constants (K_a)

Do you remember how to write an equilibrium expression
from the last chapter?
We can show the degree of dissociation of a weak acid
by its equilibrium constant.
In this case we call it a **dissociation constant** (given the symbol $\boldsymbol{K_a}$
rather than K_c because the 'a' refers to the **a**cid's equilibrium constant).
If we have an acid HX, then:

$$HX(aq) \rightleftharpoons H^+(aq) + X^-(aq)$$

$$K_a = \frac{[H^+(aq)]_{eq}[X^-(aq)]_{eq}}{[HX(aq)]_{eq}}$$

The units of K_a will be $mol\,dm^{-3}$. Can you see why?
(See page 369.)

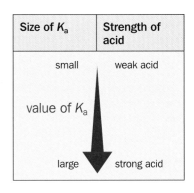

Size of K_a	Strength of acid
small	weak acid
value of K_a	
large	strong acid

- If an acid is strong, what can you say about the top line
  in the equilibrium expression? Will we have a high
  concentration of $H^+(aq)$ and $X^-(aq)$ ions?
  What about the concentration of undissociated HX on the bottom line?

So from this, you can see that we can use the value of K_a
to tell us how strong or weak an acid is. We can say that:

> **The higher the value of K_a, the stronger the acid.**

Look at the values of K_a in the table opposite:

- Which is the strongest acid in the table?
- Which is the weakest acid?

Look at the example below:

Acid	K_a at 25 °C / mol dm^{-3}
ethanoic acid	1.7×10^{-5}
chloroethanoic acid	1.3×10^{-3}
dichloroethanoic acid	5.0×10^{-2}
trichloroethanoic acid	2.3×10^{-1}

Acid	K_a at 25 °C / mol dm^{-3}
hydrochloric acid	1×10^7
nitric acid	40
hydrofluoric acid	5.6×10^{-4}
phenol	1.3×10^{-10}

- What is the pattern as we go down the table?
If we look at the structures of the molecules we can explain the pattern:

Chlorine has a relatively high electronegativity.
So the chlorine atoms are electron-withdrawing groups.
Trichloroethanoic acid has three chlorine atoms all pulling electrons
away from the acidic end of the molecule. This makes it easier
for the O—H bond to break and H^+ ions to be produced.

We can also think of the trichloroethanoate ion as the weakest conjugate base.
The negative charge is not as concentrated at one end of the ion
because of the chlorine atoms. This makes it less attractive to an H^+ ion.

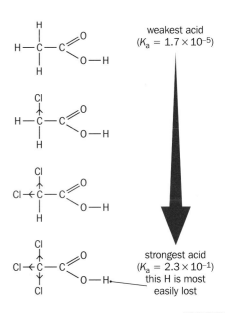

weakest acid
($K_a = 1.7 \times 10^{-5}$)

strongest acid
($K_a = 2.3 \times 10^{-1}$)
this H is most
easily lost

▷ pH of weak acids

On page 383 we worked out the pH of a 0.1 mol dm^{-3} solution
of the strong acid, hydrochloric acid.
This was straightforward because we could assume that
all the HCl molecules were dissociated.
But what happens if we have a weak acid?
As we found on page 384, a large proportion of their molecules
are undissociated. So how can we work out the pH
of a known concentration of a weak acid?

If we know the dissociation constant, we can calculate
the concentration of H$^+$ ions, and hence the pH value.
Let's look at an example:

Oranges contain citric acid – a weak acid

Example
We have a 0.10 mol dm^{-3} solution of ethanoic acid.
What is its pH value?
($K_a = 1.7 \times 10^{-5}$ mol dm^{-3} at 25 °C)

$$CH_3COOH(aq) \rightleftharpoons CH_3COO^-(aq) + H^+(aq)$$
ethanoic acid   ethanoate ion

$$K_a = \frac{[CH_3COO^-(aq)]_{eq}[H^+(aq)]_{eq}}{[CH_3COOH(aq)]_{eq}}$$

If we start with 0.1 mol dm^{-3}, at the point of equilibrium we have:

$$CH_3COOH(aq) \rightleftharpoons CH_3COO^-(aq) + H^+(aq)$$
$$(0.1 - x) \qquad\qquad x \qquad\quad x$$

(because 1 mole of ethanoic acid would give 1 mole of ethanoate ions
and 1 mole of hydrogen ions. So if x moles of ethanoic acid dissociate,
we get x moles of ethanoate ions and x moles of hydrogen ions).
Putting these values into the expression for the dissociation constant:

$$K_a = \frac{x \times x}{(0.1 - x)} = \frac{x^2}{(0.1 - x)} = 1.7 \times 10^{-5}$$

To make the calculation easier, we can assume that $(0.1 - x) = 0.1$.
We can say this because we know that x is very, very small
as ethanoic acid is a weak acid.
Therefore:

$$\frac{x^2}{0.1} = 1.7 \times 10^{-5}$$

$$x = \sqrt{1.7 \times 10^{-5} \times 0.1} = \sqrt{1.7 \times 10^{-6}} = 1.3 \times 10^{-3} \text{ mol dm}^{-3}$$

So [H$^+$] = 1.3×10^{-3} mol dm^{-3}

From this we can work out the pH:

$$pH = -lg\,[H^+]$$
$$= -lg\,(1.3 \times 10^{-3}) = -(-2.9) = 2.9$$

So the pH of a 0.10 mol dm^{-3} solution of ethanoic acid is 2.9.

ethanoic acid   hydrochloric acid
(0.1 M) weak acid   (0.1 M) strong acid

Can you see why the pH of 0.1M HCl
is 1.0? (See page 383)

▶ pH of water

If you were asked to name a neutral liquid,
you would probably say water.
Pure water at 25 °C has a pH of 7, so we can work out
the concentration of $H^+(aq)$ ions present.

$$pH = -lg\,[H^+]$$

$$7 = -lg\,(10^{-7})$$

So the concentration of $H^+(aq)$ ions is $10^{-7}\,mol\,dm^{-3}$.

Can you remember the ions that make a solution alkaline?
What can you say about the number of $H^+(aq)$ ions and $OH^-(aq)$ ions
in a neutral solution.
In a solution with a pH of 7, neither $H^+(aq)$ nor $OH^-(aq)$ are in excess.
There is an *even* balance of the ions responsible for making
solutions acidic or alkaline.
Therefore:

> **In pure water at 25 °C, $[H^+] = [OH^-] = 10^{-7}\,mol\,dm^{-3}$**

*Universal Indicator is green when
the concentration of $H^+(aq)$ ions is
$10^{-7}\,mol\,dm^{-3}$ (pH = 7)*

The ionic product of water

So even in pure water there is a very low concentration of H^+ and OH^- ions.
We can show this:

$$H_2O(l) \rightleftharpoons H^+(aq) + OH^-(aq)$$

and can write an equilibrium expression:

$$K_c = \frac{[H^+(aq)]_{eq}[OH^-(aq)]_{eq}}{[H_2O(l)]_{eq}}$$

But the concentration of a pure liquid, such as water, is constant.
It doesn't matter whether you have $1\,cm^3$ or $10\,000\,cm^3$ of water,
its concentration, the number of moles if you had $1000\,cm^3$, is the same.
This also applies to the concentration of solids.
So we can write a new equilibrium constant:

$$K_c \times [H_2O(l)]_{eq} = [H^+(aq)]_{eq}[OH^-(aq)]_{eq}$$

We call this the **ionic product of water, K_w**:

> **$K_w = [H^+(aq)]_{eq}[OH^-(aq)]_{eq}$**

At 25 °C the ionic product of water = $\mathbf{10^{-14}\,mol^2\,dm^{-6}}$
(i.e. $10^{-7} \times 10^{-7}$).

At other temperatures, the equilibrium is disturbed and a new
position of equilibrium is established. So will the pH of water always be 7?
However, we still say that water is neutral because $[H^+] = [OH^-]$.

*At 100 °C, $K_w = 5.13 \times 10^{-13}\,mol^2\,dm^{-6}$.
What is the pH of pure water at its boiling
point?*

▷ pH of alkalis

What can you say about the pH value of an alkaline solution?
On the last page we met the ionic product of water, K_w, which is a type of equilibrium constant.
We also know from our work in the last chapter that varying concentrations do not affect the value of an equilibrium constant. (See page 374.)

We can use these two bits of information to work out the pH of alkalis.
We know that at 25 °C in any aqueous solution:

Oven cleaners contain strong alkalis to break down (hydrolyse) the grease

> **$[H^+] \times [OH^-]$ will always equal 10^{-14}**

So in our first example on page 383, a solution of $0.1\,mol\,dm^{-3}$ HCl(aq) has an $H^+(aq)$ ion concentration of $0.1\,mol\,dm^{-3}$ (assuming complete dissociation).
So $[H^+] = 0.1 = 10^{-1}$.

We can say that:

$$[H^+][OH^-] = 10^{-14}$$

Putting in our value for $[H^+]$ of 10^{-1}, we get:

$$10^{-1} \times [OH^-] = 10^{-14}$$

$$[OH^-] = \frac{10^{-14}}{10^{-1}} = 10^{-13}\,mol\,dm^{-3}$$

We can use K_w when asked the pH of a strong alkali.
Like a strong acid, a strong alkali dissociates almost completely in solution. In doing so it forms $OH^-(aq)$ ions.

This Universal Indicator paper has been used to test a strong alkali

Example
What is the pH of $0.2\,mol\,dm^{-3}$ sodium hydroxide solution at 25 °C?
We can assume sodium hydroxide (NaOH), a strong alkali, dissociates completely, so we have:

$$[OH^-] = 0.2$$

Put this into the ionic product of water, $K_w = [H^+][OH^-] = 10^{-14}\,mol^2\,dm^{-6}$:

$$[H^+] \times 0.2 = 10^{-14}$$

$$[H^+] = \frac{10^{-14}}{0.2} = 5 \times 10^{-14}$$

We know that:

$$pH = -lg\,[H^+]$$

so the pH of our solution here is:

$$pH = -lg\,(5 \times 10^{-14})$$

$$= -(-13.3)$$

$$= \mathbf{13.3}$$

▷ Indicators

How many indicators can you name?
In this chapter we have recalled our use of universal indicator
to find rough values for the pH of a solution.
(A pH meter will give more accurate readings of pH.)
But often it is useful to use an indicator that has two distinct colours.
We will look at how these can be used in titrations on the next page.

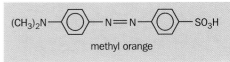

methyl orange

*What would be the formula of In⁻ for
methyl orange?*

We can think of indicators as **weak acids**.
Their molecules are quite complex. Look at the example opposite:

If we represent the indicator as HIn, we can show the equilibrium mixture
in solution as:

$$HIn(aq) \rightleftharpoons H^+(aq) + In^-(aq)$$
$$\text{red} \qquad\qquad\qquad \text{yellow}$$

If HIn is methyl orange we would have the colours shown above.
The acid form of the indicator (HIn) is red, and its conjugate base (In⁻) is yellow.
In this case, the indicator will turn red in acid and yellow in alkali.
Can you see why?

If we add acid to a solution, there is an excess of $H^+(aq)$ ions.
Therefore, the position of equilibrium moves to the left
to remove some of the $H^+(aq)$ ions.
(Think back to Le Châtelier's principle on page 358.)
The indicator will be red.

Methyl orange in acid

On the other hand, if we add alkali, the position of equilibrium
shifts to the right. This will replace some of the $H^+(aq)$ ions lost
as they are neutralised by the $OH^-(aq)$ ions added.
The indicator will be yellow.

We can write an equilibrium expression for the indicator:

$$K_{Ind} = \frac{[H^+(aq)]_{eq}[In^-(aq)]_{eq}}{[HIn(aq)]_{eq}}$$

At the point where an indicator changes between its two colours,
we can say that [HIn] = [In⁻].
So at the indicator's exact '**equivalence point**', the equation above becomes:

$$\mathbf{K_{Ind} = [H^+(aq)]} \qquad ([In^-] \text{ and } [HI] \text{ cancel each other out})$$

Methyl orange at its equivalence point

So we can tell from an indicator's K_{Ind}, the pH of the end point
that it will identify in a titration:

$$\mathbf{pH = -\lg K_{Ind}} \qquad \text{at the indicator's equivalence point.}$$

$-\lg K_{Ind}$ is sometimes given the symbol $\mathbf{pK_{Ind}}$ or $\mathbf{pK_a}$ **of the indicator.**

In fact, as we observe indicators, they appear to change colour over a range
of pH values.
On the next two pages we can see how to select the best indicator for a
particular titration.

Methyl orange in alkali

▷ pH curves

Have you ever tried to get a neutral solution by adding together a strong acid and alkali, using universal indicator?
If you have, you will remember how difficult the task is.
One drop too much of the alkali and the indicator turns purple.
One drop too much of the acid and the indicator turns red.
It takes some skill to get a green solution!

You can use a pH meter to plot the changes in pH during an acid–alkali titration.
For the different combinations of strong and weak acids against strong and weak alkalis, we get graphs like the ones below:

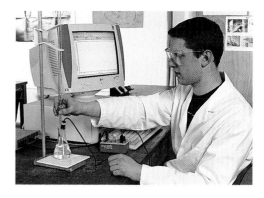

pH curves can be obtained from data logging experiments using a pH probe

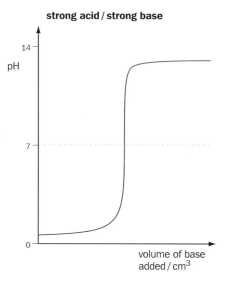

There is a large, sudden change in pH at the end point of the titration

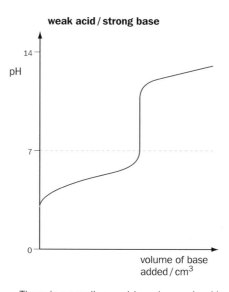

There is a smaller, sudden change in pH (mainly on the alkaline side)

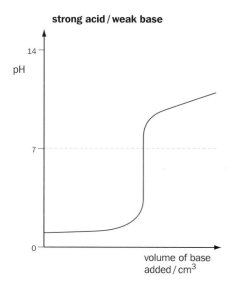

There is a smaller, sudden change in pH (mainly on the acid side)

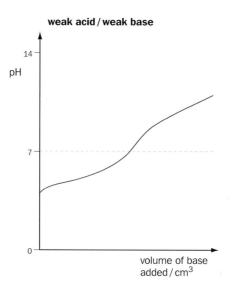

There is no sudden change in pH during the titration

▷ Choosing an indicator

As we found on page 389, indicators appear to change colour over a range of pH values.
Look at the table opposite:

If we match these ranges to the pH curves on the last page, we find that some indicators are suitable for certain titrations, but not others.
For example, if we titrate a strong acid against a weak alkali, can we use phenolphthalein to indicate the end point?
Let's look at its equivalence point and range on the pH curve:

Indicator	pK_{Ind} or pK_a	Range
methyl orange	3.7	3.2–4.4
bromocresol green	4.7	3.8–5.4
methyl red	5.1	4.8–6.0
bromothymol blue	7.0	6.0–7.6
phenol red	7.9	6.8–8.4
phenolphthalein	9.4	8.2–10.0

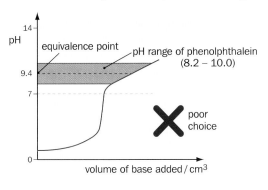
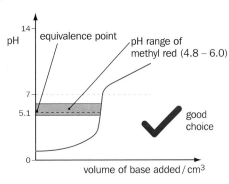

As you can see, phenolphthalein will change colour after the end point and well before its equivalence point.
Too much alkali would have to be added before the indicator changed colour.
However, methyl red would be a suitable indicator. (See graph above.)

The graphs below match some indicators from the table above to the appropriate pH curves from the last page:

> **Choose an indicator whose range lies on the vertical section of the pH curve.**

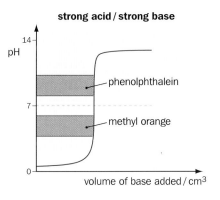
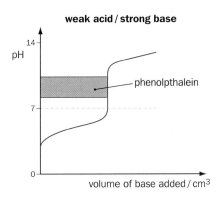

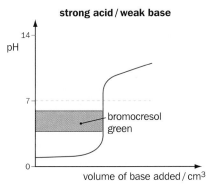
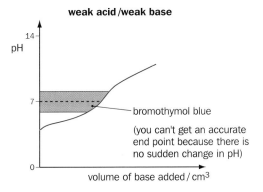

● Which titrations can be done with the greatest variety of indicators? Why?

▷ Buffer solutions

Do you know what the verb 'to buffer' means?
Where would you find buffers in a railway station?
A buffer solution 'softens' the effect of adding acid or alkali.
They **resist sudden large changes in pH**.
That's why they are so important in our blood.
The pH of blood is around 7.4. A change of half a pH unit
can be fatal. So the pH is kept constant with the help of buffer solutions.

Buffer solutions can be made in two ways:

1. From a mixture of a weak acid and one of its salts.
   For example, ethanoic acid (CH_3COOH) and sodium ethanoate (CH_3COONa),
   or carbonic acid (H_2CO_3) and sodium hydrogencarbonate ($NaHCO_3$).

2. From a mixture of a weak base and one of its salts.
   For example, ammonia (NH_3) and ammonium chloride (NH_4Cl).

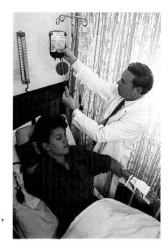

The pH value of blood must not vary too much. Buffer solutions ensure this (see page 394)

How does a buffer solution work?

Let's look at ethanoic acid and sodium ethanoate as our example.
In ethanoic acid we have the equilibrium established:

$$CH_3COOH(aq) \rightleftharpoons CH_3COO^-(aq) + H^+(aq)$$
$$\text{ethanoic acid} \qquad \text{ethanoate ion}$$

$$K_a = \frac{[CH_3COO^-(aq)]_{eq}[H^+(aq)]_{eq}}{[CH_3COOH(aq)]_{eq}} = 1.7 \times 10^{-5}\,mol\,dm^{-3}$$

As we can see from the very small value of K_a, ethanoic acid is a weak acid.
The vast majority of its molecules in solution are undissociated.
Hardly any molecules ionise to form ethanoate and hydrogen ions.
So [CH_3COOH] is high.
The sodium ethanoate is a soluble salt. It ionises completely:

$$CH_3COO^-Na^+(s) \longrightarrow CH_3COO^-(aq) + Na^+(aq)$$

So [CH_3COO^-] is also high.

a) Adding acid to the buffer solution

If we add acid, $H^+(aq)$ ions, the solution counteracts this by removing them:

$$CH_3COOH(aq) \rightleftharpoons CH_3COO^-(aq) + H^+(aq)$$

The position of equilibrium shifts to the left.
We need the sodium ethanoate to provide us with plenty of ethanoate ions
'to mop up' the H^+ ions added.

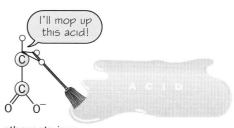

ethanoate ions
'mop up'
extra H^+ ions

b) Adding alkali to the buffer solution

If we add alkali, $OH^-(aq)$ ions, these react with any $H^+(aq)$ ions in
the solution:

$$H^+(aq) + OH^-(aq) \longrightarrow H_2O(l)$$

This shifts the position of the equilibrium above to the right to replace
$H^+(aq)$ ions.
We have plenty of undissociated CH_3COOH molecules available
because it's a weak acid.
These are ready to split up and replace the lost $H^+(aq)$ ions.

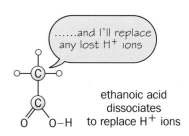

ethanoic acid
dissociates
to replace H^+ ions

▷ pH of a buffer solution

As we saw in the last example, buffer solutions have a large supply of a weak acid and its conjugate base. In this case it was ethanoic acid and ethanoate ions.

If we know the dissociation constant, K_a, of the weak acid, we can calculate the pH of the buffer solution.
Let's look at an example:

Example
A buffer solution was made up by adding equal volumes of $0.20\ \text{mol dm}^{-3}$ solutions of ethanoic acid and sodium ethanoate at $25\,°\text{C}$.
What is its pH?
(The dissociation constant of ethanoic acid is $1.7 \times 10^{-5}\ \text{mol dm}^{-3}$ at $25\,°\text{C}$.)

The original $0.2\ \text{mol dm}^{-3}$ solutions have become $0.1\ \text{mol dm}^{-3}$ on adding the equal volumes together.
We know that:

$$K_a = \frac{[CH_3COO^-(aq)]_{eq}[H^+(aq)]_{eq}}{[CH_3COOH(aq)]_{eq}} = 1.7 \times 10^{-5}\ \text{mol dm}^{-3}$$

We can assume the concentration of ethanoic acid is $0.1\ \text{mol dm}^{-3}$ because such a small proportion of its molecules dissociate.
We can also say the concentration of ethanoate ions is $0.1\ \text{mol dm}^{-3}$ because sodium ethanoate dissolves completely.
The extra ethanoate ions produced by ethanoic acid dissociating will be insignificant.
Putting these values into the equilibrium expression we get:

$$1.7 \times 10^{-5} = \frac{0.1 \times [H^+]}{0.1}$$

So $1.7 \times 10^{-5} = [H^+]$

We know from page 383 that $pH = -lg[H^+]$.
Therefore:

$$pH = -lg\,(1.7 \times 10^{-5})$$

$$= -(-4.8)$$

$$= \textbf{4.8}$$

So the pH of the buffer solution is 4.8.

In this example, where the concentration of the weak acid equals the concentration of its conjugate base,
i.e. [acid] = [conjugate base]

$$pH = -lg\,K_a$$

$$= pK_a$$

The pH of tears is kept at 7.4 by protein buffers

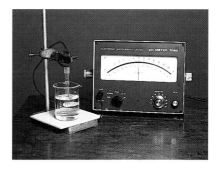
pH meters are calibrated using a buffer solution

In general for this type of buffer solution, we can find its pH using this equation:

$$\boxed{\textbf{pH} = \textbf{p}K_{\textbf{a}} + \textbf{lg}\ \frac{\textbf{[base]}}{\textbf{[acid]}}}$$

▷ Chemistry at work: Acids and bases

No bad blood!

The pH of the blood in your arteries is 7.4 and in your veins it is 7.35. If the pH falls below 6.8 or rises above 8.0 for more than a few hours, you will not survive.

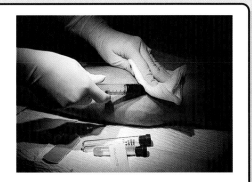

One way in which your body controls the pH of the blood is by buffer systems.
The most important of these is the is the carbon dioxide/hydrogencarbonate ion buffer system:

$$CO_2(aq) + H_2O(l) \rightleftharpoons HCO_3^-(aq) + H^+(aq)$$

If $H^+(aq)$ ions – acid – are added to the blood most will combine with hydrogencarbonate ions and the pH is only altered slightly:

$$H^+(aq) + HCO_3^-(aq) \longrightarrow H_2O(l) + CO_2(aq)$$

If $H^+(aq)$ ions are removed, they are largely replaced by the reaction of carbon dioxide with water. Again the pH is changed only slightly:

$$CO_2(aq) + H_2O(l) \longrightarrow H^+(aq) + HCO_3^-(aq)$$

A number of proteins also act as buffers in the body.
They contain both amine groups, which can remove $H^+(aq)$ ions, and carboxylic acid groups, which ionise to replace any $H^+(aq)$ ions that are removed. (See page 246.)

No bad hair days!

Have you *ever* seen the term 'pH balanced' on shampoo containers or adverts?
Have you wondered what it meant?

Hair is made from the protein keratin. This is a natural polymer made up of thousands of amino acids all joined together. (See page 248.)
Within the complex structure of hair, there are three main types of bonding keeping the protein polymers in place:

- hydrogen bonding
- salt linkages
- disulphide bonds.

These bonds are generally stable in the pH range of 4.5 to 6.0. However, at lower or higher pH values the bonds tend to break and your hair becomes damaged.
So the makers of shampoo keep its pH close to this range so that detergents will clean your hair without damaging it.

Next time you use your pH 5.5 balanced shampoo, you can rest assured that the bonds in your hair will still be intact!

No bad teeth!

Many of the 'convenience' foods we eat contain a lot of sugar.
Even a tin of baked beans contains about 25 g of sugar.

When sugar from food and drink remains on the teeth,
bacteria in the mouth convert it into an acid.
This acid immediately attacks the enamel on your teeth.
Eventually a hole or cavity is produced which requires
a visit to the dentist for a filling.

So how does chewing help?
Chewing sugar-free gum stimulates the production of saliva
which is a weakly alkaline solution.
The saliva then acts to neutralise the acid on your teeth,
preventing any further attack on the enamel.

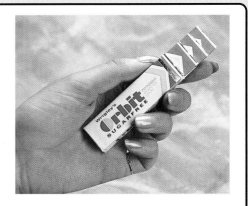

...are you sure????

If your sweets make you foam at the mouth, or purse your lips
and narrow your eyes, its probably down to some neat acid–base chemistry.

Those super-sour sweets contain a mixture of malic acid (found in apples)
and citric acid (found in lemons, limes and oranges).

Foaming bubble-gums rely on these acids reacting with
sodium hydrogencarbonate in the gum. The acids ionise
in the moisture in your mouth, forming $H^+(aq)$ ions:

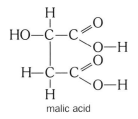

malic acid

citric acid

- Can you see which are the acidic hydrogen atoms?

The $H^+(aq)$ ions then react with the hydrogencarbonate ions
producing carbon dioxide gas, which makes the foam:

$$H^+(aq) + HCO_3^-(aq) \longrightarrow H_2O(l) + CO_2(g)$$

This is the same reaction that happens in baking powder,
which is used to help cake mix to rise.
It contains sodium hydrogencarbonate (known as bicarbonate of soda)
and a weak acid.
When water is added the two react, giving off CO_2.
The carbon dioxide gets trapped in the cake mix.
Self-raising flour has baking powder already added to it.

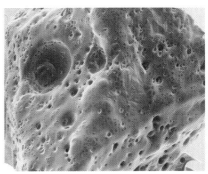

*Pieces of Pop Rock candy magnified
50 times*

And finally, we have those exploding, fizzy crystals
which tickle your tongue and make your teeth vibrate!
These have carbon dioxide gas trapped under pressure inside the solidified candy.
As the sugar dissolves in your mouth, the carbon dioxide escapes with a crack!
Then make sure you reach for the sugar-free gum!

Summary

- Acids are proton (H^+) donors.

- Bases are proton (H^+) acceptors.

- Each acid has an associated base, called its conjugate base.
  The acid and base form a conjugate pair.
  For example:

$$HX(aq) + H_2O(l) \rightleftharpoons H_3O^+(aq) + X^-(aq)$$

  acid 1   base 2   acid 2   base 1

- The pH value of a solution tells us the concentration of $H^+(aq)$ ions:

$$pH = -lg\,[H^+(aq)]$$

- The degree of ionisation of an acid's molecules is given by its dissociation constant:

$$K_a = \frac{[H^+(aq)]_{eq}[X^-(aq)]_{eq}}{[HX(aq)]_{eq}}$$

  The higher the value of K_a, the stronger the acid.

- The ionic product of water (K_w) is:

$$K_w = [H^+(aq)]_{eq}[OH^-(aq)]_{eq}$$

  At 25 °C this equals 10^{-14} mol^2 dm^{-6} in any aqueous solution.

- Indicators are weak acids (HIn).
  At the end point in a titration, $[HIn(aq)] = [In^-(aq)]$.
  Therefore

$$K_{Ind} = [H^+(aq)], \text{ and the pH of the solution is } -lg\,K_{Ind} \text{ or } pK_{Ind}.$$

  Look at the pH curves below:

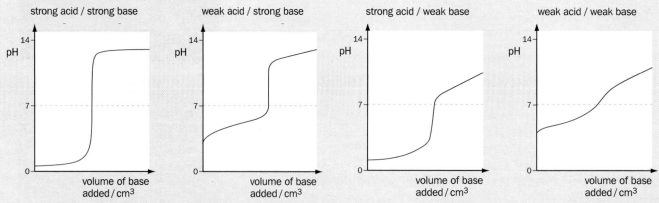

strong acid / strong base   weak acid / strong base   strong acid / weak base   weak acid / weak base

For an acid–base titration, we choose an indicator whose range
lies on the vertical section of the pH curve for that particular reaction.

- Buffer solutions resist changes in pH.
  They can be made from a mixture of either:
  a) a weak acid and one of its salts, or
  b) a weak base and one of its salts.

▶ Questions

1 Copy and complete:

Acids give away protons (better described as .... ions), whereas bases tend to .... protons.
Every acid has its .... base . For example, in the reaction:

$$HCl(aq) + H_2O(l) \rightleftharpoons H_3O^+(aq) + Cl^-(aq)$$

the .... base of HCl is .....
HCl is called a .... acid because its molecules almost all .... in water.
For a weak acid, it is useful to use its .... constant, K_a, to show its strength. The lower the value of K_a, the .... the acid.

The pH value of a solution tells us the .... of $H^+(aq)$ ions present. It is given by the formula:

pH = ...

We can use pH curves to decide on a suitable .... for a particular acid–base .....

A .... solution, such as a solution of a .... acid and one of its ...., will resist changes in pH.

2 A solution of ethanoic acid in water was compared with a solution of ethanoic acid in methylbenzene.
a) Make a table to show the results of the following tests on each solution:
blue litmus paper
sodium carbonate
magnesium ribbon
electrical conductivity
b) How does water affect the properties of ethanoic acid?
Explain your answer.
c) Describe another test that will show if a solution is acidic?

3 What is the pH value of the following solutions of strong acids:
a) 1.0×10^{-3} mol dm^{-3} hydrochloric acid
b) 0.1 mol dm^{-3} hydrochloric acid
c) 1.0 mol dm^{-3} hydrochloric acid
d) 0.01 mol dm^{-3} nitric acid
e) 0.50 mol dm^{-3} nitric acid
f) 2.5×10^{-3} mol dm^{-3} hydrochloric acid
g) 0.0045 mol dm^{-3} hydrochloric acid

4 Work out the concentration of these solutions of strong acids:
a) a solution of hydrochloric acid whose pH value is 5.0.
b) a solution of nitric acid with a pH value of 2.4.

5 a) Explain why the pH value of pure water at 25 °C is 7.
b) Explain this statement:
'The ionic product of water at 25 °C is 10^{-14} mol^2 dm^{-6}.'
c) Work out the pH of the following solutions of strong bases:
i) 0.1 mol dm^{-3} sodium hydroxide
ii) 1.0 mol dm^{-3} sodium hydroxide
iii) 0.025 mol dm^{-3} potassium hydroxide.

6 Look at the dissociation constants of these weak acids:

	K_a at 25 °C / mol dm^{-3}
chloric(I) acid, HClO(aq)	3.7×10^{-8}
bromic(I) acid, HOBr(aq)	2.1×10^{-9}
hydrocyanic acid, HCN(aq)	4.9×10^{-10}

a) What do we mean by the 'dissociation constant' of an acid? Use HCN to help explain your answer.
b) Which is the weakest acid in the table above? How did you decide on your answer?
c) Use the information in the table to find the pH of a
i) 0.10 mol dm^{-3} solution of bromic(I) acid.
ii) 0.20 mol dm^{-3} solution of chloric(I) acid.
iii) 1.5×10^{-3} mol dm^{-3} solution of hydrocyanic acid.

7 Sketch the pH curves you would expect if we titrated:
a) a strong acid with a strong base,
b) a strong acid with a weak base,
c) a weak acid with a strong base,
d) a weak acid with a weak base.

Indicators are weak acids.
e) Explain the importance of the 'equivalence point' of an indicator.
f) Why do values of pK_{Ind} help us to choose an appropriate indicator for a particular titration?
Refer to one of your pH curves sketched earlier in the question.
g) Congo red is an indicator with a pK_{Ind} value of 4.0 and a pH range of 3.0 to 5.0.
With which titration from a) to d) above would you use Congo red to indicate the end point?

8 a) Explain how a *buffer solution* made from solutions of ammonia (NH$_3$) and ammonium chloride (NH$_4$Cl) works.
b) What will be the pH of a buffer solution made up from equal volumes of 0.10 mol dm^{-3} solutions of propanoic acid and sodium propanoate?
(K_a for propanoic acid is 1.3×10^{-5} mol dm^{-3} at 25 °C.)

32 Redox: Extraction of metals

We rely on redox reactions to obtain most of the metals
that we all take for granted:

- metals such as iron, which goes on to make the steel used to make
  bicycles, cars, ships and trains;
- the aluminium used in making aeroplanes.

In this chapter we will look at the chemistry involved in getting
these metals from their raw materials – ores.

A metal's ore is the rock from which we extract the metal.

Look at these photos of two ores
and the metals we get from them:

Haematite, Fe_2O_3

Cars are made from mild
steel, an alloy of iron

▷ The Reactivity Series

The metals in ores are chemically bonded to other elements.
So how can we extract the metals?
To answer this we must understand the Reactivity Series of metals.
The Reactivity Series is like a 'league table' for metals.
The most reactive metals are at the top of the league.
The least reactive are at the bottom.

Here is a table that summarises the reactions of metals:

Bauxite, Al_2O_3

Aeroplanes are made from
alloys of aluminium

Order of reactivity	Reaction when heated in air	Reaction with water	Reaction with dilute acid
potassium sodium lithium calcium magnesium aluminium zinc iron	burn brightly, forming oxides	fizz (effervesce), giving off hydrogen; alkaline solutions(hydroxides) are formed.	explode
		react with steam, giving off hydrogen; the metal oxide is made.	fizz, giving off hydrogen
tin lead copper	oxide layer forms without burning	only a slight reaction with steam	react slowly with warm acid
silver gold platinum	no reaction	no reaction, even with steam	no reaction

Carbon can be placed just above zinc in the series.
This is a useful reducing agent used to extract metals
that are less reactive than itself.

Another non-metal, hydrogen, fits into the Reactivity Series just above copper.

▷ Extracting metals

Knowing about the Reactivity Series, we can now
start to understand how we get metals from their ores.
First of all, we will look at metals of low and medium reactivity.
This includes the most widely used of all metals, iron.

Metals of low reactivity

Most metals are found naturally in rocks called ores.
They are in compounds, chemically bonded to other elements.
However, the metals at the bottom of the Reactivity Series
can be found as the elements themselves.
We say that they are found **native**.

We can find copper, silver, gold and platinum as the metals in nature.
Copper and silver are also mined as ores.

Gold is so expensive because it is rare and so difficult to find
and separate from the waste rock.
Did you know that there is plenty of gold in the sea?
Unfortunately, it is spread all round the world.
This makes it too costly to extract from seawater.

Many metal ores contain oxides or sulphides of the metal.
Copper is found in an ore called copper chalcocite.
This has copper(I) sulphide in it.
We can get the copper from this ore just by heating it in air:

$$\underset{\text{Copper(I) sulphide}}{Cu_2S(s)} \; + \; \underset{\text{oxygen}}{O_2(g)} \; \xrightarrow{\text{heat}} \; \underset{\text{copper}}{2\,Cu(s)} \; + \; \underset{\text{sulphur dioxide}}{SO_2(g)}$$

Care must be taken to stop sulphur dioxide gas escaping from the furnace.
This gas causes acid rain.

Metals of medium reactivity

All metals above copper in the series are only found as ores.
The metal above copper in the Reactivity Series is lead.
Lead can be extracted from an ore, such as galena, which contains
lead sulphide.

When we roast copper(I) sulphide, we get copper.
However, when we roast lead sulphide, no lead is made.
Instead, we get lead oxide (plus sulphur dioxide).
The sulphur dioxide is collected and used to make sulphuric acid.
(See page 361.)

$$\underset{\text{lead sulphide}}{2\,PbS(s)} + \underset{\text{oxygen}}{3\,O_2(g)} \longrightarrow \underset{\text{lead oxide}}{2\,PbO(s)} + \underset{\text{sulphur dioxide}}{2\,SO_2(g)}$$

Then the lead oxide has to be reduced to get the lead metal.
Carbon can be used as the reducing agent in a furnace.
Carbon is more reactive than lead.
Therefore, it can displace lead from lead oxide.

$$\underset{\text{carbon}}{C(s)} + \underset{\text{lead oxide}}{2\,PbO(s)} \longrightarrow \underset{\text{carbon dioxide}}{CO_2(g)} + \underset{\text{lead}}{2\,Pb(s)}$$

This man is panning for gold in Pakistan

*The copper in these wires has been
extracted by roasting its ore. It is then
purified by electrolysis*

*Lead is used for flashings on roofs
Can you see any other lead in the photo?*

There is a link between a metal's place in the
Reactivity Series and how easy it is to extract:

> **The more reactive a metal is, the more
> difficult it is to extract chemically
> from its ore.**

▶ Extracting metals with carbon

Carbon is a non-metal. However, we can put it into the Reactivity Series of metals. It fits in between aluminium and zinc. This means that carbon can displace any metal below aluminium in the Reactivity Series. We get carbon from coal. Coal is cheap and there's plenty of it. Therefore, metals extracted using carbon are not too expensive if they have a readily available ore.

▶ Extraction of iron

Carbon is important in the extraction of iron. We use a giant blast furnace to get the iron from its ore. The raw materials are fed into the top of the furnace in a continuous process. The raw materials are:

* **iron ore** (mainly haematite, iron(III) oxide – Fe_2O_3),
* **coke** (a cheap form of carbon, made from coal),
* **limestone** (to get rid of sandy impurities).

Look at the diagram:
Can you see why it is called a **blast** furnace?
It's a bit like a huge barbecue. The temperature gets above 1500 °C. The air is blown in through pipes called tuyères.

This blast furnace is over 50 m high

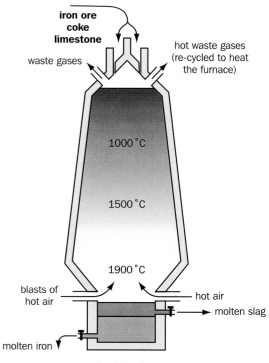

The blast furnace

Reactions in the blast furnace

1. The coke (carbon) reacts with air to make carbon dioxide:

    $$C(s) + O_2(g) \longrightarrow CO_2(g)$$

2. This carbon dioxide reacts with more coke, making carbon monoxide gas:

    $$CO_2(g) + C(s) \longrightarrow 2\,CO(g)$$

3. The carbon monoxide then reduces the iron oxide to iron:

    $$Fe_2O_3(s) + 3\,CO(g) \longrightarrow 2\,Fe(s) + 3\,CO_2(g)$$

    Some iron(III) oxide is also reduced by the carbon in coke:

    $$2\,Fe_2O_3(s) + 3\,C(s) \longrightarrow 4\,Fe(s) + 3\,CO_2(g)$$

    But why do you think the main reducing agent is CO gas?
    The iron forms as a solid which then melts near the base of the furnace.
    It sinks to the bottom of the furnace and is run off into moulds.

4. Limestone gets rid of the sandy impurities in the iron ore.
    They form a liquid **slag**.
    The limestone decomposes into calcium oxide (a base) and carbon dioxide.
    The calcium oxide reacts with the acidic oxide, SiO_2, forming the slag:

    $$CaO(s) + SiO_2(s) \longrightarrow CaSiO_3(l)$$
    calcium silicate (slag)

    Calcium aluminate ($CaAl_2O_4$) is also formed in the slag.
    The molten slag floats on top of the iron.
    The slag is tapped off, cooled and used for making roads and breezeblocks.

▷ Iron into steel

The iron from the blast furnace is impure.
It is called 'pig-iron' (after the name given to the moulds).
It contains 3–4% carbon, plus some other non-metals.
The impure iron is very brittle. It cracks easily.
Most of it gets turned into steel which is much tougher.
Steel is mainly iron (over 98%). It has a tiny amount
of carbon left in it. Other metals can also be added
to improve its properties.
There are two main steps in turning iron into steel:

1. Removing carbon and other impurities

This can be done by blowing oxygen on to molten pig-iron
using a basic oxygen converter.
Look at the diagram opposite:
Here is list of non-metal impurities found in pig-iron:

Impurities in pig-iron
carbon (3 to 5%)
silicon (1 to 2%)
phosphorus (0.05 to 1.5%)
sulphur (0.05 to 0.1%)

The carbon burns and escapes as carbon dioxide gas.

$$C(s) + O_2(g) \longrightarrow CO_2(g)$$

Notice the amount of carbon dioxide formed in producing iron and steel.
What environmental problem does this gas cause? (See page 169.)
Gases are 'scrubbed' before being released. The 'scrubbers' contain
basic compounds to react with the acidic gases given off.

Sulphur dioxide, formed by oxidising sulphur in the pig-iron,
can also be removed like this.
But we can avoid producing that pollutant by passing
magnesium powder into the molten pig-iron.
This reacts vigorously to form magnesium sulphide
which floats and can be scraped from the surface:

$$Mg(s) + S(l) \longrightarrow MgS(s)$$

This reaction, like the other redox reactions in the converter, is exothermic.
The heat given out keeps the pig-iron molten while it has
most of its impurities removed.

The phosphorus and silicon are removed in the converter by adding lime
(calcium oxide). The phosphorus(v) oxide (P_4O_{10}) and silicon dioxide(SiO_2)
aren't given off as gases. They are removed as slag:

$$6\,CaO + P_4O_{10} \longrightarrow 2\,Ca_3(PO_4)_2$$
calcium phosphate slag

2. Adding other metals

Small amounts of other metals are added to give the steel special properties.
For example, we make stainless steel by alloying iron with a little chromium
and nickel. This type of steel does not rust. It is used to make cutlery.

Steel cables strengthen a suspension bridge

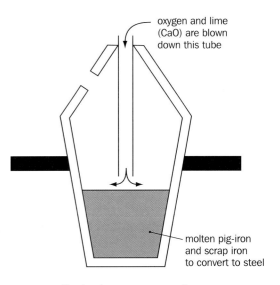

oxygen and lime (CaO) are blown down this tube

molten pig-iron and scrap iron to convert to steel

The basic oxygen converter

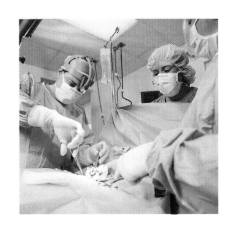

Stainless steel instruments are used by surgeons

▶ Chemical reduction of other metal ores

Tungsten (W)

Although carbon is by far the cheapest reducing agent,
we can't use it to extract *every* metal below it in the Reactivity Series.
Some metals react with carbon to form compounds called **carbides**.
For example, tungsten extracted using carbon would form
tungsten carbide, W_2C, as a stable product.
This makes the reduction worthless because you can't get the metal
pure enough to use.

The tungsten we use to make the filaments in light bulbs is extracted
by reduction using **hydrogen** gas:

$$WO_3(s) + 3\,H_2(g) \xrightarrow{\text{heat}} W(s) + 3\,H_2O(g)$$

- Why do you think it is important to control the purity
  of tungsten in light bulbs carefully?

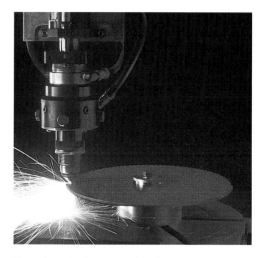

*Tungsten steels are very hard.
They are used to make cutting tools*

Titanium (Ti)

Titanium is another unreactive metal that carbon could reduce from its ore.
But like tungsten, the formation of the carbide is a problem.

Titanium finds many uses in expensive high-performance alloys.
It has to be extracted using a more reactive metal as the reducing agent.
Magnesium or sodium is used in industry to make batches
of the metal. Using reactive metals, which have already had to be 'won'
from their ores, makes titanium an expensive metal.
This is despite its main ore (ilmenite – a mixed oxide of iron and titanium)
being fairly common.

Titanium(IV) oxide is separated from the ore, then converted to
titanium(IV) chloride:

$$\underset{\text{rutile}}{TiO_2(s)} + \underset{\text{coke}}{C(s)} + 2\,Cl_2(g) \xrightarrow{\sim 1000^\circ C} TiCl_4(g) + CO_2(g)$$

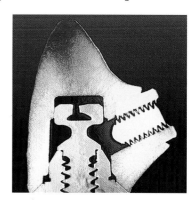

*These teeth implants and screws are
made from titanium*

(Notice that carbon is used in this stage, but not the reaction below.)
The $TiCl_4$ is a simple molecular liquid. It is purified by distillation,
then reduced with magnesium or sodium:

$$TiCl_4(l) + 4\,Na(l) \xrightarrow{\text{heat}} Ti(s) + 4\,NaCl(l)$$

- Can you write an equation for the reduction of $TiCl_4$ by magnesium?

The molten sodium chloride or magnesium chloride is tapped off.
This is called the **Kroll process**.

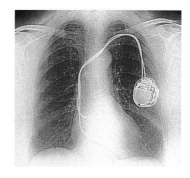

*The heart pacemaker in this baby
contains titanium*

Chromium (Cr)

Many metal objects are made from iron or steel, but rusting is a problem.
Chromium is a hard, shiny metal that resists corrosion.
It forms the final layer on beautifully shiny chrome-plated objects.
Chromium is also one of the metals added to iron to make stainless steel.
Like titanium, it is extracted by a more reactive metal.
In this case, **aluminium** is used to reduce chromium(III) oxide:

$$Cr_2O_3(s) + 2\,Al(s) \xrightarrow{\text{heat}} 2\,Cr(s) + Al_2O_3(s)$$

Chromium is used in stainless steel

▶ Chemistry at work: Uses of tungsten, titanium and chromium

Hot stuff!

Tungsten's melting point of 3410 °C is very high, even for a metal.
This makes it ideal for use as the thin resistance wire used
in the filament of a light bulb.
It can glow 'white hot' without melting.
The light bulb has the air removed from inside and replaced by
some argon gas. Why do you think this is done?
(Remember that argon is one of the noble gases.)

It is also a very dense metal.
Its actual density is 19.35 g cm^{-3}, compared with gold's 18.88 g cm^{-3}.
This has led to its use in making the shafts of darts.
This means a darts player can have a heavy dart with a thin shaft.
Why do you think this is an advantage?

The filament in this light bulb is made of tungsten

This dart has a tungsten shaft

Titanium – a good mixer!

Titanium is used in alloys with a variety of metals.
Its alloys are low-density, corrosion-resistant metals
that remain strong even at high temperatures.
For these reasons they are used in the aircraft industry.
For example, the turbines in jet engines are made from titanium alloy.

The joints in our bodies take a lot of wear and tear.
The 'ball and socket' type joints in the hip and shoulder
have to work especially hard.
Sometimes joints are attacked by arthritis.
This is a very painful and crippling disease.

Look at the photo opposite:
Now people can be fitted with replacement joints.
These are made of plastic and metal alloys containing titanium.

What properties must an alloy used inside your body have?

Aeroplanes contain titanium alloys

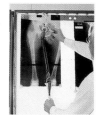

This artificial bone is made of titanium

All things bright and beautiful!

As you know, rusting can be a problem for iron or steel.
We can use chromium to protect against corrosion.
However, chromium does not stick very well to steel.
The objects are first electroplated with copper.
A layer of nickel goes on top of this.
Now the chromium has a good base to stick to.
The final layer of chromium makes the object beautifully shiny!
The object to be chrome-plated is made the cathode in an electrolytic cell:

$$\text{Cathode: } Cr^{3+} + 3e^- \longrightarrow Cr$$

▷ Extracting reactive metals

The highly reactive metals are the most difficult to extract from their ores.
Their compounds are very stable compared with their elements.

Reduction by carbon won't work.
You know carbon's place in the Reactivity Series.
It lies just under aluminium. Therefore carbon can't reduce the ores of the highly reactive metals.

However, we do have a way to get these metals.
It is called electrolysis. We looked at this on page 53.
Once you have separated the metal compound from the ore, there are two steps:

1. melt it, then
2. electrolyse it.

Both steps use up a lot of energy.
Therefore highly reactive metals are expensive to extract.

The metal ions are reduced in the electrolysis.
They gain electrons at the negative electrode (the cathode):

$$M^{z+} + z\,e^- \longrightarrow M \qquad \textbf{Reduction}$$

Remember OIL RIG, i.e. Oxidation Is Loss, Reduction Is Gain (of electrons).

Extraction of sodium

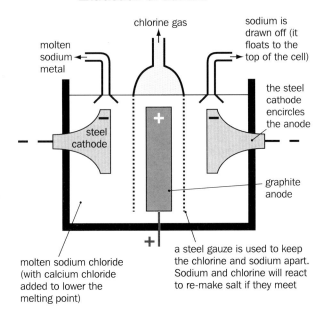

chlorine gas

molten sodium metal

sodium is drawn off (it floats to the top of the cell)

the steel cathode encircles the anode

steel cathode

graphite anode

molten sodium chloride (with calcium chloride added to lower the melting point)

a steel gauze is used to keep the chlorine and sodium apart. Sodium and chlorine will react to re-make salt if they meet

Sodium is extracted from sodium chloride in a Downs Cell

$$\textbf{At the cathode: } Na^+(l) + e^- \longrightarrow Na(l)$$

▷ Extraction of aluminium

The most important of the reactive metals is aluminium.
Aluminium has many useful properties.
It conducts heat and electricity well. It has a low density for a metal.
It does not corrode because it is protected by an oxide layer on its surface.
These have led to its use in drinks cans, overhead power cables, cooking foil and a variety of low-density alloys. These alloys are particularly useful in the aircraft industry.

Getting the ore

Aluminium is extracted from its ore **bauxite**.
This is mainly aluminium oxide.
Large amounts of bauxite are mined in Jamaica.

Look at the photo of the open-cast bauxite mine:

The impurities are removed before aluminium is extracted from its oxide.
This results in large reservoirs of brown water, stained by impurities containing iron compounds.

Look at the photo opposite:

● What effect does the aluminium industry have on our environment?
● How can we help?

Open-cast mining of bauxite

Waste is stored in reservoirs after bauxite has been purified

Electrolysis of aluminium oxide

The aluminium oxide is **_melted_**, then **_electrolysed_**.
Why do we need to melt the aluminium oxide?
(See page 53.)

Energy is saved by dissolving the oxide in cryolite (Na_3AlF_6).
This lowers its melting point (from 2045 °C to 970 °C).
What is the other major use of energy in the process?

The electrolysis is done in cells like the one shown below:

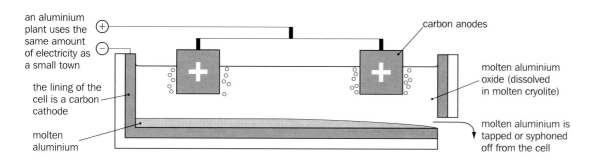

an aluminium plant uses the same amount of electricity as a small town

the lining of the cell is a carbon cathode

molten aluminium

carbon anodes

molten aluminium oxide (dissolved in molten cryolite)

molten aluminium is tapped or syphoned off from the cell

At the cathode: $Al^{3+}(l) + 3e^- \longrightarrow Al(l)$ **Al^{3+} ions are reduced.**

At the anode: $2\,O^{2-}(l) - 4\,e^- \longrightarrow O_2(g)$
then: $C(s) + O_2(g) \longrightarrow CO_2(g)$

The oxygen gas reacts with the carbon anodes,
making carbon dioxide gas. This burns away the anodes,
so they have to be replaced regularly.

The electrolysis requires huge amounts of electricity.
A typical aluminium plant needs the same electrical power
as a small town.
That's why aluminium is usually made near sources of cheap electricity,
such as a hydroelectric power station.

Recycling

The two main metals that we recycle are iron and aluminium.
Recycling helps conserve the Earth's precious resources:
not only the raw materials used in the extraction of these metals,
but also the energy saved – for example, the gas used to heat
the blast furnaces and steel-making plants or to melt aluminium oxide.
However, the scrap aluminium, mainly from drinks cans, has to be
melted before being recast, as does scrap iron. This also takes energy.
In recycling the steel from 'tin' cans, energy is also used in cleaning,
sorting and removing the thin layer of tin from the cans.
Nevertheless, a balance sheet shows that recycling metals is still worth while.

Any energy savings will also reduce the pollution released from the
extraction processes and the burning of fossil fuels, either
directly in the plants or at power stations to generate electricity.

More people now recycle aluminium

Summary

- The method we use to extract a metal from its ore depends on its position in the Reactivity Series.

- The more reactive a metal is, the harder it is to extract.

  Look at the list of metals below:

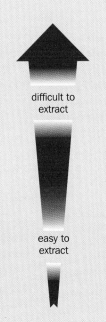

difficult to extract

easy to extract

Order of reactivity	Method of extraction
Potassium (K) Sodium (Na) Lithium (Li) Calcium (Ca) Magnesium (Mg) Aluminium (Al)	Electrolysis. The metal compound is: 1. melted, then 2. electrolysed.
Zinc (Zn) Iron (Fe) Tin (Sn) Lead (Pb)	Chemical reduction by carbon or carbon monoxide For example, $ZnO + C \longrightarrow Zn + CO$ (If the ore is a sulphide, it is roasted first to get the oxide)
Copper (Cu) Silver (Ag) Gold (Au) Platinum (Pt)	These metals can be found uncombined, as the metal itself. We say that they are found 'native'. (Copper and silver are often found as ores but they are easy to extract by roasting the ore. Once extracted, copper is purified by electrolysis.)

▶ Questions

1 Copy and complete:

The method we use to .... a metal from its ore depends on the .... of that particular metal. The highly reactive metals are extracted by ...., whereas those less reactive than carbon are extracted by .... reduction.
For example, iron is extracted in a .... furnace.
Carbon, in the form of ...., is mixed with iron ore and ..... The main reducing agent in the furnace is .... gas, although some iron(III) ... is reduced by ... .
Reduction can be defined as the loss of .... from a compound, such as iron(III) oxide. It can also be defined as the .... of electrons, as happens when a metal ion arrives at the .... electrode during electrolysis, e.g. $Al^{3+}(l) + ... \longrightarrow Al(l)$.

2 This table shows when some metals were discovered:

Metal	Known since:
potassium	1807
sodium	1807
zinc	before 1500 in India and China
copper	ancient civilisations
gold	ancient civilisations

What pattern can you see relating the metal's place in the Reactivity Series to its discovery?
Can you explain this pattern?

3 a) Draw a labelled diagram of a blast furnace.
  b) Describe, using equations, the main reactions that happen in a blast furnace.
  c) What is the main impurity in the iron we get from a blast furnace?
  d) How is iron turned into steel in a basic oxygen converter?

4 a) Tungsten is below carbon in the Reactivity Series. Why don't we use carbon to extract tungsten from its ore?
  b) Name the reducing agent used in the extraction of tungsten and give an equation to show the reaction.
  c) Describe how titanium is extracted from titanium(IV) oxide. Use equations in your answer.
  d) Explain why titanium is such an expensive metal.
  e) Which metal is used as a reducing agent in the extraction of chromium metal?
  f) Write an equation to show how we obtain chromium from chromium(III) oxide.

5 a) Draw a labelled diagram of the cell we use to extract aluminium.
  b) Why is the aluminium oxide dissolved in cryolite?
  c) Why do we have to replace the anodes at regular intervals?
  d) Write the half equation at the cathode.
  e) Discuss the advantages of recycling aluminium.
  f) List five uses of aluminium.

33 Redox: Electrode potentials

In the last chapter we saw how we can extract metals from their ores.
The method used was related to the metal's position in the Reactivity Series.
We can use this order of reactivity to predict displacement reactions.
A metal higher up the series will **displace** a metal lower down
from its compounds. For example:

$$Zn(s) + CuSO_4(aq) \longrightarrow ZnSO_4(aq) + Cu(s)$$

Can you remember what spectator ions are?
The sulphate ions do not change in the displacement reaction above.
So we can leave them out of the equation and write an ionic equation:

$$Zn(s) + Cu^{2+}(aq) \longrightarrow Zn^{2+}(aq) + Cu(s)$$

Zinc is added to copper sulphate solution

Which reactant gets reduced?
(Remember its oxidation number will be reduced.)
Which is the reducing agent?
(Remember that reducing agents GIVE electrons.)

In Chapter 10 we saw how we can add up half equations.
We can think of any redox reaction as two half equations.
One will represent reduction:

$$Cu^{2+} + 2\,e^- \longrightarrow Cu$$ | **Cu²⁺ ions are reduced to Cu.**

Zinc displaces copper ions from solution

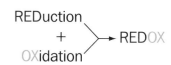

The other will be an oxidation reaction:

$$Zn \longrightarrow Zn^{2+} + 2\,e^-$$ | **Zn atoms are oxidised to Zn²⁺ ions.**

There is a tendency for any metal atom to give away electrons
and form a positive ion.
But in the example above, zinc is the stronger reducing agent.
Copper is 'forced' into the reverse reaction. Its ions accept electrons
and change into atoms.

So we can represent a metal and its ion as a reversible reaction:

$$M(s) \rightleftharpoons M^{z+}(aq) + z\,e^-$$

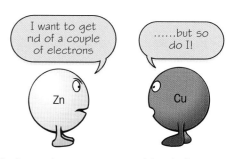

Both zinc and copper are potential reducing agents

The direction of the reaction above depends on the other reactant.
For example, if we mix magnesium and zinc sulphate, then zinc ions
will change to zinc atoms.
The more powerful reducing agent, in this case magnesium,
has a greater tendency to lose electrons:

$$Mg(s) \longrightarrow Mg^{2+}(aq) + 2\,e^-$$
$$+ \; Zn^{2+}(aq) + 2\,e^- \longrightarrow Zn(s)$$
$$\overline{Mg(s) + Zn^{2+}(aq) \longrightarrow Mg^{2+}(aq) + Zn(s)}$$

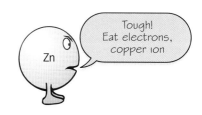

*…but zinc is the more powerful. It has a greater
tendency to lose electrons.*

▷ Half cells

We can show the direction of electron flow in metal/metal ion displacement reactions by joining two half cells.
Look at the diagram below:

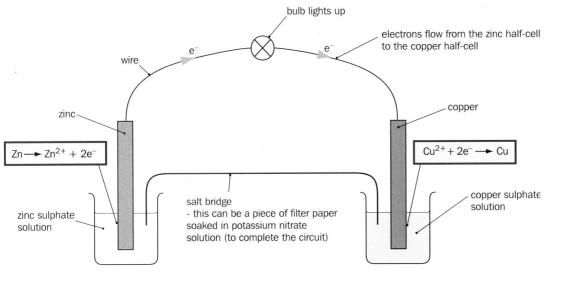

The electrons will flow through the wire from the zinc to the copper.

The current would flow in the circuit above until one of the reactants was used up.

We can replace the bulb by a voltmeter. The voltage reading will tell us the potential difference between the two metals in each half cell.
We can think of this as the difference in the tendency to give away electrons.
The bigger the voltage, the bigger the difference in their power as reducing agents.

If we use a high-resistance voltmeter that draws off hardly any current, we can measure the **maximum potential difference between the half cells**. This is called the **e.m.f. (electromotive force)** of the cell.

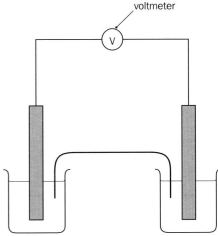

A high resistance voltmeter measures the e.m.f. of a cell (E_{cell})

Look at the examples below:

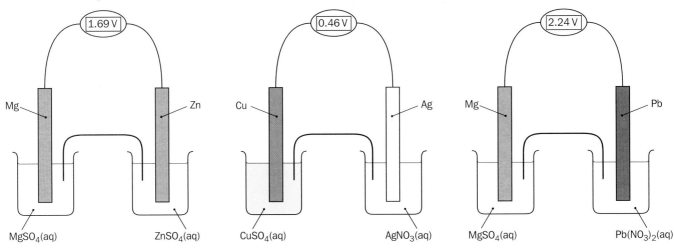

* Can you see any link between the voltage and the difference in reactivity of the pairs of metals?

▶ Cell diagrams

We don't really want to draw out a full diagram of two half cells joined together *every* time we refer to a cell.
So chemists have a shorthand way of representing a cell, called a **cell diagram**.
Look at the cell diagram below:

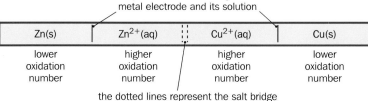

this line represents the boundary between the metal electrode and its solution

Zn(s)	Zn^{2+}(aq)	Cu^{2+}(aq)	Cu(s)
lower oxidation number	higher oxidation number	higher oxidation number	lower oxidation number

the dotted lines represent the salt bridge

A cell diagram

Notice that the higher oxidation number is always written next to the dotted line in each half cell.

By convention, the sign of the standard electrode potential is taken from the half cell written on the right of the cell.
So we can write:

Zn(s) | Zn^{2+}(aq) ⋮ Cu^{2+}(aq) | Cu(s) $E_{cell} = +1.10\,V$

or

Cu(s) | Cu^{2+}(aq) ⋮ Zn^{2+}(aq) | Zn(s) $E_{cell} = -1.10\,V$

Using E_{cell} to predict redox reactions

The sign of E_{cell} tells us which way the reaction should go.
If its sign is positive, both half cell reactions go forward:

→   →

Zn(s) | Zn^{2+}(aq) ⋮ Cu^{2+}(aq) | Cu(s) $E_{cell} = +1.10\,V$

So Zn turns to Zn^{2+}, and Cu^{2+} turns to Cu.
As we know, this reaction does happen.

If E_{cell} is negative, then the reverse changes occur.
Let's just check this with the cell diagram where $E_{cell} = -1.10\,V$.

←   ←

Cu(s) | Cu^{2+}(aq) ⋮ Zn^{2+}(aq) | Zn(s) $E_{cell} = -1.10\,V$

Can you see why knowing the convention for drawing cell diagrams is important? If we get them the wrong way round, the predictions we make from E_{cell} don't work.

We also used values for free energy (ΔG) to predict whether reactions were feasible or not in Chapter 26. But remember the predictions tell us nothing about the rate of reaction.
The same applies to E_{cell}. Its sign may indicate that a redox reaction can happen, but it could be so slow that in effect there is no reaction that we can see. The reactants are then said to be kinetically stable with respect to the products.

Two half cells connect!

$$Zn(s) \longrightarrow Zn^{2+}(aq) + 2e^-$$
$$+\ Cu^{2+}(aq) + 2e^- \longrightarrow Cu(s)$$
$$\overline{Zn(s) + Cu^{2+}(aq) \longrightarrow Zn^{2+}(aq) + Cu(s)}$$

▷ Standard electrode potentials

In all the examples seen so far we have measured the e.m.f.
of pairs of half cells joined together.
This is because you can't measure the e.m.f. of a half cell on its own.
The e.m.f. is a potential **difference**.
But it would be useful to have one half cell against which we could
compare all others.
Chemists have chosen the **standard hydrogen half cell**, sometimes called
the hydrogen electrode, as their reference point.
As such, its value is taken as zero.
Look at the diagram of the standard hydrogen half cell below:

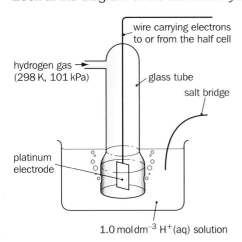

1.0 mol dm^{-3} H$^+$(aq) solution

The e.m.f. of a cell will vary depending upon the temperature,
pressure of any gases involved and the concentration of solutions.
Therefore, we need to set some standard conditions if the e.m.f.
of half cells are to be compared.
Values for half cells compared with the standard hydrogen electrode
are then called **standard electrode potentials**.
The standard conditions chosen are:

Temperature: 298 K Concentration: 1 mol dm^{-3} Pressure: 101 kPa (1 atmosphere)

A platinum electrode is always used to carry electrons to or from half cells
containing no metals.

Look at some standard electrode potentials taken from a book of data:

$$H_2(g) \rightleftharpoons 2H^+(aq) + 2e^-$$

(The equilibrium is established at the
surface of the platinum electrode. H$_2$ gas
is adsorbed on to its surface, which is
coated in finely divided platinum to speed
up the reaction by increasing its surface
area.)

	$E^{\ominus}$/V
Li$^+$(aq), Li(s)	-3.03
K$^+$(aq), K(s)	-2.92
Na$^+$(aq), Na(s)	-2.71
Mg^{2+}(aq), Mg(s)	-2.37
Al^{3+}(aq), Al(s)	-1.66
Zn^{2+}(aq), Zn(s)	-0.76
Pb^{2+}(aq), Pb(s)	-0.13
2H$^+$(aq), H$_2$(g)|Pt	0.00
Cu^{2+}(aq), Cu(s)	$+0.34$
Ag$^+$(aq), Ag(s)	$+0.80$

These all assume that the hydrogen electrode is written on the left
in a cell diagram. For example:

$$\textbf{Pt}\,|\,\textbf{H}_2\textbf{(g)}, \textbf{2H}^+\textbf{(aq)} \,\|\, \textbf{Zn}^{2+}\textbf{(aq)}\,|\,\textbf{Zn(s)} \qquad E^{\ominus}_{\text{cell}} = \textbf{-0.76 V}$$

This is part of the **electrochemical series**.
Can you see any differences from the Reactivity Series?

▷ Using standard electrode potentials

We have seen on page 409 that the e.m.f. of a cell can be used
to predict whether a redox reaction is feasible or not.
Standard electrode potentials allow us to work these out
without having to do an experiment. But remember that
they tell us nothing about the rate of a reaction.
We will now see how we can make use of the tables of data.

Reducing and oxidising agents

The tables of standard electrode potentials tell us the relative power
of reducing agents and oxidising agents.
As you saw on the last page, the tables of data are presented like this:

	$E^{\ominus}/V$
$Li^+(aq) \mid Li(s)$	-3.03
$K^+(aq) \mid K(s)$	-2.92
$Na^+(aq) \mid Na(s)$	-2.71
$Mg^{2+}(aq) \mid Mg(s)$	-2.37
$Al^{3+}(aq) \mid Al(s)$	-1.66
$Zn^{2+}(aq) \mid Zn(s)$	-0.76
$Cr^{3+}(aq), Cr^{2+}(aq) \mid Pt$	-0.41
$Pb^{2+}(aq) \mid Pb(s)$	-0.13
$2H^+(aq), H_2(g) \mid Pt$	0.00
$Cu^{2+}(aq) \mid Cu(s)$	$+0.34$
$Fe(CN)_6^{3-}(aq), Fe(CN)_6^{4-}(aq) \mid Pt$	$+0.36$
$Ag^+(aq) \mid Ag(s)$	$+0.80$
$Cl_2(aq), 2\,Cl^-(aq) \mid Pt$	$+1.36$
$[MnO_4^-(aq) + 8\,H^+(aq)], [Mn^{2+}(aq) + 4\,H_2O(l)] \mid Pt$	$+1.51$

*increasingly powerful reducing
agents (backward reaction)*

-------------------- hydrogen reference --------------------

*increasingly powerful oxidising agents
(forward reaction)*

Taking an example from near the top of the list we have:

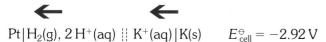

$$Pt \mid H_2(g), 2\,H^+(aq) \; \vdots \; K^+(aq) \mid K(s) \qquad E^{\ominus}_{cell} = -2.92\,V$$

As you can see, $E^{\ominus}_{cell}$ is highly negative.
Applying the rules from page 409, we can say there is a strong tendency
for the reaction $K(s) \longrightarrow K^+(aq) + e^-$ to happen.
In other words, potassium metal, $K(s)$, is a strong reducing agent.
(**R**educing **a**gents **g**ive **e**lectrons.)

If we look near the bottom of the list, we find:

$$Pt \mid H_2(g), 2\,H^+(aq) \; \vdots \; Cl_2(aq), 2\,Cl^-(aq) \mid Pt \qquad E^{\ominus}_{cell} = +1.36\,V$$

Because $E^{\ominus}_{cell}$ is so positive, there is a strong tendency for the reaction
$Cl_2(aq) + 2\,e^- \longrightarrow 2\,Cl^-(aq)$ to occur.
So we can say that chlorine, $Cl_2(aq)$, is a strong oxidising agent.
(Oxidising agents accept electrons.)

- What do you think would happen if we combined potassium and chlorine?
- Can you add up the two half-equations for the reaction?

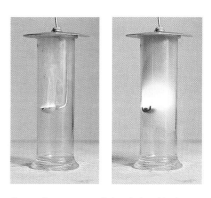

Potassium reacts violently in chlorine gas

▷ Calculating $E^{\ominus}_{cell}$

We can use standard electrode potentials to find the e.m.f. of a cell.

Example
What is the e.m.f. of the cell set up between the $Pb(s)|Pb^{2+}(aq)$ half cell
and the $Cu(s)|Cu^{2+}(aq)$ half cell under standard conditions?
The standard electrode potential of each half cell is given below:

$Pb^{2+}(aq)|Pb(s)$ $E^{\ominus} = -0.13\,V$
$Cu^{2+}(aq)|Cu(s)$ $E^{\ominus} = +0.34\,V$

There are two ways to find the e.m.f.:

1. Draw a sketch of the half cells on an electrode potential scale:

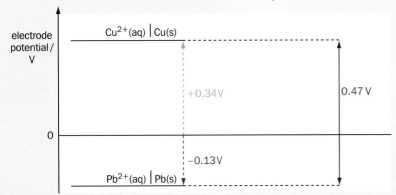

This shows the potential difference between the two half cells is 0.47 V.
We can draw the cell diagram as:

$Cu(s)|Cu^{2+}(aq) \vdots Pb^{2+}(aq)|Pb(s)$

Remember that the sign of $E^{\ominus}_{cell}$ is decided by the right-hand terminal.
In this case lead is the more negative terminal of the cell.

So $E^{\ominus}_{cell} = \mathbf{-0.47\,V}$

2. Start by drawing a cell diagram:

$Cu(s)|Cu^{2+}(aq) \vdots Pb^{2+}(aq)|Pb(s)$

Then add up the standard electrode potentials, but you have to
change the sign of the half cell drawn in reverse to that in the standard tables:

$Cu(s)|Cu^{2+}(aq) \vdots Pb^{2+}(aq)|Pb(s)$
$\quad(-0.34)\qquad + \quad(-0.13)\quad = E^{\ominus}_{cell}$
$\qquad\mathbf{-0.47\,V}\qquad\qquad = \boldsymbol{E^{\ominus}_{cell}}$

The value of $E^{\ominus}_{cell}$ predicts the direction of the redox reaction.
Because the cell, as drawn, has a negative value, the reactions

$Pb(s) \longrightarrow Pb^{2+}(aq) + 2\,e^-$ and
$Cu^{2+}(aq) + 2\,e^- \longrightarrow Cu(s)$

should happen.
(But remember only an experiment will tell us how quickly!)

● What would the value of $E^{\ominus}_{cell}$ have been if we had drawn
the cell diagram as $Pb(s)|Pb^{2+}(aq) \vdots Cu^{2+}(aq)|Cu(s)$?

By convention, we normally draw cell diagrams with the more
positive half cell on the right.

i.e. $Pb(s)|Pb^{2+}(aq) \vdots Cu^{2+}(aq)|Cu(s)$ $E^{\ominus}_{cell} = +0.47\,V$

> From standard electrode potential
> tables we get:
>
> $\quad Cu^{2+}(aq)|Cu(s) \qquad E^{\ominus} = +0.34\,V$
>
> Therefore:
>
> $\quad Cu(s)|Cu^{2+}(aq) \qquad E^{\ominus} = -0.34\,V$

Overall reaction:

$\quad Pb(s) + Cu^{2+}(aq) \longrightarrow Pb^{2+}(aq) + Cu(s)$

▶ Electrode potentials and corrosion

Corrosion of iron and steel (rusting) costs us millions of pounds
every year. So we try very hard to prevent rusting.
How many ways to protect iron can you think of?

Many methods rely on keeping water and oxygen away from the metal.
However, the most effective ways use sacrificial protection.
(See next page.)
Here we choose a metal higher up the electrochemical series
to protect the iron. Do you know a metal commonly used?
Before looking at this in more detail, we need to understand more
about rusting.

When an object rusts, iron atoms (Fe) turn into iron(II) ions (Fe^{2+}).
These ions are then further oxidised to iron(III) ions (Fe^{3+}).
The rust formed is a complex compound, best described as
hydrated iron(III) oxide or hydroxide.
Remember that both water and oxygen are needed for iron to rust.

In order for iron to rust
Both air and water's a must.
Air alone won't do,
Without water there too,
So protect it or get a brown crust!

Look at the electrode potentials below:

These painters battle continuously against corrosion

What happens if you don't oil the chain on your bicycle regularly?

	$E^{\ominus}_{cell}$ / V
$Fe^{2+}(aq)\,|\,Fe(s)$	−0.44
$[O_2(g) + 2\,H_2O(l)], 4\,OH^-(aq)\,|\,Pt$	+0.40
$Fe(OH)_3(s), [Fe(OH)_2(s) + OH^-(aq)]\,|\,Pt$	−0.56

Combining the first two half cells we get:

$$Fe(s)\,|\,Fe^{2+}(aq) \;\vdots\; [O_2(g) + 2\,H_2O(l)], 4\,OH^-(aq)\,|\,Pt$$

where $E^{\ominus}_{cell} = (+0.44) + (+0.40)$
$= +0.84\,V$

We can add the two half cell reactions up.

$$2\,Fe(s) \longrightarrow 2\,Fe^{2+}(aq) + \cancel{4e}$$
$$+\, O_2(g) + 2\,H_2O(l) + \cancel{4e} \longrightarrow 4\,OH^-(aq)$$
$$\overline{2\,Fe(s) + O_2(g) + 2\,H_2O(l) \longrightarrow 2\,Fe(OH)_2(s)}$$

So the forward reactions can occur as written
in the cell diagram.
This forms iron(II) hydroxide, $Fe(OH)_2(s)$.

The iron(II) is then oxidised to iron(III):

Again these can be added up:

$$4\,Fe(OH)_2(s) + \cancel{4\,OH^-} \longrightarrow 4\,Fe(OH)_3(s) + \cancel{4e}$$
$$+\, O_2(g) + 2\,H_2O(l) + \cancel{4e} \longrightarrow \cancel{4\,OH^-}(aq)$$
$$\overline{4\,Fe(OH)_2(s) + O_2(g) + 2\,H_2O(l) \longrightarrow 4\,Fe(OH)_3(s)}$$

$$Pt\,|\,[Fe(OH)_2(s) + OH^-(aq)], Fe(OH)_3(s) \;\vdots\; [O_2(g) + 2\,H_2O(l)], 4\,OH^-(aq)\,|\,Pt$$

where $E^{\ominus}_{cell} = (+0.56) + (+0.40)$
$= +0.96\,V$

And so iron(III) hydroxide is formed. We can think of this as a simple
form of rust.

413

▶ Chemistry at work: Preventing corrosion

We mentioned on the last page that we can prevent rusting by sacrificial protection.
In this method a metal that is more reactive than iron corrodes in preference to the iron.
The most commonly used metal is zinc.
The iron or steel object is dipped into molten zinc, and is said to be **galvanised**.

Magnesium is also used in extreme conditions.
Look at the examples of sacrificial protection on this page:

*This bin has been galvanised.
You can see crystals of zinc if you look closely at this type of bin*

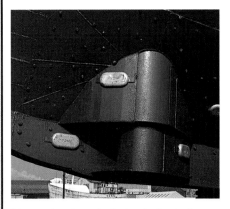

Magnesium bars bolted onto the hull of a ship

*Why are the steel legs of this pier protected by blocks of magnesium.
Why are they particularly prone to rusting?*

We can use standard electrode potentials to show why metals higher up the electrochemical series protect iron.

Look at the electrode potentials of the iron and zinc half cells:

	$E^\ominus$ / V
$Fe^{2+}(aq)\,|\,Fe(s)$	−0.44
$Zn^{2+}(aq)\,|\,Zn(s)$	−0.76

Combining these we get:

$$Zn(s)\,|\,Zn^{2+}(aq) \;\vdots\; Fe^{2+}(aq)\,|\,Fe(s)$$

$$(+0.76) \quad + \quad (-0.44) = E^\ominus_{cell}$$

$$+0.32\,V \qquad = E^\ominus_{cell}$$

So the Zn(s) is oxidised in preference to Fe(s).
Even when scratched, the zinc still provides protection for the iron.

● Draw a cell diagram for the iron and magnesium half cells.
Use the values on page 411 to work out the $E^\ominus_{cell}$.
How does your answer explain the photo opposite?

● Does tin $(Sn^{2+}(aq)\,|\,Sn(s)\ E^\ominus = -0.14\,V)$ provide sacrificial protection on a steel can? Explain your answer.
What will happen if the tin coating is scratched?

▶ Chemistry at work: Cells and batteries

Dry cells

You will be very familiar with dry cells. They are widely used in electrical items such as torches and portable radios.

A common dry cell is the Leclanché cell. It has carbon (positive) and zinc (negative) electrodes and can produce a potential difference of 1.5 volts.

When in use the outside zinc casing is used up.

$$Zn(s) \longrightarrow Zn^{2+}(aq) + 2\,e^-$$

Between the two electrodes there is a moist paste of ammonium chloride and a mixture of powdered carbon and manganese(IV) oxide. The ammonium ions are converted to ammonia and hydrogen. The ammonia dissolves in the water of the paste and the hydrogen is oxidised by the manganese(IV) oxide to water.

$$2\,NH_4^+(aq) + 2\,e^- \longrightarrow 2\,NH_3(g) + H_2(g)$$

Eventually the zinc casing is eaten away and the paste emerges through it.

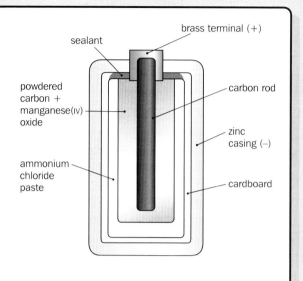

The lead–acid accumulator

Car batteries are usually lead acid accumulators made up of three or six cells. This gives a potential difference of 6 or 12 volts. This type of cell is also used to power milk floats. Unlike the dry cell their useful life can be extended by recharging them.

The negative terminal is a lead plate. When the cell is in use lead(II) ions are produced.

$$Pb(s) \longrightarrow Pb^{2+}(aq) + 2\,e^-$$

The positive terminal is lead(IV) oxide. It is in contact with the sulphuric acid electrolyte. When the cell is in use lead(II) ions are formed at this electrode also.

$$PbO_2(s) + 4\,H^+(aq) + 2\,e^- \longrightarrow Pb^{2+}(aq) + 2\,H_2O(l)$$

We can use our work on electrode potentials and tables of data to work out the e.m.f. of each cell, under standard conditions:

Lead batteries are used in cars

$$\overrightarrow{\quad\quad}\qquad\qquad\overrightarrow{\quad\quad}$$
$Pb(s)\,|\,Pb^{2+}(aq) \;\vdots\; [PbO_2(s) + 4\,H^+(aq)], [Pb^{2+}(aq) + 4\,H_2O(l)]\,|\,Pt$
$(+0.13)$ (as written) $+ (+1.46)$

so $E^{\ominus}_{cell} = +1.59\,V$

(Given a choice, we normally write the more positive half cell on the right of a cell diagram.)

The lead(II) ions formed at each electrode combine with sulphate(VI) ions from the sulphuric acid to form insoluble lead(II) sulphate.

$$Pb^{2+}(aq) + SO_4^{2-}(aq) \longrightarrow PbSO_4(s)$$

The battery in a car is used to start it. When the engine is running the battery is recharged. This is achieved by reversing the electrode reactions so as to reform lead and lead(II) oxide.

Fuel cells

Fuel cells are different from dry cells and the lead–acid accumulator because the substances from which they derive energy are continually fed in. As long as the fuel and oxygen continue to be supplied the cell will continue to operate.

One of the first fuel cells to be developed uses hydrogen and oxygen as the reactants. The negative electrode is porous graphite coated with nickel. The positive electrode is porous graphite coated with nickel and nickel(II) oxide. The purpose of the nickel and nickel oxide is to act as catalysts for the reactions that occur on the surface of the electrodes. The elelectrolyte that is contact with both electrodes is potassium hydroxide solution.

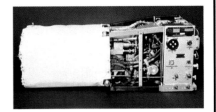

Hydrogen/oxygen fuel cell

Hydrogen gas is supplied to the negative electrode. It diffuses through the graphite and reacts with hydroxide ions to form water:

$$2\,H_2(g) + 4\,OH^-(aq) \longrightarrow 4\,H_2O(l) + 4\,e^-$$

Oxygen is supplied to the positive electrode. It diffuses through the graphite and reacts to form hydroxide ions:

$$O_2(g) + 2\,H_2O(l) + 4\,e^- \longrightarrow 4\,OH^-(aq)$$

If we add the two electrode reactions together we can see that the overall change resulting from the hydrogen/oxygen fuel cell produces water:

$$2\,H_2(g) + O_2(g) \longrightarrow 2\,H_2O(l)$$

Other fuel cells have been developed which use hydrocarbons or alcohols as the fuel instead of hydrogen. When methane is the fuel the following reactions occur.

At the negative electrode:

$$CH_4(g) + 2\,H_2O(l) \longrightarrow CO_2(g) + 8\,H^+(aq) + 8\,e^-$$

At the positive electrode:

$$2\,O_2(g) + 8\,H^+(aq) + 8\,e^- \longrightarrow 4\,H_2O$$

Overall reaction:

$$CH_4(g) + 2\,O_2(g) \longrightarrow CO_2(g) + 2\,H_2O(l)$$

Fuel cells are a very efficient way of converting chemical energy into electrical energy. About 70 per cent of the energy is converted compared with only 45 per cent in a power station. They also produce very little pollution. The drawback with them is that any impurities in the fuel or oxygen can poison the catalysts on the electrodes, making the cell less efficient.

Hydrogen/oxygen fuel cells are used in spacecraft

Hydrogen/oxygen fuel cells have been used a lot in spacecraft. The gases are light to carry and the product from the cell is used as drinking water.

Summary

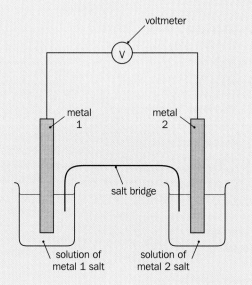

voltmeter

metal 1

metal 2

salt bridge

solution of metal 1 salt

solution of metal 2 salt

- The tendency for a half equation to occur is given by its **standard electrode potential**.

- This can be measured as the potential difference between between a half cell and the standard hydrogen half cell under standard conditions.
  For example,

$$\overset{\longleftarrow}{Pt\,|\,H_2(g),\,2\,H^+(aq)}\ \vdots\ \overset{\longleftarrow}{Mg^{2+}(aq)\,|\,Mg(s)} \qquad E^{\ominus}_{cell} = -2.37\,V$$

  The standard electrode potential in this case is negative. Therefore, as written in the cell diagram above, the half-equations will tend to go in the backward direction (from right to left as we look at the diagram).

$$Mg(s) \longrightarrow Mg^{2+}(aq) + 2\,e^-$$
$$2\,H^+(aq) + 2\,e^- \longrightarrow H_2(g)$$

  So the overall reaction will be:

$$Mg(s) + 2\,H^+(aq) \longrightarrow Mg^{2+}(aq) + H_2(g)$$

- However, standard electrode potentials will not tell us anything about the rate of a reaction.
  The $E^{\ominus}_{cell}$ can indicate that a reaction is feasible, but it may be very, very slow in practice.

▶ Questions

1 Copy and complete:

  Oxidation is the .... of electrons, whereas reduction is the .... of electrons.
  The standard .... potential of a half cell is quoted relative to the standard .... half cell.
  The standard .... potential of a cell helps to .... whether the reaction is .... or not, but it can't tell us about the .... of the reaction.

2 Copy these half equations, adding in the missing electrons.
  Then classify each half equation as oxidation or reduction:
  a) $Ag(s) \longrightarrow Ag^+(aq)$
  b) $Fe^{3+}(aq) \longrightarrow Fe^{2+}(aq)$
  c) $Br_2 \longrightarrow 2\,Br^-(aq)$
  d) $MnO_4^-(aq) + 8\,H^+(aq) \longrightarrow Mn^{2+}(aq) + 4\,H_2O(l)$
  e) Why should we always classify whole reactions involving transfer of electrons as 'redox' reactions?

3 a) Draw a labelled diagram of the standard hydrogen electrode.
  b) What are the standard conditions used to quote $E^{\ominus}$ values?
  c) Why is the platinum electrode coated in finely divided platinum in the hydrogen electrode?

4 Use cell diagram notation to represent the following half cells:
  a) zinc/zinc ions
  b) chromium/chromium(III) ions
  c) iodine/iodide ions
  d) manganate(VII) ions/manganese(II) ions

5 A student attaches a zinc half cell to a lead half cell in order to measure the e.m.f. of the cell.
  a) Draw a diagram of the apparatus the student might have used.
  b) What is used in the apparatus above to provide electrical contact between the two half cells?
  c) Draw a cell diagram to represent the cell set up by the student.
  d) Use the data on page 411 to decide the direction that electrons will flow in the cell.
  e) What would be the standard electrode potential of the cell as represented in your cell diagram in part c)?
  f) Use your answer to e) to predict the reaction that should occur in the cell. Give the ionic equation.

6 Use the data on page 411 to give the value of $E^{\ominus}_{cell}$ in the following cells as drawn below:
  a) $Pb(s)\,|\,Pb^{2+}(aq)\ \vdots\ Li^+(aq)\,|\,Li(s)$
  b) $K(s)\,|\,K^+(aq)\ \vdots\ Cu^{2+}(aq)\,|\,Cu(s)$
  c) $Na(s)\,|\,Na^+(aq)\ \vdots\ Mg^{2+}(aq)\,|\,Mg(s)$
  d) $Al(s)\,|\,Al^{3+}(aq)\ \vdots\ 2\,H^+(aq),\,H_2(g)\,|\,Pt$
  e) $Zn(s)\,|\,Zn^{2+}(aq)\ \vdots\ Cl_2(aq),\,2\,Cl^-(aq)\,|\,Pt$
  f) $Ag(s)\,|\,Ag^+(aq)\ \vdots\ Cr^{3+}(aq),\,Cr^{2+}(aq)\,|\,Pt$
  g) $Ag(s)\,|\,Ag^+(aq)\ \vdots\ [MnO_4(aq) + 8\,H^+(aq)],$
  $[Mn^{2+}(aq) + 4\,H_2O(l)]\,|\,Pt$
  h) $Pt\,|\,Fe(CN)_6{}^{4-}(aq),\,Fe(CN)_6{}^{3-}(aq)\ \vdots\ Cl_2(aq),$
  $2\,Cl^-(aq)\,|\,Pt$

▷ **Equilibrium mixtures**

1 One of the major ammonia-producing plants in the UK is located in Billingham on the North Sea coast. The source of the hydrogen needed is methane, CH_4, although water has been used in the past and could become important again in the future. The synthesis gas from which ammonia is produced has a typical composition of 74.2% hydrogen, 24.7% nitrogen, 0.8% methane and 0.3% argon.

The gas is compressed to about 200 atmospheres pressure and passed over a catalyst at a temperature of 450 °C. Under these conditions about 15% of the synthesis gas is converted into ammonia.

$$N_2(g) + 3H_2(g) \rightleftharpoons 2NH_3 \ \Delta H = -90.2 \text{ kJ mol}^{-1}$$

On leaving the converter, ammonia is removed from the unreacted gases.

Some ammonia is used to produce nitric acid. A further reaction between ammonia and nitric acid gives ammonium nitrate, which is mainly used as a fertiliser. Ammonium nitrate is potentially explosive, and great care has to be taken in its manufacture.

a) i) Suggest one reason why an ammonia plant is located at Billingham. [1]
   ii) Under what circumstances could water 'become important again in the future' as a source of hydrogen? [1]
   iii) Explain the presence of argon in the synthesis gas. [1]
b) Explain one advantage and one disadvantage of using high pressure for the production of ammonia. [3]

c)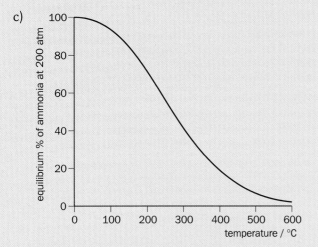

i) By referring to the graph above, discuss the use of 450 °C as a temperature and the use of a catalyst for the conversion. [4]
   ii) Give the name of the catalyst used and the type of catalysis occurring. [2]
d) Describe
   i) how ammonia is removed from the unreacted gases. [2]

   ii) what happens to the gases which have not reacted. [1]
e) Write equations for the reactions in which:
   i) ammonia is oxidised to give nitrogen monoxide (NO) and water as the first stage of nitric acid production; [2]
   ii) ammonia reacts with nitric acid. [1]
f) i) Explain why an ammonium nitrate plant is located on the same site as the ammonia production unit in Billingham. [3]
   ii) State a safety precaution which would be taken in and around an ammonium nitrate plant. [1]
   (AQA)

2 a) Sulphuric acid is produced in the UK by the Contact Process. The sulphur dioxide needed for this process is obtained by burning elemental sulphur, which is imported as a liquid.
   i) State one advantage and one disadvantage of transporting sulphur as a liquid. [2]
   ii) Write equations to show the conversion of sulphur into sulphur trioxide. [2]
b) The diagram represents a sulphuric acid converter.

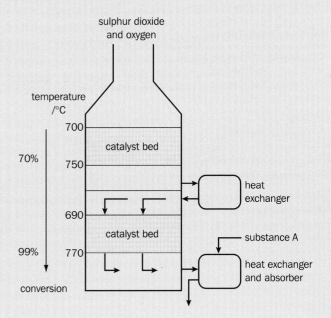

i) Is the reaction between sulphur dioxide and oxygen exothermic or endothermic? [1]
   ii) Give the name of the catalyst used in this process. [1]
   iii) Give two reasons why heat exchangers are used in the Contact Process. [2]
   iv) Why is more than one catalyst bed used? [2]
   v) Give the name of substance A, which enters the absorber, and then write an equation for the process occurring in the absorber. [3]
c) Give two reasons why a sulphuric acid plant should not be sited near a residential area. [2]
   (AQA)

3 a) Six equations are given below which show the equilibria established when the gaseous reactants, A(g) and B(g), form gaseous products, C(g) and D(g). In each case the enthalpy change in the reaction is stated.

1. $A(g) + B(g) \rightleftharpoons C(g) + D(g)$ Endothermic
2. $A(g) + B(g) \rightleftharpoons C(g) + D(g)$ Exothermic
3. $2\,A(g) + B(g) \rightleftharpoons C(g) + D(g)$ Endothermic
4. $2\,A(g) + B(g) \rightleftharpoons C(g) + D(g)$ Exothermic
5. $A(g) + B(g) \rightleftharpoons 2\,C(g) + D(g)$ Endothermic
6. $A(g) + B(g) \rightleftharpoons 2\,C(g) + D(g)$ Exothermic

Select from this list the number of the equation for which the equilibrium yield of products is always
i) increased when temperature is increased and pressure is increased.
ii) increased when temperature is increased and pressure is decreased.
iii) decreased when temperature is decreased and pressure is increased.
iv) decreased when temperature is increased but is unaffected by a change in pressure.

(AQA)

4 Each of the equations **A**, **B**, **C** and **D** represents a dynamic equilibrium.

A $N_2(g) + O_2(g) \rightleftharpoons 2\,NO(g)$ $\Delta H^\ominus = +180\,\text{kJ mol}^{-1}$
B $N_2O_4(g) \rightleftharpoons 2\,NO_2(g)$ $\Delta H^\ominus = +58\,\text{kJ mol}^{-1}$
C $3\,H_2(g) + N_2(g) \rightleftharpoons 2\,NH_3(g)$ $\Delta H^\ominus = -92\,\text{kJ mol}^{-1}$
D $H_2(g) + I_2(g) \rightleftharpoons 2\,HI_2(g)$ $\Delta H^\ominus = -10\,\text{kJ mol}^{-1}$

a) Explain what is meant by the term *dynamic equilibrium*. [1]

b) Explain why a catalyst does not alter the position of the equilibrium reaction. [2]

c) The graphs below show how the yield of product varies with pressure for three of the reactions **A**, **B**, **C** and **D** given above.

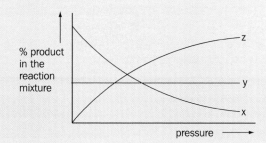

i) Identify a reaction from A, B, C and D which would have the relationship between yield and pressure shown in graphs x, y and z.
ii) Explain why an industrial chemist would not use a very low pressure for the reaction represented in graph x.

iii) Explain why an industrial chemist may not use a very high pressure for the reaction represented by graph z.

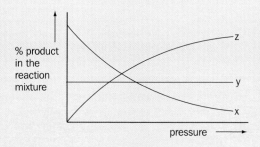

iv) Add to the above graphs a line to show how the product yield would vary with pressure if the reaction which follows curve z was carried out at a temperature higher than that of the original graph.

(AQA)

▶ Equilibrium constants

5 In the Contact Process, sulphur dioxide is oxidised to sulphur trioxide, according to the following gaseous equation.

$$2\,SO_2(g) + O_2(g) \rightleftharpoons 2\,SO_3(g)$$
$$\Delta H^\ominus = -197\,\text{kJ mol}^{-1}$$

a) Write down the expression for the equilibrium constant, K_p, for this equilibrium.
b) What determines the way in which the equilibrium constant changes with temperature? [1]
c) Equilibrium constants and rates of reaction are both affected by changes of temperature. For the equilibrium, show the effect on the rate and the equilibrium constant of increasing the temperature, using a table like the one below.

	Effect of increasing temperature
The value of the equilibrium constant	
The rate of the forward reaction	
The rate of the reverse reaction	

[3]
(OCR)

6 Dinitrogen tetroxide and nitrogen dioxide exist in the following equilibrium.

$$N_2O_4(g) \rightleftharpoons 2\,NO_2(g)$$

When 11.04 g of dinitrogen tetroxide were placed in a vessel of volume 4.80 dm³ at fixed temperature, 5.52 g of nitrogen dioxide were produced at

Further questions on equilibria and redox

equilibrium under a pressure of 100 kPa. Use these data, where relevant, to answer the questions below.

a) Calculate the number of moles of the gases N_2O_4 and NO_2 in the vessel. [2]
   (A_r values: N = 14; O = 16)

b) i) Write an expression for the equilibrium constant, K_c, for the above equilibrium.
   ii) Calculate the value of the equilibrium constant, K_c, and state its units. [4]

c) i) Write an expression for the equilibrium constant, K_p, for the above equilibrium.
   ii) Calculate the mole fraction of NO_2 present in the equilibrium mixture.
   iii) Calculate the value of the equilibrium constant, K_p, and state its units. [5]

(AQA)

7 a) When 10.0 mol of sulphur dioxide were reacted with 5.0 mol of oxygen at 450 °C, 90% of the sulphur dioxide was converted into sulphur trioxide.
   i) Calculate how many moles of sulphur dioxide, of oxygen and of sulphur trioxide were present in the equilibrium mixture.
   ii) Write down expressions for the mole fractions of each of the three gases in the equilibrium mixture.
   iii) Assuming that the total pressure of the equilibrium mixture was 200 kPa, calculate the partial pressure of each gas in the equilibrium mixture.
   iv) Write an expression for the equilibrium constant, K_p, for this reaction.
   v) Calculate the value of K_p and state its units. [9]

b) State two uses of sulphuric acid. [2]

(OCR)

8 Copper forms complexes with water, ammonia and chloride ions which co-exist in equilibria.

a) i) State Le Chatelier's principle. [1]
   ii) Concentrated hydrochloric acid is added to a solution containing $[Cu(H_2O)_6]^{2+}$ until there is a high concentration of Cl^-.

$[Cu(H_2O)_6]^{2+}(aq) + 4Cl^-(aq) \rightleftharpoons [CuCl_4]^{2-}(aq) + 6H_2O(l)$
Hexa-aquacopper(II)   Tetrachlorocuprate(II)
   pale blue   yellow

Use Le Chatelier's principle to deduce what is observed as the acid is added. [2]

b) i) The equilibrium constant, K_c, for the $[Cu(H_2O)_6]^{2+}/[CuCl_4]^{2-}$ equilibrium may be written as follows.

$$K_c = \frac{([CuCl_4]^{2-})(H_2O)^6}{([Cu(H_2O)_6]^{2+})(Cl^-)^4}$$

It is possible in aqueous solution to modify this expression to the following.

$$K'_c = \frac{([CuCl_4]^{2-})}{([Cu(H_2O)_6]^{2+})(Cl^-)^4}$$

The numerical value of K'_c for this equilibrium, at 25 °C, is 4.17×10^5. What are the units of K'_c? [2]

   ii) An equilibrium mixture, at 25 °C, contained 1.17×10^{-5} mol dm^{-3} of $[Cu(H_2O)_6]^{2+}(aq)$ and 0.800 mol dm^{-3} Cl^-. Calculate the equilibrium concentration of $[CuCl_4]^{2-}(aq)$. [3]

(OCR)

9 A chemist has discovered a new process for making a commercially important material **G**. This involves an equilibrium between two gases **E** and **F**.

$$\mathbf{E}(g) + 2\mathbf{F}(g) \rightleftharpoons \mathbf{G}(g)$$

The process is normally carried out in the factory at a pressure of 500 000 kPa and a temperature of 300 °C.

a) Write an expression for K_p for this reaction, explaining the symbols you use. What are the units of K_p?

b) The chemist carried out two experimental runs (both at 50 000 kPa) using a mixture of **E** and **F**, in the mole ratio 1 : 2. Use the results below to calculate the value of K_p for run 1.

	Run 1	Run 2
Temperature/°C	150	300
% of **E** converted	50%	70%

c) State *Le Chatelier's principle*. Explaining your reasoning, deduce the sign of the enthalpy change of this process.

d) Suggest the conditions of temperature and pressure which would give a greater yield of **G** than in either run. Explain why the conditions you suggest may be different from those used industrially. [15]

(OCR)

10 Phosphorus(V) chloride dissociates at high temperatures according to the equation

$$PCl_5(g) \rightleftharpoons PCl_3(g) + Cl_2(g)$$

83.4 g of phosphorus(V) chloride are placed in a vessel of volume 9.23 dm^3. At equilibrium at constant temperature, 11.1 g of chlorine are produced at a total pressure of 250 kPa.

Use these data, where relevant, to answer the questions that follow.

a) Calculate the number of moles of each of the gases in the vessel at equilibrium. [3]

b) i) Write an expression for the equilibrium constant, K_c, for the above equilibrium.
   ii) Calculate the value of the equilibrium constant, K_c, for the above equilibrium. [4]

c) i) Write an expression for the equilibrium constant, K_p, for the above equilibrium.
   ii) Calculate the mole fraction of chlorine present in the equilibrium mixture.

iii) Calculate the partial pressure of PCl_5 present in the equilibrium mixture.

iv) Calculate the value of the equilibrium constant, K_p, and state its units. [7]

(AQA)

▶ Acid/base equilibria

11 The table gives information about the hydrogen halides, HF to HI.

	HF	HCl	HBr	HI
pK_a	3.25	−7.00	−9.00	−11.00
Average bond enthalpy / kJ mol^{-1}	562	431	366	299

a) Explain what is meant by the term *weak acid*. [1]

b) Define the term *average bond enthalpy*. [2]

c) Using the information given in the table, state and explain the variation in the strengths of acids formed by dissolving each of the hydrogen halides in water. [3]

d) Using the information in the table, state and explain how the thermal stabilities of the hydrogen halides vary from HF to HI.
Write an equation to show the effect of heat on hydrogen iodide. [3]

(AQA)

12 a) A student used a pH meter to measure the pH of an aqueous solution containing 1.00 mol dm^{-3} of propanoic acid and 0.500 mol dm^{-3} of sodium propanoate. The value obtained at 25 °C was 4.60.

i) Write an equation to show what ocurs when propanoic acid dissolves in water. [1]

ii) Write an expression for the acid dissociation constant, K_a, for propanoic acid. [1]

iii) Deduce the value of the pK_a for propanoic acid in this experiment, showing how you arrived at your answer. [4]

iv) Calculate the value of K_a for the system. [2]

b) Given that the ionic product for water is 1.00×10^{-14} mol^2 dm^{-6} at 25 °C, calculate the pH of an aqueous solution of sodium hydroxide containing 0.00500 mol dm^{-3}. [3]

c) i) Write an expression for the acid dissociation constant, K_a, of phenol. [1]

ii) Suggest how the value of K_a for phenol compares with the value of K_a for propanoic acid. [1]

(AQA)

13 In aqueous solution, hydrofluoric acid, HF is a weak acid.

a) Given that the ionisation of HF in aqueous solution is an endothermic reaction, state whether K_a increases as the temperature is raised and explain your answer. [2]

b) 10 cm^3 of 0.50 mol dm^{-3} aqueous sodium hydroxide are added to 100 cm^3 of water at 298 K. Calculate the number of moles of sodium hydroxide added and and hence the pH of the resulting solution.
At 298 K, $K_w = 1.0 \times 10^{-14}$ mol^2 dm^{-6}

c) 10 cm^3 of 0.50 mol dm^{-3} aqueous sodium hydroxide are added to solution A, which comprises 100 cm^3 of an aqueous solution containing hydrofluoric acid (0.50 mol dm^{-3}) and sodium fluoride (0.50 mol dm^{-3}). In aqueous solution, NaF is fully ionised.
At 298 K hydrofluoric acid has pK_a = 3.45

i) Write an expression for K_a for aqueous HF. Hence calculate the pH of solution A before the sodium hydroxide has been added.

ii) Calculate the concentration of HF present in the solution formed after adding the sodium hydroxide to A.

iii) Calculate the concentration of fluoride ions present in the solution formed after adding the sodium hydroxide.

iv) Use your answers above to determine the pH of the solution formed after adding the sodium hydroxide. [10]

(AQA)

14 a) State two identical features of, and two differences between the titration curves for the separate addition of 0.75 mol dm^{-3} sodium hydroxide to 25 cm^3 samples of i) 1.5 mol dm^{-3} hydrochloric acid and ii) 1.5 mol dm^{-3} ethanoic acid. [4]

b) What characteristic features must all acid–base indicators possess? Name an indicator that could be used for both the titrations in part (a) above and explain the reasons for your choice. [4]

c) An aqueous solution of the weak acid HA, which has an initial pH of 2.50, is titrated against sodium hydroxide. When the pH reaches 4.30, [HA] = [A$^-$]. Calculate the value of the acid dissociation constant of HA and hence the original concentration of the acid in solution. [7]

(AQA)

15 a) Explain the terms *acid* and *conjugate base* as used in the Brønsted–Lowry theory of acids and bases. [2]

b) For each of the following reactions, give the name or formula of the acid and of its conjugate base.

i) $NH_3 + HCl \longrightarrow NH_4^- + Cl^-$ [1]

ii) $H_2SO_4 + HNO_3 \longrightarrow HSO_4^- + H_2NO_3^-$ [1]

iii) $NaNH_2 + NH_4Cl \longrightarrow NaCl + 2NH_3$ [1]

c) When ethanoic acid, CH_3COOH dissolves in water, a solution of a weak acid is formed.

i) Explain the difference between a *strong acid* and a *weak acid*. [2]

ii) Write an equation to show the reaction of ethanoic acid with water. [1]

iii) There are two conjugate acid–base pairs involved in the reaction in c) ii). Use the symbols A1 and B1 to label one of the acid-base pairs, and the symbols A2 and B2 to label the other pair, by writing each symbol above the species to which it refers. [2]

(AQA)

16 You should answer this question in continuous prose wherever appropriate.

a) i) With the aid of an example, explain the meaning of the terms *strong acid*, *weak acid*, *strong base*, and *weak base*.

ii) Describe and explain the use of buffer solutions. [10]

b) Assuming the temperature to be 25 °C, what is the pH of each of the following?

i) 0.05 mol dm^{-3} sulphuric acid, H_2SO_4

ii) 0.01 mol dm^{-3} sodium hydroxide [3]

($K_w = 1 \times 10^{-14}$ mol^2 dm^{-6} at 25 °C)

c) Benzoic acid, $C_6H_5CO_2H$, is a weak acid with a dissociation constant, K_a, of 6.3×10^{-5} mol dm^{-3} at 25 °C.

i) Calculate the pH of 0.20 mol dm^{-3} benzoic acid at this temperature.

ii) Draw a sketch graph of the change in pH which occurs when 0.20 mol dm^{-3} potassium hydroxide is added to 25 cm^3 of 0.20 mol dm^{-3} benzoic acid until in excess.

iii) The pK_a values of some indicators are given below.

Thymol blue	1.7
Congo red	4.0
Thymolphthalein	9.7

Which of these indicators would be most suitable for determining the end point of the titration between the benzoic acid and potassium hydroxide in ii)? Explain your answer. [8]

(OCR)

17 a) i) Define pH.

ii) Calculate the pH of 0.010 mol dm^{-3} HCl(aq) and of 0.010 mol dm^{-3} NaOH(aq). ($K_w = 1.0 \times 10^{-14}$ mol^2 dm^{-6}) [4]

b) Methanoic acid, HCO_2H, behaves as a weak acid.

$$HCO_2H \rightleftharpoons HCOO^- + H^+$$

i) Write an expression for the acid dissociation constant, K_a, for HCO_2H.

ii) A buffer solution of pH 4.4 was prepared by mixing equal volumes of methanoic acid and 0.5 mol dm^{-3} sodium methanoate, HCO_2Na. Calculate the concentration of methanoic acid that was used to produce this buffer solution. (pK_a of $HCO_2H = 3.8$) [3]

c) The following equations show acid/base reactions.

$$H_2SO_4 + HNO_3 \rightleftharpoons H_2NO_3^+ + HSO_4^-$$
$$H_2O + HS^- \rightleftharpoons H_3O^+ + S^{2-}$$

i) In **each** equation, draw a ring round a reagent which is behaving as an acid.

ii) Use **one** of the equations to explain the nature of acid/base reactions. [3]

(OCR)

18 a) Write expressions to show the meaning of the terms K_a (for an acid HA), pK_a and K_w. [3]

b) Calculate the pH of a 0.65 M solution of propanoic acid ($K_a = 1.4 \times 10^{-5}$ mol dm^{-3}). [4]

c) Select a suitable indicator for a titration of propanoic acid with sodium hydroxide. Give a reason for your choice. [2]

(AQA)

19 When ammonium salts are dissolved in water the following equilibrium is set up:

$$NH_4^+(aq) \rightleftharpoons NH_3(aq) + H^+(aq)$$

a) Write the full expression for the dissociation constant, K_a, for this equilibrium. [2]

b) The pH of a solution of ammonium chloride is 5.6.

i) Calculate the hydrogen ion concentration in this solution, showing the mathematical relationship you use. [2]

ii) What will happen to the concentration of **ammonium ions** in solution when hydrochloric acid is added to the ammonium chloride? Explain your answer. [2]

c) A mixture of ammonium chloride and ammonia solution acts as a buffer.

i) What is meant by a **buffer** solution? [2]

ii) Explain the changes which occur when a solution containing hydroxide ions, OH^-, is added to this buffer. [2]

d) The equilibrium involving ammonium ions and ammonia can be written showing the water molecules.

$$NH_4^+(aq) + H_2O(l) \rightleftharpoons NH_3(aq) + H_3O^+(aq)$$

Use the Brønsted–Lowry theory to explain whether water is acting as an acid or a base in this equilibrium. [1]

(EDEXCEL)

▶ Redox: Extraction of metals

20 Niobium, Nb, is a transition metal. From your knowledge of the extraction of other metals, suggest three different possible methods for the extraction of niobium by direct reduction of its oxide (Nb_2O_5). For each method you suggest, predict one likely advantage and one likely disadvantage.

(AQA)

21 Sodium metal is manufactured in a Downs cell, as shown in the diagram. The electrolyte is molten sodium chloride, to which some calcium chloride is added.

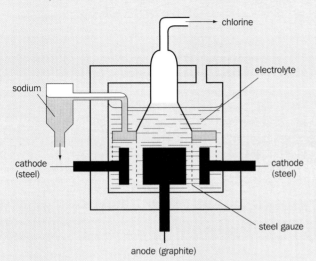

a) Give the ionic half-equation for the electrode process which is a reduction. Use oxidation numbers to justify the term *reduction*. [2]

b) Suggest **one** reason why most of the chlorine manufactured in the U.K. is **not** produced by the Downs cell method. [1]

c) Downs cell plants are sometimes situated in mountainous areas. What is the economic advantage of this? [1]

d) The anode is made of graphite, although steel is a better electrical conductor. Suggest why graphite is used rather than steel. [1]

e) Explain why the addition of calcium chloride to the electrolyte reduces the energy cost of the process. [2]

(OCR)

▶ Redox: Electrode potentials

22 Use the standard electrode potentials in the list below, as appropriate, to answer the questions which follow.

	$E^{\ominus}$/V
$MnO_4^-(aq) + 8\,H^+(aq) + 5\,e^- \longrightarrow Mn^{2+}(aq) + 4\,H_2O(l)$	+1.51
$Cl_2(g) + 2\,e^- \longrightarrow 2\,Cl^-(aq)$	+1.36
$Cr_2O_7^{2-}(aq) + 14\,H^+(aq) + 6\,e^- \longrightarrow 2\,Cr^{3+}(aq) + 7\,H_2O(l)$	+1.33
$Fe^{3+}(aq) + e^- \longrightarrow Fe^{2+}(aq)$	+0.78
$Fe^{3+}(aq) + 3\,e^- \longrightarrow Fe(s)$	−0.04
$Fe^{2+}(aq) + 2\,e^- \longrightarrow Fe(s)$	−0.44

a) The two half-cells above which involve metallic iron are joined to produce an electrochemical cell. Using standard notation, give the conventional representation for this cell, calculate its standard potential, and write an equation for the spontaneous reaction that occurs. [6]

b) Potassium manganate(VII) and potassium dichromate(VI) are both strong oxidising agents. Which of the two is not used for the quantitative estimation of iron(II) ions in a solution of iron(II) chloride? Use data from the table to justify your choice. [3]

c) Equimolar solutions of acidified potassium manganate(VII), manganese(II) sulphate, potassium dichromate(VI) and chromium(VII) sulphate are mixed and allowed to come to equilibrium.
   i) State which ion is oxidised and which is reduced.
   ii) Use half-equations to construct the equation for the overall reaction that occurs. [5]

(AQA)

23 a) List four important features of the standard hydrogen electrode. [4]

b) The redox couples $Mn^{2+}(aq)\,|\,Mn(s)$ and $U^{3+}(aq)\,|\,U(s)$ have standard electrode potentials of −1.18 V and −1.79 V respectively.
   i) What is the standard potential of an electrochemical cell formed by connecting the two half-cells under standard conditions?
   ii) Write an equation, including state symbols, for the resulting spontaneous cell reaction. [4]

(AQA)

24 The diagram shows the apparatus used to determine the standard electrode potential, $E^{\ominus}$, for zinc, i.e. $Zn^{2+}(aq)\,|\,Zn(s)$.

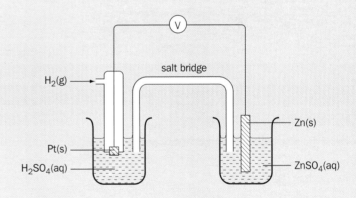

a) In this standard cell, what is the concentration of
   i) $Zn^{2+}(aq)$
   ii) $H_2SO_4(aq)$? [2]

b) State the pressure at which $H_2(g)$ is used in the hydrogen half-cell. [1]

c) The standard electrode potential of $Zn^{2+}(aq)\,|\,Zn(s)$ is −0.76 V. What temperature is used when this value is measured? [1]

(d) Name a suitable salt to be used in the salt bridge. [1]

(OCR)

Synoptic questions

1 Sodium chloride is a very important chemical feedstock used to produce sodium, sodium hydroxide and chlorine.
   a) i) How is sodium made from sodium chloride? Details of the manufacturing plant are not required. [2]
      ii) Sodium melts at about 98 °C, has a density of $0.97\,g\,cm^{-3}$ and can easily be cut with a knife. Explain these facts on the basis of the structure of sodium. [3]
   b) Sodium metal is a powerful reducing agent, and is used to make titanium using the following reaction.

   $$TiCl_4(l) + 4\,Na(l) \longrightarrow Ti(s) + 4\,NaCl(s)$$

   The table shows various properties of NaCl and $TiCl_4$.

	Melting temperature/°C	Boiling temperature/°C	Action in moist air
$TiCl_4$	−25	137	dense white fumes
NaCl	801	1413	none

   i) State the nature of bonding in each of these chlorides, and explain why each of them has the bonding you state. [2]
   ii) $TiCl_4$ is made from TiO_2 which occurs naturally as ilmenite. The ore is chlorinated using chlorine at about 1100 K. The product contains the volatile chlorides of silicon and vanadium amongst others. Name the process by which $TiCl_4$ may be separated from these other volatile chlorides. [1]
   iii) One of the main reactions in $TiCl_4$ extraction is

   $$TiO_2(s) + 2\,Cl_2(g) + C(s) \longrightarrow TiCl_4(l) + CO_2(g)$$

   The standard enthalpies of formation in $kJ\,mol^{-1}$ are as follows. $TiO_2(s)$ −940; $TiCl_4$ −804; and $CO_2(g)$ −394. Calculate ΔH for this reaction. [7]
   c) Sodium hydroxide and chlorine may be made simultaneously from brine in a diaphragm cell.
   i) Briefly indicate the conditions required and sketch the plant used, outlining the principles of its operation. [4]
   ii) Give the equation and the conditions for the reaction of sodium hydroxide with ethyl ethanoate. Which industrial process uses this *type* of reaction? [3]
   iii) Give the equation for the reaction of chlorine with cold, dilute sodium hydroxide solution, and use this reaction to illustrate the meaning of the term *disproportionation*. [4]
   (EDEXCEL)

2 Many insects communicate using chemical compounds called pheromones. Such compounds may be quite simple, and organism is extremely sensitive to their presence. Insect alarm pheromones have been studied as potential insecticides. Using the information which follows, deduce the formula for an alarm pheromone, P, in ants.
   a) P contains 73.47% carbon and 10.20% hydrogen by mass, the remainder being oxygen. The mass spectrum shows a significant peak at $m/e = 98$ but none higher than this. Find the empirical formula and molecular formula for P. [5]
   b) P decolorises bromine water readily at room temperature. 0.735 g of P dissolved in tetrachloromethane reacts with $30\,cm^3$ of a $0.250\,mol\,dm^{-3}$ solution of bromine in the same solvent. Use this information to find the nature and number of one of the types of functional group in the molecule. [3]
   c) P gives a precipitate with 2,4-dinitrophenylhydrazine and reduces ammoniacal silver nitrate solution on warming. What is the second functional group in P? Give your reasons. [2]
   d) P can be reduced by hydrogen/platinum at room temperature, or by sodium borohydride in ether. In each case, 1 mole of P adds on one mole of hydrogen, but the products are not the same. Explain these observations. [3]
   e) The carbon chain in P is unbranched, and the functional groups are adjacent on the chain. P has two stereoisomers. Draw the possible structures of P. [2]
   f) Only one of these stereoisomers is effective at persuading ants to disappear elsewhere. Suggest why this is so. [1]
   (EDEXCEL)

3 Carvone is the main flavouring material in spearmint oil.

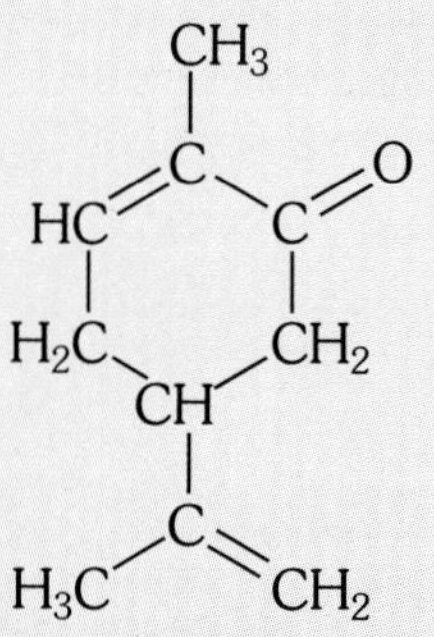

   may also be drawn as

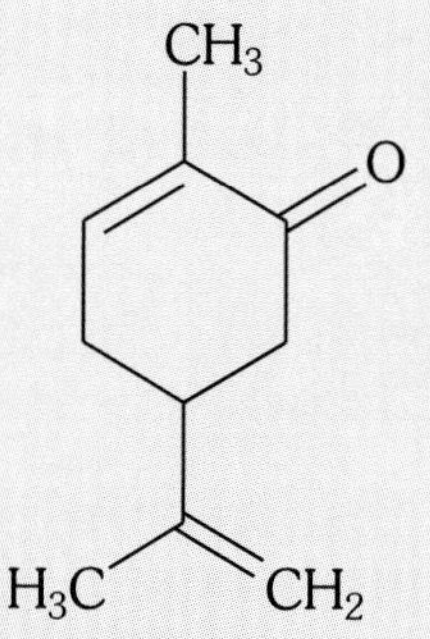

   a) Draw the structure of the product obtained when carvone reacts with
   i) 2,4-dinitrophenylhydrazine [2]
   ii) bromine [2]
   b) Explain why carvone does not react with ammoniacal silver nitrate (Tollens' reagent). [1]

c) Carvone is chiral and shows optical activity.
   i) Explain the meaning of the term chiral. [1]
   ii) Copy the structure of carvone and circle the feature of the molecule which makes it chiral. [1]
   iii) What is optical activity? [2]
d) Suggest a synthetic method, including reference to reagents and conditions, by which carvone could be converted into the following compound:

CH₃
Cl
H₃C CH₂

(EDEXCEL)

4 Phenylamine, $C_6H_5NH_2$, can be made in several ways from benzene. The flowchart shows two of these in outline.

AlCl₃/C₂H₅Cl
C_8H_{10} A
MnO₄⁻/OH⁻
$C_7H_6O_2$ B
PCl₅
C_7H_5OCl C
NH₃
C_7H_7NO D

Step 1 → NO₂
Step 2 → NH₂
Step 3 → phenylamine

a) i) Give the reagents and conditions needed for step 1. [2]
   ii) Write the mechanism for this reaction [4]
   iii) Give the reagents and conditions for step 2. [3]
b) i) In the alternative pathway identify the compounds A to D inclusive. [4]
   ii) State the reagents and conditions for step 3. [3]
   iii) Why is the first pathway commercially preferable for the manufacture of phenylamine? [1]
c) Phenylamine reacts with nitrous acid in the presence of concentrated hydrochloric acid at 0 – 5 °C to produce benzenediazonium chloride. If the temperature of this solution rises, this

compound reacts with the solvent water to give phenol, C_6H_5OH, and nitrogen gas. The rate of reaction can be followed by measuring the volume of nitrogen produced at various times, pressure and temperature remaining constant. The amount of benzenediazonium chloride remaining in the solution is proportional to $V_\infty - V_t$, where V_t is the volume of gas at time t and V_∞ is that at the end of the reaction.
   i) Give the equation for the reaction between benzenediazonium chloride and water. [2]
   ii) Some results of this experiment are shown below.

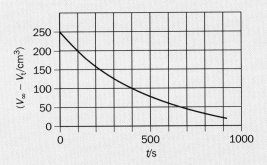

Deduce the order of the reaction with respect to benzenediazonium chloride from the graph. [4]
   iv) Is the reaction necessarily of this order overall? Explain your answer. [2]

(EDEXCEL)

5 Isomers with the formula C_4H_8 are hydrocarbons in which the carbon atoms can be linked in a straight or branched chain or in a ring.
W, **X**, **Y** and **Z** are four isomers with formula C_4H_8 but their carbon atoms are linked in different ways. Some information about them is given in the table below.

Hydrocarbon	W	X	Y	Z
Effect of adding bromine	no change	immediately decolourised	immediately decolourised	immediately decolourised
Number of peaks in NMR spectrum	1	2	3	4

a) Use the information in the table above to deduce a possible structure of each of the four hydrocarbons. Draw **displayed** formulae for **W**, **X**, **Y** and **Z** and give *brief* reasons for your deductions. [6]
b) The isomers of C_4H_8 can all be atomised as shown below.

$$C_4H_8(g) \longrightarrow 4\,C(g) + 8\,H(g)$$

Synoptic questions

Use the values of bond energies below:

Bond	Bond energy / kJ mol^{-1}
C—H	413
C—C	347
C=C	612

to calculate the value of the standard enthalpy change, $\Delta H^{\ominus}$, for the equation
i) for the isomer with carbon atoms in a ring.
ii) for any **one** other isomer.
Discuss two factors which cause these isomers to differ in stability with respect to their elements. [6]

c) Hydrocarbons are important starting materials in organic syntheses. Suggest how the following could be made from C_4H_8.

i) $H_3C-\overset{\displaystyle\underset{\textstyle O}{\|}}{C}-\overset{\displaystyle\underset{\textstyle O}{\|}}{C}-CH_3$

ii) $H_3C-\underset{\textstyle CO_2H}{CH}-CH_2-CH_3$

In each case show the structural formula of the isomer you select, and give chemical equations for all the reactions involved. Show reaction conditions where appropriate.

The infra-red spectra of the two products have one principal difference. State fully the cause of this difference and where the difference would be observed in the spectrum. [8]

(EDEXCEL)

---

6 a) The following data concerns the redox chemistry of halogen elements and sodium thiosulphate.

$$E^{\ominus}/V$$

$$Cl_2 + 2\,e^- \rightleftharpoons 2\,Cl^- \qquad +1.36$$
$$Br_2 + 2\,e^- \rightleftharpoons 2\,Br^- \qquad +1.07$$
$$2\,SO_4^{2-} + 10\,H^+ + 8\,e^- \rightleftharpoons S_2O_3^{2-} + 5\,H_2O \qquad +0.57$$
$$I_2 + 2\,e^- \rightleftharpoons 2\,I^- \qquad +0.54$$
$$S_4O_6^{2-} + 2\,e^- \rightleftharpoons 2\,S_2O_3^{2-} \qquad +0.09$$

i) What is the maximum change in oxidation number of sulphur which can be brought about by the action of sodium thiosulphate with: iodine; chlorine?
Write full ionic equations for each reaction. [5]
ii) Suggest a reason why bromine cannot be estimated by direct titration with sodium thiosulphate in the same way that iodine can. [2]

---

b) Bromine can be used to convert ethene to 1,2-dibromoethane which can then undergo further reactions as shown below:

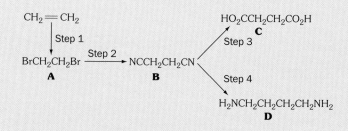

i)   Give the reagents and conditions required for each of steps 2, 3 and 4, clearly identifying the step to which you are referring. [6]
ii) Write a mechanism for the reaction in step 2. Give the type of mechanism and identify the rate determining step. [6]
iii) **C** and **D** can react together to give a polymer. Give the structural formula of this polymer showing clearly the repeat unit. [3]
iv) The polymer in b) iii) could be made more rapidly in the laboratory if **C** was first converted into another more reactive compound. Give the formula of this compound and show how it could be formed from **C**. [3]

(EDEXCEL)

---

7 a) Most metals have high melting points, and high electrical and thermal conductivities.
i)   Describe the bonding in a metal.
ii) Draw a diagram to illustrate your answer.
iii) How does the bonding account for high electrical and thermal conductivities of a metal? [3]
b) Write a short account of FOUR characteristic chemical or physical properties of transition metals and their compounds NOT mentioned in part a). Illustrate your answer with examples. [8]
c) When dilute hydrochloric acid is added to yellow sodium chromate(VI) solution, the solution turns orange.
When dilute sodium hydroxide is added to orange sodium dichromate(VI) solution, the solution turns yellow.
Use the chemical equation below to explain what is happening in these two reactions.

$$2\,CrO_4^{2-}(aq) + 2\,H^+(aq) \rightleftharpoons Cr_2O_7^{2-}(aq) + H_2O(l)$$

[3]

d) Name **two** transition metals, other than iron, and give one use of each. [2]

(EDEXCEL)

8 a) The term **acid** is used to describe a wide range of substances, some of which are listed below:

hydrofluoric acid (a solution of hydrogen fluoride) and hydrobromic acid (a solution of hydrogen bromide),

phenol and benzoic acid,

ethanoic acid and trichloroethanoic acid,

water and the ammonium ion, NH_4^+.

For each pair of substances in the list explain why the first substance is a weaker acid than the second, using data where appropriate.
In your answer you should make clear the features of each substance which allow it to be classified as an acid.   [10]

b) The formulae below show two isomeric amino acids.

$$
\begin{array}{ccc}
\text{H} & & \text{CH}_3 \\
| & & | \\
\text{C}_2\text{H}_5\!-\!\text{C}\!-\!\text{CO}_2\text{H} & \quad & \text{CH}_3\!-\!\text{C}\!-\!\text{CO}_2\text{H} \\
| & & | \\
\text{NH}_2 & & \text{NH}_2 \\
\textbf{A} & & \textbf{B}
\end{array}
$$

The structures of these acids can be investigated using spectroscopic techniques.
Use a book of data to predict the principal features in their infra-red spectra.
Low resolution nuclear magnetic resonance (NMR) spectroscopy of acid **A** produces a spectrum with 5 main peaks while the spectrum of **B** contains 3 peaks. Suggest why the isomers produce different spectra.
Which of the two spectroscopic techniques do you consider more useful for investigation of these isomers? Explain your answer.   [5]
(EDEXCEL)

9 This question is about how and why reactions occur. Experimental studies of rates give clues about reaction mechanisms, and studies of energetics indicate their direction and extent.
Explain what can be deduced from the results of these studies, illustrating your answer with references to some specific reactions.
For full credit you should consider at least four of the following:

- how measurements of rates are used to find the order of a reaction;
- how to deduce a rate equation;
- what rate equations indicate about reaction mechanisms;
- how activation energy is measured, and its significance;
- information deduced from catalysed reactions;
- information from measuring ΔH, ΔS and ΔG values.

You are not expected to discuss how to carry out particular reactions but should explain the use of the results.   [15]
(EDEXCEL)

▷ Revision skills

When you revise, you need to
balance your time between:

- learning your notes
- practising past paper questions

The next four pages concentrate mainly on how you can learn your notes
effectively so that you have a good knowledge and understanding of
chemistry when you go into the exam room.

Before you start:

- Get a copy of the syllabus (specification) from your teacher
  or the Awarding Body.

- Be clear about which topics you need to revise for the exam you are about
  to take. If you check the website at www.nelsonthornes.com you will find
  a section which will help with this.

- Work out which are your strong topics and which you will need to spend
  more time on. One way of doing this is to look at tests or exams that you
  have done in the past to identify any weaknesses.

Some helpful ideas

1. Work out your best way of learning. Some people learn best from
diagrams/videos whilst some prefer listening (perhaps to taped notes) and
making up rhymes and phrases. Others prefer doing something active with
the information like answering questions or making a poster on a topic.

If you know which way you prefer, then this will help you to get the most
out of your revision.

Work out your best way of learning!

2. Test yourself! Just reading through notes will not make them stick.
Get someone to test you on a section of work or write down some questions
testing your knowledge of the topic. A quick way of doing this is to tape the
questions and then play them back to yourself.
Check your notes if you can't answer any of the questions.

3. Teach others. If you can find someone to teach a topic to (friends or
family?) then this is sometimes the best way to learn. You and some friends
might take in turns to present a topic to each other.

4. Make sure that you understand the work! It is unlikely that you will
remember much chemistry if you do not understand it!

Having said that, there are still things that you need to learn by heart.
For example, if you don't know that alcohols contain the —OH group,
there is no way to work that out from first principles. So know your basic facts!
But don't waste your time learning data that will be given in the exam.
If you aren't sure, ask your teacher for guidance.

Teach others!

Some revision techniques

1. Get an overall view of a topic first. Before you start revising a topic, quickly read through the whole topic so that you have a general understanding of it and of how the different bits of it connect with each other. A good place to start is with the summary shown at the end of each chapter.

2. Highlight key words and phrases in your notes using hi-lighter pens in different colours.

3. Make notes. Rewriting and condensing notes is a good and active way of reading and then understanding what you need to learn.

4. Make yourself cards with notes on one side and a diagram on the other. Test yourself by looking at the diagram and seeing if you can recite the notes.

5. Visualisation. When you are memorising material, always try to get a bold and bright picture in your mind that will help you to remember. It helps if the picture is something which is very important to you because it is easily remembered (girl/boyfriend? football team? rock group?). Sometimes imagining something outrageous that can be connected to the fact may help.

Use visualisation

6. A poster. You can summarise a topic with a poster which you can put on the wall of your bedroom. Include important words and phrases in large, bold letters. If you are a *visual* person then include bright, colourful diagrams which illustrate the ideas.

7. A mind map. This is a poster which summarises a topic by showing the links between the different concepts that make it up. Making a mind map forces you to think about a topic and will help your understanding of it.

8. Use rhymes and phrases. Some people are good at rhymes or raps and this can be a way of memorising work. Phrases such as **R**ichard **o**f **Y**ork **g**ave **b**attle **i**n **v**ain, which is used to remember the colours of the spectrum (red, orange, yellow, green … etc.), can be useful.

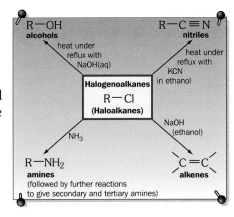

Make posters

9. Revision CD ROMs. These can be bought in many shops and often have questions for you to test yourself. They are an active way of revising which may suit you.

10. Practice calculations. You can learn the techniques involved in different types of chemical calculation as follows:

Find a worked example to look through in your notes or book.
Make sure you understand the logical steps between lines in the calculation.
Then cover the answer and try to solve the problem yourself.
If you get the answer wrong, this method can show you straight away where you went wrong. Or if you get stuck, you can reveal the next line, and then carry on.

You should then try some other problems from scratch.

▷ Organising revision

Do you have difficulty starting revision and feel that there is so much to do that you will never complete it?
Do you constantly put off revising and find other things to do?

There are ways in which you can help yourself:

1. Think about the positive effects of starting. When you have finished a session you will feel good that you have made progress and will feel less anxious about not getting enough work done.

2. Think about the negative effects of delaying. What will happen and who will be affected if you put off starting?

3. Give yourself rewards. Think of things with which you can reward yourself at the end of a session, e.g. a cup of coffee or listening to some favourite music.

4. Get help! Think of ways to involve friends and family which will make revision easier and more enjoyable.

Reward yourself AT THE END of a planned revision session!

Making a revision timetable

Some recent research suggests that some students do better in exams than others because they;

● start their revision earlier

● use better techniques for learning work such as testing themselves, rather than just reading their notes

● get help from others rather than working alone

● have a planned revision timetable which includes working on their weaknesses.

You can use these ideas to help you plan a **revision timetable**.

1. Start your revision a long time before your exams (at least eight weeks). Plan to spend quite a lot of the last two weeks before your exam on revising your weaker topics again.

2. Note down when you will cover each topic and stick to this!

3. Spend more time on your weaker areas. Try to get extra help on them from your teacher.
   (Don't just do the things you are good at already!)

4. Give yourself enough time to do past questions.

5. Arrange in some revision periods to work with someone who can help.

6. Do some social activities in between revision sessions, so that you don't go completely crazy!

What will you revise?

You will need to divide your time between:

1. Learning the work which you have covered so that you have a good knowledge and understanding of it, including knowing chemical formulae and definitions of terms such as ionisation enthalpy (energy).
2. Practising past questions so that you know what to do when you get a similar question in the exam. This can be useful in learning work, because you will often need to read your notes to help you answer a question. You can also judge where your weaknesses are.

You need to work out what is best for you – how much time should you spend on each and which should you start first?

How long should you revise for?

Research suggests that if you start revision with no thought of when you will stop, then your learning efficiency just gets less and less.

However, if you do decide on a fixed time, say 30 minutes, then you learn the most at the beginning of a session and just before you have decided to stop. This is when the brain realises that it is coming to the end of a session. (See the first two graphs.)

Which would be better, one two-hour session or four 25 minute sessions with a break of 10 minutes in between them?

The four sessions would be much better, as shown by the second graph. It is important, though, to stick to the 25 minutes and have a break, rather than just carrying on!

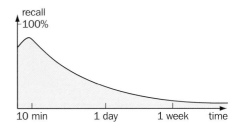

Short revision sessions are more effective

How often should you revise?

The third graph shows what percentage of revised material is remembered after you have stopped.
As it shows, you very quickly forget material which you have revised.

The first graph below shows that, if you revise work again after 10 minutes, then the amount you remember increases.

So what should you do after you have had your 10 minute break after working for 25 minutes?

You should briefly read again what you have been studying.

If you then revise this material again after a day and then after a week then you remember even more of the work, as shown by the last graph.

The trick is to briefly revise a topic again at regular intervals!

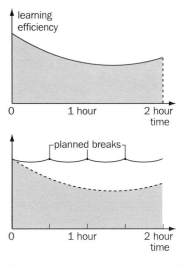

Recall falls rapidly after one revision session

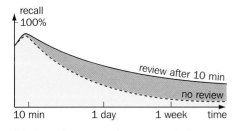

(Horizontal axes not drawn to scale!)

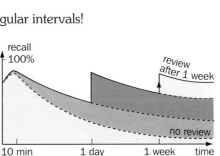

Recall improves by reviewing revised material regularly

▷ Exam technique

Before the exam

1. Make sure that you carefully check the times and dates of all your exams, so that you are not late!

2. Make sure that you know which type of paper (e.g. multiple-choice, short answer) is on which day, and which topics are being examined on which paper.

3. Make sure that you know how many questions you have to do on each paper, how long it is and whether you will get a choice of question. Plan how long you will spend on each question on a paper.

4. Make sure that you are familiar with the chemical formulae of the compounds named in your syllabus (specification).

5. On the night before the exam, it may help you to steady your nerves by briefly looking through your notes. But don't do too much!

6. Make sure that you get a good night's rest before your exam.

On the day of the exam

1. Aim to arrive early at the exam and try to get into the room as early as possible. This will help you to settle your nerves and give you time to prepare.

2. Don't drink alcohol before an exam, or eat too much or too little food.

3. Make sure that you are properly equipped with pens and pencils (and spares in case they break), a rubber, ruler, calculator (check the batteries) and a watch.

During the exam

1. Don't waste time when you get the paper! Write your name and exam number onto the front of any sheets of paper or answer booklets that you are going to use.
   Read the instructions on the front page of the exam.

2. Read each question very carefully and underline important parts.
   If you have a choice on which questions to attempt, then read *all* of the questions on the paper. Remember that some of the later parts of some questions can be easier than the first parts.

3. Don't dive into a question without reading all of it first.

4. Do not spend too long on any question! If you are stuck just leave some space so that you can go back to it later.
    It is easier to get 50% on all the questions than 100% on half of them.

5. Sometimes you may be stuck on one part of the question. Check to make sure that there are no later parts which you can do easily.

6. Write neatly and in short sentences that will be easier for the marker to understand. Try to be precise and detailed without writing too much, so that you don't waste time.

7. Make your diagrams clear and neat but do not spend a long time on them to make them perfect.

8. Check that you have done all the required questions – for example, sometimes people don't see that there is a question on the last page of the paper!

9. Check your answers! The first thing that you should check is whether an answer is much too big or too small.
    You must also check units and significant figures.

Check if your answer seems too big or too small

Some hints on answering questions

1. If an exam paper shows that a question is worth 4 marks then put down 4 points in your answer.

2. Use correct scientific words as much as possible.

3. When you do calculation questions you must show your working – for example, there is often a mark for writing down the right equation which you will get even if you don't finally get the right answer.

4. Don't forget units and to give the answer to the same number of significant figures as the numbers in the question.

5. In a multiple choice question narrow down your options by crossing out those answers which can't possibly be right. If you are then not sure … guess!

6. Even though you get no marks for doing working in multi-choice questions, you are more likely to get them right if you do careful calculations.

7. When you are asked to draw a graph, label the axes (including units) and plan a sensible scale to fill most of the grid.

8. Make sure your chemical equations are balanced. Remember to include state symbols where appropriate, especially in questions on enthalpy changes.

9. If asked for a 'reagent' in a question, give its full name (as it would appear on its bottle), e.g. sodium hydroxide solution, not hydroxide ions.

10. If a question starts with the word 'explain', marks are given for reasons. You might begin your answer with a phrase starting 'because …'.

11. If you use the word 'stable' in an answer always follow it up with the words 'with respect to …'.
    For example, 'Because glucose is kinetically stable with respect to its products of combustion'.

Practical skills

Your practical skills can be assessed by a practical examination or by your teacher as you work through the course.
In either case you need to develop your skills in 4 areas:

1. Planning
2. Implementing
3. Analysing and drawing conclusions
4. Evaluating.

These skills are grouped differently by different Awarding Bodies. So you must make sure that you know how yours will judge your level in the areas it defines. However, the following advice will be useful whichever exam you are taking.

▷ Planning

Your planning skills will be assessed in the context of work you do in your AS or A2 modules. Just like an actual research chemist, you will be able to look up information to help you plan an experiment.

You can use textbooks, data books, CD ROMs, databases, Hazcards, or any other source of useful information. This might include leaflets, posters, videos, TV programmes or results from trial runs.
You will need to plan your method *in detail*.

To get good marks you must think about:

- stating your problem and presenting your plan clearly and accurately
- which chemicals to use and how much of each you will need
- the purity of your reagents and products
- which techniques your experiment requires
- which apparatus you will use
- the precision of your measurements
- the measuring equipment that can give you the precision you require
- how many readings will be needed to get reliable results
- the range over which your readings will be taken
- the logical sequence of steps
- the control of variables (if appropriate)
- any safety issues. (You can make a risk assessment for your procedure, including the hazards involved in using any reagents or products formed and the control measures that need to be taken.)

Oxidising

Highly flammable

Toxic

Harmful

Corrosive

Irritant

You need to know these symbols when planning chemical experiments

▷ Implementing

This skill looks at the way that you carry out your experiments. You will need to be familiar with a variety of chemical techniques used for analysis, synthesis and investigation.

The techniques below might be useful, depending on the nature of your activity:

Titration
– used to find reacting quantities in solution. The first result is often approximate, then the titration is repeated until two titres are within 0.1 cm^3 of each other.

Heating under reflux
– used to heat volatile substances without losing reactants or products by evaporation

Suction filtration
– used to separate solids from solvents in a Buchner funnel and flask. (Useful in preparing and purifying organic compounds)

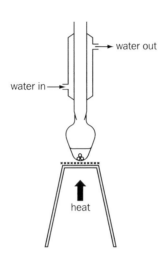

water out

water in

heat

Colorimeter
– used to monitor the concentration of coloured solutions. (See page 326.)

Separating immiscible liquids
– used to separate two liquids that do not mix in a separating funnel

Any techniques you use should be carried out skilfully, safely and with confidence. For the best marks you will not need the guidance of your teacher (but remember the need to work safely!).

Any measurements you make should be taken with care, reading the equipment to the precision allowed by the scale.
Data logging can be a useful way to gather data, particularly over long periods of time, or in very fast reactions.

You will also need to **record** your results effectively.
In a chemical investigation, this is often done in a table.
The variable that you have changed systematically (in order to find its effect) will go in the first column of your table.
This is called the independent variable.
The second column is used to record your measurements of the dependent variable.
This will often be split up so that repeat readings can be presented.
Look at the example below:

Temperature / °C	Time for cross under flask to disappear / s			
	1st test	2nd test	3rd test	Average

▷ Analysing and drawing conclusions

Once you have a set of data, then your analysis begins. The skills you use
will depend upon the data gathered or given to you. They could include:

- calculations (giving answers to the appropriate number of significant figures)
- drawing graphs (using lines of best fit and recognising anomalous results)
- interpreting graphs using mathematical techniques
- explaining trends using detailed chemical knowledge and understanding,
  together with technical language and symbols
- interpreting the chemical and physical analysis of an unknown substance.

Here is some guidance to help you with interpreting graphs and tackling calculations:

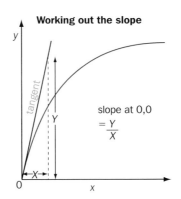

Mathematical analysis of graphs

There are two examples of lines that you need to work with:

a) straight lines
   These can always be
   described by the equation:

   $$y = mx + c$$

b) curves
   You can find the rate at which y is
   changing for any value of x by working
   out the slope at that point:

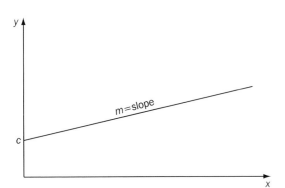

Significant figures in calculations

To get the best marks you should report the answers to any calculations
to the appropriate number of significant figures. This means that you need
to look at the accuracy of your measurements. For example, you might have
data from a thermometer read to the nearest 0.5 °C.

If the reading taken is 18.5 °C, then it is reported to 3 significant figures.
In the same experiment 25 cm^3 of solution might have been measured
using a 50 cm^3 measuring cylinder. This reads to the nearest cm^3.

So 25 cm^3 is reported to 2 significant figures. If both values are then used in a
calculation, you should only report your answer to 2 significant numbers. Your
accuracy is decided by your least accurate data.
Look at the example opposite:

How could you improve the accuracy of your answer?

Final temperature = 30.0 °C
Initial temperature = 18.5 °C
Rise in temperature = 11.5 °C

Energy given out = 25 × 4.18 × 11.5 J
               = 1201.75 J
               = 1200 J
(reported to 2 significant figures)
or 1.2 kJ

(It takes 4.18 J to raise the temperature
of 1 cm^3 of solution by 1 °C
– data given to 3 significant figures.)

> **Always use the data measured to the least number of significant
> figures to decide on the number of significant figures you include
> in the final line of your calculation**.

N.B. If your calculation involves relative atomic masses, you can assume they are
accurate. So you do not have to consider them when deciding how many significant
figures should appear in your answer.
(See page 442 for more guidance on significant figures.)

▷ Evaluation

The final skill area involves reflecting on your working methods, the quality of evidence produced and hence the strength of any conclusions drawn. In order to gain high marks you should think about:

I can't understand my low yield.

- the suitability and limitations of the methods used to generate the data
- the errors involved in your procedures, including measuring equipment used
- estimating percentage errors in order to identify the main sources of error
- suggesting how you could reduce the main sources of error
- the reliability of the data (i.e. if you or someone else were to repeat your experiment, would you get the same results?)
- suggesting how to gather more reliable data, if appropriate
- any anomalous results and explaining why they are out of line with the rest of the data
- the strength of the conclusions you can draw from a set of data

(You might consider the number of measurements or observations made. Or the range over which readings are taken. Will any generalisations made be true for readings taken outside the range within which your data lies? Is the percentage error in experimental data so great as to make your conclusions invalid?)

Considering errors

Example

A student decided to find out the enthalpy of combustion of an alcohol. He used the apparatus opposite:

He measured out 50 cm³ of water using a 100 cm³ measuring cylinder. He estimated that he could read this volume to within ±1 cm³. This gives a percentage error in his measurement of $1/50 \times 100 = 2\%$

He measured the rise in temperature of 2.5 °C using a thermometer that can be read to ±0.5 °C.
This means that there could be an error of 0.5 °C in both the initial and final temperature noted by the student. So the rise in temperature contains a potential error of 0.5 + 0.5 = 1.0 °C. This is a percentage error of $1.0/2.5 \times 100 = 40\%$.
This major source of error would be carried into the calculation of the energy given out when burning the alcohol. Once we put these values into the equation:
Energy given out = mass (which equals the volume of water used) × 4.18 × rise in temperature.
Then the errors are multiplied together.
This means that there could be as much as (2% × 40%) = 80% error in the value calculated for the energy given out!

So you can see that any evaluation must comment on this large source of error and its effect on the final answer worked out for the enthalpy of combustion. The student should also consider ways to reduce this error. Can you make any suggestions?

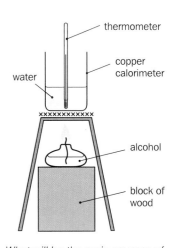

thermometer

copper calorimeter

water

xxxxxxxxxxxx

alcohol

block of wood

What will be the main sources of error carrying out the experiment as shown above?

Key Skills in Advanced Chemistry

When you study chemistry you learn about lots of chemicals
and how they react with one another. You also learn about
a variety of ways in which chemists solve problems.
But one of the best things about studying A levels (any A levels) is that
you learn how to do lots of other things which you will find useful at work
or at university even if you do not become a professional chemist.
Three important areas are using the skills of communication, number
and IT.

To recognise this, the Government has introduced a new qualification
called the Key Skills Qualification.
To get this qualification, you have to achieve three units:
- one in Communication,
- one in Application of Number, and
- one in IT.

For each unit, you have to produce a portfolio of evidence
(better known as coursework) and pass a test (like a short exam).
You can pass a unit at any Level from 1 to 4 and you should aim
as high as you can.
Level 3 is probably the right level for an A level student to aim for.

The other key skills – working with others, problem solving
and improving your own learning – are just as important
as those listed above but are not examined.

You should have practised your key skills harder!

The Qualification is separate from your A level course;
in fact, it is also available to people taking GNVQs, degrees,
Modern Apprenticeships, or any other kind of education or training.
However, the idea is that you should develop these Key Skills
and get your portfolio of evidence (as much as possible anyway)
within your A level course.
But you don't have to get all the evidence from your A levels,
and certainly not all from A level Chemistry.
Your tutor will advise you about this.

The main thing is that you should aim to develop the skills
where they are needed naturally, not force them in where they don't fit.
Chemistry is a good subject for the first three Key Skills,
because you are communicating and using numbers all the time,
and IT is becoming an ever more essential tool for research and analysis.

The next few pages give you some ideas to help you make the most
of the opportunities in A level Chemistry to become good at
the Key Skills and to get the portfolio of evidence you need.

But remember, an important part of Key Skills is that
you take the initiative yourself. So, whenever you produce a piece of work,
you should ask yourself: 'Have I used any of the Key Skills,
and are there any more Key Skills I could have used?'

Communication

Communicating our ideas to other people is one of the most important things we ever do, both in discussions and in writing. Scientists sometimes have a poor reputation when it comes to communication. But we know that some scientists communicate very well. How do they do that?

The Level 3 Communication unit (you should ask your tutor for your own copy of the Key Skills units) says that you should be able to:

- contribute to discussions, in twos and threes and in larger groups

- make a presentation to an audience (a small one will do!)

- select, read and understand quite long articles and sections from books, and take out the bits you need at the time

- write essays, reports, etc. in a way that suits what you are trying to communicate. This includes using diagrams, graphs, tables, etc. if they help you say what you want to say. In chemistry, they usually do make your work more clear.

You will do most of this in a chemistry course anyway. If you can learn how to do it at Level 3, you will be well on the way to being a good communicator, in chemistry or anywhere else.

Throughout this book you will find opportunities to develop your communication skills. There are open-ended questions that require you to research a topic and discuss issues.

For example, on page 54 you are asked for your views on the subject of adding fluoride to drinking water. Or on page 175, question 6 asks for the advantages and disadvantages of different methods we use for waste disposal. Page 261, question 11 asks about plastic pollution. If you do biology as well as chemistry, you might like to do some research on genetically modified crops. (See page 377.)

Many of the 'Chemistry at work' pages introduce you to the latest developments and would also be suitable for further research. This could be followed by a presentation to the rest of your group. Examples might include the discovery of particles in the nucleus (page 27), the formation of new elements (page 100), bucky-balls (page 64), memory metals (page 78) or conducting polymers (page 258).

Application of Number

When you start to learn chemistry you don't get very involved with numbers. But one of the things you will learn in your A level studies is that numbers are very important to chemists. It is only by making careful measurements that chemists arrived at the idea of chemical elements and compounds and were able to find chemical formulae.

You will not have to do many calculations yourself in chemistry because calculators usually do them better and get the right answer (provided that you press the right buttons). But you will need to make sure that you can cope with very large and very small numbers (e.g. 6.02×10^{23}) and that you can estimate answers well (e.g. $4 \times 10^2 - 2 \times 10^{-3}$) so that you have a check on your arithmetic.

You will also need to make sure that you can solve simple equations systematically. Look for instance, at the enthalpy calculations on page 303, and make sure that you can do them yourself and get the same answer. It often helps to write down a formula, and the numbers to be put into it, separately before starting to do the calculations.

$$\Delta H_f^{\ominus}[NH_4^+(aq)] = -132.5 \, kJ \, mol^{-1}$$

$$\Delta H_f^{\ominus}[SO_4^{2+}(aq)] = -909.3 \, kJ \, mol^{-1}$$

$$\Delta H_f^{\ominus}[(NH_4)_2SO_4(s)] = -1180.9 \, kJ \, mol^{-1}$$

Example

$$(aq) + (NH_4)_2SO_4(s) \xrightarrow{\Delta H_1} 2 \, NH_4^+(aq) + SO_4^{2-}(aq)$$

$$\Delta H_2 \nwarrow \qquad \nearrow \Delta H_3$$

$$N_2(g) + 4 \, H_2(g) + S \text{ (rhombic, s)} + 2 \, O_2(g)$$

$$\Delta H_1 = \Delta H_3 - \Delta H_2$$

$$\Delta H_3 = (2 \times \Delta H_f^{\ominus}[NH_4^+(aq)] + \Delta H_f^{\ominus}[SO_4^{2-}(aq)]$$
$$= (2 \times -132.5) + (-909.3)$$
$$= -1174.3 \, kJ \, mol^{-1}$$

So $\Delta H_1 = (-1174.3) - (-1180.9)$
$$= (-1174.3) + 1180.9$$
$$= +6.6 \, kJ \, mol^{-1}$$

But most of all you will need to practise doing calculations as you come to them during the course. Make sure that you can get correct answers to the calculations at the end of each chapter. If you can't, find out from your teacher where you went wrong then try the question again.

Many students have problems understanding where the chemistry ends and the calculations begin. In the enthalpy calculation above, for instance, it is important that you understand why some of the changes are positive and others negative; why you need to multiply some of the figures by 2; and how to use brackets, before you start to do the calculations. And remember that taking away a negative number is like adding a positive one. You then end up with a long string of numbers to punch into your calculator. Make sure you have a systematic way of doing this and stick to it. If you try to take short-cuts and leave out some stages you will probably make mistakes.

Finally, make sure that you can do the calculations that come from titrations. There is a nice simple formula for calculating results and it is a good thing to learn it by heart:

$$\text{number of moles} = \frac{\text{volume of titre (cm}^3\text{)} \times \text{concentration of solution (mol dm}^{-3}\text{)}}{1000}$$

Remember, though, that you don't necessarily have to produce all this evidence in chemistry. You should practise the skills in chemistry, but you may find that you can get the evidence more easily from another subject, such as physics. This is for you to decide, after talking it over with your teacher.

For your Application of Number portfolio, you will need to have evidence to show that you can:

- work out what numerical data you need for what you want to do

- get it from somewhere, maybe including your own measurements

- carry out the right calculations, and get the right results

- check your work and correct any mistakes

- decide what the results are telling you

- present the results in a way that suits the situation, using graphs etc. where they help make your point.

Information Technology

Information technology is about using computers to help you to do your work more quickly, to present your work more professionally, to make measurements and process the results, or to give you access to information that would be difficult to find in books. We will look at each of these in turn.

In experimental work you often find that you have a large number of measurements and have to work on them in order to find the quantity you want. The usual way to deal with these is to draw a table with suitable headings. But using a spreadsheet can often do the job more effectively. For instance, suppose you are carrying out an experiment that involves several titrations. At its simplest you could use a spreadsheet to record your results and subtract them to find the titre in each case. You could put in a formula to find the concentration directly from each titration, or you could make the spreadsheet find the average titre before finding an overall result. Setting up the spreadsheet is an excellent exercise to help you to understand how to do calculations from titrations.

You could also use a spreadsheet to process data extracted from a databook, for example to show trends across a period or down a group. You have probably learned about trends across the second or third period, but with a spreadsheet you could put in data for the other periods and draw conclusions.

You will probably not want to word-process all your work because you will have to write with a pen in your chemistry module tests and examinations. But it is a good idea to set yourself a goal to produce a piece of word-processed work at least once per month, say. Discuss this with your teacher and take his or her advice.

Computers are ideal for collecting data over a very short or very long period. Computers can be used to collect data on reactions that are complete in a one hundred millionth of a second! You will not be doing any reactions that are quite as fast as that, but computers can record changes in mass, temperature, colour, etc. much better than human beings because they do not forget to take readings, misread the thermometer, or get called away to another lesson. And they can often produce a graph or other chart as they log the data, giving you an instant picture of what is going on during the reaction. You should find some opportunities for data logging during your course. (See page 297.)

Finally, you should not ignore opportunities for finding things out on the Internet or CD-ROMs. These have a wealth of information and give you access to information which you would find difficult to assemble in any other way.

In other words, do what you have to do in chemistry anyway, but use IT so that you can do it more effectively.

Remember, though, that you also have to pass a test in each of the three Key Skills, so you have to be sure you understand all the techniques that underlie the skills and can answer questions about them under exam conditions.

Your school or college will have arrangements to help you develop your Key Skills, assemble your portfolio, and prepare for the test. Find out what these are and always ask your tutor if you are not sure what you should be doing.

Key Skills are not a soft option. They earn you UCAS points, and employers are very keen on them. Over the next few years, more and more employers are going to be expecting people to have Key Skills qualifications. Anyway, life is much easier if you are good at communicating, using numbers and using IT.

For your IT Key Skills portfolio at Level 3, you will have to have evidence that shows you can:

- decide what information you want and where you are going to get it (CD ROM? Internet? Your own experiments?)

- select the right information for what you want to do

- use spreadsheets, databases, etc. to input this data and do calculations, test hypotheses, find the answers to questions, and so on

- check that your results are accurate and make sense

- present your results effectively

Answers

Answers to end-of-chapter questions

Here are the answers to questions that require you
to do a calculation.
You should always consider the number of **significant figures** to include
in your final answer.
Look at the number of significant figures in these answers:

3.56 g (to 3 significant figures); 2400 cm³ (to 2 sig. fig.);   0.003 (to 1 sig. fig.);
0.000 20 (to 2 sig. fig.) 7.87×10^{-5} (to 3 sig. fig.)

Notice that a zero at the end of a number is significant after a decimal point.
Don't just copy all the numbers from the display on your calculator.
Choose the measurement given to the least number of significant figures
to guide your decision.

Chapter 2

Page 25
The relative atomic mass of germanium is 72.7.
The relative atomic mass of chlorine is 35.5
3 a) 204.4   b) 91.32   5 a) 79.99

Chapter 3

Page 30
1 2.5 moles   2 0.3 moles   3 40 moles   4 0.1 moles
5 0.03 moles

Page 31
6 2 g   7 70 g   8 320 g   9 9.5 g   10 0.12 g

Page 32
1 3 moles   2 0.1 moles   3 0.3 moles   4 0.005 moles
5 0.4 moles

Page 33
8.0 g of magnesium oxide.

Page 34
1 2 moles   2 0.125 moles   3 0.05 moles   4 0.3 moles
5 2.0×10^{-4} moles

Page 35
6 48 dm³   7 12 dm³   8 2.4 dm³   9 0.012 dm³
10 4.8 dm³

Page 38
1 2 moles   2 1 mole   3 0.25 moles   4 0.005 moles
5 0.025 moles

Page 40
1 CH_4 2 PbO   3 CO_2 4 Fe_2O_3 5 $CuCO_3$

Page 41
The formula of magnesium oxide is MgO.

End of chapter answers
3 a) 2 moles   b) 0.1 moles   c) 0.002 moles   d) 0.01 moles
e) 3.0×10^5 moles
4 a) 1080 g   b) 2.5 g   c) 6.4 g   d) 3 g

e) 0.0345 g (3.45×10^{-2} g)
5 a) 18   b) 17   c) 103   d) 101   e) 58
6 a) 0.25 moles   b) 0.01 moles   c) 0.01 moles
7 a) 0.1 moles   b) 5.0×10^{-3} moles   c) 4.0×10^{-3} moles
d) 1.0×10^{-3} moles   e) 0.5 moles
8 a) 0.05 moles   b) 0.1 moles
9 a) 21.25 g   b) 0.186 g   c) 0.033 g
11 a) NaCl   b) $CaCO_3$ c) KNO_2 d) Fe_2O_3 e) CO_2
12 CuO   13 0.292 mol dm⁻³   14 4.99 moles
15 60 cm³
16 b) 1.28×10^{-5} moles   c) 6.4×10^{-5} moles
d) 6.4×10^{-4} moles   e) 0.0358 g

Chapter 11

12 d) 1 : 5   f) 3.0×10^{-4} g) 1.5×10^{-3}
h) 0.060 mol dm⁻³   i) 0.91 g/100 cm³ of water

Chapter 12

8 a) C_2H_5 b) C_4H_{10}
9 a) C_2H_6O b) C_2H_6O d) ethanol

Chapter 17

3 d) -360 kJ mol⁻¹   g) 152 kJ mol⁻¹

Chapter 22

3 a) 152   b) 138   c) 1 mole   d) 88%   e) 2.1 g
f) 67%   g) 59%

Chapter 23

2 CH_4
3 a) 0.201 moles   b) 0.603 moles   c) CH_3

Chapter 24

2 b) 9660 J (or 9700 J to 2 sig. fig.)
c) 0.2 moles of each
d) -48.3 kJ mol⁻¹ (or -48 kJ mol⁻¹ to 2 sig. fig.)
3 b) 5208 J (or 5200 J to 2 sig. fig.)
c) 4.1×10^{-3} moles
d) -1270 kJ mol⁻¹ (or -1300 kJ mol⁻¹ to 2 sig. fig.)

$5 \ -104.5\,\text{kJ mol}^{-1}$ $6 \ +1.9\,\text{kJ mol}^{-1}$ $7 \ -136.9\,\text{kJ mol}^{-1}$
$8 \ +35.6\,\text{kJ mol}^{-1}$ $9 \ +95\,\text{kJ mol}^{-1}$

Chapter 25

2 e) $-1046\,\text{kJ mol}^{-1}$
3 a) i) $-2815\,\text{kJ mol}^{-1}$ ii) $-1959\,\text{kJ mol}^{-1}$
4 a) $-2527\,\text{kJ mol}^{-1}$

Chapter 26

3 a) $+179.2\,\text{J mol}^{-1}\,\text{K}^{-1}$ c) $-111.4\,\text{J mol}^{-1}\,\text{K}^{-1}$
d) $+67.8\,\text{J mol}^{-1}\,\text{K}^{-1}$ f) $-20.2\,\text{kJ mol}^{-1}$

Chapter 28

2 b) First order c) Second order d) Third order
3 c) First order d) Rate $= k[N_2O_5]$ f) $1.5 \times 10^{-4}\,\text{s}^{-1}$
g) $3.5 \times 10^{-5}\,\text{s}^{-1}$
4 c) First order with respect to propanone d) Zero order
e) Rate $= k[\text{propanone}][\text{H}^+]$ g) $\text{mol}^{-1}\,\text{dm}^3\,\text{min}^{-1}$
5 b) Rate $= k[\text{HNO}_3]$
6 a) i) First order ii) First order iii) Second order
b) Rate $= k[\text{BrO}_3^-][\text{Br}^-][\text{H}^+]^2$
7 c) Rate $= k[\text{1-bromopropane}][\text{OH}^-]$

Chapter 30

2 b) $\text{mol}^{-1}\,\text{dm}^3$ 3 d) Reaction b); units are kPa
4 b) $3.0 \times 10^4\,\text{kPa}$ c) $7.67 \times 10^{-9}\,\text{kPa}^{-2}$
5 c) $4.8 \times 10^{-4}\,\text{moles}$ d) $3.4 \times 10^{-3}\,\text{moles}$

Chapter 31

3 a) 3.0 b) 1 c) 0 d) 2 e) 0.30 f) 2.6 g) 2.3
4 a) $1.0 \times 10^{-5}\,\text{mol dm}^{-3}$ b) $4.0 \times 10^{-3}\,\text{mol dm}^{-3}$
5 c) i) 13 ii) 14 iii) 12.4
6 c) i) 4.8 ii) 4.1 iii) 6.1
8 b) 4.9

Chapter 33

5 e) $+0.63\,\text{V}$, if your cell diagram in part c) was
$\text{Zn(s)} \mid \text{Zn}^{2+}(\text{aq}) \;\vdots\; \text{Pb}^{2+}(\text{aq}) \mid \text{Pb(s)}$, or
$-0.63\,\text{V}$ if it was written $\text{Pb(s)} \mid \text{Pb}^{2+}(\text{aq}) \;\vdots\; \text{Zn}^{2+}(\text{aq}) \mid \text{Zn(s)}$
By convention, you would choose the first cell diagram,
giving a value of $+0.63\,\text{V}$.
6 a) $-2.90\,\text{V}$ b) $+3.26\,\text{V}$ c) $+0.34\,\text{V}$ d) $+1.66\text{V}$
e) $+2.12\,\text{V}$ f) $-1.21\,\text{V}$ g) $+0.71\,\text{V}$ h) $+1.00\,\text{V}$

Answers to further questions

The Awarding Bodies accept no responsibility for the answers or method of working given. These are the sole responsibility of the author.

Atoms and Structure

1 a) i) The space within an atom occupied by a pair of (or a single) electron.
  ii) The energy (enthalpy) needed to remove one mole of electrons from one mole of gaseous ions.
  b) i) See bottom of page 96.
  ii) Because electrons within the same shell (energy level) are attracted to the nucleus by increasing positive charge on the nucleus as we cross the period.
  iii) Li is much lower than He because the electron removed is from a new shell (energy level) further from the nucleus, so the force of attraction is lower.
  Be is higher than B because the electron would be removed from a full sub-shell (2s) in Be.
  N is higher than O because the electron is removed from a half-filled sub-shell (2p) in N. (Remember that this arrangement reduces the repulsion between electrons.)
  c) i) $\text{Na(g)} \longrightarrow \text{Na}^+(\text{g}) + \text{e}^-$
  ii) $\text{Mg}^+(\text{g}) \longrightarrow \text{Mg}^{2+}(\text{g}) + \text{e}^-$
  d) i) 2nd I.E. of Na would be higher because the Na$^+$ ion has 11 protons holding in 10 electrons whereas the Ne atom has only 10 protons holding in 10 electrons.
  ii) 2nd I.E. of Na would be much higher because the electron is removed from a full second shell, whereas Mg's second electron is removed from the 3rd shell, which is further from the nucleus.
2 a) The energy required to remove one mole of electrons from F$^+$(g).
  b) Steady rise for first 7 I.E.'s, then a steep rise to the 8th I.E., rising again to the 9th I.E. (See page 12 for an example.)
3 a) One less electron each time, but same positive charge on the nucleus, resulting in greater attraction.
  b) $\text{C}^{4+}(\text{g}) \longrightarrow \text{C}^{5+}(\text{g}) + \text{e}^-$
  c) There is a large increase in I.E. between the 4th and 5th I.E.'s where a new shell is broken into. The small increases in the first 4 I.E.'s show that the electrons are being removed from the same shell. Therefore, carbon has 2 electrons in the first shell and 4 electrons in the second shell.

4 Relative isotopic masses refer to the mass of a single isotope, based on a scale in which the carbon-12 isotope is given a relative mass of exactly 12. However, relative atomic masses are a weighted mean of the relative isotopic masses, taking into account the proportions of each isotope found in a naturally occurring sample of the element. Sometimes they are expressed in atomic mass units (a.m.u.) where the carbon-12 isotope is assigned a mass of exactly 12 a.m.u.
5 a) See page 23.
  b) i) Mg has 3 isotopes: ^{24}Mg (with 12 neutrons), ^{25}Mg (with 13 neutrons) and ^{26}Mg (with 14 neutrons).
  ii) $\left(24 \times \dfrac{1}{(1 + 0.127 + 0.139)}\right) + \left(\dfrac{25 \times 0.127}{1.266}\right) + \left(\dfrac{26 \times 0.139}{1.266}\right)$
  $= 24.32$
6 Same number of protons, same number of electrons, different number of neutrons.
7 a) i) The proportions of each isotope present in a naturally occurring sample of the element.
  ii) $\dfrac{(46 \times 8.02) + (47 \times 7.31) + (48 \times 73.81) + (49 \times 5.54) + (50 \times 5.32)}{100}$
  $= 47.93$
  b) i) Peak drawn at 162, which is the same height as peak at 158, and a peak at 160, which is twice the height of the other two peaks.
  ii) There are 3 possible combinations of the two Br isotopes in a Br$_2$ molecule;
  Peak at 158 is the $(^{79}\text{Br}—^{79}\text{Br})^+$ ion; peak at 160 is the $(^{79}\text{Br}—^{81}\text{Br})^+$ ion and the peak at 162 is the $(^{81}\text{Br}—^{81}\text{Br})^+$ ion.
  iii) The chances of different isotopes occurring in a Br$_2$ molecule are twice that of the same isotope appearing in a Br$_2$.
8 a) See pages 22 and 23. b) See bottom of page 26.
  c) i) 3 peaks
  ii) ^{35}Cl—^{35}Cl, ^{35}Cl—^{37}Cl, ^{37}Cl—^{37}Cl
  iii) The ^{35}Cl—^{35}Cl peak because ^{35}Cl is three times more abundant than ^{37}Cl.
9 a) $2\,\text{NaHCO}_3(\text{s}) \longrightarrow \text{Na}_2\text{CO}_3(\text{s}) + \text{H}_2\text{O}(\text{l}) + \text{CO}_2(\text{g})$
  b) $60\,\text{cm}^3$ ($0.06\,\text{dm}^3$)
  c) labelled diagram showing test tube / delivery tube / attached to syringe / heat under test tube.
10 a) 1.5 moles, $111\,\text{g}$.
  b) $\text{Ca(s)} + 2\,\text{H}_2\text{O}(\text{l}) \longrightarrow \text{Ca(OH)}_2(\text{aq}) + \text{H}_2(\text{g})$
  $60\,\text{g}$ of Ca.

11 a) Number of moles of HCl $= \dfrac{0.500 \times 38.40}{1000}$

$= 0.0192$ moles

b) 0.0192 moles

c) Number of moles of NaOH $= \dfrac{0.500 \times 50}{1000}$

$= 0.025$ moles

d) (0.025 – 0.0192) moles of NaOH reacted, i.e. 0.0058 moles. From the equation this would react with half that number of moles of ammonium sulphate.

So the number of moles of ammonium sulphate $= \dfrac{0.0058}{2}$

$= 0.0029$ moles

e) $0.0029 \times (28 + 8 + 32 + 64) = 0.3828$ g (0.383 to 3 sig. fig.)

12 a) P_2O_3 b) The relative molecular (formula) mass of the oxide

c) $P_4 + 5 O_2 \longrightarrow P_4O_{10}$ 7.3 g of P_4O_{10}.

13 a) i) 0.011 moles ii) 0.055 mol dm^{-3} iii) 132 cm^3 (0.132 dm^3)

b) 0.167 mol dm^{-3}

14 a) $PV = nRT$ b) 72.1 (See method on page 37.)

15 495 kg

16 47.6%

17 a) i) protons and neutrons (56 protons, 82 neutrons in ^{138}Ba)

ii) See CaF_2 example on page 50 (change Ca to Ba, and F to Cl).

b) i) so that electrolysis does not occur.

ii) acid $= 5.0 \times 10^{-3}$ moles, alkali $= 5.0 \times 10^{-3}$ moles

iii) $Ba(OH)_2(aq) + H_2SO_4(aq) \longrightarrow BaSO_4(s) + 2 H_2O(l)$

iv) There are no free $Ba^{2+}(aq)$ ions or $SO_4^{2-}(aq)$ ions present.

c) i) $Ba(NO_3)_2$ ii) apple green (see page 116)

18 a) i) C is $\delta+$, Cl is $\delta-$ / Cl is $\delta+$, F is $\delta-$ / H is $\delta+$, Cl is $\delta-$

ii) See page 68.

b) i) hydrogen bonds ii) dimers iii) 120

19 a) Increasingly strong van der Waals' forces as the molecules get larger.

b) There are relatively strong hydrogen bonds between H_2O molecules.

20 a) $1s^2 2s^2 2p^6 3s^2 3p^3$

b) See diagram of NH_3 at bottom of page 61 (change N to P, and H to F). Its shape is called pyramidal.

c) The central phosphorus atom is surrounded by 4 pairs of electrons in PF_3, suggesting a tetrahedral arrangement. But one of the pairs of electrons is P's lone pair which repels the bonding pairs more strongly. This pushes them closer together than in a perfect tetrahedron.

21 BF_3 – see page 60 (bond angle $= 120°$)

NF_3 – see NH_3 at bottom of page 61 (bond angle $= 106.7°$, i.e. less than the tetrahedral angle of $109.5°$)

OF_2 – See H_2O on page 71 (bond angle $= 104.5°$, i.e. less than NF_3 because O has 2 lone pairs as opposed to N's single lone pair).

22 a) It contains only one isotope. It exists as P_4.

b) P_4 has strong covalent bonds within each molecule, but weak forces between its molecules, i.e. van der Waals' forces.

c) Si atoms form a giant covalent structure, so melting requires the breaking of the strong covalent bonds.

23 a) e.g. $90°$ – SF_6, $109.5°$ – CH_4, $120°$ – BF_3, $180°$ – CO_2

b) See page 71 (bond angle $= 104.5°$)

24 CO_2. See page 58.

H ×• N •× H   H ×• Cl ×× H

(with lone pairs shown and H below N)

25 a) $104.5°$

b) Oxygen atom has 2 lone pairs and 2 bonding pairs of electrons surrounding it in H_2O. Lone pairs repel more strongly than bonding pairs (because they are held more closely to the central atom) so the O—H bonds are squeezed closer together than the usual tetrahedral bond angle of $109.5°$.

c) hydrogen bonding

d) F is more electronegative than H, so the electrons in the H—F bond are found, on average, nearer to the F atom.

e) Bond angle increases because the electrons in the lone pair will be drawn towards the HF molecule, reducing its charge density around the oxygen atom in H_2O.

26 a) BF_3 – trigonal / 3 bonding pairs of electrons repelling each other.

CH_4 – tetrahedral / 4 bonding pairs of electrons.

SF_6 – octahedral / 6 bonding pairs of electrons.

b) 4 bonding pairs of electrons repelling to maximum tetrahedral bond angle in NH_4^+. Lone pairs of electrons repel more strongly than bonding pairs, so the angle is reduced in NH_3 which has one lone pair on the N atom. Lone pair–lone pair repulsion is stronger again, and the O in H_2O has two lone pairs, resulting in the reduced H—O—H bond angle.

c) $BeCl_2$ – linear

BrF_5 – octahedral (distorted because of lone pair on Br).

27 a) i) See answer to question 24.

ii) See page 61.

b) i) Ammonia has the higher boiling temperature because the hydrogen bonds between its molecules are stronger than the dipole–dipole attraction between phosphine molecules. Therefore it requires more energy to break them and separate neighbouring molecules.

ii) Ammonia form hydrogen bonds with water, but phosphine is not polar enough to interact that strongly with water molecules.

28 a) i) There are only weak van der Waals' forces between iodine molecules so the force of attraction is easily overcome by gentle heating, allowing I_2 molecules to escape from its lattice.

ii) There are strong electrostatic forces of attraction between the oppositely charged ions in the giant structure of sodium chloride. Therefore it takes a lot of energy to separate the ions and break down the lattice.

iii) SiO_2 has a giant covalent structure, so in order to melt it, the strong covalent bonds between atoms in the lattice must be broken, which requires a lot of energy.

29 Refer to pages 62 and 75.

30 a) See page 75.

b) i) cheaper

ii) lower density which is important in the launching of satellites in orbit

31 a) i) covalent   ii) van der Waals' forces

b) i) I_2

c) There are only weak van der Waals' forces of attraction between molecules of iodine.

d) NaCl has a giant ionic structure with strong electrostatic forces of attraction between oppositely charged ions.

e) They vibrate more vigorously.

f) To vaporise the NaCl the oppositely charged ions need to become separate from each other completely in the gaseous state, unlike in the liquid where the ions are still in close proximity.

32 a) i) See page 66.   ii) See page 62.

b) Refer to pages above.

c) NaCl. See page 51 for diagram of its lattice (face-centred cubic); coordination number of both the Na^+ and Cl^- is 6.

CsCl. See question 7, page 55 or question 33 in this section for diagram of its lattice (body centred cubic); coordination number of both ions is 8. The different lattices are formed because of the greater difference in size between Cs^+ and Cl^- ions, making it more difficult to pack closely together.

d) See page 75.

33 a) Number of nearest neighbours.

b) NaCl – 6,   CsCl – 8

c) i) See bottom of page 52.

ii) Ethanol forms hydrogen bonds with water molecules, but non-polar hydrocarbon molecules do not interact with the polar water molecules.

34 a) Hydrogen – covalent bonding

b) Lithium fluoride – ionic bonding

c) Hydrogen chloride – covalent bonding

35 a) X and Y   b) Y and Z

36 a) See page 51.

b) i)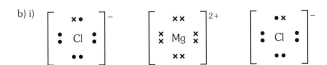

(Mg²⁺ can be represented [Mg]²⁺, i.e. with no electrons in outer shell.)

ii)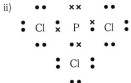

c) See diagram of ammonia, page 61 (change N to P, change H to Cl). Bond angle about 107°.

d) $[PCl_4]^+$ – tetrahedral $[PCl_6]^-$ – octahedral

The Periodic Table

1 a) Electronegativity is a measure of how strongly an atom attracts electrons to itself in a bond.

b) The attraction between the nucleus and the outer shell electrons increases as the nuclear charge increases and successive electrons are added to the same shell.

c) It decreases as the outer shell electron is further from the nucleus and it is shielded from the attractive force of the nucleus by more full inner shells.

d) Covalent. If there is a large difference in electronegativities, the bonding is likely to be ionic (e.g. electron transfer in compounds of metals and non-metals). But if the difference is small, electrons are likely to be shared, i.e. covalent bonding.

2 a) i) 2.9 or above   ii) less than 0.9

b) It does not form compounds/bonds with other elements/atoms.

3 a) Group 1, as there is a very large increase between the 1st and 2nd I.E. because the second electron is removed from a new, complete shell.

b) 13 000/14 000 kJ mol⁻¹

c) p electron

d) $T^+(g) \longrightarrow T^{2+}(g) + e^-$

e) Rises to U, falls slightly to V, then rises again to W. (See page 96 for pattern at the start of a period.)

f) M has 2 electrons in its outer shell, then a further 4 electrons are removed from its next shell. This shell must contain at least 8 electrons, and the next shell would be the first shell (holding 2 electrons) in the smallest atom possible, i.e. 2.8.2 = 12.
(The only smaller atom in Group 2 would have an electronic structure of 2.2, so would only have a maximum of 4 I.E.'s, whereas the graph shows the first 6 I.E.'s.)

4 carbon 77, fluorine 64, lithium 152, potassium 227.

5 a)

Na₂O	PCl₃/PCl₅	SO₃/SO₂
solid	liquid / solid	liquid / gas
Ionic	covalent	covalent
giant ionic	simple molecular	simple molecular

b) i) $Na_2O(s) + H_2O(l) \longrightarrow 2\,NaOH(aq)$ ii) pH = 14
 i) $SO_3(l) + H_2O(l) \longrightarrow H_2SO_4(aq)$ ii) pH = 1

c) Effervesces (fizzes) giving off misty white fumes.
$PCl_3 + 3\,H_2O(l) \longrightarrow H_3PO_3(aq) + 3\,HCl(aq)$

6 a) i) $NaOH(aq) + HCl(aq) \longrightarrow NaCl(aq) + H_2O(l)$
 ii) $Si(s) + 2\,Cl_2(g) \longrightarrow SiCl_4(g)$

b) Silicon oxide is insoluble in water. It does not react like sodium oxide, which forms an alkali with water. Its oxide is acidic in nature, so will not react with an acid such as HCl(aq).

c) $MgCl_2$ – the white crystals would dissolve. The magnesium chloride solution formed is slightly acidic (pH = 6.5) as the hydrated Mg²⁺ ion undergoes slight hydrolysis.
PCl_3 – Misty white fumes of HCl(g) are given off in a vigorous reaction. The remaining solution is acidic (pH = 2) as a solution of phosphoric(III) acid is formed and some HCl gas dissolves in the water.

7 a) i) Al_2Cl_6 or $AlCl_3$
 ii) liquid   iii) – v) reacts giving off fumes of hydrogen chloride.
 vi) simple molecular   vii) simple molecular.

b) i) fumes of hydrogen chloride given off
 ii) $SiCl_4(l) + 2\,H_2O(l) \longrightarrow SiO_2(s) + 4\,HCl(aq)$

8 a) If the values are similar – covalent
If there is a large difference in the values – ionic

b) i) Al_2Cl_6 has covalent bonding
$AlCl_3$ are hydrated crystals in which the bonding is ionic with some covalent character.
 ii) $Al_2Cl_6 + 6\,H_2O \longrightarrow 2\,Al(OH)_3 + 6\,HCl$
 iii) The pH is about 3 because the hydrated Al³⁺ ions have a high charge density and are hydrolysed producing H⁺(aq) ions:
$[Al(H_2O)_6]^{3+}(aq) \rightleftharpoons [Al(H_2O)_5OH]^{2+}(aq) + H^+(aq)$

c) ionic

d) $Na_2O(s) + H_2O(l) \longrightarrow 2\,NaOH(aq)$ pH = 14

9 a) i) I X is not P_4O_{10} or SO_2.
   II X is not Al_2O_3 (amphoteric) or SiO_2.
   III X is not MgO.
   Therefore X is Na_2O.

 ii) $Na_2O(s) + H_2O(l) \longrightarrow 2\,NaOH(aq)$
 iii) acidic – SiO_2, P_4O_{10} or SO_2
   amphoteric – Al_2O_3

b) $\dfrac{0.3}{267}$ moles of Al_2Cl_6 will give $\dfrac{6 \times 0.3}{267}$ moles of Cl⁻ ions

$(= 6.74 \times 10^{-3})$
Vol. of 0.100 mol dm⁻³ silver nitrate containing 6.74×10^{-3} moles

$= \dfrac{6.74 \times 10^{-3} \times 1000}{0.100} = 67.4\ cm^3$

10 a) P_4O_{10} b) SiO_2 c) Na_2O

11 a) See table on page 106.

b) i)   P : Cl

$\dfrac{22.5}{31} : \dfrac{77.5}{35.5} = 0.726 : 2.18$ (divide both sides by 0.726 to get simplest ratio)

$= 1 : 3$ so the empirical formula of A is PCl_3

P : Cl

$\dfrac{14.9}{31} : \dfrac{85.1}{35.5} = 0.481 : 2.40$ (divide both sides by 0.481 to get simplest ratio)

$= 1 : 5$ so the empirical formula of B is PCl_5

 ii) $PCl_3(l) + Cl_2(g) \longrightarrow PCl_5(s)$

12 a) Clean nichrome wire by dipping in conc. HCl, heat in non-luminous Bunsen flame to check wire is clean, dip wire in sample then place in non-luminous flame.

b) i) Ba^{2+}
 ii) A = barium bromide ($BaBr_2$) B = barium sulphate ($BaSO_4$)
   C = sodium bromide (NaBr) D = barium carbonate ($BaCO_3$)
   E = silver bromide (AgBr)   F = bromine (Br_2)
 iii) $BaBr_2(aq) + Na_2CO_3(aq) \longrightarrow BaCO_3(s) + 2\,NaBr(aq)$
 iv) carbon dioxide (CO_2)
 v) $2\,NaBr(aq) + Cl_2(aq) \longrightarrow 2\,NaCl(aq) + Br_2(aq)$
   a displacement/redox reaction

13 They increase in thermal stability as we descend the group.
$2\,Mg(NO_3)_2(s) \longrightarrow 2\,MgO(s) + 4\,NO_2(g) + O_2(g)$

14 a) i) X is magnesium.
   $Mg(s) + H_2O(g) \longrightarrow MgO(s) + H_2(g)$
 ii) Y is calcium
   e.g. $Ca(s) + 2\,H_2O(l) \longrightarrow Ca(OH)_2(aq) + H_2(g)$
   Z is CaO

b) Flame tests (e.g. Ca – brick red, Sr – crimson red, Ba – apple green).

15 a) i) $NaCl(s) + H_2SO_4(l) \longrightarrow NaHSO_4(s) + HCl(g)$
 ii) with NaCl – no coloured gas/vapour, with NaBr some brown vapour (Br_2), with NaI some purple/violet vapour (I_2)
 iii) The hydrogen halides become easier to oxidise as we go down Group 7, so conc. H_2SO_4 can oxidise HBr and HI, breaking the H—Halogen bond, but it does not oxidise HCl.

b) See table on page 124.

16 a) See page 68.

b) The relative molecular mass increases and the larger molecules contain more electrons, so will produce more instantaneous, induced dipoles. This means stronger van der Waals' forces between molecules.

c) There is hydrogen bonding between molecules of HF. So although it is the smallest molecule, the exceptionally high electronegativity of fluorine means that the HF molecule carries a large permanent dipole. This enables a hydrogen bond to form between the partial positively charged H atom and a lone pair from the F atom in a neighbouring molecule of HF.

17 a) starch

b) $I_2(aq) + 2 S_2O_3^{2-}(aq) \longrightarrow 2 I^-(aq) + S_4O_6^{2-}(aq)$

c) -1

d) moles of thiosulphate $= \dfrac{0.020\,00 \times 23.35}{1000} = 4.67 \times 10^{-4} \text{ mol}$

This reacts with $\dfrac{4.67 \times 10^{-4}}{2}$ moles of $I_2 = 2.335 \times 10^{-4} \text{ mol}$

(in 25.00 cm^3 of solution)

So in 1 dm^3 (1000 cm^3) of I_2 solution we would have

$2.335 \times 10^{-4} \times \dfrac{1000}{25}$

$= 9.34 \times 10^{-3} \text{ mol dm}^{-3}$

18 $I = -1$; $Mn = +7$; $O = -2$; $I = 0$; $Mn = +4$

19 a) One reactant is reduced whilst the other is oxidised in the reaction.

b) $Cl_2(aq) + 2 I^-(aq) \longrightarrow 2 Cl^-(aq) + I_2(aq)$

c) The colourless solution turns brown.

20 a) i) $I = 0$ in I_2; $I = -1$ in NaI; $I = +5$ in $NaIO_3$ ii) disproportionation

b) i) pipette (+filler)

ii) starch, turns from blue/black to colourless

iii) $\dfrac{0.0100 \times 16.7}{1000} = 1.67 \times 10^{-4} \text{ mol of thio}$

iv) $\dfrac{1.67 \times 10^{-4}}{2} = 8.35 \times 10^{-5} \text{ mol of } I_2$

v) In 10 cm^3 we had $\dfrac{8.35 \times 10^{-5}}{3}$ moles of sodium iodate

$= 2.78 \times 10^{-5} \text{ mol}$

So in the original 100 cm^3 we had $10 \times 2.78 \times 10^{-5}$

$= 2.78 \times 10^{-4} \text{ mol}$

vi) $(2.78 \times 10^{-4} \times 198) \text{ g}$ of sodium iodate $= 0.055\,11 \text{ g}$

Therefore percentage purity $= \dfrac{0.055\,11}{0.060} \times 100\%$

$= 92\%$ (to 2 sig. fig.)

21 a) See pages 147 and 333.

b) Variable oxidation states.

c) Any example, e.g. see pages 361, 362, 364.

22 a) i) See page 136.

ii) A coordinate (dative) bond forms as the ligand donates a lone pair of electrons into an empty orbital on the central metal ion.

b) They form 2 coordinate (dative) bonds with the central metal ion.

c) i) $+2$ ii) 6

iii) splitting of d orbitals changes in size slightly with different ligand.

iv) $[Cu(H_2O)_6]^{2+}(aq) + 2 \text{ en}(aq) \longrightarrow$
$[Cu(en)_2(H_2O)_2]^{2+}(aq) + 4 H_2O(l)$

23 Silver compounds tend to be white.

Silver has only one oxidation state in its compounds, i.e. $+1$.

24 F = silver nitrate G = potassium iodide

H = ammonia I = barium chloride

$2 Cu^{2+}(aq) + 4 I^-(aq) \longrightarrow 2 CuI(s) + I_2(s)$

See bottom of page 139 for copper complex reactions.

$Ba^{2+}(aq) + SO_4^{2-}(aq) \longrightarrow BaSO_4(s)$

25 a) $[CuCl_4]^{2-}$

b) i) $Fe(s) + Cu^{2+}(aq) \longrightarrow Fe^{2+}(aq) + Cu(s)$

ii) Solution loses its blue colour / pink solid forms

iii) $[Fe(H_2O)_6]^{2+}$

c) P is an anionic, tetrahedral complex ion.

Q is a cationic, octahedral complex ion.

d) i) green   ii) $Fe(OH)_3$ iii) oxygen   iv) redox

(Fe is oxidised to Fe^{2+}, then Fe^{2+} is oxidised to Fe^{3+})

26 Ge $[Ar]3d^{10}4s^24p^2$

Cr $[Ar] 3d^54s^1$

Cu $[Ar] 3d^{10}4s^1$

27 a) $Cr_2O_7^{2-} + 14 H^+ + 6 e^- \longrightarrow 2Cr^{3+} + 7 H_2O$

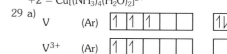

$+ \dfrac{6 Fe^{2+} \qquad 6 Fe^{3+} + 6 e^-}{Cr_2O_7^{2-} + 14 H^+ + 6 Fe^{2+} \qquad 6 Fe^{3+} + 2 Cr^{3+} + 7 H_2O}$

b) Moles of iron present $= \dfrac{0.0200 \times 20.0 \times 6}{1000} = 2.4 \times 10^{-3} \text{ mol}$

Mass of iron $= 2.4 \times 10^{-3} \times 56 \text{ g} = 0.1344 \text{ g}$

Percentage in original sample $= \dfrac{0.1344}{0.140} \times 100\% = 96\%$

28 $+5 = VO_3^-$

$+2 = Cu[(NH_3)_4(H_2O)_2]^{2+}$

29 a)

V   (Ar)

V^{3+} (Ar)

b) i) hexaaquavanadium(III) ion

ii) green

iii) octahedral

iv) coordinate/dative bonds

c) i) $+5$

ii) A. $VO_2^+(aq) + 2 H^+(aq) + e^- \longrightarrow VO^{2+}(aq) + H_2O(l)$

B. $2 VO_2^+(aq) + SO_3^{2-}(aq) + 2 H^+(aq) \longrightarrow$
$2 VO^{2+}(aq) + SO_4^{2-}(aq) + H_2O(l)$

iii) Zinc granules. The solution turns violet when complete.

30 a) They display variable oxidation states/form complex ions with ligands/often used as catalysts.

b) E.g. iron in Haber process/vanadium(V) oxide in Contact process, etc. (See table on page 146 for other examples of uses as catalysts.)

c) i)

ii)

d) i) It is reduced by 3, from $+6$ to $+3$.

ii) moles of $Fe^{2+}(aq) = \dfrac{12.15 \times 25.00}{151.91 \times 1000} = 2.000 \times 10^{-3} \text{ mol}$

iii) We need $\dfrac{2.000 \times 10^{-3}}{6}$ moles of dichromate in a $0.0200 \text{ mol dm}^{-3}$

solution. This has a volume of $\dfrac{2.000 \times 10^{-3} \times 1000}{6 \times 0.0200} = 16.7 \text{ cm}^3$

31

Fe^{2+}

Mn^{2+}

32 A = $[Co(H_2O)_6]^{2+}(aq)$

B = $[CoCl_4]^{2-}(aq)$

C = $Co(OH)_2(s)$ or $Co(OH)_2(H_2O)_4(s)$

D = $[Co(NH_3)_6]^{2+}(aq)$

E = $[Co(NH_3)_6]^{3+}(aq)$

Organic Chemistry 1

1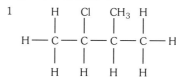

2 Empirical formula $= C_2H_4O$

Molecular formula $= C_4H_8O_2$

3 C_3H_6O

4 a) $C_8H_{18}(l) + 12.5 O_2(g) \longrightarrow 8 CO_2(g) + 9 H_2O(g)$

or $2 C_8H_{18}(l) + 25 O_2(g) \longrightarrow 16 CO_2(g) + 18 H_2O(g)$

b) carbon monoxide and carbon

c) See page 164 for possible isomers.

5 a) a hydrocarbon with no double bonds/only single bonds/the maximum number of hydrogen atoms.
  b) i) same molecular formula, but different structural formulae (i.e. same atoms present but bonded together differently)
  ii)

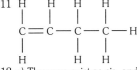

6 a) differing boiling points / petrol or gasoline fraction
  b) $C_7H_{16}(l) + 11\,O_2(g) \longrightarrow 7\,CO_2(g) + 8\,H_2O(g)$
7 See pages 170 and 171.
8 a) i) sunlight   ii) See pages 170 and 171.
  b) van der Waals' forces
  c) i) Easier to transport / fill up / store in car or re-filling station / less flammable therefore safer
     ii) aromatic hydrocarbons – carcinogenic
        tetraethyllead(IV) – lead is toxic / damages brain
9 a) sunlight   b) homolytic   c) propagation
  d) $CH_3CH_2C\overset{\bullet}{H}_2CH_2 + CH_3CH_2CH_2\overset{\bullet}{C}H_2 \longrightarrow CH_3(CH_2)_6CH_3$

  e) Thermal cracking / polymerisation of ethene are examples.
10 a) 2,2,4-trimethylpentane / C_8H_{18}
   b) $C_8H_{18}(l) + 12.5\,O_2(g) \longrightarrow 8\,CO_2(g) + 9\,H_2O(g)$
      or $2\,C_8H_{18}(l) + 25\,O_2(g) \longrightarrow 16\,CO_2(g) + 18\,H_2O(g)$
11

```
    H   H   H   H
    |   |   |   |
    C = C — C — C — H
    |   |   |   |
    H       H   H
```

12 a) They can exist as *cis*- and *trans*- forms because there is no rotation around the double bond.
   b) See diagram on page 177.
   c) geometrical isomerism
13 Free radical mechanism $C_7H_{16}(g) \longrightarrow C_2H_4(g) + C_5H_{12}(g)$
14 a) See page 162. For structures see answer to question 5. b) ii) above.
   b) See page 177.
15 A
16 A
17 See page 183.
18 $C_{10}H_{22}(g) \longrightarrow C_2H_4(g) + C_8H_{18}(g)$
19 a)

```
        Br  Br  H
        |   |   |
   H — C — C — C — H
        |   |   |
        H   H   H
```
                              1,2-dibromopropane
   b) addition by electrophile
   c) Steam/phosphoric(V) acid catalyst. (See page 200.)
      (Alternatively conc. sulphuric acid/water.)
   d)

```
                              CH_3
                              |
   n CH_2 = CHCH_3 → —(CH_2C)— n
```
   e) chlorine in sunlight
   f) free radical substitution
   g) 3-chloroprop-1-ene
20 2-methylpent-2-ene
21 a) i) See page 183, replacing Cl by Br in mechanism.
      ii) electrophilic addition
      iii) cracking of fractions from crude oil
      iv) $C_2H_4(g) + H_2O(g) \longrightarrow C_2H_5OH(g)$
         (catalyst of phosphoric(V) acid – see page 200)
   b) See table page 252.
22 a) i) A =   B =

```
        H   H              H           H
    H   |   |   H           \         /
     \  |   |  /             C = C
      C — C                  /       \
      |                     C
      C                    / \
     / \                  H   H
    H   H
```

ii)

```
   H   H   H          H           H
   |   |   |          |           |
   C = C — C — H      C ≡ C — C — H
   |   |   |                      |
   H   H                          H
```
   isomer of A – an alkene   isomer of B – an alkyne
                                (contains a C≡C bond)

iii) CH_2 – poly(ethene)

b) i) Mass of carbon $= \dfrac{1.76 \times 12}{44} = 0.48\,\text{g}$

   Mass of hydrogen $= \dfrac{0.54 \times 2}{18} = 0.06\,\text{g}$

   No. of moles of carbon $= \dfrac{0.48}{12} = 0.04$

   No. of moles of hydrogen $= \dfrac{0.06}{1} = 0.06$

   So ratio C:H is 4:6 which equals 2:3
   Therefore empirical formula is C_2H_3.

   ii) 1 mole of C has a mass of $0.54 \times 100\,(1/0.01) = 54$
      One unit of C_2H_3 has a mass of $(24 + 3) = 27$,
      so there must be two units in 54, so molecular formula $= C_4H_6$

23 a) i) It contains no double bonds/only single bonds/max. no. of H atoms.
      ii) $C_{10}H_{22}$ iii) $C_{10}H_{16} + 3\,H_2 \longrightarrow C_{10}H_{22}$ iv) $7.2\,\text{dm}^3$
   b) i) 6 double bonds   ii) $C_{30}H_{50}$

24 a)

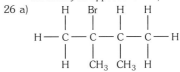

silver catalyst
explosive / flammable / toxic

b) i)

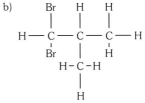

ii) $HO(CH_2CH_2O)_3H$

25 a) See answer to question 24 a) above.
   Strain in the 3-membered ring of epoxyethane, therefore bonds break easily.
   b) $CH_3CHBrCH_2CH_3$ or 2-bromobutane
   Secondary intermediate more stable than primary (or intermediate carbocation stabilised by 2 electron-donating alkyl groups in secondary as opposed to one).

26 a)

```
        H   Br  H   H
        |   |   |   |
   H — C — C — C — C — H
        |   |   |   |
        H  CH_3 CH_3 H
```
   b) nucleophilic substitution by heating under reflux with sodium hydroxide solution

27 a) Show how you work out that the empirical formula $= C_2H_4Br$
   The rel. mol. mass of C_2H_4Br is 108. We need two of these to make up the mass of 215.8 (216). Therefore the molecular formula is $(C_2H_4Br) \times 2 = C_4H_8Br_2$

b)

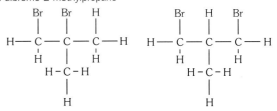

c) KOH in aqueous solution will give $CH_3CH(OH)CH_3$ (substitution).
KOH dissolved in ethanol will give $CH_3CH=CH_2$ (elimination).
d) i) cyanide ion (CN^-)
ii) nucleophilic substitution
iii) $CH_3CH(Br)CH_3 + KCN(CH_3CH(CN)CH_3 + KBr$
iv)

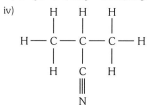

28 a) I = sodium hydroxide in water
II = sodium cyanide (potassium cyanide) in ethanol/alcohol
III = sodium hydroxide in ethanol/water
b) slower, because the C—Cl bond is stronger/shorter
c) faster, because more stable intermediate is formed
29 a) Elimination. (For mechanism see page 191.)
b)

$$CH_3 - CH_2 - \overset{\overset{\displaystyle CH_3}{|}}{\underset{\underset{\displaystyle Br}{|}}{C}} - CH_3$$

c)

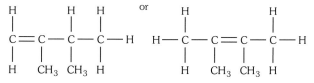

2-methylbut-2-ene   2-methylbut-1-ene

30 a) i) in sunlight
ii) free radical substitution
b) A = pentanenitrile or $CH_3CH_2CH_2CH_2CN$
B = butylamine or $CH_3CH_2CH_2CH_2NH_2$
C = butan-1-ol or $CH_3CH_2CH_2CH_2OH$
D = pentanoic acid or $CH_3CH_2CH_2CH_2COOH$
31 a) nucleophilic substitution by OH^-
b) electrophilic addition by HBr (initial attack by the electron-deficient H atom in HBr)
32 a) Moles of NaOH at start $= \dfrac{0.5 \times 50}{1000} = 0.025$

Moles of NaOH at end $= \dfrac{0.1 \times 10}{1000} = 0.001$

So (0.025 – 0.001) moles of OH^- reacted with the C_4H_9Br (rel. mol. mass = 137). Therefore (0.024×137) g = 3.288 g of C_4H_9Br were present originally.

% purity $= \dfrac{3.288}{3.5} \times 100 = 94\%$

b) The C—Cl bond is the most highly polarised because of the trend in electronegativity going down Group 7, followed by C—Br, then C—I. This suggests that the C atom is more open to attack by nucleophiles (H_2O or OH^- in hydrolysis) in chlorobutane. However, the C—Cl bond is in fact stronger than the C—Br or C—I bonds. Therefore it is more difficult to break the C—Cl bond and for chlorobutane to undergo hydrolysis. Iodobutane undergoes hydrolysis most readily as the C—I bond is the weakest of the three.
33 $C_6H_{12}O_6 \longrightarrow 2 CH_3CH_2OH + 2 CO_2$
34 a)

$$\underset{\underset{\displaystyle H}{|}}{\overset{\overset{\displaystyle H}{|}}{C}} = \underset{\underset{\displaystyle H}{|}}{\overset{\overset{\displaystyle H}{|}}{C}} - \overset{\overset{\displaystyle H}{|}}{\underset{\underset{\displaystyle H}{|}}{C}} - H$$

b) i) aluminium oxide   ii) conc. sulphuric acid

c) i) propan-2-ol

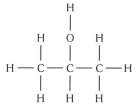

ii) Yes, because the —OH group is removed plus a H atom from an adjacent carbon. In this case both adjacent carbons are equivalent, so if H is removed from either one we still get propene.
35 a) dehydration reaction

$$H - \overset{\overset{\displaystyle H}{|}}{\underset{\underset{\displaystyle H}{|}}{C}} - \overset{\overset{\displaystyle +}{}}{\underset{\underset{\displaystyle CH_3}{|}}{C}} - \overset{\overset{\displaystyle H}{|}}{\underset{\underset{\displaystyle CH_3}{|}}{C}} - \overset{\overset{\displaystyle H}{|}}{\underset{\underset{\displaystyle H}{|}}{C}} - H$$

b) A hydrogen atom can be removed from either of the adjacent carbon atoms, so it could form two isomers:

(structures shown)   or   (structures shown)

36 a) i) tertiary alcohol   ii) secondary alcohol
b) 2-methylpropan-2-ol
c) C or D
i) $CH_3CH_2CH_2CHO$ from C   or $CH_3CH(CH_3)CHO$ from D
ii) Add dropwise to potassium dichromate(VI) and dil. sulphuric acid and distil off the aldehyde as it forms (otherwise further oxidation will produce propanoic acid).
d) i) removal of a molecule of H_2O ii) alkenes
ii) conc. sulphuric acid/heat (or pass vapour over hot aluminium oxide catalyst)
iii) Choose C or D which produce double bond at end of the molecule.
iv) B $CH_3CH_2CH=CH_2$ or $CH_3CH=CHCH_3$
There are two C atoms from which a H atom can be removed (once the —OH group is lost). In B these are not equivalent (unlike A). C and D have only one adjacent C atom to remove a H atom from.
37 a) butan-2-one $CH_3COCH_2CH_3$
b) potassium dichromate(VI) and dil. sulphuric acid
c) $CH_3CH_2CH(CH_3)O^- Na^+$
d) $CH_3CH=CHCH_3$ $CH_3CH_2CH=CH_2$
e) dehydration
38 a) i) $(CH_3)_2CHCH(OH)CH_3$ or

$$H - \overset{\overset{\displaystyle H}{|}}{\underset{\underset{\displaystyle H}{|}}{C}} - \overset{\overset{\displaystyle CH_3}{|}}{\underset{\underset{\displaystyle H}{|}}{C}} - \overset{\overset{\displaystyle OH}{|}}{\underset{\underset{\displaystyle H}{|}}{C}} - \overset{\overset{\displaystyle H}{|}}{\underset{\underset{\displaystyle H}{|}}{C}} - H$$

ii) See page 199 for mechanism.
iii) Loss of a hydrogen atom could also be from CH_3 group.
b) $(CH_3)_2CHCOCH_3$ or

$$H - \overset{\overset{\displaystyle H}{|}}{\underset{\underset{\displaystyle H}{|}}{C}} - \overset{\overset{\displaystyle CH_3}{|}}{\underset{\underset{\displaystyle H}{|}}{C}} - \overset{\overset{\displaystyle O}{||}}{C} - \overset{\overset{\displaystyle H}{|}}{\underset{\underset{\displaystyle H}{|}}{C}} - H$$

39 a) To heat under a condenser so that volatile reactants or products cannot escape for the reaction flask. The reaction is slow, therefore reactants need to be heated together for a relatively long period.
b) To remove any unreacted ethanoic acid and the sulphuric acid catalyst.
c) To remove any water present.
d) For 100% yield we would get $\dfrac{21}{60} \times 88$ g of ethyl ethanoate = 30.8 g

Therefore actual yield $= \dfrac{20}{30.8} \times 100 = 65\%$

The yield was not higher because the reaction is reversible. (There will also be handling losses at each stage in the process.)

e) sodium ethanoate and ethanol

Organic Chemistry 2

1 a) A = cyclohexane   B = hydrogen   C = nickel
   D = aluminium chloride   E = ethylbenzene
  b) Forming A is addition because the hydrogen is added to benzene ring to produce a saturated compound.
     Forming B is electrophilic substitution because one of the H atoms in benzene is substituted by the ethyl group.

2 a)

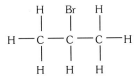

  b) One Cl atom is bonded directly to a C atom in the benzene ring. This will not be attacked by a nucleophile. However, the Cl atom bonded to the alkyl group will produce a partial positive charge on the adjacent C atom. This will be open to attack by the OH^- nucleophile.

3 a) A = cyclohexane   B = hydrogen   C = bromine
   D = iron(III) bromide / iron   E = bromobenzene
   F = conc. sulphuric acid
  b) i) NO_2^+ forms nitrobenzene, and Br^+ from the $Br_2 \rightarrow FeBr_3$ complex forms bromobenzene. This can be written as $Br^+[FeBr_4]^-$.
    ii) To prevent further attack by NO_2^+ on the nitrobenzene formed.
   iii) Used in manufacture of dyes, explosives, etc.
  c) i) 300 °C, 30 atm
    ii) $C_6H_6(l) + 3 Cl_2(g) \longrightarrow C_6H_6Cl_6(l)$

4 a) (electrophilic) addition reaction with propene

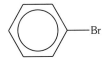

   (electrophilic) substitution reaction with benzene

  b) iron(III) bromide
  c) Propene contains a double bond in one part of its molecule whereas benzene has a complete ring of delocalised electrons spread around the whole molecule. When benzene reacts with bromine the delocalised system is preserved to maintain its stability.

5 a) i) Chloromethane (or other halogenomethane) with anhydrous aluminium chloride.
    ii) electrophilic substitution
  b) CH_2Cl $CHCl_2$ CCl_3 or

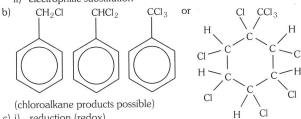

   (chloroalkane products possible)
  c) i) reduction (redox)
    ii) NH_2 which reacts with HCl present to give $NH_3^+Cl^-$

6 a) i)   C : H
      $\dfrac{90.56}{12}$: $\dfrac{9.44}{1}$
      7.55 : 9.44
         1 : 1.25
         4 : 5   i.e. C_4H_5
   ii) C_8H_{10}
  iii)

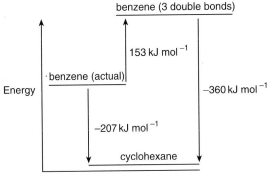

  b) i) 1,4-dimethylbenzene   ii)

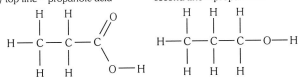

  c) i) free radical substitution
    ii) There is further attack by the highly reactive chlorine free radicals in which the remaining H atoms in the methyl group can be substituted/and there can also be addition of chlorine on to the benzene ring by a free radical mechanism (forming cyclic chloro-substituted alkanes).

7 a) $\Delta H = -156 - (-36) = -120\,kJ\,mol^{-1}$
  b) $3 \times (-120) = -360\,kJ\,mol^{-1}$
  c) Benzene is more stable than a compound containing 3 C=C bonds (by $153\,kJ\,mol^{-1}$).

```
                              benzene (3 double bonds)
                                   ↑        ↑
                                153 kJ mol⁻¹
                    · benzene (actual)
         Energy      ──────────────         −360 kJ mol⁻¹
                              ↓
                      −207 kJ mol⁻¹
                              ↓
                           cyclohexane      ↓
```

  d) Mixture of concentrated nitric acid and concentrated sulphuric acid at 55 °C.
  e) For mechanism see page 212.

8 a) top line – propanoic acid   second line – propan-1-ol

449

last line – hydrogen cyanide

H—C(H)(H)—C(H)(H)—C(H)(O—H)—C≡N

b) Orange precipitate of Cu_2O forms as the propanal is oxidised by the Cu^{2+} ion (Cu^{2+} itself is reduced to Cu^+).

c) With Tollens' reagent, a silver mirror is formed inside the heated test tube.

9 a) X = $CH_3CH_2CH_2OH$ Y = $CH_3CH_2CH(OH)CN$ Z = CH_3CH_2COOH
b) See page 224.

10 a) See page 222 for details of Fehling's / Tollens' reagent tests.
b) i) S =

H—C(H)(H)—C(H)(O—H)—C≡N

T =

(structure: H—C(H)(H)—C(H)=N—N—(2,4-dinitrophenyl with NO₂ groups))

U =

H—C(H)(H)—C(H)(H)—O—H

ii) ethane 2,4-dinitrophenylhydraz**one** / orange crystals

c) The mechanism of nucleophilic addition is described on page 224.

11 a) i) $CH_3CH_2CH_2CH_2OH + [O] \longrightarrow CH_3CH_2CH_2CHO + H_2O$
Colour would change from orange to green.
ii) Butan-1-ol gives the aldehyde and will show orange colour when heated with Fehling's solution (or silver mirror when heated with Tollens' reagent). Butan-2-ol yields the ketone, which does not react when heated with Fehling's solution or Tollens' reagent.

b) butanoic acid

c)

H—C(H)(H)—C(H)(CH₃)—C(H)(H)—OH   H—C(H)(H)—C(OH)(CH₃)—C(H)(H)—H

2-Methylpropan-1-ol is a primary alcohol and will be oxidised to the aldehyde, then carboxylic acid. However, 2-methylpropan-2-ol is a tertiary alcohol and oxidation is difficult and would require the breaking of a C—C bond.

12 a) i) reduction
ii) Changing CH_3CHO to CH_3CH_2OH involves the addition of 2 H atoms to CH_3CHO. The addition of hydrogen or the removal of oxygen is defined as reduction in organic chemistry.
b) ethanoic acid, CH_3COOH

13 a) reduction   b) oxidation

H—C(H)(H)—C(H)(H)—C(H)(H)—OH   H—C(H)(H)—C(H)(H)—C(=O)(OH)

c) (nucleophilic) addition

H—C(H)(H)—C(H)(H)—C(OH)(H)—C≡N

14 a) i) $CH_3COCl + H_2O \longrightarrow CH_3COOH + HCl$
ii)

(structure: $(CH_3CO)_2O$ acid anhydride) + $H_2O \longrightarrow 2\ CH_3COOH$

b) Care needed with a) i) because it is a vigorous reaction and acidic fumes of HCl are given off.
c) CH_3COOH and CH_3OH

15 a) i) Unequal distribution of electrons in the bond/partial charges on atoms at either end of bond because of difference in electronegativity of elements involved.
ii)

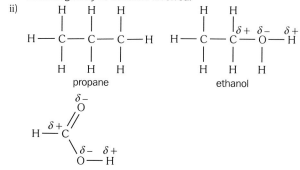

propane   ethanol

methanoic acid

b) i) van der Waals' forces which are weak, so molecules are easily separated from each other.
ii) hydrogen bonding
Methanoic acid exists as a dimer (effectively doubling its rel. mol. mass) / stronger H bonding than in ethanol.

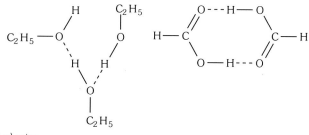

16 a) ester
b) i) G =

H—C(H)(H)—C(=O)(OH)   H = (benzene ring with OH and OH / hydroquinone)

ii) $C_6H_4(OCOCH_3)_2 + 2 H_2O \longrightarrow 2 CH_3CO_2H + C_6H_4(OH)_2$
c) M_r of F = 194, so in 19.4 g we start with 0.1 moles
From the equation in b) ii), this could give 0.2 moles of G and 0.1 moles of H.
i) 0.1 moles of H has a mass of $0.1 \times 110\,g = 11\,g$
Therefore its % yield $= \dfrac{10}{11} \times 100\% = 90.9\%$
ii) 0.2 moles of G has a mass of $0.2 \times 60\,g = 12\,g$
Therefore its % yield $= \dfrac{10}{12} \times 100\% = 83.3\%$

d) i) hydrolysis of fat by alkali   ii) soaps

17 a) solvents, plasticisers, perfume, biodiesel
b) i) 2-methylpropan-1-ol

ii) ethanoic acid

A =

$$CH_3C \overset{\displaystyle O}{\underset{\displaystyle O-CH_2-CH-CH_3}{\big\Vert}}$$
$$\underset{\displaystyle CH_3}{\big\vert}$$

iii) conc. sulphuric acid; in the same state/phase as the reactants

iv) D =

$$CH_3-\overset{\displaystyle H}{\underset{\displaystyle OH}{\overset{\displaystyle \vert}{\underset{\displaystyle \vert}{C}}}}-CH_2CH_3$$

E =

$$CH_3-\overset{\displaystyle CH_3}{\underset{\displaystyle OH}{\overset{\displaystyle \vert}{\underset{\displaystyle \vert}{C}}}}-CH_3$$

18 a) i) 2-aminobutanoic acid ii) propylamine

b) i) $CH_3CH_2CH(NH_2)COO^- Na^+$

ii) $CH_3CH_2CH(NH_3{}^+Cl^-)COOH$

19 a) i) $CH_3CONH_2 + NaOH \longrightarrow CH_3COONa + NH_3$

ii) $CH_3CH_2CN + HCl + 2 H_2O \longrightarrow CH_3CH_2COOH + NH_4Cl$

b) $CH_3CH_2NH_2 + CH_3COOH / CH_3COCl$

20 a) The lone pair of electrons on the N atom in phenylamine is drawn into the delocalised benzene ring system and the electrons are not as readily available to donate to an H^+ ion. The positive charge on the N atom once the salt has formed also tends to be reduced and stabilised by the electron-donating alkyl group in (phenylmethyl)amine.

b) $C_6H_5CN + 4 [H] \longrightarrow C_6H_5CH_2NH_2$ (See bottom of page 245 for details of reagents in this reduction reaction of the nitrile.)

c) quaternary ammonium salt

$$C_6H_5CH_2\overset{+}{N}(CH_3)_2(CH_2)_{11}CH_3 \text{ i.e.}$$

$$\text{benzene ring}-CH_2-\overset{\displaystyle CH_3}{\underset{\displaystyle CH_3}{\overset{\displaystyle \vert}{\underset{\displaystyle \vert}{\overset{+}{N}}}}}-(CH_2)_{11}CH_3$$

21 a) amine; amide

b) When dil. acid is added the amine is neutralised and the salt $C_2H_5NH_3{}^+ Cl^-$ is formed, but when alkali is added the amine $C_2H_5NH_2$ is re-formed

c) $CH_3CONH_2 + NaOH \longrightarrow CH_3COONa + NH_3$
The gas evolved is ammonia.

22 B

23 Addition polymerisation / peroxide free radical initiator.

24 a) A reaction in which many small, reactive monomer molecules combine to form a very large molecule with repeating units

b) i) (structural formula showing peptide linkage)

ii) peptide linkage, —CO—NH— grouping circled

iii) proteins

c) i) $n C_2H_4 \longrightarrow +(C_2H_4)+_n$

ii) High density poly(ethene) has straight chain polymers that can pack closely together, whereas the low density poly(ethene) has branched chains that cannot pack together well.

iii) melting temperature

iv) $\dot{C}H_2—CH_2—R$

v) Ziegler catalyst

d) i) Does not break down in nature.

ii) Plastics won't take up space in landfill sites.

25

$$+\overset{\displaystyle H}{\underset{\displaystyle H}{\overset{\displaystyle \vert}{\underset{\displaystyle \vert}{C}}}}-\overset{\displaystyle CH_3}{\underset{\displaystyle COOCH_3}{\overset{\displaystyle \vert}{\underset{\displaystyle \vert}{C}}}}+_n$$

26 a) $n CH_2{=}CHCOOH \longrightarrow +CH_2{-}CH(COOH)+_n$

b) Polystyrene – van der Waals' forces between polymers (weakest)
Orlon – dipole–dipole attraction between polymers
Perspex – dipole–dipole
Poly(propenoic acid) – hydrogen bonds between polymers (strongest)

c) i) release of toxic / cyanide gases

ii) biodegradable plastics / recycling

27 a) $H_2N(CH_2)_6NH_2$ and $ClOC(CH_2)_4COCl$

b) hydrogen chloride

c) It will be hydrolysed and the peptide links will be broken.
—$(CH_2)_4$—CONH—$(CH_2)_6$—NHCO—$(CH_2)_4$—CONH—$(CH_2)_6$—
NHCO— + 4 $H_2O \longrightarrow 2 H_2N(CH_2)_6NH_2 + 2 HOOC(CH_2)_4COOH$

28 a) i) e.g. poly(ethene) / poly(propene)

ii) e.g. Nylon / Kevlar

iii) e.g. protein / named protein / silk

iv) poly(tetrafluoroethene) / Teflon

b) i) See reactants in bottom equation on page 255.

ii) See product in bottom equation on page 255.

iii) An addition reaction accompanied by elimination of a small molecule (in this case water).

iv) The polymer will be broken down by hydrolysis.

c) They are made up of mixtures of chains of different sizes/not a single pure compound.

29 a) Step 1 – Friedel–Crafts reaction (electrophilic substitution) with chloromethane and aluminium chloride catalyst.
Step 3 – reduction with tin and conc. hydrochloric acid

b) Use reagents conc. nitric acid and conc. sulphuric acid.
If we mix conc. nitric and sulphuric acids together we generate the $NO_2{}^+$ electrophile:
$HNO_3 + 2 H_2SO_4 \longrightarrow NO_2{}^+ + 2 HSO_4{}^- + H_3O^+$
Heated with ethylbenzene to about 60 °C we can get:

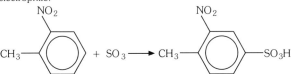

If we now add fuming sulphuric acid, the SO_3 molecule will act as an electrophile:

(structures) CH_3—benzene with NO_2 + $SO_3 \longrightarrow CH_3$—benzene with NO_2 and SO_3H

30 a) Heat with potassium dichromate(VI) and dilute sulphuric acid.

b) CH_3CH_2CHO. Add propanol dropwise to the potassium dichromate(VI) and dil. sulphuric acid, but distil off the aldehyde propanal as it forms.

c) $CH_3CH_2COOH + PCl_5 \longrightarrow CH_3CH_2COCl + POCl_3 + HCl$
Anhydrous conditions mean in the absence of water / dry because propanoyl chloride reacts with water to reform propanoic acid / PCl_5 is also hydrolysed by water.

d) F = CH_3NH_2 (methylamine).

$$H-\overset{\displaystyle H}{\underset{\displaystyle H}{\overset{\displaystyle \vert}{\underset{\displaystyle \vert}{C}}}}-\overset{\displaystyle H}{\underset{\displaystyle H}{\overset{\displaystyle \vert}{\underset{\displaystyle \vert}{C}}}}-\overset{\displaystyle O}{\overset{\displaystyle \Vert}{C}}-\overset{\displaystyle}{\underset{\displaystyle H}{\overset{\displaystyle}{\underset{\displaystyle \vert}{N}}}}-\overset{\displaystyle H}{\underset{\displaystyle H}{\overset{\displaystyle \vert}{\underset{\displaystyle \vert}{C}}}}-H$$

e) Hydrogen. G = sodium propoxide.

31 a) i) elimination ii) no rotation about the double bond

(two cis/trans but-2-ene structures)

$$\underset{\displaystyle H}{\overset{\displaystyle H_3C}{>}}C{=}C\underset{\displaystyle H}{\overset{\displaystyle CH_3}{<}} \qquad \underset{\displaystyle H}{\overset{\displaystyle H_3C}{>}}C{=}C\underset{\displaystyle CH_3}{\overset{\displaystyle H}{<}}$$

iii) Bromine water turns from yellow to colourless.

iv) The high electron density in the pi bond in alkenes makes it susceptible to attack from electrophiles. This results in addition reactions in which the pi bond breaks and new sigma (single) bonds form.

b) i) The isomers rotate the plane of polarised light in opposite directions.

ii)

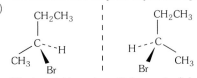

c) i) 'Electron-rich' species, with lone pair of electrons to donate.

ii) $CH_3CH_2CH(OH)CH_3$ or

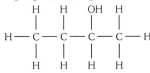

iii) Add PCl_5 – steamy, white fumes given off.

d) i) hydrolysis / saponification.

ii) Yield decreases because reaction with acid is reversible and reaches equilibrium.

e) i) ethanoic acid

ii) CH_3COOH (acid) / CH_3COO^- (base)

iii) HCl is stronger acid than CH_3COOH / CH_3COO^- is stronger base than Cl^-.

32 a) There are 3 different types of H atoms (protons), i.e. CH_3, CH_2 and CH, so there are 3 peaks. The areas under each peak are proportional to the numbers of each type of H atom (proton) – there are 12 CH_3 hydrogen atoms (protons), 2 CH_2 hydrogen atoms (protons) and 2 CH hydrogen atoms (protons), i.e. 6 : 1 : 1.

b) 2 peaks

33 a) C_2H_4O

b) One mole of X produces 2 moles of CO_2.

Therefore X must contain 2 carbon atoms.

So in this case the empirical formula is the same as the molecular formula, i.e. C_2H_4O.

34 a) ester; amine

b) i) ethanol and conc. sulphuric acid

ii) See diagram on page 188.

iii)

c)
195 – some unreacted compound B
165 – benzocaine

120 –

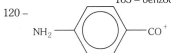

ion from fragmentation of benzocaine

d) A, because of the broad peak around 3000 cm^{-1} caused by hydrogen bonding in carboxylic acid group.

35 a) C : H : O

$\dfrac{52.13}{12}$: $\dfrac{13.15}{1}$: $\dfrac{34.72}{16}$

4.34 : 13.15 : 2.17 (divide throughout by smallest number, i.e. 2.17)

2 : 6 : 1

So empirical formula = C_2H_6O which would have a rel. molar mass of 46.

Therefore the molecular formula is also C_2H_6O in this case.

b) i) Strong intermolecular bonds formed between a hydrogen atom in one molecule and a strongly electronegative atom (O,N or F) in an adjacent molecule.

ii) CH_3CH_2OH

presence of O—H stretching frequency in i.r. spectrum, plus C—O stretching.

The shape of the OH peak indicates hydrogen bonding, which could not be present in the other structural isomer of C_2H_6O, i.e. CH_3OCH_3 – dimethyl ether.

c) 45 – $C_2H_5O^+$ 31 – CH_2OH^+ 29 – $CH_3CH_2^+$

d) i) $CH_3COOC_2H_5$ – ethyl ethanoate (an ester)

ii) dropwise, in a fume cupboard.

Energy and Rates

1 a) $C_2H_6(g) \longrightarrow 2\ C(g) + 6\ H(g)$

b) i) $4 \times (C—H) = 662\ kJ\ mol^{-1}$

C—H = $415.5\ kJ\ mol^{-1}$

ii) In ethane we have 6 C—H bonds = $415.5 \times 6 = 2493\ kJ\ mol^{-1}$

Therefore, $2924 - 2493 = C—C$

C—C = $431\ kJ\ mol^{-1}$

c) enthalpies of combustion for carbon, hydrogen and methane

2 $-\left(4.4 \times \dfrac{65.5}{1308}\right) kJ\ mol^{-1} = -220\ kJ\ mol^{-1}$

3 a) i) $9.79\ kJ\ mol^{-1}$ ($9790\ J\ mol^{-1}$)

ii) $9790 = 250 \times 4.18 \times$ rise in temp.

Rise in temp. $= \dfrac{9790}{250 \times 4.18} = 9.37\ °C$

b) i) No, because the temperature would not be high enough to denature the enzymes in the yeast.

ii) No, because although a lot more energy will be given out from the large quantities of glucose used, this energy heats up a very large volume of water, resulting in a small temperature rise.

4 a)

$$2\ SO_2(g) + O_2(g) \xrightarrow{\Delta H_1} 2\ SO_3(g)$$
$$\Delta H_2 \searrow \qquad \nearrow \Delta H_3$$
$$2\ S(s) + 3\ O_2(g)$$

$\Delta H_1 = \Delta H_3 - \Delta H_2$

$\Delta H_2 = 2 \times (-297)\ kJ\ mol^{-1}$

$\Delta H_3 = 2 \times (-395)\ kJ\ mol^{-1}$

So $\Delta H_1 = -790-(-594)$

$= -196\ kJ\ mol^{-1}$

b) The enthalpy of any element, in its most stable form at 298 K, is taken as zero by convention.

5

$$Li_2CO_3(s) \xrightarrow{\Delta H_1} Li_2O(s) + CO_2(g)$$
$$\Delta H_2 \searrow \qquad \nearrow \Delta H_3$$
$$2\ Li(s) + C(s,\ graphite) + 1\tfrac{1}{2}\ O_2(g)$$

$\Delta H_1 = \Delta H_3 - \Delta H_2$

$\Delta H_2 = -1216\ kJ\ mol^{-1}$

$\Delta H_3 = (-596)+(-394)$

$= -990\ kJ\ mol-1$

So $\Delta H_1 = -990-(-1216)$

$= +226\ kJ\ mol^{-1}$

6

$$(CN)_2(g) \xrightarrow{\Delta H_2} 2C(g) + 2\ N(g)$$
$$\Delta H_f \swarrow \qquad \nearrow \Delta H_1$$
$$2\ C(graphite,\ s) + N_2(g)$$

$\Delta H_f = \Delta H_1 - \Delta H_2$

$\Delta H_1 = (2 \times 717) + (2 \times 473)$

$= +2380\ kJ\ mol^{-1}$

$\Delta H_2 = +2121\ kJ\ mol^{-1}$

Therefore, $\Delta H_f = +2380 - 2121$

$= +259\ kJ\ mol^{-1}$

7

$$C_3H_8(g) \xrightarrow{\Delta H_1} C_3H_6(g) + H_2(g)$$
$$\Delta H_3 \searrow \qquad \nearrow \Delta H_2$$
$$3\ C(graphite,\ s) + 4\ H_2(g)$$

$\Delta H_1 = \Delta H_2 - \Delta H_3$

$= +20.2 - (-104.5)$

$= +124.7\ kJ\ mol^{-1}$

a) a pair of electrons shared between two atoms

b) the energy needed to break one mole of the bonds

c)

$$N_2(g) + 3H_2(g) \xrightarrow{\Delta H_1} 2\,NH_3(g)$$

with ΔH_3 and ΔH_2 leading to $2\,N(g) + 6\,H(g)$

$\Delta H_2 = \Delta H_3 - \Delta H_1$
$\Delta H_3 = +946 + (3 \times 436)$
$\quad = +2254\,\text{kJ mol}^{-1}$
$\Delta H_2 = +2254 - (-92)$
$\quad = +2346\,\text{kJ mol}^{-1}$

There are 6 N—H bonds broken in ΔH_2.

Therefore N—H $= \dfrac{+2346}{6} = +391\,\text{kJ mol}^{-1}$

d)

$$N_2(g) + 2\,H_2(g) \xrightarrow{\Delta H_3} N_2H_4(g)$$

with ΔH_2 and ΔH_1 leading to $2\,N(g) + 4\,H(g)$

$\Delta H_1 = \Delta H_2 - \Delta H_3$
$\Delta H_2 = 946 + (2 \times 436)$
$\quad = +1818\,\text{kJ mol}^{-1}$
$\Delta H_1 = +1818 - (+94)$
$\quad = +1724\,\text{kJ mol}^{-1}$
$\Delta H_1 = (4 \times \text{N—H}) + (1 \times \text{N—N})$
$+1724 = (4 \times 391) + (\text{N—N})$
Therefore, N—N $= +1724 - (4 \times 391)$
$\quad = +160\,\text{kJ mol}^{-1}$

a) See top of page 299.

b) i)

$$C_4H_{10}(g) + \tfrac{13}{2}O_2(g) \xrightarrow{\Delta H_c^{\ominus}} 4\,CO_2(g) + 5\,H_2O(g)$$

with ΔH_1 and ΔH_2 leading to $4\,C(\text{graphite, s}) + 5\,H_2(g) + \tfrac{13}{2}O_2(g)$

$\Delta H_c = \Delta H_2 - \Delta H_1$
$\Delta H_2 = 4 \times \Delta H_f[CO_2(g)] + 5 \times \Delta H_f[H_2O(g)]$
$\Delta H_c = 4 \times \Delta H_f[CO_2(g)] + 5 \times \Delta H_f[H_2O(g)] - \Delta H_f[C_4H_{10}(g)]$

ii) $\Delta H_f[C_4H_{10}(g)] = 4 \times \Delta H_f[CO_2(g)] + 5 \times \Delta H_f[H_2O(g)] - \Delta H_c[C_4H_{10}(g)]$
$\quad = (4 \times -394.0) + (5 \times -286.0) - (-2877)$
$\quad = -1576 - 1430 + 2877$
$\quad = -129\,\text{kJ mol}^{-1}$

a) i) $Cu(g)$ ii) $Cu^+(g)$ iii) $2\,Br(g)$

b) Standard enthalpy of formation of copper(II) bromide.

c) $\Delta H_{\text{lattice}} = -[(+338.3) + (+746.0) + (1958) + (2 \times 111.9)$
$\quad + (2 \times -324.6)] + (-141.8)$
$\quad = -2616.9 + (-141.8)$
$\quad = -2758.7\,\text{kJ mol}^{-1}$

a) i) The magnitude of the lattice enthalpy decreases as we descend a group (use data for LiF, NaF, KF, RbF and CsF to illustrate Group 1 trend and MgF_2, CaF_2, SrF_2 and RaF_2 for Group 2).

ii) The magnitude of the lattice enthalpy decreases as we descend Group 7 (use data for LiF, LiCl, LiBr and LiI).

iii) The lattice enthalpy decreases in magnitude as we descend any group of metals.

iv) The charge density of the metal decreases as its size increases as we descend a group. This is because the same charge is now spread over a larger volume.

a) The magnitude of the lattice enthalpy increases with increasing ionic charge.
The magnitude of the lattice enthalpy increases with decreasing ionic size.

b) $Cu(s) + \tfrac{1}{2}O_2(g) \longrightarrow CuO(s)$
$Cu^{2+}(g) + O_2^-(g) \longrightarrow CuO(s)$
$Cu(g) \longrightarrow Cu^+(g) + e^-$

c)

$$Cu^{2+}(g) + O^{2-}(g) \xrightarrow{\Delta H_{\text{lattice}}} Cu^{2+}O^{2-}(s)$$

with ΔH_1 and ΔH_2 from $Cu(s) + \tfrac{1}{2}O_2(g)$

$\Delta H_{\text{lattice}} = \Delta H_2 - \Delta H_1$
$\Delta H_1 = +339 + 745 + 1960 + 448 + (-141) + 791$
$\quad = +33\,942\,\text{kJ mol}^{-1}$
$\Delta H_2 = -155\,\text{kJ mol}^{-1}$
So $\Delta H_{\text{lattice}} = (-155) - (+3942)$
$\quad = -4097\,\text{kJ mol}^{-1}$

a) i) $Mg^{2+}(g) + 2\,Cl^-(g) \longrightarrow Mg^{2+}(Cl^-)_2(s)$

ii) Call unknown enthalpy change x.
From diagram we have: $-2648 = -155 - 642 - x$
$x = -155 - 642 + 2648$
$\quad = +1851\,\text{kJ mol}^{-1}$
So $\Delta H_{\text{lattice}} = -1851 - 642$
$\quad = -2493\,\text{kJ mol}^{-1}$

b) i) There is an enthalpy change of $+122\,\text{kJ mol}^{-1}$ when one mole of $Cl(g)$ atoms are formed from chlorine gas, under standard conditions.

ii) When one mole of electrons is added to one mole of chlorine atoms, under standard conditions, there is an enthalpy change of $-364\,\text{kJ mol}^{-1}$.

c) i)

$$Mg(s) + Cl_2(g) \xrightarrow{+1851} Mg^{2+}(g) + 2Cl^-(g)$$
$$\downarrow (2 \times 122)$$
$$Mg(s) + 2Cl(g)$$
$$\downarrow (2 \times -364)$$
$$Mg(s) + 2Cl^-(g) \xrightarrow{+148} Mg(g) + 2Cl^-(g)$$
with y on the right side

$y = -148 + 728 - 244 + 1851$
$\quad = +2187\,\text{kJ mol}^{-1}$

ii) Because the same positive charge on the nucleus (i.e. 12+) is now holding in 11 electrons instead of 12 electrons, reducing the distance between the outer electron and the nucleus. Therefore it is more difficult for the second electron to escape.

a)

$$PCl_3(l) + Cl_2(g) \xrightarrow{\Delta H_1} PCl_5(s)$$

with ΔH_2 and ΔH_3 leading to $P(s) + \tfrac{5}{2}Cl_2(g)$

$\Delta H_1 = \Delta H_3 - \Delta H_2$
$\quad = (-443.5) - (-319.7)$
$\quad = -123.8\,\text{kJ mol}^{-1}$

b) $\Delta S_{\text{surroundings}} = -\dfrac{\Delta H}{T} = -\dfrac{(-123\,800)}{298} = +415.4\,\text{J mol}^{-1}\,\text{K}^{-1}$

c) i) Fewer moles of product compared with reactants / and reactants are more disordered because they are in the liquid and gaseous states, as opposed to the more orderly arrangement in the solid product PCl_5.

ii) $+415.4 - (-215.6) = +199.8\,\text{J mol}^{-1}\,\text{K}^{-1}$

iii) Yes, because there is an increase in the total entropy as a result of the reaction.

d) Decreases, because position of equilibrium will shift to the left in order to lower the temperature, i.e. the endothermic backward reaction.

a) ΔG = change in (Gibbs) free energy
ΔH = change in enthalpy
ΔS = change in entropy

b) i) $\Delta G = \Delta H - T\Delta S$

Therefore, $\Delta S = \dfrac{\Delta H - \Delta G}{T}$

$\Delta S = \dfrac{-65\,200 + 55\,200}{298}$ (ΔH and ΔG expressed in J, as opposed to kJ)

$\quad = -33.6\,\text{J mol}^{-1}\,\text{K}^{-1}$

ii) ΔG is negative, so the reaction is spontaneous/feasible.
ΔH is negative, so reaction is exothermic.
ΔS is negative, so system gets less disordered as a result of the reaction.

16 a) i) No effect.
ii) Lowers the activation energy.
b) The proportion of particles with energy exceeding the activation energy increases in both cases.

17 a) i) and ii) See graph on page 332.
iii) No effect on the distribution of energies but lower activation energy means a greater proportion of molecules have sufficient energy to react when they collide.
b) The reactant(s) and catalyst are in different states.
Examples – see page 333.

18 a) and b)

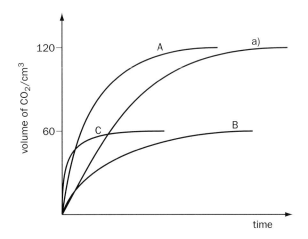

c) The minimum energy that reactant particles must possess when they collide in order for a reaction to occur. A catalyst lowers the activation energy so that a higher proportion of particles have sufficient energy to react.

19 See pages 146 and 147.

20 a) See pages 147 and 333.
b) Step 1 – bonds form between reactants and catalyst.
Step 2 – bonds within reactants break and new bonds form between reactants.
Step 3 – bonds to catalyst break and new products leave.
c) The bond formed between reactant and catalyst might be too weak. This affects step 1.
The bonds between reactant and catalyst are too strong. This affects step 3.

21 a) Greater surface area, therefore more chance of collisions.
b) Energy of collision is less than the activation energy/or particles not in correct orientation for a reaction to occur.

22 a) Peak moved to right of original curve/lower peak than on the original curve.
b) The **average** energy of molecules increases, so there are a higher proportion of molecules with energy greater than the activation energy (as shown by the increased area under the curve beyond E_A). There are more frequent and more effective collisions producing an increased rate of reaction.

23 a) second order
b) rate $= k[NO][H_2]^2$
c) $1.20 = k \times 0.002 \times (0.012)^2$
$$k = \frac{1.20}{0.002 \times (0.012)^2}$$
$= 4.17 \times 10^6 \, mol^{-2} \, dm^6 \, min^{-1}$
d) The average energy of the molecules increases and their average speed increases. There are more collisions and more of theses collisions result in a reaction because the proportion of molecules with energy greater than the activation energy increases rapidly.
e) The value of the rate constant increases.

24 a) See first diagram of apparatus on page 326.
b) i) first order
ii) s^{-1} (or min^{-1})
iii) The first step is the rate determining step because it includes N_2O_5 as a reactant, and N_2O_5 appears in the rate equation. The reactant molecules in the second and third steps do not appear in the rate equation, so these steps must happen rapidly.

25 a) i) blue/black
ii) Any iodide removed in the reaction is replaced by the iodine produced reacting with sodium thiosulphate, until the thiosulphate is used up.
b) The rate (1/time) is directly proportional to the concentration of persulphate ions (as shown by the straight line on the graph in b) i)). Therefore, the reaction is first order with respect to the concentration of persulphate ions.
c) i) rate $= k[S_2O_8^{2-}][I^-]$
ii) $mol^{-1} \, dm^3 \, s^{-1}$

26 a) i) first order with respect to [A]
ii) zero order with respect to [B]
b) rate $= k[A]$
c) $6.0 \times 10^{-3} = k \times 0.40$
$k = 1.5 \times 10^{-2} \, s^{-1}$ (i.e. $0.015 \, s^{-1}$)
d) i) A slow step in the mechanism of the reaction that influences the overall rate of the reaction.
ii) Mechanism 1 – Not possible because the slow step must involve A but not B. The first step here involves both A and B, so both A and B would appear in the rate equation.
Mechanism 2 – This is possible. The first two steps could be fast, so [B] will not appear in the rate equation. But the third step could be slow, so [A] will affect the rate and will appear in the rate equation.
Mechanism 2 – Unlikely because if the first step is slow (so that [A] appears in the rate equation), there are two A's reacting, so it is likely that the rate would depend on $[A]^2$, not just [A].

27 a) i) Experiments 1 and 2 show that if we double the concentration of $(CH_3)_3CBr$, we double the rate of the reaction, i.e. the rate is directly proportional to $[(CH_3)_3CBr]$ – first order.
However, experiments 2 and 3 show that if we double the concentration of OH^-, the rate of reaction is not affected, i.e. OH^- will not appear in the rate equation – zero order.
ii) $3.0 \times 10^{-3} = k \times 1.0 \times 10^{-3}$
$$k = \frac{3.0 \times 10^{-3}}{1.0 \times 10^{-3}}$$
$= 3.0 \, s^{-1}$
iii) rate $= 3.0 \times 4.0 \times 10^{-3}$
$= 1.2 \times 10^{-2} \, mol \, dm^{-3} \, s^{-1}$
b) $S_N 2$ mechanism for primary bromoalkanes. See bottom of page 347 for mechanism.
c) Add acidified (dil. sulphuric acid) potassium dichromate solution. The tertiary alcohol formed in part a) would not react (solution remains orange), but the primary alcohol in b) would be oxidised and the orange colour would change to green.

28 a) second order with respect to C
zero order with respect to D
initial rate $= 1.6 \times 10^{-5} \, mol \, dm^{-3} \, s^{-1}$
b) i) $CH_3COOCH_3 + OH^- \longrightarrow CH_3COO^- + CH_3OH$
ii) rate $= k[CH_3COOCH_3][OH^-]$
$$k = \frac{8.8 \times 10^{-5}}{0.020 \times 0.020} = 0.22 \, mol^{-1} \, dm^3 \, s^{-1}$$
iii) Large excess of OH^- ions present, making the concentration of OH^- ions, $[OH^-]$, effectively constant.

Equilibria and Redox

1 a) i) Near to the source of methane gas, i.e. North Sea gas.
ii) As oil and gas (fossil fuels) are used up, an alternative source of methane will be needed.
iii) Argon from the air (which is the raw material for the nitrogen gas).
b) Advantage – higher percentage of ammonia in equilibrium mixture/faster rate of reaction.

Disadvantage – higher costs (or more energy needed) in compressing gases to higher pressures/dangers involved in reactors running at very high pressures/high cost of building plant that can withstand very high pressures.

  c) i) Although the percentage of ammonia at equilibrium decreases with increasing temperature, at low temperatures the rate of reaction will be too slow to make the process economically viable. So 450 °C is chosen to give a reasonable yield of ammonia at a faster rate. The catalyst will also speed up the rate at which equilibrium is established (but won't affect the percentage of ammonia in an equilibrium mixture).

    ii) Iron, which is a heterogeneous catalyst.

  d) i) Ammonia is cooled down, condensed and run off as a liquid.

    ii) They are recycled to re-enter the reaction vessel.

  e) i) $4 NH_3(g) + 5 O_2(g) \rightleftharpoons 4 NO(g) + 6 H_2O(g)$

    ii) $NH_3(aq) + HNO_3(aq) \longrightarrow NH_4NO_3(aq)$

  f) i) Because ammonia is needed as one of the reactants itself to make ammonium nitrate. The other reactant, nitric acid, is also manufactured from ammonia. Therefore transport costs will be reduced if the ammonia can be piped to different parts of the same site.

    ii) Solid ammonium nitrate is explosive, should be isolated from people to reduce risk in the event of an accident.

2 a) i) Advantage – can be piped on and off ships easily.
       Disadvantage – cost/energy requirements of melting and keeping sulphur molten.

    ii) $S(l) + O_2(g) \longrightarrow SO_2(g)$
       $2 SO_2(g) + O_2(g) \rightleftharpoons 2 SO_3(g)$

  b) i) exothermic

    ii) vanadium(V) oxide

    iii) Energy produced in the exothermic reactions is used to heat reactants and catalyst, saving costs on fuel. They also prevent the temperature rising too high as this would reduce the percentage conversion of SO_2 to SO_3.

    iv) To increase the surface area thereby increasing its efficiency and the rate of the reaction.

    v) Substance A is concentrated sulphuric acid (98% H_2SO_4 and 2% water).
      The reaction can be shown as:
      $SO_3(g) + H_2O(l) \longrightarrow H_2SO_4(l)$
      or $SO_3(g) + H_2SO_4(l) \longrightarrow H_2S_2O_7(l)$ – called oleum.

  c) In case any sulphur dioxide is released from stacks. A fine mist of sulphuric acid could also be produced if absorption goes above 99.5%.

3 a) i) 3 (and 1 is increased by the effect of temperature only)
    ii) 5   iii) 5   iv) 2

4 a) A reversible reaction in which the rate of the forward reaction is the same as the rate of the backward reaction (concentration of reactants and products remains constant although there is continuous reaction going on).

  b) It increases the rate of both the forward and backward reactions by the same amount.

  c) i) line x = B, line y = A or D, line z = C

    ii) Reaction would be too slow/too few collisions.

    iii) Plant to withstand very high pressures would be expensive to build/danger or expense involved in compressing gases to very high pressures.

    iv) Rising curve, but below line z.

5 a) $K_p = \dfrac{p^2(SO_3(g))_{eq}}{p^2(SO_2(g))_{eq} \times p(O_2(g))_{eq}}$

  b) The enthalpy change of the reaction.

  c) top line – decreases
    middle line – increases
    bottom line – increases

6 a) moles of NO_2 = 0.12 moles
    moles of N_2O_4 = (0.12 − 0.06) = 0.06 moles.

  b) i) $K_c = \dfrac{[NO_2(g)]_{eq}^2}{[N_2O_4(g)]_{eq}}$

    ii) $[N_2O_4] = \dfrac{0.06}{4.80} = 0.0125 \text{ mol dm}^{-3}$

      $[NO_2] = \dfrac{0.12}{4.80} = 0.025 \text{ mol dm}^{-3}$

      $K_c = \dfrac{(0.025)^2}{0.0125} = 0.05 \text{ mol dm}^{-3}$

  c) i) $K_p = \dfrac{p^2(NO_2(g))_{eq}}{p(N_2O_4(g))_{eq}}$

    ii) mole fraction of $NO_2 = \dfrac{0.12}{(0.12 + 0.06)} = 0.67$

    iii) $K_p = \dfrac{(0.67 \times 100)^2}{(0.33 \times 100)} = 136 \text{ kPa}$

7 a) i)
                $2 SO_2(g) + O_2(g) \rightleftharpoons 2 SO_3(g)$
      At start   10 mol   5 mol   0 mol
      At eqm.   1 mol   0.5 mol 9 mol

    ii) Total moles = (1 + 0.5 + 9) = 10.5 moles

      Mole fraction of $SO_2 = \dfrac{1}{10.5} = 0.095$

      Mole fraction of $O_2 = \dfrac{0.5}{10.5} = 0.048$

      Mole fraction of $SO_3 = \dfrac{9}{10.5} = 0.86$ (to 2 sig. fig.)

    iii) $p(SO_2)_{eq} = 0.095 \times 200 = 19 \text{ kPa}$
       $p(O_2)_{eq} = 0.048 \times 200 = 9.6 \text{ kPa}$
       $p(SO_3)_{eq} = 0.86 \times 200 = 172 \text{ kPa}$

    iv) $K_p = \dfrac{p^2(SO_3(g))_{eq}}{p^2(SO_2(g))_{eq} \times p(O_2(g))_{eq}}$

    v) $K_p = \dfrac{(172)^2}{(19)^2 \times 9.6} = 8.5 \text{ kPa}^{-1}$

  b) See page 365 for uses of sulphuric acid.

8 a) i) See page 358.

    ii) The initial blue colour turns green (as the blue and yellow complexes mix at first), then it turns yellow when chloride ions are in excess.

  b) i) $\text{mol}^{-4} \text{ dm}^{12}$

    ii) $4.17 \times 10^5 = \dfrac{[CuCl_4^{2-}]}{1.17 \times 10^{-5} \times (0.800)^4}$

      $[CuCl_4^{2-}] = 2.0 \text{ mol dm}^{-3}$

9 a) $K_p = \dfrac{p^2(G(g))_{eq}}{p(E(g))_{eq} \times p^2(F(g))_{eq}}$

  where p = partial pressure of gases.
  Units of K_p will be kPa^{-2}.

  b)

	E	F	G
Moles at start	1	2	0
At equilibrium	0.5	1	0.5

  Total no. of moles = 2

  Mole fractions are: $E = \dfrac{0.5}{2} = 0.25$ $F = \dfrac{1}{2} = 0.5$ $G = \dfrac{0.5}{2} = 0.25$

  Partial pressures: $pE = 0.25 \times 50\,000$
                 $pF = 0.5 \times 50\,000$
                 $pG = 0.25 \times 50\,000$

  Substitute into expression for K_p:

  $K_p = \dfrac{12\,500}{12\,500} \times (25\,000)^2$
    $= 1.6 \times 10^{-9} \text{ kPa}^{-2}$

  c) See page 358.
  The sign of the enthalpy change for the forward reaction is positive, i.e. endothermic, because as the temp. is increased in Run 2, more E is converted to G in an attempt to lower the temperature.

  d) Higher temperature than 300 °C and higher pressure than 50 000 kPa. Higher pressures would be costly in term of the cost of plant to withstand such high pressures/could be dangerous/cost of energy needed to compress gases.
  If temperature too high we have increased energy costs/products might decompose.

10 a) Moles of $Cl_2 = \dfrac{11.1}{35.5} = 0.156$

Moles of $PCl_3 = 0.156$ (same as Cl_2)

Moles of $PCl_5 = \dfrac{83.4}{208.5} - 0.156 = 0.244$

b) i) $K_c = \dfrac{[PCl_3(g)]_{eq}[Cl_2(g)]_{eq}}{[PCl_5(g)]_{eq}}$

ii) $[PCl_3] = [Cl_2] = \dfrac{0.156}{9.23} = 0.0169\,mol\,dm^{-3}$

$[PCl_5] = \dfrac{0.244}{9.23} = 0.0264\,mol\,dm^{-3}$

$K_c = \dfrac{0.0169 \times 0.0169}{0.0264} = 0.0108\,mol\,dm^{-3}$

c) i) $K_p = \dfrac{p^2(PCl_3(g))_{eq} \times p(Cl_2(g))_{eq}}{p(PCl_5(g))_{eq}}$

ii) Mole fraction of $Cl_2 = \dfrac{0.156}{(0.156 \times 2) + 0.244} = 0.281$

iii) Mole fraction of $PCl_5 = \dfrac{0.244}{(0.156 \times 2) + 0.244} = 0.439$

So partial pressure $= 0.439 \times 250$
$= 109.6\,kPa$ (110 kPa to 3 sig. fig.)

iv) $\dfrac{(70.25)^2}{109.6} = 45.0\,kPa$ (to 3 sig. fig.)

11 a) The molecules of a weak acid do not dissociate completely in water. There will be a large proportion of undissociated acid molecules in solution and a low proportion of $H^+(aq)$ ions.

b) The average energy required to break one mole of bonds, using data from a range of different molecules.

c) The strength of the hydrogen halides as acids increases as we descend Group 7 (as shown by values of pK_a – the higher the value, the weaker the acid). The trend is explained by the ease with which the H—Halogen bond is broken. The bonds get weaker as we descend the group, so HI dissociates more easily than HF to produce H^+ ions.

d) The stability of the hydrogen halides decreases as we descend the group. This is explained by the trend in the average bond enthalpies, which also decrease going down the group, making it easier to break the H–Halogen bond.

$2\,HI(g) \longrightarrow H_2(g) + I_2(g)$

12 a) i) $CH_3CH_2COOH(aq) \rightleftharpoons CH_3CH_2COO^-(aq) + H^+(aq)$

ii) $K_a = \dfrac{[CH_3CH_2COO^-(aq)][H^+(aq)]}{[CH_3CH_2COOH(aq)]}$

iii) $K_a = \dfrac{0.500 \times [H^+(aq)]}{1.00} = 10 \times [H^+(aq)]$

$-\lg K_a = -\lg (0.5 \times [H^+(aq)])$
$= -\lg 0.5 + (-\lg[H^+(aq)])$ where $-\lg[H^+(aq)] = pH$
$= -(-0.30) + 4.60$
So $pK_a = 4.90$

iv) $-\lg K_a = 4.90$
$K_a = 1.26 \times 10^{-5}\,mol\,dm^{-3}$ (to 3 sig. fig.)

b) $1.00 \times 10^{-14} = [H^+][OH^-]$
$[OH^-] = 0.005\,00\,mol\,dm^{-3}$

$\dfrac{1.00 \times 10^{-14}}{0.005\,00} = [H^+(aq)]$

$200 \times 10^{-14} = [H^+(aq)]$
$2.3 + (-14) = \lg[H^+(aq)]$
$11.7 = -\lg[H^+(aq)]$
So $pH = 11.7$

c) i) $K_a = \dfrac{[C_6H_5O^-(aq)][H^+(aq)]}{[C_6H_5OH(aq)]}$

ii) The value of K_a will be lower (phenol is a weaker acid than propanoic acid)

13 a) As the temperature is raised, K_a for HF will increase. This is because more HF molecules will dissociate in an endothermic reaction, thereby lowering the temperature.

b) Number of moles of $OH^- = \dfrac{0.50 \times 10}{1000} = 0.0050$

So there are 0.005 moles in $110\,cm^3$ of solution

Therefore its concentration is $\dfrac{0.005 \times 1000}{110} = 0.045\,mol\,dm^{-3}$

$1.0 \times 10^{-14} = [H^+][OH^-]$

$\dfrac{1.0 \times 10^{-14}}{0.045} = [H^+]$

$12.65 = -\lg[H^+(aq)] = pH$

c) i) $K_a = \dfrac{[H^+][F^-]}{[HF]}$

$-\lg K_a = -\lg[H^+(aq)]$ as $[HF] = [F^-]$ and cancel out.
$3.45 = pH$

ii) 0.005 moles of OH^- are added and the HF dissociates to replace the H^+ ions removed. This leaves $(0.05 - 0.005)$ moles of HF in $110\,cm^3$ of solution.
So $[HF]$ will be $0.41\,mol\,dm^{-3}$.

iii) There were 0.05 moles of F^- ions before addition of the alkali, but after addition we have more F^- ions from the HF that has dissociated.
We have $(0.05 + 0.005)$ moles of F^- in $110\,cm^3$ of solution.
So its concentration is still $0.5\,mol\,dm^{-3}$.

iv) $K_a = \dfrac{[H^+] \times 0.5}{0.41}$

$0.82 \times K_a = [H^+(aq)]$
$-\lg (0.82 \times K_a) = -\lg[H^+(aq)]$
$-(-0.086 - 3.45) = pH$
$3.54 = pH$

14 a) Both have sudden change in pH when $50\,cm^3$ of sodium hydroxide is added.
Both finish off at the same pH in excess alkali.
Ethanoic acid starts at a higher pH value.
The sudden change in pH is not as large with ethanoic acid.

b) They are weak acids with differently coloured undissociated acid molecules and conjugate base ions.
Phenolphthalein because its equivalence point and range of colour change (between approx. pH 8 and 10) coincide with the vertical section of the pH curve between ethanoic acid and sodium hydroxide, which occurs mainly above pH 7. Therefore there will be a sharp change in colour at the end point of the reaction. It will also work for HCl and NaOH which has such a large sudden change in pH that the choice of indicator is not as critical.

c) When the pH is 4.3, $[A^-] = [HA]$ so they cancel out in the expression for K_a.
Therefore $K_a = [H^+]$
$-\lg[H^+(aq)] = pH = 4.3 = pK_a$
So $K_a = 5.01 \times 10^{-5}$
Initially the pH = 2.5
So $[H^+] = 3.16 \times 10^{-3}$
Substitute into the expression for K_a:

$5.01 \times 10^{-5} = \dfrac{(3.16 \times 10^{-3})^2}{[HA]}$

$[HA] = \dfrac{(3.16 \times 10^{-3})^2}{5.01 \times 10^{-5}}$

$[HA] = 2.0\,mol\,dm^{-3}$

15 a) An acid donates protons (H^+ ions) and its conjugate base accepts protons (H^+ ions) to re-form the undissociated acid molecule.

b) i) acid = HCl   conjugate base = Cl^-
ii) acid = H_2SO_4 conjugate base = HSO_4^-
iii) acid = NH_4^+ conjugate base = NH_3

c) i) A strong acid has a high degree of dissociation in water and produces a high proportion of $H^+(aq)$ ions. A weak acid has a high proportion of undissociated acid molecules in solution, producing fewer $H^+(aq)$ ions.

ii) $CH_3COOH(aq) + H_2O(l) \rightleftharpoons CH_3COO^-(aq) + H_3O^+(aq)$

iii)   A1   B2   B1   A2
$CH_3COOH(aq) + H_2O(l) \rightleftharpoons CH_3COO^-(aq) + H_3O^+(aq)$

16 a) i) See page 384.
   ii) See page 392.
   b) i) pH = 1 (assuming complete dissociation of H_2SO_4, i.e. 1 mole of H_2SO_4 produces 2 moles of H^+ ions)
      ii) $1 \times 10^{-14} = [H^+][OH^-]$
         $1 \times 10^{-14} = [H^+] \times 0.01$
         $$\frac{-\lg(1 \times 10^{-14})}{0.01} = -\lg(1 \times 10^{-12}) = pH$$
         $$12 = pH$$
   c) i) $K_a = \dfrac{[C_6H_5COO^-][H^+]}{[C_6H_5COOH]}$
         $$6.3 \times 10^{-5} = \frac{x^2}{0.2}$$
         $$2.4 = pH$$
      ii) See second graph on page 390.
      iii) Thymolphthalein, because its equivalence point coincides with the steep part of the pH curve, so it will change colour sharply at the end point of the neutralisation.

17 a) i) $pH = -\lg_{10}[H^+(aq)]$
      ii) $0.010 \, mol \, dm^{-3}$ HCl(aq)   pH = 2
         $0.010 \, mol \, dm^{-3}$ NaOH(aq)   pH = 12
   b) i) $K_a = \dfrac{[H^+(aq)][HCOO^-(aq)]}{[HCOOH(aq)]}$
      ii) pH = 4.4, therefore $[H^+] = 4.0 \times 10^{-5} \, mol \, dm^{-3}$
         $pK_a = 3.8$, therefore $K_a = 1.6 \times 10^{-4} \, mol \, dm^{-3}$
         $[HCOO^-] = 0.5/2$ (because equal volumes are added together, halving the concentration of each solution) $= 0.25 \, mol \, dm^{-3}$
         $$1.6 \times 10^{-4} = \frac{4.0 \times 10^{-5} \times 0.25}{[HCOOH(aq)]}$$
         $$[HCOOH(aq)] = \frac{4.0 \times 10^{-5} \times 0.25}{1.6 \times 10^{-4}} = 0.0625 \, mol \, dm^{-3} \text{ in the buffer solution}$$

         Therefore the concentration of the original solution $= 0.0625 \times 2 = 0.125 \, mol \, dm^{-3}$
         (Alternatively use the values given for pH and pK_a in equation given on page 393.)
   c) i) Ring around H_2SO_4 and $H_2NO_3^+$
         Ring around HS^- and H_3O^+
      ii) Explain acid chosen as proton (H^+) donor and base as proton (H^+) acceptor.

18 a) $K_a = \dfrac{[H^+(aq)][A^-(aq)]}{[HA(aq)]}$
      $pK_a = -\lg_{10} K_a$
      $K_w = [H^+(aq)][OH^-(aq)]$
   b) $1.4 \times 10^{-5} = \dfrac{x^2}{0.65}$ where $x = [H^+(aq)]$
      $\sqrt{1.4 \times 10^{-5} \times 0.65} = x$
      $x = 3.0 \times 10^{-3} = [H^+(aq)]$
      $pH = -\lg(3.0 \times 10^{-3}) = 2.52$
   c) Phenolphthalein because its equivalence point is above 7.

19 a) $K_a = \dfrac{[NH_3(aq)]_{eq}[H^+(aq)]_{eq}}{[NH_4^+(aq)]_{eq}}$
   b) i) $pH = -\lg[H^+(aq)]$
         pH = 5.6 so $[H^+(aq)] = 2.5 \times 10^{-6} \, mol \, dm^{-3}$

      ii) It will increase, because equilibrium will shift to the left to remove $H^+(aq)$ ions added from HCl(aq).
   c) i) A solution which resists changes in pH on addition of acid or alkali to the solution.
      ii) OH^- reacts with H^+ ions (forming H_2O), removing them from the solution, so NH_4^+ ions dissociate to replace them.
   d) Water is acting as a base because it accepts a proton (H^+ ion) from NH_4^+ when it forms H_3O^+.

20 Method 1 – heat with carbon.
   Advantage – cheap/abundant carbon/continuous process.
   Disadvantage – carbide impurity formed/CO, CO_2 pollutant gases formed.
   Method 2 – heat with a reactive metal, such as Na/Al/Mg.
   Advantage – no pollutants formed.
   Disadvantage – reactive metals are expensive/batch process/small amounts produced.
   Method 3 – electrolyse molten compound.
   Advantage – pure product formed/continuous process.
   Disadvantage – large quantities of electrical energy needed, which is expensive.
   (Another method – heat with hydrogen.
   Advantage – no pollution/pure product formed
   Disadvantage – high temperature needed/danger of explosion with hydrogen.)

21 a) $Na^+(l) + e^- \longrightarrow Na(l)$
      Sodium's oxidation number is reduced from +1 to 0.
   b) It is cheaper to electrolyse salt solution because you don't have use energy heating the salt to melt it.
   c) Cheap hydroelectric power.
   d) The iron in steel will react with the chlorine produced, but graphite does not.
   e) It lowers the melting point of the sodium chloride.

22 a) $Fe(s) \mid Fe^{2+}(aq), \, Fe^{3+}(aq) \mid Fe(s)$
      $E = +0.44 - 0.04$
      $\quad = +0.40 \, V$
      $2 \, Fe^{3+}(aq) + Fe(s) \longrightarrow 3 \, Fe^{2+}(aq)$
   b) Potassium manganate(VII) is not used as this can oxidise the chloride ions present as well as the Fe^{2+} ions in the solution. However, potassium dichromate(VI) will oxidise the Fe^{2+} ions but not the chloride ions, so would give an accurate result.
   c) i) Cr^{3+} is oxidised and MnO_4^- is reduced.
      ii) $6 \, MnO_4^-(aq) + 10 \, Cr^{3+}(aq) + 11 \, H_2O(l) \longrightarrow$
         $\quad\quad 6 \, Mn^{2+}(aq) + 5 \, Cr_2O_7^{2-}(aq) + 22 \, H^+(aq)$

23 a) Platinum electrode/coated in finely divided platinum for increased surface area to aid adsorption of hydrogen gas/hydrogen bubbled over the electrode at 298 K / 101 kPa (1 atm)/in solution of $1.0 \, mol \, dm^{-3} \, H^+(aq)$ ions.
   b) i) $U(s) \mid U^{3+}(aq), \, Mn^{2+}(aq) \mid Mn(s)$
         $+1.79 + (-1.18) = E$
         $\quad\quad +0.61 \, V = E$
      ii) $2 \, U(s) + 3 \, Mn^{2+}(aq) \longrightarrow 2 \, U^{3+}(aq) + 3 \, Mn(s)$

24 a) i) $1.0 \, mol \, dm^{-3}$
      ii) $0.5 \, mol \, dm^{-3}$
   b) 101 kPa (1 atm)
   c) 298 K
   d) potassium nitrate solution

Chemical tests

▷ Common organic functional groups

Functional Groups	Testing reagent	Results of test
Alkene ($>C{=}C<$)	Add bromine water	Bromine water is decolourised (from orange/yellow to colourless)
Hydroxyl (—OH) group	Add phosphorus pentachloride (PCl_5) at room temperature.	There is a rapid, exothermic reaction and misty fumes of hydrogen chloride are produced which turn blue litmus red.
Primary (CH_2OH), secondary ($>CHOH$) and tertiary alcohols ($\geqq COH$).	Acidified solution of potassium dichromate(VI). The alcohol is added and the mixture heated.	**Primary alcohols** – the mixture changes from orange ($Cr_2O_7{}^{2-}$) to green (Cr^{3+}) and the product is an aldehyde that will react with Tollen's reagent or Fehling's solution (see test for aldehydes below).
		Secondary alcohols – the mixture changes from orange ($Cr_2O_7{}^{2-}$) to green (Cr^{3+}) and the product is a ketone that will **not** react with Tollen's reagent.
		Tertiary alcohols – there is no reaction and the mixture stays orange in colour
Carbonyl compounds – aldehydes (—CHO) and ketones ($>C{=}O$)	2,4-dinitrophenylhydrazine at room temperature.	Both aldehydes and ketones give an orange crystalline precipitate – the dinitrophenyl hydrazone. This has a melting point characteristic of the aldehyde or ketone from which it was formed.
Distinguishing aldehydes and ketones	Fehling's solution and heat	With the clear blue Fehling's solution, aldehydes give a brick-red precipitate (Cu_2O) whilst ketones give no reaction.
	Tollens' reagent (ammoniacal silver nitrate) and heat in water bath	Aldehydes give a silver mirror on the sides of the test tube. Ketones give no reaction.
Halogenoalkanes (Haloalkanes) (R—X where X is Cl or Br or I)	Warm haloalkane in a dilute solution of alkali in ethanol. Acidify with dilute nitric acid and then add silver nitrate solution.	**Chlorides** – these give a white precipitate of silver chloride.
		Bromides – these give a pale cream precipitate of silver bromide.
		Iodides – these give a yellow precipitate of silver iodide.
Carboxylic acids (—COOH)	Add sodium hydrogen carbonate to compound and bubble gas produced through limewater.	Rapid effervescence and carbon dioxide gas produced gives a white precipitate with the limewater.
Ethanoyl (CH_3CO—) or CH_3CHOH— group	Add alkali to iodine; add a few drops of compound and warm mixture gently in a water bath.	Both reagents give a yellow precipitate of tri-iodomethane or iodoform (CHI_3) – this is commonly known as the iodoform test. The product also has an antiseptic ('hospital-like') smell.
	Add chlorate(I) ions to iodide ions; add a few drops of compound and then warm mixture gently in a water bath.	

Anions

Anion	Formula	Test	Results of test
Carbonate	CO_3^{2-}	Add hydrochloric acid and test gas produced by bubbling through limewater	Rapid effervescence and carbon dioxide produced gives white precipitate with limewater. $CO_3^{2-} + 2H^+ \longrightarrow H_2O + CO_2$
Hydrogencarbonate	HCO_3^-	Heat either solid or solution and test gas produced with limewater	Carbon dioxide gas produced gives white precipitate with limewater.
Sulphate(VI)	SO_4^{2-}	Add dilute nitric acid to solution of ion and then barium chloride solution.	Dense white precipitate of barium sulphate is produced. $Ba^{2+}(aq) + SO_4^{2-} (aq) \longrightarrow BaSO_4(s)$
Sulphate(IV) (or sulphite)	SO_3^{2-}	Add dilute hydrochloric acid.	Effervescence as sulphur dioxide gas is produced that has pungent, 'metallic taste' and decolourises acidified manganate(VII) solution. (SO_2 is toxic.)
Hydrogensulphate	HSO_4^-	Test for sulphate(VI) and then make solution and add universal indicator.	Positive test for sulphate(VI) and the U.I. turns red. $HSO_4^- + H_2O \rightleftharpoons H_3O^+ + SO_4^{2-}$
Chloride	Cl^-	Add dilute nitric acid followed by silver nitrate solution.	White precipitate formed. $Ag^+(aq) + Cl^-(aq) \longrightarrow AgCl(s)$
Bromide	Br^-	Ditto (as above)	Pale cream precipitate formed. i.e. $AgBr(s)$
Iodide	I^-	Ditto (as above)	Yellow precipitate formed i.e. $AgI(s)$
Nitrate(V)	NO_3^-	**EITHER** Add NaOH solution to compound and Devarda's alloy. Heat.	Pungent smell of ammonia gas and red litmus turns blue.
		OR Add iron(II) sulphate solution + conc. sulphuric acid with care.	Brown ring where layers meet.

Cations

Cation	Formula	Test	Results of test
Ammonium	NH_4^+	Add NaOH solution and heat.	Pungent smell of ammonia gas and red litmus turns blue.
Magnesium	Mg^{2+}	Add aqueous ammonium phosphate to solution of ion.	White precipitate formed.
Sodium	Na^+	Flame test	Deep yellow flame
Potassium	K^+		Lilac (pale pink) flame
Calcium	Ca^{2+}		Brick red flame
Barium	Ba^{2+}		Pale green (apple green) flame

Gases

Name of gas	Formula	Test	Results of test
Hydrogen	H_2	Lighted spill	Hydrogen burns with a 'pop'.
Oxygen	O_2	Glowing spill	Spill relights
Carbon dioxide	CO_2	Pass gas through limewater	Dense white precipitate formed.
Ammonia	NH_3	Smell (CARE) and blue litmus paper	Characteristic pungent smell ('smelling salts') and litmus turns blue.
Chlorine	Cl_2	Blue litmus paper	Paper turns red then quickly bleached.
Nitrogen dioxide	NO_2	Appearance	Brown colour
Sulphur dioxide	SO_2	**EITHER** Acidified potassium dichromate solution	Colour changes from orange to green
		OR Acidified potassium manganate (VII)	Colour changes from purple to colourless.

Periodic Table

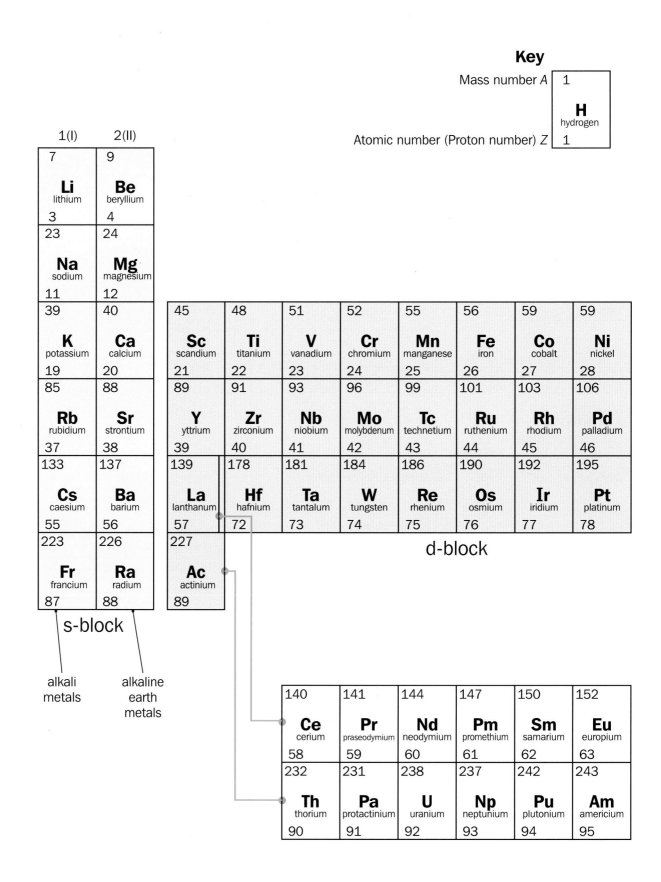

Key

Mass number A | 1

H
hydrogen

Atomic number (Proton number) Z | 1

1(I)	2(II)
7 **Li** lithium 3	9 **Be** beryllium 4
23 **Na** sodium 11	24 **Mg** magnesium 12
39 **K** potassium 19	40 **Ca** calcium 20
85 **Rb** rubidium 37	88 **Sr** strontium 38
133 **Cs** caesium 55	137 **Ba** barium 56
223 **Fr** francium 87	226 **Ra** radium 88

s-block

alkali metals
alkaline earth metals

45 **Sc** scandium 21	48 **Ti** titanium 22	51 **V** vanadium 23	52 **Cr** chromium 24	55 **Mn** manganese 25	56 **Fe** iron 26	59 **Co** cobalt 27	59 **Ni** nickel 28
89 **Y** yttrium 39	91 **Zr** zirconium 40	93 **Nb** niobium 41	96 **Mo** molybdenum 42	99 **Tc** technetium 43	101 **Ru** ruthenium 44	103 **Rh** rhodium 45	106 **Pd** palladium 46
139 **La** lanthanum 57	178 **Hf** hafnium 72	181 **Ta** tantalum 73	184 **W** tungsten 74	186 **Re** rhenium 75	190 **Os** osmium 76	192 **Ir** iridium 77	195 **Pt** platinum 78
227 **Ac** actinium 89							

d-block

140 **Ce** cerium 58	141 **Pr** praseodymium 59	144 **Nd** neodymium 60	147 **Pm** promethium 61	150 **Sm** samarium 62	152 **Eu** europium 63
232 **Th** thorium 90	231 **Pa** protactinium 91	238 **U** uranium 92	237 **Np** neptunium 93	242 **Pu** plutonium 94	243 **Am** americium 95

0 or 8(VIII)

3(III)	4(IV)	5(V)	6(VI)	7(VII)	
					4 **He** helium 2
11 **B** boron 5	12 **C** carbon 6	14 **N** nitrogen 7	16 **O** oxygen 8	19 **F** fluorine 9	20 **Ne** neon 10
27 **Al** aluminium 13	28 **Si** silicon 14	31 **P** phosphorus 15	32 **S** sulphur 16	35 **Cl** chlorine 17	40 **Ar** argon 18

64 **Cu** copper 29	65 **Zn** zinc 30	70 **Ga** gallium 31	73 **Ge** germanium 32	75 **As** arsenic 33	79 **Se** selenium 34	80 **Br** bromine 35	84 **Kr** krypton 36
108 **Ag** silver 47	112 **Cd** cadmium 48	115 **In** indium 49	119 **Sn** tin 50	122 **Sb** antimony 51	128 **Te** tellurium 52	127 **I** iodine 53	131 **Xe** xenon 54
197 **Au** gold 79	201 **Hg** mercury 80	204 **Tl** thallium 81	207 **Pb** lead 82	209 **Bi** bismuth 83	210 **Po** polonium 84	210 **At** astatine 85	222 **Rn** radon 86

p-block

halogens   noble gases

| 157 **Gd** gadolinium 64 | 159 **Tb** terbium 65 | 163 **Dy** dysprosium 66 | 165 **Ho** holmium 67 | 167 **Er** erbium 68 | 169 **Tm** thulium 69 | 173 **Yb** ytterbium 70 | 175 **Lu** lutetium 71 |
| 247 **Cm** curium 96 | 245 **Bk** berkelium 97 | 251 **Cf** californium 98 | 254 **Es** einsteinium 99 | 253 **Fm** fermium 100 | 256 **Md** mendelevium 101 | 254 **No** nobelium 102 | 257 **Lr** lawrencium 103 |

f-block

▷ Physical data of elements

Data on the first 36 elements

Element	Symbol	Atomic number	Relative atomic mass	Melting point / K	Boiling point / K	Enthalpy of atomisation / kJ mol^{-1}	Density at 298 K / g cm^{-3}
Hydrogen	H	1	1.0	14	20	218.0	0.000 09
Helium	He	2	4.0	1	4	–	0.000 18
Lithium	Li	3	6.9	454	1615	159.4	0.53
Beryllium	Be	4	9.0	1551	3243	324.3	1.85
Boron	B	5	10.8	2573	2823	562.7	2.34
Carbon	C	6	12.0	>3823	5100	714.8	3.51
Nitrogen	N	7	14.0	63	77	472.7	0.001 25
Oxygen	O	8	16.0	55	90	249.2	0.001 43
Fluorine	F	9	19.0	53	85	79.0	0.001 70
Neon	Ne	10	20.2	25	27	–	0.0009
Sodium	Na	11	23.0	371	1156	107.3	0.97
Magnesium	Mg	12	24.3	922	1380	147.7	1.74
Aluminium	Al	13	27.0	933	2740	326.4	2.70
Silicon	Si	14	28.1	1683	2628	455.6	2.32
Phosphorus	P	15	31.0	317	553	314.6	1.82
Sulphur	S	16	32.1	392	718	278.5	1.96
Chlorine	Cl	17	35.5	172	238	121.7	0.003 21
Argon	Ar	18	39.9	84	87	–	0.001 78
Potassium	K	19	39.1	336	1033	89.2	0.86
Calcium	Ca	20	40.1	1112	1757	178.2	1.54
Scandium	Sc	21	45.0	1814	3104	377.8	2.99
Titanium	Ti	22	47.9	1933	3560	469.9	4.50
Vanadium	V	23	50.9	2163	3653	514.2	5.96
Chromium	Cr	24	52.0	2130	2943	396.6	7.20
Manganese	Mn	25	54.9	1517	2235	280.7	7.20
Iron	Fe	26	55.9	1808	3023	416.3	7.86
Cobalt	Co	27	58.9	1768	3143	424.7	8.90
Nickel	Ni	28	58.7	1728	3003	429.7	8.90
Copper	Cu	29	63.5	1356	2840	338.3	8.92
Zinc	Zn	30	65.4	693	1180	130.7	7.14
Gallium	Ga	31	69.7	303	2676	277.0	5.90
Germanium	Ge	32	72.6	1210	3103	376.6	5.35
Arsenic	As	33	74.9	886	1090	302.5	5.73
Selenium	Se	34	79.0	490	758	227.1	4.81
Bromine	Br	35	79.9	266	332	111.9	3.12
Krypton	Kr	36	83.8	116	121	–	0.003 73

Data on other selected elements (in alphabetical order)

Element	Symbol	Atomic number	Relative atomic mass	Melting point / K	Boiling point / K	Enthalpy of atomisation / kJ mol^{-1}	Density at 298 K / g cm^{-3}
Astatine	At	85	210.0	575	610	90.4	–
Barium	Ba	56	137.3	998	1913	180.0	3.51
Caesium	Cs	55	132.9	302	942	76.1	1.88
Francium	Fr	87	223.0	300*	950*	72.8	–
Gold	Au	79	197.0	1337	3353	366.1	18.88
Iodine	I	53	126.9	387*	457*	106.8	4.93
Lead	Pb	82	207.2	601	2013	195.0	11.34
Mercury	Hg	80	200.6	234	630	61.3	13.59
Platinum	Pt	78	195.1	2045	4100*	565.3	21.45
Plutonium	Pu	94	242.0	914	3505	–	19.84
Radium	Ra	88	226.0	973	<1419	161.9	5*
Radon	Rn	86	222.0	202	211	–	0.009 73
Rubidium	Rb	37	85.5	312	959	80.9	1.53
Silver	Ag	47	107.9	1235	2485	284.6	10.50
Strontium	Sr	38	87.6	1042	1657	164.4	2.6
Tin	Sn	50	118.7	505	2533	304.2	7.28
Tungsten	W	74	183.9	3683	5933*	849.4	19.35
Uranium	U	92	238.0	1405	4091	535.6	19.05
Xenon	Xe	54	131.3	161	166	–	0.005 89

*Note: These values are uncertain.
The densities of francium and astatine are unknown.

Ionisation enthalpies (or ionisation energies)

Name of element	Number of electrons removed and ionisation enthalpy (energy) / kJ mol^{-1}									
	1	2	3	4	5	6	7	8	9	10
Hydrogen	1312									
Helium	2372	5251								
Lithium	520	7298	11 815							
Beryllium	900	1757	14 849	21 007						
Boron	801	2427	3660	25 026	32 828					
Carbon	1086	2353	4621	6223	37 832	47 278				
Nitrogen	1402	2856	4578	7475	9445	53 268	64 362			
Oxygen	1314	3388	5301	7469	10 989	13 327	71 337	84 080		
Fluorine	1681	3374	6051	8408	11 022	15 164	17 868	92 040	106 437	
Neon	2081	3952	6122	9370	12 177	15 239	19 999	23 069	115 382	131 435
Sodium	496	4563	6913	9544	13 352	16 611	20 115	25 491	28 934	141 367
Magnesium	738	1451	7733	10 541	13 629	17 995	21 704	25 657	31 644	35 643
Aluminium	578	1817	2745	11 578	14 831	18 378	23 296	27 460	31 862	38 458
Silicon	789	1577	3232	4356	16 091	19 785	23 787	29 253	33 878	38 734
Phosphorus	1012	1903	2912	4957	6274	21 269	25 398	29 855	35 868	40 960
Sulphur	1000	2251	3361	4564	7012	8496	27 107	31 671	36 579	43 140
Chlorine	1251	2297	3822	5158	6542	9362	11 018	33 606	38 601	43 963
Argon	1521	2666	3931	5771	7238	8781	11 996	13 842	40 761	46 188

Ionisation enthalpies (cont.)

Name of element	Number of electrons removed and ionisation enthalpy (energy) / kJ mol⁻¹									
	1	2	3	4	5	6	7	8	9	10
Potassium	419	3051	4412	5877	7975	9649	11 343	14 942	16 964	48 577
Calcium	590	1145	4912	6474	8144	10 496	12 320	14 207	18 192	20 385
Scandium	631	1235	2389	7089	8844	10 720	13 320	15 313	17 370	21 741
Titanium	658	1310	2653	4175	9573	11 517	13 586	16 259	18 640	20 833
Vanadium	650	1414	2828	4507	6294	12 362	14 490	16 760	19 860	22 240
Chromium	653	1592	2987	4740	6686	8738	15 540	17 822	20 200	23 580
Manganese	717	1509	3249	4940	6985	9200	11 508	18 956	21 400	23 960
Iron	759	1561	2958	5290	7236	9600	12 100	14 576	22 679	25 290
Cobalt	758	1646	3232	4950	7671	9840	12 400	15 100	17 960	26 600
Nickel	737	1753	3394	5300	7285	10 400	12 800	15 600	18 600	21 660
Copper	746	1958	3554	5330	7709	9940	13 400	16 000	19 200	22 400
Zinc	906	1733	3833	5730	7970	10 400	12 900	16 800	19 600	23 000
Gallium	579	1979	2963	6200						
Germanium	762	1537	3302	4411	9021					
Arsenic	947	1798	2736	4837	6043	12 312				
Selenium	941	2045	2974	4144	6590	7883	14 990			
Bromine	1140	2100	3500	4560	5760	8549	9938	18 600		
Krypton	1351	2368	3565	5070	6243	7574	10 710	12 158	22 230	

▷ Electron affinities for some elements and ions

(Energy change for process $X^{n-}(g) + e^- \longrightarrow X^{(n+1)-}(g)$)

Formula of atom or ion	Electron affinity / kJ mol⁻¹
H	−72.77
C	−122.3
N	−7
O	−141.1
O⁻	+798
P	−72
S	−200.42
S⁻	+640
F	−328.0
Cl	−348.8
Br	−324.6
I	−295.4

▷ Enthalpy of formation of selected compounds

Name of compound	Formula	Enthalpy of formation $\Delta H_f^{\ominus}$ / kJ mol⁻¹
Lithium fluoride	LiF	−616.0
Beryllium iodide	BeI_2	−211.0
Strontium iodide	SrI_2	−558.1
Sodium oxide	Na_2O	−414.2
Sodium fluoride	NaF	−573.6
Water	H_2O	−285.8

Enthalpy of formation (cont.)

Name of compound	Formula	Enthalpy of formation $\Delta H_f^{\ominus}$ / kJ mol^{-1}
Carbon dioxide	CO_2	-393.5
Carbon monoxide	CO	-110.5
Hydrogen chloride	HCl	-92.3
Ammonia	NH_3	-46.1
Rubidium bromide	$RbBr$	-435.3
Magnesium oxide	MgO	-601.7

▷ Enthalpy of combustion of selected organic compounds

Name of compound	Formula	Enthalpy of combustion $\Delta H_c^{\ominus}$ / kJ mol^{-1}
Methane	CH_4	-890.3
Ethane	C_2H_6	-1559.7
Propane	C_3H_8	-2219.2
Butane	C_4H_{10}	-2876.5
Octane	C_8H_{18}	-5470.2
Ethanol	C_2H_5OH	-1367.3
Propan-1-ol	C_3H_7OH	-2021.0
Ethanoic acid	CH_3COOH	-874.1
Propanoic acid	C_2H_5COOH	-1527.2
Ethene	C_2H_4	-1410.8
Benzene	C_6H_6	-3267.4

▷ Dissociation constants for some acids

Name of acid	Formula	Equilibrium	Dissociation constant (K_a) at 298 K / mol dm^{-3}	pK_a
Sulphuric	H_2SO_4	$H_2SO_4 \rightleftharpoons HSO_4^- + H^+$	very large	
Nitric	HNO_3	$HNO_3 \rightleftharpoons H^+ + NO_3^-$	40	-1.4
Hydrofluoric	HF	$HF \rightleftharpoons H^+ + F^-$	5.6×10^{-4}	3.3
Methanoic	$HCOOH$	$HCOOH \rightleftharpoons HCOO^- + H^+$	1.6×10^{-4}	3.8
Ethanoic	CH_3COOH	$CH_3COOH \rightleftharpoons CH_3COO^- + H^+$	1.7×10^{-5}	4.8
Propanoic	CH_3CH_2COOH	$C_2H_5COOH \rightleftharpoons C_2H_5COO^- + H^+$	1.3×10^{-5}	4.9
Chloroethanoic	$CH_2ClCOOH$	$CH_2ClCOOH \rightleftharpoons CH_2ClCOO^- + H^+$	1.3×10^{-3}	2.9
Dichloroethanoic	$CHCl_2COOH$	$CHCl_2COOH \rightleftharpoons CHCl_2COO^- + H^+$	5×10^{-3}	1.3
Trichloroethanoic	CCl_3COOH	$CCl_3COOH \rightleftharpoons CCl_3COO^- + H^+$	2×10^{-1}	0.7
Phenol	C_6H_5OH	$C_6H_5OH \rightleftharpoons C_6H_5O^- + H^+$	1.28×10^{-10}	9.9
Trichlorophenol	$C_6H_2Cl_3OH$	$C_6H_2Cl_3OH \rightleftharpoons C_6H_2Cl_3O^- + H^+$	1×10^{-6}	6.0
Carbonic	H_2CO_3	$H_2CO_3 \rightleftharpoons HCO_3^- + H^+$	4.3×10^{-7}	6.4
Hydrogencarbonate	HCO_3^-	$HCO_3^- \rightleftharpoons CO_3^{2-} + H^+$	4.8×10^{-11}	10.3
Benzoic	C_6H_5COOH	$C_6H_5COOH \rightleftharpoons C_6H_5COO^- + H^+$	6.46×10^{-5}	4.19

Index

A

absolute zero of temperature   298
absorption spectrometry   278–81
acid anhydrides   229, 233, 268
acid chlorides   229, 231, 232–3, 268
acid rain   103
acid/alkali titrations   39, 43, 390–91
acid/base equilibria   380–95
acidic oxides   103–4
acids 115, 380, 381
   Brønsted–Lowry theory   382
   Lewis acid   382
   strong and weak   380, 384, 385, 386
   see also carboxylic acids
activation energy   321, 325
   effect of catalysts   332
active site (enzyme)   334
acyl chlorides *see* acid chlorides
acylation   242
   Friedel–Crafts   214
addition polymers   252–3
addition reactions   178–83, 215, 223–4
aerosol propellants   192
agrochemicals *see* fertilisers; pesticides
air bags   345
'alcohol' *see* ethanol
alcoholic drinks   195, 335
alcohols   158, 159, 160, 195–201
   physical properties   195
   protonation   198
   reactions   197, 233, 266
      with carboxylic acids   197, 231, 374
      dehydration   199
      nucleophilic substitution   198–9
      oxidation   196
      test for   458
aldehydes   158, 160, 196, 221–7, 267
   test for   143, 222
alkali metals *see* Group 1 elements
alkaline earth metals *see* Group 2 elements
alkalis   99, 388
alkanes   159, 166–74
   combustion   168
   cracking   172, 176, 184
   physical properties   167
   reforming   172, 173
   substitution reactions   170–71
   see also plastics
alkenes   176–85, 199
   reactions   178–83, 250, 252–3, 266
   test for   178, 458
   uses   176
alkyl groups   158
alkylation   242
   Friedel–Crafts   214, 265
allotropes   63–4, 299
alloys   76, 95, 149

alpha particles   26
   bombardment experiments   9, 18
aluminium
   extraction   104, 404–5
   recycling   405
aluminium chloride   107
   catalyst   214
aluminium oxide   104, 404–5
amides   158, 160, 233, 242, 244–5, 269
amines   158, 160, 189, 239–42
   preparation   241
   reactions   233, 242–3, 269
      as bases   240
amino acids   158, 160, 246–7, 248
ammonia
   manufacture *see* Haber process
   partition between solvents   371
   reactions   189, 233
   shape of molecule   61
   solubilities of silver halides in   124
   test for   459
ammonium ion   59
   test for   459
ammonium nitrate   364, 366
ammonium phosphate   366
amphoteric oxides   92, 104
amylase   334
anaesthetics   187, 193
analgesics   270, 271
analysing data   436
Answers   442–57
antacids (indigestion remedies)   114, 118, 381
antibiotics   270
anticancer drug   149
antifreeze   185, 201
antipyretics   270
arenes   *see* aromatic hydrocarbons
aromatic hydrocarbons   209–19, 267
asorbic acid   380
aspirin   270–71
asymmetric molecules   247
atactic polymers   252
atomic mass units (a.m.u.)   21
atomic number (proton number)   18
   and Periodic Table   88–90
atomic radii   96, 108, 123
atomic spectra   10, 11
atoms
   structure   8–16
   visualisation   27
autocatalysis   148
auxochromes   279
Avogadro, Amedeo   30
Avogadro constant   30
Ayers, Joseph   79
azo dyes   218, 243, 262

B

baking powder   395
balanced equations   29, 30
barium   113, 114
barium sulphate   118, 459
bases   191
   Brønsted–Lowry theory   382
basic oxides   103–4
basic oxygen converter   400
batteries (car)   415
bauxite   104, 398, 404
benomyl   219
benzamide   233
benzene
   reactions   267
      addition   215
      electrophilic substitution   211–14
   structure   209
benzene ring   209–10
benzenediazonium ion   243
benzenesulphonic acid   213
beryllium   113, 114
beryllium chloride, shape of molecule   60
beryllium oxide   118
bidentate ligands   140
biodegradable polymers   256, 259
biodiesel   237
blast furnace   33, 400
bleaches   124, 127, 128
blood
   pH   392, 394
   see also haemoglobin
body-centred cubic structures   77
Bohr, Niels   10
boiling points
   alkane isomers   167
   chlorides   106
   elements   97
   oxides   105
bomb calorimeter   295
bond angles   60–61
bond dissociation enthalpies   187, 304–5
bond lengths   187
   in benzene   210
   in carboxylic acids   230
   in halogenoalkanes   187
bond polarity   69, 188
bonding, and physical properties   80, 97, 105, 106
Born–Haber cycles   310–17
boron trifluoride, shape of molecule   60
Bosch, Carl   362
Brady's reagent   225
breath tests   285
bromine   120, 122
   extraction from seawater   130
   oxidation states   126–7

bromine water   178–9, 358–9
bromoalkanes, mechanism of
    hydrolysis   347
bromobenzene   213
Brønsted–Lowry theory   382
buckminsterfullerenes   64
bucky-balls   64–5
buffer solutions   246, 392–3, 394
butanedione dioxime   141
butanone   227
butenes, isomerism   177

C

caesium   98–9
calcium   112, 113
    reactions   115
calcium carbonate   115, 117, 118
    decomposition   323
    see also limestone
calcium hydroxide   115, 116
calcium oxide   116, 117
calcium sulphate   118
cannabis   272
carbocations   181–3, 190
carbon   92, 398
    reducing agent   399, 400
    see also diamond; fullerenes; graphite
carbon dioxide   58, 103, 105, 110
    greenhouse gas   169
    limewater test for   115
carbon monoxide   169, 174, 400
    poisoning   143, 169
carbon tetrachloride   69, 107
carbonates   110, 117
    see also calcium carbonate
    tests for   459
carbonyl compounds   221–8
    see also aldehydes; ketones
carboxylic acids   158, 160, 196, 229–31
    hydrogen bonding in   71, 229
    reactions   230–31, 268
        with alcohols   197, 231, 374
        test for   458
    see also fatty acids
β-carotene   279
Carothers, Wallace   254
catalase   334
catalysts   146–8
    in industry   250, 253, 333
    and reaction rate   332
    see also enzymes
catalytic converters   143, 147, 169, 333
catalytic cracking   176, 184
cell diagrams   409
cells (electrical)   408–10, 415–16
CFCs see chlorofluorocarbons
Chadwick, James   19
chain isomers   163
chalcocite   399
chalcopyrite   149
chalk   117, 118
charge density   54, 72
chelation   141
chemical plant, siting   366
chemical shifts   282

Chernobyl nuclear accident   130
chewing gum   395
chiral centres   247
chlordane   377
chloric(I) acid   127, 128, 129
chlorides   42, 106–7
chlorine   57, 120
    determination in water   123
    manufacture   128
    oxidation states   126–7
    preparation   121
    reactions
        with alcohols   198
        with alkanes   170–71
        with benzene   215
        with halides   122–3
        with iron   122
    test for   124, 459
    uses   120, 128–9
chloroalkanes   198
chlorobenzene   213
chlorofluorocarbons (CFCs)   192
chloroform (trichloromethane)   69, 187
chromate(VI) ion   144
chromium   15
    extraction   402
    hydrated ions   139
    ion formation   133
    oxidation numbers   134
    uses   403
chromophores   278
cisplatin   149
cis–trans isomerism   137, 177
citric acid   380, 381, 395
closed systems   357
cobalt, hydrated ions   139, 146
'cobalt chloride' paper   136
cocaine   272
codeine   272
collision theory   328
colorimeter   326, 435
coloured ions   135, 138, 142
combustion   168–9, 178
complex ions   135, 136–43, 242
    naming   140
    shapes   137
condensation polymers   254–5
condensation reactions   225
conducting polymers   258
conjugate pairs (acid–base)   382, 384
Contact process   361
coordinate (dative) bonding   59, 136, 240
coordination number   136–7
copper   15
    extraction   399
    hydrated ions   139
    mass spectrum   24
    uses   149
copper alloys   149
copper complexes
    pigment   142
    substitution reactions   141
corrosion   413–14
coupling reactions   243
covalent bonding   56–72
cracking   172, 176, 184

crude oil   245
    fractionation   167
crystals, ionic compounds   52
cycloalkanes   166
cycloalkenes   176
cyclohexane   215

D

d-block elements   89, 90, 92, 132–49
    coloured compounds   135, 138
    complex formation   136–7, 141, 142–3
    electronic structures   133
    ion formation   133
    oxidation numbers   133, 134–5
    physical properties   132
    uses   132
    see also metals
d sub-shells   11, 13–15, 142
Dalton, John   8
data logging   297, 326, 435
data pages   462–5
dative (coordinate) bonding   59, 136, 240
DDT   219
dehydration reactions   199, 245
delocalised electrons   74, 75, 210, 211, 230, 243
diamond   62, 94, 95, 299
diaphragm cell   128
diatomic molecules   57, 120
diazotisation   243
dichloromethane   193
dichromate(VI) ion   144, 145, 196
2,3-dihydroxybutanedioate (tartrate)   146
dimers   71, 229
2,4-dinitrophenylhydrazine (Brady's reagent)   225
diols   201
dioxins   174
disorder   318
displacement reactions   122–3, 407
displayed (structural) formulae   159, 161
disproportionation reactions   127
dissociation constant
    acids K_a 230, 385–6, 465
    bases K_b 241
dissolving   316
Döbereiner, Wolfgang   88
dolomite   117
dot and cross diagrams   50, 57, 58, 59
double bonds   58
Downs Cell   404
drugs   149, 270–72
dyes   218, 243, 279
dynamic equilibria   357

E

EDTA^{4-} (ligand)   140, 141
electrochemical series   410
electrode potentials   407–16
electrolysis   53, 128, 404–5
electrolytes   53
electromotive force (e.m.f.)   408, 409, 412
electron affinity   311, 456
electron density map, benzene   210

electron transfer 46–7
electronegativity 68, 93, 123, 188
electronic structures 10–15, 90, 91
    d-block elements 133
    Group 2 elements 112
    Group 7 elements 120
electrons 8, 9
    delocalised 74, 75, 210, 211, 230, 243
    density map 210
    energy levels 10–11, 279
    lone pairs 61, 140
    shells 10–11
    sub-shells 11–15
electrophiles 180
electrophilic addition reactions 181
electrophilic substitution reactions 211–14, 216–17
electroplating 143
elements
    Dalton's list 8
    new (artificial) 100
    patterns in properties 88
    see also Periodic Table
elimination reactions 191
empirical formulae 40, 41, 275
enantiomers 247
endothermic reactions 296, 307, 360
energetic stability 300
enthalpy of atomisation $\Delta H_{at}^{\ominus}$ 299, 304, 462–3
enthalpy changes (ΔH) 295–307
enthalpy of combustion $\Delta H_{c}^{\ominus}$ 299, 465
enthalpy cycles 300–301
    see also Born–Haber cycles
enthalpy of formation $\Delta H_{f}^{\ominus}$ 299, 300–301, 302–3, 456–7
enthalpy of hydration 316
enthalpy of ionisation see ionisation enthalpies
enthalpy level diagrams 147, 296, 301, 305, 312, 325
enthalpy of neutralisation 297
enthalpy of reaction $\Delta H^{\ominus}$ 298, 302
enthalpy of solution 303
entropy change (ΔS) 318–21
entropy (S) 141, 316, 318
enzymes 241, 248, 334–5
    immobilised 336
epoxyethane 185
equilibria 141, 357–67
    acid/base 380–95
    factors affecting position 358–60
    in industry 361–4
equilibrium constants, factors affecting 368–75
Equilibrium Law 368
error 437
esters 158, 160, 197, 229, 231, 233, 234–6, 268
ethane-1,2-diamine (en) 140, 141
ethanedioate titrations 148
ethane-1,2-diol 185, 201
ethanoic acid 230, 384, 386
    in buffer solutions 392–3
    hydrogen bonding in 71
ethanoic anhydride 233

ethanol 195, 264, 272
    in breath 285
    fuel 200
    industrial production 200
ethanoyl chloride 232–3
ethanoyl group, test for 458
ethene 58, 176, 191, 200
    uses 185
ethylbenzene 214
evaluating practicals 437
exothermic reactions 296, 307, 360

F

f-block elements 89, 92
face-centred cubic close-packed structures 77
fatty acids 235, 237
feasibility of reaction 302, 322
Fehling's solution 222
fermentation 195, 200, 335
Fermi, Enrico 100
fertilisers 364, 366, 376
'fingerprinting' 277, 280–81
fire extinguishers 110
fireworks 306
flame retardants 187, 192
flame tests 116, 459
fluorides 54
fluorine 120, 122, 127
food flavourings 197, 236
food preservatives 230, 236
formalin 221, 226
formulae
    empirical 40, 41, 275
    molecular 41
    structural (displayed) 159, 161
fractional distillation (crude oil) 167
fragmentation (mass spectrometry) 277
free energy changes (ΔG) 322–3
free-radical reactions 170–71, 192, 215, 253
Friedel–Crafts reactions 214, 265
fructose 227
fuel cells 416
fuels 174
    waste plastics 174
    see also oil; petrol
fullerenes 64–5
functional group isomers 163
functional groups 158
fundamental particles see sub-atomic particles
fungicides 215, 219

G

galvanising 414
gas constant 36
gases 36, 319
    moles of 34
    volumes of 35
'gasohol' 200
Geiger and Marsden's experiment 9, 18
gemstones 138
genetically modified crops 377
geometrical isomers 177
germanium 88, 92, 95
giant covalent structures 62–3
giant ionic structures 51

giant metallic structures 74–5, 77
Gibbs, J. Willard 322
glass 109, 110
    photochromic 134
global warming 169
glucose 227
glues 236, 257
glycerides 235
goitre 130
gold 75, 399
graph work 339, 436
graphite 94–5, 299
    structure 63
gravimetric analysis 42
greenhouse effect 169, 200
Grignard reagents 266
Group 1 elements 98–9
    flame tests 116
Group 2 elements 112–18
    flame tests 116
    hydroxides 115, 116
    ionisation energies 112–13
    oxides 116
    physical properties 113
    reactions 114–15
Group 4 elements 92, 93
Group 7 elements 120–30
    as oxidising agents 121–2
    reactions 121, 122, 124
    reactivity 122, 123
    van der Waals forces in 67
gypsum 118

H

Haber process 360, 362–3, 376
    catalysis in 146, 147, 362
haematite 398
haemoglobin 143, 169
halates see oxohalogen compounds
half cells 408
half equations 121, 127, 144–5
    combining 121, 145, 148, 407
half-life (reactant) 342
halide ions, test for 124, 143
haloalkanes see halogenoalkanes
halogenoalkanes 158, 160, 187–93
    reactions 266
        elimination reactions 191
        nucleophilic substitution reactions 188–90
    test for 458
halogens see Group 7 elements
halothane 187, 193
herbicides 219
Hess's Law 300
heterogeneous catalysts 147, 333
heterolytic fission 181, 190
1,2,3,4,5,6-hexachlorocyclohexane 215
hexagonal close-packed structures 77
Hofmann degradation 244, 265
homogeneous catalysts 146–7, 148, 333, 334
homologous series 159
    'stepping down' 265
    'stepping up' 264

homolytic fission 170, 253
hydrated ions 52, 59, 107, 138–9, 316
hydrocarbons 166
   see also alkanes; alkenes; arenes
hydrochloric acid 380, 381, 384, 386
hydrogen
   reactions
      with alkenes 179
      with benzene 215
      with carbonyl compounds 223
   reducing agent 398, 402
   test for 320, 459
hydrogen bonding 70–71
   in alcohols 195
   in amides 244
   in amines 239
   in carboxylic acids 229
   in hydrogen halides 70
   in polyamides 255
hydrogen halides 125
   boiling points 68, 70
   hydrogen chloride 381, 382
      see also hydrochloric acid
   hydrogen iodide, decomposition 343,
      368–9, 370
   preparation 125
   reactions 178, 179, 180–83, 198–9
hydrogen ions 381, 382, 383
hydrogen peroxide 146, 334
hydrogencarbonate ion 459
hydrogensulphate ion 459
hydrolysis
   bromoalkanes 347
   epoxyethane 185
   esters 234
   hydrated ions 138
   non-metal chlorides 107
hydroxynitriles 224

I

ibuprofen 271
ideal gas equation 36–7
ilmenite 402
implementing practical skills 435
indicators 39, 389, 391
   starch 39
   universal 383, 387, 388
indigestion remedies *see* antacids
infra-red spectrometry 280–81, 285
initial rate of reaction 327
insecticides 215, 219, 377
insulin 248
integration trace in n.m.r. spectra 283
intermediate bonds 72
intermolecular forces 66–7, 68
internal energy changes (ΔU) 295
iodine 120
   oxidation states 126–7
   structure 66
   titration with thiosulphate 123, 129
   uses 130
iodoform reaction 223
ionic bonding 46–8
ionic compounds 46–54
ionic equations 115

ionic product of water Kw 387
ionic radii 108
ionisation enthalpies 12, 93, 96, 311, 312,
   463–4
   alkali metals 99
   chromium and vanadium 134
   Group 2 elements 112–13
ions 47–8, 49
   charges/tests for 459
   hydrated 52, 59, 107, 138–9, 316
   polarisation 72, 313
iron 109
   catalyst 146, 147
   conversion to steel 401
   extraction 400
   Fe(II)/Fe(III) differentiation 139
   hydrated ions 138, 139
   ion formation 133
   recycling 405
   uses 132
iron(III) chloride 138
isomerism 137, 162, 177
   geometric 177
   optical 247
   structural 162–4
isotactic polymers 252
isotopes 20, 21, 22
   labelling with 197
isotopic abundance 24–5
I.U.P.A.C. rules for nomenclature 160

K

Kekulé, Friedrich August 209
kerosene 168
ketones 158, 160, 196, 221–7, 267
Kevlar 254, 256
Key Skills in chemistry 438
kinetic stability 318, 325
kinetics *see* reaction kinetics
Kroll process 402
Kroto, Sir Harry 64

L

lasers 16
lattice enthalpy 310–16
lava lamps 193
Le Châtelier's principle 358, 374, 375
lead 93
   extraction 399
lead chromate, pigment 142
lead–acid accumulator 415
Leclanché cell 415
leptons 27
Lewis acids 382
Lewis bases 382
ligands 136, 140, 141, 242
lime kilns 117
limestone 110, 117, 118, 400
limewater 115
linear complexes 137
linear molecules 60
liquids 36, 319
lithium 98–9
lithium tetrahydridoaluminate(III) 223,
   231, 245

lone pairs (electrons) 61, 140, 240
luminescence 16
Lycra 257
Lyman Series 11

M

magnesium 112, 113, 414
   reactions 112, 114, 115
   reducing agent 402
   test for ion 459
magnesium bromide 130
magnesium carbonate 117
magnesium hydroxide 114
magnesium nitrate 117
magnesium oxide 54, 103, 105, 118
   lattice enthalpy 314–15
magnetic resonance imaging 285
malachite 149
malic acid 395
manganate(VII) ion 135, 144, 145, 148,
   178, 196, 217
manganese, ion formation 133
margarine, manufacture 179, 333
Markovnikov's Rule 182
mass number (nucleon number) 20
mass spectrometry 22–3
   spectra 24–5, 26, 276–7, 285
Maxwell–Boltzmann distribution 328
melting points
   d-block elements 132
   elements 97
   Group 2 elements 113
   ionic compounds 52
memory metals 78–9
Mendeleev, Dmitri 88–9
metaldehyde 226
metallic bonding 74
metalloids (semi-metals) 92
metals 74–5, 92, 93
   extraction 398–402
   see also alloys
methanal 221, 226
methane 174, 366
   chlorination 170–71
   intermolecular forces 66
   shape of molecule 60
methanoic acid 229, 230
methanol 201
methyl orange 389
methylbenzene 217
MIBK (methyl isobutyl ketone) 226
Midgley, Thomas 192
molarity 38
mole fractions 372
molecular formulae 41
molecular ions 25, 276
molecules, shapes 60–61, 69
moles 30
   calculations using 30–43
Monastral blue pigment 142
monodentate ligands 140
monomers 250
morphine 272
MRI (magnetic resonance imaging) 285
multidentate (polydentate) ligands 140, 141

N

native metals   399
neutralisation   381
neutrons   19, 27
Newlands, John   88
nickel
    catalyst   333
    hydrated ions   139
nickel complexes   141
nicotinamide   244
Nitinol   78–9
nitrates   117
nitration   212
nitric acid   380
    manufacture   146, 364
    uses   365
nitriles   158, 160, 189, 245, 269
nitrobenzene   211, 212, 217, 218
nitrogen oxides   174, 342, 364, 376
    equilibrium mixture   359–60, 370
nitronium ion   212
nitrous acid (nitric(III) acid)   243
nomenclature
    complex ions   140
    organic compounds   160–61
non-metals   92, 93
nuclear fission   26
nuclear magnetic resonance
        spectroscopy   282–4, 285
nuclear power   26
nucleon number see mass number
nucleophiles   188, 189, 242
nucleophilic addition reactions   223–4
nucleophilic attack   231, 234, 242
nucleophilic substitution reactions   188–90,
        198–9
nucleus (atomic)   9, 18–20, 27
nylon   251, 254–5

O

octahedral complexes   137
octahedral molecules   61
octane   166
octane numbers   172
oil
    fractionation of crude   167
    and global stability   173
    refining   172, 173, 245
optical isomers   247
orbitals   13, 14, 15
orders of reaction   341–4
ores   398
organic analysis   274–85
organic compounds
    defined   158
    nomenclature   160–61
organic synthesis   262–72
oxidation   109, 196, 222, 407
oxidation numbers (states)   126–7
    and redox reactions   144
    variable 126–7, 133, 134–5
oxides   103–5, 107, 110, 116
oxidising agents, determination   123
oxohalogen compounds   127

oxygen, reactions   113, 376
ozone   169, 192

P

p-block elements   89, 90, 92
    see also Group 7 elements
p sub-shells   11, 13–15
paracetamol   271
Parathion®   219
parent ions see molecular ions
partial pressures   372
particle accelerators   27, 100
partition coefficients   377
peptide links   248, 254
perfumes   236
Period 2 elements
    atomic and ionic radii   108
    chlorides   106
    ionisation enthalpies   96
    oxides   104–5
    structures   97
Period 3 elements
    atomic and ionic radii   108
    chlorides   106, 107
    oxides   104–5
    structures   97
Periodic Table   88–99, 460
    groups   91
    periods   91
periodicity   96
    and chemical properties   103–9
    and physical properties   96–7
perspex   226
pesticides   120, 215, 219, 377
PET   257
petrol   172–3
pH   43, 383, 386–8, 393
pH curves   390–91
pH meters   390, 393
pharmaceuticals see drugs
phenol   213, 216
phenylamine   218, 241, 243
phosphorus(III) chloride   107
phosphorus(V) chloride   198, 458
    shape of molecule   61
photochemical reactions   329
photochromic glass   134
photographic materials   124, 143
pi (π) bonds   180
pigments   142
planar molecules   60
Planck's constant   142
planning practical work   434
Plaster of Paris   118
plasticisers   237
plastics   193, 250–51
    disposal of waste   174
Platforming   173
platinum, uses   149
platinum complexes see cisplatin
Plum Pudding model of atom   8
poisoning of catalysts   147
polar bonds   69, 188
polar molecules   52, 68–9
polarimeter   247

polarisation, ions   72, 313
pollution
    from acid rain   103
    from combustion   168–9
    from greenhouse gases   169
    from ozone   169
    from pesticides   219
    from waste disposal   174
poly(3-hydroxybutyrate)   259
polyalkenes see poly(ethene);
        poly(phenylethene); polypropene
polyamides   255, 256
poly(chloroethene) (PVC)   183, 252
polydentate ligands see multidentate ligands
polyesters   231, 255, 257
poly(ethene) (polythene)   250, 251
poly(ethenol)   259
polymerisation   252–5
polymers   226, 250–59
poly(phenylethene) (polystyrene),   236, 252
poly(propene)   251, 252
poly(tetrafluoroethene)   252
polyurethane   257
position isomers   162–3
potassium   98–9
potassium chloride   366
potassium nitrate   366
practical skills   434–7
propanal   221, 264
propane-1,2-diol   201
propane-1,2,3-triol (glycerol)   235, 237
propanone   221, 226
proteases   248
proteins   246, 248, 394
proton acceptors   382
proton donors   382
proton number see atomic number
protons   18, 27

Q

quarks   27
quaternary ammonium salts   239

R

racemates   247
radioactivity   9
rapeseed oil   237
rate constant (k)   340, 341, 343
rate determining steps   346
rate equations   338–44
    determination   342–4
rates of reaction   325–36, 345
    factors affecting   329–32
        see also catalysts
reaction kinetics   325–36, 338–47
reaction profiles see enthalpy level diagrams
reactivity
    Group 1 elements   99
    Group 2 elements   114–15
    Group 7 elements   122
Reactivity Series   398, 399
recycling
    glass   110
    metals   405
    plastics   174, 257

redox reactions   109, 121, 398–405
   transition metals   144–5
reduction   109, 196, 400, 402, 404, 407
reflux, heating under   188, 199, 435
reforming   172, 173
refrigerants   192
relative atomic mass   21, 24, 30
relative formula mass   31–2
relative molecular mass   31
resonance   209, 230
reversible reactions   356–7, 407
   see also equilibria
revision skills   428–31
robots   79
rockets   63, 118, 306, 307
rubber, vulcanisation   251
rubidium   98
rusting   109, 413
Rutherford, Ernest   9, 18

S

s-block elements   89, 90, 92
   see also Group 1 and 2 elements
s sub-shells   11, 13–15
sacrificial protection   413
salts   380
saponification   235
saturated hydrocarbons   166
scandium   133
scanning probe microscopy   27
semi-metals (metalloids)   92
shampoo, pH balanced   394
sigma (σ) bonds   180
significant figures   436, 442
silicon   92, 95
silicon dioxide   62, 104, 105, 110
silicon tetrachloride   107
silk   254
silver, extraction   143
silver complexes   143
silver nitrate solution   124
silver plating   143
simple molecular structures   66–7
slag   400
smart polymers   258
smoke alarms   26
S_N1 mechanism   190, 347
S_N2 mechanism   190, 347
soaps   235
sodium   98–9, 197
   atomic spectra   12
   extraction   404
   reducing agent   402
sodium benzoate   230, 236
sodium carbonate   110
sodium chlorate(I)   127
sodium chloride   54, 121
   electrolysis of molten   404
   electrolysis of solution   128
   lattice enthalpy   310–11
   uses   54, 110
sodium hydroxide, manufacture   128
sodium oxide   103
sodium tetrahydridoborate(III)   223, 267

sodium thiosulphate   123, 129
solder   95
solids   36, 319
solvents   193, 236
spectator ions   115
spectrometry   278–85
   infra-red   280–1, 285
   nuclear magnetic resonance   282–4, 285
   ultraviolet   278–9
   visible-range   279
   see also mass spectrometry
square planar complexes   137
stainless steel   401
standard conditions   298
standard electrode potentials $E^{\ominus}$ 410–13
standard enthalpy changes   298–9
standard hydrogen electrode   410
starch indicator   39
steel   109, 132, 398, 401
stereoisomers   137, 177
strontium   113
structural formulae   159, 161
structural isomers   162–4
structure, and physical properties   80, 97,
      105, 106
study skills   428–33
sub-atomic particles   19, 20, 27
   see also electrons; leptons; neutrons;
      protons; quarks
substitution reactions
   alcohols   198–9
   alkanes   170–71
   aromatics   211–4, 216–7
   complex ions   141
   halogenoalkanes   187–90
sugars   227
sulphonation   213
sulphur   66
sulphur dichloride   107
sulphur dioxide   103, 174, 361
sulphur trioxide   103, 361
sulphuric acid   103, 380
   manufacture   361
   uses   365
sulphur(VI) fluoride, shape of molecule   61
surfactants   185, 239
syndiotactic polymers   252

T

tartrate see 2,3-dihydroxybutanedioate
TCP (trichlorophenol)   213
'Teflon'   193
temperature scales   298
Tencel   256
Terylene   255
tetrahedral complexes   137
tetrahedral molecules   60
tetramethylsilane (TMS)   282
thermal cracking   184
thermoplastics   251
thermosets   251
Thomson, J.J.   8
tin   93, 95
titanium   402, 403
   ion   138

titrations   39, 43, 123, 129, 390–1, 435
TMS (tetramethylsilane)   282
TNT (trinitrotoluene)   217
Tollens' reagent   143, 222
transition metals   110, 133
   catalysts   146–7
   redox reactions   144–5
trichloroethanoic acid   385
trichloromethane (chloroform)   69, 187
trigonal bipyramidal molecules   61
trigonal planar molecules   60
tungsten   402, 403

U

ultraviolet spectrometry   278–9
unidentate ligands   140
universal indicator   383, 387, 388
unsaturated hydrocarbons   176
   test for   178
   see also alkenes
uranium-235, nuclear fuel   26

V

van der Waals' forces   67, 167, 251
vanadium, oxidation numbers   134
vanadium(V) oxide   361
videotape manufacture   227
visible-range spectrometry   279

W

waste disposal   174, 193
water
   acid–base properties   381, 382
   cobalt chloride test for   136
   greenhouse gas   169
   hydrogen bonding in   71
   ionic product   387
   pH   387
   reactions
      with acid chlorides   232
      with chlorides   107
      with Group 2 elements   114–15
      see also hydrolysis
water purification   120, 129
wavenumbers   280

X

X-ray crystallography   51
X-ray diffraction   210

Y

yeast   335
yields, calculating   263

Z

Ziegler catalysts   250, 253
zinc   133, 414
zwitterions   246

Acknowledgements

I would like to thank the following people for their help and support in writing this book. Each one has made their contribution and added value to my initial efforts: John Hepburn, John Bailey, Adrian Wheaton, Derek Denby, Margaret Ferguson, David Waistnidge, Tom Keogh, Geoff Morrison, Claire Penfold, Michael Penfold, Carol Stretch, Judy Ryan, Mike Wooster, Andy Raw and Patrick McNeill.

Acknowledgement is made to the following Awarding Bodies for permission to reprint questions from their examination papers.

AQA
OCR
EDEXCEL
Northern Ireland Council for the Curriculum Examinations and Assessment (NICCEA)
Welsh Joint Education Committee (WJEC)

Illustration acknowledgements

Adams Photolibrary 95BC, 132M David Simpson, 183 Nance Fyson, 254B, 325B, 413T Advertising Archives 215T, 216TR, 236CT Aquafilm Ltd 259B BASF (UK) 362M Biopol 259T Body Shop 262 BP Amoco 173T British Steel 33B Britstock IFA 168B Nowitz Chubb Fire 58T Colorsport 403b David Hoffman Photolibrary 217, 377B Nick Cobbing Dr Robert Shoemaker, Towson University 395B Ecoscene 118b Peter Hulme, 321 Chirich Gryniewicz Flexon 78T Frank Lane Picture Agency 219T Panda/H. Fadigati Geoscience Features 52, 98B, 113a, b, d, 149TCL, TCR, 398TL Groupal Ltd 104T, 404T Growbag 306T, M, BR Simon Roberts Holt Studios International 14B, 219B Nigel Cattlin Honda 110T ICI 54MT, 146 Chemicals and Polymers, 215B Agrochemicals, 323, 364, 366T ICN Bureau UK 251 Image Bank 94T Marks Product, 95TC Steve Dunwell, 201B Alvis Upitis, 361, 395BM Barros and Barros Image Select 209B Ann Ronan, 362T Dr L.F. Haber Impact Photos 118e Tom Webster, 187T Caroline Penn, 272T Giles Askham Insurance Institute for Highway Safety 345T International Centre for Conservation Education 405 J. Allen Cash Photolibrary 95B, 129B Janine Wiedel Photolibrary 272B Johnson Matthey 333 Leslie Garland Picture Library 383B Andrew Lambert, 414BL Ian Cartright Martyn Chillmaid 26T, 32, 35B, 39, 51T, 58B, 59, 62T, 63T, BR, 75T, 98T, 99B, 103T, M, 107, 112, 113c, 114, 115, 116B, 118a, 120C, 122, 124CL, CM, CR, 127, 130B, 134, 136, 133B, 139, 141, 143C, B, 145, 170, 176, 178, 179, 185, 187B, 193, 197, 200T, 213, 214, 216TL, B, 221T, 222, 223, 224, 225, 226, 227, 232, 234, 235, 236T, CB, B, 237T, 239, 240, 242, 248T, 250, 252, 253, 256 (courtesy Marks & Spencer), 257T, 270M, B, 271, 275. 297, 307T, 310, 326, 327, 330, 331, 332, 333B, 334, 338, 356, 357, 371, 380T, 381, 384, 386, 387, 388, 389, 390, 393B, 394B, 395T, TM, 399M, 407, 411, 413B Mary Evans Picture Library 362B NASA front cover, 415T National Gallery, London 142 NDC 78B New Media 99T (reproduced from the award-winning CD ROM, *Chemistry Set 2000* published by New Media Press, Henley-on-Thames) Nordic Track 246T Novosti (London) 26M, 130TB Oxford Scientific Films 43T Make Price/Survival Anglia, 195B Bernd Schellhammer, 229B Densey Clyne Panos Pictures 129T Sean Sprague, 264 Paul Smith Perkin Elmer 278 Popperfoto 174B Professor D. Williams, Imperial College, London 51B Raychem 258C Rex Features Photolibrary 168T R.G.Williamson Robert Harding Picture Library 76T Charlie Westerman, 184 Tom Carroll/Phototake NYC, 399T Paulo

Koch, 403a Greg Voight/International Stock, 414T   Roche 233 Science Museum 8B   Science Photolibrary 8T Northwestern University, 10 Department of Physics/Imperial College, 16T Will and Deni McIntyre, CL Tim Malyon, CR Rosenfeld Images Ltd, 22, 24 Geoff Tompkinson, 26B NASA, 30, 64 Geoff Tompkinson, 65T Biosyn Technologies Inc., B Ken Eward, 66 Claude Nuridsany and Marie Perennou, 76BR Lawrence Livermore National Laboratory, 88, 95T Sinclair Stammers, 100T Los Alamos National Laboratory, M, B Jean Collombet, 103B Will McIntyre, 113e Ross Lappa, 116M Andrew McClenaghan, 118d CNRI, 120R, L, 121 Charles D. Winters, 143T Antonia Reeve, 149TL Martin Land, 169B Astrid and Hanns-Frieder Michler, 245T Will and Deni McIntyre, 248B Saturn Stills, 248C J.C. Revy, 270T Charlotte Raymond, 282T, B James King-Holmes, 285B Alfred Pasieka, 322, 325T Erich Schrempp, 345B Eye of Science, 358, 380B marcelo Brodsky, 381T Dr Jeremy Burgess, 400 Martin Bond, 402TM Volker Steger, 403d Heini Schneebel, 415M NASA   Still Pictures 147 Andre Moslennikov/Sweden, 173B, Pierre Gleizes Stock Boston 345M Tom Wurl   Stockmarket 229T Norbert Schafer, 243C Geprge Disario, 398TR George Schiarone   Stone 168R Robert Brons/BPS, 29 Rick Iwasaki, 43B Ben Deborne, 45 Hugh Stilton, 56 Christopher Bissell, 57T Frank Herholdt, 62B Robert Frerck, 75BL Jack Veary, BR Bob Thomason, 76BC Martyn Goddard, 110B Richard Kaylin, 124B Antonia Deutsch, 130T Richard Passamore, 149TR Lester Lefkowitz, 160 Dennis O'Clair, 166 Jon Riley, 169T Paul Chesley, 172B Kristian Hilsen, 178T Peter Cade, 274 Ben Osborne, 306BL Ary Diesendruck, 335 Jon Riley, 402BM UHB Trust, 414BR Oliver Benin   Sygma 42   Sylvia Cordaiy Photolibrary 123 Johnathon Smith, 195T Chris Parker   Telegraph Colour Library 54MB Elke Hesser, 128 Colorific/Louis Psihoyos/Matrix, 149M S. Benbon, 209T Mel Yates, 218 Jamie Baker, 258T Hugh Burden, 314 Michael Yanashita, 366B Jean Louis Batt, 393T Genna Naccache, 394 R. Chapple   Tesco 230B   Topham Picturepoint 54B, 117B, 200M Cameramann International Ltd, 221B, 239T, 241B, 255, 257B, 285T Press Association   Travel Ink Photolibrary 117T Angela Hampton   TRIP 94T A. Tjagny-Rjadno, 110M H. Rogers, 125 J. Drew, 138T, 172T H. Rogers, 200B A. Tovy, 201T Tony Freeman, 254 R. Winstanley, 256TL M. Melia, TR A. Woodward, 295 Eric Smith, 392 P. Kaplan, 398BL H. Rogers, 399B H. Rogers, 402T M. Zarember, 404B D. Saunders   UK Copper Plumbing and Heating Systems Board 74T   William Huber 79   www.jewellers.net 149B www.johnbirdsall.co.uk 230T

Thanks are also due to the staff and pupils of:

The Leys High School, Redditch
Arrow Vale Community High School, Redditch
New College, Bromsgrove and
St George's Sixth Form College, Birmingham

who assisted with the photographs in the book.